HISTORY
of
WASHINGTON COUNTY
PENNSYLVANIA

From Its First Settlement

to the

PRESENT TIME,

First under Virginia as Yohogania, Ohio, or Augusta County until 1781, and Subsequently under Pennsylvania;

with

Sketches of All the Townships, Boroughs, and Villages, Etc.;

And to Which Is Added

a Full Account of the Celebrated Mason and Dixon's Line, the Whiskey Insurrection, Indian Warfare, Traditional and Local Historical Events

Whatever makes the past, the distant, or the future preponderate over the present, advances us in the dignity of thinking beings. —Dr. Johnson

Alfred Creigh, LL.D.

HERITAGE BOOKS
2009

HERITAGE BOOKS
AN IMPRINT OF HERITAGE BOOKS, INC.

Books, CDs, and more—Worldwide

For our listing of thousands of titles see our website
at
www.HeritageBooks.com

A Facsimile Reprint
Published 2009 by
HERITAGE BOOKS, INC.
Publishing Division
100 Railroad Ave. #104
Westminster, Maryland 21157

Entered according to Act of Congress, in the year 1870, by
Alfred Creigh, LL.D.
In the Office of the Clerk of the District Court of the
United States in and for the Western District of Pennsylvania

Copyright © 2001 Willow Bend Books

— Publisher's Notice —
In reprints such as this, it is often not possible to remove blemishes from the original. We feel the contents of this book warrant its reissue despite these blemishes and hope you will agree and read it with pleasure.

International Standard Book Numbers
Paperbound: 978-1-58549-677-8
Clothbound: 978-0-7884-8150-5

TO THE CITIZENS

OF

WASHINGTON COUNTY, PENNSYLVANIA,

WHOSE DEVOTION TO PATRONIZE AND ENCOURAGE

MORALITY, LITERATURE, PATRIOTISM, AND RELIGION

IS NOT SURPASSED

BY ANY BODY OF CITIZENS IN THE

AMERICAN UNION,

This Volume

IS RESPECTFULLY DEDICATED

BY THEIR FELLOW-CITIZEN,

ALFRED CREIGH.

Ellendale Villa,
Washington, Pa., June 29, 1870.

PREFACE.

For the last nine years, the author of this volume has been engaged in collecting and arranging materials for the history of Washington County, a county whose existence (not, however, in its present organized chartered form) is coeval with the chartered rights both of Pennsylvania and Virginia. These States claimed control over its territory, until the disputed question was finally settled and adjusted by extending the celebrated Mason and Dixon's line, in 1785, although the chartered history of Washington County dates back to 1781.

There has been a growing desire, for the last few years, among the people of this and other counties to investigate and become acquainted with their local history. It is eminently proper and praiseworthy in any people to rescue from oblivion memorials of unpublished facts, reminiscences, and traditions; to call to memory the primitive days of our forefathers, their frontier life and hardships, their struggles with the red men of the forest, and to collect and preserve valuable and interesting statistical information and reliable facts which will tend to perpetuate their history.

Under such influences, and at the request of a committee of my fellow-citizens, I entered the hitherto untrodden field to collect all these memorials, and now present them for your consideration and approval. I do not intend to convey the meaning that it is entirely perfect; it will take time and more diligent research to procure the memorials which have not yet been published; but this volume is intended to be the starting-point from which the future historian can gain reliable facts. I have been particularly careful not to give any traditionary facts, without being corroborated by authentic documents or strong circumstantial evidence.

To natives and their descendants of Washington County, settled in distant places, this volume will prove of great interest, recalling

PREFACE. 5

to memory old associations, friends of former years, and the recollection of events and incidents passed from memory.

The causes which led to the preparation of this history of Washington County may be gathered from the perusal of the following correspondence:—

WASHINGTON, January 9, 1861.

DR. ALFRED CREIGH,

DEAR SIR: Our "old men" are fast passing away, and with them, unless soon rescued, will be lost many facts connected with the early settlement and history of our borough and county. Many accounts are doubtless in existence which are also liable to be lost when the present possessors cease to own them.

We believe it to be the duty of some one to gather unpublished facts, reminiscences, memorials, and traditions of the early settlement of the county, and present them to the public in an historic form. A history of Washington Borough and County would prove deeply interesting to the present inhabitants and to their children scattered all over the land. As a work of future reference, it would be invaluable. Knowing your zeal and perseverance in matters of this kind, we would respectfully suggest that you undertake this work. We will cheerfully aid you in obtaining facts and gaining access to documents.

We believe that sufficient numbers of the book could be sold to repay you for your labor. Hoping you will comply with the request,

We remain yours, &c.,

ALEXANDER WILSON,	JOHN L. GOW,
JOHN H. EWING,	THOS. W. GRAYSON,
C. M. REED,	G. W. MILLER,
J. L. JUDSON,	DAVID AIKEN,
JOHN R. DONEHOO,	WM. VANKIRK,
WM. HOPKINS,	FREEMAN BRADY, JR.,
JAMES B. RUPLE,	W. S. MOORE,
H. A. PURVIANCE,	JAMES W. KUNTZ,
WM. HUGHES,	R. H. KOONTZ,
A. H. ECKER,	GEO. S. HART,
WILLIAM SWAN,	W. A. MICKEY,
W. H. HORN,	H. J. VANKIRK.

REPLY.

WASHINGTON, January 21, 1861.

GENTLEMEN: Your letter of January 9th is now before me, and after mature deliberation upon its contents, I shall avail myself of preparing, and at the earliest opportunity of presenting to the public a full history of Washington Borough and County. The reminiscences, memorials, and traditions which exist in this county will make an interesting work, more especially as this was the *first* county which was organized in Pennsylvania after the Declaration of Independence.

PREFACE.

It is true that the history which I am about to write will require untiring diligence, unwearied perseverance, and industrious research, yet with the *promised* aid of yourselves and the co-operation of my fellow-citizens who may be in possession of any facts or traditions tending to elucidate our history, I have no fear of the result. As Washington County was the *first* organized, let her likewise be the *first* in the State to inaugurate a system by which, every county, following her example, will present their separate histories to the American people, whereby incalculable good will result not only to the State of Pennsylvania, but to the rising generation.

With sentiments of respect and esteem, I remain yours truly,

ALFRED CREIGH.

To ALEXANDER WILSON, Esq., and others.

The materials for the work have been derived chiefly from the Colonial Records and Archives of the State, the records of the county and borough, files of newspapers, pastors of churches, and kind friends who felt a deep interest in procuring for my use these memorials. To the committee who addressed me on the subject, to my friend Hon. James Veech, of the city of Pittsburg, am I particularly indebted for the use of his notes on Washington County, and the Mason and Dixon question; to David S. Wilson, Esq., who aided me by his counsel and research, and to Rev. Dr. James I. Brownson who, from the moment of its undertaking, felt a deep and abiding interest in its publication, with many others, I return my sincere thanks, fondly trusting that the work may meet the approval of all my fellow-citizens; fully convinced that any imperfections will be overlooked by the reader, in the contemplation of the variety of subjects presented for his consideration.

Where any error is discovered, I shall be thankful to the reader to inform me by letter of the inaccuracy, and I shall have it corrected in a subsequent edition, my desire being to give a faithful, truthful, and reliable history of Washington County.

CONTENTS.

CHAPTER I.
WASHINGTON COUNTY—ITS PRIMITIVE HISTORY UNDER VIRGINIA.

Spottsylvania County; its boundaries—Orange County—Frederick County; its boundaries—Augusta County; its boundaries—District of West Augusta—Justices' Courts—Oath of allegiance—Oath of supremacy—The test oath—Oath of abjuration—Youghiogheny County; its boundaries, courts, and court-houses, and punishments—Pillory and stocks described—Whipping-post and ducking-stool—Ohio County; its boundaries and court-house—Monongalia County—Courts and roads—Orphan children—Taverns—Continental money—Ferries—Attorneys-at-law—Sheriffs and deputy-sheriffs—Surveyors—Military officers—Grist-mills—Salts—Cotton, and wool cards—Counterfeit money—Allegiance—Naturalization—Passports—Benevolence of Youghiogheny County—Marriage extraordinary—Reflections 9

CHAPTER II.
A GENERAL OUTLINE HISTORY OF PENNSYLVANIA.

History of Pennsylvania, from the date of its charter to the present time, embracing a list of all the Indian titles to lands—Historical and statistical facts—The date of the formation of each county of the State, with the number of acres and population in each, and a list of the Governors from the accession of William Penn, its proprietor, in 1681 to 1870 27

CHAPTER III.
ORIGINAL ACT ESTABLISHING WASHINGTON COUNTY.

Divisions by the formation of townships—Its original and present townships and boroughs—Its present boundaries with topographical and geographical description and its streams—Its early religious element and the religious agreement of 1782—Marriage custom and ceremony—School-houses 39

CHAPTER IV.
PROCEEDINGS OF THE SUPREME EXECUTIVE COUNCIL.

A brief history of the Provincial Conference—The Constitution of 1776; the Council of Censors; the Convention of 1789; the Constitution of 1790; the action of the Legislature of 1825; with regard to a convention, and the vote of the people; the Convention of 1837; the Constitution of 1838, and the full proceedings of the Supreme Executive, from 1781 to 1791, which relates to Washington County . . . 54

CHAPTER V.
TOWNSHIPS AND BOROUGHS IN WASHINGTON COUNTY.

The history of the Townships and Boroughs in their chronological order, detailing interesting events in each—Also the history of churches and the present state of education in each township and borough . . 87

(7)

CHAPTER VI.
ELECTED OFFICERS OF WASHINGTON COUNTY FROM 1790.

Members of Congress—Senators and Representatives—President Judges—Associate Judges and Deputy Attorney-Generals—Attorneys-at-Law—Prothonotaries—Registers—Recorders—Clerk of the Courts—Sheriffs—Coroners—Commissioners—Clerks to Commissioners—Treasurers—Auditors—Notary Public—Directors of the Poor—Deputy Surveyor-General—Justices of the Peace 250

CHAPTER VII.
MILITARY HISTORY OF WASHINGTON COUNTY.

Brig.-Gen. Clark's expedition in 1781—Col. David Williamson's expedition in 1782—Col. William Crawford's expedition in 1782—Whiskey Insurrection in 1791-4—Outrage on the Chesapeake Frigate, 1807—War of 1812—Texas Revolution, in 1836—Mexican War in 1846—Southern Rebellion in 1861 278

CHAPTER VIII.
HISTORY OF ASSOCIATIONS, AND EVENTS WHICH TRANSPIRED IN WASHINGTON COUNTY 341

APPENDIX.

CHAPTER I.
THE VIRGINIA AND PENNSYLVANIA CONTROVERSY, FROM 1752 TO 1783.

The date of the earliest settlements by Virginians and Pennsylvanians—The difficulties between the Governors of both States arising from these settlements—The names of the first settlers—The various acts of Capt. Connolly as the representative of Virginia in claiming Fort Duquesne (Pittsburg) as within Virginia—His treason—Commissioners appointed by both States to run a temporary line until the Revolutionary War would terminate—The action of both States approving of the same, and the necessity of erecting Washington County 3

CHAPTER II.
THE MASON AND DIXON'S LINE.

Its full history—the line run by Charles Mason and Jeremiah Dixon—the claim of Pennsylvania—the claim of Lord Baltimore—the appointment of commissioners—the labors of Mason and Dixon ended in 1767—new commissioners appointed in 1783 by the States of Virginia and Pennsylvania—letter from Joseph Reed on the scientific apparatus to be used—report of the joint-commissioners—report of the Pennsylvania commissioners—cost of running the line—the western line of Pennsylvania run by commissioners appointed by both States, and the report of the commissioners thereupon—the origin of the Pan Handle in West Virginia 24

CHAPTER III.
INDIAN HISTORY OF WESTERN PENNSYLVANIA AND VIRGINIA.

Names of all the tribes of North America in 1764—Those inhabiting Western Pennsylvania and adjoining territory—Letters on the Indian wrongs from 1765 to 1780—Rice's fort—Letters from Dr. J. C. Hupp on Miller's block-house—Captivity and escape of Jacob Miller, and the cruel murder of five of Miller's friends—Vance's fort—Well's fort—Lindley's fort 38

CHAPTER IV.
WHISKEY INSURRECTION. . . . 59

HISTORY OF WASHINGTON COUNTY.

CHAPTER I.

WASHINGTON COUNTY—ITS PRIMITIVE HISTORY UNDER VIRGINIA.

Spottsylvania County; its boundaries—Orange County—Frederick County; its boundaries—Augusta County; its boundaries—District of West Augusta—Justices' Courts—Oath of allegiance—Oath of supremacy—The test oath—Oath of abjuration—Youghiogheny County; its boundaries, courts, and court-houses, and punishments—Pillory and stocks described—Whipping-post and ducking-stool—Ohio County; its boundaries and court-house—Monongalia County—Courts and roads—Orphan children—Taverns—Continental money—Ferries—Attorneys-at-law—Sheriffs and deputy sheriffs—Surveyors—Military officers—Grist-mills—Salt—Cotton, and wool cards—Counterfeit money—Allegiance—Naturalization—Passports—Benevolence of Youghiogheny County—Marriage extraordinary—Reflections.

To trace the history of Washington County from its primitive existence, the historian should give facts, but the inferences and reflections should be left to the reader. It will be our province, therefore, to examine into the history of the colony of Virginia from its first settlement on the 25th day of March, 1584, to the 23d day of August, 1785, at which date the commissioners of the States of Virginia and Pennsylvania entered into conciliatory measures whereby that portion of Western Pennsylvania claimed by Virginia became vested in our own State.

Our chartered rights, therefore, are deduced from charters granted by the reigning King of England, either to the colony of Virginia in 1584, or to the colony of Pennsylvania in 1681, as the records will demonstrate.

In 1584 Sir Walter Raleigh obtained letters patent for discovering unknown countries, by virtue of which he took possession of that part of America which he afterwards named VIRGINIA, in honor of Queen Elizabeth. He attempted its settlement, but failed. He took an active part in many enterprises in England; and, among the number, he endeavored to place Arabella Stewart on the throne, and for this conspiracy was tried and condemned, on November 17, 1603, to be hanged, drawn, and quartered. Notwithstanding his conviction and sentence, he was not executed, but was confined in the Tower as a prisoner, where he remained many years, devoting his time to writing the *History of the World.* On the accession of James I. to the crown, Raleigh was released, and sent on a mining expedition to South America, with the necessary number of men and ships, of which Spain was informed; but the expedition failing, and one of the Spanish towns being destroyed by fire, the Spanish ambassador demanded satisfaction by the return and death of Raleigh. He was, therefore, immediately seized, and, without any new trial, was beheaded on his former conviction, on the 29th of October, 1618, to appease the anger of Spain.

In 1606 James I., by virtue of his prerogative as king, divided the colony of Virginia between two companies: the southern company was granted to Thomas Gates and others, and called the London Company; the northern company was called the Plymouth Company. This grant embraced all the lands in Virginia from Point Comfort, along the sea-coast, to the northward two hundred miles, and from the same point, along the sea-coast, to the southward two hundred miles, and all the space from this precinct on the sea-coast up into the land, west and northwest, from sea to sea, and the islands within one hundred miles of it. Subsequently, on the 12th day of March, 1612, by other letters patent, the king added all islands in any part of the ocean between the thirtieth and forty-first degrees of latitude.

On the 24th of July, 1621, the colony of Virginia established a form of government, subject to the approval of the "General Quarter Court of the Company in England." To this was added the proviso that no order of the Council in England should bind the colony *unless* ratified in the General Assembly of Virginia. Thus early in our country's history was introduced those principles of republicanism, which eventually secured to us our present form of government.

The king and the Company, however, quarrelled, and he suspended their powers by the Proclamation of July 15, 1624. King James I. having died on 27th March, 1625, Charles I. took the government into his own hands. He made extensive grants of plantations in a high state of cultivation, and also woodlands, in the colony of Virginia, to his particular friends, Lord Baltimore and Lord Fairfax, to the former of whom he even granted the separate and sole right of jurisdiction and government. Charles I. having been deposed by Oliver Cromwell in 1650, and assuming the title of Protector, he considered himself as standing in the place of the deposed king, and as having succeeded to all the kingly powers, without as well as within the realm, and therefore assumed control over the American colonies. Virginia, however, had expressed herself as opposed to Cromwell and his parliament, and invited Charles II. (the son of the deceased king), who was then an exile in Breda, Flanders, to come into Virginia and become their king, but on the eve of embarking, in 1660, he was recalled to the throne of England, on the 29th of May, of the same year. After Charles II. had ascended the throne, and desirous of giving a substantial proof of the profound respect he entertained for the loyalty of Virginia, he caused her *coat-of-arms to be quartered with those of England, Ireland, and Scotland*, as an independent member of the empire. Hence the origin of the term *Old Dominion*. It also derives this term from the fact that it was the first of the English settlements in the limits of the British colonies.

Having thus exhibited the chartered rights of the colony of Virginia for sixty-six years, let us retrace our steps to the year 1634, when the colony of Virginia was divided into eight shires or counties. Six of these were situate between the James and York rivers, viz.: Henrico, Charles City, James City, York City, Warwick, and Elizabeth City shires. The Isle of Wight Shire was between the James and Caroline rivers, while the Northampton or Accomac Shire was on the eastern shore. From these eight original shires or counties have been erected the one hundred and fifty-eight counties of the Old Dominion, fifty-six of which are situate west of the Blue Ridge Mountain, which is broken by the Potomac River at Harper's Ferry, and traverses the State in a line of about two hundred and sixty miles, separating it into the two great divisions of Eastern and Western Virginia.

Spottsylvania County.

The territory of Washington County, Pennsylvania, was, according to the original chartered rights of Virginia, claimed as belonging to the county of Spottsylvania. This county was formed from parts of Essex, King William, and King and Queen counties, in 1720, during the reign of King George I. It was named in honor of Alexander Spottswood, who was then Governor, and also in commemoration of the fact that he made the *first* discovery of the passage over the Appalachian Mountains.

The preamble to the act erecting this portion of Western Virginia into a county reads thus: That the frontier toward the high mountains is exposed to danger from the Indians, and the late settlements of the French to the westward of the said mountains, therefore it is enacted, that SPOTTSYLVANIA bounds upon Snow Creek up to the mill; thence by a southwest line to the North Anna River, thence up said mountains, *as far as convenient*, and thence by a line to be run on the northwest side thereof, so as to include the northern passage through the said mountains, thence down the said river until it comes against the head of the Rappahannock River and down that river to the mouth of Snow Creek, which tract of land shall become the COUNTY OF SPOTTSYLVANIA, from May 1, 1721.

By the act of 1730, Williamsburg was declared to be the county town, and the same act, on account of the large area of territory to be travelled by the judicial officers, provided that the burgesses should be allowed for four days' journey, in passing and returning.

In 1712, Virginia was divided into forty-nine parishes, which act also determined the salary of each clergyman, but in 1730 St. George's parish was divided by a line running from the mouth of the Rappahannock to the Pamunkey River, the upper portion to be called St. Mark's, and the lower portion St. George's parish.

In 1734 the names of these parishes were changed, St. George's was called *Spottsylvania* and St. Mark's was named *Orange*, and all settlers beyond the Shenandoah River were exempted for three years from the payment of public and parish dues. It is apparent, therefore, that the first settlers endeavored to mould their religious government and make it conform as near as possible to the church of England.

Orange County.

In 1734, Spottsylvania County was divided, and from it Orange County was formed, which comprised the whole of the colony of Western Virginia.

Frederick and Augusta Counties.

In 1738, the act of legislature erected two more counties out of the extensive county of Orange, by naming one *Frederick*, and the other *Augusta*. Frederick County was bounded by the Potomac on the north, the Blue Ridge on the east, and a line to be run from the head spring of Hedgeman to the head spring of the Potomac, on the south and west. Augusta County was to embrace the remainder of Virginia west of the Blue Ridge.

Augusta County.

In October, 1776, the legislature of Virginia passed an act to ascertain the boundary between the county of Augusta and the district of West Augusta, and to divide said district into three distinct counties.

District of West Augusta.

The preamble to the act, which embraces much historical information, is in these words: Whereas, it is expedient to ascertain the boundary between the county of Augusta and the district of West Augusta—Be it therefore enacted by the General Assembly of the Commonwealth of Virginia, that the boundary between the said district and county shall be as follows: beginning on the Alleghany Mountains, between the heads of the Potomac, Cheat, and Green Briar Rivers (Haystack Knob, or north end of Pocahontas County), thence along the ridge of mountains which divides the waters of Cheat River from those of Green Briar, and that branch of the Monongahela River called Tyger's Valley River, to the Monongahela River; thence up the said river, and the west fork thereof, to Bingerman's Creek, on the northwest side of the said west fork; thence up the said creek to the head thereof; thence in a direct course to the head of Middle Island Creek, a branch of the Ohio, and thence to the Ohio, including all the waters of said creek in the aforesaid DISTRICT OF WEST AUGUSTA, all that territory lying to the northward of the aforesaid boundary, and to the westward of the States of Pennsylvania and Maryland, shall be deemed, and is hereby declared to be, within the DISTRICT OF WEST AUGUSTA.

At a court of the District of West Augusta, held at Fort Duquesne (Pittsburg), September 18th, 1776, the court decided that on the passage of the ordinance, they became a separate and distinct jurisdiction, from that of East Augusta, and as such, West Augusta assumed and exercised independent jurisdiction over its entire territory.

After the thirteen colonies had declared themselves free and independent, the General Assembly of Virginia passed an act on the 20th of August, 1876, enabling the present magistrates to continue the administration of justice until the same can be more amply provided for.

JUSTICES' COURTS.

Justices' courts were organized by John Eare, of Dunmore, his majesty's Lieutenant and Governor-in-Chief of Virginia, as early as December, 1774. He also issued, the same year, a commission adjourning the county court of Augusta, from Staunton to Fort Dunmore. This fort was originally called Fort Pitt, but in 1773 the British government abandoned it, and Dr. John Connelly took possession of it *in the name* of Virginia, and named it Fort Dunmore. It is evident, therefore, that as late as three years before the Declaration of Independence, Pittsburg and the surrounding country was claimed as belonging to the district of West Augusta. This interresting question will be fully discussed in the Appendix, Chapter II., wherein we shall treat of and examine the celebrated Mason and Dixon's line.

George Croghan, Edward Ward, John Stephenson, Isaac Cox, George M'Cormick, Joseph Beckett, John Campbell, Dorsey Pentecost, John Connelly, John Gibson, George Vallandigham, Thomas Smallman, William Crawford, and William Goe took the usual oaths to his majesty's person and government, subscribed the abjuration and test oaths, as also the usual one of justices of the peace, justices of the county court in chancery, and justices of the oyer and terminer. As these oaths are peculiar in their character I shall add them.

Oath of Allegiance.—I, A. B., do sincerely promise and swear that I will be faithful, and bear true allegiance to his majesty King George the Third. So help me God.

Oath of Supremacy.—I, C. D., do swear that I from my heart abhor, detest, and abjure as impious and heretical, that damnable doctrine and position, that princes excommunicated and deprived by the Pope, or any authority of the See of Rome, may be deposed or murdered by their subjects, or any other whatsoever. And I do declare, that no foreign prince, person, prelate, State, or potentate, hath or ought to have any jurisdiction, power, superiority, pre-eminence or authority, ecclesiastical or spiritual, within this realm. So help me God.

The Test Oath.—I, E. F., do declare that I do believe there is not any transubstantiation in the Sacrament of the Lord's Supper, or in the elements of bread and wine at or after the consecration thereof, by any person or persons whatever. So help me God.

Oath of Abjuration.—I, G. H., do truly and sincerely acknowledge, profess, testify, and declare in my conscience before God and the world, that our Sovereign Lord, King George the Third, is lawful and rightful king of this realm and all other his majesty's dominions thereunto belonging.

And I do solemnly and sincerely declare that I do believe in my conscience that the person pretended to be Prince of Wales during the life of the late King James, and since his decease pretending to be and takes upon himself the style and title of King of England, by the name of James the Third, or of Scotland by the name of James the Eighth, or the style and title of King of Great Britain, hath not any right or title whatsoever to the crown of this realm or any other the dominions thereunto belonging, and I do renounce, refuse, and abjure any allegiance or obedience to him.

And I do swear that I will bear faith and true allegiance to his majesty King George the Third, and him will defend to the utmost of my power against all traitorous conspiracies and attempts whatsoever, which shall be made against his person, crown, or dignity, and I will do my utmost endeavors to disclose and make known to his majesty and his successors all treason and traitorous conspiracies which I shall know to be against him or any of them.

And I do faithfully promise to the utmost of my power to support, maintain, and defend the succession of the crown against him, the said James, and all other persons whatsoever, which succession (by an act entitled an act for the further limitation of the crown and better securing the rights and liberties of the subject) is and stands limited to the Princess Sophie, late Electress and Duchess Dowager of Hanover, and the heirs of her body being Protestants—and all these things I do plainly and sincerely acknowledge and swear, according to these express words by me spoken and according to the plain and common sense and understanding of the same words, without any equivocation, mental evasion, or secret reservation whatsoever, and I do make this recognition, acknowledgment, abjuration, renunciation, and promise heartily, willingly, and truly upon the true faith of a Christian. So help me God.

After this digression we shall resume our narrative of the district of West Augusta, which, by an act of the General Assembly of Virginia, from and after November 8th, 1776, was divided into three counties, viz: *Youghiogheny, Ohio,* and *Monongalia*—to each of which we will refer *seriatim.*

YOUGHIOGHENY COUNTY.

The boundaries of this county lay to the northward of the following lines, and began at the mouth of Cross Creek, running up its several sources to the head thereof; thence southeastwardly to the nearest part of the dividing ridge (which divides the waters of the Ohio from those of the Monongahela); thence along the said ridge to the head of Tenmile Creek; thence east to the road leading from Catfish Camp (Washington) to Red Stone Old Fort (Brownsville); thence along the said road to the Monongahela River; thence crossing the river to the said Fort; thence along Dunlap's old road to Braddock's road, and with the same to the meridian of the head fountain of the Potomac (west line of Maryland), shall be called and known by the name of YOUGHIOGHENY COUNTY.

This act defined the qualifications of electors and various essential matters for the future prosperity and government of these new counties. Electors were required to be free white male persons over twenty-one years of age, residing in the county and State one year, and in possession of twenty-five acres of land with a house thereon; claiming an estate for life in the said land in his own right or in the right of his wife.

COURTS AND COURT-HOUSE.

The electors were required to meet on the 8th day of December, 1776, at the house of Andrew Heath, on the Monongahela River, to choose the most convenient place for holding courts for the county of Youghiogheny. Notices for election were to be given by the sheriff, ministers, and rectors in the same manner as for representatives to serve in the General Assembly. The law also provided that if prevented holding the election on the day aforesaid, by rain, snow, or rise of waters, the sheriff was authorized to adjourn to that day week, or as often as so prevented.

The electors met at the appointed time and selected the farm of Andrew Heath as the most convenient place. This farm is on the Monongahela River (now Washington County) nearly opposite and a little above Elizabethtown, Alleghany County.

The court directed Thomas Smallman, John Canon, and John Gibson, or any two of them, to provide a house at the public expense for the use of holding the court, and that the sheriff contract with the workmen to put the same in repair.

The original records show that the court directed Isaac Cox to contract with some person or persons to build a complete *bar* and other work in the inside of the court-house to be completed by the next court.

On the 24th of November, 1778, Messrs. Kuykendall and Newall were authorized to contract with some person to junk and daub the court-house, and provide locks and bars for the doors of the gaol, and to build an addition to the eastern end of the court-house and gaol, sixteen feet square, one story high, with good, sufficient logs, a good cobber roof, a good outside chimney, with convenient seats for the court and bar, with a sheriff's box, a good iron pipe stove for the gaol room, and that they have a pair of *stocks*, *whipping-post*, and *pillory* erected in the court yard.

The ancient laws of Virginia declared that the court in every county shall cause to be set up near the court house a pillory, pair of stocks, a whipping-post, and a ducking-stool in such place as they shall think convenient, which not being set up within six months after the date of this act, the said court shall be fined five thousand pounds of tobacco.

PUNISHMENTS.

In 1780 Andrew Heath was ordered to have the court-house and gaol repaired and to erect a *pillory* and *stocks*. It appears that the price paid for these articles of punishment at this time was two thousand dollars, continental money, to Paul Matthews, the contractor, which amount was equivalent to three hundred and seven dollars.

On the 24th of June, 1778, the court ordered Colonel William Crawford and David Shepherd to lay out the *prison bounds* for the county of Youghiogheny, and make report to the court. This committee subsequently reported the prison bounds to be as follows, viz: Beginning at a large black oak standing easterly from the court-house and marked with six notches, and extending thence southeasterly by a line of marked trees to a white oak near and including the spring; thence northerly by a line of marked trees, including the house of Paul Matthews, to a white oak; thence by a line of marked trees to the place of beginning, which prison bounds were approved by the court and ordered to be recorded.

Paul Matthews, whose house was included in the prison bounds, was appointed the gaoler, and for the year 1778 was allowed seventy-five pounds five shillings and tenpence for furnishing prisoners with victuals and finding iron for criminals.

On the 24th of January, 1780, the following curious entry is made in the minutes of the court: Ordered, that Isaac Justice, John Chamberlain, William Bruce, and William Maybell be allowed one hundred and twenty-five pounds of tobacco for seven days' attendance as a guard on a prisoner, and eighty-four dollars each for finding their own provisions, and the sheriff was directed to pay the same.

At the same sitting of the court we find that Andrew Heath was directed to have the upper story of the gaol put into order for a *jury room.*

We have spoken of the corporeal punishments inflicted upon criminals, which consisted of the pillory, the stocks, the whipping-post, and the ducking-stool, each of which I shall describe for the benefit of those who are unacquainted with these relics of barbarism.

The PILLORY is one of the most ancient corporeal punishments in England, France, Germany, and other countries. As early as 1275, by a statute of Edward I., it was enacted that every stretch-neck or *pillory* should be made of convenient strength, so that execution might be done upon offenders without peril to their bodies. The pillory consisted of a wooden frame erected on a stool with holes and folding boards for the admission of the head and hands. The heroes of the pillory have not been the worst class of men, for we find that a man by the name of Leighton, for printing his *Zion's Plea against Prelacy,* was fined £10,000, degraded from the ministry, pilloried, branded, and whipped through the city of London, in 1637, besides having an ear cropped and his nostrils slit. The length of time the criminal stood *in and upon the pillory* was determined by the judge.

The STOCKS was a simple arrangement for exposing a culprit on a bench, confined by having his ankles made fast in holes under a movable board. Sometimes the stocks and *whipping-post* were connected together, the posts which supported the stocks being made sufficiently high were furnished near the top with iron clasps to fasten round the wrists of the offender and hold him securely during the infliction of the punishment. Sometimes a single post was made to serve both purposes, clasps being provided near the top for the wrists when used as a whipping-post, and similar clasps below for the ankles when used as stocks, in which case the culprit sat on a bench behind the post, so that his legs, when fastened to the post, were in a horizontal position.

On the 23d of February, 1775, Luke Joliff was tried for deserting from the militia with a stand of arms and preventing the Indians from returning prisoners held by them. He was courted at Fort Dunmore (Pittsburg), and sentenced to receive five hundred lashes with a cat-o'-nine-tails on his bare back, well laid on, at such hours and in such manner as not to endanger life and member.

At a court held in Washington County, June, 1786, Richard Burke was convicted of larceny and sentenced to seventeen lashes at the public whipping-post well laid on, between 4 and 6 o'clock P. M., to restore the goods and pay fine and costs.

For the purpose of restraining evil, men suffered in the stocks, but women in *ducking-stools.* This punishment was extensively used in the sixteenth and seventeenth centuries. The following description was given by an intelligent Frenchman in the year 1700: He says this method of punishing scolding women is funny enough.

They fasten an armed chair to the end of two strong beams, twelve or fifteen feet long and parallel to each other. The chair hangs upon a sort of axle, on which it plays freely, so as always to remain in the horizontal position. The scold being well fastened in her chair, the two beams are then placed, as near to the centre as possible, across a post on the water-side, and being lifted up behind, the chair, of course, drops into the cold element. The ducking is repeated according to the degree of shrewishness possessed by the patient, and has generally the effect of cooling her immoderate heat, at least for a time.

The ducking-stool for Youghiogheny County was erected at the confluence of the Ohio and the Monongahela rivers on February 22d, 1775.

We are glad, however, in this enlightened age, that all these varied punishments are done away with, especially the one for the weaker, if not always the gentler sex.

While on the subject of punishments in Youghiogheny County, we may add that many persons were fined from five to twenty shillings for drunkenness, profane swearing, &c., &c., while the sheriff, George McCormick, received one pound, seventeen shillings and sixpence for executing a negro boy on the 28th of November, 1788, belonging to James Decamp.

Previous to the ratification of the report of the surveyors by the legislature of Virginia, October 8th, 1785, Ohio County had been formed from Youghiogheny by the line of Cross Creek. On the settlement of the boundary question, that portion of Youghiogheny County lying north of Cross Creek was added to Ohio County, being too small for a separate county; and the county of Youghiogheny became extinct; hence Hancock and so much of Brooke as lies north of Cross Creek was the last of the ancient Youghiogheny County.

Other facts connected with Youghiogheny County we shall reserve until we give the boundaries of Ohio and Monongalia Counties, the former of which is intimately connected with Washington County.

OHIO COUNTY.

Ohio County originally constituted a part of the district of West Augusta. Its boundaries, according to the act of Assembly of October, 1776, were as follows—that from and after the 8th of November, 1776, all that part of the said district lying within the following lines, to wit, beginning at the mouth of Cross Creek, thence up the same to the head thereof; thence southeastwardly to the nearest part of the ridge which divides the waters of the Ohio from those of Monongahela; thence along the said ridge to the line which divides the county of Augusta from the said district; thence with the said boundary to the Ohio; thence up the same to the beginning, shall be known by the name of Ohio County.

The electors of Ohio County were to meet at the house of Ezekiel

Dewit, on the 8th of December, 1776, to choose the most convenient place for holding courts in said county. It is said that for some time the courts of this county were held at Black's Cabin, on the waters of Short Creek, on January 16, 1777, at or near where West Liberty is.

Rev. Dr. Smith says: The first court for the county of Ohio was held at Black's Cabin. There is every reason to believe that this was the first civil court held in the valley of the Mississippi. On the 7th of April, 1777, the court ordered a court-house and jail to be erected. The first attorneys admitted to practise in the court were Philip Pendleton and George Brent, on the 2d November, 1778. Mr. Pendleton was appointed the commonwealth's attorney.

In a work by the Rev. Joseph Smith, D. D., entitled "Old Redstone," which contains historical sketches of Western Presbyterianism—its early ministers, its perilous times, and its first records, we find that the Presbytery of Redstone met on the 25th of October, 1782, at Dunlap Creek, and one minister was appointed as a supply at Ohio court-house. This place, says the Rev. Dr. Smith, was some miles west of the present town of Washington, and was a seat of justice under the government of Virginia, as all Washington County, together with Fayette and Greene and a large portion of Allegheny and Westmoreland counties was claimed by that State and considered a part of Augusta County, Virginia. The records show no other appointment for a supply at this place.

MONONGALIA COUNTY.

This was the third county into which the district of West Augusta was divided. It was northward of the county of Augusta, westward of the meridian of the head fountain of the Potomac, and to the eastward of the county of Ohio.

The Monongalia court-house was on the farm of Theophilus Phillips from 1776 to 1782 (now owned by Everhart Bierer), near New Geneva in Fayette County. By an act of the General Assembly of Virginia of May, 1783, it declares that by reason of the late extension of Mason and Dixon's line the court-house of Monongalia had fallen within the limits of Pennsylvania, therefore, the house of Zachwell Morgan (the present location of Morgantown, Virginia) should be made the future place of holding courts until a court-house should be erected.

The county lines of Youghiogheny, Ohio, and Monongalia were adjusted in the summer of 1778 by Col. William Crawford, Richard Yeates, Isaac Leet, William Scott, and James McMahon.

COURTS.

The courts of each judicial district were required to administer and dispense justice, establish ferries, confirm roads when reported necessary, bind out orphan children, grant letters of administration, probate wills, appoint subordinate officers, grant tavern licenses, record marks, try crimes and misdemeanors, and perform such duties as would advance the interests of the community.

When the court met at Fort Dunmore, originally Fort Pitt, on the 21st of February, 1775, many questions were presented to them at this and their subsequent sittings, some of which we shall give to gratify the taste of the antiquarian, and as calculated to throw some light on our early history.

ROADS.

Viewers appointed to report a road from Fort Dunmore to Fort Dunfield; from Gist's to Fort Dunmore and Paul Freeman's on Shirtee (Chartiers) Creek, by James Devore's ferry. From P. Mountz mill by Arbergus ferry and from thence to CATFISH CAMP (now Washington). This road ran from Mountz mill by way of Beeler's ferry; thence to the east fork of Chartiers' Creek; thence to Catfish Camp. From Fort Dunmore to Becket's Fort the points were from Becket's Fort to James Wilson's; thence to the Monongahela River; thence to the head of Sawmill Run; thence to Fort Pitt (Pittsburg); from the court-house to Pentecost's mill on Chartiers' Creek. This road began at the court-house on Andrew Heath's farm; thence to Spencer's Point; thence near Richardson's school-house; thence through Gabriel Cox's land; thence crossing Peters' Creek near to John Cox's; thence to Joshua Wright's; thence to William Stephenson's; thence to Thomas Crook's; thence to said mill. This road confirmed April 24, 1778. From Catfish Camp (Washington) to Pentecost's mill; confirmed May 26, 1778. Overseers were Thomas Ashbrooke and John McDowell. From Froman's mill on Mingo Creek to the road leading from the court-house to Pentecost's mill, between the plantations of Johnson Wrights and John Johnston. From Fort Dunmore to Dunfields, to join Dunfields on Chartiers' Creek. From old Redstone fort (Brownsville) to Conrad Walker's, foot of Laurel Hill. From Thomas Gist's to Paul Freeman's on Chartiers' Creek. From Redstone old fort (Brownsville) to Chartiers' Creek and to Paul Freeman's. From the mouth of the Youghiogheny River at McKee's ferry to the road from Devore's ferry to Reno's, near Sampson Beaver's and to Freeman's mill. From Fort Dunmore to Charles Brice's on Raccoon Creek. From Dorsey Pentecost's by Peter Barrackman's ferry to Fort Dunmore. From Major William Crawford's to near the forks of Indian Creek. From the foot of Laurel Hill at Conrad Walter's, by William Teagarden's ferry on the Monongahela to the mouth of Wheeling Creek. The points of this road were from the confluence of Wheeling Creek to the confluence of Tenmile Creek, on the Monongahela River; thence to Walter's. In the construction of roads the tithables (that is, all persons between the ages of 16 and 45) within three miles of the proposed road, were required to work upon the road under supervisors appointed to superintend the making and grading of the same.

ORPHAN CHILDREN.

The orphan children were bound out by the court as apprentices. They were required to serve until they arrived at the age of twenty-one; were instructed in some art; taught to read and write, and arithmetic as far as the rule of three; given two suits of clothing, and if brought up on a farm, each male also received an axe, maul, nugs, and wedges.

TAVERNS.

Taverns were licensed by the court of Youghiogheny County, and in 1778 we find that the court fixed the following bill of prices for the keepers of taverns. Whiskey by the half pint, two shillings; whiskey made into toddy, two shillings and sixpence; beer per quart, two shillings and sixpence; hot breakfast, three shillings; cold breakfast, two shillings and sixpence; dinner, four shillings; supper, three shillings; lodging with clean sheets, one shilling and sixpence; stabling with hay and fodder, five shillings; corn per quart, ninepence; oats per quart, sixpence. But in 1781, when continental money was depreciated, the prices were changed by the court, who ordered tavern keepers to sell at the following rates: For half pint of whiskey, $4; breakfast or supper, $15; dinner, $20; lodging with clean sheets, $3; one horse over night, $3; one gallon of corn, $5; one gallon of oats, $4; strong beer per quart, $6. The rates of license were published by the crier of the court, and also set up in the most public places.

CONTINENTAL MONEY.[1]

While upon the subject of finances, as there will be occasion to refer to the continental money, I may add that this money was issued by Congress to carry on the Revolutionary War, for the redemption of which the faith of the colonies was pledged. I therefore give the dates and amounts of issues from a reliable source.

1775, June 22, $2,000,000. Other emissions from this date to 1780, amounting to $200,000,000, had been issued and none redeemed.

1777, January, paper currency 5 per cent. discount, and in July 25 per cent., but before the end of the year, $3 in paper would not command a silver dollar.

1778, April, $4 in paper to one dollar in coin. September, $5 to one in coin, and December, $6 50 to one dollar in coin.

1779, February, $8 50, May $12, and September $18 to one in coin, and before the close of the year a paper dollar was worth but four cents.

1780, March, one dollar in paper worth 3 cents; May, a dollar worth but two cents, and in December, $74 in paper was worth one dollar in silver.

FERRIES.

The court licensed the following persons to establish ferries at different localities within the county of Youghiogheny, from 1775 to 1779.

Henry Heath, on his own plantation on the Monongahela River. William Lynn, on the Monongahela River, from his house to the land of Francis Hall. Michael Cressay, at Redstone, old fort (Brownsville), to the land of Indian Peter. James Devore, from his house on the Monongahela River, to the mouth of Pigeon Creek. To Samuel Sinclair, who lives in the forks of the Monongahela and Youghiogheny rivers, to have a ferry over each of the rivers. Jacob Bausman, across the Monongahela River, from his house to the town opposite (fort Dunmore). Christopher Carpenter, across the Monongahela River, for the purpose of conveying over the militia men on muster days. William Anderson, on the southeast side of the Monongahela River, to the lands of Andrew Heath. The prices established by the court for ferriage were, fourpence half penny for any head of neat cattle, and the same for a foot person; two shillings and sixpence for a man, and the same for a horse.

ATTORNEYS AT LAW.

The lawyers were required to take the abjuration, test, and other oaths to which I have referred. The record gives the following persons as having complied therewith during the years 1775 and 1776.

George Brent, Philip Pendleton, George Rootes, David Semple, James Berwick, Andrew Ross, Henry Peyton, John G. Jones, Charles Simms, Samuel Irwin.

SHERIFFS AND DEPUTY SHERIFFS.

During the years 1775 and 1780, John Christian and Joseph Horton, George McCormick, Matthew Ritchie, William Harrison, Benj. Kuykendall, Thomas Smallman, and Edward Ward exercised the office of sheriff, and Patrick McElroy, Francis Worm, David Steel, William Hawkins, Hugh Sterling, John Dossman, John J. Wood, Richard Burns, that of deputy sheriff.

SURVEYORS.

David Steel, William Crawford, Edward Sharp, Gabriel Green, Samuel Finch, John Harry, and Daniel Leet were appointed surveyors, who acted as such for several years.

On the 17th of April, 1776, Daniel Leet produced a commission from the College of William and Mary to be Surveyor of the County of Augusta, which embraced the county itself and the district subsequently divided into three counties. He took the usual oaths in open court, and gave as his securities for the fulfilment of the duties of his office, George Rice and George McCormick, Esquires.

It appears that in the early history of our country, these certificates or commissions from a college were absolutely necessary, for in examining the records of Culpepper County, Virginia, is the following record: 20th July, 1749 (O. S.), George Washington, Gent., produced a commission from the President and Master of William and Mary College appointing him to be a surveyor of Culpepper County, which was read, and thereupon he took the usual oaths to his majesty's person and government, and other oaths according to law.

Military Officers.

All military officers were required, in open court, to take the test and other oaths. Among the list of officers commissioned is the name of the notorious *Simon Girty*, who subscribed these oaths February 22d, 1775, in Pittsburg, and yet proved recreant to all his obligations, renounced civilized life and assisted the Indians in torturing the noble and heroic Col. William Crawford, at Sandusky, in 1782, where he suffered the most terrible death which Indian ingenuity could devise.

Grist-Mills.

Before a mill could be erected, so tenacious was the law of the rights of individuals, that it required the sheriff to summon twelve freeholders of the vicinage to meet on the land to determine if any of the adjoining lands would be affected by the back-water from the dam, and the jury there assembled were to value the damages and make report to the court. Applications were made by the following persons, and confirmed by the court, establishing mill-seats at the localities designated: Paul Froman on Mingo Creek; Col. John Campbell on Campbell's Run emptying into Chartiers' Creek on the west side near the mouth of Robinson Run; Nicholas Pease on Chartiers' Creek; Basil Brown on Big Redstone Creek; Dorsey Pentecost on the eastern branch of Chartiers' Creek. These mills were erected from 1777 to 1781.

Salt.

The early condition of the inhabited country west of the Laurel Hill can be easily imagined from the decree of the court in reference to this article.

In 1778, November 24, the court ordered that Isaac Cox be empowered to account with all persons that hath neglected any business relation to this (Youghiogheny) county's *salt*, lodged with Israel Thompson, of Loudon County, and that he receive the remainder of said salt and transport it to this county and issue the same to the inhabitants to whom it is due, at six pounds ten shillings per bushel, and the profits thereon shall be his full satisfaction for his said services, and that the said Colonel Cox shall also pay all demands on said salt, either for the original purchase or otherwise.

On September 29, 1779, the court ordered that Col. John Canon have the *public salt*, which now lies at Alexandria, brought up to this (Youghiogheny) county and distribute it to the persons entitled to receive it, and that he be authorized to contract for the carriage on such terms as he can, taking care in the distribution to fix the price so as to raise the money due thereon for the original cost. January 3, 1780, Benjamin Kuykendall was directed to bring up two hundred bushels of salt from Alexandria on the same principles.

COTTON AND WOOL CARDS.

Intimately connected with the foregoing subject was that of cotton and wool cards, provided for at the public expense, under the direction of the court, as the sequel will show.

May 27, 1778, the court ordered Isaac Cox, Thomas Freeman and Andrew Swearingen, to distribute the CARDS assigned for this county, upon proper and suitable satisfaction produced to them. On the 24th of June, of the same year, Col. John Stephenson and Isaac Cox were directed to distribute one-half of the foregoing cards to the battalion of Col. Stephenson. In the distribution of the cards the Committee were instructed to conform to the Governor's letter of November 26, 1777, which provided that if there are more women in either battalion, the Committee were to supply according to the number of persons who had the right to obtain the same.

COUNTERFEIT MONEY.

The law authorized the court to appoint suitable persons to decide upon counterfeit money. Accordingly, we find that in 1779 Thomas Gist, Thomas Warren, and John Irwin, of Pittsburg, Matthew Ritchie and Dorsey Pentecost, of the then county of Westmoreland, but in 1781 were residents of Washington County, were appointed and sworn in as judges of counterfeit money

ALLEGIANCE.

1778, June 22d. Rev. Edward Hughy produced a license from the Presbytery of Londonderry, in the kingdom of Ireland, to preach the Gospel of Jesus Christ, which was read in open court, whereupon the said Edward Hughy came into court and took the oath of allegiance and fidelity to this commonwealth. The Presbytery of Donegal reported to the Synod of Philadelphia, May 19th, 1773, that they had received the Rev. Mr. Hughy as a member, and that on May 14th, 1774, they had suspended him for unchristian conduct and character.

1778, August 28th. Rev. William Renno, a minister of the Gospel, also came into court and took the required oaths.

NATURALIZATION.

In the office of the Secretary of State, at Harrisburg, is a list, showing the names of those who were naturalized in the year 1765. The requisitions were entirely different to those of the present time, and were then considered as a *religious rite* or ceremony. The certificate of the Prothonotary reads thus:—

I do hereby certify that at a Supreme Court held at Philadelphia, before William Allen, William Coleman and Alexander Stedman, Esqs., judges of the same court, from the 24th of September to the 26th of October, 1765, between the hours of nine and twelve o'clock in the forenoon of each day, the following persons being foreigners, and having inhabited and resided for the space of seven years in his majesty's colonies in America, and not having been absent out of the said colonies for a longer space than two months at one time, during the said seven years, and having produced to the said court certificates of their having taken the *Sacrament of the Lord's Supper* within three months before the said court, took and subscribed the oaths, and did make and repeat the declaration, according to the directions of an act of Parliament, made in the thirteenth year of the reign of his late majesty, King George II., entitled "An act for naturalizing such foreign Protestants and others therein mentioned, as are settled or shall settle on any of his majesty's colonies in America, and therefore were admitted to be his majesty's natural born subjects of the kingdom of Great Britain.

EDWARD SHIPPEN, Prothonotary.

PASSPORTS.

The court, upon application, granted passports, indorsing the character of good and true citizens. To preserve the form used I subjoin one.

1778, May 26th. Tacitus Gillard, Esq., came into court, and procured a passport from the Board of War, and desired that the same might be entered on the minutes of the court of Youghiogheny County, as a testimonial of his allegiance and fidelity to the United States of America, which is granted, and is as follows:—

WAR OFFICE, YORKTOWN, October, 15, 1777.

To all Continental officers, and others whom it may concern:

Tacitus Gillard, Esq., late an inhabitant of the State of South Carolina, being on his way to Florida, or some of the countries or places on this side thereof, or adjacent thereto, where he purposes to form a settlement; and having applied for a passport to enable him to go and travel through the parts of the country in allegiance to and in amity with the United States of America, and having produced the testimonial of his having taken the oaths of allegiance and fidelity to the said States; *these* are to permit the said Tacitus Gillard, Esq., freely to pass with his family, servants, attendance, and effects down the Ohio River, and all persons are desired not to molest the said Tacitus Gillard, Esq., and his family, servants, and effects on any account or pretence whatever.

By order of the Board of War.

RICHARD PETERS, Secretary.

Benevolence of Youghiogheny County.

The court felt it to be their duty to provide for the soldiers' widows and the orphans of soldiers, who had been engaged in the Continental service, and they accordingly appropriated out of the county funds, a monthly allowance for the purpose. A few examples will suffice.

Eleanor Lindsey was allowed for herself and her five children, five pounds per month; John Sherley's widow, forty shillings per month; Bridget Blackstone, three pounds per month; and William Shaw's wife and six children, six pounds per month.

Marriage Extraordinary.

1778, April 28th. Thomas Gist came into court, and being sworn on the Holy Evangelists of Almighty God, sayeth that in the year of our Lord 1772, in the month of April, to the best of his recollection, in the presence of Joseph Beeler, John Stephenson, and George Read, he solemnized the rite of matrimony between Isaac Meason and Catharine Harrison, according to the rites and ceremonies of the Church of England, he, the said deponent, being a magistrate in the State of Pennsylvania, and that he was under an *oath not to divulge* said marriage, except lawfully called on for that purpose.

John Stephenson and Joseph Beeler came into court, and being sworn, sayeth that they were present at the marriage of Isaac Meason and Catharine Harrison, in the year 1772, in the month of April, and was under a promise not to divulge said marriage, unless legally called upon, or death of either of the parties.

And the said Joseph Beeler says that there was a pre-engagement between the said Isaac and Catharine, that upon divulging the said marriage, *contrary to the will of the said Isaac, that said parties should be absolved from any obligation to each other as man and wife.*

Reflections.

In bringing our first chapter to a close, we need but remark that the early or primitive history of this section of the country has almost passed from the minds of the present generation of men. The footprints of time are visible everywhere, and occasionally we procure a solitary landmark, isolated and alone. These we have collected together to perpetuate them as relics of the past. Neither is it to be expected that our forefathers would devote their time and attention in recording facts for future generations. The difficulties they had to encounter, the toils they were required to endure, the constant dread of Indian massacre, all united to prevent faithful and reliable facts from being preserved to guide the historian.

The advantage to be derived from this chapter is that we became acquainted with the topography of the country, its boundaries, streams, laws, customs, and names of the leading public characters, and thus we are enabled to localize facts, events, and persons.

CHAPTER II.

A GENERAL OUTLINE HISTORY OF PENNSYLVANIA.

History of Pennsylvania, from the date of its charter to the present time, embracing a list of all the Indian titles to lands—Historical and statistical facts—The date of the formation of each county of the State, with the number of acres and population in each, and a list of the Governors from the accession of Wm. Penn, its proprietor, in 1681 to 1870.

ON the 4th of March, 1681, Charles the Second granted to William Penn a charter for the Province of Pennsylvania, the king having a regard to the memory and merits of William Penn's father in divers services, and particularly in his late conduct, courage and discretion, under James, Duke of York, in that signal battle and victory fought and obtained against the Dutch fleet, commanded by Heer Von Opdam, in the year 1655. In consideration thereof, King Charles II. granted to William Penn, his heirs and assigns, all that tract or parcel of land in America, with all the islands therein contained, as the same is bounded on the east by Delaware River, from twelve miles distance, northwards of New Castletown, unto the three and fortieth degree of northern latitude, if the said river doth extend so far northward, but if the said river shall not extend so far northward, then by the said river so far as it doth extend, and from the head of the said river the eastern bounds are to be determined by a meridian line to be drawn from the head of said river, unto the said three and fortieth degree. The said land to extend westward five degrees in longitude, to be computed from the said eastern bounds, and the said land to be bounded on the north by the beginning of the three and fortieth degree of northern latitude, and on the south by a circle drawn at twelve miles distance from New Castle northward, and westward unto the beginning of the fortieth degree of northern latitude, and then by a straight line westward to the limits of longitude above mentioned. This charter is in the office of the Secretary of Pennsylvania, and is written on parchment in the old English handwriting. Each line is underscored with red ink, the borders are gorgeously emblazoned with heraldic devices, and on the top is a portrait of his majesty. This document is nearly two hundred years old.

Under the provisions of this charter, William Penn, by and with the advice, assent, and approbation of the freemen of the said country, had authority to ordain, make, and enact laws. Accordingly, on the 25th of April, 1682, William Penn framed a form of government for the Province of Pennsylvania. It consisted of a preface and twenty-four articles, confirming, unto the freemen thereof, their liberties, franchises, and property.

On the 24th October, 1682, William Penn arrived with an additional number of colonists at New Castle, (now in the State of Delaware), and entered into a solemn covenant with the Indians by purchasing their lands and giving them full satisfaction. It must be remembered that William Markham, his deputy, had preceded him to America, and had entered into negotiations with the Indians on July 15, 1682, but it was stipulated therein that this act was to be publicly ratified by William Penn on his arrival. Consequently, the Sachems and their tribes, with Penn and his colonists, met at Coaquannoc (Philadelphia), but the treaty was confirmed at Shackamaxon (Kensington), under the ELM TREE.

In connection with the subject of lands, their extent and limits as purchased from the Indians, it will be proper to remark, that from the arrival of William Markham, deputy of William Penn, until the year 1792, a period of one hundred and ten years, the whole right of soil of the Indians within the charter bounds of Pennsylvania, has been extinguished by the follow thirty-three treaties and purchases:—

1.—1682, July 15. Deed for lands between the falls of Delaware and Neshaming Creek, confirmed by William Penn, October 24, 1682, under the elm tree.
2.—1683, June 23. Deed for lands between Pennepack and Neshaming, and to run two days' journey with a horse, backward up into the country.
3.—1683, June 25. *Wingebone's* release for lands on the west side of Schuylkill, beginning at the first falls and backward on the same as far as his right extended.
4.—1683, July 14. Deed for lands between Schuylkill and Chester Creek.
5.—1683, July 14. Deed for lands between Schuylkill and Pennepack.
6.—1683, September 10. *Kake Tappan's* deed for his half of all his lands between Susquehanna and Delaware, on the Susquehanna side.
7.—1683, October 18. *Machaloha's* deed for lands between the Delaware River and Chesapeake Bay, and up to the falls of the Susquehanna.
8.—1684, June 3. *Manghenghsin's* release for his land on Perkioming.
9.—1684, June 7. *Richard Mettammicont's* release for lands on both sides Pennepack on Delaware River.
10.—1685, July 30. Deed for lands between Pennepack and Chester

Creek, and back *as far as a man can go in two days* from a point on Conshohocken hill.
11.—1685, October 2. Deed for lands between Duck and Chester creeks, and backward from Delaware, *as far as a man could ride in two days with a horse.*
12.—1692, June 15. Acknowledgment of satisfaction for land between Neshaming and Poquessing creeks, and back to the bounds of the Province.
13.—1696, January 13. *Dongan's* deed to William Penn for lands on both sides of Susquehanna, from the lakes to the Chesapeake Bay.
14.—1697, January 5. *Taming's* deed for the lands between Pennepack and Neshaming, *and as far back as a horse can travel in two summer days.*
15.—1700, September 13. Deed of the Susquehanna Indians for the lands on both sides of the Susquehanna and next adjoining the same, and comprising Dongan's deed (No. 13)
16.—1701, April 23. Ratification of Dongan's deed and the deed of September 13, 1700 (No. 14), by the Susquehanna, Shawnese, Potomac, and Conestogoe Indians.
17.—1718, September 13. Deed of release by the Delaware Indians, for the lands between the Delaware and Susquehanna rivers, from Duck Creek to the Lehigh hills.
18.—1720, December 16. Controversy respecting the boundary of the lands, arising from the distance which a man and horse can each travel in a day, and satisfactorily arranged by deed.
19.—1726, May 31. Deed for lands on both sides of Brandywine Creek.
20.—1732, September 7. Deed for lands between Lehigh hills and Kittatinny Mountains, between Schuylkill and its branches, and the branches of Delaware.
21.—1736, October 11. Deed for the river Susquehanna and the lands on both sides thereof, eastward to the head of the branches, or springs running into the Susquehanna, and westward to the setting of the sun, and from its mouth to the Kittatinny hills.
22.—1736, October 25. The preceding deed declared by the Indians to include the lands on the Delaware, and northward to the Kittatinny hills.
23.—1737, August 28. Deed comprising the *walking* purchase, or, *as far as a man can go in a day and a half* from the westerly branch of Neshaming up the Delaware.
24.—1749, August 22. Deed for lands from the Kittatinny Mountain to Mahanoy Mountain, and between Susquehanna and Delaware on the north side of Lackawaxen Creek.
25.—1754, July 6. Deed at Albany for the lands on the west side of Susquehanna, from Kittatinny Mountain, to a mile above the mouth of Penn's Creek, thence northwest and by west, as far as the Province extends to its western boundaries.

26.—1758, October 23. Deed of surrender of part of the purchase of 1754, and new boundaries declared and confirmed from Penn's Creek, northwest and by west, to Buffalo Creek, then west to Alleghany Mountain, and along the east side thereof, to the western boundary of the Province.

27.—1768, September 5. The end of Nittany Mountain assumed as a station, per deed made, and surveys not usually made north thereof.

28.—1768, November 5. Deed at Fort Stanwix, commonly called the new purchase.

29.—1784, October 23. Deed explaining the boundary at the treaty at Fort Stanwix and Pine Creek, declared to have been the boundary designed by the Indians.

30.—1784, December 21. Deed declaring Lycoming to be the boundary.

31.—1785, January 21. Deed at Fort Stanwix and Fort McIntosh, for the residue of the lands within the Commonwealth, made October 23, 1784, and January 21, 1785.

32.—1789, January 9. Indian cession of lands at Presque Isle.

33.—1792, March 3. It is necessary to state that on the 3d of October, 1788, an Act was passed authorizing the Supreme Executive Council to draw on the State Treasurer for a sum of money for defraying the expense of purchasing of the Indians, lands on lake Erie. It is usually called the purchase of the triangle from the United States. This triangle contains two hundred and two thousand one hundred and eighty seven acres of land.

To the student of Pennsylvania history, these facts are worthy of rememberance, because it gives the date and extent of the purchases made from the Indians. We shall now turn our attention to the government of the Province of Pennsylvania, when in its infancy.

On December, 1682, William Penn, in accordance with the sixteenth article of the frame of his government, assembled all the freemen of this Province at Chester (then called Upland), as well as those of the three territories (as they were called), of Newcastle, Kent, and Sussex. At this purely democratic meeting, an act of union passed, annexing the three lower counties (now the State of Delaware) to the Province of Pennsylvania, in legislation.

The Proprietor, by and with the consent of the first Assembly, divided the *Province* of Pennsylvania into three counties, and named them PHILADELPHIA, BUCKS, and CHESTER, while the *Territories* retained the names of New Castle, Kent, and Sussex. For each of the counties and territories, sheriffs and other proper officers were appointed by the Proprietor; but the Council and Assemblymen were elected by the people.

On March 10th, 1683, the Council and Assemblymen met in Philadelphia; each county having returned *three* members for the Council and *nine* for the Assembly.

In the year 1684, William Penn returned to England, leaving commissioners with a President to administer the government during his absence. But this mode of government not proving satisfactory to the three lower counties, its form was changed in 1691; William Markham was appointed Deputy Governor by William Penn. It was at this period that separate legislatures were formed and the Provinces became finally separated.

In August, 1699, William Penn sailed from England to Pennsylvania, and reassumed the reins of government to the entire satisfaction of the people. On the 28th of October, 1701, he presented the Council and Assembly with a new charter of privileges, and having appointed Andrew Hamilton Lieutenant-Governor, sailed for England. This charter continued the supreme law of the Province until the Declaration of Independence was promulgated July 4th, 1776. A court then assembled at Philadelphia, July 8th, 1776, to form a constitution for the State of Pennsylvania, and on the 28th of September following, a constitution was adopted by representatives for the city of Philadelphia and the counties of Philadelphia, Bucks, Chester, Lancaster, York, Cumberland, Berks, Northampton, Bedford, Northumberland, and Westmoreland, being all the counties (eleven in number) which then composed the State of Pennsylvania. It is eminently proper to remark that Benjamin Franklin was President of the Convention which formed the first Constitution for Pennsylvania. Immediately upon his taking his seat, the representatives unanimously passed a resolution inviting the Rev. William White (who afterwards officiated for many years as Bishop of the Protestant Episcopal Church of this diocese) to perform divine service for the Convention, to jointly offer up their prayers to Almighty God to afford His divine grace and assistance in the important and arduous task committed to them as the representatives of the people of Pennsylvania, and to offer up their praises and thanksgiving for the manifold mercies and the peculiar interposition of His special providence in behalf of the injured, oppressed, and insulted United States.

This Constitution was the supreme law of the State, from September 28th, 1776, the date of its final adoption, until September 2d, 1790, when a SECOND constitution was formed by the representatives of the people. On the 9th of October, 1838, a THIRD constitution was adopted by the people; the same having been submitted by a' vote of the Convention which had previously assembled to make the necessary amendments.

Having thus briefly narrated a concise history of the State, and to which we shall often have occasion to refer in the history of Washington County, I shall now turn our attention to the boundaries of Pennsylvania for the like reason.

HISTORY OF WASHINGTON COUNTY.

Pennsylvania extends from north latitude 39° 43′ to north latitude 42°; from 2° 17′ east to 3° 31′ west from Washington city. It is bounded, in common with the State of Delaware, from the Delaware River by a circular line, around New Castle County to the northeast limits of Cecil County, Maryland, . . 24 miles.
Due north to the northeast angle of Maryland, . . 2 "
Along the northern limits of Maryland, . . . 203 "
In common with Virginia, from the northwest angle of Maryland to the southwest angle of Green County, . 59 "
Due north in common with Ohio and Brooke counties of West Virginia to the Ohio River, . . . 64 "
Continuing the last noted limit in common with the Ohio to Lake Erie, ... 91 "
Along the southeast shore of Lake Erie to the Western limit of New York, ... 39 "
Due south, along Chautauque County of New York, to north latitude, 42° . . . . 19 "
Thence due east in common with New York, to the right bank of the Delaware River, ... 230 "
Down the Delaware to the northeast angle of the State of Delaware, ... 230 "

Having an entire outline of . . . . 961 "

The greatest length of Pennsylvania is due west from Bristol, on the Delaware River, to the eastern border of Ohio County in West Virginia, through three hundred and fifty-six minutes of longitude along north latitude, 40° 09′ This distance, on that line of latitude, is equal to two hundred and eighty American statute miles.

The greatest breadth is one hundred and seventy-six miles, from the West Virginia line to the extreme northern angle on Lake Erie, it being one hundred and seventy-five miles. It contains forty-four thousand three hundred and seventeen miles; or twenty-eight million three hundred and sixty-two thousand eight hundred and eight acres of land.

The following table will exhibit the population of Pennsylvania, both as a Province and a State, from 1731, at periods of ten years.

1731— 10,000.	1780— 128,293.	1830—1,348,170.
1740— 14,325.	1790— 474,373.	1840—1,724,033.
1750— 21,000.	1800— 602,545.	1850—2,314,897.
1760— 31,667.	1810— 810,091.	1860—2,905,215.
1770— 39,665.	1820—1,049,313.	

I shall now close this general history of the State of Pennsylvania, by giving the names of each county; the date of its formation; the number of acres in each, with their respective population, premising the following tabular statements, with the remark, that Cameron County was not organized until after the census of 1860 had been taken, and the population is included in the counties of Clinton,

HISTORY OF WASHINGTON COUNTY. 33

Elk, McKean, and Potter, from which it was taken; while with the part of Venango which was added to Forest by act of Assembly approved October 31st, 1866, the population was transferred but not ascertained.

Name.	Date of Formation.		Acres.	Populat'n.
1. Philadelphia	Mar. 10, 1682,	one of Penn's original counties	80,640	565,529
2. Chester	Mar. 10, 1682,	" " "	472,320	74,578
3. Bucks	Mar. 10, 1682,	" " "	387,200	63,578
4. Lancaster	May 10, 1729,	from a part of Chester	608,000	116,314
5. York	Aug. 19, 1749,	" " Lancaster	576,000	68,200
6. Cumberland	Jan. 27, 1750,	" " Lancaster	348,160	40,098
7. Berks	Mar. 11, 1752,	from a part of Philadelphia, Chester, and Lancaster	588,800	93,818
8. Northampton	Mar. 11, 1752,	from a part of Bucks	240,000	47,904
9. Bedford	Mar. 9, 1771,	" " Cumberland	636,160	26,736
10. Northumberland	Mar. 27, 1772,	from a part of Cumberland, Berks, Bedford, and Northampton	292,480	28,922
11. Westmoreland	Feb. 26, 1773,	from a part of Bedford, and in 1785 part of the Indian purchase of 1784 was added	672,000	53,736
12. Washington	Mar. 28, 1781,	from a part of Westmoreland	573,440	46,805
13. Fayette	Sept. 26, 1783,	" " Westmoreland	527,360	39,909
14. Franklin	Sept. 9, 1784,	" " Cumberland	480,000	42,126
15. Montgomery	Sept. 10, 1784,	" " Philadelphia	303,080	70,500
16. Dauphin	Mar. 4, 1785,	" " Lancaster	357,760	46,756
17. Luzerne	Sept. 25, 1782,	" " Northumberland	896,000	90,244
18. Huntingdon	Sept. 20, 1787,	" " Bedford	537,600	28,100
19. Allegheny	Sept. 24, 1788,	from a part of Westmoreland and Washington	482,560	178,831
20. Mifflin	Sept. 19, 1789,	from a part of Cumberland and Northumberland	236,800	16,340
21. Delaware	Sept. 26, 1789,	from a part of Chester	113,280	30,597
22. Somerset	April 17, 1795,	" " Bedford	682,240	26,778
23. Greene	Feb. 9, 1796,	" " Washington	389,120	24,343
24. Wayne	Mar. 26, 1796,	" " Northampton	460,800	32,239
25. Lycoming	April 13, 1796,	" " Northumberland	691,200	37,399
26. Adams	Jan. 22, 1800,	" " York	337,920	28,006
27. Centre	Feb. 13, 1800,	from a part of Mifflin, Northumberland, Lycoming, and Huntingdon	688,000	27,000
28. Armstrong	Mar. 12, 1800,	from a part of Alleghany, Westmoreland, and Lycoming	408,960	35,797
29. Beaver	Mar. 12, 1800,	from a part of Alleghany and Wash'n	298,240	29,140
30. Butler	Mar. 12, 1800,	" " Alleghany	502,400	35,594
31. Crawford	Mar. 12, 1800,	" " Alleghany	629,760	48,755
32. Erie	Mar. 12, 1800,	" " Alleghany	480,000	49,432
33. Mercer	Mar. 12, 1800,	" " Alleghany	416,000	36,850
34. Warren	Mar. 12, 1800,	" " Alleg'y and Lycoming	551,040	19,190
35. Venango	Mar. 13, 1800,	" " Alleg'y and Lycoming	330,240	25,043
36. Indiana	Mar. 30, 1803,	from a part of Westmoreland and Lycoming	492,800	33,687
37. M'Kean	Mar. 20, 1804,	from a part of Lycoming	716,800	8,859
38. Clearfield	Mar. 26, 1804,	from a part of Lycoming and Northumberland	761,600	18,759
39. Jefferson	Mar. 26, 1804,	from a part of Lycoming	412,800	18,270
40. Potter	Mar. 26, 1804,	" " Lycoming	384,000	11,470
41. Cambria	Mar. 26, 1804,	from a part of Huntingdon, Somerset, and Bedford	428,800	29,155
42. Tioga	Mar. 26, 1804,	from a part of Lycoming	714,240	31,044
43. Bradford*	Feb. 21, 1810,	" " Luzerne and Lycoming	751,360	48,734
44. Susquehanna	Feb. 21, 1810,	" " Luzerne	510,080	36,267
45. Schuylkill	Mar. 1, 1811,	" " Berks and Northamp.	485,400	89,510
46. Lehigh	Mar. 6, 1812,	" " Northampton	232,960	43,753
47. Lebanon	Feb. 16, 1813,	" " Dauphin and Lancast.	195,840	31,831
48. Columbia	Mar. 22, 1813,	" " Northumberland	275,840	25,065
49. Union	Mar. 22, 1813,	" " Northumberland	165,120	14,145
50. Pike	Mar. 26, 1814,	" " Wayne	384,000	7,655
51. Perry	Mar. 22, 1820,	" " Cumberland	344,960	22,793
52. Juniata	Mar. 2, 1831,	" " Mifflin	224,640	16,986
53. Monroe	April 1, 1836,	" " Northampton and Pike	384,000	16,758

* Previous to March 24, 1812, this county was called Ontario.

Name.	Date of Formation.	Acres.	Populat'n.
54. Clarion	Mar. 11, 1839, from a part of Venango and Arms'ng.	384,000	24,988
55. Clinton	June 21, 1839, " " Lycoming and Centre	591,360	17,723
56. Wyoming	April 4, 1842, from a part of Northumberland and Luzerne	261,760	12,540
57. Carbon	Mar. 13, 1843, from a part of Northampton and Monroe	256,000	21,033
58. Elk	April 18, 1843, from a part of Jefferson, Clearfield, and McKean	446,720	5,915
59. Blair	Feb. 26, 1846, from a part of Huntingdon and Bedford	380,160	27,829
60. Sullivan	Mar. 15, 1847, from a part of Lycoming	275,200	5,637
61. Forest	April 11, 1848, " " Jefferson and Venango	284,800	898
62. Lawrence	Mar. 25, 1850, " " Beaver and Mercer	229,120	22,999
63. Fulton	April 19, 1850, " " Bedford	268,800	9,131
64. Montour	May 3, 1850, " " Columbia	94,720	13,053
65. Snyder	Mar. 2, 1855, " " Union	187,520	15,035
66. Cameron	Mar. 29, 1860, from a part of Clinton, Elk, M'Kean, Potter (not organized when census was taken.)	268,480	

Pennsylvania has been called the KEYSTONE STATE from the fact of having six of the old original States on each side of her. It is not my province to speak of her majestic mountains, her beautiful rivers and lakes—the variety of her soil—the salubriousness of her climate—and her agricultural, manufacturing, and commercial interests. Mine is a humbler sphere, confined henceforth in this volume exclusively to the history of WASHINGTON COUNTY—the *first* county formed by the legislature of Pennsylvania after the Declaration of Independence had been promulgated to all nations, and Pennsylvania had assumed her rank and place as a free and independent State ; and therefore named after the immortal WASHINGTON. With this remark, we can truthfully say that our citizens therefore will be pre-eminently proud of the character of Washington County, whether viewed in a moral, educational, political, or religious view.

In concluding this chapter I shall add a list of the chief magistrates, or governors, from 1681 to the present time, as being more immediately connected with the general matters therein contained.

ACCESS.   NAMES.   EXIT.

1.—1681. William Penn, Proprietor.   August, 1684.
2.—1684. Thomas Lloyd, Pres't of Governor's Council.   December, 1687.
3.—1687. Thomas Lloyd, Robert Turner, Arthur Cook, John Symcock, and John Eckley appointed Deputy Lieutenants by William Penn.
4.—1688. Capt. John Blackwell, Lieutenant-Governor.   1690.
5.—1690. Thomas Lloyd, Deputy and Lieutenant-Governor.   1693.
6.—1693. Benjamin Fletcher, Captain-General and Lieutenant Governor of New York, Pennsylvania, and the county of New Castle and territories.   September, 1698.
7.—1698. William Markham, Lieutenant-Governor.   1700.
8.—1700. William Penn again acted as Governor to   November 1, 1701.
9.—1701. Andrew Hamilton, Deputy-Governor.   February, 1703.
10.—1703. Edward Shippen, President of Council   " 1704.
11.—1704. John Evans, Deputy-Governor,   " 1709.
12.—1709. Charles Gookin, "   May 31, 1717.
13.—1717. Sir William Keith, "   June 22, 1726.
14.—1726. Patrick Gordon, "   August 5, 1736.

HISTORY OF WASHINGTON COUNTY.   35

ACCESS.   NAMES.   EXIT.
15.—1736. On the death of Governor Gordon, the Council consisted of James Logan, Samuel Preston, Anthony Palmer, Clement Plumstead, Thomas Lawrence, Ralph Asheton, Samuel Hasill, and Thomas Griffits, who elected James Logan President of Council.   June, 1738.
16.—1738. George Thomas, Lieutenant-Governor.   " 1747.
17.—1747. Anthony Palmer, President of Council.   November, 1748.
18.—1748. James Hamilton, Lieutenant-Governor.   October, 1754.
19.—1754. Robert Hunter Morris   "   August, 1756.
20.—1756. William Denny   "   November, 1759.
21.—1759. James Hamilton   "   October, 1763.
22.—1763. John Penn, son of Rich'd Penn, Deputy-Governor. May, 1771.
23.—1771. Richard Penn, Governor.   August, 1773.
24.—1773. John Penn,   "   July, 1775.

Under the Council of Safety.

25.—1775. Benjamin Franklin, President of the Council,   August, 1776.

Under the Constitution of September 28, 1776.

26.—1776. Thomas Wharton, President of the Supreme Executive Council.   October, 1777.
27.—1777. Joseph Read, President of the Supreme Executive Council.   November, 1781.
28.—1781. William Moore, President of the Supreme Executive Council   November, 1782.
29.—1782. John Dickson, President of the Supreme Executive Council.   November, 1785.
30.—1785. Benjamin Franklin, President of the Supreme Executive Council. November, 1788.
31.—1788. Thomas Mifflin, President of the Supreme Executive Council.   September, 1790.
When the Constitution went into operation.

Popular Vote of Candidates for Governor under the Constitution of September 2, 1790.

ELECTION.   MAJORITY.
32.—1790. Thomas Mifflin, ... 27,725
          Arthur St. Clair, ... 2,803   24,522
                                Whole number, 30,528

32.—1793. Thomas Mifflin, ... 19,590
          F. A. Muhlenburg, ... 10,700   8,890
                                Whole number, 30,290

32.—1796. Thomas Mifflin, ... 30,029
          F. A. Muhlenburg, ... 10,011   20,018
                                Whole number, 40,040

33.—1799. Thomas McKean, ... 37,244
          James Ross, ... 22,643   14,601
                                Whole number, 59,887

36   HISTORY OF WASHINGTON COUNTY.

ELECTION.   MAJORITY.
33.—1802. Thomas McKean, ... 47,879
          James Ross, ... 17,037 ⎫
          Scattering, ...   94 ⎭ 30,748

                    Whole number, 57,472

33.—1805. Thomas McKean, ... 43,644
          Simon Snyder, ... 38,483 ⎫
          Samuel Snyder, ...   395 ⎭   4,766

                    Whole number, 82,522

34.—1808. Simon Snyder, ... 67,975
          James Ross, ... 39,575 ⎫
          John Spayd, ...   4,006 ⎬
          Scattering, ...   8 ⎭ 24,386

                    Whole number, 111,564

34.—1811. Simon Snyder, ... 52,319
          William Tilghman, ...   3,609 ⎫
          Scattering, ...   1,675 ⎭ 47,035

                    Whole number, 57,603

34.—1814. Simon Snyder, ... 51,099
          Isaac Wayne, ... 29,566 ⎫
          George Littimore, ...   910 ⎬
          Scattering, ...   18 ⎭ 20,605

                    Whole number, 81,593

35.—1817. William Findley, ... 66,331
          Joseph Hiester, ... 59,272 ⎫
          Scattering, ...   11 ⎭   7,048

                    Whole number, 125,614

36.—1820. Joseph Hiester, ... 67,905
          William Findley, ... 66,300 ⎫
          Scattering, ...   21 ⎭   1,584

                    Whole number, 134,226

37.—1823. J. Andrew Shultz, ... 89,928
          Andrew Gregg, ... 64,211 ⎫
          Scattering, ...   8 ⎭ 25,709

                    Whole number, 154,147

37.—1826. J. Andrew Shultz, ... 72,710
          John Sergeant, ...   1,175 ⎫
          Scattering, ...   1,174 ⎭ 70,361

                    Whole number, 75,059

HISTORY OF WASHINGTON COUNTY.

ELECTION.			MAJORITY.
38.—1829.	George Wolf,	78,219	
	Joseph Ritner,	61,776 ⎫	
	Scattering,	12 ⎭	16,433
	Whole number,	140,007	
38.—1832.	George Wolf,	91,335	
	Joseph Ritner,	88,165	3,170
	Whole number,	179,500	
39.—1835.	Joseph Ritner,	94,023	
	George Wolf,	65,804 ⎫	
	H. A. Muhlenberg,	40,586 ⎭	
	Whole number,	200,413	

Of these votes Messrs. Wolf and Muhlenberg had . . . 106,390
Joseph Ritner, ... 94,023

Thus making Joseph Ritner a minority Governor by . . . 12,377

Under the Constitution of October 9, 1838.

40.—1838.	David R. Porter,	127,821	
	Joseph Ritner,	122,325	5,496
	Whole number,	250,146	
40.—1841.	David R. Porter,	136,504	
	John Banks,	113,473 ⎫	
	F. Julius Lemoyne,	763 ⎬	
	Scattering,	23 ⎭	22,245
	Whole number,	250,763	
41.—1844.	Francis R. Shunk,	160,322	
	Joseph Markle,	156,040 ⎫	
	F. Julius Lemoyne,	2,566 ⎭	1,716
	Whole number,	318,928	
41.—1847.	Francis R. Shunk,	146,081	
	James Irvin,	128,148 ⎫	
	E. C. Reigart,	11,247 ⎬	
	F. Julius Lemoyne,	1,861 ⎬	
	Scattering,	6 ⎭	4,819
	Whole number,	287,343	
42.—1848.	William F. Johnston,	168,522	
	Morris Longstreth,	168,225 ⎫	
	E. D. Gazzam,	48 ⎬	
	Scattering,	24 ⎭	225
	Whole number,	336,819	

ELECTION.				MAJORITY.
43.—1851.	William Bigler,	186,499		
	William F. Johnston,	178,034	⎫	
	Kimber Cleaver,	1,859	⎬	6,539
	Scattering,	67	⎭	
	Whole number,	366,459		
44.—1854.	James Pollock,	203,822		
	William Bigler,	166,991	⎫	
	B. Rush Bradford,	2,194	⎬	34,604
	Scattering,	33	⎭	
	Whole number,	373,040		
45.—1857.	William F. Packer,	188,846		
	David Wilmot,	146,139	⎫	
	Isaac Hazelhurst,	28,168	⎬	14,527
	Scattering,	12	⎭	
	Whole number,	363,165		
46.—1860.	Andrew G. Curtin,	262,349		
	H. D. Foster,	230,239		32,110
	Whole number,	492,588		
46.—1863.	Andrew G. Curtin,	269,506		
	George W. Woodward,	254,171	⎫	
	Scattering,	2	⎬	15,333
	Whole number,	523,679		
47.—1866.	John W. Geary.	307,274		
	Hiester Clymer,	290,096		17,178
	Whole number,	597,370		
48.—1869.	John W. Geary,	290,552		
	Asa Packer,	285,956		4,596
	Whole number,	576,508		

Although the State of Pennsylvania has had but forty-eight governors, yet from the numbers attached to their names we learn some have filled the office two and even three terms.

We shall close this chapter by giving an extract from the 41st chapter of the acts of the first General Assembly of Pennsylvania, passed December 7th, 1682, from which it appears that the first settlers began the year in March, and repudiated the heathen names as now applied to the days of the week, evidently demonstrating that our forefathers were governed by a religious sentiment in our organization as a colony. The following is a literal copy:—

"And bee it enacted by the authority aforesaid, that ye days of ye week and ye months of ye year shall be called as in Scripture, and not by heathen names (as are vulgarly used), as ye first, second, third daies of ye week, and first second and third months of ye year, beginning with ye day called Sunday and ye month called March."

CHAPTER III.

ORIGINAL ACT ESTABLISHING WASHINGTON COUNTY.

Divisions by the formation of townships—Its original and present townships and boroughs—Its present boundaries with topographical and geographical description and its streams—Its early religious element and the religious agreement of 1782—Marriage custom and ceremony—School-houses.

HAVING in the preceding chapters confined myself to the primitive history of what is now known as Washington County, originally belonging to Virginia, and also a general outline history of Pennsylvania, and thereby laid the foundation stone upon which to erect the superstructure, I shall now proceed with the general history of Washington County.

On the 28th of March 1781, the legislature of Pennsylvania passed an act for erecting part of the county of Westmoreland into a separate county, and the reasons given in the preamble to said act are in these words: Whereas, the inhabitants of that part of Westmoreland County which lies west of the Monongahela River, have represented to the Assembly of this State the great hardships they lie under, from being so far remote from the present seat of judicature and the public offices; for to remedy these inconveniences they therefore passed the act of separation. The act is in eighteen sections (the preamble being numbered the first), which we will refer to, either at length or by giving a summary of the contents of each separately.

Section second gives the boundaries of Washington County as follows: all that part of the State of Pennsylvania west of the Monongahela River, and south of the Ohio, beginning at the junction of the said rivers, thence up the Monongahela River aforesaid, to the line run by Mason and Dixon; thence by the said line due west to the end thereof; and from thence the same course, to end of five degrees of west longitude, to be computed from the River Delaware; thence by a meridian line, extended north, until the same shall intersect the Ohio River, and thence by the same to the place of beginning (the said lines from the end of Mason and Dixon's line to the Ohio River to be understood as to be hereafter ascertained by commissioners now appointed or to be appointed for that purpose), shall be and the same is hereby declared to be erected into a county, henceforth to be called Washington.

Section third gives the same rights and privileges to the inhabitants as enjoyed by other counties in the State.

Section fourth authorizes the trustees to take assurance of ground whereon to erect a court-house and prison, and divide the county into townships, before July 1st, 1781.

Section fifth empowers the inhabitants to elect Inspectors, two Representatives for the Assembly, one member of the Supreme Executive Council, two persons for Sheriff, two for Coroner, and three Commissioners. The election was ordered to be held at the house of David Hoge, at the place called CATFISH CAMP, now Washington.

Section sixth. Justices of the Supreme Court to have like powers and authorities in Washington County.

Sections seventh and eighth provide for an election for justices of the peace, to be held on the 15th of July, 1781, for the various townships, after judges and inspectors have been elected.

Section ninth. Justices of the peace authorized to hold courts of General Quarter Sessions and Gaol Delivery.

Section tenth. James Edgar, Hugh Scott, Van Swearingen, Daniel Leet, and John Armstrong appointed commissioners to purchas. ground for a court-house, as provided for in section four.

Sections eleventh and twelfth provide for the mode of defraying the expenses of the public buildings.

Section thirteenth. For the continuance of suits commenced in the original county.

Sections fourteenth, fifteenth and sixteenth provide for the appointment of a collector of the excise, his powers and fees.

Section seventeenth directs the Sheriff and Coroner of Westmoreland County to officiate until those officers could be chosen in the new county.

Section eighteenth directed the amount of the security to be given by the Sheriff and Treasurer.

DIVISION OF WASHINGTON COUNTY.

The inhabitants of Washington County, with those of Westmoreland, considering their counties were too extensive, and that they were subject to many inconveniences from their being situated at so great a distance from the seat of justice, conceived that their interests and happiness would be greatly promoted by being erected into a new and separate county; the legislature, on the 24th of September, 1788, gratified their requests, and erected *Alleghany County.* We shall give the original boundaries of this new county, so that we can trace on the map, the territory which was struck off from Washington County. Beginning *at the mouth of Flagherty's Run, on the south side of the Ohio River, from thence, by a straight line, to the plantation on which Joseph Scott, Esquire, now lives, on Montour's Run, to include the same; from thence, by a straight line, to the mouth of Miller's Run, in Chartiers' Creek; thence by a straight line, to the mouth of Perry's Mill Run, on the east side of Monongahela River; thence up the said river to the mouth of Becket's*

Run; thence by a straight line to the mouth of Sewickley Creek, on Youghiogheny River; thence down the said river to the mouth of Crawford's Run; thence by a straight line to the mouth of Bush Creek, on Turtle Creek; thence up Turtle Creek to the main fork thereof; thence by a northerly line until it strikes Puckety's Creek; thence down the said creek to the Allegheny River; thence up the Allegheny River to the northern boundary of the State; thence along the the same to the river Ohio, and thence up the same to the place of beginning. The above portion of the line *italicized* is the portion taken from Washington County.

But the inhabitants of Washington County still seemed desirous of having justice administered to them at their very doors, again petitioned the legislature to annex a certain part of this to Allegheny County; and on the 17th of September, 1789, the General Assembly believing their prayer to be just and reasonable, granted their request. The boundaries of that part of Washington, annexed to Allegheny County, began at the river Ohio, where the boundary line of the State crosses the said river; from thence in a straight line, to White's mill, on Racoon Creek; from thence by a straight line, to Armstrong's mill, on Miller's Run, and from thence by a straight line, to the Monongahela River, opposite the mouth of Perry's Run, where it strikes the present line of Allegheny County.

By this act of annexation, the whole of *Dickinson* and part of *Cecil township* became part of Allegheny County; according to a decision of the Supreme Executive Council. Peter Kidd and John Beaver were authorized to have the boundary lines marked, each being allowed twenty-five shillings per day, out of the treasury of Allegheny County.

On the 9th of FEBRUARY, 1796, another portion of the territory of Washington County was erected into GREENE County. The boundary line began at *the mouth of Tenmile Creek, on the Monongahela River; thence up Tenmile Creek to the junction of the north and south forks of said creek; thence up said north fork to Colonel William Wallace's mill; thence up a southwesterly direction to the nearest part of the dividing ridge between the north and south forks of Tenmile Creek; thence along the top of the said ridge to the ridge which divides the waters of Tenmile and Wheeling creeks; thence a straight line to the head of Enlow's branch of the Wheeling;* thence down said branch to the western boundary of the State; thence south along the said line to the southern boundary line of the State; thence east along said line to the river Monongahela, and thence down the said river to the place of beginning.

The words *italicized* form the southern line separating Washington and Greene counties.

The officers of Washington County were authorized to exercise the duties of their office in the new county (except justices of peace) until similar officers were appointed. Washington and Greene were to elect, jointly, four representatives; while Washington, Allegheny, and Greene were to compose the congressional district.

On the 22d of January, 1802, by authority of the legislature of Pennsylvania, the following alteration took place in the line between the counties of Washington and Greene; beginning at the present line, on the ridge that divides the waters of the Tenmile and Wheeling creeks, near Jacob Bobbett's; thence a straight line, to the head-waters of Hunter's fork of Wheeling Creek, and thence down the same, to the mouth thereof, where it meets the present county line.

The act of the same date declares that so much of the county of Greene, which, by the act, is reunited to the county of Washington, as lies west of the road called Ryerson's Road, is hereby annexed to Findley township, and shall hereafter be a part of the district called Stevenson's election district, and that part thereof, which lies east of said road is hereby annexed to Morris township, and shall hereafter be a part of the Washington elected district.

The Governor was authorized to appoint two commissioners to run and mark the aforesaid line; the expense to be borne equally out of the treasury of both counties.

By the erection of Greene County, Morgan, Cumberland, Franklin, Greene, and Rich Hill townships became component parts of Greene County.

On the 12th of March, 1800, an act was passed by the General Assembly, erecting parts of Washington and Alleghany counties into a new county, to be called BEAVER. The boundary line began at the mouth of the Sewickley Creek on the Ohio River; thence up the said creek to the west line of Alexander's district of depreciation lands; thence northerly along the said line, and continuing the same course to the north line of the first donation district; thence westerly along the said line to the western boundary of the State; thence southerly along the said boundary, across the Ohio River to a point in the said boundary, *from which a line to be run at right angles easterly will strike White's mill on Racoon Creek, and from such point along the said easterly line to the said mill; thence on a straight line to the mouth of Big Sewickley Creek, the place of beginning.* (The words *italicized* is the boundary line between Washington and Beaver counties). The expense of running the line was to be borne by Beaver County.

ORIGINAL TOWNSHIPS.

The organic act authorized the trustees to divide the county into a suitable number of townships. In accordance therewith, the trustees subdivided it into thirteen townships, in commemoration of the thirteen States which formed the United States. Their names in alphabetical order were: 1. Amwell; 2. Bethlehem; 3. Cecil; 4. Cumberland; 5. Donegal; 6. Fallowfield; 7. Hopewell; 8. Morgan; 9. Nottingham; 10. Peters; 11. Robison; 12. Straban; 13. Smith.

These townships went into operation on the 15th of July, 1781, by the provisions of the act of the legislature and the election of township officers.

As the county became more thickly settled, the people felt the necessity of forming new townships and boroughs. This power was confined to the legislature until the 24th of March, 1803, when it was transferred to the courts of Quarter Sessions, although it appears that in some few cases the courts had exercised it.

By the erection of new counties out of Washington, whole townships and parts of townships were cut off, and at the present time, May, 1870, we find that Washington County has eleven boroughs and thirty-one townships within her limits.

We shall now add this list with their respective organizations, from the formation of Washington County.

o. t.* 1.—Amwell township, formed July 15, 1781.
o. t. 2.—Bethlehem " " "
o. t. 3.—Cecil " " "
o. t. 4.—Cumberland " " "
o. t. 5.—Donegal " " "
o. t. 6.—Fallowfield " " "
o. t. 7.—Hopewell " " "
o. t. 8.—Morgan " " "
o. t. 9.—Nottingham " " "
o. t. 10.—Peters " " "
o. t. 11.—Robison " " "
o. t. 12.—Straban " " "
o. t. 13.—Smith " " "
t. 14.—Somerset township, formed April 3, 1782.
t. 15.—Greene " " "
t. 16.—Dickinson " " September 15, 1785.
b. 1.—Washington, (town,) formed February 6, 1786.
t. 17.—Hanover township, ". March 11, 1786.
t. 18.—Franklin " " July 16, 1787.
t. 19.—Findley " " May 6, 1788.
t. 20.—Morris " " March 13, 1788.
d. t. 1.—East Bethlehem " " January 18, 1790. (See Bethlehem township.)
d. t. 2.—West Bethlehem township, formed January 18, 1790. (See Bethlehem township.)
t. 21.—Chartiers township, formed March 12, 1790.
t. 22.—Cross Creek " " March 23, 1790.
t. 23.—Canton " " June 10, 1791.
d. t. 3.—Pike Run " " January 8, 1792.
d. t. 4.—Rich Hill " " March 13, 1793.
t. 24.—Buffalo " " May 8, 1799.
b. 7.—Cannonsburg " " February 22, 1802. (See Chartiers township.)

---

* Explanation of letters—o. t. means original townships; d. t. divided townships; b. boroughs.

HISTORY OF WASHINGTON COUNTY.

T. 25.—Mount Pleasant township, formed May 12, 1806.
B. 10.—West Middletown borough, formed March 27, 1823.
D. T. 5.—East Findley township, formed December 24, 1828. (See Findley township.)
D. T. 6.—West Findley township, formed December 24, 1828. (See Findley township.)
D. T. 7.—North Straban township, formed May 2, 1831. (See Straban township.)
D. T. 8.—South Straban township, formed May 2, 1831. (See Straban township.)
B. 8.—Claysville borough, formed April 2, 1832.
T. 26.—Carrol township, formed September 30, 1834.
B. 4.—Greenfield borough, formed April 9, 1834. (See Pike Run township.)
T. 27.—Union township, formed March 31, 1836.
D. T. 9.—East Pike Run township, formed March 9, 1839.
D. T. 10.—West Pike Run township, formed March 9, 1839.
B. 3.—Monongahela City, formed April 1, 1837. (See Carrol township.)
B. 2.—Millsborough, formed April 16, 1840. (See Bethlehem township).
B. 5.—West Brownsville borough, formed April 2, 1852. (See Pike Run township.)
B. 6.—Beallsville borough, formed February 16, 1852. (See Pike Run township.)
T. 28.—Allen township, formed June 14, 1853.
T. 29.—Jefferson " " June 16, 1853.
B. 9.—California borough, formed November 26, 1853. (See Pike Run township.)
T. 30.—Independence township, formed May 19, 1855.
T. 31.—Franklin " " August 13, 1855.
B. 11.—Bentleysville borough, formed May 2, 1868. (See Somerset township.)

Of these boroughs and townships we shall give a detailed account in Chapter V. as far as we have been able to ascertain their history, and particularly those which now embrace this county.

Its Boundaries.

The present limits of Washington County, therefore, may be thus defined geographically—bounded on the north by Beaver County, northeast by Allegheny County, east by Westmoreland and Fayette counties, south by Greene County, and west by the State of West Virginia. Its greatest length is thirty-two miles, its mean width, twenty-eight miles, containing 896 square miles, or 573,440 acres of land, in latitude 40°10'21" north, and longitude from Washington 3°12'53" west. Its population in 1790 was 23,866; in 1800, 28,293; in 1810, 36,289; in 1820, 40,038; in 1830, 42,860; in 1840, 41,279; in 1850, 44,939, and in 1860, 46,805.

Topographical Description.

This county is watered by many streams (which will be given in a separate chapter), but suffice it to say, however, that many valleys are formed, of greater or less width and depth, by their indentation, hence, the county presents a rolling character, and although not belonging to the class called mountainous, yet may be termed hilly. These hills are cultivated to the very tops, and in point of agriculture and grazing are not inferior to any in the State. The undulating surface of the county presents scenery unsurpassed and picturesque, supporting thousands of sheep, and is truly deserving the name of being the largest wool-growing county in the State, and the second in the United States for the quality of the wool.

GEOLOGICAL DESCRIPTION.

In a geological view, the rocks belong to the upper series of our bituminous coal formation, consisting of alternate strata of sandstone, shales, and limestone, with interposed beds of coal from three to six or eight feet it thickness. These nearly level strata extend over the whole surface of this and a great part of the adjoining counties, are sometimes cut through by the deep valleys of the streams and exposed in varied succession in the steep banks and along the hill sides, in situations favorable to access and affording great facilities for mining and quarrying. Coal for domestic consumption is abundant in every part of the county and along the bank of the Monongahela. It is mined in great quantities and sent down the Ohio River in boats.

STREAMS.

We add a list of the streams of this county, with their tributaries and localities.

The MONONGAHELA RIVER, which flows through the eastern part of Washington County, rises in Randolph County, Virginia, at the foot of the Laurel Mountain, and flowing northwardly for about three hundred miles, empties into the Allegheny River at Pittsburg and forms the Ohio. It is nearly four hundred yards wide at its mouth, and is navigable for light boats sixty miles, to West Brownsville, in this county, and for small boats nearly two hundred miles from its mouth. Its principal tributaries are the Youghiogheny and Cheat rivers, which enter into it on the east side, but on the west side, in Washington County, are *Tenmile Creek, Pigeon Creek, Baker and Fish Pot runs, Pike Run, South Fork and Maple Fork, Mingo Creek.*

TENMILE CREEK empties into the Monongahela River at Clarksville, Greene County; the *north fork* of this creek rises in Morris township and waters the townships of East and West Bethlehem, Amwell and Morris, its tributaries being *Middle Fork, Craft's Fork, Road's Fork, Hoosang's Fork, McFarlane's Fork, Bane's Fork,* with Kembler's and McGiffin's Run. Coniconick empties into Craft's Fork at Prosperity. Its Indian name is *Cusuthee.*

LITTLE NORTH FORK, with its tributaries, Brush Run, Camp's Fork, Carter's Run, Daniel's Run, Hawkin's and Plumb Hill forks, empties into it. On both branches of Tenmile Creek are many grist and saw-mills.

PIGEON CREEK empties into the Monongahela at Monongahela City. It rises by two branches in Somerset township and flows northeast through Fallowfield township. Its length is about fifteen miles.

MINGO and LITTLE MINGO creeks rise in Nottingham township, and flow east to the Monongahela.

BAKER AND FISH POT runs empty into it in East Bethlehem township.

PETERS' CREEK and its branch called *Pine Branch*, Fry's Branch, and Bruce's Run, empty into the Monongahela River.

CHARTIERS' CREEK flows a north-northeast course of thirty-five or forty miles and empties into the Ohio River five miles above Pittsburg. Its tributaries are Catfish Run, Braddock's Run, Weirich's Run, Leet's Run, north branch of Chartiers', Quail's Run, Little Chartiers' Creek and its tributaries, Vance's, Little's, Pollock's, McCorkle's, Kenny's, and Brush runs on the east and west side of this creek, emptying into the Ohio River below Pittsburg. Miller's Run rises in Mount Pleasant township and empties into Little Chartiers' Creek. Robeson's Run rises about two miles north of Candor and empties into Racoon. This creek flows through the townships of Robinson, Cecil, Mount Pleasant, Chartiers', Canton, North and South Strabane, Somerset, Amwell, and Morris.

This creek derives its name from Peter Chartiers, who went among the Indians on the Ohio and tributary streams to deal for peltries. He was an influential Indian interpreter, and joined the French Indians on the Ohio, to the injury of Pennsylvania. Chartiers had a trading station on or near the mouth of the creek. Governor Thomas, in 1745, said that the perfidious blood of the Shawnees partly runs in his veins.

BIG AND LITTLE RACOON rise in Mount Pleasant township; the former near Hickory, and the latter near David Lyle's, in the vicinity of Prospect Church. The tributaries of these creeks are Boyd's, Burgett's, Cherry Valley, Bailey's, Painter's, Patrick's, and Brimner and Brush runs. These different streams water the townships of Hanover, Robeson, Smith, and Mount Pleasant.

HARMAN'S CREEK rises in Smith township, and with its tributaries of Tucker and Buffalo runs, empties into the Ohio River near Georgetown, watering the townships of Smith, Hanover, and Cross Creek. Its length is about twelve miles.

INDIAN or KING CREEK (northeast branch) and Tomlinson's Run rise in Hanover township near Florence.

CROSS CREEK rises in Mount Pleasant township and runs northwest to the Ohio River, a few miles above Wellsburg, West Virginia. Its tributaries are Stewart's Run—the *middle* fork, with Smiley's Run, Lyle's Run; the *North* Fork rises near Cross Creek Village. This

HISTORY OF WASHINGTON COUNTY. 47

creek flows through the township of Mount Pleasant, Cross Creek, and empties into the main branch of the creek at Patterson's mills.

BUFFALO CREEK rises in East Findley; its tributaries are Brushy Run, Mill Run, Indian Camp Run, Buck Run, and Dutch Fork. These streams flow through the townships of East Findley, Donegal, Hopewell, and Buffalo, and the creek itself empties into the Ohio River.

WHEELING CREEK rises in East Findley, having for its tributaries Templeton's and Enslow's Fork, Hunter's Fork, and Tucker's Fork; these streams water East and West Findley townships.

LITTLE WHEELING CREEK rises in Donegal township; *Middle* Wheeling Creek, in West Findley township; these two creeks meet at Triadelphia and empty into Wheeling Creek at Shepherd's mills.

EARLY RELIGIOUS ELEMENT.

Our first settlers were composed of the Scotch-Irish element, those who emigrated from the west of Scotland and the north of Ireland, while many others came from Cumberland and York counties, where the same element prevailed, and not a few from Virginia. These early pioneers, one hundred years ago, crossed the rugged steeps of the Allegheny Mountains, the boisterous waves of the swift-flowing rivers, and penetrated into an unknown wilderness to secure the blessings of civil and religious liberty. No county in the State of Pennsylvania, or probably in the United States, can boast of a purer, better, more intelligent and devoted company of Christians than those who settled in Washington County. Military men are praised for their heroic deeds, statesmen for understanding the great principles of government; but in this instance, men from all nations meet together around one common altar, and declare in the very commencement of their labors, their religious principles—in other words, they laid the corner stone of the religion of Jesus when they first settled Washington County, by entering into solemn engagements. These engagements were binding not only upon the males, but upon the females also. Whole families united in the league or covenant, and the principles of Presbyterianism which they brought with them, as well as those of other religious sects, are so intimately interwoven with our political affairs, that our civil and religious interests are carefully guarded by their descendants.

To illustrate the positions I have assumed, I add a religious agreement entered into between these early pioneers, which I received from the Rev. John T. Fredericks, pastor of the Presbyterian Church at Burgettstown, Washington County; and before giving it I will give the causes which led to its adoption. This " Religious Agreement," entered into on the 14th day of February, 1782, is in the hand-writing of James Edgar, Esq., deceased, who was an Associate Judge of this county. He with five others left York County in 1779—all members of the Presbyterian Church. They made an agreement to locate near each other, so that they might secure to themselves and their families the ordinances and preaching of the gospel, and be the means of collecting a church with like principles together, as they themselves professed.

These families left their eastern homes and travelled through Tygart's Valley and crossed the Monongahela River at Parkinson's Ferry (now Monongahela City). Mr. Hugh Scott, one of the six, settled west of this place; another where Buffalo Church and Village now stand; James Edgar in Cross Creek township, on the farm now owned by Finley Scott, Esq.; another settled near to Briceland's Cross Roads (now Florence); and another, Patrick McCullough, in what became Mill Creek Congregation, in Beaver County; yet no two settled together, but in contiguous neighborhoods, and each had the pleasure of seeing a church of their denomination to which he belonged erected to God and dedicated to his glory. At the time of this "Religious Agreement" there were no altar and no church but the forts and the woods, in which God was worshipped with pure hearts, and in the beauty of holiness and the purity of truth. This ADVANCE GUARD of the church met, and while the minister officiated, and prayer and praise went up from pure hearts, sanctified by the grace of God, they grasped the faithful rifle to defend themselves against the insidious attacks of the Indians. The Rev. Dr. John Stockton, in his fortieth anniversary sermon, says: "In these forts (Wells' and Vance's) social and afterwards public worship was kept up for seven years, especially in summer and autumn, the seasons when the Indians were out west to make their raids, and it was a common thing for men to go to these meetings armed with their trusty rifles, and to stand guard during the services." Dr. Stockton also adds, that the Rev. James Powers "preached the first gospel sermon under an oak tree just outside the gate of Vance's Fort. It was on this occasion that Dr. Powers baptized the child of Mr. Marquis, which was the first person who received that rite in that region of country."

With these remarks we now add the document itself, with the list of names attached, many of whose descendants are living lives of virtue, of honor, and of honesty, around and near the old family hearthstones, consecrated by the prayers of many an aged father and mother, who have crossed the Jordan of death, and beckon their descendants to the ineffable joys of the spirit world.

RELIGIOUS AGREEMENT.

We, and each of us, whose names are underwritten, being chiefly the inhabitants of the western frontier of Washington County, considering the many abounding evils in our own hearts and lives, as also the open and secret violation of the holy law of God, which dishonors His name and defiles and ruins our country; such as ignorance, unbelief, hardness of heart, contempt of God in his ordinances, law, and gospel (in particular in setting our hearts upon the creature in one line or another more than upon God), breach of his Sabbath, disobedience to parents, backbitings, entertaining bad thoughts, and receiving groundless evil reports of others, unfaithfulness to God for His mercies, profaning His name, uncleanness, lascivious songs, filthy discourse, promiscuous dancing, drunkenness, defraud, deceit, over-reaching in bargains, gaming, horse racing, cock fighting, shooting for prizes, lying, covetousness, discontent, fretting against the dispensations of God's providence, unfaithfulness for God (in suffering sin to remain on our neighbor unreproved), denying God in the neglect of family and secret worship, catechizing and instruction of our children and servants or slaves, vexatious wranglings, and law suits, together with innumerable evils, provoking God to send down heavy judgments on our land, and to withhold or withdraw His gracious presence, and unfit our soul for enjoying any solid happiness, which we desire to acknowledge with shame and sorrow of heart before God, and do in the strength of God and depending on His Grace for support, solemnly promise (to our power, according to our various places and stations) to engage against, both in ourselves and others, as providence shall give us opportunity, and prudence direct.

In witness whereof, we have hereunto set our hands, this 14th day of February, 1782. (N. B. This is not to be a barrier to prevent any from signing at any time hereafter.)

Robert McCready, William Vance, John Stone, James Edgar, William McCandless, Robert Dunbar, John Robinson, John Donahey, Matthew Hilles, Benjamin Bearkus, John McMillen, Samuel Hindman, George McCulloch, John Ekin, Moses Wallace, David Thompson, Henry McBride, John Dodds, John Strain, James Barr, Thomas Hanna, James Dabbin, Thomas Strain, Samuel Jefferey, Alex. McCandless, Samuel Leeper, James Matthews, William Smith, Thomas Bay, Ebenezer Smith, John Cowen, Thomas Barton, Hugh Sherer, Hugh Newel, Arthur Campbell, John Stephenson, Samuel Johnston, James Loop, John Hustein, William Thompson, William Reno, William Rannells, Henry Graham, William Hughes, William Campbell, Patrick McCormick, John Singer, Joseph Patterson, Daniel C. McCoy, David Kerr, John Morrison, John Stone, William Park, William Smiley, George Marquiss, Mary Marquiss, Thomas Marquiss, Joseph Vance, John Marquiss, William Wallace, Samuel Reed, James Marshall, Elias Newkirk, John Cooper, William McCullough, Alexander Wright, James Jackson, Agness Jackson, Mary Cowen, Sr., Mary Cowan, Jr., Martha Dunbar, Prudence Matthews, Elizabeth E. Hughes, Janet McCandless, Anne Vance, David Rannells, Elizabeth McCullough, Ruth Rannells, Annie Park, Mary Johnston, Martha Edgar, Mary Graham, John Hughes, Gabriel Walker, Alexander Kidd, Jean Patterson.—86. The above signed the first day. Attached is a second additional clause, with 28 names added to the first list. The second clause and names read thus:—

We desire to acknowledge the goodness of God, who hath continued his precious gospel with us in purity, and especially for his late gracious outpourings of divine influence on many parts of the land, and especially here where we were so sunk in carnal security and wordly mindedness, floating along with the flood of vanity. And we desire to lament our barrenness and leanness under these gracious favors, and we do now, in the strength of God, relying on His grace, resolve that we will seek to the Lord for help to improve these precious favors, and knowing that some do oppose the work, and aspersing it as a delusion, &c., we will be guarded in our conduct, careful of our company, and we believe that it is the duty of awakened sinners next to their supplication to the throne of grace, to lay open their case to ministers and experienced Christians, lest Satan and corruption might get the advantage of them, and that we will be careful and watchful to perform the duties required by Christian rules in the families we belong to, as we stand related severally as parents and children, husbands and wives, masters or mistresses, and servants.

Signed in 1786 by Angas Sunderland, Jane Sunderland, Thomas Bay, Elizabeth Bay, Mary Patterson, Sarah Vance, Jean Marquis, Martha Rannells, Robert Morgan, Margaret Marshall, Susannah Patterson, Robert Marshal, Elizabeth Thompson, Tabitha Kirk, Sarah Marquis, Susannah Parke.

May 31, 1787, Thomas Hays, Jos. Colville Vance, William Huston, John M. Cloan, Joseph Wiley, Catharine Edgar, Catharine Phillis, John Sanders, Andrew Ferguson, Elizabeth McMillen, Mary Edgar, Sr., Hannah Huston.

To which names are added these words, "Whole number 114—dead 26." James Edgar, Esq., makes a note below the additional clause of these words, " I believe this additional clause was made on the second day's signing."

Time would fail me were I to give a history of most of these men whose names were subscribed to this religious agreement. Many of them filled high and important stations in church and State, and have bequeathed to their posterity a priceless inheritance. Their descendants linger among us, and the rural cemeteries of Cross Creek, Buffalo, Racoon and Burgettstown, contain the remains of those of whom it can be truthfully said, " Blessed are the dead who die in the Lord."

MARRIAGE CUSTOM AND CEREMONY.

In connection with the church, I shall add a sketch of an old-fashioned wedding party, from the rare work of Rev. Dr. Dodridge, such as was practised by the first settlers.

When neighborhoods became in some degree settled, and boys and girls had grown to manhood and womanhood, mutual love resulted in marriage, which was celebrated different from weddings of the present day. An eye-witness and a participant gives the following glowing description of a wedding day among our early settlers:—

In the morning of the *wedding day* the groom and his attendants assembled at the house of his father for the purpose of reaching the mansion of his bride by noon, which was the usual time for celebrating the nuptials, which for certain must take place before dinner.

Imagine an assemblage of people, without a store, tailor, or mantua-maker within a hundred miles, and an assemblage of horses without a blacksmith or saddler within an equal distance. The gentlemen dressed in shoepacks, moccasons, leather breeches, leggings, linsey hunting shirts, and all home made. The ladies dressed in linsey petticoats and linsey or linen bed-gowns, coarse shoes, stockings, handkerchiefs, and buckskin gloves, if any. If there were any buckles, rings, buttons, or ruffles, they were the relics of old times, family pieces from parents or grandparents. The horses were caparisoned with old saddles, old bridles or halters, and pack-saddles, with a bag or blanket thrown over them. A rope or string as often constituted the girth as a piece of leather.

The march, in double file, was often interrupted by the narrowness and obstructions of our horse-paths, as they were called, for we had no roads, and these difficulties were often increased, sometimes by the good and sometimes by the ill-will of neighbors, by felling trees and tying grape-vines across the way. Sometimes an ambuscade was formed by the wayside, and an unexpected discharge of several guns took place, so as to cover the wedding party with smoke. Let the reader imagine the scene which followed this discharge, the sudden spring of the horses, the shrieks of the girls, and the chivalric bustle of their partners to save them from falling. Sometimes, in spite of all that could be done to prevent it, some were thrown to the ground. If a wrist, elbow, or ankle happened to be sprained, it was tied with a handkerchief, and little more was thought or said about it.

Another ceremony took place before the party reached the house of the bride. When the party were about a mile from the place of their destination, two young men would single out to run for the bottle of whiskey, the worse the path, the more logs, brush, and deep hollows, the better, as these obstacles afforded an opportunity for the greater display of intrepidity and horsemanship. The start was announced by an Indian yell, logs, brush, muddy hollows, hill and glen, were speedily passed by the rival ponies. The bottle was always filled for the occasion, so that there was no use for judges, for the first who reached the door was presented with the prize, with which he returned in triumph to the company. On approaching them, he announced his victory over his rival by a shrill whoop. At the head of the troop he gave the bottle *first* to the groom and his attendants, and then to each pair in succession to the rear of the line, giving each a dram, and then putting the bottle in the bosom of his hunting shirt, took his station in the company.

The ceremony of the marriage preceded the dinner, which was a substantial backwoods feast of beef, pork, fowls, and sometimes venison and bear meat, roasted and boiled, with plenty of potatoes, cabbage, and other vegetables. During the dinner, the greatest hilarity prevailed, although the table might be a large slab of timber hewed out with a broadaxe, supported by four sticks set in auger holes, and the furniture, some old pewter dishes and plates, the rest, wooden bowls and trenchers; a few pewter spoons, much battered about the edges, were to be seen at some tables. The rest were made of horns. If knives were scarce, the deficiency was made up by the scalping knives, which were carried in sheaths, suspended to the belt of the hunting shirt.

After dinner the dancing commenced, and generally lasted till the next morning. The figures of the dancers were three and four handed reels or square sets and jigs. The commencement was always a square four, which was followed by what was called jigging it off, that is, two of the four would single out for a jig, and were followed by the remaining couple. The jigs were often accompanied with what was called "cutting out," that is, when either of the parties became tired of the dance, on intimation, the place was supplied by some one of the company without any interruption of the dance. In this way a dance was often continued till the musician was heartily tired of his situation. Towards the latter part of the night, if any of the company, through weariness, attempted to conceal themselves for the purpose of sleeping, they were hunted up, paraded on the floor, and the fiddler ordered to play "hang out till to-morrow morning."

About nine or ten o'clock a deputation of the young ladies stole off the bride and put her to bed. In doing this it frequently happened that they had to ascend a ladder instead of a pair of stairs, leading from the dining and ball-room to the loft, the floor of which was made of clapboards lying loose and without nails. This ascent one might think would put the bride and her attendants to the blush, but as the foot of the ladder was commonly behind the door (which was purposely opened for the occasion), and its rounds at the inner end were well hung with hunting shirts, petticoats, and other articles of clothing, the candles being on the opposite side of the house, the exit of the bride was noticed but by few.

This done, a deputation of young men in like manner stole off the groom, and placed him snugly by the side of his bride. The dance still continues, and if seats happen to be scarce, which was often the case, every young man when not engaged in the dance was obliged to offer his lap as a seat for one of the girls, and the offer was sure to be accepted. In the midst of this hilarity, the bride and groom were not forgotten. Pretty late in the night some one would remind the company that the new couple must stand in need of some refreshments. Black Betty, which was the name of the bottle, was called for, and sent up the ladder. But sometimes black Betty did not go alone. I have many times seen as much bread, beef, pork, and cabbage sent along with her, as would afford a good meal for a half dozen hungry men. The young couple were compelled to eat and drink more or less, of whatever was offered them.

In the course of the festivity, if any wanted to help himself to a dram, and the young couple to a toast, he would call out, "Where is black Betty? I want to kiss her sweet lips." Black Betty was soon handed to him, then holding her up in his right hand, he would say, "Here's health to the groom, not forgetting myself, and here's to the bride, thumping luck and big children." This, so far from being taken amiss, was considered as an expression of a very proper and friendly wish, for big children, especially sons, were of great importance; every big son being considered as a young soldier.

It often happened that some neighbors or relations not being asked to the wedding took offence, and the mode of revenge adopted was that of cutting off the manes, foretops, and tails of the horses of the wedding company.

On returning to the infare, the order of procession and race for black Betty was the same as before. The feasting and dancing often lasted for several days.

SCHOOL-HOUSES.

The school-house was considered as necessary to the prosperity of a settlement as the church, and the requirements of the schoolmaster were, that he could read, write, and cipher as far as the double rule of three. When such a man offered himself, the neighbors would employ him, and immediately set about the erection of school-house. One would give the ground, some would cut the logs, some would haul them to the appointed place, others would put them up. In the erection of the school-house, a log would be kept out the entire length to answer the purpose of a window. The fireplace was built with logs, with a stone back wall calculated for a back log six feet long. The chimney was built with what was then called "cat and clay chimney." The seats were made of small trees, cut about twelve feet long and split, the flat side dressed smooth with the axe, and legs put in the round side, which stood on an earthen floor. In summer time the dust would be sometimes two inches deep, hence the scholars for amusement would amuse themselves by "kicking up the dust" (which is likely the origin of the expression), to the great annoyance of the schoolmaster, who would use his cat-o'-nine-tails very freely.

In old times, they had a custom which is now, we believe, entirely laid aside. About a week before Christmas the larger scholars would meet in the night to *bar out* the master. On his arrival at the school-room he would endeavor to force his way in, but finding his efforts unavailing, he would enter into an agreement to give them holiday between Christmas and New Year's, give a gallon of whiskey, and lots of ginger-cakes on Christmas day, and play corner ball with the scholars on that occasion.

CHAPTER IV.

PROCEEDINGS OF THE SUPREME EXECUTIVE COUNCIL.

A brief history of the Provincial Conference—The Constitution of 1776; the Council of Censors; the Convention of 1789; the Constitution of 1790; the action of the Legislature of 1825; with regard to a convention, and the vote of the people; the Convention of 1837; the Constitution of 1838, and the full proceedings of the Supreme Executive, from 1781 to 1791, which relates to Washington County.

SUPREME EXECUTIVE COUNCIL.

BEFORE proceeding with the acts of this body, as connected with Washington County, it is necessary to give a history of its rise and origin, as interwoven with the Constitution of 1776.

A provincial conference of committees of the several counties of Pennsylvania convened at Carpenter's Hall, in Philadelphia, on 25th of June, 1776, in consequence of a circular letter from the committee of the city and liberties of Philadelphia, inclosing the resolution of the Continental Congress of the 15th of May, 1776. Returns of delegates were laid before this provincial conference from the city of Philadelphia, and the counties of Philadelphia, Bucks, Chester, Lancaster, Berks, Northampton, York, Cumberland, Bedford, Northumberland, and Westmoreland (these ten counties then composing the province). Thomas McKean was chosen President, Joseph Hart, Vice-President, and Jonathan B. Smith and Samuel C. Morris, Secretaries.

The President directed the reading of the resolution of the 15th of May, 1776, passed by the Continental Congress, which was in these words:—

Whereas, his Britannic majesty, in conjunction with the Lords and Commons of Great Britan, has, by a late act of Parliament, excluded the inhabitants of these United Colonies from the protection of his crown; and whereas no answer whatever to the humble petitions of the colonies for the redress of grievances and reconciliation with Great Britain has been or is likely to be given, but the whole force of that kingdom, aided by foreign mercenaries, is to be exerted for the destruction of the good people of these colonies; and whereas it appears absolutely irreconcilable to reason and good conscience for the people of these colonies now to take the oaths and other matters necessary for the support of any government under the crown of Great Britain, and it is necessary that the exercise of every kind of authority, under the said crown, shall be totally suppressed, and all the powers of government exerted under the authority of the people of the colonies, for the preservation of interval peace, virtue and good order, as well as for the defence of their lives, liberties, and properties, against the hostile invasions and cruel depredations of their enemies; therefore,

Resolved, That it be recommended to the respective assemblies and conventions of the United Colonies, where no government sufficient to the exigencies of their affairs has been hitherto established, to adopt such government as shall, in the opinion of the representatives of the people, best conduce to the happiness and safety of their constituents in particular and America in general.

The Conference adopted the resolution, and resolved to adopt a new government in the province of Pennsylvania, on the authority of the people only.

The Convention appointed Monday the 8th day of July, 1776, for electing members in the different counties to said Convention, and fixed Monday the 15th of July, 1776, for the assembling of the delegates.

On the 15th of July, 1776, delegates from the city of Philadelphia and the ten counties of the State as above specified, met in Philadelphia, and organized by electing Dr. Benjamin Franklin, President; Col. George Ross, Vice-President; John Morris, Secretary. The Convention terminated their session on the 28th of September, 1776, and adopted a constitution, containing a *declaration of rights* and the *frame of government*. The commonwealth was to be governed by an Assembly of the representatives of the freemen of the State, a President and Council. In the House of Representatives the *supreme legislative power* was vested, but in the President and Council the *supreme executive power* was vested, under the title of SUPREME EXECUTIVE COUNCIL.

The first Constitution of Pennsylvania, adopted July 15, 1776, provided that this council should consist of twelve persons, chosen from the counties then in existence, but provided that in case of the formation of new counties, such county or counties shall elect a councillor. The Council was required to meet annually at the same time and place with the General Assembly.

The duties of the President and Executive Council (five of whom constituted a quorum) were to appoint all officers, civil and military, except such as were chosen by the people or the General Assembly, and to fill vacancies, grant pardons, remit fines, grant reprieves, see that the laws were faithfully executed, &c. &c. &c. Two justices of the peace for each district were elected for seven years.

The Constitution also provided that a COUNCIL OF CENSORS should be elected by the people on the second Tuesday of October, 1783, and in every seventh year thereafter, whose duty was to inquire if the Constitution had been preserved inviolate, whether the different branches of government had performed their duties faithfully, and whether the taxes were justly laid, &c. &c., and to call a convention to amend any article of the Constitution which might be defective.

The first *Council of Censors* met on November the 10th, 1783, when *Washington County* was represented by James Edgar and John McDowell. After examining the Constitution and its operation, they appointed several committees and adjourned to June 1, 1784, and after hearing the opinions of the members, they passed a resolution by a vote of fourteen to ten, that there was no absolute necessity to call a convention to alter, explain, or amend the Constitution, but drafted an address to the people on the necessity of supporting the Constitution by giving it a fair and honest trial, and if at the end of seven years it did not answer the desired purpose, to make the necessary change.

On the 24th of March, 1789, a resolution was adopted by the General Assembly by a vote of forty-one to seventeen, that it was necessary to call a convention to revise, alter, and amend the Constitution, and for this purpose the authority was given to the people to elect delegates for that purpose, to meet in Philadelphia on the 24th of November, 1789.

This Convention met at the day appointed, with delegates from the city and county of Philadelphia, and the counties of Bucks, Chester, Lancaster, York, Cumberland, Berks, Northampton, Bedford, Westmoreland, Washington, Fayette, Franklin, Montgomery, Dauphin, Luzerne, Huntingdon, Delaware, Northumberland, and Alleghany (there being twenty counties in the State). The delegates from WASHINGTON County were Alexander Addison, John Hoge, David Reddick, and James Ross. Thomas Mifflin was elected President. This convention adjourned on the 26th of February, 1790, to assemble on the 9th of August following, after having adopted a constitution, which was ordered to be printed for the consideration of the people of Pennsylvania. The reason given for a change is thus explained by Thomas McKean. The balance of the one, the few, and the many, is not well poised in the State; the legislature is too powerful for the executive and judicial branches. We have now but one branch; we must have another branch, a negative in the executive, stability in our laws, and permanency in our magistracy, before we shall be reputable, safe, and happy.

The delegates reassembled at the time and place appointed, and after a careful review and an investigation of the Constitution, adopted the same on *September* 2, 1790, by a vote of sixty-one to one, and was officially proclaimed as such.

In the Constitution of 1790, the legislative power was vested in the Senate and House of Representatives, and not in the House of Representatives alone, as in the Constitution of 1776.

The supreme executive power was vested in the Governor, while in the Constitution of 1776 it was in the President and Supreme Executive Council.

The Constitution of 1790 going into effect, the Supreme Executive Council was abolished, and on the 22d of April, 1794, an act was passed vesting all the powers of the late Supreme Executive Council in the Governor, unless otherwise vested by law. On the 28th of March, 1825, an act was passed by the legislature to ascertain the opinion of the people relative to the call of a convention.

On the second Tuesday of October, 1825, the people, by ballot, decided against the proposed convention. On the second of May, 1837, a State Convention assembled at Harrisburg to amend the Constitution. Hon. John Sergeant, of Philadelphia, was chosen President. This Convention continued in session until the July following, when it adjourned and reassembled in October. In the following December the Convention removed to Philadelphia and finally closed their labors on the 22d of February, 1838. The proposed amendments to the Constitution were adopted by the people at the annual October election of the same year.

I shall now proceed to give extracts from the proceedings of the Supreme Executive Council, on subjects referring to Washington County.

Philadelphia, Monday, April 2, 1781.

Present: His Excellency Joseph Reed, Esq., President, the Vice-President, and members of the Supreme Executive Council.

The Council taking into consideration the act of Assembly passed the 28th inst., entitled "An act for erecting part of the county of Westmoreland into a special county" called by the name of WASHINGTON.

Resolved, That Thomas Scott, Esq., be appointed and commissioned to be the Prothonotary of the said county of Washington.

Resolved, That James Marshal, Esq., be appointed and commissioned to be Lieutenant of the county of Washington, and that John Cannon and David Lite (Leet) be appointed and commissioned to be the sub-Lieutenants of the said county.

Philadelphia, April 4, 1781.

Present: His Excellency Joseph Reed, Esq., President, and Executive Council.

James Marshal, Esq., appointed by the Honorable House of Assembly to be Register for the Probate of Wills and granting letters of administration, and Recorder of Deeds for the county of Washington, and by this Board to be Lieutenant of the said county, attended in council and took the several oaths necessary to qualify him for the said offices respectively.

Philadelphia, April 20, 1781.

Present: His Excellency Joseph Reed, Esq., President, and Executive Council.

Ordered, That Colonel James Marshal, Lieutenant of the county of Washington, be authorized and directed to call out forty men of the militia of that county, or if the militia shall not be organized sufficient for that purpose, to raise the said number of men for the purpose of escorting and guarding the commissioners appointed to run the line between this State and Virginia, during the time they shall be on that service, and that he be authorized to call on the commanding officer at Fort Pitt for ammunition for that purpose.

Col. Daniel Broadhead was commandant at Fort Pitt.

Philadelphia, August 23, 1781.

Present: His Excellency the President and Executive Council.

Returns of Justices for the following townships in the county of Washington were received and read, by which it appears that the following gentlemen were elected:—

Peters township. John Douglass and Robert Thompson.

Nottingham township. Benjamin Parkinson and Joseph Parkinson.

Strabane township. (In which is the place called Catfish Camp, ordered by law to be the seat of justice). Daniel Leet, Henry Taylor, John White, Nicholas Little, Alexander Eddy, and David Clark.

Amwell township. Abner Howell and John Craig.

Donegal township. Samuel Mason and Samuel Williamson.

Hopewell township. William Scott and John Marshall.

Fallowfield township. John Parker, John Hall, east end, and John Stevenson and Patrick McCullough, west end of said township.

Smith's township. Samuel Johnston and James Edgar.

Cecil township. Matthew McConnell and John Reed.

On consideration,

Resolved, That Henry Taylor, William Scott, John Craig, John White, Daniel Leet, John Marshall, John Douglass, Benjamin Parkinson, John Reed, Abner Howell, Matthew McConnell, Samuel Johnston, and Samuel Mason, be appointed and commissioned justices of the peace, of the court of Common Pleas, and of the Orphans' Court of the county of Washington, and that a general commission be issued accordingly.

Philadelphia, October 11, 1781.

Present: The Honorable the Vice-President and Executive Council.

The Council took into consideration a resolve of Congress of the 24th of September last, appointing Brigadier-General William Irvine to the command of Fort Pitt, and thereupon

Ordered, That agreeably to the said recommendation, the Lieutenant of the county of Washington be ordered to call forth, agreeably to law, upon his requisition, such militia as may be necessary for that post and the protection of the county.

Philadelphia, Nov. 19, 1781.

Present: His Excellency the President, the Vice-President, and Executive Council.

Dorsey Pentecost, councillor elect for the county of Washington, attended in council and took the oath of allegiance and oath of office required by the Constitution, and thereupon took his seat at the Board as a member thereof.

Philadelphia, Nov. 21, 1781.

Present: His Excellency the President, Vice-President, and Executive Council.

A return of an election said to have been held at the house of Ezekiel Roe, in Bethlehem township in Washington County, for electing justices of the peace for said township, was presented and read, and on inquiry, it appeared that the said election was not appointed by a justice of the peace for the said county, where a "vacancy had happened," the case provided for by law, but in consequence of a neglect to choose according to the directions of the law, wherefore the said election is void.

The Council therefore proceeded to the choice of a justice of the peace for the said township of Bethlehem, agreeably to the directions of the act of Assembly, entitled "A further supplement to an act entitled, 'an act directing the mode and time of electing justices of the peace for the city of Philadelphia, and the several counties in this commonwealth, and for other purposes herein mentioned,'" and appointed Thomas Crooks, Esq.

Ordered, That he be commissioned accordingly.

IN COUNCIL.   *Philadelphia,* Nov. 24, 1781.

A free conference being had, it appeared to be the sentiments of the Council and of the Committee, that an additional company is necessary for the defence of Washington County, and to complete the four companies now established, and that it might be proper to make application to Congress for such assistance from the United States as would render an incursion into the Indian country prudent and practicable.

IN COUNCIL.   *Philadelphia,* Nov. 30, 1781.

A petition from Thomas Bay, of Washington County, praying to be reimbursed for sundry expenses he has been at in raising twelve volunteers in the spring of the year 1780 for the defence of the said county was read, and thereupon

Resolved, That the said petition be presented to the General Assembly.

A return of the general election of the county of Washington was read, by which it appears that the following gentlemen were duly elected, viz: *Councillor,* Dorsey Pentecost; *Representatives,* James Edgar and John Cannon; *Sheriffs,* Van Swearingen and Andrew Swearingen; *Coroners,* William McFarlane and William McComb; *Commissioners,* George Vallandingham, Thomas Crooks, and John McDowell.

On consideration,

Resolved, That Van Swearingen be appointed sheriff of the county of Washington, and that William McFarlane be appointed coroner of the said county, and that they be commissioned accordingly.

Van Swearingen, Esq., sheriff elect for the county of Washington, now offers Andrew Swearingen and Richard Yeates as sureties for the faithful performance of the duties of his office of sheriff, according to law, and the same are approved.

IN COUNCIL.   *Philadelphia,* Dec. 6, 1781.

Resolved, That William Scott of Cross Creek, and Andrew Heath be appointed agents of forfeited estates in the county of Washington.

IN COUNCIL.   *Philadelphia,* Dec. 11, 1781.

Ordered, That Col. Lewis Farmer be directed to purchase the following articles of clothing for the company of rangers to be raised in Washington County.* Fifty coats, fifty waistcoats, fifty pair of overalls, fifty hats, one hundred shirts, one hundred pairs of shoes, and fifty blankets.

The Hon. Dorsey Pentecost, Esq., presented to the Board a state of the accounts of James Marshal, Esq., Lieutenant of the county of Washington, agreeably to the 19th section of the militia law of this State, and the same being considered,

Resolved, That the said accounts be transmitted to the Auditors of the public accounts.

Philadelphia, Dec. 1, 1781.

A letter from John Conner, Esq., of the 10th inst., inclosing his commission of sub-Lieutenant of the county of Washington, and praying this Board to accept his resignation thereof, was read, and on consideration,

Resolved, That the same be accepted.

* See December 27, 1781.

On consideration,   *Philadelphia*, Dec. 19, 1781.

Ordered, That Captain Joseph Stiles, commissary of military stores, be directed to deliver to the Hon. Dorsey Pentecost, Esq., five hundred weight of gunpowder, one thousand weight of lead, and one thousand flints, to be forwarded to Col. James Marshal, Lieutenant of the county of Washington, for the defence of the frontiers of the said county.

Philadelphia, Dec. 20, 1781.

An order was drawn on the Treasurer in favor of the Honorable John Piper, Esq., for the sum of three pounds specie and the sum of nineteen pounds specie, being money advanced by him for the carriage of Captain Boyd's Company of Rangers in Bedford County, and for the carriage of powder and lead for the counties of WASHINGTON, Westmoreland, and Bedford.

The Honorable Dorsey Pentecost, Esq., presented to the Board his account for 31 days' attendance in Council from the 19th of November to the 20th of December inst., at 25 shillings per day   £38.15

Mileage. 350 miles coming from Washington County at 1 shilling per mile   17.10

Balance specie   £56.05

And therefore an order was drawn on the Treasurer in favor of the Honorable Dorsey Pentecost, Esq., for the sum of fifty-six pounds, five shillings specie, amount of the said account.

Philadelphia, Dec. 24, 1781.

The Council took into consideration the appointment of sub-Lieutenants for the county of Washington, agreeably to the militia laws of this State; and William McCleary, William Parker, George Vallandingham, and Matthew Ritchie being recommended; on consideration,

Resolved, That William McCleary, William Parker, George Valandingham, and Matthew Ritchie be appointed sub-Lieutenants of the county of Washington, and that they be commissioned accordingly.

Philadelphia, Dec. 27, 1781.

The Council, taking into consideration the appointing officers for the Ranging Company for the county of Washington,

Resolved, That John Hughes, Esq., be appointed and commissioned to be Captain of a company of Rangers to be raised in the county of Washington, and that Gabriel Peterson be appointed Lieutenant and James Morrison, Ensign of the said company, and that they be commissioned accordingly.

Philadelphia, Dec. 29, 1781.

On consideration of the proposals made by John Cannon, Esq., for supplying the militia and Rangers of the county of Washington which may be employed for the defence of the frontiers of said county

Ordered, That twelve pence per ration, in specie, be allowed for the rations delivered at such places as the said troops may from time to time be stationed within the said county of Washington.

The rations to consist of

One pound of bread; one pound of beef or three-fourths pound of pork; one gill of whiskey per day and one quart of salt and two quarts of vinegar, to every hundred rations.

Eight pounds of soap and three pounds of candles to every seven hundred rations.

Philadelphia, Jan. 5, 1782.

Resolved, John Hughes be appointed Captain, Gabriel Peterson Lieutenant, and James Morrison Ensign of the Company of Rangers to be raised in the county of Washington for the defence of the frontiers.

Resolved, That the sum of two hundred and fifty pounds specie be paid into the hands of Henry Taylor, Esq., to be by him delivered out to Captain John Hughes, Lieutenant Peterson, and Ensign Morrison for the purpose of recruiting the company of Rangers for the county of Washington.

Philadelphia, Jan. 8, 1782.

The Council, taking into consideration the exposed situation of the frontier counties, the probability of invasions of them by parties of Indians, and the impossibility of obtaining particular orders from the Council for calling out in due time the militia of the said counties in such cases,

Ordered, That the Lieutenant of the county of Washington be authorized and empowered to call out such and so many militia, according to law, as they may judge necessary for repelling the enemy.

Philadelphia, Jan. 29, 1782.

An order was drawn on the Treasurer in favor of John McCashem for the sum of ten pounds specie for paying for the transportation of clothing for the ranging companies of Washington and Westmoreland counties from Philadelphia to Shippensburg.

Philadelphia, Feb. 26, 1782.

A letter from the Commissioners of the Taxes of the county of Washington, respecting the collection of the taxes was received and read, and on consideration ordered that the same be transmitted to the General Assembly of the State.

Philadelphia, March 5, 1782.

Ordered, That Captain Joseph Stiles, Commissary of Military Stores, be directed to deliver to the Honorable Dorsey Pentecost one thousand flints, fifty stand of arms, and fifty pouches, to be forwarded to the Lieutenant of the county of Washington for the use of the Ranging company to be raised in the said county.

Philadelphia, March 9, 1782.

An order was drawn on the Treasurer in favor of the Honorable Christopher Hayes, Esq., for the sum of eighteen pounds fifteen shillings specie for paying for the transportation of arms and ammunition from the city to Conocheague for the defence of the frontiers of Washington, Westmoreland, and Bedford counties.

Philadelphia, March 18, 1782.

The Honorable Dorsey Pentecost, Esq., presented to the Board the following account, viz.,

Dr. The State of Pennsylvania in account with Dorsey Pentecost, Esq., For attendance in council from the 20th of December, 1781, to the 23d of March, 1782—94 days at 17s. 6. £82.5

And thereupon an order was drawn on the Treasurer in favor of the Honorable Dorsey Pentecost, Esq., for the sum of eighty-two pounds, five shillings specie, amount of the said account.

Philadelphia, March 30, 1782.

Ordered, That James Alison be appointed sub-Lieutenant of the county of Washington in the room of Daniel Leet, who has resigned.

Philadelphia, March 30, 1782.

The Board being informed by letter and a return inclosed, on the 4th of February last, from Col. James Marshal, Lieutenant of the county of Washington, that there were irregularities in the election of some of the militia officers of the said county, and others had refused to serve,

Resolved, That the said Lieutenant be directed to proceeded with all convenient speed, to fill up the said vacancies agreeably to law, in order that commissions may issue.

Philadelphia, April 2, 1782.

An order drawn on the Treasurer in favor of the Honorable Dorsey Pentecost, Esq., for the sum of twelve pounds ten shillings specie, to be paid to Adam Poe for taking an Indian scalp in the county of Washington, agreeably to the proclamation of the Board.

Philadelphia, April 3, 1782.

A return of justices for the township of Somerset, in the county of Washington, was received and read, by which it appears that Wm. Parker and John Stevenson were duly elected justices for the said township, thereupon

Resolved, That William Parker, Esq., be appointed a justice of peace for the county of Washington, and commissioned accordingly.

Philadelphia, April 6, 1782.

Ordered, That the Lieutenant of the county of Washington be authorized and required to call into service, and put under the direction of Alexander McClean, Esq., such number of militia as the said McClean may judge necessary for guards to the commissioners for running the line between the States of Virginia and Pennsylvania, not exceeding one hundred.

Philadelphia, April 8, 1782.

The Honorable Dorsey Pentecost, Esq., presented to the Board the following account for his attendance in council, from the 24th of March, till the 9th of April, 1782; 17 days at 17s. 6d. £14 17s. 6d.

Thereupon an order was drawn on the Treasurer in favor of the Honorable Dorsey Pentecost, Esq., for the sum of fourteen pounds seventeen shillings and sixpence specie, amount of the above account.

Philadelphia, April 15, 1782.

A return of justices from Robinson township in the county of Washington was received and read, by which it appears that Alexander Wright and James Ervins were duly elected justices for said township, thereupon,

Resolved, That Alexander Wright be appointed a justice of peace for the county of Washington, and commissioned accordingly.

WHEREAS, It hath been represented to this Board, that the freeholders of the townships of Cumberland and Morgan in the county of Washington (*now Greene*) have each of them neglected to *choose* two fit persons, on the 15th day of July, 1781, agreeable to the act of Assembly passed the 28th of March, 1781, entitled an "Act for erecting part of the county of Westmoreland into a separate county" to serve as justices of the peace.

AND WHEREAS, By a clause in an act of Assembly entitled "A further supplement to the act entitled 'an act directing the mode and time of electing justices of the peace for the city and the several counties of the commonwealth, and for other purposes therein mentioned,' passed August 31, 1778," it is enacted that where the freeholders of any district, county, town, township, or ward within this commonwealth have refused or neglected, or shall hereafter refuse or neglect to elect justices of the peace, agreeably to the directions of the before recited acts, or of the further provisions herein made, that then it shall and may be lawful to and for the President or Vice-president in council, to commission a suitable number of justices of the peace to fill up such vacancies agreeably to the number settled in the aforesaid recited acts, therefore

Ordered, That John Minor be appointed a justice of the peace for the township of Cumberland, and Levi Karrod be a appointed a justice of the peace for the township of Morgan in the county of Washington, and that commissions be issued accordingly.

IN COUNCIL.   *Philadelphia,* April 17, 1782.

An order was drawn on the Treasurer in favor of John Cannon, Esq., for the sum of one hundred pounds specie, in part of contract for supplying the troops stationed in the county of Washington with provisions, for which he is to account.

The Honorable Dorsey Pentecost, Esq., presented to the Board the following account for his attendance in council, viz.:—

From the 9th till the 17th of April, 1782, 8 days at 7s. 6d. $7.00, and thereupon an order was drawn for the amount of said account.

IN COUNCIL.   *Philadelphia,* June 12, 1782.

An order was drawn on the Treasurer in favor of Captain John Hughes of the company of Rangers to be raised in the county of Washington, for the sum of sixty-five pounds specie, being two months pay for himself, Lieutenant Gabriel Peterson and Ensign James Morrison, officers of the said company for which they are to account.

Ordered, That Captain John Hughes, of the company of Rangers to be raised in the county of Washington, be directed to give a bounty, not exceeding nine pounds specie, for such recruits as he may raise till his company be completed.

IN COUNCIL.   *Philadelphia,* July 12, 1782.

Ordered, That the Lieutenant of the county of Washington be directed not to call out a greater number than one hundred militia at any one time for the defence of the frontiers of the county, but by special order of this Board.

IN COUNCIL.   *Philadelphia,* July 25, 1782.

Ordered, That a special commission of Oyer and Terminer and General Gaol Delivery, directed to the Honorable Christopher Hayes and Dorsey Pentecost, Esquires, and Edward Cooke, Esq., be now issued to the county of Washington, for the trial of divers persons now confined in the gaol of the said county charged with high crimes and misdemeanors.

IN COUNCIL.   *Philadelphia,* August 14, 1782.

Ordered, That the county of Washington be directed to make out and return to the Board pay rolls of moneys due to the militia of the said county, with the proper vouchers for the same.

IN COUNCIL.   *Philadelphia,* September 28, 1782.

Ordered, That the Lieutenant of the county of Washington be directed to call out no more militia after the expiration of the time of those now in service; his Excellency George Washington having received intelligence that the British have called in all the savages, and that no more parties are to be permitted to be sent out against the frontiers.

IN COUNCIL.   *Philadelphia,* October 26, 1782.

A letter from Thomas Scott, Esq., of Washington County, with a return of justices for Cumberland township in said county, was received and read, by which return it appears that William McCleary and John Armstrong were duly elected justices. On consideration: *Ordered*, That the said letter and return lie on the table for consideration.

IN COUNCIL. *Philadelphia*, October 26, 1782.

The Council resumed the consideration of the letter from Thomas Scott, Esq., and the return of justices for Cumberland township, Washington County; and thereupon,

Ordered, That a letter be written to the said Thomas Scott, Esq., informing him that Council think it not quite prudent to issue a commission upon so old a return as that in which Mr. Edgar is mentioned, unless a petition from the people of the district had supported the sentiment expressed in his letter; and that they have also thought it best to delay their decision on the return now received, as they are informed it is probable that one of the gentlemen named therein may be returned a member of the General Assembly; but when that point is known, the Council will nominate and issue the commission, so as to forward it by the first opportunity.

IN COUNCIL. *Philadelphia*, November 26, 1782.

Petition of David Hoge was read, stating that he had conveyed a piece of land to the commissioners to build a court-house and prison in Washington County, and praying the said commissioners may be ordered to report their proceedings as soon as may be to this Board. (See March 14, 1783.)

IN COUNCIL. *Philadelphia*, December 4, 1782.

A return of the general election for the county of Washington was received and read, by which it appears that the following gentlemen were duly elected:—

Representatives. Matthew Ritchie and William McCleary. *Sheriffs.* Van Swearingen and Andrew Swearingen. *Coroners.* William McFarlane and John Marshall. *Commissioner.* George McCormick. And the same being considered,

Ordered, That Van Swearingen, Esq., be appointed sheriff of the county of Washington, and that William McFarlane be appointed coroner of the said county, and that they be commissioned accordingly.

Van Swearingen, Esq., sheriff elect for the county of Washington, offers Matthew Ritchie and John Cornaghan as sureties for the faithful discharge of the duties of his office of sheriff of the said county, according to law, which the Council approve.

IN COUNCIL. *Philadelphia*, February 15, 1783.

An order was drawn on the Treasurer, in favor of Col. John Cannon, for ninety-five pounds six shillings, balance of his account for rations furnished to the militia and rangers in Washington County, from February, 1782, till February, 1783.

IN COUNCIL. *Philadelphia*, March 5, 1783.

A petition from Anne Browne, Jean McCulloch, Frances Morgan, Agnes Reed, Catharine Pecas, Leah Norris, Anne Straight, Hannah Russel, Nancy Peckerol, Elizabeth Shanks, Elizabeth Palmer, and Mary Patterson, convicted of fornication and bastardy, in the county of Washington, and sentenced each of them to pay a fine of ten pounds to the use of the State, praying remission of their fines, was read, and thereupon

Ordered, That the fines adjudged to be paid to the use of the State by the persons before mentioned, be remitted.

In Council. Philadelphia, March 6, 1783.
An order was drawn on the Treasurer in favor of the Honorable Dorsey Pentecost, for sixteen pounds, for three hundred and twenty miles' riding to Philadelphia, at one shilling per mile.

In Council. Philadelphia, March 14, 1783.
A report from Hugh Scott, Daniel Leet, Van Swearingen, and John Armstrong, of the county of Washington, appointed by an act of General Assembly of the 28th of March, 1781, to purchase a piece of land in said county, thereon to build a court-house and prison, was received and read, setting forth that, agreeably to the directions of the said act, they have purchased from David Hoge a piece or parcel of land, within one mile of the centre of said county, for the purpose expressed in the said act, and submitting the same to the approbation of the Council; whereupon,
Ordered, That the said report be accepted and approved accordingly.

In Council. Philadelphia, March 17, 1783.
Ordered, That an order be drawn on the Treasurer in favor of Captain John Hughes, Lieutenant Gabriel Peterson, and Ensign James Morrison, of the company of rangers in the county of Washington, to be charged to their account;
Ordered, That a letter be written to Henry Taylor, Esq., of the said county, requesting him to pay to the non-commissioned officers and privates of Captain John Hughes' Company of Rangers two months' pay.

In Council. Philadelphia, March 21, 1783.
An order was drawn on the Treasurer, in favor of Mr. Matthew Ritchie, for twenty-five pounds specie, to be paid by him to Alexander Wright and William Minor, being the reward allowed by proclamation of Council for two Indian scalps taken in the county of Washington.
The Council taking into consideration the proclamation of the 22d day of April, 1780, offering a reward for Indian scalps, and the reasons upon which the same was founded no longer continuing,
Resolved, That the same be made null and void, anything therein contained to the contrary notwithstanding.
Ordered, That the foregoing resolution be sent to the Lieutenants of the county of Washington.

In Council. Philadelphia, March 22, 1783.
Resolved, That Council has no further use for the service of Captain John Hughes, commanding the Washington County Rangers, after the 5th of April next. That Captain Hughes be informed that Council return him thanks for the service he has rendered the State while in their employ.
An order was drawn in favor of Captain John Hughes, for thirty pounds specie, being two months' pay advanced to him, for which he is to account, to be paid out of the fund appropriated to the frontier defence.

In Council. Philadelphia, March 25, 1783.
An order was received on the Treasurer in favor of Honorable Dorsey Pentecost, Esq., for forty pounds, seven shillings and six pence, specie, amount of his account for his attendance in council from the 10th of February till the 26th of March, 1783.

In Council. Philadelphia, April 1, 1783.
The Comptroller General's report upon the account of James Marshall, Esq., Lieutenant of the county of Washington, was read and approved.

IN COUNCIL.   *Philadelphia*, May 1, 1783.
   Ordered, That Capt. Joseph Stiles, Commissary of Military Stores, be directed to deliver four hundred and fifteen pounds of powder and eight cwt. weight of lead, to Col. Christopher Hays, for the use of the militia of Washington and Westmoreland counties.
   Ordered, That letters be written enjoining it upon the Lieutenants of the said counties not to issue any part of this ammunition upon the receipts of the officers commanding corps, and that the same obligation be carried down to the private soldier.

IN COUNCIL.   *Philadelphia*, May 24, 1783.
   A letter from John Cannon, Esq., contractor for the subsistence of the Washington Rangers, was read.

IN COUNCIL.   *Philadelphia*, May 29, 1783.
   The Comptroller General's report upon the account of Thomas Scott, Esq., Prothonotary of Washington County, was read and approved.

IN COUNCIL.   *Philadelphia*, June 6, 1783.
   Ordered, That the Washington Ranging Company be immediately discharged from the service of the State, but that in settlement of accounts they be entitled to pay and rations till the first day of July next. The eldest officer of the company lately commanded by Capt. John Hughes, is therefore directed to put all his vouchers, &c., into the hands of Captains Boyd and Stokely. The corps is also informed that Council, under a sense of their many services, will take some early moment to call the attention of the Assembly to their situation, and that no disposition or good offices shall be wanting to render it as easy as possible.

IN COUNCIL.   *Philadelphia*, August 27, 1783.
   A letter was delivered to the Clerk of the General Assembly from Thomas Scott, Prothonotary of Washington County, in reply to several letters from Council upon the subject of the late communication from Virginia.

IN COUNCIL.   *Philadelphia*, August 28, 1783.
   The Comptroller General's report upon the accounts of James Pollock and William Cocheran, Esqs., was read and approved.

IN COUNCIL.   *Philadelphia*, September 23, 1783.
   An order was drawn on the Treasurer in favor of the Honorable Dorsey Pentecost, Esq., for thirty-one pounds, fifteen shillings, in full for his attendance in council to this day, inclusive, and his mileage.

IN COUNCIL.   *Philadelphia*, October 6, 1783.
   The Honorable Dorsey Pentecost, Esq., sent in a resignation of his seat at this Board, which was read and accepted.

IN COUNCIL.   *Philadelphia*, October 7, 1783.
   The following report from the Comptroller General was read and approved, upon the accounts of Thomas Scott, Esq., Prothonotary of Washington County, for tax arising from writs in said county.

IN COUNCIL.   *Philadelphia*, October 10, 1783.
   An order was drawn on the Treasurer in favor of Honorable Dorsey Pentecost, Esq., for fifteen pounds fifteen shillings specie, in full for his attendance in council till the 6th inst., inclusive.

IN COUNCIL.   *Philadelphia*, October 31, 1783.
   Resolved, That Dorsey Pentecost, Esq., be appointed a Judge in, and President of, the Court of Common Pleas for the county of Washington.

IN COUNCIL.   *Philadelphia,* November 10, 1783.
   The return of the General Election held in the county of Washington was received and read, by which it appears that the following gentlemen were duly elected, viz :—
   Censors. James Edgar, John McDowell.
   Councillor. John Neville.
   Representatives. John Stephenson, Matthew Ritchie.
   Sheriffs. Van Swearingen, Andrew Swearingen.
   Coroners. William McFarlane, William McComb.
   Commissioner. Demas Lindley.
   On consideration, *Ordered,* That Van Swearingen be appointed sheriff, and William McFarlane coroner of the county of Washington, and that they be commissioned accordingly.
   Van Swearingen, Esq., now offers John Neville, Andrew Swearingen, and Dorsey Pentecost, Esqrs., of the county of Washington, as sureties for the faithful performance of the duties of his office for the said county, according to law, which the Council approve.

IN COUNCIL.   *Philadelphia,* November 14, 1783.
   A representation from the magistracy of Washington County, upon the complaints of John Campbell and John Coxe, was read.

IN COUNCIL.   *Philadelphia,* November 20, 1783.
   The following order was drawn on the Treasurer, viz: In favor of John Cannon, Esq., for two hundred and seventy-four pounds five shillings, in full, for rations furnished to Rangers and militia in Washington County till August 1783, inclusively, to be paid out of the frontier fund.

IN COUNCIL.   *Philadelphia,* January 20, 1784.
   The Comptroller General's report upon the account of James Marshall, Esq., Lieutenant, and James Allison, late sub-Lieutenant of Washington County, was read.

IN COUNCIL.   *Philadelphia,* March 26, 1784.
   The Comptroller's report upon the account of Samuel Beeler for provisions furnished to the Washington County militia, was read and approved.

IN COUNCIL.   *Philadelphia,* March 30, 1784.
   The Comptroller's report upon the account of Matthew Ritchie, late sub-Lieutenant of the county, was read and approved.

IN COUNCIL.   *Philadelphia,* April 5, 1784.
   The report of the Comptroller-General upon the account of Colonel William Parker, late sub-Lieutenant of Washington County, was read and approved.

IN COUNCIL.   *Philadelphia,* June 10, 1784.
   John White attended, and Council agreed to allow him twenty-one pounds ten shillings for riding express to the counties of Washington, Westmoreland, Bedford, Cumberland, York, Lancaster, and Chester, with dispatches to the several sheriffs of said counties, for calling the General Assembly, and thereupon an order was drawn in his favor for fifteen pounds specie in part of said sum.

IN COUNCIL.   *Philadelphia,* July 23, 1784.
   A letter from James Marshall, Esq., Lieutenant of the county of Washington, was read.

IN COUNCIL   *Philadelphia*, August 12, 1784.
The Comptroller General's report upon the accounts of Hon. John McDowell and James Edgar, Esqs., and orders drawn on the Treasurer for the sum of thirty-three pounds five shillings each, in full for their attendance severally, till the 10th inst. inclusively, as members of the Council of Censors, to be paid according to resolution of Assembly of the 22d of November, 1783.

IN COUNCIL.   *Philadelphia*, September 10, 1784.
The record of the conviction of Thomas Richardson of burglary in the county of Washington, was read and considered; upon which it was
Resolved, That execution of the sentence of the court be made and done upon him, the said Thomas Richardson, on Saturday, the 2d day of October next, between the hours of ten of the clock in the forenoon and two of the clock in the afternoon of the same day, at the most proper and public place within the said county.

IN COUNCIL.   *Philadelphia*, September 25, 1784.
An order was drawn upon the Treasurer of the State in favor of James Edgar, Esq. (for fifty-six pounds eighteen shillings), a member of the Council of Censors, for his wages, for attendance in the said Council until this day, to be paid according to the resolution of the General Assembly, dated the 22d day of November, 1783.

IN COUNCIL.   *Philadelphia*, September 27, 1784.
An order was drawn on the Treasurer in favor of Henry Taylor, Esq., for the sum of two pounds five shillings specie, for his services in paying the Ranging Company of Washington County, late commanded by Captain Hughes, agreeably to the Comptroller-General's report.

IN COUNCIL.   *Philadelphia*, September, 28, 1784.
The Comptroller-General's reports upon the following accounts were read and approved: For provisions furnished to the Washington County militia by William Campbell, Richard Elson, John Smith, William Rankin, Thomas Cherry, John Nichols, Henry Enoch, David Shepherd, Thomas Rankin, Stephen Treacle, Demus Lindley, James Marshall, Jr., and George Atkinson.

IN COUNCIL.   *Philadelphia*, September 29, 1784.
The Comptroller-General's report upon the account of Captain Craig Ritchie, for the pay of his company of Washington County militia—also upon the account of William McCleary, Esq., sub-Lieutenant of the county of Washington, was read—and approved September 30, 1784.

IN COUNCIL.   *Philadelphia*, October 6, 1784.
Matthew Ritchie and John Cannon, Esqs., were appointed justices of the county Court of Common Pleas in and for the county of Washington.

IN COUNCIL.   *Philadelphia*, October, 19, 1784.
A petition from divers inhabitants of Washington County, complaining of the conduct of the commissioners of taxes in said county, in laying the taxes in a partial manner to the great injury of the petitioners, was read and thereupon
Ordered, That a copy of said complaint be transmitted to the said commissioners, and that they be directed to explain to Council their conduct with respect to the petitioners (which was accordingly done).

IN COUNCIL.   *Philadelphia*, October 26, 1784.
Upon the petition of Rachel Cotton, convicted of fornication in the county of Washington, it was
Ordered, That her fine be remitted.

IN COUNCIL.   *Philadelphia*, November 1, 1784.
The return of the general election held in the county of Washington was received and read, by which it appears the following gentlemen were duly elected:—
Representatives. Matthew Ritchie, John Stevenson.
Sheriffs. James Marshall, Daniel Leet.
Coroners. William McCombs, Robert Benson.
Commissioner. James Allison.
On consideration,
Ordered, That James Marshall, Esq., be appointed and commissioned to be sheriff of said county of Washington, and that William McCombs, Esq., be appointed and commissioned coroner of said county. James Marshall, Esq., offered John Hoge and John Stevenson, Esqs., as sureties for the faithful discharge of the duties of his office of sheriff for the said county, according to law, which the Council approved.
James Marshall's resignation of his office of Register and Recorder of Deeds in and for the county of Washington was read.

IN COUNCIL.   *Philadelphia*, Nov. 3, 1784.
A bond was executed in Council by James Marshall, John Stevenson, and John Hoge, in the sum of one thousand pounds, for the said James Marshall's faithful performance of the duties of his office of sheriff of the county of Washington according to law.
James Marshall's resignation of the office of Lieutenant of the county of Washington, was read and not accepte

IN COUNCIL.   *Philadelphia*, Nov. 10, 1784.
The Comptroller-General's report upon the account of Col. James Marshall, Lieutenant of the county of Washington, by which it appears that a balance of eight hundred and twenty-six pounds eighteen shillings and three pence, specie, is due to him, was read and approved and an order drawn in his favor for the sum of fifty pounds specie, in part of the said balance.

IN COUNCIL.   *Philadelphia*, Nov. 16, 1784.
The Comptroller-General's report upon the account of Captain John Hughes, late of a company of rangers raised in the county of Washington, was read and approved.

IN COUNCIL.   *Philadelphia*, Nov. 17, 1784.
A dedimus potestatem was issued to Thomas Scott and Thomas Stokely, Esqs., of the county of Washington.

IN COUNCIL.   *Philadelphia*, Nov. 19, 1784.
Thomas Stokely, Esq., was commissioned to be register of, and probate of wills, and granting letters of administration, and recorder of deeds in the county of Washington, in consequence of an appointment to those offices by the General Assembly.

IN COUNCIL.   *Philadelphia*, January 22, 1785.
The Comptroller-General's report upon the account of Ensign James Morrison, of Captain John Hughes' company of rangers of the county of Washington, was read and approved, the balance due to him being ninety pounds.

IN COUNCIL.   *Philadelphia*, Jan. 25, 1785.
An order was drawn upon the Treasurer in favor of Lieut. James Morrison, late of Capt. John Hughes' company of rangers in Washington County, for the sum of fifteen pounds, being two months' pay, for which he is to be accountable.

IN COUNCIL.   *Philadelphia*, Jan. 27, 1785.
The Comptroller-General's report upon the following accounts were read and approved, viz :—
Of Jonathan Hennard and David Ruble, for provisions furnished to the Washington County militia.
Of Dorsey Pentecost, Esq., for disbursements in raising Capt. Hughes' company of rangers.
Of William Marshall, for losses sustained in the Indian expedition of 1781.
Of the pay due the non-commissioned officers and privates of Captain Hughes' company.
Of Lieut. Gabriel Peterson, for pay in the said company.

IN COUNCIL.   *Philadelphia*, Feb. 11, 1785.
Henry Vanmetre elected justice of the peace for Cumberland township, and commissioned according to law.

IN COUNCIL.   *Philadelphia*, Feb. 24, 1785.
The Comptroller-General's report upon the account of Captain Andrew Swearingen's ranging company, for pay from March to November, 1781.

IN COUNCIL.   *Philadelphia*, March 1, 1785.
The return of an election of justices of the peace for the district of Fallowfield and county of Washington, was read and postponed.

IN COUNCIL.   *Philadelphia*, March 2, 1785.
The Comptroller-General's reports upon the following accounts were read and approved, viz :—
Of Craig Ritchie and Andrew Munroe, for horses lost in the Sandusky expedition.
Of Lieut.-Col. George Vallandingham, for militia services.
Of the aforesaid Capt. Craig Ritchie for rations due him from the 20th of May to the 20th of June, 1782.
Of Van Swearingen, Esq., for provisions furnished the ranging company of Andrew Swearingen, captain, and for seven thousand one hundred and forty rations furnished the militia of Washington County, from April 1st to September 2d, 1782.
Of John Smilie, for a horse and rifle lost in the Sandusky expedition.
Of James Curry and John Geiger, for team hire in transporting baggage of the troops employed in escorting the convention army in 1778.

IN COUNCIL.   *Philadelphia*, March 3, 1785.
The Comptroller-General's report upon the account of Joseph Holmes, of the county of Washington, for provisions furnished himself when on militia service, was read and approved.

IN COUNCIL.   *Philadelphia*, April 7, 1785.
William Graham was appointed collector of excise for Washington, Westmoreland, and Fayette counties.

IN COUNCIL.   *Philadelphia*, April 27, 1785.
On consideration,
Ordered, That General Neville be authorized upon his return to Washington County, to place some fit person in possession of the buildings at

Fort McIntosh (near Beaver, Pa.), with directions to keep them and the public timber upon the adjoining land in a state of as much preservation as possible.

IN COUNCIL. *Philadelphia*, May 3, 1785.

A letter to John Story, Esq., additional commissioner for settling accounts (of this State with the United States), requesting him to enter upon the execution of his office as soon as possible in Washington County, and Westmoreland and Fayette, unless circumstances shall hereafter require any alteration of this direction.

IN COUNCIL. *Philadelphia*, May 7, 1785.

An order was drawn upon the Treasurer in favor of Dorsey Pentecost, Esq., for three pounds specie, being money advanced by him to Mr. William Croghen, for the transportation of two hundred and fifty pounds from this city to the county of Washington, and its deposit in the hands of the lieutenant of said county.

IN COUNCIL. *Philadelphia*, May 20, 1785.

The fine imposed upon Annie Essicks, of Washington County, upon being convicted of fornication, was remitted.

IN COUNCIL. *Philadelphia*, Aug. 30, 1785.

The Comptroller-General's report upon the account of William Shearer, of the county of Washington, for a horse lost in the Sandusky expedition, was read and approved.

IN COUNCIL. *Philadelphia*, Sept. 22, 1785.

A return of a magistrate for the township of Donegal, and county of Washington, was read. (See Feb. 6, 1786.)

A certificate from the Court of General Quarter Sessions of the peace of the county of Washington, accompanied by a petition from the inhabitants of the town of Washington, that it is become necessary and proper, and will be useful that the aforesaid town of Washington be erected into a district for the election of a justice of the peace, was read and approved, agreeably to law. (See Feb. 6, 1786.)

A return of officers chosen to command the troops of Washington County light horse was read and approved, and commissions directed to issue.

IN COUNCIL. *Philadelphia*, October 26, 1785.

A return of the general election for the county of Washington was received and read.

IN COUNCIL. *Philadelphia*, December 15, 1785.

James Marshall, Esq., was commissioned sheriff and William McCombs coroner for the county of Washington; David Reddick and John Hoge, Esquires, were offered as securities for James Marshall and accepted.

IN COUNCIL. *Philadelphia*, February 6, 1786.

William Johnstone, Esq., was appointed a justice of the peace upon a return of an election of justices for the district of Donegal, in the county of Washington, and commissioned accordingly; to this commission was added that of a justice of the Court of Common Pleas.

On motion of Mr. Neville:—

The town of Washington was this day erected into a distinct district for the election of justices of the peace, agreeably to a certificate of the court of the county of Washington.

IN COUNCIL.   *Philadelphia*, March 8, 1786.
A certificate of the court of Washington County, for dividing the township of Smith, in the said county, was read. (See September 2, 1786.)

IN COUNCIL.   *Philadelphia*, April 19, 1786.
The Comptroller-General's report upon the following accounts was read and approved:—
Of Hugh Sprouls, of the county of Washington, for a horse lost in the Sandusky expedition. Of Joseph Brown, of said county, for rations furnished to the militia employed on the said expedition. Of Thomas Brown, of said county, for rations furnished as aforesaid. Of William McGlaughlin, of said county, for pork furnished for the use of the militia when in service on the frontiers of Washington County, in 1782.

IN COUNCIL.   *Philadelphia*, July 25, 1786.
John Craig, Esq., of the county of Washington, was appointed collector of excise for the county aforesaid, and for the counties of Westmoreland and Fayette, in the room of William Graham, resigned.

IN COUNCIL.   *Philadelphia*, September, 2, 1786.
A certificate of the division of the township of Smith, in the county of Washington, by the Court of Quarter Sessions of the Peace held at Washington, for the county aforesaid, on the 5th of January last, was read and order taken that the decision be confirmed, agreeably to the decree of the said court.

IN COUNCIL.   *Philadelphia*, October 24, 1786.
A return of the general election for the county of Washington was received and read, by which it appears that David Reddick was duly elected *counsellor;* James Marshall and William Wallace, sheriffs, and William McComb and Joseph Wherry, coroners for the said county.

IN COUNCIL.   *Philadelphia*, November 20, 1786.
David Reddick, Esq., took his seat at this Board, agreeably to a return of the general election for the county of Washington (read on the 24th of October last), having previously taken several oaths of qualification.

IN COUNCIL.   *Philadelphia*, November 21, 1786.
A certificate of the division of Peters township, in the county of Washington, by the Court of General Quarter Sessions held at Washington, for the county aforesaid, the last Tuesday in September, 1784, was read and order taken that the decision aforesaid be confirmed, agreeably to the decree of the said court.

John Hoge and Thomas Scott, Esquires, were appointed and commissioned justices of the peace for the district of Washington, in the county of Washington. John Hoge and Thomas Scott were also appointed and commissioned justices of the Court of Common Pleas in and for the county of Washington.

James Marshall, Esq., was appointed and commissioned sheriff, and Wm. McCombs, coroner of the county of Washington. John Hoge and David Reddick, Esqs., were accepted as sureties for Mr. Marshall.

IN COUNCIL.   *Philadelphia*, November 25, 1786.
An order was taken upon motion, that as Dorsey Pentecost, Esq., late judge of the Court of Common Pleas and president of that court for the county of Washington has removed from the county aforesaid and is now settled in a neighboring State, that he be suspended in the offices aforesaid.

IN COUNCIL. Philadelphia, December 12, 1786.
Ordered, That the commission of Collector of Excise for the counties of Washington, Westmoreland, and Fayette be revoked, and that John Dodd be appointed collector for the county of Washington, and Joseph Douglass for that of Fayette.

IN COUNCIL. Philadelphia, Dec. 20, 1786.
An order was drawn upon the Treasurer in favor of the Hon. David Redick, Esq., for twenty-three pounds five shillings in full for his attendance in council until this day inclusively.

IN COUNCIL. Philadelphia, Feb. 9, 1787.
The Comptroller-General's report upon the account of James Marshall Esq., Lieutenant of Washington County from November, 1784, until November, 1786, was read and approved.

IN COUNCIL. Philadelphia, Feb. 12, 1787.
An order was drawn upon the Treasurer in favor of Col. James Marshall for three hundred and seventy-eight pounds ten shillings and nine pence, in part of the balance due upon his account as Lieutenant of the county of Washington, according to the Comptroller General's report, to be paid out of the fund arising from militia fines.

IN COUNCIL. Philadelphia, March 21, 1787.
An order was drawn upon the Treasurer in favor of the Hon. David Redick, Esq., for forty pounds five shillings in full, for his attendance in council until this day, inclusively.

IN COUNCIL. Philadelphia, April 12, 1787.
An order was drawn upon the Treasurer in favor of the Hon. David Redick, Esq., for thirty-five pounds in full for his attendance in council from the 21st of March to the 14th of April inclusively, and his mileage.

IN COUNCIL. Philadelphia, Aug. 18, 1787.
The fine of ten pounds imposed upon Ruth Grenaugh, convicted of fornication and bastardy in the county of Washington, was remitted upon her petition and a recommendation in her favor.

IN COUNCIL. Philadelphia, Sept. 3, 1787.
On motion ordered, Thomas Stockley, Esq., was appointed and commissioned a justice of the Court of Common Pleas in and for the county of Washington.

IN COUNCIL. Philadelphia, Sept. 14, 1787.
Monday next was assigned for going into the consideration of the return of the proposed road through the western counties of the State and Pittsburg, together with the several petitions against it, and the Secretary was directed to request the members of the General Assembly from the counties of Washington, Westmoreland, Fayette, and Bedford to meet council on that day to give them some information upon the subject.

IN COUNCIL. Philadelphia, Sept. 1787.
The members of the General Assembly from the counties of Washington, Westmoreland, Fayette, and Bedford, attended in the council chamber agreeably to the request of the council of the 14th inst., and a conference was held upon the subject of the proposed road from Miller's Spring into Cumberland County to Fort Pitt.

IN COUNCIL.   *Philadelphia*, Sept. 25, 1787.

Joseph Scott, Esq., was appointed and commissioned a justice of the peace for the district of Robinson township, in the county of Washington, and also appointed and commissioned a justice of the Court of Common Pleas in said county.

IN COUNCIL.   *Philadelphia*, Oct. 5, 1787.

An order was drawn upon the Treasurer in favor of the Hon. David Redick, Esq., for fifty-two pounds fifteen shillings in full, for his attendance in council until the 4th inst., inclusively, and his mileage.

IN COUNCIL.   *Philadelphia*, Nov. 2, 1787.

An order was drawn upon the Treasurer in favor of Col. James Marshall, Lieutenant of Washington County, for thirty-seven pounds two shillings and six pence, to be paid by him to Abraham Enslow, Frederick Crow, Stephen Gapen, Peter Clawson, William Crawford, Jesse Vanmetre, W. Harrod, Sr., Michael Dougherty, John Flora, John Heaton, William Tarpine, Harrod Newland, Robert Flora, Alexander Brown, and Peter Dailey for their services in watching the movements of Indians, and protecting the frontiers from Indian depredations in the year 1782, agreeably to the act of Assembly, dated December 1781.

IN COUNCIL.   *Philadelphia*, Nov. 12, 1787.

It appearing from intelligence received from Washington County that the Indians have murdered some of the inhabitants of the said county, and that the people there are in want of arms and ammunition,

Resolved, That one hundred stand of arms, four hundred weight of powder and eight hundred weight of lead, and one thousand flints be purchased by the Comptroller General, and sent to the Lieutenant of Washington County.

IN COUNCIL.   *Philadelphia*, Nov. 15, 1787.

WHEREAS, It is represented to the Board that the Indians have recently committed divers depredations on the frontier settlements in this State, therefore,

Resolved, That the Lieutenants of the several frontier counties may, from time to time, order into actual service for the protection of the inhabitants, such part of the militia of their respective counties as may appear to them, or any of them, necessary, not exceeding at any one time the proportion allowed by law.

IN COUNCIL.   *Philadelphia*, December 3, 1787.

An order was drawn upon the Treasurer in favor of the Honorable David Redick, Esq., for forty-five pounds, in full for his attendance in council to this day, inclusively.

IN COUNCIL.   *Philadelphia*, December 4, 1787.

Resolved, That the Lieutenants of the city and the several counties within the State, be directed to collect all the public arms within their respective counties, have them repaired, and make return to council, with the accounts and vouchers necessary for payment.

IN COUNCIL.   *Philadelphia*, May 6, 1788.

Two certificates of the division of Cumberland and Morgan townships, and of the township of Donegal, in the county of Washington, by the Court of General Quarter Sessions of the Peace of the said county, in order for the more convenient election of justices of the peace, were received, read, and ordered to be filed. (See August 7, 1788.)

'Samuel Glassgow, Esq., was appointed and commissioned a justice of the peace and a justice of the Court of Common Pleas in and for the county of Washington, upon a return made according to law, for the district of the township of Hanover.

IN COUNCIL. *Philadelphia, June 6, 1788.*

An order was drawn upon the Treasurer in favor of the Honorable David Redick, for thirty-one pounds five shillings, in full of his account for attendance in council from the 5th day of May until the 5th of June, 1788, inclusively, and his mileage.

IN COUNCIL. *Philadelphia, June 30, 1788.*

William Wallace, Esq., was appointed and commissioned a justice of the peace, and of the Court of Common Pleas in and for the county of Washington, upon a return made according to law, for the district of Somerset.

IN COUNCIL. *Philadelphia, August 5, 1788.*

An order was drawn in favor of David Redick, Esq., for the sum of fifty-three pounds fifteen shillings, in full of his account for his attendance in council from the 6th day of June until the 5th of August, 1788, and his mileage from Philadelphia to Washington County.

IN COUNCIL. *Philadelphia, August 7, 1788.*

Two certificates from the Court of General Quarter Sessions of the Peace for the county of Washington, that a division of the district of the townships of Cumberland and Morgan, and of the district of the township of Donegal, in the said county, agreeably to act of Assembly, dated the 31st of March, 1784, for the election of justices of the peace, is become proper and will be useful, which were received and read on the 6th of May, were this day taken into consideration, and the division, as made by the said court, was confirmed.

IN COUNCIL. *Philadelphia, August 8, 1788.*

An order was drawn upon the Treasurer in favor of the Honorable David Redick, Esq., for four pounds ten shillings, in full for his attendance in council from the 6th until the 12th of this month, both days included.

IN COUNCIL. *Philadelphia, August 23, 1788.*

An order was drawn upon the Treasurer in favor of Col. James Marshall, Lieutenant of Washington County, for seventy-seven pounds eighteen shillings and four pence, payable out of the moneys arising from militia fines, being in full of two several accounts for militia services on the frontier of the said county in September and October, 1787, and in March, April, and May, 1788, according to the Comptroller General's report.

An order was drawn upon the Treasurer in favor of James Chambers and William Marshall, for fifty pounds nineteen shillings and seven pence, payable out of the militia fines of the county of Washington, in full of their accounts for repairing the public arms belonging to the said county, according to the Comptroller-General's report.

IN COUNCIL. *Philadelphia, September 30, 1788.*

Henry Taylor, Esq., was appointed and commissioned a justice of the peace for the district of the township of Strabán; James Edgar a justice of the peace for the district of the township of Smith, and William McFarlane a justice of the peace for the district of the township of Amwell, in the county of Washington, upon returns made, according to law, for the said several districts. They were also appointed and commissioned justices of the Court of Common Pleas in and for the county of Washington.

On motion,
Ordered, That the said Henry Taylor be appointed and commissionated President of the Court of Common Pleas, of the Court of General Quarter Sessions of the Peace and Jail Delivery, and of the Orphan's Court of Washington County.

Two returns of justices from the districts of the townships of Cecil and Dickinson, in the county of Washington, were read and not allowed, as the whole of Dickinson, and part of Cecil district, has been struck off to the county of Allegheny.

IN COUNCIL. *Philadelphia*, October 15, 1788.

The oath, directed by the Constitution was administered to the Hon. David Redick, Esq., to qualify him for the exercise of his office of Vice-President of this board.

IN COUNCIL. *Philadelphia*, November 7, 1788.

Returns of elections of justices of the peace, lately held in several districts of Nottingham, Hopewell, and Findley, together with a petition against the latter, were also received and read.

IN COUNCIL. *Philadelphia*, November 8, 1788.

The return of an election of justices of the peace for the district of Findley township, in Washington County, which was read yesterday, was read the second time, together with a petition from several freeholders, resident in said district, complaining of illegal proceedings at said election, whereupon it was

Ordered, That John Hoge, Thomas Scott, and William McFarlane, Esqrs., justices of the peace in and for the county of Washington, living near the said district, be authorized and directed to investigate the facts stated in the said petition, upon the oaths of such witnesses as may be adduced, and make report thereof to this Board in manner and form prescribed in and by an act of Assembly, entitled "An act to remedy the defects of the several acts of Assembly heretofore made for regulating the elections of justices of the peace throughout this State, &c.," passed the 31st day of March, 1784. (See March 31, 1789.)

John Reed and Hugh Scott, Esqrs., were appointed and commissionated justices of the peace and of the Court of Common Pleas, in and for the county of Washington, the former for the district of the township of Cecil, and the latter for the district of the township of Nottingham, upon returns made according to law from the said several districts.

IN COUNCIL. *Philadelphia*, Nov. 10, 1788.

William Smiley, Esq., was appointed and commissioned a justice of the peace, and of the Court of Common Pleas, in and for the county of Washington, upon a return made according to law for the district of the township of Hopewell.

IN COUNCIL. *Philadelphia*, Nov. 25, 1788.

An order was drawn upon the Treasurer in favor of the Hon. David Redick, Esq., for seventy-two pounds seven shillings and four pence in full of his account for his salary as Vice-President from the 14th of October until the 4th of November, 1788, and for his pay as Councillor until this day, including his mileage and cash paid for postage of letters on public business.

IN COUNCIL. *Philadelphia*, Dec. 6, 1788.

On motion,
Resolved, That Monday the 8th inst. be assigned for going into the appointment of a sheriff for the county of Washington.

IN COUNCIL.   *Philadelphia*, Dec. 8, 1788.
Mr. Wood's motion for appointing a sheriff for the county of Washington was referred to Col. Miles, Col. Smith, and Col. Wood.

IN COUNCIL.   *Philadelphia*, Dec. 23, 1788.
On motion,
Resolved, That the Secretary employ two proper persons to ride to the counties of Washington, Westmoreland, Fayette, Bedford, Huntingdon, Northumberland, Cumberland, Luzerne, Franklin, and Dauphin, to bring to Council from those counties the returns of electors for the choice of President and Vice-President of the United States, and that he assign to the said expresses their proper counties, give them the necessary instructions, and direct the said expresses to set off on Monday next.

IN COUNCIL.   *Philadelphia*, Dec. 27, 1788.
James Dunwood was employed as one of the persons to ride to the counties of Washington, Westmoreland, Fayette, Bedford, Huntingdon, Cumberland, Franklin, and Dauphin agreeably to the minutes of the 23d inst., and it was agreed to allow him two dollars and a half in specie per diem while he is employed in the said business.

IN COUNCIL.   *Philadelphia*, Dec. 31, 1788.
The return of members to represent this State in the Congress of the United States having been received by Council from the city of Philadelphia, and the several counties, except the county of Fayette,
Resolved, That for the information of the public, the following state of the returns be published.

Fred. A. Muhlenberg	8707	John Allison	7067
Henry Wynkoop	8246	Stephen Chambers	7050
Thomas Hartley	8263	William Findley	6586
George Clymer	8094	William Irvine	6492
Thomas Fitzsimmons	8067	Charles Pettit	6481
Thomas Scott	8068	William Montgomery	6348
Peter Muhlenberg	7417	Blair McClerrachan	6223
Daniel Hiester	7403	Robert Whitehill	5850

IN COUNCIL.   *Philadelphia*, Jan. 17, 1789.
A return of the general election of sheriffs and coroners held in and for the county of Washington, in October, 1788, was received and read, and David Williamson, Esq., thereupon appointed and commissionated sheriff, and Robert Benham coroner of the said county.
William Parker and Josiah Scott, of the county of Washington, were offered and accepted as sureties for the said David Williamson's faithful performance of the duties of his office of sheriff for the county aforesaid according to law.

IN COUNCIL.   *Philadelphia*, Feb. 3, 1789.
Resolved, That the several returns of electors for choosing a President and Vice-President of the United States, which have been transmitted to Council, be referred to Mr. McClay and Mr. Smith to inspect the same and report to Council the names of the ten highest to vote, which being done, a proclamation was issued embracing the names of the following electors: Edward Hand, John Arndt, Lawrence Keene, James O'Hara, Samuel Potts, George Gibson, Coleman Read, James Wilson, David Grier, and Alexander Grayson.

78   HISTORY OF WASHINGTON COUNTY.

IN COUNCIL.   *Philadelphia*, Feb. 17, 1789.
The report of the Committee to whom was referred the letter from Thomas Scott, Esq., with the proceedings of the General Assembly thereon, was read and adopted as follows, viz :—
Resolved, That the letter from Thomas Scott, Esq., of the 20th of January last, together with the proceedings of the General Assembly on the same subject, be transmitted by the earliest opportunity to the said Thomas Scott, with an intimation that it would be agreeable to Council if he would endeavor to serve during the first session of Congress, or until his place can be supplied without expense to the State at the next annual election.

IN COUNCIL.   *Philadelphia*, Feb. 28, 1789.
Eleazer Jenkins, Esq., was appointed and commissioned a justice of the peace and of the Court of Common Pleas in and for the county of Washington upon a return made according to law for the district of the township of Bethlehem in said county.

IN COUNCIL.   *Philadelphia*, March 12, 1789.
Absalom Baird and John Douglass, Esqs., were appointed and commissionated justices of the peace, the former for the district of the town of Washington, and the latter for the district of the township of Peters in the county of Washington, upon returns made according to law from the said districts.
The said Absalom Baird and John Douglass, Esqs., were also appointed and commissionated justices of the Court of Common Pleas in and for the said county of Washington.

IN COUNCIL.   *Philadelphia*, March 12, 1789.
Upon consideration of the report of the Committee to whom was referred the petition and recommendation in favor of William Stewart, Aaron Lyle, James Ross, James McClellan, John Donat, Josias Gamble, Samuel Agnew, Robert Ralston, William Campbell, Joseph Wells, Samuel Hanna, and John Rankin for remission of the fines which have been imposed upon them by the last Court of Oyer and Terminer held in the county of Washington upon their being convicted severally of a riot in said county,
Resolved, That the several fines due to the Commonwealth, imposed upon the petitioners as aforesaid, be remitted.

IN COUNCIL.   *Philadelphia*, March 18, 1789.
An order was drawn upon the Treasurer in favor of Hugh Spear, for five pounds seventeen shillings, in full, of his account for hauling public arms and ammunition from Philadelphia to the county of Washington, for the defence of the western frontiers.

IN COUNCIL.   *Philadelphia*, March 24, 1789.
Mr. Redick, member of this Board, was offered and accepted as surety for Thomas Scott, Esq., Prothonotary of the county of Washington, in the room of John Neville, Esq., who was approved by the Board on the 19th instant as surety for Mr. Scott.
On motion,
Resolved, That a *dedimus potestatem* issue to Thomas Scott, Thomas Stokely, John Hoge, and Absalom Baird, Esqs., of the county of Washington.

IN COUNCIL.   *Philadelphia*, March 25, 1789.
An order was drawn in favor of Peter Daily for three pounds fourteen shillings and eleven pence, payable out of the militia fines of Washington County, being the amount of his account for thirty-one days' militia service

as a ranger on the frontiers of Washington County, by order of the Lieutenant of said county, and for subsistence during the said service.

Also, in favor of Abraham Inlow, Edward Sergent, Andrew Farley, and Alexander Burns, for fourteen pounds nineteen shillings and eight pence, amount of their several accounts for thirty-one days' militia service each, on the frontiers of said county, by order of the said Lieutenant, from the 25th of March till the 25th of April, 1788, inclusively, and for subsistence during the said term, payable out of the militia fines as aforesaid.

In favor of Thomas Orr, John Lesnet, John Vance, and Hercules Roney, for fourteen pounds nineteen shillings and eight pence, payable out of the moneys arising from militia fines as aforesaid, amount of the several accounts for militia services from the 8th of April till the 8th of May, 1788, inclusive, and for subsistence as aforesaid.

In favor of Abner Braddock and Francis Braddock, for seven pounds nine shillings and ten pence, payable out of the moneys arising from militia fines, amount of their several accounts for militia services from the 8th of April till the 8th of May, 1788, inclusive, and for subsistence as aforesaid.

IN COUNCIL. *Philadelphia*, March 28, 1789.

WHEREAS, Thomas Scott, Esquire, Prothonotary of the county of Washington, hath informed this Council by letter that he hath been elected a representative of this State in the Congress of the United States, and that he is on his way to New York to take his seat as such;

AND WHEREAS, The said Thomas Scott, Esquire, by the acceptance of his appointment as representative in Congress, is incapable of discharging the duties of prothonotary of the county aforesaid; and it is therefore proper that a prothonotary for the said county should forthwith be appointed in his room and stead:

Resolved, That Alexander Scott, son of the said Thomas Scott, Esquire, be and he is hereby appointed Prothonotary of the county of Washington in the room and stead of Thomas Scott, Esquire.

James Marshall, David Redick, and Thomas Scott, Esquires, were offered and accepted as sureties for Alexander Scott, Esquire, Prothonotary of the county of Washington.

IN COUNCIL. *Philadelphia*, March 30, 1789.

Agreeably to the Comptroller-General's reports, orders were drawn upon the Treasurer for the following sums, payable out of the moneys arising from militia fines of Washington County.

For one pound nineteen shillings, amount of pay due to seven men of the Washington County militia, two days in July, 1787, and four pounds nineteen shillings and four pence, pay due to the seven men of the said militia from the 8th to the 10th of June, 1788, for militia services.

For five pounds twelve shillings, amount of pay due to Captain Thomas Axtell's company of said militia in actual service two days to the 19th day of October, 1787.

For one hundred and thirty-seven pounds seventeen shillings, amount of pay due to Captain Eleazer Jenkin's company of said militia in actual service from August the 6th to the 20th of September, 1788.

For ninety-three pounds nine shillings and four pence, amount of pay due to Captain James Scott's company of said militia in actual service for two days to Sept. 1787.

For sixty pounds eight shillings and two pence, amount of pay due to Lieutenant Jonathan Ross's company of said militia, in actual service from July 17th to August 13th, 1788.

For two pounds ten shillings, amount of pay due to a party of said militia for six days in actual service, ending the 22d of October, 1787, and for two pounds fifteen shillings, amount of pay due to seven men of said militia, for seven days' actual service, ending the 1st of November, 1787.

For fifty-three pounds fourteen shillings, amount of pay due to Ensign Sampson Nicholas's company of said militia from June 9th to July 15th, 1788.

For nine pounds, amount of John Custard's account for a horse lost on the Sandusky expedition under Colonel Crawford in 1782.

For seven pounds, amount of Richard Hale's account of a gun taken into actual service and lost in 1782, in the expedition under Colonel Crawford.

IN COUNCIL. *Philadelphia*, March 31, 1789.

A report from John Hoge and Thomas Scott, Esquires, two of the justices who were appointed by Council on the 8th day of November last to investigate the complaint against an election of justices of the peace held in Findley township, in the county of Washington, on the 23d of September, 1788, was read, by which it appears that notice of the time of holding the said election was not given according to law; therefore,

Resolved, That said election of justices of the peace in the township of Findley be set aside and made void, and that a writ under the lesser seal be now issued for holding a new election of justices of the peace in and for the said township, on the 28th day of July next, according to law.

IN COUNCIL. *Philadelphia*, April 8th, 1789.

On motion,

Resolved, That Thomas Ryerson be appointed and commissionated a justice of the Court of Common Pleas in and for the county of Washington.

IN COUNCIL. *Philadelphia*, April 27, 1789.

An order was drawn upon the Treasurer in favor of the Honorable David Redick, Esq., for fifty-six pounds in full of his account for attendance in Council until the 1st day of May, 1789, inclusively, and for mileage coming from Washington County to Philadelphia.

IN COUNCIL. *Philadelphia*, May, 15, 1789.

The account of Thomas Scott, Esq., Prothonotary of Washington County, for fees upon tavern licenses received from July to September, 1788, amounting to nineteen pounds eight shillings, was read and approved.

IN COUNCIL. *Philadelphia*, May 20, 1789.

The petition of Elisha Mills, of the county of Washington, praying remission of a fine of ten pounds, payable to the use of the Commonwealth, to which he has been sentenced by the Court of General Quarter Sessions of the Peace of the said county, upon being convicted of fornication, was read and an order taken that the prayer of the said petitioner be granted.

IN COUNCIL. *Philadelphia*, June 17, 1789.

Two orders were drawn in favor of the Hon. David Redick, Esq., one for forty-four pounds fifteen shillings, in full of his account for his attendance in Council from May 2 to June 19, 1789, inclusively of his mileage from Philadelphia to Washington city, and the other for thirty-three pounds and eight pence, being a balance due upon an account settled by the Comptroller and Register-General, for his services and expenses, in surveying two islands in the rivers Ohio and Allegheny, and for surveying and dividing the reserved tract of land opposite Pittsburg into town and out lots, agreeably to the order of Council dated November 28, 1787, and an act of Assembly dated September 11, 1787.

IN COUNCIL.   *Philadelphia,* August 3, 1789.
A petition and representation from a number of inhabitants of Washington County, complaining that Thomas Stokely, the Register and Recorder of that county has been absent for upwards of six months from the county, and praying Council to appoint some person in his room to hold and exercise those offices until the General Assembly of the State shall meet, was received and read.

IN COUNCIL.   *Philadelphia,* September 2, 1787.
The following account of Thomas Rogers was read and approved, for provisions furnished to Captain William Leet's company of Washington County militia from the 15th of April to the 16th of May, 1782, amounting to three pounds six shillings and ten pence, and for provisions furnished to Captain William Hogeland's company of the said militia, in April, 1782, amounting to one pound fourteen shillings and four pence.

IN COUNCIL.   *Philadelphia,* September 29, 1789.
The following account of Thomas Rankin, of Washington County, for his services on the frontiers in 1781, amounting to ten shillings, was read and approved.

IN COUNCIL.   *Philadelphia,* Nov. 6, 1789.
A return of the general election held in the county of Washington on the second Tuesday of October last, was received and read, by which it appears that the following gentlemen were duly elected: Henry Taylor, *councillor;* David Williamson and William Wallace, *sheriffs;* Samuel Clark and Sashbazer Bentley, *coroners;* whereupon
Resolved, That David Williamson be appointed and commissioned *sheriff,* and Samuel Clark, *coroner,* of the county of Washington.
William Parker and John Leman were offered and accepted as sureties for the sheriff of the county of Washington.

IN COUNCIL.   *Philadelphia,* November 30, 1789.
John Minor, Esq., was appointed and commissionated a justice of the peace, and of the Court of Common Pleas in and for the county of Washington, upon a return made according to law from the district of the township of Greene in the said county.

IN COUNCIL.   *Philadelphia,* December 1, 1789.
An order was drawn upon the Treasurer, in favor of John Cannon, Esq., for fifty-three pounds ten shillings, for his attendance in Council from the 7th to the 11th of February and from the 10th of August until the 2d of October, 1789, and his mileage coming to Philadelphia and returning to Washington County.

IN COUNCIL.   *Philadelphia,* December 3, 1789.
Henry Taylor, councillor elect for the county of Washington, appeared, and being qualified as the Constitution and the act of Congress of the first of June last directs, was admitted to his seat at the Board.

IN COUNCIL.   *Philadelphia,* December 5, 1789.
A letter from Daniel Broadhead, Esq., Surveyor-General, dated November 23, 1789, nominating agreeably to act of Assembly of the 8th of April, 1785, Messrs. Presley Neville and Matthew Richie, as "deputy surveyors of a district late part of Washington County, part whereof has since been erected into a separate county called Allegheny, bounded by the great road leading from Fort Burd to the town of Washington, late Catfish Camp, from thence to the nearest head-waters of Buffalo Creek, thence

down the said creek to the line of the State, thence along the same to the River Ohio, thence up the same to the mouth of the Monongahela River, and thence up the same to the beginning," was received and read, and thereupon

Resolved, That the Board concur with the said nomination.

IN COUNCIL. *Philadelphia*, December, 8, 1789.

General John Gibson and John Neville, Esqs., were offered and accepted as sureties for Messrs. Presley Neville and Matthew Richie, deputy surveyors of part of Washington and Alleghany counties.

A petition from Margaret Jeffries, now confined in the workhouse of this city for larceny, praying remission of the fine, payable to the use of the State, and the punishment at hard labor, to which she was sentenced for the said offence, was read, and Mr. Taylor, member of Council, having informed the Board that the petitioner had agreed to enter into an indenture of service to him, and that he will send her to the county of Washington, if Council are pleased to pardon her, thereupon

Resolved, That the said Margaret Jeffries be and she is hereby pardoned.

IN COUNCIL. *Philadelphia*, December 9, 1789.

A certificate of the division of the township of Cecil, in the county of Washington, by the Court of Quarter Sessions, for the more convenient election of justices of the peace, which was read on the first day of September last, was this day read the second time, and an order taken that the said division for the purpose aforesaid be, and the same is hereby confirmed, according to the bounds and limits following, that is to say, beginning at Chartiers' Creek, at the junction or mouth of Brush Run, and continuing up the same as high as to Matthew Johnston's, to include his farm in the upper division; thence leaving James Read's farm to the lower division, directly to include GENERAL WASHINGTON's and Henry Guy's land in the upper division, and immediately to intersect to outside line of the township.

[In the Western Telegraph and Washington Advertiser, the following advertisement is published under date of Aug. 26, 1795. LAND FOR SALE. A tract of land of about three thousand acres, late the property of General Washington, lying on Miller's Run, in Washington County, Pennsylvania, of an excellent quality, rich, level, well timbered, and well watered, with a suitable proportion of meadow land, will be sold by the subscriber, living in Washington. There are thirteen farms cleared and cultivated on the land, and to accommodate purchasers, it will be divided into small tracts.   MATTHEW RICHIE.]

IN COUNCIL. *Philadelphia*, Dec. 10, 1789.

The Comptroller and Register General's reports upon the following accounts were read and approved, viz:—

Of Demus Lindley, for seven thousand and fifty-four weight of flour issued by him, from June the 14th until the 21st of November, 1788, to the Washington County militia, in actual service on the frontiers, by order of the Lieutenant of said county, amounting to forty-four pounds one shilling and nine pence, for which sum an order was drawn on the Treasurer for the sum, payable out of the militia fines of Washington County. (See March 4, 1790.)

Of Adam Miller, for one month's service as a spy, watching the motions of the Indians on the frontiers in the year 1788, amounting to two pounds fifteen shillings, for which sum an order was drawn on the Treasurer as aforesaid.

Of Ensign Isaac Lindley, for the pay of his company of Washington

County militia, for nine days' militia service on the frontiers, in October, 1787, amounting to four pounds nine shillings, for which sum an order was drawn upon the Treasurer, payable as aforesaid.

Of George Tompoh, for his provisions employed as a militia man on the frontiers of Washington County, and for a blanket, a pack saddle, and two bags, lost on the said expedition, under Colonel Crawford in 1782, amounting to two pounds seven shilling and sixpence.

Of John Hill, for a saddle, blanket, two bags, and a wallet or knapsack, lost on the said expedition, amounting to four pounds two shillings and sixpence.

Of Robert Taylor, for thirty days' provisions due him while employed on the said expedition, amounting to one pound two shillings and sixpence.

Of Richard Hopkins, for a horse lost on said expedition, amounting to four pounds.

Of John Turvey, for thirty days' provisions due to him while employed on the said expedition, amounting to one pound two shillings and sixpence.

A certificate of the division of Hopewell township, in the county of Washington, by the Court of Quarter Sessions, for the more convenient election of justices of the peace, agreeably to the act of Assembly, passed the thirty-first day of March, 1784, which was read on the first day of September last, was this day read the second time, and an order taken that the said division for the purpose aforesaid, be, and the same is hereby confirmed according to the bounds and limits following, that is to say, beginning at a certain spring on the head-waters of Cross Creek, which rises about ten perches from the township of Straban, between the dwelling houses of James Anderson and Timothy Spencer, thence down the south branch thereof to Wells' mills, thence down the creek to the State line.

IN COUNCIL.   *Philadelphia*, Dec. 17, 1789.

The Comptroller and Register-General's reports upon the following accounts were read and approved, viz:—

Of Robert Walker, Jr., of Washington County, for provisions furnished by him for the Sandusky expedition under Colonel Crawford, in the year 1782, amounting to one pound two shillings and sixpence.

Of Captain John Reed, for the pay of his Washington County militia, in actual service against the Indians, by order of the Lieutenant of said county, from the 24th of September to the 29th of October, 1788, amounting to forty-six pounds seven shillings, for which sum an order was drawn upon the treasurer in favor of the said Captain John Reed, payable out of the militia fines of said county.

Of Lieutenant Alexander Kidd, for the pay of his company of the said militia in actual service as aforesaid, from the 22d of October to the 24th of November, 1788, amounting to forty pounds sixteen shilling and eight pence, for which sum an order was drawn upon the Treasurer in favor of the said Alexander Kidd, payable out of said fines.

IN COUNCIL.   *Philadelphia*, Dec. 28, 1789.

Upon the second reading of the return of an election of justices of the peace, held in the township of Findley, in the county of Washington, on the 28th of July last, with a petition against it,

Resolved, That William Smith, Esq., be appointed and commissionated a justice of the peace and of the Court of Common Pleas in and for the said county of Washington, he having a majority of votes.

IN COUNCIL.   *Philadelphia*, Jan. 11, 1790.

James Bell, Esq., was appointed and commissionated a justice of the peace and of the Common Pleas in and for the county of Washington, upon a return made according to law, from the district of the township of Morgan in said county.

IN COUNCIL. *Philadelphia*, Jan. 18, 1790.
A certificate from the Court of Quarter Sessions of Washington County, of the division of Bethlehem township in the said county, by a straight line run from Peter Drake's to Weise's mills, for the more convenient election of justices of the peace, agreeably to act of Assembly passed the thirty-first day of March, 1784, was read the second time, by which it appears that the said division has become proper and will be useful, it was thereupon
Resolved, That the same be confirmed.

IN COUNCIL. *Philadelphia*, Jan. 22, 1790.
An order was drawn upon the Treasurer in favor of Hon. Henry Taylor, Esq., for the sum of forty-nine pounds fifteen shillings, in full for his attendance in council, from the 3d day of December, 1789, until the 22d day of January, 1790 (deducting six days' absence), and his mileage coming to Philadelphia and returning to Washington County.

IN COUNCIL. *Philadelphia*, Jan. 25, 1790.
Mr. Ross and Mr. Addison, members of Convention, and Mr. Ryerson, member of Assembly for the county of Washington, attended and produced in writing, a statement of the depredations committed by the savages within that county from time to time, and submitting the same to the consideration of Council, whereupon
Resolved, That Mr. Findley, Mr. Miles, and Mr. Taylor, be appointed a committee to confer with the said gentlemen, upon the subject of a defence for the western counties against the Indians, and that they make report to Council.

IN COUNCIL. *Philadelphia*, Feb. 13, 1790.
A letter from Daniel Broadhead, Esq., Surveyor-General, of the 2d day of February inst., informing Council that he has appointed Messrs. David Redick and John Hoge deputy surveyors of a district bounded and described as follows, viz: Northerly by the great road leading from Fort Bird to the town of Washington, thence by a direct course to the nearest head-waters of Buffalo Creek, and down the said creek to the State line, easterly by the Monongahela River, southwardly by the continuation of Mason and Dixon's line, and westerly by the State line aforesaid, and submitting the said appointments to Council for their approbation, agreeably to act of Assembly, passed the 8th day of April, 1785, was received and read, and thereupon
Resolved, That Council approve of the said appointments, and that Col. James Marshall and Andrew Swearingen be accepted as sureties for the said deputy surveyors.

IN COUNCIL. *Philadelphia*, Feb. 18, 1790.
The Comptroller and Register-General's reports upon the following accounts were read and approved, viz:—
Of Joseph Brown for one month's pay as a volunteer militia-man, while stationed at one McDonald's, for the defence of the frontiers of the county of Washington, in August, 1782, amounting to five pounds five shillings.
Of Samuel Brown for forty days' pay as a militia-man in Captain Robert Miller's Company, stationed on the frontiers of said county in the year 1782 and 1783, amounting to four pounds.
Of Alexander Lashley for a horse which was taken into public service

and lost on the Sandusky expedition against the Indians, under Col. Crawford, in the year 1782, valued at twelve pounds, and allowed.

Of George Sharp for bacon and flour furnished the militia of Washington County under his command, on the frontiers of said county, in March, 1785, amounting to two pounds four shillings.

IN COUNCIL. *Philadelphia*, March 4, 1790.

Upon the second reading of the report of the Committee to whom was referred the application for a new order in favor of Demus Linsley :—

Resolved, That the order which was granted to him for forty-four pounds one shilling and ninepence, on December 10, 1789, on the militia fines of Washington County, be cancelled, and that a new order for the same be issued, payable out of the militia funds of the county of Lancaster.

IN COUNCIL. *Philadelphia*, March 8, 1790.

A letter from Thomas Ryerson, Esq., member of Assembly, relative to the defence of the western frontiers, against the invasion of the Indians, was received and read, whereupon it was

Resolved, That to-morrow be assigned for taking into consideration the several papers now before the Council, on the subject of a frontier defence.

IN COUNCIL. *Philadelphia*, March 22, 1790.

A letter from his Excellency, the President of the United States, dated the 15th inst., in answer to the letter from the President of this State, of the 10th, which inclosed the representatives from some of the inhabitants of Washington County, respecting the mischiefs which have been committed for several years past by the Indians in that county, was received and read, and the same was transmitted to the General Assembly in a letter from the President to the Speaker.

IN COUNCIL, *Philadelphia*, April 6, 1790.

An order was drawn upon the Treasurer in favor of the Honorable Henry Taylor for the sum of fifty-five pounds ten shillings in full of his account for his attendance in council, from the 23d day of January until the 6th day of April, 1790, inclusively.

James Archer, Esq., was appointed and commissionated a justice of the peace and of the Court of Common Pleas in and for the county of Washington, upon a return made according to law, from the district of the township of Franklin, in the said county.

IN COUNCIL. *Philadelphia*, April 19, 1790.

A letter from Henry Knox, Secretary of War, of the 15th inst., inclosing a copy of a letter which has been forwarded by him to the Lieutenant of Washington County in this State, authorizing him to embody any number of men, not exceeding eighty, for a temporary security to the frontiers of this State, was received and read.

IN COUNCIL. *Philadelphia*, August 19, 1790.

Resolved, That the Lieutenant of the county of Washington be directed to transmit to Council as soon as may be, a return of the officers of the militia of the said county in order that commissions may issue to them, and that the Secretary write to the said Lieutenant and inclose him a copy of this resolution.

IN COUNCIL. *Philadelphia*, August 24, 1790.

James Mitchell, John Cannon, and Henry Graham, Esquires, were appointed and commissionated justices of the peace and of the Court of Common Pleas in and for the county of Washington, upon returns made to Council of elections held, according to law, in the following districts, viz: James Mitchell elected in the district of Peters township; John Cannon in the district of Chartiers, and Henry Graham in the district of Cross Creek.

IN COUNCIL. *Philadelphia, August* 28, 1790.

The report of the Comptroller and Register-Generals upon the following accounts was read and approved :—

Of Moses Cook, for a horse which was lost on the Sandusky expedition against the Indians, in the year 1782, amounting to fifteen pounds.

Of James Brownlee, for flour furnished to the militia of Washington County, in the month of May, June, and July, 1787, under the command of Colonel Marshall, amounting to nine pounds three shillings and three-pence.

IN COUNCIL. *Philadelphia,* September 4, 1790.

It having been determined at a conference of members of the General Assembly; the members of the Supreme Executive Council; the Judges of Supreme Court, Judges Shippen and Wilson; the Attorney-General of the State, and Alexander Wilcocks and Jared Ingersoll, Esquires, Attorneys-at-law, that the powers of the legislature of the present year expired on Thursday the second instant, and that the office of State Treasurer and Register-General of the accounts of this commonwealth, and of Register of Wills and a Recorder of Deeds in each county of this State, in like manner expired on the said day; therefore

Resolved, That by virtue of the powers vested in this Board by the Constitution of this State,

Thomas Stokely be and hereby is appointed Register for the Probate of Wills and granting Letters of Administration, and Recorder of Deeds, in and for the county of Washington.

IN COUNCIL. *Philadelphia,* September 22, 1790.

The following accounts were read and approved, viz :—

Of Thomas Scott, Esq., Clerk of the Peace of the county of Washington, for moneys received by him for fees upon tavern licenses from December, 1788, until June, 1789, amounting to thirty-nine pounds twelve shillings, which sum hath been paid into the treasury.

Of Daniel Beam, for his pay for sixty days' service as a Ranger on the frontiers of Washington County, in the militia, in the months of April and June, 1788, and for provisions during the same time, amounting to five pounds ten shillings.

IN COUNCIL. *Philadelphia,* November 10, 1790.

Andrew Swearingen and Gabriel Blakely were offered and accepted as sureties for Thomas Stokely, Esq., who was, on the 4th day of September last reappointed Register for the Probate of Wills and granting Letters of Administration, and Recorder of Deeds, in and for the county of Washington.

IN COUNCIL. *Philadelphia,* December 11, 1790.

A letter from John Hoge, Esq., informing council that at the last general election held in the district composed of the counties of Washington and Fayette, he has been elected to represent that district in the Senate of this State, and requesting that Council would be pleased to accept his resignation of the offices of justice of the peace, and of the Court of Common Pleas for the county of Washington, which he now holds, previous to his taking his seat, was read, whereupon it was

Resolved, To accept the said resignation.

IN COUNCIL.   *Philadelphia,* December 14, 1790.
It being represented to Council that William Wallace, Esq., Sheriff of the county of Washington, and Samuel Clarke, Coroner of the said county of Washington, are prevented from attending in Philadelphia to enter into negotiations and to give bonds with sureties, as the act of Assembly of the 5th of March last directs; thereupon

Resolved, That a commission under the great seal be issued to Alexander Scott and Dr. Absalom Baird, of the said county, authorizing them to take from the said sheriff and coroner the said recognizances and bonds, in the manner prescribed in and by the said act of Assembly, and that the said commissioners make a report to council of their proceedings in the premises.

Thomas Scott and John Hoge, Esqrs., were accepted as sureties for the said William Wallace, and John Hoge, and Henry Taylor, Esqrs., as sureties for the said Samuel Clarke.

IN COUNCIL.   *Philadelphia,* December 20, 1790.
The following order was drawn upon the Treasurer, viz:—

In favor of the Honorable Henry Taylor, for forty-four pounds ten shillings, for attendance in council from the 14th of November to the 21st of December, and mileage coming to Philadelphia and returning to Washington County.

The Constitution of 1790 going into effect, the office of Supreme Executive Council was abolished. But very few persons having access to the twenty-eight octavo volumes which compose our colonial records and archives, I concluded to incorporate in this volume every fact contained therein in relation to Washington County, so that in the future it could be referred to.

CHAPTER V.

TOWNSHIPS AND BOROUGHS IN WASHINGTON COUNTY.

The history of the Townships and Boroughs in their chronological order, detailing interesting events in each—Also the history of churches and the present state of education in each Township and Borough.

WE now proceed to the history of the townships of Washington County, which have been enumerated in chapter three, commencing with the thirteen original townships, and placing them in alphabetical order; these townships having been organized on July 15th, 1781. When one of the original townships has been subdivided, or boroughs formed therein, we shall place its history with the township from which it was taken, yet giving a separate history. New townships and boroughs we shall place in chronological order.

HISTORY OF WASHINGTON COUNTY.

AMWELL TOWNSHIP.

In the original record of this county its name is written "Aimwell." At the date of its organization, July 15th, 1781, it was bounded on the north by Strabane township, east by Bethlehem township, south by Morgan township (a township of Greene County since 1796), and on the west by Donegal.

Its present boundaries are South Strabane on the north, Morris and Franklin on the west, West Bethlehem on the east, and Greene County on the south. On the 19th of June, 1838, part of Amwell was annexed to Strabane township, and at the May term of court in 1856, the township lines between Amwell and Morris were changed and confirmed. It is centrally distant from the borough of Washington ten miles. Its population in 1860 was 2042, of which seven were colored. Its greatest length is ten miles, breadth four and one-half miles.

This township is drained by the north fork of Tenmile Creek, by the little North fork and Bane's fork of the same creek. It contains four stores, one distillery, and ten schools, employing five male and five female teachers, the former receiving thirty-eight dollars and thirty-eight cents, and the latter thirty-three dollars and five cents each per month, with five hundred and nineteen scholars, of which two hundred and eighty-six are males and two hundred and thirty-three are females—the tuition costing each scholar per month eighty-three cents. Amount of tax levied for building purposes, four hundred and thirty-eight dollars and ninety-five cents—total amount levied for school purposes, two thousand four hundred and thirty-nine dollars and fourteen cents; amount received from the State appropriation one hundred and eighty-three dollars and thirty cents. The towns are AMITY and CLARKTOWN (TENMILE VILLAGE.)

Amity is about ten miles from the county seat, and is on Bane's fork of Tenmile Creek and on the road leading from Washington to Waynesburg, containing thirty-four dwellings, two stores, a Presbyterian church* under the care of Rev. J. W. Hamilton, and a Methodist Protestant church, the pastor of which is Rev. F. A. Day.

This town was located about the year 1790 by Daniel Dodd, Esq., a brother of the Rev. Thaddeus Dodd, who owned the land, formed the plan, and numbered the lots. The position being central, on the main thoroughfare to Greene County, a hewed log Presbyterian church, stores, tavern, and dwelling houses were soon erected. At that early date the churches were destitute of heating apparatus, and the church-going members sat in their pews with their great coats and mittens, while the women were muffled up—not in furs, but in home-made dresses and comfortable shawls. Here we may remark, that both before and after preaching by Rev. Dodd, the male part of the congregation used to resort to the tavern to warm themselves, the house being now occupied as a private dwelling by Squire Clutter, no tavern being licensed in the place. In those early days athletic

---

* See pp. 217, 218.

sports were much more in vogue than at present; long bullets, the ball alley, and target shooting were the favorite exercises, and the party losing paid their forfeit by ordering drinks for all hands.

MORMONISM.

The village of Amity, in all coming time, will be regarded as the Mecca of Mormonism. It was in the year 1816 that the Rev. Solomon Spaulding, a graduate of Dartmouth College, settled in this rural village, with a view to banish *ennui*. He was (what is familiarly known as) an antiquarian, and travelled far and near to investigate, scientifically, Indian mounds, and everything else connected with American antiquities, for the purpose of tracing the aborigines to their original source, a portion of one of the lost tribes of ancient Israel. While pursuing these investigations, and to while away the tedious hours, he wrote a romance, based upon fiction; his investigations and history at the same time leaving the reader under the impression that it was found in one of these mounds, and through his knowledge of hieroglyphics he had deciphered it. As time and circumstances would permit, he would often read to his friends in Amity portions of his fabulous and historical romance.

Rev. Spaulding resolved to publish it under the name of "The Manuscript Found," and actually entered into a contract with a Mr. Patterson, of Pittsburg, to publish the same, but from some cause the contract was not fulfilled. The manuscript remained in the possession of Mr. Patterson between two and three years before Mr. Spaulding reclaimed and recovered it. In the mean time a journeyman printer of the name of Sidney Rigden copied the whole of the manuscript, and hearing of Joseph Smith, Jr.'s, digging operations for money through the instrumentality of necromancy, resolved in his own mind that he would turn this wonderful manuscript to good account and make it profitable to himself. An interview takes place between Rigden and Smith, terms are agreed upon, the whole manuscript undergoes a partial revision, and in process of time, instead of finding money, they find CURIOUS PLATES, which, when translated, turn out to be the GOLDEN BIBLE, or BOOK OF MORMON, which was found under the prediction of Mormon in these words (see Mormon Bible, p. 504): "Go to the land Antum, unto a hill which shall be called Shin, and there have I deposited unto the Lord all the sacred engravings concerning this people." Oliver Cowdery, David Whitmer, and Martin Harris, certify that they have seen these selfsame plates which were deposited by Mormon—that they were faithfully translated by the gift and power of God, because God's voice declared it unto them, that the work was true, and to place the testimony of its truthfulness beyond a peradventure, eight witnesses, viz: Christian Whitmer, Jacob Whitmer, Peter Whitmer, John Whitmer, Hiram Page, Joseph Smith, Sr., Hiram Smith, and Samuel H. Smith (almost all of the witnesses belonging either to the Whitmer or Smith family), testify that Joseph Smith, Jr., the translator, showed them the plates of gold, that they handled them with their own hands, saw the curious engravings, and that the plates were of curious workmanship. Such is the account of the most stupendous imposture which has been perpetrated for many centuries, but more especially upon so intelligent a nation as the American people. An imposture, at which the religious world stands amazed, paralyzing the marriage vow, and defying the power of the general government.

To place this question beyond the possibility of a doubt, and to demonstrate the fact that the Book of Mormon was originally written in Amity, Washington County, Pa., I shall take the testimony of living witnesses, whose characters are beyond reproach, and beloved by the entire community as persons whose veracity cannot be questioned, and whose intelligence has no superior. The testimony I shall offer is a letter from the Rev. J. W. Hamilton, pastor of the Presbyterian church in Amity, Pa.—a letter from Joseph Miller, Sr., the intimate and confidential friend of Rev. Solomon Spaulding, and lastly, a letter from the wife of Rev. Spaulding, which was originally published thirty-one years since, or in 1839.

1. Letter of Rev. J. W. Hamilton

BOOK OF MORMON.

Some time since I became the owner of the book of Mormon. I put it into the hands of Mr. Joseph Miller, Sr., of Amwell township. After examining it he makes the following statement concerning the connection of Rev. Solomon Spaulding with the authorship of the book of Mormon.

Mr. Miller is now in the seventy-ninth year of his age. He is an elder in the Cumberland Presbyterian Church. His judgment is good and his veracity unimpeachable. He was well acquainted with Mr. S. while he lived at Amity. He waited on him during his last illness. He made his coffin, and assisted to bury his remains where they now lie, in the Presbyterian graveyard at Amity. He also bailed Mr. S.'s wife when she took out letters of administration on his estate.

Mr. Miller's statement may be relied on as true.   J. W. Hamilton.

2. Letter of Jos. Miller, Sr.

When Mr. Spaulding lived in Amity, Pa., I was well acquainted with him. I was frequently at his house. He kept what is called a tavern. It was understood that he had been a preacher; but his health failed him and he ceased to preach. I never knew him to preach after he came to Amity.

He had in his possession some papers which he said he had written. He used to read select portions of these papers to amuse us of evenings.

These papers were detached sheets of foolscap. He said he wrote the papers as a novel. He called it the "Manuscript Found," or "The Lost Manuscript Found." He said he wrote it to pass away the time when he was unwell; and after it was written he thought he would publish it as a novel, as a means to support his family.

Some time since, a copy of the book of Mormon came into my hands. My son read it for me, as I have a nervous shaking of the head that prevents me from reading. I noticed several passages which I recollect having heard Mr. Spaulding read from his "Manuscript." One passage on the 148th page (the copy I have is published by J. O. Wright & Co., New York) I remember distinctly. He speaks of a battle, and says the Amalekites had *marked* themselves with *red* on the foreheads to distinguish them from the Nephites. The thought of being marked on the forehead with red was so strange, it fixed itself in my memory. This together with other passages I remember to have heard Mr. Spaulding read from his "Manuscript."

Those who knew Mr. Spaulding will soon all be gone, and I among the rest. I write that what I know may become a matter of history; and that it may prevent people from being led into Mormonism, that most seductive delusion of the devil.

From what I know of Mr. Spaulding's "Manuscript" and the book of Mormon, I firmly believe that Joseph Smith, by some means, got possession of Mr. Spaulding's "Manuscript," and possibly made some changes in it and called it the "Book of Mormon." JOSEPH MILLER, SR.

March 26, 1869.

3. LETTER OF MRS. DAVIDSON, FORMERLY MRS. SPAULDING.

THE MORMON BIBLE.

Joseph Miller, Esq., an old and highly respected citizen of Amwell township, sends us by hand of Rev. J. W. Hamilton, of Amity, the following communication, which originally appeared in a magazine entitled the *Evangelist of the True Gospel*, published at Carthage, Ohio, in 1839.

Mr. Miller has, on various occasions heretofore, furnished us with many interesting incidents connected with the career of Solomon Spaulding, and the origin of the so-called Mormon Bible. The present contribution, which consists of a statement from the wife of Mr. Spaulding, seems to furnish conclusive evidence that the "Manuscript Found," written by her husband, and the "Book of Mormon," are one and the same.

Origin of the "Book of Mormon," or "Golden Promise."—As this book has excited much attention, and has been put by a certain new sect in the place of the Sacred Scriptures, I deem it a duty which I owe to the public to state what I know touching its origin. That its claims to a divine origin are wholly unfounded, needs no proof to a mind unperverted by the grossest delusions. That any sane person should rank it higher than any other merely human composition, is a matter of the greatest astonishment; yet it is received as divine by those who dwell in enlightened New England, and even by those who have sustained the character of devoted Christians. Learning recently that Mormonism has found its way into a church in Massachusetts, and has impregnated some of its members with its gross delusions, so that excommunication has become necessary, I am determined to delay no longer doing what I can to strip the mask from this monster of sin, and to lay open this pit of abominations.

Rev. Solomon Spaulding, to whom I was united in marriage in early life, was a graduate of Dartmouth College, and was distinguished for a lively imagination and a great fondness for history. At the time of our marriage he resided at Cherry Valley, New York. From this place we removed to New Salem, Ashtabula County, Ohio, sometimes called Conneaut, as it is situated upon Conneaut Creek. Shortly after our removal to this place his health sunk, and he was laid aside from active labors. In the town of New Salem there are numerous mounds and forts, supposed by many to be the dilapidated dwellings and fortifications of a race now extinct. These ancient relics arrested the attention of the new settlers, and became objects of research for the curious. Numerous implements were found, and other articles evincing great skill in the arts. Mr. Spaulding being an educated man, and passionately fond of history, took a lively interest in these developments of antiquity, and in order to beguile the hours of retirement, and furnish employment for his lively imagination, he conceived the idea of giving *an historical sketch of this long lost race.* Their extreme antiquity of course would lead him to write in the *most ancient style,* and as the Old Testament is the most ancient book in the world, he imitated its style as nearly as possible. His sole object in writing this *historical romance* was to amuse himself and his neighbors. This was about the year 1812. Hull's surrender at Detroit occurred near the same time, and I recollect the date from that circumstance. As he progressed in his narrative, the neighbors would come in from time to time to hear portions read, and a great interest in the work was excited among them. It claimed to have been written by *one of the lost nation,* and to have been *recovered from the earth,* and assumed the title of "Manuscript Found." The neighbors would often inquire how Mr. S. progressed in deciphering the manuscript, and when he had a sufficient portion prepared he would inform them, and they would assemble to hear it read. He was enabled, from his acquaintance with the classics and ancient history, to introduce *many singular names,* which were particularly noticed by the people, and could be easily recognized by them. Mr. Solomon Spaulding had a brother, Mr. John Spaulding, residing in the place at the time, who was perfectly familiar with this work, and repeatedly heard the whole of it read.

From New Salem we removed to Pittsburg, Pennsylvania. Here Mr. S. found an acquaintance and friend in the person of Mr. Patterson, an editor of a newspaper. He exhibited his manuscript to Mr. P., who was very much pleased with it, and borrowed it for perusal. He retained it a long time, and informed Mr. S. that if he would make out a title page and preface, he would publish it, and it might be a source of profit. This Mr. S. refused to do, for reasons which I cannot state. Sidney Rigdon, who has figured so largely in the history of the Mormons, was at this time connected with the printing-office of Mr. Patterson, as is well known in that region, and as Rigdon himself has frequently stated. Here he had ample opportunity to become acquainted with Mr. Spaulding's manuscript, and to copy it if he chose. It was a matter of notoriety to all who were connected with the printing establishment. At length the manuscript was returned to its author, and soon after we removed to Amity, Washington County, Pa., where Mr. S. deceased in 1816. The manuscript then fell into my hands and was carefully preserved. It has frequently been examined by my daughter, Mrs. M'Kinstry, of Monson, Massachusetts, with whom I now reside, and by other friends. After the "Book of Mormon" came out, a copy of it was taken to New Salem, the place of Mr. Spaulding's former residence, and the very place where the "Manuscript Found" was written. A woman-preacher appointed a meeting there; and, in the meeting, read and repeated copious extracts from the "Book of Mormon." The historical part was immediately recognized by all the older inhabitants as the identical work of Mr. Spaulding, in which they had been deeply interested before. Mr. John Spaulding was present, who is an eminently pious man, and *recognized perfectly* the work of his brother. He was amazed and afflicted that it should have been perverted to so wicked a purpose. His grief found vent in a flood of tears; and he arose on the spot, and expressed in the meeting his deep sorrow and regret that the writings of his sainted brother should be used for a purpose so vile and shocking. The excitement in New Salem became so great that the inhabitants held a meeting and deputed Dr. Philastus Hurlbut, one of their number, to repair to this place and to obtain from me the original manuscript of Mr. Spaulding, for the purpose of comparing it with the Mormon Bible, to satisfy their own minds, and to prevent their friends from embracing an error so delusive. This was in the year 1834. Dr. Hurlbut brought with him an introduction and request for the manuscript signed by Messrs. Henry Lake, Aaron Wright, and others, with all of whom I was acquainted, as they were my neighbors when I resided in New Salem.

I am sure that nothing could grieve my husband more, were he living, than the use which has been made of his work. The air of antiquity which was thrown about the composition doubtless suggested the idea of converting it to purposes of delusion. This historical romance, with the addition of a few pious expressions and extracts from the Sacred Scriptures, has been construed into a new Bible, and palmed off upon a company of poor deluded fanatics as divine. I have given the previous narration, that this work of deep deception and wickedness may be searched to the foundation, and its author exposed to the contempt and execration he so justly deserves.

MATILDA DAVIDSON.

The Rev. Solomon Spaulding was the first husband of the narrator of the above history. Since his decease she has been married to a second husband, by the name of Davidson. She is now residing in this place, is a woman of irreproachable character, and an humble Christian, and her testimony worthy of implicit confidence.

A. ELY, D. D.,
Pastor Congregational Church, Monson.
D. R. ELY,
Principal of Monson Academy.

TENMILE VILLAGE.

I have been favored with the following description of Clarktown, or Tenmile Village, by J. C. Milliken, M. D., one of our most successful physicians in this county :—

This town is situated in the southern part of the county, near the line of Greene County, on North Tenmile Creek. It is one of our neatest country villages, with one main street and another running across it at nearly right angles ; the houses are generally neatly painted, with yards in front ornamented with evergreens, shrubbery, and flowers. The town contains one large flour and saw-mill, one blacksmith shop, one dry-goods store, one carriage and wagon factory, one shoemaker shop, two physicians, and a population of about two hundred and twenty. It contains a Masonic lodge, and a school-house capable of containing one hundred scholars, in which the usual branches are taught nine months in the year.

EARLY SETTLERS.

Of the *early settlers* in this part of the county, as well as the adjoining county of Greene, we desire to speak. The first settlers were squatters who purchased the land from the native Indians for a gun, trinket, or gewgaw, of whom were John Rutman and Dennis Smith, the former dying at the age of ninety-nine and the latter at one hundred and four; these two, with William Gordon, Russel Reese, John Lorrison, and John James constituted the principal original settlers.

From the year 1770 to 1790 they were followed by a different kind of men, who patented their lands and obtained them legally; these early pioneers were Nathaniel McGiffin, David Evans, James Milliken, Abel McFarland, George Cooper, and John Bates, some of whom served in the Revolutionary war with marked distinction with Washington, La Fayette, Green, Marion, and Sumpter.

FORTS.

For their protection these early settlers erected two forts, one called *Fort Milliken*, situated on a beautiful mound on the farm of Mrs. Samuel Braden, the other was named *Fort McFarland*, and located on the farm of Peter Garrett. There was a third fort or blockhouse on the farm now owned by Nehemiah Woodruff, Esq., where many bones, arrows, wares, and trinkets are unearthed by the farmer's plough. The mound that encircled the area of this third fort until recently was covered with large trees, and in the immediate vicinity are numerous burying-grounds of the Indians.

CHURCHES.

In the fall of the year 1831 the Revs. A. M. Bryan, John Morgan, A. Chapman, R. Burrow, and R. Donnel came as missionaries to proclaim the doctrines of the Cumberland Presbyterian Church. They held a camp-meeting on Abel Milliken's farm near Fort Milliken. In May, 1832, another camp-meeting was held, and another in January, 1833; the result of these camp-meetings was the organization of a church on the 22d of January, 1833, which was called *Pleasant Hill*. The church is built of brick, and located about half a mile from the village.

The following pastors have officiated, viz: Rev. John Morgan, for one year and a half; Rev. Alexander Robinson, one year; Rev. S. P. Allen, one year; Rev. E. Howland, six months; Rev. Milton Bird, five years; Rev. James McFarland, six months; Rev. John Carey, twelve years; Rev. Philip Axtell, four years; Rev. Stephen Winget, ten years; Rev. Jesse Adams, two years. Rev. Philip Axtell is the present incumbent.

NORTH TENMILE BAPTIST CHURCH.

Is situated on a ridge two miles north of Tenmile village. Its history runs back as far as the year 1772. In their first labors they were much troubled with the Indians, and were often compelled to hold their meeting in Fort McFarland. Their present church is the third which has been erected on the same ground. The Rev. James Sutton was their *first* regular pastor; he was chosen February

4, 1774; he served for seven years. His successor was Rev. Joh Corbly, who remained for two years. He was followed by Rev. David Sutton. How long he preached cannot be ascertained, because the church records are lost, and our next preacher of which we have any sure knowledge was Rev. Charles Wheeler, who became the pastor in 1831 and served five years. In 1836, Rev. A. B. Bowman became the pastor and resigned in 1839, when the Rev. Levi Griffith was elected, and officiated until 1842. His successor was Rev. F. Downey, who served until 1846, then followed Rev. Wm. Whitehead for eighteen months; Rev. S. Kendall Lenning, for six and a half years; Rev. T. C. Gunford, for one year; Rev. W. Scott, for six months; Rev. B. P. Ferguson, for two and a half years; Rev. J. Boyd, for three years. In 1865, Rev. W. B. Skinner became pastor, who remained until 1867. His successor, until 1868, was Rev. S. Kendall, who was followed by the present incumbent, Rev. C. W. Tilton.

American Patriotism.

On February 6, 1839, the citizens of Amwell township met and elected John Carter President, and Samuel L. Hughes Secretary. The object of the meeting was to adopt measures to check the bitterness of party strife, sink the character of the politician, and arise superior to party dictation and party influence, by assuming the character and attributes of an American patriot.

Bethlehem Township

Was one of the original townships, organized July 15, 1781. It was at that period bounded by Straban and Fallowfield townships on the north, the Monongahela River on the east, Amwell and Franklin townships on the south, and Amwell on the east.

Application was made to the Court of Quarter Sessions on March 13, 1788, to divide the township into East and West Bethlehem townships, and on the 18th of January, 1790, the court directed the division to be made by a straight line running from Peter Drake's to Weise's mill.

On the 29th of March, 1788, before the division of the township, we find Michael Simon and Anne Ottia his wife conveying to the trustees of the Dutch Presbyterians two and a fourth acres of land situate on Brush Run, a branch of Tenmile Creek, to be used for divine worship, and teaching of school, and a burial-ground.

April 12, 1792, Joseph Townsend and wife conveyed to James Crawford, Nathaniel Heald, Abraham Smith, John Townsend, John Heald, and Isaac Jenkinson, as trustees of the Quaker Westland meeting-house, a certain lot of ground, containing twenty acres, for a meeting-house, burying-ground, and other necessary purposes, in consideration of twenty pounds, Pennsylvania currency. This land is on the draws of the Monongahela River and Twomile Run.

East Bethlehem Township.

It is bounded north by East and West Pike Run, east by the Monongahela River, south by Greene County, and west by West Bethlehem. It is centrally distant from Washington eighteen miles, its greatest length, nine miles, breadth, four and a half miles. The National road crosses the river by a bridge in the northeast angle of this township. On this road are *Frederickstown* and *Millsborough*, but have been erected into separate boroughs.

East Bethlehem has five stores, one distillery, and ten schools, employing three male and seven female teachers; the average monthly salary of the former is $36.66, and of the latter $33.14. The number of scholars is four hundred and thirty, of which two hundred and twenty-eight are males, and two hundred and two are females; the cost of tuition per month, $1.18 per scholar; amount levied for school purposes, $1792.39; received from the State appropriation, $175.89. Population in 1860, white, 1825; colored, 37, amounting to 1862.

August 25th, 1843, an alteration was made and confirmed by the court on the division line between West Pike Run and East Bethlehem townships.

November 30th, 1848, the court, upon petition and hearing the report of viewers, attached all that part of East Bethlehem to East Pike Run except West Brownsville, which is north of the National road. At the August term, 1861, the line between East and West Bethlehem was changed, so as to include Thomas Martindale in East Bethlehem.

Fredericktown

Is on the west bank of the Monongahela River, below the great bend, two miles north of the mouth of Tenmile Creek, eight miles above Brownsville, and twenty miles southwest of Washington. It was laid out by Frederick Wise, on August 21, 1790, although the land was patented March 22d, 1788, under the name of sugar-tree bottom. In laying out the town, the proprietor reserved one acre of ground for a cemetery, and lot No. 44 for a school-house, upon which a brick edifice has been erected, containing one graded school with two departments.

The town was surveyed and laid off by Isaac Jenkinson; lots measured 60 by 180, having Water, Main, and Bank streets running parallel with the river, and Washington, Walnut, and Sycamore running at right angles to the former; each street being 50 feet wide except Main, which is 60. The proprietor of the town entered into an agreement with Isaac Jenkinson and others September 20, 1793, recorded in the Recorder's office of this county, that no distillery for the destruction of grain or fruit shall be at any time erected on the premises, by or under said Wise or any purchaser of his or their purchase.

In 1793 a public library was established, which continued in operation until the 31st day of July, 1825, when it was closed and the books sold.

The town contains a population of 320 inhabitants; a stoneware pottery, manufacturing 30,000 gallons annually; a grist and sawmill; two hotels; a rectifying distillery; fifty dwellings; and salt works, the well being 520 feet deep.

About a mile below Fredericktown is a curious cave called the *Panther's den*. It enters the hill half way from its base, by a small fracture or rent in the rock. After going a few yards through a narrow and descending passage, you enter a wide but low room in which you can walk nearly upright; to the roof of this room the exploring party found bats hanging in a stupid kind of sleep. By clambering up another fracture in the rock, they entered another room; they were required to roll themselves through this room, and entered a third by a narrow and descending passage, occasioned by another rent in the rock. This room was high enough to walk upright in, and was divided by a partition of petrifactions, formed by the drippings of water through the roof. The party explored it about forty yards.

David S. Wilson, Esq., of Washington, has kindly permitted me to copy the following letter, the original of which is in his possession, and is a proud monument to the citizens of Fredericktown and its vicinity, showing their devotion to our government in its infant state. The letter is in the hand-writing of John Adams, President of the United States.

To the inhabitants of Fredericktown and its vicinity, in the county of Washington and the State of Pennsylvania—

Gentlemen: Your memorial to the President, Senate, and House of Representatives has been presented to me by Judge Addison, for which I return you my thanks.

From the beginning of the world, the elements of division of opinion among the people have existed; the distinctions of the wise and foolish, learned and ignorant, industrious and idle, strong and weak, virtuous and vicious, have ever prevailed, and while these continue men will think differently. One would imagine that under a constitution of their own choice they might agree, but we find that they do not; to be sure to seek shelter under a foreign power is another thing; they must be depraved and lost, who are capable of this. Very few, if any, whose blood was first distilled from the American soil can be of the number; these will very generally pledge themselves to a cordial attention to every duty incumbent on citizens of a free and independent Republic.   JOHN ADAMS.

Philadelphia, July 7, 1798.

MILLSBOROUGH

Was incorporated as a borough on April 16, 1840. Its population in 1860 was 292. It is 21 miles distant from Washington, and is situate in East Bethlehem township, and was laid out by Jesse Bomgarner in the year 1700 (the land being patented June 3, 1769) on the north bank of Tenmile Creek, at its confluence with the

Monongahela River, at which there is a ferry. The streets are 50 feet wide—lots, 60 by 180 feet. The houses, generally frame, and some brick; yet a few of the old landmarks (log houses) still remain to remind the inhabitants of the days of "Auld Lang Syne." There are sixty dwelling-houses and three churches, viz., a Cumberland Presbyterian, under the care of Rev. J. S. Gibson; a Methodist Episcopal, under charge of Rev. Mr. Hill, and a Methodist Protestant Church; two cabinet-makers, five stores, two cooper shops, one blacksmith shop, two foundries, one hotel, one wagon manufactory, a steam grist-mill, a saw mill, and one rectifying distillery in this borough. Mill Street is the principal street, being 60 feet wide, while the remaining streets, Ferry, Walnut, Water, and Morgantown, are but 40 feet. Three of these run east and west, and the others intersect them at right angles.

Millsboro' has two school-houses with 82 scholars, 34 males and 48 females; cost of tuition per month is $1.09; amount of taxes levied for school purposes, $2.77; State appropriation, $36.66.

Half a mile from the town, on the opposite side of the river, is a rock of about twenty feet square, upon which are curious hieroglyphics which can scarcely be deciphered. The rock is of a sand-stone character, and upon it are impressions of Indians, animals, pipes, feet, heads, claws, &c.

The Monongahela River at this place is slack water, twenty miles up the river from this point, as far as Geneva. Steamboats ply this river and carry freight to and from Pittsburg, and supply this and the adjoining counties and West Virginia. An old water grist-mill still remains, to which the inhabitants in the old times came fifty miles.

WEST BETHLEHEM TOWNSHIP

Is bounded on the north by Somerset, on the east by Somerset and E. Bethlehem, on the south by Greene County, and on the west by Amwell and S. Strabane. This township is centrally distant from Washington 15 miles. In 1860 it contained a population of 1961, of which 4 were colored. It has 13 schools, with 652 scholars, of which 324 are males and 228 females; the cost of tuition per month being 98 cents; the total amount of tax levied for school and building purposes, $2421.97; the State appropriation being $193.83. Its length is 10 miles; its breadth, 6 miles.

The towns are HILLSBOROUGH and ZOLLARSVILLE. *Hillsborough* is on the National Road, midway between Washington and Brownsville, 11 miles from each. It contains 38 dwellings, 3 preachers, 5 physicians, 3 shoe shops, 2 saddle and harness shops, 1 hotel, 1 blacksmith shop, 1 wagon-maker shop, 1 cabinet-maker, 2 carpenters, 4 stores, a Presbyterian and Methodist Episcopal church. It is elevated 1750 feet above tide water—917 feet above the Monongahela River at Brownsville, and 1002 feet above the Ohio at

Wheeling. It was laid out by Stephen Hill and Thomas McGiffen, Esq., deceased, and has a population of 180 inhabitants.

The land upon which Hillsborough (now called Scenery Hill) was laid out, was patented September 15, 1784, by Wm. Hill, Esq., and named Springtown, and contained 393⅞ acres, for and in consideration of three pounds five shillings and sixpence. This tract is now divided thus: the land upon which the town is laid out, and the respective farms of Oliver Lacock, Valentine Kinder, John Taylor, and Joseph W. Cowan, Esqrs. The aggregate value of these tracts is estimated at $75,000.

The first church in Hillsborough was erected about 1850 by the Presbyterians and Lutherans; the second church, by the Methodists, in 1852, by Hiram Winnett. Before their erection divine service was performed in the school-house. The Methodist denomination has had the efficient services of Revs. J. White, Geo. S. Holmes, Wakefield, Hudson, Yarnall, and many others who have labored successfully in the cause of their Divine Master. The Methodist church has about eighty members.

The first postmaster was the late Samuel Stanley. He worked at the carpenter business in 1810 at the large storehouse of Oliver Lacock; settled and became a resident of the place, and died ten years since at an advanced age. As a man, a citizen, a Christian, and a Freemason, he had no superior. His daughter fills his place in the post-office department.

Zollarsville is on the north branch of Tenmile Creek, 16 miles from Washington. It was laid out by Stephen Ullery in 1856, and is a small and thriving village. Near the residence of ex-sheriff E. R. Smith is the remains of an Indian fort. The entrenchment around the fort, which can yet be traced, is about 100 feet from the fort. Bones, pipes, arrows, &c., have been found. None of the inhabitants of the surrounding country can trace its origin; but a tree was lately cut down within the inclosure of the grounds of the fort, and its age, according to the mode of computing the age of trees, amounted to about 300 years. Coal is found at 180 feet, and salt water at 400 feet.

There is a Methodist Episcopal church northwest of Zollarsville, and a Dunkard Baptist church near Mr. Wherry's.

This township has a number of grist and saw-mills.

Half a mile below Hillsborough there was erected an Episcopal church, under the supervision of Rev. Joseph Dodridge (but the site can only now be traced), near George Taylor's, Esq.

CECIL TOWNSHIP.

This was the third of the original townships formed July 15, 1781. Its boundaries were Robinson township on the north; Peters, Dickinson, and Strabane on the east; Amwell on the south; and Smith and Hopewell on the west.

By the act of Assembly of September 24, 1788, a part of this township, with the whole of Dickinson, was ceded to Allegheny County, at which time the county was formed and confirmed by the Supreme Executive Council, September 30, 1788. An application was made to the Court of Quarter Sessions of this county, praying for a division of the township, beginning at Chartiers' Creek at the junction of the mouth of Brush Run, and continuing up the same as high as to Matthew Johnston's, to include his farm in the upper division, thence leaving James Reed's farm in the lower division, directly, to include GENERAL WASHINGTON'S and Henry Guy's land in the upper division, and immediately to intersect the outside line of the township.

December 9, 1789, the Supreme Executive Council confirmed the same, and the township thus formed was called *Chartiers*.

Cecil township is now bounded by Robinson township and Allegheny County on the north, Peters township and Allegheny County on the east, Chartiers and North Strabane on the south, and Mount Pleasant and Chartiers on the west. Its greatest length is $7\frac{1}{2}$ miles, breadth, $4\frac{1}{2}$ miles. Miller's branch of Chartiers' Creek passes southeast through the middle of the township, upon which are several mills. Its population in 1860 was 959, of which but one is colored. It contains three stores. The township line between this and Mount Pleasant township was adjusted and confirmed by the court.

The only town in this township is *Venice*, 12 miles from Washington, named, by its founder, after the famous maritime city of Italy. We cannot say with the poet,

> "From out the wave her structures rise
> As from the stroke of the enchanter's wand,"

there being but 26 dwelling houses, a Presbyterian church south of Venice, with a parsonage attached. There is another Presbyterian church east of the place.

This township has seven schools with two male and five female teachers, receiving a monthly salary of $35.00, having 210 scholars, of which 112 are males and 98 females, tuition costing each scholar per month $1.35. Amount of taxes levied, $1991.11, and receiving from the State appropriation, $98.67.

GEN. WASHINGTON'S LAND.

From our county records we learn the history of this land. A patent was issued July 5, 1775, by John, Earl of Dunmore, Lieutenant and Governor-General of the colony of Virginia, to George Washington, for *two thousand eight hundred and thirteen* acres of land, in Augusta County, in the State of Virginia, on the waters of Miller's Run, one of the branches of Shirtee Creek, which is a branch of the Ohio River. Gen. Washington held this land until June 1, 1796, when he conveyed the same to Matthew Richie, Esq., of this county, in consideration of the sum of twelve thousand dollars. Witnesses to the deed were James Ross, Esq., and Charles Lee, the

HISTORY OF WASHINGTON COUNTY.

deed being acknowledged in Philadelphia by the grantor, before James Biddle, President of the Court of Common Pleas of the first district. The payments on the land were $3180 cash, and the balance, $8820, in three equal annual payments with interest.

Matthew Richie, Esq., in his advertisement to sell the land after he had purchased it, says, there are thirteen farms cleared and cultivated on the land, which is of excellent quality, rich, level, well timbered, and well watered.

Gen. Washington came to visit his lands (which were, when patented, in Augusta County, Virginia), and brought ejectments for their recovery. During his stay, the mother of James Reed (silversmith, formerly of this place) cooked a dinner on or near the lands for the General, and on his return stayed one night with Col. John Cannon, the proprietor of Canonsburg.

Before the sale to Matthew Richie, Esq., the record of the court shows that suit was instituted for the recovery of this land.

Smith.   His Excellency George Washington, Esq., No. 110.   *vs.*

Breckenridge.   { Samuel McBride, James McBride, Thomas Biggart, Wm. Stewart, Brice McGehan, John Reed, John Glen, James Scott, William Hillis, and Matthew Johnson.

Ejectment served. Hugh M. Breckenridge, Esq., appears, pleads *non cul*, and enters into the common rule and rule for tryal next term. March, 1785. Removed *per certiorari*. Clerk, £1. 4. 4. Sheriff, £4. 19. Mileage, 5 shillings.

Our court records also have the name of the illustrious Benj. Franklin as plaintiff. April 1, 1788.

Ross.   { Benjamin Franklin, Esq., President of the Supreme Executive Council,   *vs.*

Bradford.   David Williamson, Andrew Swearingen, and Thomas Stokely.

Summons. Debt £1000, served on each. Entered by plaintiff's attorney, J. Ross.

The suit was brought against David Williamson, who was elected sheriff of this county October 26, 1787, and his securities.

The United Presbyterians have a church formed by the union of the Associate and Associate Reformed churches in 1858. The Associate congregation of Miller's Run was organized in September, 1849, the Rev. A. Anderson, D. D., and Rev. Thomas Beveridge, D. D., officiated respectively as pastors from November, 1849, to June, 1855.

The U. P. congregation of Venice was organized in 1858; the Rev. A. R. Anderson has officiated as pastor from April 17, 1860, till the present time, with a membership of 182.

CUMBERLAND TOWNSHIP

Was the fourth of the thirteen original townships, which was organized by the trustees of the county on July 15, 1781. It was bounded by Morgan township on the north, Mason and Dixon's line on the south, the Monongahela River on the east, and the State line on the west.

Fort Jackson was situate in this township, on Tenmile Creek, just below Waynesburg. The waters of Muddy Creek flow through this township, upon and near which so many Indian murders were committed. Garrard's Fort was situate on Big Whitley Creek.

By the erection of Greene County, on the 9th day of February, 1796, this township became a component part thereof, Greene County, at its organization, being composed of Cumberland, Franklin, Greene, Morgan, and Rich Hill townships. These five townships have been subdivided into the following townships, viz: 1. Aleppo; 2. Centre; 3. Cumberland; 4. Dunkard; 5. Franklin; 6. Gilmore; 7. Greene; 8. Jackson; 9. Jefferson; 10. Marion; 11. Monongahela; 12. Morris; 13. Morgan; 14. Perry; 15. Rich Hill; 16. Spring Hill; 17. Washington; 18. Wayne, and 19. Whitely, whose population in 1860 was 23,816, and whose territory embraces 364,460 acres of land.

DONEGAL TOWNSHIP

Was organized July 15, 1781, by the trustees of the county, and ranks fifth in alphabetical order out of the thirteen.

It was originally bounded by Smith township on the north, Morris township on the east, Mason and Dixon's line on the south, and the State line on the west.

On the 6th of May, 1788, an application was made to the court for a division of the township, who granted it and ordered a copy to be forwarded to the Supreme Executive Committee, and on the 7th of August following it was confirmed by the Council, by the name of *Finley* township.

Its present boundaries are Independence township on the north, East and West Findley on the south, Buffalo and East Findley on the east, and West Virginia on the west. It is centrally distant from Washington, twelve miles, its greatest length is eight miles, breadth, six and a half miles. The township is drained by the Dutch Fork of Buffalo Creek, Bush Run, and Castleman's Run. The National road runs southwest through it, upon which lie *Claysville* on the east, and *West Alexander* on the west.

In 1860 its population was 1690, of which thirteen are colored. It contains nine stores, nine schools, employing seven male and two female teachers, the former receiving $39.48, and the latter, $36.00 per month, having 376 scholars, of which 205 are males, and 171 females. Cost of tuition per month, $1.25; amount levied for school purposes, $1776.69; levied for building purposes, $1332.52, and receiving from the State appropriation, $146.25.

West Alexander is on the western boundary of this township, fifteen miles southwest of Washington, containing ninety-two dwellings, an academy, a Presbyterian church and parsonage, and a Methodist Episcopal church.

This town was laid out by Charles De Hass, on May 12, 1817;

the sale of lots took place the 10th of June following. Three miles east of this place is a Roman Catholic church. It was first built of logs, on land given by Mr. Dougherty, at which time the Rev. Mr. Horner officiated. The log chapel has been removed and a brick edifice erected.

The Hempfield Railroad passes through this township from its eastern to its western boundary, through the borough of Claysville and West Alexander.

On September 7, 1795, Thomas Stokely, of Washington, and Jesse Evans, of Fayette County, conveyed three acres and forty-eight perches, in consideration of seven shillings and sixpence, to James Armstrong, William Gaston, William Bower, Samuel Byers, and John White, trustees of the Presbyterian church belonging to the Ohio Presbytery and now supplied by Rev. John Brice. It appears from a deed executed May 30, 1796, that the same trustees purchased the same property from William Smith, William Slater, and James Stevenson, trustees of the Associate Congregation of Three Ridges (near West Alexander). This land was originally conveyed by Robert Humphreys and wife to the trustees of the Associated church, and is described as being in the townships of Finley and Donegal, although Humphreys claimed his title under the Virginia law. The question of title, however, was referred to John Hoge, Isaac Leet, and James Edgar, who awarded it to the Presbyterian church, called the Three Ridges. Its pastors have been Rev. John Brice, Rev. Mr. Stephenson, Rev. John McCluskey, and Rev. W. H. Lester.

CLAYSVILLE.

The town of Claysville is in Donegal township, and was erected into a borough the second day of April, 1832, and the lots sold on the 8th of May following. Each lot is fifty by two hundred feet deep, with suitable and convenient streets and alleys to each block. The town is on the National road from Cumberland to Wheeling, beautifully located, well watered, in a fertile section of the county, and with a good population.

It has eighty-five dwellings, two churches—a Presbyterian and Methodist Episcopal—a tannery, a steam mill, four stores, one confectionery and one distillery, with a population of four hundred and sixty-seven; two schools employing one male and one female teacher, ninety-two scholars, thirty-eight males and fifty-four females, tuition costing per month seventy-two cents; amount levied for building purposes five hundred and sixty-four dollars and thirty cents; receiving from the State appropriation forty dollars and nineteen cents; amount levied for school purposes, five hundred and sixty-four dollars and thirty cents.

Presbyterian Church.

The Presbyterian church at Claysville was organized September 20th, 1820. Its first house of worship was a frame building. Its present house of worship is of brick, and was erected during the summer of 1830, at a cost of about three thousand dollars. The first pastor was Rev. Thomas Hoge, of Washington. His pastorate continued fifteen years, at the close of which he removed to Philadelphia. His successor was the Rev. Peter Hassinger, who officiated for four years. From 1838 to 1846, the church had only supplies. On the first Sabbath of October, 1846, the Rev. Alexander McCarrell, the present pastor, entered upon his duties, and breaks the bread of life to a devoted Christian people. This church has a Sabbath-school connected with it.

Donegal township has always been noted for its morality and high-toned religious sentiment, as the following notice will show: the dockets of the justices of that period exhibit the fact that many persons were brought to trial and fined.

WHEREAS, A number of the inhabitants of the vicinity of Three Ridges (West Alexander) have entered into an association and formed an acting committee for the purpose of aiding and assisting the civil authority in the suppression of evil and immorality, they take this method of informing the public that after the date hereof, all persons driving wagons, pack-horses, or unlawfully travelling through said vicinity, or doing other things contrary to the penal laws of this State, may expect to be dealt with as the law directs.

W. SMITH, *Secretary*.   JOHN McPHERSON, *President*.

The United Presbyterian church of West Alexander is composed of the Associate and the Associate Reformed congregations of West Alexander.

The Associate Congregation was organized in 1839. Rev. Joseph Shaw was pastor from June 20th, 1843, until April 20th, 1852. Rev. James Murch from September, 1853, until 1858. The pastors of the Associate Reformed Congregation, previous to 1859, were Rev. Joseph Buchanan and Rev. G. D. Bradford.

In 1859, these two congregations were united under the pastorate of Rev. Josias Stevenson. The present membership of the congregation is one hundred and eighty.

The Associated Reformed Presbyterians had a church at West Alexander, in which Rev. Alexander McCoy officiated as pastor in 1800. His successors were Rev. William Patterson and Rev. William Shaw in 1845. During Mr. Shaw's pastorate the church became Seceders, and afterwards United Presbyterians, whose pastor was Rev. J. Stevenson.

FALLOWFIELD TOWNSHIP

Was the sixth of the original townships of this county. Its original bounds were Nottingham on the north; the Monongahela River on the east; Bethlehem township on the south, and Strabane township on the west. Its present limits are Nottingham and Carroll on the north; the Monongahela River, Allen, and Carroll townships on the east; E. and W. Pike Run and Allen on the south; and Somerset and Nottingham on the west. It is centrally distant from Washington, 17 miles. The population in 1860 was 897, of which 30 were colored. Its greatest length 8½ by 6 miles.

It contains two stores, seven school-houses, employing 3 male and 4 female teachers, with 267 scholars, 165 male and 102 female; the tuition costing $1.15 cts. per month; amount of tax levied for school purposes, $1050.15 cts.; the State appropriation was $81.90. The male teachers receive monthly, $35.16; the female, $34.75.

The towns in this township are Jonestown and Ginger Hill. Jonestown is six miles from the Monongahela River, on the State road leading from Canonsburg to Bellvernon; it was laid out by John Jones, in 1828, and has a population of about fifty.

Ginger Hill is on the Williamsport and Washington Turnpike, and in the northern part of the township, near the township line.

There are four churches in this township: The Presbyterian Church on Maple Creek, two miles from Jonestown, founded in 1842. The pulpit was first filled with supplies; Rev. J. W. Kerr was elected its first minister; the ministers who have succeeded him were the Rev. James Carson, Rev. A. Virtue, Rev. Thomas Vaneman, and Rev. W. Hanna.

The Methodist Episcopal Church is on the State road from Jonestown to Bellvernon, four miles from Jonestown. The church was built in 1849, and has had the successive ministerial labors of the Rev. Warren Long, Rev. T. M. Hudson, Rev. J. G. Sansom, Rev. Geo. W. Cranage, Rev. John Spencer, Rev. David Sharpe, Rev. J. W. Kessler, Rev. Henry Neff, Rev. D. B. Campbell, Rev. J. W. Weaver, Rev. Charles H. Edwards, and Rev. McClure.

The Methodist Episcopal Church, in the upper end of the township, was erected in 1836, on the road leading from Bentleysville to Monongahela City; it is called Pigeon Creek Methodist Episcopal Church. Its first preacher was the Rev. Samuel E. Babcock; his successor was the Rev. Wm. Tipton.

The first church built under the direction of the Rev. Mr. Babcock was of brick, 30 by 40 feet, but a new one has been erected about 200 yards from the site of the first one; its dimensions being 42 by 60 feet; 18 feet to the square, with a basement for Sunday school, lecture-room, &c.

A Disciple Church was established, and a church built in 1866, on the farm of Dutton Shannon, Esq. It is a brick edifice 30 by 40 feet; Rev. Samuel Fry being its pastor.

The township has one tannery; two grist-mills; one distillery; two manufacturers of sorghum; five saw-mills; one extensive vineyard.

HOPEWELL TOWNSHIP

Is the seventh of the thirteen original townships organized by the trustees of Washington County, July 15, 1781.

At its formation, it was bounded on the north by Smith township; on the east by Robinson and Cecil; on the south by Donegal; on the west by Virginia.

On the 1st day of September, 1789, an application was made to the court for a division, which was subsequently confirmed by the Supreme Executive Council, on December 10th, 1789. This division was formed by running a line, commencing at a certain spring on the head-waters of Cross Creek, which rises about ten perches from the township of Strabane, between the dwelling-houses of James Anderson and Timothy Spencer; thence down the south branch thereof to Wells' mill; thence down the creek to the State line. This division formed *Cross Creek* township.

The present boundaries of this township are Cross Creek and Mount Pleasant on the north; Mount Pleasant and Canton on the east; Buffalo on the south, and Independence on the west. It is centrally distant from Washington 12 miles; its greatest length six miles; breadth three and a half miles. Its population 1213, of which 87 are colored.

It contains six schools, employing one male and five female teachers; receiving as their monthly pay $30.00; having 197 scholars, 110 males and 87 females; tuition costing per month, $1.15. Amount levied for school purposes $1563.67; receiving from the State appropriated $78.78.

This township is drained by the waters of Buffalo and Cross creeks.

The towns are *West Middletown, Buffalo Village,* and *Egypt* or *Midway.*

West Middletown being a borough, we shall speak presently of it in connection with this township.

Buffalo Village is on a fork of Buffalo Creek, seven miles southwest of Washington, and contains twenty dwellings.

Midway is on the Pittsburg and Steubenville Railroad, which passes through this township, and is destined to be a place of considerable importance.

In the Register's office of this county, in the will of the Rev. Joseph Smith, of Hopewell township, made July 28, 1788, he bequeaths to each of his beloved children a Bible, to be paid out of his personal estate, and by so doing "mean to intimate to them as I am a dying man and in the sight of God, that it is ten thousand times more my will and desire that they should find and possess the pearl of great price hid in the field of Scriptures, than enjoy anything else which I can bequeath to them, or even ten thousand worlds, were they composed of the purest gold, and all brim full of the richest jewels, and yet be ignorant of the precious treasures in God's Word that are entirely hid even from the most eagle-eyed and quick-sighted men that are properly of this present world."

Upper Buffalo Presbyterian Church.

In connection with the name of this great and good man, we may state that he was elected first pastor of this church, organized June 21, 1779, on the eastern part of Hopewell township, at Buffalo Village, lying north of Brush Run.

Rev. Smith served until April 19, 1792. The Rev. Thomas Marquis, of Cross Creek church, served as a supply, by the sanction of Presbytery, until March 9, 1800, when the Rev. John Anderson accepted a call, and entered upon his pastoral labors; his labors ceased June 18, 1833, and his successor is the Rev. John Eagleson, D. D., its present popular pastor, who was ordained January 19, 1834, and zealously labors in the promotion of his Master's cause. Thus, in the course of ninety years, but *four* ministers have filled the pulpit, one of whom is still living.

Pleasant Hill Female Seminary

Is located in this township, and was organized in 1846, near the borough of West Middleton. It is on the dividing ridge between the waters of Buffalo and Cross creeks, enjoying the advantages of a country location, salubrity of air and water, delightful rural scenery, and above all, retirement, which is essentially necessary to study. It is surrounded by a highly moral and industrious population, engaged generally in agriculture, hence the advantage is, that the faculty of the seminary are not compelled to impose formal restraints upon young ladies, nor to cause them to incur inordinate expense in relation to appearance or dress.

This seminary has large and convenient buildings, halls for the literary societies, libraries, philosophical apparatus.

The seminary is under the control and management of Mrs. Martha McKeever, who is fully competent to sustain the institution as well as to oversee and provide for the pupils committed to her charge. She has as assistants, Rev. T. A. Crenshaw, Miss Kate M. Bigger, Aurie T. Burkett, John M. Bigger, Esq., Miss Ella E. McKeever, Miss Eliza McFadden, Mrs. G. B. Crenshaw.

West Middletown Borough

Is situated in Hopewell township, and was erected into a borough on the 27th day of March, 1823.

It is in the northwest part of the township, eleven miles from Washington.

It contains ninety-two dwelling-houses, six stores, one confectionary, the usual number of the mechanical professions, one extensive machine shop, one tannery, a United Presbyterian church, and a Wesleyan Methodist Protestant church, a Disciple church, with Rev. T. A. Crenshaw, pastor of the Disciple church at Middletown, and a colored Methodist church, and a population of about eight hundred. It contains two schools, with one male and one female teacher, the former receiving $56.00, and the latter $31.00 per month, with ninety-six scholars, fifty-two males and forty-four females, tuition costing eighty-seven cents per month. Amount of tax levied for shool purposes, $701 00, receiving from the State $42.50.

The pastors who have filled the pulpit of the United Presbyterian church of West Middletown, were Rev. S. Findley, D. D., Rev. William Wallace, D. D., Rev. S. Taggert, from 1835 until the present time. It has a membership of 128.

ROBERT FULTON.

But few of the present generation are aware that the celebrated Robert Fulton, of steamboat notoriety, owned a farm in Hopewell township, in this county. The farm contained about eighty-four acres, and the patent granted by the State to Rev. Joseph Smith, December 12, 1785. On May 6, 1786, Thomas Pollock sold it to Robert Fulton, and his father, mother, and three sisters resided on it. After the death of his father the widow and three daughters resided upon it. About 1799 his mother died. In 1814 Robert Fulton made his will in the city of New York, and among other legacies he left to his sister Elizabeth, married to a Mr. Scott, one thousand dollars and the above farm, with all the stock, during her life, and at her death to be sold and divided. To his sister Isabella Cooke he left two thousand dollars, and to each of the children of his deceased sister Mary Morris he left five hundred dollars. Both Mrs. Cooke and Mrs. Morris resided in the town of Washington.

MORGAN TOWNSHIP.

This was the eighth of the thirteen original townships organized July 15, 1781. It was bounded on the north by Amwell township, on the east by Bethlehem, on the south by Cumberland, and on the west by Donegal and the Virginia line.

On the 9th of February, 1796, with Cumberland, Franklin, Greene, and Rich Hill townships, was struck off from Washington County, and formed Greene County.

NOTTINGHAM TOWNSHIP

Was the ninth of the original townships organized July 15, 1781. It was then bounded on the north by Peters township, on the east by the Monongahela River, on the south by Fallowfield township, and on the west by Strabane township. Its present boundaries are, Peters on the north, Union and Carroll on the east, Fallowfield and Somerset on the south, and N. Strabane on the west. It is centrally distant east from Washington borough 13 miles. In 1860 the population was 916, of which 8 were colored. It is drained by Peters Creek on the north, Mingo and Little Mingo Creeks on the south. Its greatest length is 6 miles; breadth 4 miles.

It contains five stores, five schools, employing three male and two female teachers, the former at $32 per month and the latter at $28, having 214 scholars, of whom 96 are males and 108 females; cost of tuition per month 81 cents; amount levied for school purposes $970.89; received from State appropriation $80.34.

Its town is Dunningsville, a small village with a population of sixty.

The Old School Presbyterian church of Fairview is situated on the headwaters of Peters Creek in this township. It was organized by an order of the Presbytery of Ohio on the petition of James McClane, at the instance of Rev. George Marshall, by a committee consisting of Revs. C. G. Braddock, Robert McPherson, and J. Hazlett, Feb. 24, 1860, with twenty-one members. The organization was perfected in the district school-house near where the church now stands, and which was occupied as a church until the new building was completed.

The church from its organization until September, 1861, received the services of Rev. Geo. Marshall, Rev. James Black, Rev. George Birch, Rev. S. M. Nebling, and Rev. John Aiken, at which date the Rev. John Ewing became the regular pastor. He served acceptably until April 1, 1864, when he resigned, and the pulpit was supplied by Rev. Mr. Gray until September 9, 1864, when Rev. William Hanna took charge of the congregation. He was the first installed pastor, and served until April 1, 1869, when the pastoral relation was dissolved, since which time Rev. Wm. Brown has been supplying the pulpit.

The following persons have been ordained ruling elders, viz : Liverton Thomas, John P. Cochran, William Rees, and Jonathan Caseber. The trustees are James McClane, James Roney, and William Thomas. The building committtee consisted of James McClane, John P. Cochran, and Samuel Hamilton. There is a Sabbath school connected with the church.

A United Presbyterian church, called Mount Prospect, has been established at Munntown, under the care of Rev. J. Balph, which promises to do much good in the dissemination of evangelical truth. It was organized in January, 1860, and the pulpit filled by supplies until September 29, 1864, when Rev. Mr. Balph took charge of it. It has a membership of about one hundred and thirty-two.

The most extensive establishment in any township of this county is that carried on by Kammerer Brothers. Besides a very large store, embracing general merchandise of every variety, they have a flour-mill in which forty barrels are made in ten hours. The building is stone, thirty-six by fifty-six feet, three stories high, with a tile roof, running it by a forty horse power engine. In connection with the store and flour-mill they carry on a distillery. Its capacity is forty bushels per day, or one hundred and fifty gallons.

PETERS TOWNSHIP

Was the tenth of the original thirteen townships formed by the trustees July 15, 1781, appointed for that purpose by the act forming Washington County.

In September, 1784, a petition to the Court of Quarter Sessions was presented, asking for a division of the township, which was indorsed by the court, and afterward confirmed by the Supreme Executive Council on the 21st day of November, 1786. This division formed *Dickinson* township, taken out of its northern part, which township was struck off to Allegheny County. Its original boundaries were the Monongahela River on the north and east, Nottingham on the south, Robinson and Cecil on the west. It is now bounded by Allegheny County on the north, Union township and Allegheny County on the east, North Strabane and Nottingham on the south, and Cecil and North Strabane on the west. Its greatest length is six miles; breadth three and a half miles. The population of this township in 1860 was 934.

The towns are BOWER HILL and Thompsonville. These are small but thriving villages, with post-offices at each.

Peters township contains two stores, has five schools, employing three male and two female teachers who each received $30 per month, with 300 scholars, of whom 166 are males and 134 females, tuition costing per month 68 cents. Amount levied for school purposes $1555.50, and receiving from the State appropriation $90.09.

LUSUS NATURÆ.

On September 29, 1798, upon Esquire Mitchell's farm in Peters township, a child was born with two natural heads, one affixed to each shoulder, the body perfect, but no parts of generation. The child was dead born, and appeared to have been dead some days previous to its birth.

The UNITED PRESBYTERIANS have a church in this township called *Peters Creek*. It was organized in 1808, and the following pastors have respectively filled the pulpit, viz: Rev. R. Bruce, D. D., from December 14, 1808, to December 16, 1816. Rev. Alex. Wilson, from October 8, 1817, to May 4, 1839. Rev. James Brown, D. D., from September 10, 1840, to December 5, 1843. Rev. J. C. Herron, from October 15, 1845, to January 4, 1853. Rev. J. B. Whitten, from October 6, 1854, to January 17, 1856. Rev. A. Y. Houston, from March 19, 1857, to June 16, 1868. Rev. John Patterson, from July 13, 1868, until the present time. This church has a membership of 134.

CENTRE PRESBYTERIAN CHURCH

Is located in Peters township, on land donated by David Bell. The Presbytery of Ohio, at a meeting held at Bethany church, Allegheny County, April 16, 1828, granted the request of a number of persons living within the bounds of the congregations of Bethel, Bethany, Chartiers' and Mingo creeks, and allowed them to erect a meeting-house, in order that they might enjoy the *occasional* administration of the ordinances among them. A brick meeting-house, forty by fifty feet, was immediately erected, costing twelve hundred dollars.

On the 29th of August, 1829, the congregation was regularly organized by Dr. Matthew Brown. At a meeting of Presbytery, held at Canonsburg, January 5, 1830, Centre congregation obtained permission to call a pastor. On May 4, 1830, Rev. John H. Kennedy, Professor of Mathematics in Jefferson College, was elected the pastor, and entered upon his pastoral duties, but was not installed until June, 1831. On account of ill health he resigned in 1840.

Rev. Alexander B. Brown became stated supply in 1841 and officiated until 1845, when he resigned, and Rev. W. H. Orr, Professor in Jefferson College, was chosen in the same year. He officiated about seven years, and near the close of his pastorate, in 1851, a new brick building was erected, located a few rods south of the old structure, on a more elevated piece of ground. It cost two thousand dollars.

The Rev. J. W. Hamilton became pastor in 1852 and served about two years and six months.

Rev. Alexander B. Brown, D. D., having resigned the Presidency of Jefferson College and removed to the country, in 1856, preached occasionally at Centre church, and at length, in 1858, became pastor. His health failing, Dr. Brown resigned the pastorate December 16, 1862.

Rev. Francis J. Collier, a licentiate of the Presbytery of Philadelphia, was called in October, 1863, began to labor in November, and was ordained and installed April 27, 1864. He is pastor at the present time.

In connection with the church there is a Sabbath school, having eight teachers and about ninety scholars, which holds its sessions every year during the summer months. The church is in a prosperous condition. The number of members is one hundred and sixty ; the number of families about seventy ; the number of elders, *seven.* The church is neatly painted, papered, and carpeted. It is heated by furnaces. The yard surrounding the building is securely inclosed and tastefully ornamented.

ROBINSON TOWNSHIP

Was the eleventh of the original townships formed by the trustees, July 15th, 1781. It was then bounded by the Ohio River on the north, the Monongahela River on the east, Cecil township on the south, and Smith township on the west; but its large proportions have been considerably decreased, and it is now bounded by Allegheny County on the north and east, North Strabane and Nottingham on the south, and Hanover and Smith on the west, centrally distant from Washington borough, north sixteen miles. Its greatest length is ten miles ; breadth three miles.

Population in 1860, eight hundred and forty, of which twenty-three are colored. It is drained on the north by Racoon Creek, on the east by branches of Chartiers' Creek and Montour's Run. The pike from Pittsburg to Steubenville runs through this township. On December 22d, 1836, the lines between Robinson, Cecil, Mount Pleasant, and Smith were adjusted and confirmed by the court. It has five stores, five schools, with one male and four female teachers—the former receiving $34, and the latter $30 per month, with 156 scholars (76 males and 80 females), tuition costing $1.20 cents per month; the tax levied being seven hundred and forty-two dollars and eighty-four cents; the State appropriation, eighty-eight dollars and ninety-two cents; amount levied for building purposes, ten hundred and fourteen dollars and fourteen cents. The towns are Candor* and Havelock Station.

1793, January 19th. John Clark and Jane his wife conveyed to William Rankin, Peter Kidd, William McCandless, Matthew Bailey, John Dunlap, and Alexander Wright, trustees of Racoon congregation, in consideration of nine pounds specie, all that lot of ground whereon the congregation has erected their church, under the pastoral care of Rev. Joseph Patterson, containing seven acres strict measure.

UPPER RACOON PRESBYTERIAN CHURCH

Is located in Robinson township. Rev. Joseph Patterson was installed as the first pastor, November 11th, 1789, and remained as such until October 16th, 1816. He was succeeded by the Rev. Moses Allen the 27th of May, 1817, who officiated until October 16th, 1839. Rev. Clement N. McKaig was ordained his successor, June 14th, 1841, and served until Rev. John W. Kerr became its pastor in 1862 and resigned in 1865. The pulpit is filled with supplies.

There is a tradition in the northern part of this county in regard to the Rev. Mr. Patterson, verified by the most substantial aged men of our county, which I shall relate. Mr. Patterson was a great and good man—prompt to his word and conscientious in the discharge of his every duty. A subscription was being made up to erect a meeting house, and the day appointed for its payment. The day arrived and he was disappointed in not receiving the promised money which would liquidate his subscription, amounting to six dollars. Nevertheless he concluded to attend the meeting at the schoolhouse (the place appointed), and make such a statement as would be satisfactory. He accordingly started with his gun on his shoulder. Wending his way along to the meeting, he arrived at a beautiful grove, where God and nature seemed to invite him to pour out his soul in prayer and by faith to look up for the blessing. In the midst of this devotional exercise, and when his soul was earnestly engaged in prayer, he heard a rustling among the leaves. He opened his eyes, and, behold, a panther was approaching him. He raised his rifle and

---

* *Candor* is in the southern part of the township and has forty dwelling houses, with a population of two hundred and ten. Havelock Station is on the railroad, on the property belonging to the estate of Col. McDonald. This road passes through the southern part of the township into Smith.

killed the wild animal. He took the scalp and skin with him to the meeting as a trophy of his victory. He sold them for six dollars, and was thereby enabled to redeem his subscription.

There is a United Presbyterian church not far from the Allegheny County line under the care of Rev. J. C. Rankin.

ROBINSON U. P. CHURCH

Was organized in 1833. The Rev. William Wilson officiated from 1833 to 1842. Rev. John Scott, D. D., from September 19th, 1843, to June, 1845. Rev. James G. Rankin, from September, 1849, to November, 1868. The Rev. W. R. McKee has accepted a call and commenced his pastorate in 1869. It has a membership of one hundred and thirty-seven.

STRABANE TOWNSHIP

Was the twelfth of the original thirteen townships. It was bounded by Cecil on the north, Nottingham and Fallowfield on the east, Bethlehem on the south, and Cecil on the west. On the 22d of September, 1785, the Court of Quarter Sessions of this county received a petition from the citizens of the town of *Washington*, praying that it might be set apart as a separate district from this township. The court recommended the petition to the Supreme Executive Council, and in February, 1786, the request was confirmed. On October 7, 1830, the township was again divided into North and South Strabane townships. It is drained by Chartiers' and Little Chartiers' creeks. The town of Washington was originally in this township.

An alteration of the boundary lines was confirmed by the court between this and Amwell township, at the October term in 1830, the line running from the house of Thomas Hastings to the mouth of the lane at or near Peter Dager's.

CHARTIERS PRESBYTERIAN CHURCH.

June 20, 1798, Josiah Haines conveyed two and a fourth acres of land to the Presbyterian congregation, holding the principles of the Presbyterian church as adopted in 1788, and on the 26th of June following, Craig Ritchie, Esq., attorney of Samuel Gilpin, of Cecil County, Maryland, conveyed to the trustees of the same church seven acres and three-fourths (the remaining two and a fourth acres) of the ten acres being exchanged by the said trustees for other land more convenient.

The trustees were enabled to hold land as a body politic in law, an act of incorporation having been procured February 15, 1798. The first trustees were Robert Hill, William Kerr, James McCreedy, William Hays, John Mercer, James Morrison, George Craighead, James Bradford, and John Cotton. The following members of the congregation (February 15, 1798) petitioned for the charter: John McMillen, John McDowell, Craig Ritchie, Moses Coe, Robert

Hill, William Cochran, George Craighead, William Kerr, Robert Hughes, James Foster, James Allison, John Johnston, William Welch, James Officer, Hans McClean, Abraham De Haven, Robert Welch, Robert Bowland, William Hays, John Macahey, Wm. Hartapee, Nicholas Smith, Daniel Kirkpatrick, James Wishart, John Donnell, William Gault, Alexander Frazer, John Lindsey, Thomas Brysland, Samuel Logan, Thomas Bracker, John McClain, James Gaston, John Crawford, George McCook.

This church is now, by a division of the township, in North Strabane. It is one mile south of Canonsburg, on the road leading to Monongahela City.

It is supposed that this church was organized by Dr. John McMillan, soon after his ordination, in 1776, as he received a call from both this and Pigeon Creek church. He continued its pastor until April 21, 1830. His successor was Rev. F. Leake, who was installed July 12, 1831, and served until June 21, 1843. He was succeeded by Rev. Alexander A. Brown (son of Rev. Matthew Brown), September 3, 1844, and continued to officiate until January 11, 1848. Rev. Robert White was installed September 6, 1848, and died December 14, 1848. The Rev. Joseph R. Wilson became the pastor on the 20th of June, 1849, and resigned his pastoral care January 15, 1851. Their present pastor, Rev. William Ewing, was installed January 14, 1852. This church is one of the oldest west of the Allegheny Mountains.

In a public newspaper of this county of May 12, 1796, a meeting of Dr. Millan's church was held, and after the religious service of Thursday was over, Dr. Millan intimated that business of a public nature and of great importance required the consideration of the meeting. He was chosen Chairman, and Craig Ritchie, Esq., Secretary. The Chairman then stated the present critical state of the country and the danger of an Indian and perhaps a British war, when, after discussion, the following resolutions were adopted :—

Resolved, unanimously, That, in the opinion of this meeting, the interests of this county require that the British treaty should be carried into execution with good faith.

Resolved, unanimously, That a petition be circulated and signed, and sent to the House of Representatives to this effect.

Resolved, unanimously, That the following petition be adopted.

To the Honorable the House of Representatives of the United States :—

The petition of sundry inhabitants of the western counties of Pennsylvania, humbly showeth : Having lately, with great cordiality and good intentions, very generally united in a petition, that the House of Representatives would concur in the execution of the British treaty, we had believed that no further expression of our wishes would be necessary. But it having been suggested that the Spanish treaty was the main object of our petition, and that we were indifferent as to the British treaty, and seeing our apprehensions that the British treaty might be defeated were but too well grounded, and are not yet removed, we feel ourselves constrained by a regard both to safety and duty, again to address your honorable House.

We consider the British treaty as peculiarly advantageous to us and essential to our enjoying the blessings of liberty and peace. Its ratification made it a solemn national act, according to the terms of the Constitution, binding the people and every branch of government, and we consider its execution necessary for public faith which we regard, interest which we pursue, and peace which we cherish. We therefore pray that the House of Representatives will concur with the other branches of government in a full and faithful execution of the treaty between the United States and Great Britain.

This petition being signed by all present, the meeting also passed the following:—

Resolved, That the Chairman be requested to write to his brethren, the ministers, on this side of the mountains, requesting them to call their congregations together as soon as possible, on some week day, and take their sentiments on this interesting subject.

In connection with the history of this church we will mention a providential incident. The Rev. Dr. John McMillan, in 1802, and who was pastor of this church, met with a severe trial, both of his faith and patience, as well as his Christianity. His biographer gives the following account of this domestic affliction: Two young ministers of great promise had married two of his daughters. The Rev. John Watson, the first President of Jefferson College, under the charter, had married his second daughter, Margaret. The Rev. William Moorehead had married his eldest daughter, Jane. For a time the prospect for enlarged domestic and social enjoyment shone brightly on the doctor and his family, but by the Allwise, yet deeply mysterious providence of God, these two ministers, who had been married to two sisters, by their father, on the same day, took sick on the same day, died on the same day, and were buried in the same grave at the Chartiers Presbyterian church. The two funeral processions, one coming from the house of Dr. McMillan, the other from the village of Canonsburg, met at the same point where the roads united, a few hundred yards from the graveyard.

NORTH STRABANE TOWNSHIP.

By a decision of the Court of Quarter Sessions on the 2d day of May, 1831, Strabane township was divided into North and South Strabane. This township is bounded on the north by Cecil, Peters, and Chartiers; on the east by Peters and Nottingham; on the south by Somerset and South Strabane; and on the west by Chartiers and South Strabane. Its greatest length is 6 miles; breadth $6\frac{1}{2}$ miles. In 1860, the population was 1213, of which 48 are colored.

Munntown is the only town in the limits of the township with a population of sixty.

The township has two stores, six schools, with two male and four female teachers, each receiving per month $30, with 285 scholars, of whom 130 are males and 155 are females; cost of tuition per month 77 cents. Amount levied for school purposes, $1463.06; received from the State appropriation $119.34.

Col. Geo. Morgan

Lived and died at the "Morganza" farm, two miles below Canonsburg, in this township. He was appointed Indian agent as early as 1776, and held the appointment until 1779, when he resigned. During the time he held the office, he made Pittsburg his head-quarters. History represents him as a man of unwearied activity, great perseverance, and familiar with Indian manners and habits. He won their confidence by his frank manner, soldierly bearing, generosity, and strict honesty. After an eventful military life, being an officer in the United States army, he retired to his Morganza farm, and devoted himself to agricultural pursuits, and the high honor belongs to North Strabane township of one of her sons (Col. Morgan), on the 7th of February, 1786, receiving a gold medal from the Philadelphia Society, for Promoting Agriculture, for furnishing the best Essay on a Farmyard. Hon. Timothy Pickering, in the letter forwarding the medal, says: "It is the first premium ever given in America in agriculture." The medal is in the possession of David T. Morgan, Esq., of Washington, Pa. It is of gold, one and three-fourths inches in diameter; on the obverse side, a farm-house with a man ploughing with two oxen; on the reverse, the motto, "Venerate the Plough."

South Strabane Township.

This township was formed May 3, 1831, by a division of Strabane township, and is bounded on the north by North Strabane and Chartiers; on the east by Somerset and W. Bethlehem; on the south by Franklin and Amwell, and on the west by Washington, Canton, and Franklin. Its greatest length is 9 miles; breadth 4½ miles. In 1860, the population was 1063, of which 53 are colored. It contains seven schools with seven female teachers, who receive thirty dollars per month, having 232 scholars (126 males and 106 females); tuition costing $1.46 per month. Amount levied for school purposes $1189.12; received from the State appropriation $103.35.

The towns are Cloakeyville and Williamsburg, although sometimes called Martinsburg. The former is situated on the Williamsport and Washington turnpike, six miles from Washington, and the latter on the national road two miles east of the borough of Washington. On the 28th of February, 1863, the lines between Canton and South Strabane were confirmed by the court.

November 8th, 1857, the township lines between Canton, Chartiers, and South Strabane were confirmed by the court, the question having been referred to a vote of the people.

Smith Township.

This was the thirteenth, or last township organized July 15, 1781, at the organization of Washington County.

The original boundaries were the Ohio River on the north; Robinson and Cecil townships on the east; Hopewell on the south, and Virginia on the west.

On the 5th day of January, 1786, an application was made to the court for a division, which being sanctioned, a certificate was sent to the Supreme Executive Council who, on the 11th of March, 1786, confirmed the decree of the court, and *Hanover* township was thereby erected. October 7, 1830, part of the division line between Hanover and Smith townships was confirmed by the court.

At the May session of the court, held in 1856, the boundary lines between Cross Creek and Smith were changed and confirmed.

Its present boundaries are Hanover and Robinson townships on the north; Robinson and Mount Pleasant on the east; Cross Creek and Mount Pleasant on the south; Jefferson, Hanover, and Cross Creek on the west. Its greatest length eight miles; breadth six miles. It is centrally situated northwest from Washington borough sixteen miles.

It is drained northwest by Racoon Creek and its branches. Population in 1860, 1417, of whom twenty-four were colored.

It contains fourteen stores, ten schools, with five male and five female teachers, the former receiving $43.33 per month and the latter $33; having 394 scholars, of whom 203 are males and 191 females; tuition costing per month, $1.33. Amount of tax levied for school purposes, $2730; received from the State appropriation $131.04.

The Pittsburg and Steubenville Railroad passes through the township.

The towns are *Burgettstown, Bulger, Bavington,* and *Whitetown coal works.*

On February 28, 1795, George Burgett laid out Burgettstown on the south fork of Racoon Creek, one mile north of the centre of the township. Then it was called West Boston, but the neighbors desiring to honor the founder of their village called it Burgettstown.

It is seventeen miles northwest of Washington, and on account of its locality, being on the Pittsburg and Steubenville Railroad, has become one of the most important towns of our county. The Rev. J. T. Fredericks laid out an addition to the town in 1865, whereon is the railroad station. The lots are selling rapidly and the town increasing by the erection of good and substantial buildings, and an energetic and thriving community.

Bulger is a small village near Bulger station, about three miles northwest of Burgettstown.

Bavington is in the northeast corner of the township, and *White-*

town coal works is on the railroad, and laid out on Mr. Simpson's farm.

On the 10th of June, 1810, Captain John Bavington of this township attempted to cross the Ohio River at Kelley's Ferry on a flatboat (the mouth of Harman's Creek) with a wagon loaded with whiskey and flour and four horses. When half way across, by the stamping of the horses, one of the boards became loosened, the boat filled with water, the load sank, and Capt. Bavington and the ferryman were drowned. When the bodies were found Capt. B had his whip firmly grasped in his hand. The depth of the Ohio River did not cover the bows of his wagon. He was buried at the cross roads near Florence.

Presbyterian Church.

In the year 1845, a petition was sent to the Presbytery of Washington, for the organization of a church at Burgettstown, which prayer was denied, and an appeal taken to the Synod of Wheeling, who granted the request and directed the Presbytery to organize the church. This was effected October 18, 1849, and Reverend Joel Stoneroad was elected the pastor. In October, 1850, he was succeeded by the Rev. James P. Fulton, and remained its pastor until 1857; and in the spring of 1858 the Rev. James T. Frederick, the present pastor, was called, and ordained in October following.

In 1860 the church was enlarged and refitted.

There are two *United Presbyterian* churches in this township, the former in Burgettstown. It was organized about 1809, the Rev. W. C. Brownlee, D. D., was pastor from May 3, 1809, to September 1, 1812; Rev. Alexander Donnan, from July 6, 1819, to May 12, 1840; Rev. R. J. Hammond from 1845 to April 15, 1856; Reverend S. H. Graham is the present pastor.

It has a membership of 160.

Centre U. P. Church was organized in 1859. Rev. D. S. Kennedy has been its pastor from September 4, 1862, until the present time, with a membership of 150.

There was, many years since, on the farm of David Leech, Esq., on the road leading from Hickory to Burgettstown, about half way, a United Presbyterian church called Mount Vernon, but the organization does not now exist.

Poets.

Smith township has the honor of contributing more poetry to the intellectual world than any township or borough in the county.

Mr. David Bruce, a native of Scotland, emigrated to America in 1784, and in the year 1794 he settled in Burgettstown as a merchant.

In his leisure moments he devoted his time to composing poems, written in the Scottish dialect, under the signature of the Scots Irishman, which were first published in the Western Telegraph, published in Washington by John Colerick, who afterwards embodied them into a valuable work on account of their merit. In these poems Mr. Bruce displays a vivid imagination, and both wit and satire are at his command, while patriotism flows in gentle and harmonious strains.

The dedication of the work is to the Hon. Alexander Addison, President of the Court of Common Pleas of the 5th district. The concluding verse reads thus:—

> An' when your enemies hae gaen
> To that *black hole* was made by sin,
> May ye your honorable *seat* maintain,
> *Right* to dispense,
> Wi' mind discriminating, keen,
> An' manly sense.

In writing of Washington retiring from public life, he says:—

> His parting precepts ever dear,
> A father's love, a father's care
> On every heart impress;
> Illum'd by Wisdom's purest ray,
> Their light directs the surest way
> To peace and happiness.
>
> On earth will future bards rehearse
> His deeds in never-dying verse,
> And when all mortal things shall cease,
> And time has run his span;
> In regions of eternal spring,
> The blest their heavenly harps will string,
> And to seraphic airs will sing
> The friend of peace and man.

In the year 1800 Mrs. Sally Hastings removed from Donegal township, Lancaster County, to this county, and composed many fugitive pieces of poetry, which she afterwards collected into a volume, together with her diary, and published in the year 1808. Her family commenced their journey on Oct. 7, 1800, in the mode then used—a wagon—to travel two hundred and eighty miles, and, after twenty-three days' journey, arrived in Washington County, of which she says, "The inhabitants appear to be a sober, rational, and even courteous people, who prefer convenience to parade, and partake those blessings which bounteous Providence allots them, without ambition, envy, or stupidity." On October 31 the family left Canonsburg for their new home in Smith township, and having arrived on the land, she thus writes, "I shall take a seat on the trunk of a tree, while the men are cutting a road to the house, and endeavor to describe the spot of which I am now to consider myself an inhabitant."

> Great Nature, in her loose arrray,
> Derives from art no foreign aid;
> The lofty oak, the spreading bay,
> With shade still deepening into shade.

> The moss, the ivy, and the vine
>   Increase the awful gloom profound,
> Whilst hills and lonely wilds combine
>   To shed fantastic terrors round.

Time would fail me were I to undertake to make extracts from this volume of poems written by Sally Hastings—one must suffice to demonstrate that nature forms the poet, and breathes into the mind beautiful ideas, magnificent conceptions, and eternal thoughts.

> That hand that wheels the spheres, upon the tree
> Was nail'd, and torn and crucified for me !
> Here let eternal wonders ceaseless rise !
> The creature lives—the Great Creator dies !!
> And dies for whom ?—Oh, wonder ever new !—
> My guilty soul, your Maker dies for you ! ! !
> The Lord of Life, who breath and being gave,
> And immortality to all that live,
> He dies—how can He die ?—'tis wonder new—
> Yet in His hand He holds death's fatal keys—
> Heaven, earth, and hell his sov'reign will obeys.

Somerset Township

Was erected into a township by the Court of Quarter Sessions, and afterwards confirmed by the Supreme Executive Council, on April 3, 1782. It was bounded by Strabane, Peters, and Nottingham townships on the north; the Monongahela River on the east; Fallowfield and Bethlehem on the south, and Amwell and Strabane on the west.

Its present boundaries are North Strabane and Nottingham on the north; Fallowfield and West Pike Run on the east; West Bethlehem and West Pike Run on the south, and West Bethlehem and S. Strabane on the west. It is centrally distant from Washington 12 miles. Its greatest length is 10 miles—breadth, 6 miles. It is drained by the the north and south forks of Pigeon Creek on the east, and by branches of Little Chartiers' Creek on the west.

In 1860 its population was 1723, of which 62 were colored. The Williamsport and Washington turnpike runs along the northern boundary. It contains four stores, nine schools, with six male and three female teachers, the former receiving $35 and the latter $30; having 348 scholars (180 male and 168 female), tuition costing $1.14 per month. Amount of tax levied for school purposes, $1347, and receiving from the State appropriation $111.93.

The towns in the township are *Bentleysville* and *Vanceville*.

The Borough of Bentleysville.

This town was laid out by Shesbazzar Bentley, Jr., on the 4th of March, 1816, on the waters of Pigeon Creek. It is 25 miles from Pittsburg, 9 miles from Monongahela City, 10 miles from Brownsville, and 15 miles from Washington. Shortly after the town was laid out the Presbyterian, Methodist, and Baptist families united

HISTORY OF WASHINGTON COUNTY. 121

and erected a union church, which was destroyed by fire about the year 1828.

In 1848 the Methodist Episcopal church was built, in which Rev. J. B. Yarnall officiates.

On May 2, 1868, by a decree of the court, it became a borough, and contains 36 dwelling-houses, 3 stores, 1 school-house with two apartments, a literary society, 2 grist and saw-mills, 1 steam tannery, and has a population of about 300.

Vanceville is a small village, having about twelve houses, and is situated on the south branch of Pigeon Creek.

PIGEON CREEK PRESBYTERIAN CHURCH.

The diary of the Rev. John McMillan throws much light upon the early history of this church, in which it is stated :—

1775, the fourth Sabbath of August, preached at John McDowell's. Monday, rode about six miles to Patrick McCullough's, on Pigeon Creek. Tuesday, preached at Arthur Forbes's, and lodged with Patrick Scott. Patrick McCullough lived on the farm now owned by David McNary, Esq., and Arthur Forbes's farm is the property of Frederick Whitely, and Patrick Scott's residence is the property of Adam and Samuel Wier. The sermon alluded to was the first sermon preached within the bounds of the Pigeon Creek congregation, and on that day of August, 1869, the congregation celebrated its centennial anniversary.

Rev. John McMillan returned to his father's home, at Foggs' Manor, in October, 1775, but returned and preached at Pigeon Creek on the 4th Sabbath of January, 1776, and on the following Sabbath at Chartiers. He returned to the east in the following March, and was ordained by the Presbytery of Donegal, which met at Chambersburg, June 19, 1776, to take charge of Pigeon Creek and Chartiers congregations, having received a call from these churches April 23, 1776. His connection with Pigeon Creek church ceased early in the spring of 1794, and the Rev. Boyd Mercer was called to its pastorate April 22, 1794, and served until 1799. Rev. Andrew Gwin was installed in 1800, and the pastoral relation was dissolved in 1817. He was succeeded by Rev. Andrew Wylie, D. D., January 24, 1822, and ceased to act in September, 1829. The church had no regular pastor until September 26, 1831, when Rev. W. C. Anderson was elected. He was ordained and installed April 17, 1832, and served until July 15, 1836. His successor was Rev. Ebenezer S. Graham, called September 30, 1837, and installed the following month, and the pastoral relation was dissolved in October, 1842.

The congregation did not elect a pastor until April 8, 1844, when James Sloan, D. D., was elected, and he was subsequently installed in the December following. The pastoral relation was dissolved in October, 1862. His successor was Rev. S. M. Henderson, called

June 5, 1863, ordained and installed November 4, 1863, and pastoral relationship closed April 24, 1867. The present efficient and honored pastor is the Rev. John S. Marquis, who was called March 2, 1868, and installed on June 5, 1868. As a successful laborer in his Master's cause, for humility and charity, and in dispensing gospel truth, he has no superior in the bounds of the Presbytery. To him am I indebted for the history of this church, which was planted in the wilderness more than one hundred years ago, and has proven itself a fruitful vine.

The *first* ELDERS of the church were Patrick McCullough, Patrick Scott, Hugh Cotton, and Hugh Scott. This session was subsequently increased by the election and ordination of James Smith, John Hosack, James Kerr, Joseph Vaughn, John Stevenson, William Ferguson, Robert Moon, and John Atkinson.

July 17, 1836, John Vance, Samuel Gamble Samuel Ritchey, Dr. Boyd Emery, William Kerr, and David Riddle, Esqrs., were ordained.

February 13, 1849, Andrew Smith, James Vance, John Leyda, Greer McIlvaine, and John Scott were elected, and ordained April 8, 1849.

March 3, 1856, William Smith, William Ramsey, and Edward Paden were elected, and ordained elders April 14, 1856.

March 5, 1860, Alexander Hamilton, Zechariah Peese, James Rankin, and John C. Messenger were elected elders, and ordained April 8, 1860. At the present time the session consists of Messrs. Greer McIlvain, William Smith, William Ramsey, Edward Paden, Alexander Hamilton, Zechariah Peese, and John C. Messenger.

The *first* DEACONS of the church were ordained March 7, 1864, and consisted of Messrs. Isaac V. Riddle, James Jones, William Barkley, and William Davis. This church has 306 communicants.

It is worthy of remark that the *first meeting* of the Presbytery of Red Stone was held in this church, on September 19, 1781, the foling ministers being present: Rev. John McMillan, Rev. James Power, and Rev. Thaddeus Dodd, with Joseph Neil, Demas Lindley, and Patrick Scott as ruling elders.

The *first* church was a cabin of round logs, with a clap-board roof. It stood within the present graveyard, and was neither *chunked* nor *daubed* the first winter after its erection.

The *second* was built of stone, and stood in the graveyard. The aisles were earthen, with a floor of boards under the pews. Every family had a pew or bench, according to their own wishes, hence there was a great variety of pews, benches, &c.

The *third* building was erected in 1829. Proposals having been issued, on March 14, for a brick meeting-house, 56 by 70 feet (15 feet to the square). The Building Committee or the trustees were John Atkinson, Henry Vance, Samuel Gamble, and W. Paden.

SABBATH SCHOOL.

The Sabbath school was organized in 1822. Hon. Joseph Lawrence first brought the subject of a Sabbath school to the notice of the congregation. John C. Messenger, Esq., is the present superintendent, and it has 225 scholars.

OTHER CHURCHES.

A Methodist Episcopal church was built in 1849, on the road from Hillsborough to Bentleysville. It is a neat frame building. Rev. J. B. Yarnall is the officiating minister.

Within one mile of Vanceville is a Baptist and a Disciple church, on the road from Bentleysville to Washington. The Rev. Mr. Hardzoth occupies the pulpit of the latter church, and the Rev. Mr. Skinner the Baptist pulpit.

Pigeon Creek U. P. Church was organized in 1820. Rev. Alexander Wilson was pastor from its organization until January 10th, 1834; Rev. Bankhead Boyd from September 24, 1834, to 1860; Rev. D. S. Littell from October 17th, 1861, to the present time—with a membership of one hundred and sixty-four.

GREENE TOWNSHIP

Was erected into a township on the 3d of April, 1782, by the Court of Quarter Sessions and approved by the Supreme Executive Council. Its boundaries were as follows: Beginning at the mouth of Little Whitely Creek and running therewith to the dividing ridge between that and Big Whitely Creek; thence with that ridge between Big Whitely and Muddy Creek to Mason and Dixon's line; thence to the Monongahela River; thence by the river to the place of beginning. It had Cumberland township on the north; the Monongahela River on the east; Mason and Dixon's line on the south; Virginia on the west. By the act of February 9th, 1796, this township, with Cumberland, Morgan, Franklin, and Rich Hill townships, was struck off from Washington County to form Greene County.

Jarrett's Fort was built in this township.

The town of Greensburg, Greene township, Washington County (but afterwards Greene County), was laid out by Elias Stone on the 31st day of May, 1791. Greensburg is situated on the Monongahela River, on a part of a tract of land called "Delight," patented to Elias Stone and Elizabeth his wife, in 1787. Each lot contains eighty-one perches; streets forty feet wide. Lot number sixty was appropriated for public use and at the discretion of the inhabitants. The town contains eighty lots. The names of the streets, counting from the Monongahela River, were Water, Front, Second, Third, and Fourth streets. Counting from the eastern side of the town were Diamond, Stone, Clear, Walnut, Minor's, and County streets. Lot number sixty was at the corner of Third and County streets.

DICKINSON TOWNSHIP.

The Court of Quarter Sessions made application to the Supreme Executive Council to organize this township, and on September 17th,

1775, by its action ratified the application of the court with the following boundaries—the Monongahela River on the north and east; Nottingham and Peters on the south; Robinson and Cecil on the west.

By an act of the legislature passed September 24th, 1788, Allegheny County was erected into a county, part of which was taken from Washington County. The proceedings of the Supreme Executive Council of September 30th, 1788, says: "Two returns from the districts of the townships of Cecil and Dickinson, in the county of Washington, were read and not allowed, as the whole of *Dickinson* and part of *Cecil* district has been struck off to the county of Allegheny."

WASHINGTON.

The town of Washington originally belonged to Strabane township, one of the thirteen original townships of the county, erected in July, 1781. On the 25th of September, 1785, the Court of Quarter Sessions, upon a petition of the citizens requesting to be formed into a separate election district, indorsed the application, and the Supreme Executive Council confirmed the proceedings of the court on the 6th of February, 1786. From its being originally a portion of Strabane township, so many have been the changes that its present chartered boundaries are Canton and South Strabane on the north, South Strabane on the east, Franklin and South Strabane on the south, Canton and Franklin on the west, being now entirely surrounded by new townships.

The original name of this town was BASSETT, which was laid out by David Hoge, Esq., of Cumberland County, the survey being made by David Reddick, Deputy Surveyor, October 13, 1781. Another plot states that a true copy of the plan remains in the hands of John Lukens, Surveyor General, which was made November 4, 1784, by Edward Lynch, Deputy Surveyor. This second plot was made prior to the sale of David Hoge to his sons John and William. On the 18th of October, 1781 (five days after the town was laid out), David Hoge, Esq., the proprietor, conveyed to James Edgar, Hugh Scott, Van Swearingen, Daniel Leet, and John Armstrong, as trustees of Washington County, a lot for a court house and prison, in the town of Bassett, containing two hundred and forty feet square, being bounded by Monongahela (now Market) Street on the east, Ohio (now Beau) Street on the north, lot No. 123 on the west, and Johnston's (now Cherry) Alley on the south.

The name of the town was permanently changed to Washington on the 4th of November, 1784, the date at which the second plot was made, although we have the evidence of receipts for lots being given by the proprietor in October, 1781, both as Bassettown and Washington, for in the deed of David Hoge to John and William Hoge, of November 7, 1785, it is stated that the said David conveys to his sons, John and William, a tract of land in Washington

County, on the waters of Chartiers' Creek, and known by the name of *Catfishes Camp*, containing eight hundred acres, which was to include the town of WASHINGTON, excepting the southwest fourth of said town, which said David reserved for himself. Subsequently, however, on the 10th of March, 1787, he also conveyed the remaining southwest fourth of the town to his sons, John and William. This deed also mentions the fact of the name of the streets being changed, based upon the second plot of 1784.

The act of the General Assembly of March 28, 1781, directs the electors to meet at the house of David Hoge at the place called *Catfishes Camp*, to hold their elections and courts until a court house shall be built.

To understand the Hoge purchase, we will state that there were three tracts of land originally surveyed and purchased by David Hoge, as follows: One from Martha Hunter, dated November 4, 1769, containing three hundred and thirty-nine acres and sixty-nine perches, and called "MARTHA'S BOTTOM." The second was purchased from Joseph Hunter, November 11, 1769, containing three hundred and thirty-one acres and twenty-one perches, called "GRAND CAIRO," and the third from Abraham Hunter, surveyed and purchased November 11, 1769, containing three hundred and thirty-one acres and twenty-one perches, called "CATFISHES CAMP."

The town of BASSETT was laid out on a portion of the two tracts of land known by the name of Grand Cairo and Catfishes Camp, but most generally known by the latter name. It was laid out by David Reddick, Esq., at the request of David Hoge, Esq., on October 18, 1781; it then embraced all the lots within Walnut Street on the north, College Street on the east, Maiden Street on the south, and West Alley on the west, containing two hundred and ninety-one lots.

Upon the plot of the town of BASSETT are the following memoranda: Lots marked A for a court-house and prison. This is the same public square now occupied with a court house, prison, &c. &c. Lots B, C, D were reserved by Mr. Hoge. B included the lots from Pine Alley, the residence of the late John L. Gow, deceased, to the corner of Main and Ohio (Beau) streets, the residence of William Smith, Esq. C included the lots from the Fulton House, owned by Messrs. Little and Melvin, to Johnston's (now Cherry) Alley, or the house occupied by Alexander Murdoch, Esq. D all the lots from Pine Alley, the property of the heirs of William L. Oliver, deceased, to the corner of Main and Ohio (now Beau) streets, or the iron hall front, owned by William Smith, Esq. The plot also states that the two principal streets, viz., Monongahela (Main) Street and Ohio (Beau) Street, are sixty-six feet wide. The lots are sixty feet front by two hundred and forty feet deep. B, C, D were each divided into six lots of forty feet front and two hundred and forty deep. Lot 171, on the corner of Race and Chartiers streets (now Chestnut and Second), and at present owned by

Mrs. E. H. Turner, was given gratis for a place of public worship, while lot 172, directly opposite and owned by William H. Taylor, was appropriated for a school-house. Lot 43 was presented to General Washington. This lot is on the corner of Gay and Chartiers (now Belle and Second) streets, and with the adjoining lot, 42, is owned by the First Presbyterian church. This lot was the site of the old red school-house, in which many of our citizens were educated under George K. Scott, deceased, while lot 102, which was presented at the same time and occupying the opposite corner, being the southwest corner of the college square, is owned by David S. Wilson, Esq.

The plot of BASSETT has marked upon it three springs, designated by the letters a, b, c. a is a spring given for the use of the town; b and c are springs. Where the spring run is parted, the water sinks under ground. One of these springs is on the corner lot owned by Jacob Koechline, on the corner of Main and Maiden streets, and in the cellar of his brick house. The other two springs are on the property of Wm. Huston, the adjoining lot, south of Mr. Koechline's. In the year ———, when Judge Baird erected his steam mill at the foot of Main Street, the water for running the mill was conveyed by wooden pipes from this spring, and several of the lot owners through which it passed had fountain pumps connected with these pipes. Catfishes Camp is marked upon it, near the spring on the property of Patrick Bryson, deceased.

In addition to the foregoing memoranda, at the northwest corner of the plot and outside of the limits of the town of Bassett, is the letter A and the words, "Great plain given by Mr. Hoge for a common, about seventy or eighty acres." In an examination of the minutes of the Town Council of June 6, 1811, is the following record :—

WHEREAS, A portion of the ground heretofore considered as a *common* has been sold and is about to be improved, to the prejudice of the rights of the borough and to the serious injury of several of the inhabitants, therefore

Resolved, That a committee be appointed to call on the proprietors of the town and the surviving commissioners who negotiated with Mr. David Hoge, the original proprietor, and obtain such information respecting the claims of the borough to said property as may be procured. Messrs. Alexander Reed, John Wilson, and Robert Anderson were appointed the committee. The burgesses were also instructed to give notice to all persons who are or may attempt building, inclosing, or improving, in or on the reputed commons or property of the borough, to desist therefrom. The minutes of the Council do not show that the Committee ever reported.

David Hoge having sold all his interest to his sons, they extended the original limits of Bassett by adding thereto on the EAST of College Street to the alley, called BREWERY ALLEY, commencing at the eastern end of Maiden Street and running to Walnut Street. Also adding on the SOUTH, from Maiden Street to Hazel Alley, forty building lots and many outlots.

A small stream running through the southern and western part of Washington bears the name of *Catfish Run*. It will also be remembered that the tract of land purchased from Abraham Hunter was called Catfishes Camp, and before even *Bassett* was laid out the few hamlets which occupied the southern part of Washington were called Catfish. The stream, the land, and the town all derived their name from a celebrated Indian Chief, whose Indian name was Tingoocqua or Catfish, who belonged to the Kuskuskee tribe of Indians, and occupied the hunting grounds between the Allegheny Mountains and the Ohio River.

In the records of the Provincial Council of Pennsylvania, we find him participating in a conference meeting held in Philadelphia, Dec. 4th, 1759, at which Governor Hamilton and his council with chiefs from the Wyoming, Delaware, and Kuskuskee Indians were present. At this council the Indian chief CATFISH made the following speech, after taking four strings of wampum and holding two of them separate in his fingers, thus spoke :—

I have not much to say; I am only a messenger. I came from the Kuskuskees. The nation that I belong to as well as many others to the west of us, as far as the setting of the sun, have heard that you and Teedyuscung (Chief of the Delawares) sat often together in council and at length agreed upon a peace, and we are glad to hear that the friendship and harmony, which of old always subsisted between our and your ancestors, was raised up again and established once more. This was very agreeable to us, and we came here to see if what was related was true, and we find it is true, which gives us great satisfaction. [*Then taking hold of the other two strings he proceeded.*]

Brother. Now that Teedyuscung and you have, through the goodness of Providence, brought about a peace, we entreat you to be strong; don't let it slip; don't omit anything to render it quite secure and lasting; hold it fast; consider our aged men and our young children, and for their sakes be strong, and never rest till it be thoroughly confirmed. All the Indians at Allegheny desire you to do so, and they will do all they can likewise. [*Gave a string of wampum.*]

Brother. We make eleven nations on the west of the Allegheny who have heard what you and Teedyuscung have concluded at the treaty of Easton (in 1758), and as we all heartily agreed to it and are determined to join in it, we have opened a road to where Teedyuscung lives, and we the messengers, have travelled much to our satisfaction on the road which he has made from his habitation to this town (Philadelphia). We have found it a very good road, and all our nations will use this road for the time to come. We say nothing of the Six Nations. We do not reckon them among the eleven nations. We leave you to treat with them yourselves, we make no road for them. This is your own affair. We only tell you we do not include them in anything we say. I have done. [*Gave four strings of wampum.*]

At what period Catfish settled in this part of the country tradition gives us no account. We know, however, from our aged citizen, Col. George Kuntz, whose father removed from the east to Washington in 1788, that he knew the old chief when he had a camp in the rear of the lot on which William Huston's inn now stands, near the three springs (which I have spoken of as being designated on the plan of Bassettown). Afterwards he moved his camp near to the spring now called Patrick Bryson's spring; from thence he removed his camp to Shirl's woods; from thence he went to Ohio and died.

Local tradition has falsely placed his tomb in the graveyard at Washington, Pa., marked by a large unhewn stone; but such is not the fact. This stone was procured by Alexander Lytle, Esq., deceased, on the Williamsport road, and had it placed at the grave of his wife. His daughter Harriet, on her death-bed, requested that the bodies of her father, and mother, and family, with the same stone, be taken to the cemetery. The circumstance, however, gave rise to a few verses, written by a young man named Hiram Kaine, Esq., a printer by profession, yet unassuming as a poet. To preserve his memory, therefore, who composed these verses, and who in his own language desired not to obtain popularity in the drawing-rooms of the wealthy, but in the workshops and homesteads of his native place, was the reason why he tuned his rude unlettered harp.

The Grave of Catfish.

1. A fitting monument was that
    For one so proud and stern—
   More striking than a marble bust
    Or consecrated urn!

2. Unbending as that massive rock,
    You braved the battle storm,
   And reared amidst its fiercest shock
    Thy dark, majestic form.

3. Thou needst not fear the pale face race,
    Who slumber by thy side;
   They cannot tear the home from thee,
    Which living they denied.

4. The unlettered stone above thy head
    Is not more still than they,
   The marble not more motionless
    That tells us where they lay.

5. The rank green grass is twining,
    Its wreath above thy head,
   As it ever richly twineth
    Round dwellings of the dead.

6. Oh! does thy spirit ever come,
    To gaze upon this mound,
   And tread upon the springing grass
    Above the hallowed ground?

7. Dost ever wander o'er the hills
    Where once thy tribe did roam,
   And curse the race who on their graves
    Have built themselves a home?

8. Thou hearest not, dark Chieftain—
    Thy funeral song is sung,
    The emblems of thy power have flown,
    Thy last war-whoop hath rung.

9. But yet thy name, by kindred ghosts,
    Is heard by yonder rill,
    As comes its murmuring midnight chime
    In echoes from the hill.

When *Bassettown* was laid out, David Hoge, in October, 1781, issued tickets to purchasers of lots in these words:—

No. 15.   *Bassettown*, October, 1781.

This will entitle Charles Dodd to receive a sufficient title, subject to one dollar a year in specie, for a lot marked in the original plan of said town, 58, provided there shall be erected thereon, on or before the thirtieth day of October, 1784, a house eighteen feet square at least, with a stone or brick chimney therein.   DAVID HOGE.

On the 21st of July, 1784, this lot, with the house, was sold to John Dodd, for £300 Pennsylvania currency. It is situated on Main Street and the corner of Strawberry Alley, now owned by Jas. G. Strean, upon which is erected a three-story house, iron front, occupied by Mr. Robert F. Strean's hardware store and the *Reporter* printing office.

William Darby, Esq., in the year 1845, and then in the 71st year of his age, in speaking of Bassettown (now Washington), said: In the fall of 1782, the site where Washington now stands was a vast thicket of black and red hawthorn, wild plums, hazel bushes, shrub oaks, and briers; often I have picked hazel-nuts where the court-house now stands. The yell of the savage rung in fancy's ear and alas too often in the heart of the dying victim. The whole country was a dense forest, only broken by small patches, with dead trees, made so by the axe of the early pioneer.

Bassettown, under the proprietorship of David Hoge, improved but slowly, there being but two deeds on record prior to its sale in 1785, one to James Marshall, February 8, 1785, and the other to Charles Dodd, July 21, 1784. After John and William Hoge had purchased the town, and added the addition thereto of all the lots south of Maiden Street, and divided the land into outlets, a new impetus was given to the town, and lots sold rapidly and houses were speedily erected thereon.

In this connection, we may add that Robert Fulton, of steamboat notoriety, held three lots in Washington. While sojourning in London, in 1793, he directed Mr. Hoge to make deeds of these three lots to his three sisters, Mrs. David Morris (No. 4), Mrs. Isabella Cook (No. 118), Mrs. Peggy Scott (No. 125).

In looking over the original lot-holders, and up to the date of incorporation, we find the names of John, William, and David Hoge, Dr. Moore, William Horton, James Marshall, Charles and John Dodd,

Absalom Baird, S. Darley, Anthony Horseman, J. Lochman, Jos. Harris, Rev. John Casper Sinclair, Thomas and David Acheson, Van Swearingen, D. G. Mitchell, Leonard Boyer, Thomas Hutchinson, D. Moody, Mary Miller, Philip Milsach, Thomas Stokely, Hugh Mears, Margaret Scott (sister of Robert Fulton), D. Blackmore, Hugh Workman, Edward Lynch, Wm. Findley, Alexander Addison, M. Collins, Thomas Bristor, John Standley, T. Woodward, Reasin Beall, Robert Fulton, David Morris, Archibald Kerr, John Wilson, Alexander Reed, John Flake, Daniel Moore, James Goudy, James White, James Gilmore, Isabella Cooke (sister of Robert Fulton), James W. McBeth, Stephen Way, Matthew Ritchie, Hugh Wiley, Robert Hazlett, James Ross, William Meetkirke, Daniel Kehr, Abraham Lattimore, Joseph Seaman, James Orr, J. Purviance, Gabriel Brakeny, Stephen Wood, Hugh and Samuel Workmen, Patrick Bryson, Daniel and Jonathan Leet.

But what changes have been wrought since! The town from several hundred inhabitants has increased to many thousand, its manufacturing, commercial, educational, moral, and religious interests have all been largely developed. The second generation of these pioneers have also been gathered to their fathers, and while the old landmarks remain to point out their homes, where brotherly love, truth, and friendship reigned supreme, the graveyard and the cemetery point to their sacred ashes. Amid the multiplicity of changes, we find the original property only remain in the descendants of John Wilson, Alexander Reed, David Acheson, and Patrick Bryson.

The citizens of Washington knew that their town was inferior to but few of the towns of Pennsylvania, but that it was destitute of many useful improvements, which could not be accomplished without being incorporated as a borough. Their streets were not regulated, and, during some of the winter months, not being piked, were almost impassable; the sideways were not paved, neither was there public spirit enough to purchase a fire-engine to make provision against *fire*. In the midst of these discouragements and difficulties, a town meeting was called on February 6, 1795, to consider the necessity of petitioning the legislature for an act of incorporation. The people met and discussed the question, but the principal objection was that the taxes would be greatly increased, and that a few men would have the control and direction of the borough affairs. These sentiments prevailed, and the question was ventilated through the *Western Telegraph*, then published at Washington. A writer, who signs himself " Tom Stick in the Mud," thus sarcastically writes upon the subject: "For my part I've lived all my born days, and my posterity before me and my children after me, up to the eyes in mud and never a bit the worse for it, and I can't see why other people should think themselves better stuff than we. I loves fun, and, at our end of the town, it would sometimes make you die with laughing to see your calico-carcassed, spindle-shanked folks sticking fast in a crossing-place and leaving their shoes behind them."

"A BACHELOR," in answering the foregoing communication, gives one reason why the town should be incorporated, in these words : "It would prevent emigrants and strangers from giving as accurate a description of the ladies' ankles as I myself can do. I can tell any of them whether they are flat-footed, beef-shanked, knock-kneed, or whether either of them or not. Oh ! how I have shaken my sides to see them straddling through the mud up street to a tea drinking. I hope, therefore, that the people will see that a corporation is absolutely necessary." Notwithstanding this newspaper description, the town, however, was not incorporated until the 13th day of February, 1810.

The act of incorporation defines its boundaries as follows :—

"Beginning at a post on the land of James Ashbrook; thence by land of Robert Anderson, Thomas Officer, and others, south seventy-seven degrees west one hundred and fifty-nine and one-half perches to a post; thence by land of Thomas Jones, William Hoge, and others, south fourteen and three-fourth degrees east one hundred perches to a post; thence by land of James Ashbrook, William Sherrard, and others, south thirteen degrees east sixty-three and one-half perches to a post; thence by land of John Hoge, south fifty-one and one-half degrees east twenty-nine perches to a post; thence by land late of John Simonson, Hugh Workmen, and others, north seventy-seven degrees east one hundred and twenty perches to a post; thence by land of Thomas McFadden, Daniel Kehr, and others, north, four and one-half degrees west eighty-four perches to a post; thence by land of Robert Hazlett, Isaiah Steen, and others, north ten degrees west one hundred and two perches to the place of beginning."

This act gives them authority to elect officers, make and enforce laws, hold property, and perform such acts as are usual to corporate boroughs.

On the 27th of March, 1852, the borough authorities were instructed to apply to the Court of Quarter Sessions for the admission of the borough of Washington to the benefits and privileges of a charter under the act of Assembly of the 3d of April, 1851, which was subsequently confirmed by the court on the 18th of May, 1852.

This general act provides, in Section 30, for the enlargement of borough limits, by not less than twenty of the freeholder owners of lots petitioning the council, and they declaring by ordinance that the limits have been enlarged.

June 10th, 1854, and 6th of January, 1855, the borough limits were extended to the present lines. At the May term in 1855, the borough was divided into two wards by Main Street, named respectively the East and West Wards.

With these preliminary remarks, we may now state that the borough of Washington is situated near the centre of Washington County, on the National road, twenty-four miles from Brownsville and thirty-two miles from Wheeling; twenty-seven miles from Pittsburg and twenty-two miles from Monongahela City. Its population in 1860 was 3587 (but in 1870 about 4500). Its situation is salubrious, and from its position locally adapted to become a manufacturing centre. Bituminous coal underlies the town and valley, while a railroad of seven miles would not only add Canonsburg to Washington, but develop for manufacturing purposes all the coal which exists on Chartiers' Creek.

The streets are rectangular, and are all sixty feet wide except Main and Beau streets, which are sixty-six feet wide.

Before entering upon a history of the public buildings we shall give a list of the burgesses and town council, treasurers and town clerks, since the date of its charter to the present time—I have therefore prepared them from the official record for future reference, knowing that our borough history would be incomplete and imperfect without such a record.

BURGESSES.

1.—1810. Alexander Reed, John Wilson.
2.—1811. Re-elected.
3.—1812. David Morris, Thomas Officer.
4.—1813. Re-elected.
5.—1814. Daniel Moore, James Orr.
6.—1815. David Shields, John Wilson.
7.—1816. Alexander Murdoch, Alexander Reed.
8.—1817. John Wilson, David Morris,
9.—1818. James Blaine, James Shannon.
10.—1819. James Blaine, John Gregg.
11.—1820. Re-elected.
12.—1821. Re-elected.
13.—1822. Re-elected.
14.—1823. James Orr, James Ruple.
15.—1824. James Ruple, Daniel Moore.
16.—1825. Re-elected.
17.—1826. Hugh Workman, James Orr.
18.—1827. Re-elected.
19.—1828. Re-elected.
20.—1829. James Orr, John Kuntz.
21.—1830. Re-elected.
22.—1831. George Kuntz, James Orr.
23.—1832. John S. Brady, John Wilson.
24.—1833. Archibald Kerr, John Wilson.
25.—1834. James Orr, John S. Brady.
26.—1835. Archibald Kerr, James Ruple.
27.—1836. John R. Griffith, James Ruple.
28.—1837. Re-elected.
29.—1838. John L. Gow, James Ruple.
30.—1839. James Blaine, John R. Griffith.
31.—1840. Robert Officer, John S. Brady.
32.—1841. Robert Officer, George W. Brice.
33.—1842. Re-elected.
34.—1843. Robert Officer, Thomas McGiffin.
35.—1844. Isaac Leet, James Langley
36.—1845. Mathew Griffin, Sample Sweeney.
37.—1846. L. P. Hitchcock, John L. Gow.
38.—1847. William McKennan, Alexander Murdoch.
39.—1848. James Ruple, James Langley.
40.—1849. Collin M. Reed, Alfred Creigh.
41.—1850. William Hopkins, Collin M. Reed.
42.—1851. Alex. W. Acheson, Peter Reimund.

43.—1852. Alex. W. Acheson, Hugh W. Reynolds.
44.—1853. William Workman, Charles W. Hays.
45.—1854. Charles W. Hays, James Spriggs.
46.—1855. Alexandel Murdoch, Samuel Cunningham.
47.—1856. Jacob Slagle, James Brown.
48.—1857. James B. Ruple, William Hopkins.
49.—1858. James W. Kuntz, James Rush.
50.—1859. Re-elected.
51.—1860. James W Kuntz, Thomas J. Walker.
52.—1861. James W. Kuntz, James Rush.
53.—1862. Re-elected.
54.—1863. James W. Kuntz, Alfred Creigh.
55.—1864. Andrew Brady, James Rush.
56.—1865. Re-elected.
57.—1866. Charles Hayes, William Smith.
58.—1867. H. J. Vankirk, John Hoon.
59.—1868. John D. Boyle, John McElroy.
60.—1869. John D. Boyle, J. Y. Hamilton.

Municipal elections changed by the legislature March 16, 1869, and directed to be held in October of each year. In Washington borough the burgess and two councilmen were directed to be elected, and the subsequent year the assistant burgess and three councilmen—these officers to continue in office two years.

61.—1869. John D. Boyle, Theodore F. Slater.

TOWN COUNCIL.

1.—1810. Hugh Wilson, Thomas Acheson, Hugh Workman, Robert Anderson, and Parker Campbell.
2.—1811. Re-elected.
3.—1812. John Scott, Matthew Dill, Hugh Workman, Parker Campbell, and Thomas McGiffin.
4.—1813. Thomas McGiffin, Parker Campbell, Daniel Moore, James Orr, and Hugh Workman.
5.—1814. Parker Campbell, Thomas Officer, Thomas McGiffin, Hugh Workman, and David Morris.
6.—1815. James Orr, Parker Campbell, Hugh Workman, Thomas McGiffin, and Daniel Moore.
7.—1816. Thomas McGiffin, James Lattimore, James Blaine, Parker Campbell, and George Baird.
8.—1817. Alexander Reed, James Blaine, James Lattimore, James Orr, and Thomas H. Baird.
9.—1818. Thomas M. T. McKennan, Hugh Workman, John Wilson, James Garret, and William Hunter.
10.—1819. Hugh Workman, John Wilson, William Hunter, Thomas M. T. McKennan, and James Garret.
11.—1820. Re-elected.
12.—1821. Thomas M. T. McKennan, John Wilson, David Eckert, James Stevens, and John Koontz.
13.—1822. Re-elected.
14.—1823. Hugh Workman, Thomas M. T. McKennan, Jacob Stagle, John Wilson, and James Stevens.
15.—1824. Archibald Kerr, Thomas Good, James Lattimore, Thomas M. T. McKennan, and James Kerr.
16.—1825. Re-elected.
17.—1826. Thomas M. T. McKennan, Thomas McGiffin, George Kuntz, John S. Brady, and John Wilson.

18.—1827. Thomas M. T. McKennan, George Kuntz, John Wilson, Jacob Slagle, and George L. Morrison.
19.—1828. Thomas M. T. McKennan, George Kuntz, Jacob Slagle, John K. Wilson, and Samuel Hazlett.
20.—1829. Thomas M. T. McKennan, Jacob Slagle, George Kuntz, William Robinson, and William Hunter.
21.—1830. John K. Wilson, Thomas M. T. McKennan, James Shannon, William Robinson, and John Wilson.
22.—1831. William Baird, William Robinson, John Wilson, James Shannon, and John K. Wilson.
23.—1832. Re-elected.
24.—1833. Hugh Workman, Isaac Leet, George Kuntz, Thomas Officer, and John Morrow.
25.—1834. Isaac Leet, John Morrow, George Kuntz, John K. Wilson, and Thomas Officer.
26.—1835. James Shannon, Isaac Leet, John K. Wilson, John L. Gow, and John Wilson.
27.—1836. Isaac Leet, Andrew Shearer, John N. Dagg, John Morrow, and John Bradfield.
28.—1837. John L. Gow, John N. Dagg, Andrew Shearer, John Morrow, and George Black.
29.—1838. George Black, John R. Griffith, Robert Officer, Andrew Shearer, and John Morrow.
30.—1839. Alexander W. Acheson, John Best, Henry Langley, James H. Pattison, and Peter Wolfe.
31.—1840. Alexander W. Acheson, Peter Wolfe, John Morrow, Adam Silvey, and Oliver Lindsey.
32.—1841. Alexander W. Acheson, Peter Wolfe, Oliver Lindsey, James Brown, and Matthew Griffin.
33.—1842. Re-elected.
34.—1843. Alexander W. Acheson, George Lonkert, George W. Brice, John Grayson, and John S. Brady.
35.—1844. Oliver Lindsey, John Best, John R. Griffith, Peter Wolfe, and Jacob Kissler.
36.—1845. William Smith, Oliver Lindsey, John Best, Peter Kennedy, and David Wolfe.
37.—1846. John Morrow, James Brown, Joseph Henderson, Thomas Logan, and George Lonkert.
38.—1847. James M. Hutchinson, James Brice, T. W. Grayson, Alfred Thirkield, and Robert O cer.
39.—1848. John Morrow, William Hopkins, Charles W. Hays, George Black, and James Rush.
40.—1849. Peter Kennedy, William Hopkins, Charles W. Hays, Jacob Slagle, and Oliver Lindsey.
41.—1850. John Bausman, Philip Kuhn, Jacob Kissler, John S. Brady, and Thomas B. Bryson.
42.—1851. Sample Sweeny, Oliver Lindsey, Freeman Brady, Sr., Collin M. Reed, and Thomas W. Grayson.
43.—1852. Freeman Brady, Sr., Oliver Lindsey, William McKennan, John Wiley, and James Brown.
44.—1853. John Morrow, William R. Oliver, James Rush, John Wiley, and William T. Fleming.
45.—1854. Jacob Kessler, J. L. Judson, James D. Best, Dr. M. H. Clarke, and Collin M. Read.

HISTORY OF WASHINGTON COUNTY. 135

46.—1855. Thomas W. Grayson, T. S. McKinley, H. W. Reynolds, A. R. Frisbie, and John McClelland.
47.—1856. L. W. Stockton, Dr. J. R. Wilson, Simon Cort, John McElroy, and Th. B. Bryson.
48.—1857. James W. Kuntz, Charles W. Hays, Thomas B. Bryson, John McAllister, and S. R. Witherow.
49.—1858. John Prigg, Jacob Goldsmith, N. F. Brobst, David Wolf, and W. H. Stoy.
50.—1859. James Walton, James W. Humphreys, William T. Fleming, Charles W. Hays, and Jackson Spriggs.
51.—1860. Re-elected.
52.—1861. Charles W. Hays, Freeman Brady, Jr., Andrew Brady, John Prigg, and Alexander Frazer.
53.—1862. Charles W. Hays, Thomas D. O'Hara, Andrew Brady, John Prigg, and Samuel Beatty.
54.—1863. John Prigg, John Naghtan, James Walton, John W. Lockhart, and W. T. Fleming.
55.—1864. Jacob Miller, Thomas Seamans, Alphew Murphy, A. J. Caton, and P. Waldron.
56.—1865. Ira Lacock, John Naugtan, G. Jackson Dagg, Wm. H. Drury, A. H. Ecker.
57.—1866. Thomas Walker, T. J. Hodgins, Nelson Vankirk, William Fitzwilliam, and David Aiken.
58.—1867. James C. Acheson, Thomas McKean, Charles V. Grier, Alex. Seaman, John Hallam.
59.—1868. William Taylor, John Templeton, G. O. Jones, Robert Davis, and Samuel Hazlett.
60.—1869. Alfred Creigh, A. B. Caldwell, J. L. Judson, A. C. Morrow, and James Huston.

By act of the legislature, March 16, 1869, three councilmen were to be elected biennially with the assistant burgess, at the October election in 1869, term of service to commence April, 1870, which resulted in the election of

61.—1870. George S. Hart, Martin Luther, and James Huston.

TREASURERS.

1810—12.	Daniel Moore.	1863—65.	George Kuntz.
1813—15.	Alexander Reed.	1866.	David Aiken.
1816.	Daniel Moore.	1867.	John C. Hastings.
1817—19.	John Barrington.	1868.	John Aiken.
1820—35.	John Gregg.	1869.	L. R. W. Little.
1836—56.	George Kuntz.	1870.	M. G. Kuntz.
1857—62.	George Baird.		

TOWN CLERKS.

1810—11.	David Shields.	1848—50.	William J. Wilson.
1812—14.	Samuel Cunningham.	1851—54.	Joseph O'Hara.
1815—16.	John Cunningham.	1855—62.	William B. Rose.
1817—31.	John Marshall.	1863.	Ashford Engle.
1832—33.	Samuel Doak.	1864.	Henry Brown (2 mos.).
1834.	Henry Langley.	1864—65.	Thaddeus Stanton.
1835—40.	George W. Brice.	1866.	I. Goodrich Ruple.
1841—42.	Robert K. Shannon.	1867.	John Aiken.
1843—44.	Henry M. Brister.	1868.	Joseph A. McKee.
1845—46.	James McKinley.	1869.	John Waldron.
1847.	David Wherry.	1870.	Wesley Wolf.

Public Buildings.

The public buildings in Washington Borough consist of the court-house, containing the court, jury, and library room, and the public offices, the gaol, the old market house, town hall, containing an audience room, council chamber, post office, citizens' library, engine house, and market house, Washington and Jefferson college, First Presbyterian church, Methodist Episcopal church, United Presbyterian church, Methodist Protestant church, Trinity Episcopal church, German Evangelical Lutheran church, Second Presbyterian church, Roman Catholic church, Cumberland Presbyterian church, Disciples of Christ, Baptist church, African Methodist Episcopal church, Wright's Chapel (African), Franklin Bank of Washington, Female Seminary, Union School building, Washington gas works, Washington cemetery, Washington coal works.

Court-House.

On the 18th of October, 1781, David Hoge, of Cumberland County, conveyed to James Edgar, Hugh Scott, Van Swearingen, Daniel Leet, and John Armstrong, a piece of land in the town of "Bassett" for the use of the inhabitants of Washington County, to erect thereon a court-house, prison, &c., for and in consideration of the good-will he beareth to the inhabitants, and also the sum of five shillings. The ground conveyed is thus described: Situate in Bassettown, fronting and extending along Monongahela (Main) Street, 240 feet, and in the same manner along Ohio (Beau) Street, 240 feet; thence with the lot marked in the original plan, 123 (now owned by Robert Boyd, Esq.); thence with Johnston's (Cherry) Alley 240 feet to the Monongahela Street aforesaid. The witnesses to the deed were Henry Taylor and David Reddick, which was recorded in the Recorder's office February 7, 1785.

The organic law of the county, dated March 28, 1781, section 9, directed the courts to be held at the house of David Hoge, Esq., until a court-house shall be built or otherwise provided for. The courts were held at the designated place until 1783. The courts were afterwards held at the house of Charles Dodd in 1783, at the house of James Wilson in 1784, and John Dodd's from 1785 to 1787, each of these persons receiving a stipulated rent. The house of Charles Dodd was upon the lot now owned by James G. Strean, Esq., but afterwards John Dodd bought the same property. The house rented from James Wilson was on the lot where Mr. William H. Drury resides. The courts were held there but one year, and returned to Mr. Dodd's. The gaol occupied the first floor and the court the second. It was in this court-house that Thomas Richardson was tried for larceny in 1784, convicted, and subsequently *hanged*, an account of which we shall give in Chapter VIII.

In 1783 the commissioners began the erection of a log court-house and other public buildings, which were not completed until July, 1787. In 1784 a tax of £500 was laid for the purpose of building a court-house, and in 1788 an additional sum of £150 to pay the balance on the same, the whole amounting to £650. This LOG court-house, the *first* which was erected, was occupied until the winter of 1790-91, when it was destroyed by fire. Rev. Thaddeus Dodd taught a' classical school in this court-house, and afterwards kept by David Johnston. It was during the time Mr. Johnston kept school therein that it was burned. He afterwards took charge of the Canonsburg Academy. The commissioners, on the 1st of January, 1792, laid a tax of £1500 to erect a brick court-house and other public buildings.

Local traditions have placed our first court-house at many points, sometimes in different parts of our town, sometimes at Razortown, on the Middletown road, and sometimes on Mr. William Gabby's farm. We have investigated all these traditionary reports, and will give a solution to the whole, remarking that not much confidence can be placed in tradition without being sustained by history.

No other places for holding courts were ever held in Washington County except at the places designated, the records showing of whom the several houses were rented in the town of Washington.

Our readers must bear in mind that Washington and the adjoining counties were claimed by Virginia, of which I have already given the history, that the line separating Ohio and Youghiogheny counties, Virginia, ran near the western limits of the borough of Washington. Youghiogheny County occupied the territory east of this line, and Ohio County west of it. The court-house of Youghiogheny County was on the farm of Andrew Heath, nearly opposite Elizabethtown, Allegheny County, while that of Ohio County was on the farm of William Gabby, two miles west of this place. Mr. William Gabby assures me that the logs of the court-house were used by his father in the erection of a kitchen, and that the court-house stood between the brick house (now occupied by his son James) and the barn, near the spring. John Gabby, Esq., received his deed for the same farm as early as the spring of 1784. In corroboration of this statement, I quote from the writings of Rev. Dr. Joseph Smith, who says, "One of these Virginia court-houses (west of the Monongahela River) stood a few miles west of the present town of Washington. Washington itself did not exist, but a few miserable hamlets, called CATFISH, after the Indian chief of that name who once dwelt there. In the records of the Presbytery of Red Stone, also bearing date October 16, 1782, a minister was appointed as a supply to preach at Ohio County court-house, a seat of justice under the government of Virginia.

The traditional story of a court-house at Razortown is a myth, mentioned in the life of Patrick Gass; being an aged man when he wrote his life, he mistook the Gabby farm, two miles west of Washington, and placed it two miles northwest of this place. Having thus disposed of the court-house question, we resume our narrative, and shall speak of the second court-house which was erected on the public square.

The second court-house was erected of brick, being commenced in 1792, in the centre of the public square. The cost of this court-house may be thus estimated :—

				£	s.	d.
1792, Nov.	6.	Paid James Marshall for materials for public buildings		60	0	0
" "	7.	" John Benjamin and William Reed in full to date for court-house, &c.	.	807	11	1
" "	7.	" William Gray for measuring and calculating public buildings . . .		6	6	1
1793, Jan.	8.	" Messrs. Reeds, in full, for work done court-house and jail . . .		157	8	10
" March 23.		" Alexander Cunningham for materials	.	12	14	8
				£1044	0	8

" April 10. John Reed was directed to build a wall around the public buildings, which he had completed on November 6, 1793.

1794, Feb. 28. Messrs. Price and Leet reported to the commissioners the price of the carpenters' and joiners' work of the court-house.

" March 4. A tax for £550 was levied for finishing the mason work, and plastering the jail.

" July 7. Bill for cleaning court-house and jail-yard, twenty-four dollars and seventy-one cents, approved and paid.

" Sept. 3. A bill of John and James Reed for three hundred and thirty-four dollars and eighty cents ordered to be paid for work done.

" July 19. The commissioners employed carpenters to work on the cupola of the court-house, finish the same, and have the vane gilded.

This court-house was improved in 1819 by an addition thereto, the commissioners having awarded the contract to Thomas H. Baird, Esq., who gave as his securities David Shields and George Baird, Esqs. October 18, 1836, a county meeting was held in the court-house to take action with regard to the erection of a court-house and other public buildings, which meeting, after a full discussion, resolved that the question should be determined by a vote of the electors of the county, who decided against its erection. But on March 9, 1839, the grand jury considered the erection of a new court-house, and the question was laid over to the next grand jury, who indorsed the proposition. The commissioners then certified that a new court-house would cost $12,000, and the repairs, $5000, and the subsequent grand jury sanctioned its erection, as the public buildings were unfit for public purposes ; and the whole of the public square should be entirely changed, and present an appearance which would be alike creditable to the county and have all the conveniences which the wants of the people required. Before, however, giving a description of the improvements which were made, it will be interesting to many unacquainted with the buildings which were upon the public square to state what buildings occupied it.

Commencing on the corner of Main and Beau streets, and going south, was the market-house, with a superstructure containing six rooms (a full description of which will be found under the title of "Market House"); next to and adjoining the market-house was the engine-house; then an alley, which led directly into the kitchen of the sheriff's house, through which access was had to the jail; next was the sheriff's office and house attached, and the prothonotary's office; then came the court-house. On the south of the court-house were the clerk of the court's and register's offices; adjoining which was a small shop of Alfred Galt (watchmaker, well known as an eccentric genius) and three offices, from which a rent was derived—these filled up the square.

These three offices on the southeastern corner of the public square, and immediately in front of the present market-house, were leased, on a ground-rent of twenty years, on the 1st of June, 1817. Each office was required to be in size 22 by 24 feet (with an alley 10 feet in the rear), to be built of brick, and range with the other public buildings. No. 1, next to the court-house, was leased to William Hunter, Esq., at $3.01 per foot per annum. No. 2 was leased to John Neal, Esq., and No. 3, on the corner of the street and alley, to David Shields, Esq., each at $2.54 per foot.

We now resume the history of the THIRD or present court-house. On the 22d July, 1839, Jehu Jackson, Matthew Linn, and Andrew Shearer advertised to receive sealed proposals until July 15, 1839, at 10 o'clock A.M., for the erection of new public buildings, according to the plan adopted, for the accommodation of the courts and offices of the county, and for the safe keeping of the records; and a house for the sheriff. On the 16th July, 1839, the carpenter work was awarded to Henry Shearer, Esq.; the stonework, to Freeman Brady, Esq.; the cut-stonework, to Alexander Ramsey, Esq.; furnishing and laying the brickwork, to David White, Esq.

On the 25th of September the commissioners caused all the old buildings to be removed from the public square, except the offices on the southeast corner of the square, whose leases had expired, in which the public offices should be temporarily kept. In addition to these two rooms the commissioners also rented the corner room of the "Round Corner," now occupied by James C. Acheson. They also leased the Methodist Protestant church from James L. Porter and Charles E. Jones (trustees), from the 29th of August, 1839, to the 29th August, 1843, for the sum of $200, in which the courts should be held, with the privilege of leaving the same when the new court-house should be finished.

On the 25th of September, 1840, the commissioners, Matthew Linn, Andrew Shearer, and James Pollock, Esqs., articled with

Freeman Brady and David White, Esqs., to build the jail walls, and, with David Hall and William Wylie, to plaster the court-house.

1842, May 27. The statue of Washington was ordered to be placed upon the dome of the court-house, and, on the 15th of October, James Sterret, of Allegheny County, James Chambers and William E. Erret, of Washington County, were selected to measure the carpenter work.

On December 9th, 1842, the commissioners contracted with William McFarlane and William E. Erret to build a portico to the sheriff's house, for which they were to receive one hundred and seventy-five dollars.

The cost of the court-house of 1839 was twenty-nine thousand eight hundred and eight dollars, to which is to be added the sheriff's house, costing four thousand five hundred and sixty-eight dollars, amounting in all to $34,376.

We shall now advert to the improvements made on the public square in 1867–8 and 9. Neither the court-house nor jail answered the purposes of their erection; the former required an arbitration room, library room, and sheriff's office, and jury room, and the latter an entire new building. The commissioners, consisting of Messrs. Jos. W. Cowan, Thos. J. Bell, and Jas. Walker, on the 23d of July, 1866, authorized J. W. Barr, Esq., a superior architect of Pittsburg, to inspect the county jail, with a view of repairing or rebuilding the same. The jail undergoing a thorough inspection by Mr. Barr, he gave it as his opinion that it was unfit for use, upon which the commissioners very judiciously decided that he should submit a plan for a new jail with the probable cost, and another for repairing the same.

On the 24th of August, 1866, the commissioners submitted these plans to the grand jury, who unanimously approved the erection of a new jail, and the plan thereof was submitted to the Secretary of the Commonwealth, who approved of the same. It being too late in the season to commence so large a building, it was postponed until February 28, 1867, when the new Board of Commissioners, consisting of Thomas J. Bell, James Walker, and Samuel Weirich, Esqs., resolved to proceed to the erection of the jail under the approval of the grand jury and the direction of the court.

On March 5th, 1867, the commissioners, accompanied by David S. Wilson, Esq., their attorney (who was desirous of submitting certain other improvements in connection with the court-house, by which all the necessary rooms could be obtained, and the jail connected with the court-room), went to Pittsburg, to confer with Messrs. Barr and Moser in regard to the plans and specifications and estimates of the new county prison, and the improvements therewith connected.

March 22d, 1867, the commissioners, after having adopted the present plan, and under the instructions of David S. Wilson, Esq., appointed Messrs. Barr and Moser general superintendents of the work, to be allowed one per cent. of the cost of the jail as their compensation. Nelson Vankirk, Esq., was appointed superintendent and foreman under Messrs. Barr and Moser, his compensation being $5 per day; Samuel Hargraves, superintendent of the brick and mason work, at $5 per day. The general superintendents were authorized to select all the materials, and Messrs. Vankirk and Hargraves, in their respective departments, were to employ and superintend all the hands necessary for its completion, but subject to the inspection and condemnation of the commissioners and general superintendents.

On the 23d of April, 1867, the contract for the brick was awarded to Chas. V. Grier and Joshua R. Forest, with John Hallam as security.

The new prison and extension to the court-house, including sheriff's office, arbitration room, library room, &c., cost forty-eight thousand five hundred dollars.

The stone wall inclosing public square, grading, and improvements to sheriff's house, cost thirty-five hundred dollars, amounting in the aggregate to fifty-two thousand dollars. Before the jail was finished, and in the northeast corner, about ten feet from the ground, a box, containing much valuable information, was deposited in the wall by A. T. Baird and C. M. Ruple, Esqs., on September 6, 1867, generally relating to county and borough affairs.

MARKET-HOUSE.

In the spring of 1795 the citizens of the town of Washington held a public meeting, at which it was unanimously resolved, that the wants of the people required a market-house, and to carry this resolution into effect, the meeting appointed two of their prominent citizens (Alexander Addison, Esq., and Dr. Absalom Baird) to procure the necessary amount of subscriptions, and employ competent workmen to erect a market-house.

On the 8th of September following, the market-house was finished and occupied, the commissioners having granted the northeast corner of the public square, on the corner of Main and Beau streets, for that purpose. It was opened under the following regulations: That public markets should be opened on Wednesday and Saturday of each week; that they should be kept open from early dawn to 10 o'clock A. M. of the appointed days, and, by agreement of the citizens, no provision or produce of any kind was to be purchased within the prescribed hours, except at the market-house only.

The committee having discharged the duty enjoined upon them, and the market-house fulfilling the expectations of the people, yet they were compelled to issue the following notice on November 24th, 1795:—

"We, whose names are hereunto annexed, state to all concerned in the market-house of Washington, that the expenses of building it amount, as it appears by the several bills in our hands, to . . $202.96
We have received for subscriptions only . . . 126.81

There is, therefore, due to us 76.15

"We submit it to all interested in the market-house, whether they ought not immediately to pay into our hands severally, according to the ability and inclination of every individual, a further contribution to reimburse us for what we have laid out for this building, which is a common benefit to all. There are yet some arrears unpaid of the subscription, but much is not expected from them, and if all were paid, it would be proper to have a small sum in reserve for occasional repairs, which will always be wanting to a public building like this, which being as it were the property of no particular person, no one thinks it his duty to preserve it. The delinquent subscribers are informed that the subscription papers are lodged in the hands of William Meetkirk, Esq., who will receive payments, and unless payments are made before the 1st day of December next, he will issue process against the delinquents. ALEXANDER ADDISON.
ABSALOM BAIRD."

This notice had the desired effect, the delinquents paid their indebtedness, and the citizens with commendable zeal paid the balance by additional subscriptions.

Immediately after the borough was incorporated, in 1810, the Council passed wholesome laws to regulate the markets. Yet the wants of the people required a larger and better market-house, consequently the town council, on the 23d day of October, 1813, appointed a committee consisting of Parker Campbell, James Orr, and Thomas McGiffin, Esquires, to report on the expediency of erecting a new market-house on the same ground. This committee reported (on the 30th of October) favorably, and on the 6th of Nov. following, the chief burgess was directed to call a meeting of the inhabitants on the 12th of November, to consider the subject. It appears, however, that the minds of the people were greatly agitated at this time on account of pecuniary affairs, the war and other matters; and action thereon was indefinitely postponed.

On the 16th of January, 1815, another meeting of the citizens was convened, when the usual officers were appointed and the following resolution adopted :—

"*Resolved*, That it is expedient to change the site of the market-house from the north to the south side of the public square, for the purpose of erecting a banking-house on the northeast corner of said square, and for the better accommodation of the citizens at large; provided, however, that no change or alteration in the present site of the market-house shall take place until the consent of the proper authority shall be first had and obtained to erect a banking-house on the northeast corner of the public square, and a market-house on the southeast corner of said square, nor until arrangements be made and a contract entered into for the building of said banking-house on that ground." Alexander Murdoch, Thomas H. Baird, and James Orr, Esquires, were appointed to procure the necessary authority and grant for said market-house and banking-house from the legislature and commissioners of the county.

Subsequently the Committee ascertained that the public square was to be used only *for public purposes*, and if diverted from that the property would revert to the original owners; accordingly the project was abandoned.

On the 21st of June, 1816, however, and at the request of the citizens, the commissioners granted to the borough permission to erect a market-house on the following plan, viz: On a range with the public offices and parallel with Main Street, to front on Main Street 53 feet and on Beau Street 130 feet, according to diagram adopted.

On November 2, 1816, the commissioners, consisting of John Reed, David Little, and Jonathan Knight, made a second grant, giving permission to the borough to erect another story upon the pillars or frame of the market-house, provided that one room should be used as a council room, and that after the expiration of twenty-five years, or at any time thereafter, the borough shall, upon receiving the sum originally expended in building the market-house, deliver the same to the commissioners for the use of the county.

On the 5th of November following, the citizens met at the court-house to consider the expediency of erecting a superstructure or story on the pillars of the market-house, and after a full discussion the burgesses and Council were instructed to erect said superstructure in the manner contemplated by the commissioners. The Council thereupon convened and appointed Parker Campbell, Alexander Murdoch, and Thomas McGiffin a committee with authority to borrow not exceeding two thousand dollars, for the purpose specified, which amount they procured from the branch Bank of Philadelphia established in Washington. The contract for the building of the superstructure was given to James Ruple, Esq.

On the 20th of October, 1817, possession of the market-house rooms was given to the burgesses and Council, who rented the same on the 25th to the following persons: No. 1, Robert Estep; No. 2, John Purviance; Nos. 3 and 5, Thomas H. Baird; No. 4, John McCluney; No. 6, Matthew Brown. Subsequently some of these rooms were occupied as school-rooms, and the mention of the names of Philip Potter, Stephen Wood, George Freeby, and Henry Williams will recall to the recollection of many of our inhabitants the incidents of school-life, the rod and the cat-o'-nine-tails. At one time one of the rooms was occupied by the venerable Judge Grayson, who was then editor of the Washington *Examiner.*

After many years it appears that the spirit of enterprise seized upon our citizens, and they awoke from their Rip Van Winkle sleep by being admonished by the commissioners of the county, in 1839, that the lease of the market-house grounds would soon expire, and that the public square would be occupied by a new court-house, suitable buildings for sheriff, &c. A meeting of the Town Council was called July 15, 1839, and Messrs. Alexander W. Acheson, Henry Langley, and John R. Griffith were appointed a committee to examine the lease and to make inquiries in regard to changing the site to the south side of the public square.

On the 2d of August, the Town Council called a meeting of the citizens, whereupon the following preamble and resolutions were adopted :—

WHEREAS, The commissioners of the county are about to erect new public buildings for the use of the county, and in the execution of their plan of erection it will be necessary to remove the borough market-house to make room for the erection of a contemplated sheriff's house, therefore

Resolved, That the burgesses and Council are hereby authorized to make such arrangements with the county commissioners for the exchange of the present market ground for a site or location on the south side of the public square, and obtain from said commissioners a perpetual lease of the same for the use of the borough.

The Council at their meeting on November 25th, appointed Henry Langley, Esq., to meet the commissioners on the subject of the removal of the market-house, who subsequently reported that the commissioners would in due time make a lease. In December following, however, Messrs. A. W. Acheson, James Blaine, and Henry Langley were directed to view the ground, ascertain the probable expense of erecting a market-house, and how to dispose of the old one. The Committee, on the 8th of January, 1840, reported a plan which was adopted, and on the 6th of February, the Committee entered into contract with John Wilson and John W. Seamans, Esquires, for building the same, the price being settled at *nine hundred and fifty dollars*. Messrs. James Blaine, John R. Griffiths, and J. H. Pattison were authorized to sell the old market-house, which they accordingly did, and made report thereof to the Council. To the burgesses and Council of 1839–40, therefore, were we indebted for the market-house which adorned the southern part of our public square, the stalls of which were first leased August 2, 1840.

The reason of the market-house being set so far back from a range with the other public buildings was owing to a lease made by the commissioners of 66 feet of ground on Main Street, and running back about 40 feet, upon which was erected three offices, the lease of which did not expire until after the market-house was erected.

TOWN HALL.

The first effort for the erection of a town hall was made May 5th, 1842, when the commissioners of that date executed a lease to the borough of Washington for all the public ground south of a line commencing at the curb-stone on Main Street, nine feet south of the new court-house, and running back until it strikes a lot of William Smith's, and now owned (1870) by Robert Boyd, Esq., *on condition of their erecting a town hall.*

March 23d, 1843. The Council called a meeting of the citizens to ascertain their views on the expediency of erecting a town hall, and engine-house, which, after discussion, was decided affirmatively, and the Council appointed Robert Officer, John S. Brady, and Thomas

McGiffin to report a plan and the probable cost. A plan was prepared by Mr. Erret and adopted by the Council; but on the 6th day of May, 1843, the citizens called a public meeting and refused its sanction to the erection of a town hall.

No further efforts were made until the year 1868, when the question was again agitated, and the burgess and Council called a meeting of the citizens to ascertain the public sentiment on this question. Many urgent reasons were given for its erection, but that which operated upon the public mind was the generous offer of Dr. Francis J. Lemoyne, who proposed to donate ten thousand dollars for the purchase of a public library if a fire-proof vault was made for its reception in said building. The question was referred to a vote of the people, and decided affirmatively. The term of office of the burgess and Council elected March, 1868, was about expiring, and the plans and erection of the town hall were committed to the Council of 1869, consisting of John D. Boyle, Burgess; J. Y. Hamilton, Assistant Burgess; and Alfred Creigh, J. L. Judson, A. B. Caldwell, A. C. Morrow, and James Huston, Councilmen. A plan and specification, as drawn and prepared by J. Kerr, of Pittsburg, was adopted. Messrs. Boyle, Creigh, and Judson were appointed the Building Committee, and Messrs. Boyle, Caldwell, and Morrow the Finance Committee.

It is eminently due to the Council of 1868, consisting of John D. Boyle, burgess; John McElroy, assistant burgess; Samuel Hazlett, Robert H. Davis, William Taylor, John Templeton, and George O. Jones, to state that the citizens of the borough are indebted to them for taking the incipient measures of the erection of a town hall. On February 16th, 1869, they procured legislative action authorizing the commissioners to lease a portion of the public ground to erect thereon a town hall, to be used as a post-office and for other purposes; and also an additional act on February 17th, 1869, authorizes the burgess and Council to borrow thirty-thousand dollars to be applied to the erection of a town hall, at seven and three-tenths per cent. per annum; the said bonds not liable to be taxed for county, municipal, or school purposes.

The contract for excavating the cellar, executing the cut-stone, stone, and brickwork, was awarded to Andrew Brady; the oak timber to William B. Cundall; the carpenter work was given to J. Noble Porter; the manufacture of the brick to Andrew Ford; the pressed brick to Samuel Hutson; the tinwork to Jesse Jordan; the ventilators to Jacob Miller; the plastering to Thomas Dagg and Jeremiah Marshall, and the painting to Col. Samuel Bulford. In connection with this subject it is proper to remark that the brickwork was sub-let by Mr. A. Brady to Messrs. James Huston and John Dye, and the cut-stonework to Edward Little.

The town hall is a substantial brick edifice of the Franco-Italian style, fronting fifty-six feet on Main Street and extending back one hundred feet, with a cellar underneath the whole building.

The *first* floor is occupied by the post-office and vestibule, a reading room, a library room with a fire-proof vault in which the library is kept, an engine-house, and a market-house.

The *second* floor consists of the council chamber and an audience room with a gallery, capable of seating one thousand persons.

As the post-office is now permanently located in the town hall, I shall give the names of the postmasters as far back as can be ascertained, and the year in which they entered upon the duties of their office.

1797.	William Meetkirke.	1844.	Jonathan D. Leet.
1801.	Daniel Moore.	1848.	James M'Dermot.
1805.	Hugh Wylie.	1851.	George W. Aiken.
1828.	Joseph Henderson.	1852.	David Acheson.
1829.	Thomas Morgan.	1856.	Freeman Brady.
1839.	Samuel Workman.	1860.	James M'Dermot.
1840.	Robert Colmery.	1865.	William C. Wylie.

On September 18, 1869, the corner-stone was laid by U. S. Grant, President of the United States, and so rapid was the work carried forward, that on April 1, 1870, the post-office room was finished and occupied. We give below the ceremonies of laying the corner stone, and matters connected therewith.

A desire being expressed on the part of many citizens that the President should be present, and deposit a box containing curiosities in the corner stone of the town hall, the following correspondence between the Burgesses and Council and President Grant took place:—

WASHINGTON, PA., September 17, 1869.

GENERAL U. S. GRANT, President of the United States:

HONORED SIR: The undersigned, the Burgesses and Councilmen of the borough of Washington, representing its citizens, would respectfully solicit you to deposit within the corner stone of the town hall, now in process of erection, on Saturday next (September 18th), a box containing the memorials of the present and the past, so that future generations may learn our history to the present time, when these memorials shall come to light.

The occasion is one worthy of your consideration, because this was the first county and town named after the Revolutionary struggle in honor of the illustrious Washington, who was first in peace, first in war, and first in the affections of his countrymen; and you, honored sir, as his successor, both as President and Commander-in-Chief, will add additional interest to the many interesting reminiscences which cluster around our ancient borough by complying with our request.

With sentiments of high esteem we remain truly yours,

JOHN D. BOYLE, *Chief Burgess.*
I. Y. HAMILTON, *Ass't Burgess.*
ALFRED CREIGH,
A. B. CALDWELL,
JAMES HUSTON, } *Council.*
J. L. JUDSON,
A. C. MORROW,

[REPLY.]

WASHINGTON, PA., September 17, 1869.

John D. Boyle, Chief Burgess; I. Y. Hamilton, Assistant Burgess; Alfred Creigh, A. B. Caldwell, James Huston, J. L. Judson, A. C. Morrow, Councilmen:

GENTLEMEN : Your letter of this date, requesting me in behalf of the citizens to deposit within the corner stone of the Town Hall now in process of erection, on Saturday, September 18th, 1869, a box containing memorials of the present, is received.

It will afford me pleasure to comply with this request—enhanced pleasure, because your county and town were named in express honor of the Father of our Country (whose name they bear), whose name is revered by every American citizen who loves his country.

With great respect, your obedient servant,

U. S. GRANT.

The time fixed for the ceremonies above alluded to was 2½ o'clock on Saturday afternoon.

About two o'clock Burgess Boyle and Dr. Creigh, a member of Council, proceeded in a carriage to Mr. Wm. Smith's residence, to accompany the President to the public square. Upon the arrival of the President the Washington brass band, being on the ground, played a national air, after which Major Ewing announced the programme. Rev. W. A. Davidson, D. D., was then introduced, and asked the blessing of Heaven upon the undertaking being inaugurated, and returned thanks for the success and prosperity of the country. David S. Patterson, Esq., counsel for the Council, was then introduced, and delivered the following pertinent, terse, and eloquent remarks:—

The speaker said he would confine himself to a brief statement of facts, rather than attempt any formal or lengthy address. A town was laid out on the site of our present substantial and beautiful borough, in October of the year 1781, by David Hoge, and named Bassettown. Three years later it was sold to the two sons of its founder, and they gave it its present name in honor of the one who had just led a brave people to independence. In 1810 the little village obtained a borough charter. Favored by its fortunate location on the line of what was then the great national thoroughfare from East to West, its citizens enjoyed the privilege of greeting all the distinguished statesmen of the West, on their journeys to and from the national capital. Almost on the very spot where we are gathered to-day her glad people extended a joyful greeting and cordial welcome, in succession, to Presidents Monroe, Jackson, John Quincy Adams, Harrison, Polk, and Taylor.

For twenty years past the railroads have whirled statesmen and traffic over other routes, leaving our town to a lagging inland growth; but the evidences of both public and private improvement, during the last year, seem laden with better hopes. The work on the public edifice with which the people had determined by their votes to ornament the public square, having progressed to the point of laying the corner stone, the borough authorities had wisely determined to deposit beneath that stone a box, containing contributed memorials of the present and the past, so that coming generations might learn our history to the present time, when these memorials shall come to light. With equal wisdom had they embraced the opportunity afforded by the presence of General Grant amongst us to have that collection of testimony to the future deposited by the hands of a no less distinguished personage than the President of the United States himself. The speaker said there was a peculiar fitness in this feature of the ceremonies, in view of the fact that this was the first town named, after the first great struggle for independence, in honor of the illustrious hero who became the first President of the United States, and first Commander-in-Chief of her army and navy. What a happy thought was it, then, that secured on this pleasant occasion the presence and aid of the distinguished hero of the nation's last great struggle—the present, living successor of the good Washington, both as President and Commander-in-Chief.

The speaker, in conclusion, turned to President Grant, and addressed him as follows : " And now, most honored sir, the craftsmen having reported the foundation ready for the corner stone, and that stone being exactly squared and now ready to be placed in its proper position, by virtue of the authority of the Burgesses and Council of the borough of Washington, this box of memorials is delivered into your hands, to be deposited beneath it."

At the conclusion of Mr. Patterson's speech, the President silently took the box from the hands of Dr. Creigh and deposited it within the corner stone, after which the band struck up a lively tune, and the Committee of Reception escorted the President to the court room, where, after some introductory remarks by Messrs. Ewing and Hopkins, the citizens generally came forward and "shook hands." After remaining in the court room about an hour, the President retired to the residence of Mr. Wm. Smith.

List of articles which the box contained, and which was deposited in the corner stone (northeast corner) of the town' hall, collected by Dr. Alfred Creigh :—

Borough Affairs.—Charter, by-laws, and ordinances of the borough of Washington ; roll of present officers elected April, 1869; roll of officers from 1810 to the present time, prepared by Alfred Creigh ; blank borough bonds, upon which funds were raised for the erection of the town hall ; carpenter work awarded to J. Noble Porter, with the names of all the carpenters ; mason and brickwork awarded to Andrew Brady, with the roll of his workmen ; the manufacture of the brick awarded to Andrew Ford—the pressed brick to Samuel Hutson—the oak timber to W. B. Cundall, and the tinwork to Jesse Jordan ; register of voters in the borough (also the names of all females owning property), with their respective occupations and residence ; letter of John D. Boyle, Chief Burgess, to his successor when the box shall be opened ; autograph of General U. S. Grant—letter from the Burgesses and Councilmen, and his reply, and notices of his arrival and reception ; autographs of the President and Associate Judges of Washington County, together with those of the Prothonotary, Register, Recorder, Clerk of the Courts, Commissioners and their Clerk, with the impressions of the respective seals of each office, as well as the autographs of the Borough and County Treasurers, High Sheriff, and District Attorney ; list of pastors, church officers, and trustees of the churches of the borough ; list of the school directors of the Union school, with the name of the superintendent, as well as of the teachers and scholars, with their ages, including the colored school ; officers of the First National Bank of Washington, with the seal; history of Washington cemetery; catalogue of Washington Female Seminary, 1868-69 ; catalogue of Washington and Jefferson College, 1868-69 ; proceedings of semi-centennial celebration of Washington college in 1856 ; premium list of Washington County Agricultural Society, 1869 ; Directory of First Presbyterian church, with the history of the Sabbath school from its organization ; forms used in the banking houses of W. Smith & Son and Samuel Hazlett ; officers of the Washington Gas Company ; specimen of men's and boys' wear in 1869, of woollen goods, presented by A. B. Caldwell & Co., and W. Smith & Son; specimen of ladies' dress goods, and three styles of bonnets as worn in 1869, and presented by A. B. Caldwell & Co.; engravings representing gentlemen's, boys' and girls' fashion of clothing and ladies' style of bonnets for 1869, by S. Shaler and Mrs. G. Lonkert; specimen of domestic goods (for ladies) manufactured in Washington County; specimen of every variety of paper collars, by Geo. Metzner & Co.; specimens of Saxony wool, raised in Washington County, and presented by Maj. Jacob Morgan, I. Y. Hamilton, and Col. S. Beatty; style of carriage, buggies, and velocipede, by S. B. Huyes & Co.; style of mowers and reapers, with descriptive pamphlets, by J. T. Kirk; specimen of sewing machines, with descriptive pamphlets, by J. T. Kirk; a bottle of pure Monongahela rye whiskey, by J. C. Ruple; Insurance agencies in Washington, by David and J. Aiken; specimen of cotton raised in Washington, by Miss Ellen Griffith; by-laws of Washington Lodge, 164, with its officers since 1819—of Washington Chapter, 150—of Council No. 1 of Royal and Select Masters—of Jacques DeMolay Commandary No. 3 of K. T.; by-laws of Lodge 81 of I. O. O. F.; by-laws of Harmony Lodge 575 of Good Templars, with a list of officers and members; Jacob Goldsmith's advertisement; specimen of cigars manufactured by W. L. Ruple; autographs and history of Samuel Cunningham and George Freeby; set of artificial teeth manufactured by Dr. S. Fulton.

Coins, Ancient and Modern.—This class consists of a great variety presented by Miss Clara McCracken, R. M'Ilvaine Drury, A. C. Morrow, John Harter, David Aiken, W. H. Drury, John A. Templeton, J. R. Kelley, Jesse Jordan, and John Wilson; American coin ranging from 1776 to the present time.

Currency.—Bank of Washington and Franklin Bank of Washington, by D. S. Wilson, Esq.; twelve and a half cent note issued by Frederick Maryland in 1840, by J. A Templeton; postal currency prior to April, 1868, by D. S. Wilson; postal currency since April, 1868, by W. C. Wiley; Confederate money from $5 to $500, by J. A. Templeton; Continental money, by Dr. W. S. Mitchell; Continental money, by S. M. Hall.

General matters.—Specimen of the registry system of the Post Office Department, by W. C. Wiley; seal of the State of Pennsylvania and of the Secretary of State, by D. S. Wilson; blanks, &c., used in the U. S. Revenue office, by John E. Bell; pamphlet containing acts on stamp duties, by J. B. Ruple; National Tax law, by M. L. A. McCracken; History of Washington County, title page and contents, by Alfred Creigh; An Inviting Call to the Children of Israel, by F. Hood; Pittsburg Business Directory of 1867, by John D. Boyle; almanacs, religious and medical, by Messrs. C. M. Reed, F. Hood, S. M. and J. A. Templeton; Vicksburg paper at its surrender, by J. B. Ruple; stamps placed on cigar boxes, by J. C. Ruple; engraved plate of names, &c., by J. and S. Post; History of Knighthood in two volumes, by Alfred Creigh.

Curiosities.—A piece of cloth from the pall of Henry Clay, deceased, by D. S. Wilson, Esq.; a portion of the hair of Gen. Anthony Wayne, who died in 1796, by D. S. Wilson, Esq.; a piece from the weeping willow which hangs over the grave of Napoleon at St. Helena; a shell from the Bay of Biscay; a piece of the great tree in California, a Japanese writing desk, and some postal rebel stamps, by J. R. Kelley, Esq.; two pair of revolutionary shoe-buckles, by W. T. Creigh.

Newspapers.—Western Telegraph, edited by Colerick & Co., of 1797 Washington Examiner of 1829, by John Grayson; Our Country of 1840, by T. J. Morgan; the Tiny Buffer of 1840, by W. Duane Morgan; Washington Examiner of 1843, by T. W. Grayson; and the Loco Foco of 1844, by R. W. Jones, presented by Messrs. Swan & Ecker; the American Union of 1856, by J. B. Musser; Washington Examiner of 1860, by A. H. Ecker and J. R. Donehoo; Washington Review of 1866, by Wm. Swan; and Washington Tribune of 1865, presented by W. T. Creigh; Washington Review and Examiner of September 14, 1869, and Washington Reporter of September 14, 1869; The Revolution, by Mrs. Cady, and Harper's Bazar, by Geo. Metzner.

WASHINGTON AND JEFFERSON COLLEGES.

On the 24th of September, 1787, the legislature of Pennsylvania passed an act incorporating and endowing Washington Academy. The trustees were Rev. John McMillan, Rev. Joseph Smith, Rev. Thaddeus Dodd, Rev. John Clark, Rev. Mr. Henderson, Rev. John Corby, Judge Allison, and J. McDowell, Col. Marshall, and Thomas Scott. On the 15th of December following, Thomas Scott and Col. Marshall, two of the trustees, addressed a letter to Benjamin Franklin, as President of the Supreme Executive Council, respectfully soliciting the warrant for 500 acres of the donation lands which were appropriated by the legislature, and also requesting him to direct the surveyor-general to lay off these lands, which were located in what is now known as Beaver County, and were sold to James Allison about 1835.

In 1789 the Academy went into operation with twenty students under Rev. Thaddeus Dodd, who was its first principal, in the upper rooms of the court-house. He continued to teach until the winter of 1790, when he returned to his congregation in Amwell township, where he had previously opened a classical school in 1782, the first institution west of the Allegheny Mountains in the great valley of the Mississippi. James Hughes, John Brice, Daniel Lindley, Robert Marshall, and Francis Dunlaney were his first scholars; the school house was near his dwelling. It continued in operation three and a half years. His successor in 1790 was Mr. David Johnston, who, upon the destruction of the court-house, accepted the situation in the Canonsburg Academy, as its first principal, in July, 1791. June 14, 1796, Mr. James Dobbins, of York, was elected and served until 1804, when Benjamin Mills became the principal, who officiated as such until Washington Academy was incorporated into a college.

In 1790, Benjamin Franklin, Esq., presented to the Board of Trustees fifty pounds, to be applied to the purchasing of a library, which was the foundation of the college library.

On November 19, 1792, William Hoge, Esq., for the love he bears to useful learning, and for the promotion of the useful arts, sciences, and literature, presented to the trustees of Washington Academy four lots of ground, being 240 feet square, in the eastern extremity of said town, bounded on the east by the outside line of the town (now College Street), on the south by Belle Street, on the west by lot No. 104, and on the north by Cherry Alley, fronting on Belle Street 240 feet, and running back to Cherry Alley 240 feet, being lots numbered on the plan of the town, 105, 106, 107, and 108. These lots are the southeast corner of the present college campus, which, however, now embraces two entire squares, bounded by Beau Street on the north, Belle Street on the south, College Street on the east, and Second Street on the west, containing fourteen lots from No. 102 to 115 both inclusive. I shall enumerate these lots and from whom purchased or derived by gift, in their order.

No. 102 was the gift of David S. Wilson, Collin M. Reed, Joseph Mc-Knight, Joseph Henderson, Esqs., and Dr. Thomas McKennan.
" 103 and 104 were purchased by the trustees, May 9, 1833, from John Sheaffer, Esq.
" 105, 106, 107, and 108 was the gift of William Hoge, November 19, 1792, being the original academy grounds.
" 109 was purchased from David Shields, August 4, 1835.
" 110 was purchased from Daniel Moore, October 23, 1837.
" 111 was purchased from Henry Langly, executor of Samuel Marshall, deceased, July 1, 1835.
" 112 was purchased from George Mitchell, March 27, 1837.
" 113 was purchased from Rev. David Elliott, June 27, 1836.
" 114 was purchased from John Wilson (carpenter), January 10, 1838.
" 115 was purchased from the School Directors, March 8, 1837.

To these lots were added Cherry Alley, which separated the two squares. The college campus has a front of 500 feet by 420 in depth, or about five acres.

April 8, 1793, the trustees were authorized by the legislature to locate all or any part of the granted lands westward of the Allegheny and Ohio rivers.

In 1793 the trustees erected buildings on the four original lots (105, 106, 107, 108), thirty by thirty-five feet, two stories high, for the use of the Academy. This is the centre part of the southern block of buildings. The hall in this building was originally used by the Presbyterians as a place of worship.

February 16, 1796, the trustees made application to the legislature, praying for a donation to erect additional buildings. On the 2d of May, 1797, the legislature generously donated three thousand dollars to complete the buildings, on the condition that ten indigent students should be educated for a period not exceeding two years each.

WASHINGTON COLLEGE.

On March 21, 1806, Washington College was incorporated and all the property belonging to the Academy was vested in the trustees of the college and their successors. Depending on its own resources, the college, under judicious management, prospered, and so gratified were the friends of literature throughout the State, that the legislature, in 1820, granted a donation of five thousand dollars, payable in annual payments of one thousand dollars each.

This was followed in 1831 by another donation of five hundred dollars annually, for five years, to qualify young men for the higher duties of life, and especially qualify such as should become teachers.

WASHINGTON COLLEGE AS A SYNODICAL COLLEGE.

On November 9, 1852, by an agreement between the Board of Trustees and the Synod of Wheeling, Washington College became a SYNODICAL College, by which the trustees and professors were first nominated by the synod and were required to be confirmed by the trustees. The synod was also required to keep the college in operation by means of a permanent *endowment fund*, but the property was to remain in the hands of the trustees as heretofore, under the charter.

It will be proper at this time to give the plan of this endowment fund. It was placed under the control and management of a board of seven members, the corporate style being "The Board of Trustees of the College Endowment Fund of the Synod of Wheeling." It was chartered by the State of Ohio. Its treasury was established at Steubenville, and the proceeds were to be paid to the trustees of the college.

The plan of endowment was as follows:—

1. Twenty-five dollars paid shall entitle the subscriber to two years' tuition in any department of the college.

2. Fifty dollars paid shall entitle the subscriber to the tuition of one student during the entire course in the college proper, or to four years' tuition of one student in such departments of the institution as he may prefer.

3. One hundred dollars paid shall entitle the subscriber to a family scholarship, embracing the tuition of all his sons during the entire course in the college proper, or to four years' tuition of each of his sons, in such department of the institution as he may prefer; and for every additional one hundred dollars paid he shall have the privilege of designating the sons of any additional family he may choose.

4. Two hundred dollars paid by an individual, association, or congregation, shall entitle said individual, association, or congregation, to a perpetual scholarship, transferable, as other property, to which the subscriber or subscribers may appoint any individual whom they may select.

5. Five hundred dollars paid shall entitle the subscriber or subscribers to a perpetual scholarship transferable as other property.

The subscription upon this endowment was not to be considered as binding until sixty thousand dollars shall be subscribed, when certificates should be issued by the trustees of the college endowment fund.

In pursuing this history we shall next take up the action of the Board of Trustees of Washington College, held September 6, 1864, who passed the following preamble and resolutions:—

WHEREAS, The Synod of Wheeling, with which Washington College is connected, and several other synods of the Presbyterian church, in October last, made a formal and earnest proposition to the trustees of Jefferson and Washington colleges for the union of these two institutions upon some equitable basis, accompanying the said proposal with an offer, pledged by a responsible person, of $50,000 towards the endowment of the united college, and further proposed that the question of the location of the college proper, rendered difficult by local interests and feelings, be left to the decision of a disinterested and impartial board of arbitrators to be chosen jointly.

AND WHEREAS, The public mind seems now more than ever not only to approve but to demand such an union for the sake of the claims of education in this region of country:

Therefore this Board deem it due to themselves and to all concerned, without the slightest design to reflect upon any other party, to make known the fact that at a meeting held shortly subsequent to the reception of the proposition of the synod, they, by a unanimous vote, accepted the proposition with its conditions, agreeing to abide by any decision of the question thus fairly made. Also to declare that after a conference of a committee appointed by this Board with a like committee of the Board of Jefferson College on the subject of the proposed union, which was fruitless of success, owing to the declared unwillingness of the Jefferson Board to submit the *question of location* to the judgment of any persons outside of their own body, or in any way to imperil the interests of Canonsburg in regard to this question, or even to negotiate at all, except on the admitted condition that the college proper shall be located at that place. We are still, as we have from the first been, willing to adopt the proposal of *disinterested arbitrament* as originally made, and to join in asking such legislative sanction of a settlement so made, as the nature of the case may require; and farther, to set it forth as the deliberate judgment of this Board in harmony with the public voice, that the interests of education, as well as of the State and church, would be promoted by a proper union of these two colleges.

1. *Resolved*, That in order that the attitude of the Board in regard to the question at issue may not be misunderstood, the Secretary be directed to report the foregoing statement to the Synod of Wheeling, and also to publish the same in the Presbyterian Banner.

2. *Resolved*, That the Board approve the action of the faculty and local trustees in proposing to the faculty and local trustees of Jefferson College to unite in an effort to obtain a portion of the State agricultural fund on condition of a union of the colleges as calculated to facilitate the desirable end in the manner proposed by the synods.

WASHINGTON AND JEFFERSON COLLEGES CONSOLIDATED.

It may justly be remarked that from the year 1807 the records of the trustees of Jefferson and Washington colleges (situated but seven miles apart, the former at Canonsburg and the latter at Washington), looked forward to a united college. It is unnecessary in a work of this character to go into the details of the consolidation;

suffice it to say, that to accomplish the consolidation of these two rival institutions, the Rev. Dr. C. C. Beatty, of Steubenville, in 1864, proposed to give fifty thousand dollars if a union were effected. The trustees and alumni of both institutions, after preliminary meetings, were fully convinced of its necessity, and labored incessantly to bring about the desired union, and to enable the reader to judge impartially and decide for himself upon the merits of the initiative proceedings, we give the following preliminary proceedings, which eventuated in their consolidation.

On September 7th, 1864, the Alumni Association of Washington College held its annual meeting. The records of that body are given in these words: "The Rev. Francis J. Collier, of Canonsburg, appeared as one of a committee appointed by the Alumni Association of Jefferson College, and presented the following series of resolutions adopted by that body touching a union of Washington and Jefferson colleges."

1. *Resolved*, That the good of the community, the cause of education, and the welfare of the country, and the best interests of the kingdom of Christ imperatively demand the union of Washington and Jefferson colleges.

2. *Resolved*, That it is with profound gratification that we learn that a plan has been agreed upon by the officers of the colleges depending for its consummation upon the appropriation by the legislature of the State, of a liberal portion of the funds for agricultural colleges and their use.

3. *Resolved*, That in view of the fact stated, we hereby respectfully and earnestly petition the legislature of the State to take early and liberal action in this behalf. So far as we can understand the case, *justice does seem to demand* that no small part of the funds in the hands of the legislature for distribution ought to be appropriated for the benefit of this part of the State.

4. *Resolved*, That a committee of three be appointed to present these resolutions to the Alumni Association of Washington College, and in connection with a committee from that association, to the Board of Trustees of the colleges and to the legislature.

The committees appointed in pursuance of this 4th resolution were, Rev. George P. Hay, of Baltimore, Rev. F. J. Collier, of Canonsburg, and R. B. Patterson, Esq., of Greensburg, on behalf of the Jefferson Alumni.

The Rev. James I. Brownson, W. S. Moore, and Hon. Robert R. Reed, of Washington, on behalf of the Washington Alumni.

The following is the action of the Washington Alumni Association:—

WHEREAS, at a meeting of the Alumni of Jefferson College, on the 3d of August last, it was resolved, "that the good of the community, the cause of education, the welfare of the country, and the best interests of the kingdom of Christ imperatively demand the union of Washington and Jefferson colleges"—AND WHEREAS, it is understood that committees of the Boards of Trustees of the two colleges have lately been appointed to confer on the subject of union, but after trial have failed thus far to agree upon a plan of union—AND WHEREAS, a wish has been expressed at this meeting in behalf of the Alumni of Jefferson College, by one of their number acting as a member of a committee appointed for that purpose, for our co-operation in efforts to bring about the desired consummation—therefore

Resolved, That inasmuch as a suggestion has been made through the papers, of a convention of the Alumni of both colleges to assemble at an early day in the city of Pittsburg, for the consideration of the whole subject of the union, this association heartily approve such suggestion.

Resolved, That a committee consisting of Rev. Dr. James I. Brownson, Hon. R. R. Reed, and William S. Moore, be appointed to co-operate with the Alumni of Jefferson College in calling a convention, and to take such other action as in their judgment may be proper to further the proposed object.

The call for the convention read thus:—

To the Alumni of Jefferson and Washington colleges:—
The undersigned, representing jointly, though unofficially, the Alumni of Jefferson and Washington colleges, and believing that they express a wish very common, if not universal among the sons of the colleges, do hereby invite their brethren, the alumni of both, to meet in convention at the city of Pittsburg, on Tuesday, the 27th day of September inst., at 4 o'clock P.M., in the lecture room of the First Presbyterian church, to take such action as may be deemed advisable to further the consolidation of the two colleges. It is earnestly hoped that all the alumni, who possibly can, will be present at the proposed convention, as it is believed that the question of union will probably be decided within the next few weeks.

On behalf of Jefferson College.—Boyd Crumrine, Francis J. Collier, Alonzo Linn, D. A. French, James G. Dickson, A. C. McClelland, David McKinney, Robert P. Nevin, A. Williams, Thomas Ewing, J. P. Penney, John M. Kirkpatrick, Jacob H. Miller, James P. Sterritt, John M. Kennedy, James J. Kuhn, W. G. Hawkins, Jr., T. J. Bigham, Algernon C. Bell, David W. Bell, James Veech, James Allison, and R. Patterson.

On behalf of Washington College.—James I. Brownson, William S. Moore, Thomas McKennan, John H. Ewing, William McKennan, D. S. Wilson, A. T. Baird, N. Ewing, R. R. Reed, James Black, Marcus Wishart, David Reed, Thomas C. Lazear, Marcus W. Acheson, J. M. Gallagher, S. J. Wilson, J. S. Morrison, A. P. Morrison, W. A. Childs, and O. H. Miller.

This call was also indorsed thus:—

The undersigned approve the object of the proposed convention, and unite in the above call.

J. W. SCOTT, *President Washington College.*
D. H. RIDDLE, } *Profs. Canonsburg.*
WM. SMITH,

In pursuance of this call, a large majority of the alumni of both colleges met in the lecture-room of the First Presbyterian church, Pittsburg, on September 27, 1864, and organized by appointing the Rev. Dr. Chester, of Philadelphia (not an alumnus of either college) President, Thomas Ewing, Esq., Aaron Williams, D. D., and Samuel J. Wilson, D. D., Secretaries.

The meeting was opened with prayer.

A list of the alumni of both colleges was then taken and *sixty-*

nine alumni of Jefferson College, and *sixty-six* of Washington College were enrolled.

On motion of Rev. James I. Brownson, the following gentlemen were appointed a committee on business, viz: John K. Ewing, W. McKennan, Esq., and S. J. Wilson, D. D., of Washington College, and Loyal Young, D. D., D. McKenney, D. D., and R. P. Nevin, Esq., of Jefferson College.

Papers being now called for, Rev. F. J. Collier, on behalf of Jefferson College, and A. W. Acheson, Esq., on behalf of Washington College, read extended papers proposing plans of union, which were reported to the Business Committee.

While the Business Commitee were preparing their report a friendly discussion on the whole subject of the proposed union took place, in which Rev. Watson Hughes, J. E. Caruthers, F. J. Collier, John M. Smith, Geo. Frazer, John H. Ewing, Esq., James I. Brownson, and others took part. The report was read the same evening at an adjourned meeting, and action on the same continued until the next day.

The report of the committee read as follows:—

We, Alumni of Washington and Jefferson colleges, seriously wishing to promote the best interest of education and religion, having met in convention and discussed in a candid and fraternal spirit the proposed union of the colleges, do express our views as follows:—

1. *Resolved,* That we see the hand of Providence pointing to the union of the two ancient colleges whose sons we are, and fixing the present as the time for the happy consummation by such evident facts as these: The great and constantly increasing number of literary institutions in the land; the urgent need in Western Pennsylvania of an eminently influential and richly endowed college; the desire for a union of Jefferson and Washington colleges, soon to be made more apparent by the completion of a connected railway; the very unsatisfactory condition of their antiquated buildings; the reduced number of students, partly the result of our national troubles: the inadequacy of the old salaries to meet the demands of the times and afford to professors a competent support; the difficulty of obtaining aid for either institution in its separate existence; the several offers made by liberal and reliable men to furnish large amount of funds in case a union is effected, and depending also upon that event, the possible donating by our legislature of a valuable grant of land given by Congress to the State for the advancement of agricultural knowledge.

2. *Resolved,* That inasmuch as the fund which constitutes the present endowments of Washington and Jefferson colleges, were contributed for educational purposes by men of various religious creeds, justice urgently demands, and in our opinion also very deservedly, and in case of a union, the institution, which being thoroughly Protestant and evangelical in its government and teachings, should not be under the control of any ecclesiastical body.

3. *Resolved,* That the following be the plan of union recommended. for the adoption of the trustees of the two colleges:—

The two institutions shall be united and consolidated under the name of Washington and Jefferson College. All the real estate, college property, and funds of each of said colleges, shall be transferred to, and be invested in, the united institution.

The scholarships heretofore granted by either of said colleges shall be respected and their terms fulfilled by the united colleges.

The Board of Trustees of the united college shall consist of twenty-one members—to be elected as follows, to wit: The present Board of Jefferson College shall choose ten persons, and the present Board of Washington College shall choose ten persons, and the said twenty persons so chosen shall constitute the Board of Trustees of the united college, and shall have power to fill the remaining vacancy, and vacancies thereafter arising from death, resignation, or otherwise, shall be filled by the said Board.

The control and management of the property and funds of the united college, as well as the election of the President and professors, and the conducting of its business generally, shall be vested in and exercised by the Board of Trustees.

At the place where the college proper shall not be located, that is to say, at either Washington or Canonsburg, there shall be established as an integral part of the united college, two distinct and separate departments—one to be called the Preparatory Department and the other the Scientific Department of the college. The Preparatory Department to be of a high grade, and of such a character as to fully prepare students for admission into the Freshman Class of the college proper, or to the Scientific Department. The Scientific Department to afford such instructions in the higher English branches—natural sciences, belleslettres, mathematics, civil and military engineering, mechanic arts, and modern languages as may be necessary to fully prepare young men seeking education therein, for the degree of S.B. shall be conferred upon the graduates of said department. If practicable, an Agricultural Department shall be connected with the Scientific Department.

To overcome a difficulty which seems to be otherwise insuperable, the location of the college proper shall be determined by lot, in a mode to be agreed upon by the Boards of the two colleges. Before the lot shall be cast appropriate legislation shall be procured to effect the consolidation of the colleges agreeably to the foregoing plans, as a fundamental basis of the union, and providing that as said lot shall result the location of the college shall be finally and irrevocably fixed and determined; and thereupon the real estate, property, and funds of each of said colleges shall be *ipso facto* vested in and become the property of the united college; the charters of the said colleges shall cease and determine, and their respected existence be merged in the united institution.

4. *Resolved,* That in case our hopes are realized, commodious buildings shall be erected in the best style of modern architecture and furnished with everything essential to the comfort and convenience of the professors and students.

5. *Resolved,* That on account of their eminent ability, their exemplary demeanor, their faithful services, and their self-sacrificing spirit, the President and Professors now installed in the colleges which we represent, are entitled to our highest admiration and esteem, and we will accordingly take pleasure in mentioning their superior claims and commending them to the favorable consideration of the new Board of Trustees, whose duty it will be to reorganize and enlarge the present faculties in the event of a union being consummated.

6. *Resolved,* That we pledge as individuals our earnest and constant efforts to furnish money and appliances to the united college, and to persuade young men to seek instruction there in preference to any other institution.

7. *Resolved,* That a committee be appointed to make known our pro-

ceedings to the Board of Trustees of Jefferson and Washington colleges, and to urge them to convene at an early day, and take action concerning the matter which we so unanimously recommend, stating as a strong reason for promptness, the determination on the part of Dr. Beatty to withdraw and not renew his most generous and long-standing offer of $50,000, if there is no immediate prospect of a union; and in case said Boards adopt the recommendations of this convention that the said convention be further empowered to co-operate with the said Boards in securing such legislative action as may be requisite to carry into effect the plan proposed, and also to secure for the Agricultural Department a liberal proportion of the Congressional grant of lands.

8. *Resolved*, That in the judgment of this meeting it is extremely desirable that the continued co-operations of all the religious denominations heretofore patronizing these colleges should be secured, and it is therefore recommended to the old Boards, in selecting the persons who shall constitute the new Board, to give a due representation to such of the ecclesiastical denominations as are now represented in the Board.

The report and resolutions were UNANIMOUSLY adopted, and, in accordance with the seventh resolution, the Rev. Dr. Jacobus and the Business Committee, who drafted the report and resolution, were appointed to make known the proceedings to the trustees of both colleges.

Accordingly, on the 4th of March, 1865, an act of incorporation was passed by the legislature uniting these colleges, with the combined name of both. By this arrangement the senior, junior, and sophomore classes were placed at Canonsburg, and the freshmen class with the scientific and preparatory department at Washington. This experiment after a trial of four years failed, because the machinery was entirely too complicated. The people were losing confidence in its usefulness, and the public mind was discussing the question of a united and consolidated college. The trustees of both institutions, feeling the responsibility which rested upon them as the custodians of private and public funds, as well as of the church, commenced taking the preparatory steps for a consolidated college. Accordingly, on April 4, 1866, the Rev. Jonathan Edwards, D. D., was formally inaugurated as the first President of the united college, with an able corps of learned professors. But even this dividing of interests—this separation of faculty and students—did not answer the desired end, because it produced alienation, jealousy, and even distrust, and the trustees felt the necessity of an absolute consolidation of both colleges at the same location. A committee of five was appointed to consider and report upon the whole subject, Washington and Canonsburg being represented by one member.

To aid the trustees and their committee in the momentous question before them, the alumini of Jefferson College held a meeting at Canonsburg, August 5, 1868, at which a series of resolutions were adopted urging immediate consolidation as necessary to the success of the college, and pledging the acquiescence of the alumni in whatever decision the Board of Trustees might reach relative to the location of the college.

The Committee of the trustees in due time made a report recommending a modification of the charter, which amendment was carefully prepared by Hon. James P. Sterritt (an alumnus of Jefferson College), chairman of the Committee. On this subject we shall give the words of a committee who addressed the citizens of this county on this important question :—

"The legislature, in passing it, February 26, 1869, made only a single change, which limited the competition for the site of the college to the State of Pennsylvania. The Board of Trustees, in adopting this amendment before its enactment by the legislature, and then in accepting it after its passage, were unanimous, with the exception of one member, who resides at Pittsburg—all the members residing at Canonsburg and Washington voting for it."

This act authorized the trustees, by a vote of not less than two-thirds of the members present, to fix the location of the consolidated college at Canonsburg, Washington, or some other place within this commonwealth. If the trustees did not determine its permanent location within sixty days after the passage of this act, then the governor was to appoint five commissioners, four of whom should agree. The trustees were also authorized to place as much of the property as was necessary in the hands of seven local trustees, to the place losing the college, as would be necessary to establish an academy, normal school, or institution of a lower grade than a college.

April 20, 1869. The trustees, in accordance with the act, met this day in Pittsburg to determine the question, twenty-seven members being present out of the thirty trustees. Although several places wished its locality, the question was finally limited to Canonsburg and Washington—the former offering a subscription of sixteen thousand dollars, and the latter fifty thousand. On the first ballot (one member having withdrawn) *sixteen* voted for Washington, and *ten* for Canonsburg. On the eighth ballot it was decided by a two-third vote in favor of Washington—thus finally settling the question, and consolidating Jefferson and Canonsburg Colleges as one college.

From the furnished report of each college, at the time the union was perfected, we find the endowment fund of each college was as follows :—

Jefferson College Endowment.

James O'Hara's mortgage,	$60,000.00
James Robb's mortgage,	5,000.00
Stock in Bank of Pittsburg,	850.00
Stock in Canonsburg Saving Bank,	820.00
In Treasury,	400.00
	$67,070.00
Liabilities of Jefferson College,	10,296.79
Real Assets,	56,773.21

Washington College Endowment.

Five-twenty bonds, U. S.,	$25,150.00
Premium on same, 5 per cent.,	1,257.50
Interest for four months,	1,056.25
Seven-thirty bonds, U. S.,	3,600.00
Interest accrued on same,	32.40
J. C. Ramsey's note, secured by mortgage and interest,	5,450.00
W. S. & H. Woodruff's note,	1,250.00
	$37,796.15
Sundry notes, with interest,	6,124.50
	$43,920.65

By a late report, it appears that the endowment fund of the consolidated college is as follows:—

Jefferson College fund,	$56,099.29
Washington College fund,	42,698.33
Rev, Dr. C. C. Beatty, donation,	50,000.00
Citizens' subscription of Washington,	50,000.00
	$198,797.62

From a gentleman acquainted with both endowment funds, I learn that the interest accruing on both is about equal, the *one* being invested generally in bonds and mortgages upon real estate, while the *other* is in government securities, which, although differing in the amount of the capital, say $12,852, yet the interest is square.

The trustees of Canonsburg and some of its citizens, dissatisfied with the recent action of the Board of Trustees, and believing that the act consolidating the union of Washington and Jefferson colleges as invalid and unconstitutional, not only sued out an injunction from the Circuit Court, but brought suits in the Supreme Court of Pennsylvania, for the result of which we refer to the following pages:—

At the September term of the Circuit Court of the United States, held at Williamsport, Pa., in the year 1869, Judge McCandless granted a preliminary injunction, restraining the Board of Trustees from removing the collegiate department of Washington and Jefferson colleges from Canonsburg to Washington, concurrently with the bill. In the Circuit Court the following bills in equity were filed by the friends of Canonsburg in the Supreme Court of the Western District of Pennsylvania, viz: The Trustees of Jefferson College *vs.* Washington and Jefferson College; David C. Houston and others *vs.* Washington and Jefferson College; Francis J. Collier and others *vs.* Washington and Jefferson College. The case was fully prepared by James Veech. George Shiras, Jr., and Boyd Crumrine, Esqs., for plaintiffs, and M. W. Acheson and D. S. Wilson, Esqs., for defendants. The oral argument, however, before the Supreme Court was opened by George Shiras, Jr., for the complainants, who was followed by M. W. Acheson and D. S. Wilson, Esqrs., for the respondents, and James Veech, Esq., closed the argument for the complainant.

The following arguments were presented by the counsel for complainant.

1. Canonsburg is the place for the performance of the scholarship contracts.
2. The legislature could not relieve the corporation from the full and complete performance of the scholarship contracts at Canonsburg. The power reserved in the charter of 1802 does not authorize a repeal of the charter nor any alteration of it, other than as the powers and privileges conferred upon the trustees.
3. Legislation could not be accepted by the trustees, which infringes upon their contracts.
4. The act of 1869 is invalid, because it does not aver injurious results from the act of 1865, and does not protect the right of corporators, and delegates the power to fix the location of the college.
5. The assent of donors (scholarship holders) is demanded to authorize any change in the charter of Jefferson College.
6. The act of 1865 was a contract between the trustees of the two colleges, or at least evidences such contract, and the agreement thus evidenced is violated by the act of 1869.

To this the respondents replied by giving the following statement of facts:—

That Jefferson and Washington colleges were separate institutions of learning, located respectively at Canonsburg and Washington, both in the county of Washington, and seven miles distant from each other. Jefferson College was incorporated by an act of Assembly passed January 15, 1802, and Washington College by an act passed March 28, 1806.

On the 4th of March, 1865, the legislature passed an act to unite the colleges and erect them into one corporation under the name of Washington and Jefferson College, and providing for the instruction of the senior, junior, and sophomore classes at Canonsburg, and the other class and department at Washington.

On the 26th day of February 1869, a supplement to the act was passed, providing for the concentration of all the departments of the college at one place, and under this act they were located at Washington.

The trustees of Jefferson College and Francis J. Collier, and others, in their several bills, assail the act of February 26th, 1869, as unconstitutional, and David C. Houston and others in their bill assail both the acts of March 4th, 1865, and February 26th, 1869, as invalid and unconstitutional.

Messrs. M. W. Acheson and D. S. Wilson submitted arguments to the court tending to establish the following proposition:—

1. That the corporation, the trustees of Jefferson College in Canonsburg, in the county of Washington, was, by the very terms and nature of its political existence, subject to dissolution by a surrender of its corporate franchises.
2. That by the acceptance of the act of March 4th, 1865, Jefferson College surrendered its corporate franchises, and therefore ceased to exist.

3. That the general and unconditional power to alter its charter is distinctly reserved by the legislature, and is an integral part of the contract between the State and the corporation.

4. That this power may be exercised whenever the legislature deems it expedient to do so, and such exercise of it does not impair the contract between the State and the corporation.

5. That the rights of the plaintiffs, growing out of their contracts with Jefferson College are subject to the power of the legislature to alter the charter of that institution.

6. That the legislature was therefore constitutionally competent to transfer the location of Jefferson College to Washington, and by consequence to fix that as the place of performance of the plaintiffs' contract.

7. That in any aspect of the case the complainants are not entitled to the remedy by any injunction.

At the opening of the Supreme Court of Pennsylvania, in Philadelphia, on January 3d, 1870, Chief Justice Thompson delivered the unanimous opinion of the Supreme Court of the State in the several cases involving the right of the Board of Trustees to consolidate all the departments of the Institution at this place.

DAVID C. HOUSTON, JOHN JOHNSON, et al.
vs.
WASHINGTON AND JEFFERSON COLLEGE.

THE TRUSTEES OF JEFFERSON COLLEGE IN CANONSBURG
vs.
WASHINGTON AND JEFFERSON COLLEGE.

FRANCIS J. COLLIER, WM. JEFFREY, et al.
vs.
WASHINGTON AND JEFFERSON COLLEGE.

The unanimous opinion of the court was delivered at Philadelphia, January 3, 1870, by Chief Justice Thompson.

These three bills, relating to the same institution, and involving considerations common to all, were argued together, and as they can be most satisfactorily disposed of together, we now propose to do so.

The first of them raises the question whether the contracts of scholarship between the complainants and others, and Jefferson College, did not interpose a constitutional barrier to any legislative grant of authority to the trustees of the college to surrender its former charter and accept a new one, by which the college was eventually removed from Canonsburg to Washington, in the same county.

The second is by the Trustees of Jefferson College, in which the same question is raised by them; and

The third is by some of the members of the Board of Trustees of Washington and Jefferson College, in which they complain of the defendant, that its trustees are, under pretence of authority conferred by the act of 26th February, 1869, about to violate the provisions of the act of 4th March, 1865, by which Washington and Jefferson College was authorized to provide for the instruction of the Senior, Junior, and Sophomore Classes at Canonsburg, and students in the Freshman Class and in the Scientific and Preparatory Department, and the Department of Agriculture and Art in Washington, and, in disregard thereof, about to unite all the classes at Washington, and to remove thither the library and other movable property of the college, and to sell or dispose of its real estate, charging that such intended acts and doings would be, and are, in contravention of the rights, duties, and obligations conferred by the act of 4th March, 1865, referred to.

Each of these cases was set down, and all were heard together, on bills and answers. The argument took a wide range, and counsel had an attentive hearing, such as the magnitude of the seeming consequences of a determination of the controversy demanded. The questions presented, however, were not numerous or complex; and notwithstanding the possible discontent which may for a time follow the displacement of an ancient and cherished institution of learning, if the law require it, we must so determine. We do not make the law.

A question to be answered in passing on the merits of the first of these bills is, could Jefferson College surrender its charter, with the consent of the legislature, and accept a new one consolidating it with another institution or college of the same nature and kind, without the consent of the holders of scholarships in the college?

The general right of a private corporation to surrender its franchises may possibly have exceptions, but undoubtedly this is the rule. This is generally described as an inherent right, which would necessarily defeat any attempt by legislation to enforce upon a corporation qualities of perpetuity. Such a thing would be impossible in the nature of things. Corporations, like individuals, die by the decay or loss of their vital functions, and this effectually defies authority to render them perpetual. A surrender of a franchise is the voluntary death of the corporation, and is one mode by which it may cease to exist. (19 John. 474; 8 Pte. 381.) If anybody ever did dispute the right of a corporation to surrender its franchises of its own mere motion, it is not likely that such a contest about the question could be maintained long where both parties (the State and the corporation, the grantor and the grantee) consent to it absolutely or on condition. This I take to be incapable of being disputed, and the history of this college will show that this is just what has transpired in its case. It is indisputed in the pleadings.

But, independently of this mutual consent, there is in the act of the 15th of January, 1802 (the original act of incorporation of Jefferson College), a reservation of a right to do all that was done by the legislature by the act of 1865. In the 5th section of the original act it is provided "that the constitution of the said college hereby and herein declared and established shall be and remain the inviolable constitution of said college forever; and the same shall not be altered or alterable by any ordinance or law of the trustees, nor in any other manner than by an act of the legislature of the commonwealth." In the Commonwealth vs. Bonsall, 3d Wharton 559, a provision like this was held to be a good reservation of the right of the legislature to change and alter the charter of the corporation of the "Public School of Germantown." The reservation in that act of incorporation was in the same words almost as those used here; there is not a shade of difference in their meaning, and but a single literal difference. Granting the rule to be that a private charter of the date of 1802 could not be changed by the legislature without the assent of the corporators, or by virtue of the right reserved that such charter stand on the footing of contracts, we have no difficulty here, for there is not only assent here, but a sufficient reservation of the right to sustain the action of the legislature in the enactment of 1865. So far as that act is concerned, nobody objected to its passage, nor to what was done under it, in consolidating Washington and Jefferson Colleges into one body. The holders of the scholarships now complaining made no objection, and we must presume them to have been satisfied. What was done was not done in a corner, and they do not allege they were uninformed of it. Thus the surrender of the charter of Jefferson College, and the acceptance of the new one, may strictly be said to have been with the assent, in point of fact, of the trustees, the legislature, and the scholarships. This is an assent of every interest to the new organization, and ought to silence all complaints by any person having a legal right to complain or interfere. But in order to meet the objection of the holders of scholarships in the Jefferson College directly on the merits of their objection, which is that their contracts are impaired by the acts of 1865 and 1869, let us consider it and see whether there is anything sound in it. If I understand it, it is supposed that these scholarships are impaired in value by the establishment of Washington and Jefferson College, at the town of Washington, some seven miles distant from Canonsburg, under the authority of the act of 26th February, 1869. It may be noticed that these scholarships are, as stated in the certificates, for the endowment of Jefferson College. This designation does not alter the matter. They are contracts for tuition in consideration of a prepaid subscription, and as ordinary contracts are to be interpreted. This is their effect, no more and no less.

By the act of March, 1865, Jefferson and Washington Colleges were consolidated under a new charter, accepted by both. The legislature was careful in granting the new charter to avoid the very question now introduced; and, to do entire justice to the holders of certificates and scholarships, and others, provided as follows: " All the several liabilities of the said two colleges or corporations, by either of them suffered or created, including the scholarships heretofore granted by and now obligatory upon each of them, are hereby imposed upon and declared to be assumed by the corporation hereby created; which shall discharge and perform the same without *diminution* or *abatement*." The whole and entire of these contracts are thus saved in their identity and integrity. This was one of the terms of acceptance of the new charter, and there is no pretence even now that it is not obligatory on the new institution, and may be enforced against it, after acceptance of the charter, by every means known in the law applicable to or under the original charter. The nature of the new college as an institution of learning, the subjects and mode of instruction, organization, and even the professors, I believe, are the same as they were in Jefferson College. There is no pretence of impairment of these contracts on grounds of dissimilarity of instruction, or capacity on part of the new institution to impart it. In passing I may say that no objection, on any grounds, was made to the change during the three years in which the college acted partly at Canonsburg and partly at Washington, under the most cumbrous and unheard of arrangement for a college.

It is not therefore on either of these grounds that these scholarship contracts can be, or are claimed to be impaired, but another and different ground is insisted on, namely, that the contract for tuition, &c., contained therein, was to be performed at Canonsburg and not elsewhere.

When we recur to the contracts there is no word or provision to this effect in them, or in the plan or prospectus put forth to induce investments in them. No doubt it was expected, from the fact that Jefferson College was located at Canonsburg, that that was to be the place of the performance of the contract. On the face of the contract—and there is nothing but this in the case—the contracts are personal to the corporation, and it could perform or offer performance anywhere, whether at Washington or Canonsburg. The contracts are complete so as to bind both contracting parties without designating the place. The party liable to perform, like in any other personal contract, is liable on it wherever found. It was not even an incident of the contract that it was to be performed at Canonsburg. It was an expectancy perhaps—even that we do not know—we simply infer it, not from the contract, but from the situation of the contracting parties. We all know that even the incidents of contracts may be changed without impinging on the constitutional prohibition against impairing contracts. Stay laws which change the remedy and rights of the parties, to some extent at least, have from time to time been passed in this and other States, and they have been uniformly sustained, wherever the contract did not specially provide to the contrary. Chadwick vs. Moore, 8 W. & S. 50, Bunn, Raiguel & Co. vs. Gorgas, 5 Wright 441, Bilmyer vs. Evans et al. 4 Wright, 324, contain all that need be cited on this point, and in regard to the distinction noticed. In these cases, and in every one of the kind, it has been usual to present the argument that the contract having been made in view of the remedy existing at the time for its enforcement, it was a part of it, or at least an inseparable incident of it, and to permit it to be controlled by a new rule was to impair the contract. These are instances, it must be admitted, very near the outer verge of legislative power, but they have been always sustained, and in these apparently objectionable features are incomparably stronger than anything which can be assumed or predicated of the contracts in question.

The argument in support of the plaintiff's position, not being sufficiently self-sustaining, an equity is invoked to its aid. That, as a consideration in the question before us, is outside of the case, excepting as it may serve to illustrate the argument. This equity is that the subscribers for scholarships made them in view of their proximity to Jefferson College, and the convenience of maintaining scholars at home while attending upon a collegiate course of instruction, and that they will be deprived of this advantage by the removal of the college to Washington. As nothing of this appears by the contracts, and there is no proof of it *aliunde*, it may or it may not be so. It may have induced some or all to subscribe, but this is surmise. Certain it is it could have had no effect on subscribers for perpetual scholarships, for the college in such cases finds boarding, lodging, and tuition to the scholar, and it is no matter to the subscriber where that may be done as far as expense is concerned. This is a matter of indifference to him. But disappointed expectations, the motive in entering into a contract, do not affect the existence of the contract. All that may occur and the contract remain in full vigor. No constitutional provisions extend to cure this oft necessary result. We must not at this point overlook the great fact, in any contract, that it is always made in view of, and subject to, the natural or legal contingencies affecting it, or to which the contracting parties may be subject. If a contract be made with a corporation, to be executed in the future, the contingencies of existence must be regarded as having been in view as much as between man and man. The risk is taken by both parties. They know themselves to be subject to such contingencies, and not the contingencies subject to them. It must be presumed that the subscribers to these scholarships knew that the legislature might, with the assent of the corporation, alter its fundamental law, or might do it on the terms of the reservation already referred to, and thus defeat their motive for subscribing, and that it had power to do so, only preserving their contract. This might be done, and this the law presumes all parties to have known. Therefore in no sense could just expectation even have been disappointed by the act of removing the college to Washington. The case of the Genesee College and the opinion of Judge Johnson, at chambers, I presume, have been considered. The occasion of the delivery of that opinion was upon a motion to vacate an injunction order restraining the removal of the college at Lima to Syracuse, pending litigation as to the right to remove. It is true, he seems to have gone beyond the limits of the question somewhat, and discussed the question of scholarships, injecting the force of a contract into the motives for subscribing, but as I understand the case (no facts being reported with the opinion furnished us on a separate leaf) the contest was between the scholarships and the college, unaffected by the authority of the legislature. This might make a material difference between that case and the one in hand. I incline to think it would. Be that as it may, if the case goes further than this, while we acknowledge great respect for the learned jurist who delivered the opinion, we cannot follow it to the extent claimed here.

Lastly, the argument in this case culminates in an assumption that the legislature and corporation of Jefferson College, and so of any other corporate body, may be controlled in changing, altering, repealing, and surrendering the charter by the contractors with the corporation. The one may consent and the other act upon such consent and yet this may be set aside by outside parties. This position is only true of corporations generally to the extent of leaving intact contracts and preserving legal remedies, obviously no more. That is always provided for by the legislature. The 10th section of Art. 1 of the Constitution of the United States would probably require this, although the 16th section, of Art. 1 of the Constitution of the State, expressly provides only that in repealing or revoking charters by the legislature, no injury be done to the corporators. But we need not elaborate this consideration, as both the contract and remedy are preserved in this case.

In conclusion, as far as the first of these cases is concerned, it must be recollected that Washington and Jefferson College was incorporated by act of 4th March, 1865, and located for certain specified purposes, both at Canonsburg and Washington, and that the act was accepted by both of the old institutions to be consolidated. Thenceforth the corporation is under that act. The act of 24th February, 1869, therefore, providing for its removal, as the trustees or a majority might decide, was clearly within the constitutional power of the legislature, sec. 16, Art. 1, Constitution of Pennsylvania, and being assented to, is valid beyond question or controversy.

For all these reasons the bill in this case is not sustained, and must be dismissed.

Bill dismissed at the costs of the plaintiffs.

2. As to the second of the above-mentioned bills, viz: The Trustees of Jefferson College in Washington and Jefferson College, but little is required to be said. We have virtually decided it in holding, as we have done in the first of these cases, that, by the acceptance of the act of 1865 in connection with Washington College, it ceased to exist under its original charter. There is therefore now no such Board as the trustees of Jefferson College, with the right of suit in the name of that corporation. (8 Pet. 281.) Consequently the plea of the defendant is sustained, and this bill must be dismissed.

Bill dismissed, and Wm. Jeffrey, who filed it, is ordered to pay the costs, no other name appearing of record as complainant, and there being no legal Board of Trustees such as that which purports to the plaintiff in the bill.

3. The third and last of these bills is filed by a minority of the Board of Trustees of Washington and Jefferson College, and they claim that the act of Assembly of 1869, authorizing the removal of the college as consoli-

dated by the act of 1865, in obedience to the decision of the requisite number of trustees, is unauthorized for the reason, it is alleged that it infringes the contracts of scholarship with the Jefferson College, which they assume could only be performed by the college at Canonsburg. This question we have disposed of in our views in regard to the first of these cases. We need not repeat them, but refer to them as showing that the ground of unconstitutionality is not tenable. It is difficult to discover wherein the act of 1869 is obnoxious to the charge made, and the act of 1865, which was not complained of by the plaintiffs, was not. By that act the Freshmen class and preparatory department of the college were to be at Washington, and the Senior, Junior, and Sophomore classes were to be taught at Canonsburg. Now, unless the scholarships exclude the Freshman and Preparatory department of the college—which they do not—there was just the same impairment of the contract, if any, of scholarships in obliging scholars to go to Washington for tuition in the Preparatory department and Freshman class as to require them to go there to pass through the remainder of the course. Yet this objection was not made by the plaintiffs or anybody else. This, I admit is rather *argumentum ad hominem* than an illustration of the question on principle, but that, we think, we have already done.

To another charge in the bill the respondents answer that they intend to remove the classes of the college to Washington, the place fixed as the site of the college, under the provisions of the act of 1869, and to dispose of the realty strictly pursuant to the authority of the act; and as this was not replied to by the complainants, it must be taken to be true; and as we have already, in the first of these cases, held the act of Assembly of 1869 to be constitutional, it follows that this bill also must be dismissed at the cost of the complainants.

Ordered, That the several bills of the several plaintiffs herein considered be dismissed at the costs of the several plaintiffs in the said bills respectively, and that it be so entered in each of the cases.

The decision being thus rendered in favor of Washington, the Board of Trustees, through their attorneys, went into the Circuit Court at Erie immediately, and moved to dissolve the injunction, which motion resulted in its dissolution, thereby removing the restraint that had been imposed upon the Board, and permitting them to put all the departments of the institution in operation at Washington.

An appeal, however, has been taken from the decision of the Supreme Court in the case of D. C. Houston and others to the Supreme Court of the United States, which is now pending.

WASHINGTON AND JEFFERSON COLLEGE.

The Board of Trustees held a special meeting at Washington on the 1st inst. The object of the meeting was to take proper steps to put the college in effectual operation, now that the injunction granted by the Circuit Court of the United States had been removed. The injunction was allowed by his Honor, Judge M'Candless, as announced by him at the time, simply to afford the complainants an opportunity, by means of equity suits in the Supreme Court of Pennsylvania, to test the legality of the action of the Board of Trustees in consolidating the several departments of the college at Washington. The Supreme Court having unanimously sustained the action of the Board by their late decision at Philadelphia, Judge M'Candless promptly dissolved the injunction, thus leaving the Board of Trustees free to perfect the organization of the college as provided by the amended charter.

This has been done accordingly, and the undersigned were appointed a committee by the Board to announce the result to the public. The higher classes in the college proper have been restored and are now in full operation, and the prospect of success in all the departments of the institution is highly flattering. The Board have assurance of additions to the Senior, Junior, and Sophomore classes by the return of some of their members who repaired to other colleges during the pendency of the injunction. From recent letters and inquiries, a considerable accession to the present number of students is confidently expected. There are now enrolled and in actual attendance eighty-five students. In view of the obstacles now so happily surmounted, this fact furnishes the most gratifying assurance of undiminished public confidence, and is a good omen of future and permanent success.

We are gratified to state that, with but comparatively few exceptions, we have had the steadfast approval and warm sympathy of the joint alumni. This has been our source of strength; and now that the unexpected and extraordinary attempt to break down our college union has signally failed we can turn with assured confidence to the repeated pledges of the joint alumni to sustain the consolidated college in the higher and wider sphere of usefulness upon which it has just entered.

The Committee having in charge the nomination of a President have been instructed to act promptly, and to convene the Board as soon as they are ready to make a nomination.

In the mean time the college has been placed in the charge of the Rev. J. J. Brownson, D. D., as President *pro tem.*, to whom the Board is specially indebted for consenting to occupy the position temporarily, as well as for the good service he has heretofore rendered the college as Vice-President *pro tem*. With him are associated in earnest work, Professors Linn and Jones, formerly of the department at Canonsburg, and Professors Woods and Vose, of that at Washington, as well as Professor Simonton, lately inducted into the chair of mathematics. The full amount of instruction demanded by the academical and scientific courses of study is now given by these gentlemen, and preparations are in process for the enlargement of the laboratory and the employment of an assistant in laboratory practice. It is the design of the Board to enlarge the faculty hereafter to meet the advancements and wants of the college.

The Committee on buildings and improvements were instructed to proceed to the discharge of the duty assigned them, and have their reports ready to lay before the Board at their next meeting.

Arrangements entered into by the Franklin, Washington, Philo, and Union Literary Societies of the college, whereby they are to be consolidated under the names of the "Franklin and Washington" and "Philo and Union" Societies, were approved by the Board, and a committee appointed to co-operate with said societies in carrying into effect the proposed design.

In order to correct an erroneous impression derived from newspaper publications, we desire to state for public information, that the allowance of the appeal from the decree of the Supreme Court of Pennsylvania, by a Judge of the Supreme Court of the United States, does not imply an approval of said appeal on its merits. It is simply and only an authorization of the removal of the case into the Supreme Court of the United States, which any judge of that court is bound to allow in a case in which the constitutional validity of a State law is drawn in question, and involves no commitment whatever in regard to the merits, or even to the consideration of such a question.

We have only, therefore, to express our assured conviction that the judgment of that court, even should the case be prosecuted, will be concurrent with that of the Supreme Court of our own State. Abiding in this faith and confidence, the Board will continue to go forward in the work of complete and efficient organization of the college in all its departments, thereby worthily commending it to the support and patronage of the friends of education.

February 2, 1870.

JOHN EAGLESON,
A. W. ACHESON, } *Committee.*
J. R. JOHNSTON,

List of Presidents and Professors from Organization in 1806.

PRESIDENTS.

1806.—December 13. Rev. Matthew Brown, D. D., April 13, 1817.
1817.—April 13. Rev. Andrew Wylie, December 9, 1828.
(The college was closed for two years.)
1830.—February 26. Rev. David Elliott, D. D., December, 1831.
1831.—December 31. Rev. David McConaughy, D. D., October 12, 1849,
(who continued until May, 1850.)
1850.—May 6. Rev. James Clark, D. D., July, 1852.
1852.—July. Rev. James I. Brownson, D. D., pro tem., September, 1853.

Synodical College.

1853.—September. Rev. John W. Scott, D. D., 1866.

Under the Union of Jefferson and Washington College.

1865.—March 4. Rev. D. H. Riddle, D. D., pro tem., April 4, 1866.
1866.—April 4. Rev. Jonathan Edwards, D. D., April 20, 1869.

Under Consolidated College of Jefferson and Washington, at Washington.

1869.—April 21. Rev. Samuel J. Wilson, D. D., pro tem.
Rev. James I. Brownson, D. D.

VICE-PRESIDENTS.

1856.—Rev. Wm. P. Alrich,
1859.—Rev. James Black, D. D., 1866.
1868.—Rev. James I. Brownson, D. D.
1868.—Rev. John W. Scott, D. D., February 23, 1869.

PROFESSORS.

1806.—James Reed, Professor of Mathematics and Natural Philosophy, 1823.
1806.—Isaiah Blair, M. D., Professor of Medicine, 1828.
1815.—John Reed, Professor of Ancient Languages, 1817.
(Prior to this period the languages were taught by tutors, viz: Andrew K. Russell, Christopher Rankin, and T. M. T. McKennan.)
1817.—Rev. Francis McFarland, Professor of Ancient Languages.
1818.—Rev. James Rowland, Professor of Ancient Languages.
1819.—Mays Smith, Professor of Ancient Languages.
1820.—Rev. Guerdon Gates, Professor of Ancient Languages.
1821.—Rev. John Stockton, Professor of Ancient Languages.
1822.—Rev. John Graham, Professor of Ancient Languages.

1823.—James Workman, Professor of Mathematics.
1824.—John W. Scott, Professor of Mathematics.
1830.—William D. Smith, Professor of Ancient Languages.
1830.—Rev. William P. Alrich, Professor of Mathematics.
1831.—Rev. J. Holmes Agnew, Professor of Ancient Languages.
1831.—John L. Gow, Esq., Professor of English Literature.
1832.—Joseph Ritner, Esq., Professor of French, Civil Engineering, and Natural Science, 1833.
1833.—Wm. K. McDonald, Esq., Professor of Belles Lettres and Political Economy, 1836.
1834.—Rev. R. H. Lee, Professor of Ancient Languages, 1837.
1837.—Rev. R. H. Lee, Professor of Political Economy, 1854.
1837.—Rev. D. Ferguson, Professor of Ancient Languages, 1844.
1840.—Robert Milligan, Professor of English Literature, 1851.
1844.—Rev. Nicholas Murray, Professor of Ancient Languages, 1853.
1846.—John L. Gow, Professor of Constitutional and Municipal Law, 1851.
1846.—James King, M. D., Professor of Anatomy, Physiology, and Hygiene, 1851.
1851.—Rev. James W. McKennan, Professor of English Literature and Ancient Languages, 1854.
1851.—Robert Milligan, Professor of Natural Science, 1852.
1853.—Rev. E. C. Wines, Professor of Ancient Languages.
1853.—Rev. Samuel J. Wilson, Professor of Ancient Languages.
1854.—Rev. W. J. Martin, Professor of Natural Sciences, 1858.
1858.—Wm. H. Brewer, Professor of Natural Sciences, 1859.
1859.—Rev. James Black, Professor of Ancient Languages, 1868.
1860.—Alexander Muckle, Professor of Natural Sciences.
1861.—Rev. Henry Woods, Professor of Ancient Languages.
1861.—George W. Miller, Professor of Mathematics.
1862.—Rev. Joseph Waugh, Professor of Mathematics.
1864.—W. J. Brugh, Professor of Mathematics, 1866.
1865.—R. D. Wylie, Professor of Mathematics, 1866.
1865.—Rev. E. F. Farrier, Professor of English Literature, 1867.
1866.—Geo. B. Vose, Professor of Mechanics and Civil Engineering.
1866.—C. M. Dodd, Professor of Latin.
1866.—Rev. Alonzo Linn, Professor of Greek and Latin Literature.
1865.—D. Kirkwood, LL. D., Professor of Mathematics and Astronomy, 1867.
1866.—Samuel Jones, Professor of Natural Philosophy and Chemistry.
1866.—E. H. Twining, Professor of Natural Sciences, December 23, 1869.
1867.—Rev. J. S. Roberts, Professor of Mathematics and Astronomy, Dec. 23, 1868.
1868.—S. F. Peckham, Professor of Natural Science, 1869.
1869.—J. S. Simonton, Professor of Mathematics and Astronomy.

(For the history of Jefferson College see Canonsburg, title, Chartiers township.)

In connection with Washington College are two literary societies, viz: the Union Literary Society, and the Washington Literary Society, each of which has large and valuable libraries.

The Union Literary Society was founded November 10, 1809, by Jonathan Kearsley, Andrew Stewart, Joseph B. Becket, John Stephenson, Thos. S. Cunningham, and John McKennan.

The founders adopted as the motto of the Society, "*Deo juvante in ardua nitimur.*"

The Washington Literary Society was founded February 22, 1814, by Alexander Gilleland, F. J. Lemoyne, William Heaton, James Page, A. O. Patterson, Robert McLean, Andrew Page, Jacob Wolf.

The motto of the Society is "*Doctrina vim promovet insitam.*"

JAMES MONROE,

President of the United States, arrived in Washington May 4, 1817, accompanied by Gen. Brown and his aid Major Worth, General McComb and his aid Captain Root, and Governor Lewis Cass of Detroit. They were conducted to David Morris's hotel by a committee of arrangement appointed by the citizens, and escorted by Capt. McCluney's company of infantry.

The President the next day left for Canonsburg and Pittsburg, accompanied by Gen. Sutton, Col. Hill, and Maj. Dunlap.

PRESIDENT MONROE.

During the presidency of Rev. Andrew Wylie, James Monroe, President of the United States, visited Washington on May 4th, 1817. He was received and welcomed to the hospitalities of the place. Dr. Wylie addressed him in the following language :—

HONORED SIR: It is with no small degree of pleasure that I present to your Excellency, in behalf of the trustees, faculty, and students of Washington College, our sincere congratulation on your safe arrival at this place.

It would be superfluous to attempt, by our feeble testimony, to add to the evidence of that universal satisfaction with which an enlightened and happy people behold your Excellency placed in the highest office that their grateful suffrages can bestow. The public expression of this satisfaction is infinitely remote, both from the interested adulation of sycophants, and the constrained applauses of the slaves of arbitrary power. It is the voice of nature, the utterance of the heart, the spontaneous effusion of the souls of freemen, too dignified to feign what they do not feel, and too intelligent and generous not to appreciate your past distinguished services to the republic, and the unequalled advantages of that government whose executive functions you are called to discharge. Participating in this universal sentiment, permit us to join in the public expression of it.

A kind Providence bestows upon us liberty, abundance, and health, and we acknowledge, as a blessing which enhances all the rest, the exercise of that spirit of benign wisdom which sheds its radiance on the commencement of your administration. We hail its orient lustre as the precursor of a still happier day than any we have yet seen—may not its brightness be obscured by the mists of prejudice, nor its serenity disturbed by the storms of faction!

As friends in literature and mental refinement, which require for their successful cultivation a state of concord where all the charities of nature, unembittered by party rancor, have free scope for exercise, we cannot but notice, with peculiar satisfaction, every influence calculated to produce such a state. An influence of that happy character we recognize in that *liberal policy* which dictated, and which everywhere attends, your journey through the different sections of the United States. Inferior in its harmonizing tendency to no influence but that of the religion of Immanuel, may it meet no obstacle in the minds of the people to prevent its having its full effect in allaying the jealousies of party, and increasing the action of those moral ties which, still more than those of interest, are requisite to bind together this confederated republic.

We are especially sensible of the honor you have done us by visiting this western region, which is but just commencing its ascent in the scale of improvement. Those institutions which are calculated to accelerate this ascent are but in their infancy; yet we believe your Excellency will view them with some degree of interest, especially such as have for their object the cultivation of the mind, since this is the source to which all those improvements which render a people great, respectable, or happy, must be referred. That your Excellency may have the happiness of contemplating the progress of our beloved country in virtue, literature, arts, and power, becoming still more rapid in every successive year of your administration, and that you may enjoy a life prolonged amidst the choicest gifts and blessings of Heaven, honored sir, is our fervent desire.

To which PRESIDENT MONROE replied:—

SIR: I accept with unfeigned pleasure this expression of your sentiments in behalf of the trustees, faculty, and students of Washington College. The object of my present tour round a very considerable extent of our maritime and inland frontiers was that I might be enabled, from a personal knowledge of the state of our country, to discharge my official duty by providing for its best interests. In this journey I have derived great satisfaction in contemplating the increased prosperity of our beloved country, and observing those indications of patriotism and harmony which so generally prevail among my fellow-citizens, and which this movement has tended to draw forth.

The sentiments expressed in your address do honor to yourself and to the literary institution over which you preside, and are not, I am persuaded, the language of adulation, but a just expression of your esteem for our happy Constitution, which secures to us our civil and religious rights, and is so well calculated to answer every object of the social compact.

In providing for the prosperity and happiness of a country, a careful attention to literary institutions and the education of youth ought ever to occupy a high place. To the youth we must look with an eye of deep interest—they are the hope of our country—and I cannot omit mentioning the peculiar gratification I have received from observing the growth of literary institutions, and the attention which is paid to the instruction of youth, and which is certainly the best and most permanent basis on which our privileges, civil and religious, can be founded.

For the notice you have taken of the few services that I have been enabled to render to my country—for the friendly wish expressed for the prosperity of the republic under my administration, as well as for my personal comfort and happiness, I pray you, sir, to accept my thanks, and permit me to reciprocate my best wishes for the prosperity of the institution over which you preside, and for the happiness of the trustees, faculty, and students, that the College of Washington may not only retain its present celebrity, but that under your direction it may be growing in a state of progressive and rapid improvement, is my sincere desire.

Accept, sir, for yourself, the trustees, faculty, and students of Washington College, the assurance of my respect.

First Presbyterian Church.

We are chiefly indebted to the Rev. Dr. James I. Brownson, the present efficient and highly esteemed pastor of this church, for the historical facts contained in the following history of this church.

Previous to the organization of the Presbyterian church the Presbyterians who resided in the town of Washington, in October, 1781 (at the time it was laid out), held their membership in the church of Chartiers, near Canonsburg, under the care of Rev. Dr. McMillan. From this period to 1793 Presbyterial supplies preached in the courthouse. However, when the stone academy, now the central building of the old college, was erected, it served both for educational purposes and religious worship. A place of worship, however, being procured, an organization was effected in 1793, by the consent of the Presbytery of Ohio, and Andrew Swearingen, Joseph Wherry, Robert Stockton, and William McCombs were ordained as the first elders.

This being the first regular organization of the Presbyterian church, it would be well to remark as an historical fact that the records of the Presbytery of Redstone show that Alexander Addison, a licentiate from the Presbytery of Aberlour, Scotland, and afterwards the distinguished president judge of this judicial district, preached in Washington in December, 1785, when application was made for him as a stated supply, which request was granted April 18, 1786, until the meeting of the Synod.

This church having placed itself under the care of the Presbytery of Ohio, which was organized in 1793, the Rev. James Welsh occupied the pulpit as a stated supply from April, 1794, for one year. Rev. Thaddeus Dodd, Rev. Boyd Mercer, Rev. John Anderson, and Rev. Samuel Potter officiated occasionally as supplies. On the 23d of October, 1800, William McCamant and Robert Anderson were appointed commissioners from the church to attend a meeting of the Presbytery, and were authorized by the Washington congregation to take such steps as would procure the settlement of Rev. Thomas Ledlie Birch, as there were a number of his old hearers and neighbors from Ireland in the congregation. The Presbytery of Philadelphia indorsed his papers, and also many distinguished divines in the east. It appears, however, that the Presbytery did not receive such satisfaction as would induce them to give him the charge; yet he continued to exercise his ministry in Washington, under an appeal to the General Assembly. In January, 1801, at a meeting of the Presbytery at Cross Creek, the Rev. Birch underwent another examination of his experimental acquaintance with religion, but was rejected. The Presbytery then appointed supplies, and a portion of the church retained Rev. Mr. Birch. The Rev. Birch also preached in Pittsburg one Sabbath in each month, for which they paid him one hundred dollars per annum, while his salary in Washington was six hundred dollars. On the 26th

April, 1801, the congregation appointed John Wilson, Samuel Young, and William Smylie commissioners to present their complaint and supplication to the General Assembly in the May following. The letter was signed by Samuel Whann, James Chambers, William McCamant, Hon. Henry Taylor, Dr. Absalom Baird, and Robert Anderson, in which they state all the circumstances, and repel the idea of an attempt to establish a congregation within the bounds of an old organized congregation, which the Presbytery deems irregular, and contrary to the order of the Presbyterian church.

This committee also state a fact to the General Assembly worthy of being recorded to show the state of religion at that period in Washington—"We doubt not but that your humanity and zeal for the gospel will be moved at hearing of our state. Our town, the most populous in this part of the continent, is in the centre of a close settled country, not less than sixteen miles square. *The Lord's Supper never was dispensed during the last fifteen years,* and our families not even comforted by one ministerial visit, until lately by the Rev. Mr. Birch; and not more than two or three solitary supplies in a season, until now they are sent to us from a spirit of contention. We therefore humbly and respectfully supplicate that you will be pleased to take the Rev. Thomas Ledlie Birch under your protection, and take such steps towards the settlement of our congregation as your wisdom shall seem meet, as many of our principal members, now grown weary from all their attempts to obtain a gospel minister, being so many times frustrated, have declared that if Rev Mr. Birch is obliged to leave us they will withdraw, and in consequence we must nearly cease from being a worshipping society."

The General Assembly having examined Rev. Mr. Birch on his experimental acquaintance with religion decided, May 26, 1801, that they find no obstruction against any Presbytery to which he may apply, taking him up and proceeding with him agreeably to the rules and regulations in this case made and provided.

At the first meeting of the Presbytery at Buffalo, however, July, 1801, a majority of the Washington congregation petitioned the Presbytery to take Rev. Mr. Birch under their care, in accordance with the decision of the General Assembly; but the Presbytery resolved to have nothing farther to do with the Rev. Mr. Birch as to his trials for the gospel ministry, as well as from the general report which prevailed with respect to his imprudent and irregular conduct.

This led to an open rupture between the friends of the Rev. Mr. Birch and the congregation of Washington, represented by its elders, Messrs. Swearingen, Stockton, Wherry, and McComb. These four elders procured the Washington Academy in January, 1802, for religious worship, while it was closed against the adherents of the Rev. Mr. Birch. The Rev. Thomas L. Birch was buried in the old Presbyterian churchyard, in Buffalo township, where he was settled as pastor. This unchristian strife ceased after much unchristian conduct on both sides, and peace and tranquillity were restored through the instrumentality of a gifted young man who preached in the stone academy in the spring of 1805. That young divine was the Rev. Matthew Brown, a graduate of Dickinson College, who, by his urbanity of manners, Christian conduct, unassuming habits, and being an able and eloquent minister in defence of the principles of his Divine Master, received a unanimous call, and was ordained October 16, 1805 —the Rev. Mr. Snodgrass having preached the sermon from 1 Tim. iv. 16, and Rev. John Anderson delivering the usual charges. Immediately after his installation Rev. M. Brown commenced the undertaking of raising funds for the erection of a suitable place of worship. He was pre-eminently successful, and through his indefatigable labors and noble exertions a brick building, seventy by fifty-five feet, capable of seating 600 persons, was erected in the southwest part of the town, on lots Nos. 6 and 7 on First Street. It is the same building which is now used by the Messrs. Hayes & Co. for a coach and carriage factory. Lot No. 6 was purchased from Andrew Swearingen, executor of Van Swearingen, deceased, for $20, and No. 7 from Samuel Wherry for five pounds—the titles of these lots being vested in Joseph Wherry, John Simonson, Parker Campbell, Hugh Wilson, and Daniel Moore, trustees of the congregation. The cost of its erection was $3000, although for several years it was used with unplastered walls, without pulpit and pews, and a permanent floor, the necessary funds being wanted to complete it. The Lord's Supper was first administered in it in June, 1807, and it was occupied as a house of worship for the last time September 7, 1851, when the Rev. James I. Brownson preached a sermon, Psalm xlviii. 9: "We have thought of thy loving kindness, O God, in the midst of thy temple."

This history of this church edifice, from its erection to 1851, embraces the history of all the regularly settled ministers of the Presbyterian church of Washington.

1. Rev. Dr. Matthew Brown was its first pastor from its erection until April 15, 1823, a period of about eighteen years, when he resigned in order to accept the Presidency of Jefferson College. During his ministry, or from 1806 to 1816, he was the first President of Washington College.

The members of session inducted at different times during Dr. Brown's pastorate were James Brice, Josiah Scott, William Sherrard, Hugh Wylie, Thomas Stockton, Thomas Officer, Robert Johnston, Thomas Fergus, Obadiah Jennings, James Orr, and Dr. John Wishart.

2. His successor was the Rev. Obadiah Jennings (formerly one of Dr. Brown's elders), who had been a distinguished lawyer and also pastor of the First Presbyterian Church of Steubenville, Ohio. He was elected its pastor and his election approved by Presbytery on the 8th of October, 1823, and installed on the 23d of the same month. In 1828 he resigned and accepted a call from the Presbyterian church of Nashville, Tennessee, and died in 1832.

During his incumbency Charles Hawkins, Robert Colmery, Jacob Slagle, Robert Officer, Adam Wier, and Alexander Ramsey were added to the session.

In 1824, this church was transferred to the Presbytery of Washington (which, however, was formed October 18, 1819), having been included heretofore in the Presbytery of Ohio.

3. The Rev. Samuel C. Jennings (nephew of Rev. Obadiah Jennings), filled the pulpit as a stated supply for one year.

4. In the summer of 1829 a call was tendered to Rev. David Elliott, of Mercersburg, Pennsylvania, which he accepted, and was installed in the fall of 1829. He served until 1836, when he was elected to the chair of Theology in the Western Theological Seminary.

During Rev. Dr. David Elliott's pastorate, Hugh Fergus and Samuel Vance were made ruling elders.

5. In November, 1837, Rev. Daniel Deruelle entered upon the duties of pastor, and labored until October, 1840, when he resigned and accepted an agency in the General Assembly's Board of Missions. He died in 1858.

6. Rev. James Smith, of Scotland, succeeded Rev. D. Deruelle, in December, 1840, and continued its pastor until April, 1844, when ill health compelled him to resign. He returned to his native country and died March 12, 1845, leaving in the hearts of his people in Washington the inheritance of his labors, the result of his devotion to their eternal interests, looking forward to that period and to that eternal city, when and where he would present them faultless at his Father's throne.

7. In the fall of 1845, Rev. William C. Anderson, D. D., accepted a call from this church, and although not installed, he preached until January 9, 1846, when he removed to Dayton, Ohio, and is at present laboring in New Albany, Indiana.

8. In 1847, Rev. John B. Pinney was elected pastor and served until April, 1848, when he resigned to accept the agency of the New York State Colonization Society.

During his pastorate George Baird, James Boon, Joseph Henderson, and Dr. Robert R. Reed were set apart as elders, and Isaac Hewitt, John Wilson, John K. Wilson, and John Grayson, Jr., as deacons.

It is proper to remark at this place, that the reverend and venerable Dr. David M'Conaughy having accepted the Presidency of Washington College, in May, 1832, the pulpit was chiefly occupied by him as a supply when there was no regular pastor.

9. On the 1st of January, 1849, the Rev. James Irwin Brownson was installed pastor of the church, since which time he has been officiating at its altar, offering prayers and thanksgivings to God for his loving kindness and tender mercies to his flock over which the Holy Ghost has made him overseer.

On the 5th of August, 1855, Isaac Hewitt, James Ewing, and Dr. John Wilson Wishart were ordained elders, and on the 12th of the same month, H. H. Clark, John Wiley, and James C. Acheson were ordained deacons.

On the 16th of January, 1859, John Wiley, H. H. Clark, and Dr. Thomas McKennan were set apart as ruling elders, and Jackson Spriggs and David P. Lowary as deacons.

On the 12th day of June, 1864, Thomas McKean, Edward G. Cundall, Jr., James C. Acheson, and John Hoon (who had previously been an elder in the Presbyterian church at Claysville), were installed elders, and Samuel Beatty, William Praull, and M. Wilson McClain as deacons.

January 19, 1868, John B. Miller was installed a deacon.

December 19, 1869, William Davis, Sr., M. Wilson McClain, and William Praull were ordained elders, and William Davis, Jr., and Geo. W. McCombs installed deacons.

The *second* house of worship was erected on the corner of Second and Belle streets, on lots No. 43 and 42, the former of which was given by the proprietor of the town, David Hoge, to General Washington, while the opposite corner (lot 102) was presented to Mrs. Martha Washington. This building was ninety feet long and sixty-five feet wide, and, including the gallery, would contain from eight hundred to one thousand persons. It was dedicated to the Triune God, September 11, 1851. The dedicatory sermon was preached by Rev. Dr. James I. Brownson, the pastor, from 1 Kings viii. 27–30. He was assisted in the exercises by Rev. Elisha P. Swift, D.D., of Allegheny City, Rev. Dr. D. McConaughy, and Rev. James Clark, D.D., President of Washington College. The church contained one hundred and fifty-four pews, besides a gallery. The basement contained a lecture-room and Sabbath school-room. The whole building, including the purchase of the lot, cost $12,000.

We come now to speak of the *third* house of worship. Early in the spring of 1868 the congregation determined to make certain improvements to the church, which, according to the estimates of Messrs. Barr & Moser, architects, of Pittsburg, would cost about $8000. In removing the roof it was found that it would be necessary to take down the walls to the foundation. The basement, after examination, was decided to be most solid and enduring, and upon it the trustees resolved to erect the present beautiful superstructure, which is unsurpassed for architectural beauty and symmetry by any church, and is an ornament to the place. The carpenter work was awarded to Mr. Nelson Vankirk, the stonework to Mr. Hargraves, the brickwork to James Houston and John Dye.

Being built upon the foundation of the second church, it is ninety by sixty-five feet, with proportionate height of ceiling. The walls and ceiling are beautifully frescoed. The pews, pulpit, and woodwork are in imitation of walnut; the windows of stained glass; the spire rises in height 143 feet; the building is covered with slate; the tower contains a bell costing $500, upon which are the words "Holiness to the Lord." The cost of the building, or rather the present improvements, are $20,600. The lots could not be purchased and a similar building erected for less than $40,000. The church is lighted by a chandelier with eighteen burners, and forty-two additional lights. Each pew is provided with a cushion and carpeted, the cost of furnishing the church was $1800; while the matting for the Sabbath school-room cost $220.

This *third* edifice was dedicated on March 27, 1869, with the following exercises :—

A portion of Scripture was read and prayer offered by Rev. J. R. Johnson, of the U. P. Church; a sermon from Psalm xcii. 13, and an historical address by the pastor, Rev. James I. Brownson, D.D.; prayer by Rev. Mr. Caldwell, of Second Presbyterian Church. It was thus dedicated and set apart for the worship and service of the Triune God, WITHOUT ANY DEBT RESTING UPON IT. An offering thus made cannot but receive the approval, acceptance, and blessing of the Redeemer of the world.

THE SABBATH SCHOOL

Of the First Presbyterian Church was organized June 15, 1816, although a general Sabbath school for all denominations was opened

February 11, 1814, a meeting of the citizens having been called to take the preliminary measures. The meetings of this general Sabbath school, however, were held in the Presbyterian church.

The persons who have filled the office of superintendent were William C. Blair, James Williamson, Charles Hawkins, Peter De-Haven, George Baird, John W. Scott, Abner Leonard, G. Holmes Agnew, William McCombs, John McClintock, Henry Williams, Dr. Robert R. Reed, who filled the office for twenty-six years, and James C. Acheson, many of whom were students of Washington College, and became ministers in the Presbyterian Church.

The school is under the care of one superintendent, J. C. Acheson; one assistant superintendent, Dr. Thomas McKennan; a secretary and treasurer, Thomas McKean; a librarian, A. T. Baird, with two assistants, Alex. Brown and A. M. Todd; having ten male teachers, twenty female teachers, and three hundred and five scholars. The average attendance is 210 upon each Sabbath. The infant school, under the care of Miss Maria McKean and Miss Martha Wiley, contains eighty-six scholars.

Methodist Episcopal Church.

At what precise date the Methodist Episcopal denomination was established in Washington, the records of the church do not state, but the memory of some of our oldest inhabitants informs us that itinerant Methodist preachers occasionally preached in the court-house and school-houses about 1798. It is worthy of remark here with regard to the origin of Methodism in this place, that about this period, Robert Hazlett and his wife (the parents of our esteemed fellow citizen, Samuel Hazlett, now deceased), left Carlisle to settle in Washington. As they were descending Gallows Hill, the old road from Fort Redstone leading to Washington, the husband remarked to his wife, that as they were about to make new acquaintances, he hoped she would avoid those of the Methodist persuasion. She in a truly Christian spirit replied, that with the blessing of God she would seek them out and adhere to them through evil and through good report. Her subsequent Christian life, her devotion to the church of her choice, and the undying influence she has left to Methodism and her family, is the best evidence of her change of heart and acceptance with her Redeemer. She died in 1844, and has ever been recognized as the principal agent in introducing and fostering Methodism. The first official meetings took place about the year 1800, as the deed of property is the official evidence on this subject.

As early as February 5, 1801, John Hoge and wife conveyed to Thomas Lackey, Abraham Carier, Abraham Johnston, Titus Rigby, and John Cooper, trustees of the Methodist Episcopal church, for and in consideration of the sum of ten dollars, lot No. 194. This lot was on the corner of Chestnut and First streets, and now owned by Parker Thompson. Mr. Hoge, in his deed to the trustees, binds them to erect a church for the use of the members of the Methodist

Episcopal church, according to the rules and discipline of said church as adopted by the ministers and preachers at their general conference, and in further trust that they shall at all times forever hereafter permit such ministers and preachers of the said M. E. church and *none others*, to preach and expound God's holy word therein. He also provided in the same deed, that if any of the trustees advanced money for the use of said church, the sum shall be raised by mortgage or by selling the property, after giving notice to the pastor in charge, the surplus to be at the disposal of the next yearly conference.

We have ascertained by our venerable friend, John Harter, Esq., whose whole lifetime has been devoted to Methodism, that Mr. Hoge in making out his deed, conveyed lot No. 124, instead of lot 193, and that after the log church was erected on lot 193, the deed was changed by the following act of the legislature. On the 5th of January, 1811, the legislature authorized the trustees of the Methodist Episcopal church to convey the right of the said church in lot No. 194, in consideration of lot No. 193, to be conveyed by said Hoge for the use of the church. Accordingly we find that John Hoge and wife, on the 11th of January, 1812, did convey to James Chambers, Thomas Lackey, Abraham Johnston, James Shannon, and Israel Brown, lot No. 193, bounded by Chestnut Street on the north, lot 192 on the east, Pine Alley on the south, and First Street on the west, for and in consideration of one dollar, and under the same restrictions as lot No. 194 on the opposite corner was held.

The congregation erected upon lot 193, a log church (long since weather boarded), which yet stands upon the corner and is occupied as a dwelling ; the trustees after the erection of the brick church having made the change.

The log church being to small for the growing congregation, they erected in the year 1816, a substantial brick building, fifty-five by forty feet in the centre of the same lot, fronting First Street, with a gallery round the same, at an expense of six thousand dollars, the brickwork having been done by Wm. Richardson, and the carpenter work by James Orr and John Wilson. After this church had been occupied for thirty-one years, the interest of the church and the increase of population, demanded that a more appropriate house and one better arranged with Sabbath-school and class-rooms should be erected. Accordingly on November 22d, 1847, the congregation appointed a committee to procure subscriptions and select a suitable location. On the following 6th of December, the Committee reported that they had purchased lot 85 from Mrs. Abbot for $400, and exchanged the parsonage property on Beau Street, with John R. Griffith, for lot No. 84, adjoining the former lot, making a front of 120 feet by 240 feet deep. These lots are on Belle Street (formerly Wheeling Street), east of Main.

The Committee estimated the cost of the church at $3864, of which over $2000 were subscribed.

On December 8, 1847, the trustees resolved that when the subscriptions should reach $2800, and with the proceeds of the sale of the brick church (then occupied) they could erect both the church and a parsonage. A building committee, consisting of Rev. Edward Birkett, John Harter, Samuel Hazlett, Samuel Mounts, Alexander Sweeny, and George Lonkert, were appointed to receive proposals for a church edifice, to be fifty feet wide and seventy feet long, with a basement appropriately divided, and J. W. F. White was appointed treasurer of the building funds. Subsequently, however, Samuel Hazlett, Esq., and John Harter resigned, and J. S. Sheaffer was added to the Committee. After the sale of the old church property to the school directors, on April 1, 1848, at which time possession was given, the Building Committee awarded the contracts as follows: The bricklaying and furnishing all the materials to Absalom Huston, for $1628.25, and the foundation at $1.50 per perch, and the range work at 40 cents per foot; the carpenter work and painting to Messrs. Kuhn and Davis, for $2205; the plastering to William Wiley & Son, for $360; the aggregate amounting to $4825.65, including the purchase of the $400 lot.

The trustees also awarded the following contracts for the erection of the parsonage: The carpenter and brickwork to Messrs. Prigg and Dye, for $1067.50, and the plastering to William Wiley & Son, for $100, amounting to $1167.50, to which must be added $55.75 for additional work, making the aggregate amount $1223.25. The church was finished on December 31, 1848 (being fifty by seventy feet and containing seventy-two pews), and was dedicated to God by Rev. Bishop Hamlin. The entire cost of church and parsonage, including purchase and exchange of lots, furnishing church, making stone wall, fence, and pavement, amounted to $7845.78, of which amount the Ladies' Sewing Society furnished $400.

On the 18th of May, 1848, an act of incorporation was procured from the court, constituting Samuel Hazlett, Alexander Sweeny, John Harter, John Sheaffer, Joseph Reynolds, William Wiley, A. B. Wolf, George Lonkert, and Samuel Mounts, as trustees. Upon the organization of the trustees, Samuel Hazlett was elected President and Samuel Mounts Secretary.

It is worthy of remark that during the erection of the church edifice, and through the kindness of the pastor and members of the Cumberland Presbyterian church, the Methodists occupied their meeting-house one-half the time each Sabbath, until the church was finished.

We shall now proceed to give the list of ministers who have officiated in the Methodist Episcopal church since the year 1801, with their respective dates:—

1801. Rev. William Munroe.
1802. " Archibald McElroy and Rev. William Lambden.
1803. Rev. John Monroe.
1804. " Jacob Dowal and Daniel Hitt.
1805. Rev. Jacob Young.
1806. Rev. Thornton Fleming.
1807. " Daniel Hite.
1808. " James Reiley.
1809. " Wm. Brandeberry.
1810. " John White.
1811. " Jacob Gruber.
1812. " Amos Barnes.

1813. Rev. John West.
1814. " William Barnes.
1815. " John Connelly.
1816. " James Laws.
1817. " Joshua Monroe.
1818. " Thornton Fleming.
1819. " George Brown.
1820. " John Baer.
1821. " George Brown.
1822-3. Rev. Henry Furlong.
1824. Rev. Charles Cooke.
1825. " Jos. G. Sansom.
1826-7. Rev. Asa Shinn.
1828. Rev. Alfred Brunson.
1829. " Daniel Limerick.
1830-1. Rev. John Waterman.
1832. Rev. Daniel Limerick.
1833. " J. G. Sansom.
1834-5. Rev. Wesley Kenney
1836-7. " Robert Boyd.
1838. Rev. James Mills.
1839-40. Rev. George S. Holmes.
1841-2. Rev. S. R. Brockunier.
1842-3. " Charles Thorn.
1844-5. " Charles Cook.
1846. Rev. Thomas Hudson.
1847-8. Rev. Edward Birkett.
1849-50. Rev. Wesley Kenney.
1851-2. Rev. Franklin Moore.
1853. Rev. James Henderson.
1854. " Edward Birkett.
1855-6. Rev. Charles A. Holmes.
1857-8. " A. G Williams.
1859-60. Rev. William Cox.
1861-2. Rev. Hiram Sinsabaugh.
1863-4. " Hiram Miller.
1865-6. " J. S. Bracken.
1866. Rev. Hiram Sinsabaugh.
1867. " W. B. Watkins.
1868-70. Rev. W. A. Davidson, D.D.

In August, 1809, Rev. Dr. Kendree, bishop of the church, and Rev. Francis Asbury, preached in Washington. In 1818 Washington was set apart as a new district, Rev. Asa Shinn being appointed presiding elder, and Rev. Thornton Fleming minister in charge.

Sabbath School.

In connection with the M. E. church is a Sabbath school, under the efficient management of V. Harding, Esq., as Superintendent, assisted by W. J. Wilson, as Assistant Superintendent, with Samuel Hazlett, Treasurer, Joseph M. Spriggs as Secretary, and J. Nick Hainer, Wm. Underwood, A. H. Litle, and John Seaman, as Librarians. The school was organized March 1, 1825. Engaged in the benevolent work of imparting Christian instruction to the youth of the church, are nine males and fifteen females, together with two additional females teaching the infant school, numbering twenty-six teachers, with three hundred and thirty scholars.

In 1831, when John Harter, Esq., was Superintendent of the Sabbath school, he organized the Missionary Sabbath school by the scholars pledging to pay one cent monthly for this purpose. At the end of the year it amounted to $7.87; at the present time the sum contributed amounts to near $300.

United Presbyterian Church.

The history of this church may be dated to the 27th day of November, 1815, when the first meeting was held. An adjourned meeting of the *Seceder* body, friendly to the erection of a house of public worship, was subsequently held at the house of Major James Dunlap, on December 22, 1815, to make the necessary arrangements. At this meeting the following persons were elected but not ordained elders, viz : Samuel Fergus, William Wylie, and John McClelland. These things transpired when under the control of the *Seceders*, but no house of worship was erected, nor congregation definitely established because Samuel Fergus had become a prominent member of an organization styled the *Associate Reformed Church*.

This body purchased lot No. 64, originally owned by Col. D. Williamson, on Belle Street, and erected thereon a brick church, but not having funds to finish the church it was sold by the sheriff to the *Associate* Church, who purchased and finished it. Its *first* minister was Rev. David Carson, who was elected Professor of Hebrew and Church History in the Theological Seminary of the Associate Presbyterian Church, located at Canonsburg, which had received a charter from the legislature, April 8, 1833. He preached occasionally in Washington, but was elected pastor of the church on July 1, 1834, and died September 25, 1834. His successor was the Rev. Thomas Beveridge, D.D., who officiated from February 2, 1836, to September 16, 1849, when he resigned, he being a professor in the Theological Seminary, and its transfer to Ohio occasioned his resignation. The church called Rev. Thomas Hanna, D.D., November 16, 1849, which he filled to his death, October 1, 1862. His successor, the present pastor, is the Rev. J. Rankin Johnston, elected March 18, 1863. During the pastorate of Rev. Dr. Hanna, or in the year 1858, the Seceders (or Associates) and the Union (or Associate Reformed bodies) united as the *United Presbyterian Church*, and in 1863, five years after the union, its General Assembly consisted of seven synods, fifty-four presbyteries, four hundred and sixty-two ministers, six hundred and seventy-one congregations, fifty-seven thousand five hundred and fourteen communicants, and three theological seminaries.

Through the influence of Rev. J. Rankin Johnston and the zeal of the members, the United Presbyterian Church erected a new and beautiful church on Belle Street near Main Street, on lot No. 55, originally owned by Samuel Clark. It is built of brick, sixty by eighty feet, with a gallery, and contains one hundred and eight pews. It has in addition to the audience room (which is twenty feet high, an arched ceiling of a six feet raise) a basement story of twelve feet, containing a lecture and Sabbath school room. The walls of the church are frescoed. The cost of the church was $22,500.

The *Eldership* of the church consists of William Gabby, Sample Sweeny, John G. Clark, Dr. M. H. Clark, and Joseph McNary.

The *Trustees* are John E. Bell, Lewis Barker, J. P. Fergus, A. W. Pollock, Ebenezer Rodgers, and James Leiper.

SABBATH SCHOOL.

This church has a Sabbath school, organized in 1850, with six male and twelve female teachers, and one hundred and twenty scholars, with a library of seven hundred and twenty volumes.

Methodist Protestant Church.

When this denomination was organized in 1833, its meetings were held in the court-house until 1836, when the church removed into its own edifice erected on Beau Street, on lot No. 123, now owned by R. Boyd, Esq. The edifice was built of brick, thirty-five by forty-five feet, with a basement story for class and Sabbath school; the trustees being James L. Porter, Wm. S. Hutchinson, Wm. Hunter, S. B. Robinson, and Charles E. Jones. The lot was the bequest of William Hunter, deceased, who in his will, dated April 23d, 1839, said: "It is my desire that my executors make a deed to the trustees of the Methodist Reformed Church for a part of the lot on which their church is built, sixty by ninety feet. It is however distinctly understood, that on the completion of the above title I am to be clear from all responsibilities, either in a private capacity or a trustee of said society."

On April 20th, 1841, Robert Officer, executor of William Hunter, dec'd, executed a deed to Charles E. Jones, John R. Griffith, William Bushfield, W. S. Hutchinson, and James L. Porter, trustees of said church. The church was incorporated January 5th, 1850—its trustees being James L. Porter, John R. Griffith, Peter Kennedy, Simon Wolf, and David Schultz. The church was destroyed by fire in 1851, and on November 19th of the same year, the trustees, consisting of John R. Griffith, I. D. Seaton, James T. Dagg, Peter Kennedy, and Simon Wolf sold and conveyed the lot to George W. Brice, Esq.

The second church edifice was also erected on Beau Street and nearly opposite the former, on lot No. 148. It was commenced November 1st, 1851, under the supervision of the following trustees, (one of the original trustees having resigned): John R. Griffith, I. D. Seaton, James T. Dagg, Peter Kennedy, and A. B. Houston. James T. Dagg was appointed general superintendent. The building is of brick, forty-eight by sixty-eight feet, having sixty-seven pews with a basement divided into class-rooms and for Sabbath-school purposes. The cost of the lot and building was $7200, and on its completion was dedicated to Almighty God in 1853, by the name of "Avery Chapel." It was named after that distinguished philanthropist and eminent Christian, Charles Avery, who by deeds and words assisted in its erection, and a marble slab bearing his name is placed in the front wall of the church by direction of a resolution of the board of trustees, adopted June 27th, 1852.

The following persons have officiated as pastors of this church since its organization in 1833:—

1833.	Rev.	W. Russell.	1840.	Rev.	Nelson Burgess.
1835.	"	Enos Woodward.	1842.	"	J. B. Roberts.
1836.	"	John Burns.	1843.	"	John Cowell.
1837.	"	J. Woodruff.	1844.	"	James Robinson.
1838.	"	James Porter.	1845.	"	Samuel Clawson.
1839.	"	W. Hughes.	1847.	"	J. C. Hazlett.

1848. Rev. G. B. M'Elroy.
1850. " F. A. Davis.
1852. " Val. Lucas.
1853. " Noble Gillespie.
1854. " S. J. Dorsey.
1855. " John Scott.
1857. " W. H. Phipps.
1859. " J. D. Herr.
1860. Rev. W. M. Smith.
1862. " W. Wallace.
1863. " Henry Palmer.
1865. " D. I. K. Rine.
1867. " J. D. Herr.
1868. " W. Griffiths.
1869. " A. S. Woods.
1870. No settled pastor.

This church has a Sabbath school under the care of Peter Kennedy, with 4 male and 5 female teachers and 55 scholars.

TRINITY EPISCOPAL CHURCH.

Before entering upon the immediate history of this church it would be proper to remark that the beautiful and impressive ceremonials of the Episcopal Church had been performed in Washington as early as 1810. From my notes I find there was a meeting of the Protestant Episcopal clergymen in that year, and among other resolutions they passed the following resolution :—

Resolved. That the Rev. Dr. Joseph Dodridge open a correspondence with the Right Reverend Bishop White, of Pennsylvania, for the purpose of obtaining through him permission from the General Convention of the Protestant Episcopal Church to form a diocese in the western country, embracing the western counties of Pennsylvania, Western Virginia, and the State of Ohio, to elect a Bishop.

In 1812 Rev. Wm. David, of Somerset, Pennsylvania, preached occasionally in a school-house near the site of the Baptist Church, on Belle Street.

Time rolls by and several families settled in Washington, who brought with them the religious principles of their choice, and in which they had been educated. They were not numerous enough to establish a church, and although they united with other Christian associations, yet the germ was planted in early life, and they looked forward to the period when it would both bud and blossom like Aaron's rod.

In 1843 the Rev. Enos Woodward, of Brownsville, sent word to the Episcopalians that he would occasionally preach to them if a suitable place could be obtained. The college chapel was had through Professor R. H. Lee, and the fourth Sunday of each month the services of this church were performed by Rev. E. Woodward. On November 12th, 1843, he, with the assistance of Rev. Mr. Dyer, of Pittsburg, administered the Lord's Supper to their communicants, the first time which this rite had ever been given according to the ceremonies of the Protestant Episcopal Church in this place as far as we can ascertain.

While these few Episcopalians were thus meeting time and again, they were visited by Rev. K. J. Stewart, of Connellsville (who preached both in the court-house and Cumberland Presbyterian church), who advised the erection of a church, and also the propriety of the members holding a prayer-meeting, asking God to direct them in such measures as would secure a house in which their principles would be taught, and in accordance with God's holy word. They met at the house of Professor Lee, and after earnest and importunate prayer, so strong was their faith that before the services were ended, a committee consisting of Mrs. F. A. Barlow, Prof. R. H. Lee, R. P. Lane, M. D., and James R. Shannon were appointed a committee to solicit subscriptions, while the Rev. Stewart promised that he would bring the subject before a special convention which was shortly to assemble at Uniontown, and also the Bishop. The effect of that prayer-meeting was the erection of the church, of which we shall now give a full account.

On April 22d, 1844, a meeting of the congregation was held to effect a permanent organization. Rev. Enos Woodward was called to the chair, and Prof. R. H. Lee was appointed Secretary. After a mutual exchange of sentiments the meeting resolved that it was expedient to organize a Protestant Episcopal Church in Washington, and the following persons associated themselves together under the name, style, and title of the "Parish of Trinity Church," viz: Richard Henry Lee, Joseph Grey, Curtis P. Brown, Abigail M. Brown, Mary C. Brown, Seth T. Hurd, Daniel Brown, William Howe, Hugh H. Reynolds, R. P. Lane, Anna E. Lee, Eliza H. Hill, Francis H. Lee, Eliza M. Crafts, Letitia Poole, James R. Shannon, John Bulling, R. Foster, Samuel Potter, Harriet Bulling, F. Anika Barlow, Rebecca Burton, Harriet Burton, Flora Lee, J. Bowman Sweitzer, James M'Corkle, Leslie Carrons.

The church being thus organized, they elected R. H. Lee, R. P. Lane, Leslie Carrons, Joseph Gray, Wm. Howe, James R. Shannon, and Hugh H. Reynolds as the vestry, and the Rev. Enos Woodward as the pastor, to which he consented.

On the 13th May, 1844, the church procured an act of incorporation from the court.

Rev. E. Woodward officiated as the rector of the church from its organization until May, 1845, when he resigned, and was succeeded by Rev. E. J. Messenger, who preached until the following August, when he tendered his resignation to become a missionary, went to Africa, and died March 28, 1846. From their organization to August, 1845, the church occupied the college hall; but after this period they removed to the Lutheran church. The pulpit was filled by supplies and Prof. Lee as a lay reader, from 1845 to 1850. In June, 1850, the congregation resolved to build a church, and for this purpose they purchased lot No. 160 on the east end of Beau Street, and directly opposite the college edifice, from David Shields, for four hundred dollars. William McKennan and James R. Shannon, Esqs., were appointed the Building Committee, with full power to act. They awarded the carpenter work to Frederick Hayes, the mason work to Messrs. William Cline and A. B. Houston. It was opened for divine worship December 15, 1850, when a sermon was preached from Genesis, chapter xxviii. verse 17, by Rev. Samuel Clements, who had become the rector, and took charge of the church on December 1, 1850. The cost of this church edifice was $2725 15, including the price of the lot. The furniture of the church was presented by several donors; the carpets by Trinity Church, of Pittsburg, the chancel furniture by Christ Church, of Brownsville, the lamps by the Female Episcopal School of Philadelphia, and the chairs by St. Andrew's Church, of Philadelphia.

The entire indebtedness of the church edifice being liquidated, the Rt. Rev. Bishop Alonzo Potter consecrated the church on September 10, 1854. March 31, 1855, the Rev. Samuel Clements resigned, and Prof. R. H. Lee was elected a lay reader, to officiate as such according to the forms and canons of the church. In January, 1856, Rev. George Hall accepted the rectorship of the church, having been previously elected, and served until December, 1856, when he resigned, and Prof. R. H. Lee was again elected lay reader.

In February, 1858, Prof. R. H. Lee was ordained a deacon by Rt. Rev. Bishop Potter, and in the following October was ordained a priest by Rev. Bishop Bowman, Assistant Bishop, and took charge of Trinity Church as its rector. Rev. R. H. Lee served the church as a faithful and consistent ambassador of Christ until January 3, 1865, when he exchanged the church militant for the church triumphant.

The devoted friends of Rev. Dr. Lee have placed in a niche in the west wall of the chancel of the church, a beautiful marble tablet, containing the following appropriate and touching inscription to his memory:—

In memory of Rev. Richard Henry Lee, LL. D., Rector of this Parish from A. D. 1858 to A. D. 1865. Born in Fairfax County, Virginia, A. D. 1794. He received a classical education at Dickinson College, Pennsylvania, and graduated with high honors at an early age. Devoting himself to the legal profession, he practised in the courts of his native State until the year 1834, when he accepted the Professorship of Ancient Languages in Washington College, Pennsylvania, a position which he exchanged in 1837 for the chair of Belles Lettres and Political Economy in the same institution. In 1854 he resigned his connection with the college, and was shortly afterwards commissioned Lay Reader by the Bishop of Pennsylvania. He was ordained Deacon, February 10, 1858, and became Rector of this Parish, which owes to him, under God, its origin and organization. On Sunday, October 31, 1858, he was ordained Priest. He labored in his holy office faithfully and lovingly until the close of his life.

He died January 3, 1865, aged 71 years, and was gathered unto his fathers, having the testimony of a good conscience, in the communion of the Catholic Church, in the comfort of a reasonable religious and holy hope, in favor with God, and in perfect charity with the world.

It is proper to remark that during the rectorship of Rev. Dr. Lee, the church edifice had been found so defective that it became necessary to erect another, more durable and more commodious. In consequence thereof the congregation, with commendable zeal, erected the present beautiful Gothic church, at an expense of $3697 20, which is now estimated worth $10,000, which was consecrated by Bishop Potter November 17, 1863. During the time of its erection church services were held in the court-house.

The successor of Rev. Dr. Lee was James McIlvaine, who was commissioned lay reader until Rev. James A. Brown became the rector, December 22, 1865, and served until December 23, 1867, when he resigned, to enter upon a larger field of labor. His successor was Jacob B. McKennan, Esq., who was commissioned as lay reader by the Bishop on January 1, 1868.

The present vestry of the church consists of Wm. McKennan, Wm. W. Smith, James McIlvaine, Jacob B. McKennan, Jr., Wm. B. McKennan, H. H. Reynolds, Hugh Q. Miller, and Samuel Hargraves.

On October 17, 1869, Rev. J. K. Mendenhall preached his first sermon in Trinity church, and was ordained November 5, 1869, Rector of the parish, by Rt. Rev. Bishop J. D. Kerfoot, Bishop of the diocese. The church purchased a bell weighing 2040 pounds; the tenor bell of a peal of bells, which was placed in its proper position in the bell-tower, between the church and parish school-house, and first rung January 16, 1870.

Sunday School.

On June 9, 1844, a Sunday school was established, with Professor Lee as its superintendent, having four male and five female teachers. This school has an excellent library.

Parish School-house.

The congregation resolved, on August 29, 1868, to erect a parish school-house on the church property in the rear of the church. This praiseworthy object, through the liberality of its members, was completed, February 27, 1869, at an expense of nine hundred and twenty-three dollars and sixty-six cents.

Bequest to Trinity Church.

On the 11th of May, 1865, Wm. L. Bowman, son of James Bowman, Esq., of Brownsville, died in the 26th year of his age. When a student of law in Washington, he became a communicant in this church; and so greatly attached was he to the church in which he devoted his life, his heart, his all to his Redeemer, that he manifested his love for it by providing in his will that his executors should pay the legal representatives of the church two thousand dollars, the interest of which should be annually applied to the rector's salary, and the principal invested for this purpose.

German Church.

The German Evangelical Lutheran and Reformed church is bounded by Walnut Street on the north; lot No. 262 on the east; Spruce Alley on the south, and lot No. 265 on the west; the church owning lots Nos. 263 and 264, upon which is a frame meeting-house and attached thereto is a burial-ground. These lots were sold by John and William Hoge to Thomas Woodward August 29, 1786, and conveyed by him to Peter Snyder September 12, 1787. On May 5, 1812, P. Snyder and wife sold to Jacob Weirich, Lewis Hewitt, David Sedicker, and Christian Hornish, trustees and managers of the German Lutheran and Presbyterian Church.

On October 13, 1840, they procured an act of incorporation from the court, authorizing the election of nine trustees, and incorporated as the German Evangelical Lutheran Church.

We shall give the respective ministers of the church as far as we have been able to ascertain them; although the records of the church are very unsatisfactory, we must depend alone upon oral testimony.

The first minister was the Rev. Mr. Monesmith; his successor was the Rev. Henry Weygandt, who officiated for sixteen years. In 1832, Rev. Abraham Winters, of the United Brethren, filled the pulpit; his successor was Rev. John Brown, a Lutheran; after him was Rev. Charles Swissler, a Reformed German preacher. He was succeeded by Rev. Mr. Doubert; his successor Rev. Mr. Beckerman, a Lutheran. Then followed the Rev. H. B. Miller, from 1830 until March 14, 1836, when Rev. Abraham Weills occupied the pulpit for eighteen years, or until 1854. His successors were Rev. C. G. Fredericks, Rev. T. Hartley, Rev. P. Sweigert, and Rev. Z. H. Gable.

This church has lately been refitted, and although the people have been scattered, our German population are uniting in the noble effort of resuscitating the waste places of this branch of Zion, so that the church of their fathers may again take its place among those of our ancient borough, dispensing evangelical truths.

SECOND PRESBYTERIAN CHURCH.

On the 9th day of December, 1860, a meeting of the First Presbyterian Congregation of Washington was held in the church to consider the necessity of enlarged church accommodations, and appointed the following Committee to report at an adjourned meeting on December 27, 1860. The Committee consisted of Collin M. Reed, D. S. Wilson, Thomas McKean, Robert F. Strean, Jackson Spriggs, Dr. J. W. Wishart, J. D. Chambers, and William Hughes. The congregation met at the time appointed to hear the report of the Committee. A majority of the Committee reported that the only feasible plan for increasing church accommodations was another church organization, and suggested the following preamble and resolution :—

Believing it to be our duty to furnish the means of hearing to all who may desire or can be constrained to listen to the preaching of the divine message; that said accommodation is not furnished at our present church, and any increase of sittings is impracticable and inexpedient, and that the size of our congregation justifies the recommendation of the formation of a new congregation as the only effectual remedy in the present exigency, therefore

Resolved, That in the opinion of this congregation the interest of religion would be promoted by the organization of a Second Presbyterian congregation in Washington, and whenever any number of persons will signify their willingness to engage in a new church enterprise, this congregation will lend them all the aid, comfort, and encouragement in its power, and to that end do now appoint a committee to co-operate with them in the accomplishment of this object. The Committee appointed were Collin M. Reed, Thomas McKean, John Grayson, Jr., H. H. Clarke, and W. B. Cundall.

This committee had a conference with the session of the First Presbyterian church on February 2, 1861, for the purpose of fulfiling the above-mentioned wishes of the congregation, and requested the session to designate two or more members of their number who may favor the project, and carry out the desire of the congregation. In view, therefore, of the congregation's action in initiating the movement, a movement prompted by a sincere regard for the interest of religion and the advancement of Presbyterianism in this community, the session unanimously

Resolved, That as the Committee requested the session, if in accordance with their views, to designate two of their number to go off, and the session having learned that the two members desired by the persons favorable to this movement are Dr. John W. Wishart and H. H. Clarke, therefore, if these brethren should feel themselves assured that such is their duty, whilst retaining unabated and unqualified confidence and Christian affection for them as brethren, and also expressing our sorrow at the thought of their separation from our number, yet we cannot withhold our consent, and will follow them with our prayers for the blessing of the Master upon themselves individually, and upon the enterprise with which they are to be connected.

Resolved, That we recommend to the members of the church and congregation, so far as they may severally feel enabled and inclined, to lend this movement all the aid, comfort, and encouragement in their power.

An application was accordingly made to Presbytery on March 12, 1861, for the organization of a Second Presbyterian church, which held a *pro re nata* meeting in the First Presbyterian church, Rev. Dr. John W. Scott being moderator, and Rev. W. B. Keeling clerk.

Dr. John W. Wishart, representing one hundred petitioners, of whom thirty-six were communicants, presented the necessary papers, when, on motion of Rev. James I. Brownson, the prayer of the petitioners was granted.

On motion of Rev. N. B. Lyon, the new organization was styled the Second Presbyterian church.

On motion of Collin M. Reed, the following persons were designated as ruling elders, viz: Dr. J. W. Wishart, H. H. Clarke, Wm. B. Cundall, and John Grayson, Jr.

On motion of H. H. Clarke, David Aiken and Wm. J. Matthews, were elected deacons.

A constitution was adopted and the following gentlemen were elected trustees, viz: Collin M. Reed, Andrew Brady, Norton McGiffin, William Blair, and John Baird.

The Rev. R. V. Dodge, of Wheeling, was unanimously chosen the pastor, and the trustees directed to procure the college hall for the meetings of the congregation, until more satisfactory arrangements could be made.

Notwithstanding all these preliminary movements, the church was not at that time organized, but the members returned to the *first* church, as the following minutes of the church record show. A meeting of the session of the first church was held September 7, 1861, and adopted the following preamble and resolution :—

WHEREAS, On the 12th day of March, 1861, the session dismissed a number of members of this church to be organized into a Presbyterian church; AND WHEREAS, in the present disturbed state of the country and the depressed condition of money matters, there would seem to be no possibility of such organization being carried forward; and whereas, the present church relations of the persons so dismissed are peculiar and embarrassing to all parties, therefore it was unanimously

Resolved, That this session do most cordially invite the persons thus dismissed to renew their former relation to this church, assuring them of a most hearty welcome to our fellowship and to a participation in the cares and responsibilities of private and official membership, as heretofore.

The hindrances being removed, the members generally composing the Second Presbyterian church held a congregational meeting on April 7th, 1864, and unanimously resolved to proceed at once to carry out the object originally contemplated by their organization. A unanimous call was given to Rev. R. V. Dodge, who accepted the same, and on the 15th day of May, 1864, he preached his introductory sermon in Smith's Hall, the present place of worship, but was not installed as pastor until October 4, 1864.

On June 26, 1864, the first communion was administered.

During the pastorate of the Rev. R. V. Dodge, H. H. Clarke, Esq., was installed; and W. B. Cundall and John Grayson, Jr., were ordained elders on June 19, 1864; H. J. Vankirk and Wm. Blair were installed as deacons. April, 1868, Freeman Brady, Jr., and Morgan Hayes were installed as deacons.

Rev. R. V. Dodge resigned his charge May, 1868, and the Rev. J. C. Caldwell was elected June 1, 1868, and installed August 1, 1868.

February 14, 1869, Robert Boyd and Hugh McClelland were installed elders; and Freeman Brady and John B. Vowell were ordained elders.

Rev. J. C. Caldwell officiated as minister until December 28, 1869, when he resigned. On April 12, 1870, Rev. Henry Wood, Professor in Washington and Jefferson College, was elected.

SABBATH SCHOOL

The 2d Presbyterian church has a Sabbath school connected therewith, having an excellent library. It was organized July 17, 1864, by a vote of the congregation, which was held May 23, 1864.

The first officers of the school were John Grayson, Jr., superintendent; H. H. Clarke, assistant-superintendent; John Baird and W. Blair, librarians; H. J. Vankirk, treasurer and secretary. Its present officers are Robert Winters, superintendent; H. H. Clarke, assistant-superintendent; J. B. Vowell, Charles Butts, and James McCollum, librarians; H. J. Vankirk, treasurer; B. McCollum, secretary. The school has ten male and ten female teachers, with 150 scholars. It has also an infant school, under the care of Miss Anastasie Morgan, having upon the roll 82 members.

The Board of Trustees consists of Col. W. Hopkins, Charles Hayes, A. B. Caldwell, A. Winters, and M. G. Koontz.

The number of members connected with the church is two hundred and fourteen.

ROMAN CATHOLIC CHURCH.

The first account we have of preaching by this denomination in Washington was on February 1, 1824, at the house of Matthew Blake, by the Rev. P. Rafferty, although preaching was held previously at Williamsport, now Monongahela City, in this county. After an interval of ten years, or in 1834, the Rt. Rev. Bishop Francis Patrick Kenrick, who had already established a chapel near West Alexander, on the 27th of March, 1825, and to which the members of this church were attached, on account of the distance, made Washington a missionary station, and sent the Rev. S. Mazzuchelli as the first missionary. He preached at the Old Good tavern, the sign of the black horse, south of Catfish Run. The property is now owned by Dr. F. J. Lemoyne. In this house mass was celebrated for the first time in Washington, and also preaching.

This denomination at that time were all German Catholics, except Michael Kaine, deceased (the father of C. C. Kaine, formerly one of the editors of the "*Examiner*"), who was an Irishman. Shortly after this period the congregation was visited by Bishop Kenrick, but the preaching was held in the court-house. In 1836 the bishop made another visit, and confirmed many in the faith of the church— this being the first time the rite was held here. June 21, 1837, Bishop Kenrick preached in the German Lutheran church. In 1835, however, the bishop sent the Rev. Mr. Gallagher to this missionary field, which embraced this place, Waynesburg, and Brownsville. Rev. Gallagher officiated until 1843. His successors were Rev. James Kearney in 1844, Rev. Mr. Duffy in 1845, Rev. Jerome Kearney in 1846, Rev. Mr. Gallagher in 1847, Rev. Dennis Kearney in 1848, Rev. Mr. Reynolds in 1849, Rev. Wm. Lambert in 1850, Rev. Mr. McGowan in 1851, Rev. Daniel Hickey in 1852—who died at West Alexander in 1854—Rev. James Farran in 1854, Rev. Francis Joseph O'Shea in 1855, Rev. Jerome Kearney in 1856, Rev. Francis Joseph O'Shea in 1857, Rev. Dennis Kearney in 1858, Rev. Wm Noland in 1859, Rev. F. J. O'Shea in 1861, Rev. Patrick

Shehan in 1862, Rev. John P. Tenney in 1864, Rev. John Scanlon in 1866, and Rev. Thomas McEnrue in 1868.

In the fall of 1841 a lot was purchased for a chapel on the national pike, nearly opposite the gas-works, where the house of John D. Martin now stands; but, after its purchase, so strong was the opposition to Catholicism that several of the purchasers of the adjoining lots gave the proprietor notice that they would not build upon them if the church was established in that part of the town. The matter was finally adjusted by the Rev. M. Gallagher and Ephraim Blaim, Esq.—the church waiving her interest in the lot.

On the 5th of March, 1842, a lot was bought on the east end of Belle Street from John M. Davis, of Pittsburg (the present site of the chapel), being forty by sixty feet, for sixty dollars. The purchase money was subscribed by the following persons, viz : Anthony Renz $10, Francis Egan $10, William Erret $10, James Rush $10, Michael Metzner $5, Michael Kirchner $10, and Rev. M. Gallagher $10.

Mr. Anthony Renz and Marie Jane his wife presented an adjoining lot of twenty by eighty feet, on March 22, 1842. Both deeds were made to Bishop Kenrick in trust for the church.

The church was commenced in 1843, and finished in 1844. The carpenter-work was performed by Henry B. Roswell and Wm. McIlvaine; the mason-work by James Hamilton, at a cost of twenty-five hundred dollars. Although preaching was held in it, the chapel was not entirely completed and consecrated until 1854, when it was dedicated and consecrated by Rev. Bishop Wheelin.

Bishop Kenrick felt a deep interest in the prosperity of this church, and visited it four times; in addition to the places he preached which we have mentioned, he also preached once in the Lutheran church and once in the court-house.

At the confirmation held in 1836, there were but eight families, consisting of sixteen persons, enrolled themselves under the banner of the church; in 1869 there are forty families, and the church has three hundred members.

It is worthy to remark that Mrs. Carrol, a member of the denomination, died and was buried in the lot, and her grave is beneath the altar of the church.

CUMBERLAND PRESBYTERIAN CHURCH.

Rev. Robert Donnell, Rev. Reuben Burrow, and Rev. Alfred Bryan, regularly ordained ministers of the Cumberland Presbyterian Church, on the 29th of September, 1831, met in the court-house at Washington, and organized the church, by receiving into its communion Abel M. S. Gordon, William Fleming, Charles Andrew, J. Huper, Elizabeth Wiley, Mary Jordan, Ann Jordan, Martha Mahaffey, and Amelia Mahaffey.

On the 30th October, 1831, this church held its second meeting in the Baptist Church, when the Rev. Alfred Bryan was assisted by Rev. John Morgan, and twenty-nine persons were added to the church.

On the 27th of November, its third meeting was held in the courthouse, and ten persons were added. On January 23, 1832, Rev. A. Bryan was assisted by Rev. Milton Bird, and six persons received. February 24, 1832, an election for ruling elders was held. Peter Wolfe, Moses Little, and A. M. S. Gordon were elected and ordained ruling elders. December 25, 1832, John Hewitt and Andrew Bell were elected and ordained elders. 1835, June 14, the church dedicated by Rev. Alfred Bryan. September 21, 1835, James McDowell; March, 1838, James Guttery, Ezekiel Tharp, and William Smith; 1844, Odel Squier; 1851, William Smith, were elected elders.

March 24, 1832, Samuel McFarland, Alex. Ramsey, John Wilson, William Smith, were elected trustees. March 24, 1846, William Smith, Matthew Griffin, Joseph Martin, and Ezekiel Tharp. January 11, 1858, Hugh Munnel, John Guthery, James McElree, and H. B. McCollum.

The first Board of Trustees were authorized to procure a house of worship.

In 1834, Samuel McFarland erected the church edifice on Belle Street, from voluntary contributors and his own private funds, and in 1856, it appears the church was in debt to him $970. The reason given on the records why the church did not prosper, was their failing in their contract on this occasion, and also promising preachers more than they gave them.

The ministers who have been ordained as pastors were Rev. S. M. Aaston, Rev. J. Shook, Rev. J. Eddy, Rev. Milton Bird, Rev. A. T. Reese, Rev. W. E. Post, Rev. S. E. Hudson, Rev. S. Murdock, Rev. P. Axtel, Rev. Robert Martin, Rev. J. C. Thompson, Rev. A. S. Robertson, Rev. Frederick Wall, Rev. John R. Brown, Rev. Weaver, and Rev. John Edmiston.

In 1867, from a variety of causes, the church did not meet, there being no pastor, and the people united with other churches. The building is rented to the Disciple Church.

"DISCIPLES OF CHRIST."

Before giving a history of the different church organizations in this county, we would prefix the following account of this religious denomination:—

In their associated organization they are called the Church of Christ, or the Christian Church, but in their individual religious capacity "Disciples of Christ." As early as 1803 a church was constituted in the Pigeon Creek settlement, under the labors of Rev. Matthias Luce, the Rev. Speers, and others, taking the Holy Scriptures for their rule of faith and practice. The record itself styles this organization "The Gospel Church." This church was afterwards called the Baptist church, the cause of its origin being brought about by Rev. Charles Wheeler, who, in an effort to introduce the creed of that denomination, said, "Those that subscribed to the creed would be known and recognized as the regular Baptist Church of Pigeon Creek, those who would not, as Campbellites."

In 1807, Rev. Thomas Campbell emigrated to the United States (a member of the General Associate Synod of Scotland) and was received by the Presbytery of Chartiers. So zealous was he in the advocacy of the all-sufficiency of the Holy Scriptures designed expressly for the edification and perfection of the Christian church, that he felt it to be his duty to remonstrate against the doctrines and commandments of men in the form of creeds, confessions, and catechisms, arguing therefrom that Protestant denominations had usurped more or less the forms, the teachings, and the preachings of the divinely commissioned apostles. This teaching was opposed by his co-presbyters, and on the 17th of August, 1809, a meeting was held on the head waters of Buffalo, in this county, in which a declaration and address of the Christian Association of Washington was adopted "for the sole purpose of promoting simple evangelical Christianity, free from all mixture of human opinions and inventions of men." In its declaration, this society "by no means considers itself a church, nor does it at all assume to itself the powers peculiar to such a society, nor do the members as such consider themselves as standing connected in that relation, nor us at all associated for the peculiar purposes of church association, but merely as voluntary advocates for church reformation. Notwithstanding these principles as announced in the declaration and address, we find here, on the 4th day of May, 1811, organized a number of those who belonged to the (Buffalo) Christian Association, into a church with no other creed but the Bible.

While upon this subject, we may remark that at a meeting of the Synod of the Presbyterian Church, held October 4, 1810, Rev. Thomas Campbell, formerly a member of the Associate Synod, but representing himself as a member of the *Christian Association of Washington*, applied to be taken into Christian ministerial standing. The records show that Rev. Mr. Campbell was heard at length, but the Synod unanimously resolved that however specious the plan of the Christian Association, and however seducing its professions, as experience of the effects of similar projects in other parts has evinced their baleful tendency and destructive operations on the whole interests of religion by promoting divisions instead of union, by degrading the ministerial character, by providing free admission to any errors in doctrine, and to any corruptions in discipline, whilst a nominal approbation of the Scriptures as the only standard of truth may be professed, the synod are constrained to disapprove the plan and its natural effects. It was also resolved that Rev. Mr. Campbell's request to be received into ministerial and Christian communion cannot be granted. The Synod's disapprobation was not on account of moral character, but on account of his peculiar views, as being inconsistent with the standards of the Presbyterian church.

Afterwards Rev. Thomas Campbell sought to persuade his brethren to a stricter observance of the literal teachings of the New

Testament. Meeting, therefore, with opposition, and being driven to a closer examination of the Scriptures, he continued to impart the light which dawned upon his own mind to his hearers, and following out their own convictions they soon found themselves drifting away, not only from church standard, but from every other organization built upon what they styled a human platform. He found all his proposals to his Presbyterian friends as embodied in the Buffalo declaration and address rejected, and himself and friends cut off from all church privileges, hence they sought a closer union to Christ, by announcing that they believed that the primitive apostolic mode of worship could be attained without the embittered feelings of selfishness engendered by sectarian strife. Consequently, on the 4th of May, 1811, a number of those who had belonged to the Christian association were organized into a church with no other creed but the Bible.

At this meeting Thomas Campbell was appointed elder, his son Alexander was licensed to preach the gospel, and John Dawson, George Sharp, William Gilchrist, and James Foster were chosen deacons.

Upon the basis of the declaration and address, elder Thomas Campbell formed two congregations, one at Cross Roads, six miles northwest of Washington, Penna., and the other on Brush Run, eight miles southwest of the same place.

This denomination has the following churches in Washington County, one in Washington, formerly at Martinsburg, two miles east of the borough, one at Pigeon Creek, one at Maple Creek, one at Peters Creek, one at West Middleton, one at the Dutch Fork, one at Independence, and one at West Findley.

Washington Cumberland Church.

The church in Washington worships regularly in the Cumberland Presbyterian church, having leased the same for this purpose. It was originally organized at the house of Richard B. Chaplin, in Washington, on Thursday evening, the 12th day of May, 1831. The persons present on that occasion were Richard B. Chaplin, Samuel Marshall, Henry Langley, Frederick Huffman, and Franklin Dunham, Mrs. Sophia Chaplin, Jane McDermot, Hannah Acheson, and Hannah Marshall, who, after mature deliberation, formed themselves into a church, having for their rule of faith and practice the Holy Scriptures, and submitting themselves to the teachings of Jesus Christ and the apostles. They also appointed R. B. Chaplin and Samuel Marshall to preside at their meetings for worship and to administer the ordinances.

On May 15, 1831, the church met at R. B. Chaplin's house for the first time, and the brethren and sisters broke the loaf and partook of the wine, in commemoration of the sufferings and death of Christ. Since which time they continued to meet at the house of Samuel Marshall, and the school-house on the farm of Henry Vankirk, Sr., four miles south of Washington, until the fall of 1836, when they removed to the brick meeting house in Williamsburg, where the church continued to meet until June, 1867, when they removed to Washington, to hold their meetings in the Cumberland Presbyterian church.

The ministers who have regularly officiated were Professor Robert Milligan, of Washington College, and Rev. L. P. Streater, when the church was at Williamsburg, but since its removal to Washington, Rev. J. B. Crane took charge of it in 1867, and Rev. T. A. Crenshaw in 1869.

BAPTIST CHURCH.

This church was regularly constituted on October 14, 1814, in Washington, by delegates previously appointed by each of the Baptist churches of Peters Creek, Tenmile, and Uniontown, with such others as should meet as an advisory council. *Peters Creek church* was represented by Rev. David Phillips, Charles Daily, and Joseph Phillips; *Tenmile Creek* by Rev. Matthias Luse; *Uniontown church* by Rev. William Brownfield.

On the 15th of October, 1814, the Rev. Charles Wheeler was ordained to the ministry and received the imposition of hands by Rev. D. Phillips, M. Luce, and W. Brownfield.

This church adopted the covenant and constitution as expressed in the Confession of Faith adopted by the Philadelphia Baptist Association.

On the 25th of March, 1811, the legislature passed an act to confirm the title of the First Baptist church to lot No. 77, on Belle Street, in the town of Washington.

The members of the congregation met at the brick school-house in the rear of the lot, on November 17, 1817, to take into consideration the building of a house of worship, when a subscription paper was opened and a committee appointed to procure subscriptions. February 1, 1819, the subscribers were notified to pay their subscriptions without delay to John Barrington and Hugh Wilson, as the church edifice was finished. This is the plain substantial brick church which stands on the western end of Belle Street.

Rev. Charles Wheeler was pastor of the church from 1814 to 1839. Rev. Mr. Anderson was his successor, and resigned in March, 1842. Rev. C. T. Johnson was elected October 15, 1842, and served until September 9, 1843, when he was succeeded by Rev. J. B. W. Tisdell, who preached until October 2, 1846. His immediate successor was the Rev. Thomas Swain, who resigned September, 1850. Rev. George W. Young took charge of the congregation December 19, 1850, and upon his resignation he was followed by Rev. Malachi Taylor, who was installed December 5, 1855; he resigned and Rev. John Boyd became his successor, April 16, 1858, who preached until January, 1860, when the Rev. William Wood supplied the pulpit until the election of Rev. Robert Telford, on February 18, 1866, but he resigned June 10, 1868, since which time the church has had no regular minister, but is occasionally supplied.

In connection with the Baptist church, we might add that a meeting of the stockholders of the brick school-house erected upon the Baptist church lot was held on the 27th of May, 1816, to establish a Female Baptist Seminary, when a constitution was adopted. The seminary was subsequently opened by Rev. Charles Wheeler, assisted by Miss C. Cairns.

A. M. E. CHURCH

Was organized in the year 1818. Of its history all I could glean were the names of its founders, viz: Benjamin Dorsey, George Bolden, John Clouby, Caleb Eddy, Hark Lives, Margaret Cramer, Hannah Smith, Terry Robinson, Maria Conner, Betsy Phillips, and Chloe Warfield. They have a neat frame church with a Sabbath school connected.

Wright's Chapel (an African church) has a small building near the former, with a Sunday school.

BRANCH BANK OF PHILADELPHIA.
BANK OF WASHINGTON.
FRANKLIN BANK OF WASHINGTON, and
FIRST NATIONAL BANK OF WASHINGTON.

These four institutions have existed in our town, and we shall speak of them separately.

The *Bank of Philadelphia* was chartered March 5, 1804. By additional legislation on March 3, 1809, it was permitted to establish eight branches, provided the people of the place in which it was proposed to be located would sanction it. Washington was selected, and its citizens sanctioned its establishment. Its original charter was limited to 1814, but afterwards extended to May 1, 1824.

They erected a banking-house on the corner of Main Street and Strawberry Alley (now owned by David Aiken, Esq.), which cost $11,700, and sold it when the bank closed to the Bank of Washington. Parker Campbell was President, and John Neale Cashier. It existed from 1810 to 1822.

BANK OF WASHINGTON.

On the 10th of January, 1814, the people of Washington County, in general meeting assembled, considered the expediency of establishing an original bank, with a capital stock of five hundred thousand dollars; shares to be valued at fifty dollars each. The people sanctioned the project, and the grand jury indorsed it in the following words: "We conceive it to be our duty to countenance and encourage all institutions, companies, or associations that have for their end the genuine interests of the county. They conceive the contemplated association called the Bank of Washington, is of that character. They, therefore, earnestly recommend it to the attention of the legislature, and pray that a charter of incorporation be granted to said bank." This indorsement was signed by Daniel Leet, foreman, and eighteen grand jurors. This influence had the desired effect upon the legislature, for we find that they passed a general banking law on the 24th of March, 1814, dividing the State into twenty-seven districts, limiting its charter for eleven years, or until the year 1825.

Thomas H. Baird was elected President, and John Barrington Cashier; the capital stock to be not less than one hundred and fifty thousand dollars, or more than two hundred and twenty thousand. The Directors named to sell stock on May 4, 1814, were Thomas Patterson, David Shields, Thomas McGiffin, Thomas Hoge, Alexander Murdoch, Daniel Moore, and Parker Campbell.

In January, 1818, the Bank of Washington forfeited its charter, but it was afterwards revived, February 2, 1818, the causes having been removed; but on March 23, 1818, it was rechartered under the name of the

Franklin Bank of Washington.

It must be borne in mind that this is not the present institution, of which we shall speak presently. On account of the mismanagement of its finances, and continued lawsuits, it ceased to exist, although the legislature was required from time to time to extend its charter.

Franklin Bank of Washington.

On March 9, 1836, an act was passed incorporating the Franklin Bank of Washington, and appointed as Commissioners Alexander Reed, Daniel Moore, William Hunter, Robert Officer, Thomas McGiffin, F. J. Lemoyne, David Eckert, Jacob Slagle, Henry Langley, John K. Wilson, Thomas McCall, William Brownlee, George Wilson, Samuel Murdoch, Walter Craig, Samuel McFarland, James Stevens, Thomas Morgan, John Cooke, Enoch Wright, William Smith, Joseph Henderson, Alexander Sweeney, Samuel Mount, C. M. Reed, Aaron Fenton, James Ruple, George Black, John Morgan, James Watson, John S. Brady, and T. M. T. McKennan. These Commissioners met, and on April 30th, appointed Robert Officer, David Eckert, and Dr. F. J. Lemoyne to sell eight hundred shares of the capital stock of the Bank, it being limited to five hundred thousand dollars. The amount being sold on May 19, the balance of the stock was disposed of.

September 15, 1836, the stockholders held an election for directors, which resulted in the selection of Alexander Reed, Daniel Moore, Daniel Houston, David Eckert, William Hunter, Samuel Murdoch, Nathan Pusey, William Brownlee, Thomas McCall, Robert Wylie, John S. Brady, Aaron Fenton, and George Wilson.

The directors elected Alexander Reed, President, and John Marshall, Cashier. On account of the decease of Alexander Reed, the directors, on September 22, 1842, elected Daniel Houston, who served as President until December 21, 1843, when T. M. T. McKennan, Esq., was elected. Mr. McKennan having deceased, Collin M. Reed was elected July 29, 1852, and filled the office until the Bank became the First National Bank.

John Marshall continued as Cashier until March 16, 1857, when James McIlvaine, the present incumbent, was elected. On April 20, 1837, Samuel Cunningham was elected Clerk.

FIRST NATIONAL BANK.

The Franklin Bank of Washington was reorganized by the stockholders as the First National Bank of Washington, on January 1, 1865, with C. M. Reed as President, James McIlvaine as Cashier, Samuel Cunningham as Clerk. On May 1, 1865, Andrew S. Ritchie, Esq., was appointed Teller. The capital stock of the Bank is one hundred and fifty thousand dollars, with a surplus fund of seventy thousand dollars. It owns a fine two-story brick banking-house, on Main Street and Bank Alley, valued at four thousand five hundred and sixty-eight dollars. The first Board of Directors of the First National Bank were C. M. Reed, A. W. Acheson, J. S. Brady, M. H. Clark, William Davis, H. H. Clark, John H. Ewing, Joseph Henderson, Thomas McKean, Jacob Slagle, Alexander Seaman, John Stewart, and James Watson.

BANKING HOUSES.

There are two banking houses also in Washington, William Smith and Son, and Samuel Hazlett, both of which are extensively engaged in their legitimate business.

WASHINGTON FEMALE SEMINARY.

The origin of this seminary can be truthfully dated to the 26th November, 1835, when the following citizens met at the house of T. M. T. McKennan, Esq., to take the initiatory movement to organize a female seminary in this borough. The citizens referred to were Rev. David Elliott, John Harter, John Wilson, James Reed, Wm. J. Wilson, William Hunter, Jacob Slagle, Robert Officer, William Smith, David Eckert, John Koontz, and T. M. T. McKennan. Rev. Dr. D. Elliott appointed Chairman, and T. M. T. McKennan, Secretary. Many other citizens were, from business and professional duties, prevented from attending the *first* meeting, but their devotion to the establishment of a female seminary was afterwards evinced by their zeal and perseverance in advancing its interests. Their names are Alexander Reed, Dr. F. J. Lemoyne, Thomas Morgan, Samuel Mount, Samuel McFarland, John Grayson, John H. Ewing, James Brice, John K. Wilson, Dr. James Stevens, Alexander Ramsey, James Ruple, Alex. Sweeney, Wm. Sample, James

McCadden, John Marshall, Andrew Shearer, Dr. John Wishart, Samuel Hazlett, George Kuntz, Robert Wylie, Rev. Dr. D. McConaughy, James McCoy, Joseph Lawrence, Dr. Robert R. Reed, John L. Gow, Samuel Cunningham, Collon M. Reed, John S. Brady, Hugh W. Wilson, D. Houston, Dr. H. Buchanan, Sample Sweeney, John Bausman, Daniel Moore, James G. Strean, Rev. Thomas Hanna, Dr. R. P. Lane, N. F. Brobst, Joseph Templeton, Samuel Vance, Hon. Abraham Wootring, Wm. Brownlee, James and Henry Langley, Wm. McKennan, George Lonkert, Samuel Clokey, Wm. Gabby, Rev. James I. Brownson, Dr. M. H. Clark, Dr. John W. Wishart, Dr. Thomas McKennan, Thomas McKean, and V. Harding, who have been its warm and steadfast friends, promoting its interests pecuniarily, by subscription to stock and otherwise, as the records of the Board of Trustees constantly show. It is eminently due, therefore, that their names should be perpetuated, many of whom will appear in its history as its trustees.

At the meeting of the 26th of November, referred to, and after a full interchange of opinion, Messrs. Jacob Slagle, John Koontz, and David Eckert were appointed to ascertain if a suitable place could be procured for opening a seminary in the spring of 1836, while Messrs. T. M. T. McKennan, Wm. Hunter, John Harter, Dr. F. J. Lemoyne, and Thomas Morgan were authorized to confer with Alexander Reed, Esq., on the prospect of purchasing lots for the erection of a seminary on the east end of Maiden Street.

The Committee to procure a suitable place reported on November 30th that the Masonic Hall, which stood on the eastern end of the lot, upon which was the residence of John Grayson, Esq., with an entrance from Maiden Street, east of Main, could be rented, whereupon the same committee were instructed to rent the same, based upon the encouraging fact that Messrs. David Eckert, James Reed, and Samuel Mount had ascertained that between thirty and forty scholars would be obtained, the tuition of which would yield between six and seven hundred dollars. While these committees were making the preliminary arrangements about a suitable place and tuition, the Committee on the purchase of ground upon which to erect seminary buildings reported that Mr. Alexander Reed would sell the lots for the contemplated purpose.

The friends of the establishment of the seminary believing that its varied interests would be better promoted by procuring the sale of stock, in which every citizen would feel a deep interest, appointed Dr. F. J. Lemoyne, Alexander Sweeney, and James Reed to ascertain what amount could be procured, who, on December 18, 1835, reported the sale of eighty-five shares, equivalent to $4250.

With such encouraging prospects Messrs. F. J. Lemoyne, T. M. T. McKennan, Samuel McFarland, and Thomas Morgan were instructed to procure two suitable persons for teachers. This committee, at a subsequent meeting, reported that they had procured the services of Mrs. Francis Biddle, and had given her authority to select an assistant. Her stipulated salary to be six hundred dollars, clear of rent, fuel, furniture, and incidental expenses. The trustees also resolved that all excess over the six hundred dollars, derived from tuition, and the payment of all incidental expenses, should be paid to Mrs. Biddle in addition to her salary.

T. M. T. McKennan, Esq., chairman of the Committee to confer with Alexander Reed, Esq., on the purchase of his lots, reported December 18, 1835, that Mr. Reed would sell the lots for two hundred and fifty dollars, and the price of the fencing, which would be about fifty dollars; which report was accepted, and the trustees instructed to purchase the lots.

The lots being secured, and $4250 subscribed, Messrs. Alexander Sweeney, James Reed, and W. J. Wilson were appointed to obtain plans, &c., for the contemplated seminary buildings; and, on the 14th March, 1836, the stockholders held their first meeting for a permanent organization, under the articles of association which had been prepared by Rev. Dr. McConaughy, Alexander Reed, and Dr. F. J. Lemoyne. The building committee delayed making a report until March 14, 1836, when they reported and recommended that a *building committee* be elected, with full power to adopt a plan, obtain sealed proposals for work and materials, contract for sinking a well and putting a pump therein, to have a general superintendence, and draw upon the treasurer to meet the necessary expenses. This well-matured recommendation met the unanimous approval of the trustees, and the following persons were elected said committee, viz: Dr F. J. Lemoyne, James Reed, James Ruple, Robert Officer, and James Brice.

John Harter was appointed treasurer, instructed to collect one-fifth part of each share of stock, and pay the same out to the order of the building committee. He served as such until July 30, 1836, when Alexander Sweeney was appointed, and served until October 26, 1837, when John Grayson was elected. Messrs. John Koontz, David Eckert, John Grayson, R. H. Lee, and Rev. Dr. D. Elliott were instructed to provide suitable furniture, and act as a board of trustees and visitors for the present year. The trustees directed the building committee, on July 30, 1836, to call in the remaining instalments in such proportions as may be necessary to defray the expenses of the new buildings and premises.

On the 14th of February, 1837, the stockholders adopted a new constitution, having in view the necessity of procuring an act of incorporation from the legislature. This constitution contained fifteen articles, vesting certain powers in the board of trustees—to consist of nine members, elected annually by the stockholders; to fill vacancies, to provide the mode of election on shares of stock, to employ a principal, and manage the preliminary affairs of the institution, placing the edifice and appurtenances under the care of the principal and trustees; the principal to have charge of the domestic affairs of the seminary, under the sanction of the trustees; the principal and her assistants to instruct the scholars in such a course of studies as the trustees would approve; dividing the seminary into three classes, and requiring three years' study to complete the course and receive a diploma; the trustees to establish the price of tuition, fees, &c.; the treasurer to be elected by the stockholders, and dividends to be declared when the institution is free of debt, and an annual report to be made. Such were its provisions, which instrument, after discussion, was unanimously adopted.

Under the constitution an election for nine trustees was held February 17, 1837: the Board consisting of Dr. F. J. Lemoyne, John Marshall, Jacob Slagle, Dr. John Wishart, Rev. D. McConaughy, Joseph Lawrence, Dr. Robert R. Reed, John L. Gow, and Alexander Reed. While upon the subject of trustees I shall at this time add the names of those who have filled and are now filling the office :—

September 26, 1837, Dr. F. J. Lemoyne, Dr. R. R. Reed, Jacob Slagle, Rev. Dr. D. McConaughy, were re-elected, and John H. Ewing, James Brice, John Grayson, Samuel Hazlett, and Samuel Cunningham constituted the Board.

December 11, 1850, Dr. Wilson Addison and Mr. Ross, executors of the estate of Mrs. Jane Addison, deceased, executed a deed for four feet of ground adjoining the seminary lot, which enabled the trustees to adopt a plan for the building so as to occupy the ground up to the Addison grant.

On the 14th of April, 1838, the legislature incorporated the Washington Female Seminary, and appointed as trustees Rev. Dr. D. McConaughy, Dr. F. J. Lemoyne, Dr. John Wishart, John Grayson, Jacob Slagle, Dr. R. R. Reed, John Marshall, John L. Gow, and Joseph Lawrence.

April 4, 1839, John Grayson and John L. Gow were instructed to prepare an address to the citizens of the surrounding counties of Pennsylvania, Virginia, and Ohio in reference to the prospects of the seminary.

November 18, 1839, John L. Gow resigned the office of trustee, and Alexander Sweeney was appointed.

March 1, 1838, the trustees signed a memorial to the legislature asking an appropriation of $1000 per annum, for five years, which was granted, the law requiring the payment to be made *quarterly*, and the treasurer was authorized from time to time to receive the same.

December 7, 1841, Dr. R. R. Reed and John Marshall tendered their resignations as trustees, and T. M. T. McKennan and Collin M. Reed were appointed.

July 14, 1846, John H. Ewing was appointed a trustee in the room of Joseph Lawrence, Esq.

December 13, 1849, the trustees ordered a perpetual insurance of $6000 on the seminary buildings.

August 24, 1858, on account of the death of the Rev. D. D. McConaughy and T. M. T. McKennan, Esq., the Board proceeded to fill the vacancies by the election of Rev. James I. Brownson and Dr. M. H. Clark.

December 17, 1858, Dr. John Wishart resigned his trusteeship, and on January 19, 1859, Dr. John Wilson Wishart was elected to fill the vacancy; at the same time Dr. Thomas McKennan was elected in place of Hugh W. Wilson, deceased.

January 12, 1866, Alexander Sweeney having died, V. Harding was elected, and Dr. John Wilson Wishart having resigned Thomas McKean was elected.

With this necessary digression we shall return again to the general history of the seminary, commencing at the period before the charter was obtained, and when arrangements were being made to complete and furnish the seminary. At the meeting of June 8, 1837, it was stated that if the whole amount of $4250 were paid in, it would require an additional one thousand dollars; whereupon Messrs. James Brice, Alexander Reed, Samuel McFarland, T. M. T. McKennan, and Samuel Hazlett were appointed to sell additional stock, who, on the 22d of June following, reported that they had obtained seven shares, equal to eight hundred and fifty dollars. Being thus encouraged the trustees directed the building committee to have the buiding painted, provide suitable furniture, and borrow $500, and to pledge the new stock for its payment.

At a meeting of the trustees held December 18, 1840, the trustees taking into consideration the increase of pupils and the healthy state of the Seminary, determined that it was both expedient and necessary to erect additional buildings, they therefore appointed Dr. R. R. Reed, Dr. John Wishart, and T. M. T. McKennan, to sell new stock for that purpose. So successful were the committee, that on January 28, 1841, the Board appointed Dr. F. J. Lemoyne, John Grayson, and Dr. R. R. Reed, to receive plans for the proposed building and issue sealed proposals for the work and materials. On the 8th of March, 1841, the execution of the work was awarded to Messrs. Wm. Allen and Thos. Cooper, for the sum of $3231.59, but Mr. Allen removing from town, Henry Shearer was substituted in his place. The contractors were required to have the buildings finished by October 20, 1841. An insurance was placed upon the building amounting to $5000, and $200 appropriated for this purpose. Dr. Jno. Wishart, Alexander Sweeney, and Jacob Slagle, appointed to contract for the furnishing of the additional building.

January 28, 1846, Messrs. T. M. T. McKennan, Dr. F. J. Lemoyne, and C. M. Reed were appointed to obtain subscriptions of new stock to erect an east wing to the building, and on February 28th they reported the sale of twenty-six shares, equal to $1300. This amount not being considered sufficient to justify the trustees, the question was postponed and renewed at a meeting of the stockholders on February 3, 1848, when various plans were suggested and the whole question postponed for the action of a future meeting. While the trustees and stockholders were deliberating upon the necessity of erecting additional buildings, a fire occurred on December 1, 1848, destroying the new building which had been previously erected. The Franklin Fire Insurance Company, having been notified of the fact, telegraphed that the loss would be promptly met, and on December 13th Dr. F. J. Lemoyne, T. M. T. McKennan, and Sample Sweeney were appointed to sell additional stock, who reported the sale of forty-three shares, equal to $2150. The trustees met on February 17, 1849, and appointed Dr. F. J. Lemoyne, John H. Ewing, Sample Sweeney, James Brice, and James Ruple a building committee to borrow money and make a contract for the erection of the west wing to the Seminary building. On the 18th of May the committee report that they have contracted with Robert Ramsey for the erection of the west wing and an additional story on the old building, for the sum of $4900, to be completed by October 1, 1849. On January 30, 1850, the building committee made a final report and received a vote of thanks for the able manner in which they had discharged their duties.

In connection with the subject of the erection of the buildings and purchase of the lots and other incidental expenses, I might add that on January 19, 1859, John Grayson, Esq., treasurer, reported the institution free from debt, there being a balance in his hands of $590. Since this time the stockholders have been receiving a dividend upon their shares of stock, and a contingent fund has been established.

Principals of the Seminary.

1. Mrs. Frances Biddle.

On April 9, 1836, Rev. Dr. D. Elliott, Prof. Richard H. Lee, John Grayson, David Eckert, and John Koontz, trustees of the Seminary, published an address, stating that some time during the present month a female seminary for the education of young ladies, under the direction of *Mrs. Frances Biddle*, an experienced teacher, highly recommended by competent persons as a lady well qualified for the superintendence of a female institute. She will be aided by a well educated female assistant. The course of education will be extensive, embracing the various branches taught in the best female seminaries. Mrs. Biddle opened the seminary 21st of April, 1836, assisted by Miss Mary Clark, and during her term of office had also as assistants, Miss Henrietta M. Post (afterwards Mrs. U. W. Wise), and Miss Sarah Chapman (afterwards Mrs. Collin M. Reed).

On the 2d day of January, 1840, Rev. Dr. McConaughy, Dr. R. R. Reed, and John Grayson were instructed to confer with Mrs. Biddle on the present and future prospects of the Seminary, who reported on the 24th, that the Principal intended to resign her office at the close of the present session in March, which she accordingly did, and her resignation was accepted. On the September previous of 1839, three years having elapsed since the organization of the Seminary, the first class of young ladies graduated, consisting of six in number.

2. MISS SARAH R. FOSTER (MRS. SARAH R. F. HANNA).

After the trustees had received notice of the resignation of Mrs. Biddle, Rev. Dr. McConaughy, Dr. F. J. Lemoyne, and John Marshall were appointed to obtain information of a suitable person for Principal of the Seminary. This committee, on the 14th of March, 1840, reported that they had procured the desired information, and would recommend Miss Sarah R. Foster, of Cadiz, Ohio, as pre-eminently possessing all the qualifications which would insure thorough education and perpetuate the institution. These recommendations being entirely satisfactory, Miss Foster was unanimously elected on the terms embraced in the existing contract with Mrs. Biddle. Dr. F. J. Lemoyne, Jacob Slagle, and John Marshall were appointed to execute the contract and publish the election and acceptance of a Principal, the studies and terms of tuition.

Miss Henrietta M. Post and Miss Laura Simmons were appointed as assistants, with the consent of the Principal. During the period Miss Foster presided over the Seminary and to the present time, as Mrs. Hanna, highly educated and accomplished assistant teachers have aided her in the discharge of her arduous duties.

On the 27th day of Sept., 1848, Miss Sarah R. Foster was united in marriage to the Rev. Thomas Hanna, pastor of Seceder Congregation, and on the 11th of March following he was elected by the trustees Superintendent of the Seminary, which office he held until his death, which occurred February 9, 1864. Mrs. Hanna, however, has always filled and exercised the office of Principal with marked ability and pre-eminent success, which is owing to her unwavering energy, kindness, and efficiency, joined with her judicious selection of assistants.

In connection with this subject we shall add the whole number who have graduated yearly since the first class graduated in September, 1839, which numbered six, the remainder having graduated under Mrs. Hanna, numbering in all five hundred and ten graduates, whose parents reside in fifteen States of the Union, thereby demonstrating that the fame of Washington Female Seminary is not confined to State bounds.

OFFICERS OF THE BOARD OF TRUSTEES.

Rev. Dr. David McConaughy was the *first President*, and served until his death. His successor was the Rev. Dr. James I. Brownson, who was elected August 30, 1858.

The *Treasurers* were elected in the following years: 1st. John Harter, March 14, 1836. 2d. Alexander Sweeney, July 30, 1836. 3d. John Grayson, October 26, 1837. 4th. James Brice, March 31,

1838. 5th. John Grayson re-elected May 12, 1838. And 6th. Thomas McKean, January 8, 1867.

The following gentlemen have filled the office of *Secretary* by election, viz: T. M. T. McKennan, at the organization. 2d. Samuel Cunningham, October 26, 1837. 3d. John L. Gow, May 12, 1838. 4th. Dr. F. J. Lemoyne, December 7, 1841. 5th. Collin M. Reed, January 14, 1842. 6th. V. Harding, January 8, 1867.

The present Board of Trustees consists of Rev. Dr. James I. Brownson, *President;* Thomas McKean, *Treasurer;* V. Harding, *Secretary;* and John Grayson, Jacob Slagle, Collin M. Reed, John H. Ewing, Dr. M. H. Clarke, and Dr. Thomas McKennan.

In connection with the name of Hon. John Grayson, a member of the Board of Trustees, and who served as treasurer for thirty years, the Board at its meeting on January 16, 1867, presented him with an elegant family Bible. I might add also that John Grayson and Jacob Slagle, Esquires, are the only two trustees who have served thirty years each as a trustee, and their devotion to the interests of the Seminary, with their fellow laborers, the Principal and her assistant teachers, continues unabated.

We cannot better close our remarks upon the origin, progress, and success of the Washington Female Seminary, both as regards the intelligence of its teachers and the acquirements of the young ladies, mentally and morally, than by quoting an extract from the address of Rev. James I. Brownson, D. D., at the Quarter Centennial Celebration held on the 27th of June, 1866, who, in speaking of Mrs. Hanna, the efficient and beloved Principal of the Institute, said:—

"But especially Mrs. Hanna is here, almost as you last saw her; with the same clear voice, firm step, commanding presence, kindly heart, and wise and firm yet tender administration, which, in your school days, brought you at the same time under the power of fear and love; and, as you can see for yourselves, she is after all not *much older.* All the period of your absence she has borne you in memory and heart, and now she waits to tell you all about your alma mater, its fluctuations of prosperity and trial, its struggles and triumphs, and to hear your full history from your own mouth."

Union School Building.

This building is placed on a lot two hundred and forty feet square, on the west end of Beau Street, and west of the college. The plan was submitted by John Chislett, Esq., of Pittsburg. It is seventy-four by eighty-four feet, three stories high, the first and second fourteen feet each, and the third fifteen feet, the elevation of the first floor being three feet.

The *first* floor has four rooms, with a hall. These rooms contain closets for books, clothes-rooms, broad double stairways, and the necessary apparatus for heating and ventilation. The *second* floor is divided in like manner, while the *third* floor has a hall of forty by seventy feet, with two rooms.

The hall is used for public examination, declamation, &c. The building cost about $16,000, and the furniture $2500.

Since the erection of this building the following gentlemen have filled the office of Principal, viz: Alexander M. Gow, Rev. David P. Lowary, Alexander Wishart, Rev. L. P. Streator, D. F. Patterson, Rev. W. J. Wilson.

The borough of Washington contains twelve schools; number of months taught are ten. The schools employ one male and eight female teachers, male teachers receiving $81.50, the females $33 per month. The colored children are taught by a male teacher in another building. There are 496 male scholars, and 506 females, amounting to 1002 scholars enrolled, although about 831 are the average number in attendance. The cost of tuition per month is 58 cents; amount levied for school purposes, $4740; for building purposes, $1600; total amount, $6685. The State appropriation was $330.33; the debt remaining on school is $7087.90.

WASHINGTON GAS WORKS.

The first meeting for the establishment of gas works in the borough of Washington was held on the 26th of August, 1856. The citizens engaged in the enterprise; procured a charter, which designated as its managers Collin M. Reed, Jos. Henderson, Simon Cort, Jacob Slagle, Charles W. Hays, Freeman Brady, Jr., J. L. Judson, Jas. W. Koontz, and Alexander Seaman. This Board of Managers procured the sale of stock, and by the terms of the charter, a new Board was elected January 18, 1857, consisting of Samuel Hazlett, C. M. Reed, Dr. F. J. Lemoyne, William Smith, Jacob Miller, Alexander Wilson, and Joseph Henderson. After its organization Messrs. Lemoyne, Hazlett, and Miller were appointed to purchase a suitable lot of ground, erect the necessary buildings, and contract with Mr. Stephenson for their erection.

The company has a capital stock of twenty thousand seven hundred and seventy-five dollars, divided into eight hundred and thirty-one shares of twenty-five dollars each.

The estimated value of the gas works is thirty thousand dollars. The officers are C. M. Reed, President; John C. Hastings, Secretary and Treasurer.

WASHINGTON CEMETERY.

A desire among the people of Washington and its vicinity to have an appropriate place for their honored dead led to the organization of the Washington Cemetery Company. An application was made to the court, and on the 3d day of March, 1853, a charter was granted to the following corporators, viz: Samuel Cunningham,

James Watson, †George Lonkert, John D. Chambers, Hon. Alex. W. Acheson, †James Brown, Joseph Henderson, † R. F. Cooper, †James Ewing, †John L. Gow, John H. Ewing, Dr. John W. Wishart, Hon. Wm. McKennan, David S. Wilson, O. B. McFadden, Alex. Murdoch, William Hopkins, S. B. Hays, John Hall, Franklin Nichol, and Dr. M. H. Clark.

The charter obtained, named the following persons as the Board of Managers: Rev. Thos. Hanna, D. D., John L. Gow, Hon. Alex. W. Acheson, William Hopkins, James Watson, Jas. Brice, and D. S. Wilson, who were authorized to purchase land, fill vacancies, and perform such other acts as would promote the interest of the cemetery.

The legislature passed an act that all the lots should be forever exempt from taxation and free from seizure, levy, and sale, and also provided for its general protection. The company owns fifty acres of land, and have sold lots amounting to twenty-two thousand dollars, which has been appropriated to the erection of a superintendent's house, fencing and improving the grounds, as originally laid out by Mr. Chislett. So devoted have the lot-holders been to beautifying and adorning the resting-place of those who were near and dear to them, that the estimated value of the improvements is two hundred thousand dollars. While the larger portion of the lot-holders reside in the borough, yet the people of the county feel interested in this cemetery, and here deposit their friends in an appropriate resting-place, which we may well call the great city of the illustrious and honored dead.

The managers of the company have generously appropriated grounds for the burial of the soldiers who died in defence of the Constitution, and in these grounds the soldiers' monument is to be erected, which will add another beautiful structure to the many which already can be seen, calling to remembrance the virtues of those who have passed into the spirit-land, and whose names are engraved not only upon marble, but upon the tablet of the memory of human hearts.

WASHINGTON COAL COMPANY.

This company is situate in the western limits of the borough, the owners of which are Messrs. Parkin, Marshall & Co., who on August 24, 1864, commenced sinking a shaft for bituminous coal, with which our county abounds. They were successful on the 12th day of August, 1865, being one year engaged in the enterprise before their wishes were both realized and gratified. The perpendicular depth of the shaft is three hundred and fifty feet, but at an angle of forty-five degrees, which is the descent to the coal, by a stationary engine and cars, it is five hundred feet. The company employ thirty hands, digging daily one thousand bushels, and the improvements, with the coal right, are estimated as worth thirty thousand dollars.

† Those to whose names a cross is prefixed, have since died, and are buried in the cemetery, except R. F. Cooper, who died on the battle-field.

As it will be interesting to my geological readers to know the various strata through which the workmen passed, I shall give them as detailed to me by Mr. Parkin, the senior partner. Passing down below the soil and clay four feet, was blue clay, then five feet of gravel, then eighteen inches of black slate, like roofing slate, then a four feet bed of limestone, next fifteen feet of a blue clay or schale like fire-proof brick is made of, then an eight inch vein of coal, next six feet of gray schale like fire-proof clay, then five feet of freestone, then one hundred and seventy feet of gray limestone between beds varying from six inches to three feet. In this, however, is twenty feet of white limestone, about the centre of the foregoing depth of one hundred and seventy feet. In this white limestone, which is one hundred and fifty feet from the surface, are salt springs. Immediately below the gray limestone is twelve feet of black slate, such as is found at Cook's Mill, two miles north of Washington, then eight feet of gray limestone of a soft nature, then five feet of gray flinty limestone (the hardest they had met with), fifty feet of blue schale, and mixed with iron, until they reached sandstone, which was fifteen feet deep, mixed with fossils of various kinds, then three feet of slate, under which was a vein of pure bituminous coal of five feet six inches.

HANOVER TOWNSHIP.

By reference to the history of Smith township we learn that this township was a part thereof, but on the 11th day of March, 1786, after application had been made to and certificate granted by the court, the Supreme Executive Council confirmed the action of the court. When formed into a township its boundaries were the Ohio River on the north and east, Smith township on the south, and Virginia on the west. It will be remembered that after a part of Beaver County was taken off Washington, a part of Hanover township was thereby struck off. Yet each county retained the original name of Hanover for one of its townships.

It is bounded by Beaver County on the north, Robinson and Smith on the east, Jefferson and Smith on the south, and West Virginia on the west.

The turnpike road from Pittsburg to Steubenville on the Ohio River runs westerly through the township, and upon it is *Florence*, called originally Briceland's Cross Roads. The Pittsburg and Steubenville Railroad runs through its southern part. This township contains several valuable grist and saw-mills, also ten stores, fourteen schools, employing six male and eight female teachers, with 494 scholars (274 males and 220 females); the male teachers receive $37 50 per month, and the females $26 25; the tuition costing per month for each scholar $1 16. Amount levied for school purposes $2552 92; from State appropriation $182 91.

Its population in 1860 was 2090, of which 38 were colored. Its greatest length is 11, breadth 7 miles.

In this township resided the celebrated Adam Poe, who lived in a cabin about two miles west of Florence, situate on a little knoll on the farm of the late John Fulton, deceased.

Its towns are *Florence, Paris, Murdocksville.*

On the 14th day of August, 1814, a town was laid out by James Briceland and Moses Proudfit, who named it Florence. It was originally named Briceland's Cross Roads, from the fact of the Pittsburg and Steubenville pike crossing the Washington and Georgetown road at this point, where James Briceland kept an hotel. It is twenty-six miles from Pittsburg, sixteen from Washington, and twelve from Steubenville.

PRESBYTERIAN CHURCH.

The Cross-roads Presbyterian Church is located at Florence. It was organized originally at a place called King's Creek, in 1786, but the location was changed to its present site in 1798. The church has had as its pastors Rev. Elisha McCurdy, who was installed in June, 1800; Rev. Daniel Dernelle, in 1836; Rev. Wm. Burton, in 1838; Rev. James W. McKennan, in November, 1839; Rev. Joel Stoneroad, in 1842; Rev. J. S. Wylie, in 1850; Rev. Oliphant M. Todd, November 9, 1852; Rev. J. P. Caldwell, in 1860; Rev. Andrew W. Boyd, in 1864; and Rev. David M. Miller, in May, 1867, its present efficient and highly esteemed pastor, who informs me that the number of families connected therewith numbers eighty-nine, with a Sabbath school of one hundred and twenty children. This was one of the churches that shared in the great revival which took place at the beginning of the present century, which was accompanied by what was known as the "falling exercises."

The United Presbyterians have a church on King's Creek, near Florence. The present pastor is Rev. James L. Purdy, with a membership of eighty.

Paris is in the western part of the township, and contains about thirty-five dwellings, a Presbyterian church under the care of the Rev. Fulton Magill, and a United Presbyterian church, which has had the ministerial labors of Rev. Mr. Galloway, Rev. Mr. Backus, Rev. J. Y. Calhoon, and Rev. James C. Campbell, with a membership of one hundred and twenty. It has also one extensive threshing-machine manufactory, cabinet-makers, blacksmiths, shoemakers, &c.

Murdocksville is in the northeast part of the township.

August 26, 1811, in Pittsburg, two officers had a dispute, and they resolved to settle their difficulties by fighting a duel. Arrangements were made that the affair should be settled in Virginia. One of the parties travelled as far as Briceland's Cross-roads (Florence) the first day, and in the morning rose by daylight and practised with his pistol. One of the shots struck the headstone of Capt. Bavington, and can be seen at this day. After breakfast he left for the designated spot. The same day his antagonist left Pittsburg, but when he came near to the place called the old North Star, formerly kept by Joseph Crawford as a tavern, he was thrown from the sulky and had his leg broken. The wounded officer was taken back on a litter to Pittsburg, by soldiers sent for that purpose. Thus ended this duel.

July 3, 1793. We give the substance of a lease between George McCormick and Solomon Hule and Sarah his wife; the former conveying to the latter on lease, one hundred acres of land, on the waters of King (or Indian) Creek, in Hanover township. The rent required was one bushel of Indian corn yearly, and the taxes to be paid on four hundred acres, and at the expiration of three lives the land to revert to George McCormick and his heirs.

FRANKLIN TOWNSHIP.

On the 16th of July, 1787, the Supreme Executive Council, upon the proper certificate of the Court of Quarter Sessions of Washington County, formed this township, adopting as its boundaries Amwell township on the north, Cumberland on the east, Greene on the south, and Donegal on the west.

With Cumberland, Morgan, Greene, and Rich Hill, this township constituted Greene County by an act passed February 9, 1796.

FINLEY TOWNSHIP

Was formed out of Donegal on the 6th of May, 1788. Its boundaries were Donegal on the north, Franklin, Cumberland, and Greene on the east, Mason and Dixon's line on the south, and Virginia on the west.

It was subdivided into East and West Finley December 24, 1828, by a decree of the court. The history of each we shall give after referring to some other subjects.

About the year 1807 there existed in this township several religious sects, of which we shall speak, to show the influence which superstition has upon the human mind. The leader of this sect was a man by the name of Sergeant. He professed to have a revelation direct from heaven, through the ministry of an angel, in which was communicated to him the very convenient doctrine that there was *no hell*. He preached in that and the adjoining townships for about three years, and had many followers. Firmly believing in this doctrine, and concluding that there was no punishment hereafter, he committed forgery and was imprisoned in Cumberland, Maryland. However, before he committed this crime his fame as a minister had preceded him to Wheeling, and thither he went and preached. His services were interrupted by a lawyer, and Sergeant instituted suit against him for disturbing the solemnity of the sanctuary and the religious services in which he and his followers were engaged. The trial came off; the lawyer was acquitted and the HALYCONITES were declared not to be a religious sect. It was immediately after this he was arrested and sent to Cumberland, Maryland, for trial. As soon as the lawyer heard of this, he composed the following poetry, which is still repeated from memory by some of the old inhabitants of Finley township. The lawyer styles himself *St. David's son*, and Sergeant, St. Bones. It reads as follows:—

1. Saint Bones, to show that all his ways
   Demand the most unbounded praise,
   Returned St. David's son to court,
   Of which St. Bones became the sport,
       With all the Halycon union.

2. Saint David's son did prove full well,
   St. Bones did preach there is no hell;
   It was thus decided by the laws
   That his was not a Christian cause,
       With all the Halycon union.

3. Saint David's son to Bacchus bows,
   And in his temple pays his vows;
   Being thus inspired he moves along,
   Amidst the enthusiastic throng
       Who compose the Halycon union.

4. Now adieu, St. Bones, whene'er you die,
   Directly to heaven you will fly,
   But father Abraham, with a club,
   Will beat you down to Belzebub,
       With all the Halycon union.

This lawyer, whose name we are not authorized to give, wrote another piece upon this man Sergeant—upon his confinement—which we also give as a relic of the olden times. The lawyer represented the devil as saying:—

1. Now I'll away to Cumberland
   To see a friend in iron bands;
   To see a friend in awful dwell,
   Who always preached there was no hell.

2. He took his leave, away did go,
   He found his friend both mean and low,
   He found his friend in iron band,
   Which put the Devil to a stand.

3. Oh, now, dear son, what brought you here?
   Oh, father, pray, don't be severe;
   The truth to you I won't deny,
   They put me here for forgery.

4. Oh, now, dear father, if you can,
   Release me from these iron bands—
   Release me now—don't let me swing,
   And I'll to you new subjects bring.

5. Oh, yes, dear son, that I can do,
   And soon he burst the bands in two.
   For this here thing you shall not swing,
   This day I'll crown you HALYCON King.

This was a death-blow to the Halyconites, but on their ruins arose a more wonderful sect. Among the followers of Sergeant was an old lady by the name of Rhoda Fordyce, who, in addition to the doctrine that there was no hell, taught that it were possible for persons to live entirely on a vegetable diet, such as parched corn, sassafras buds, &c. &c., for a certain number of days and then be bodily translated to heaven. This sect was called Rhodianites, after their founder.

A man by the name of Parker, it is said, in attempting to carry out this doctrine, was absolutely starved to death in the house of this woman Fordyce. She kept the body concealed in her house for three days and three nights, and as he did not make the ascension in his lifetime, it was not probable that he would after death. The neighbors, missing Parker, and knowing the influence she was exercising upon his mind, went to the house and were refused admittance. They broke the door open, found the body and buried it.

To the doctrine of passing bodily to heaven, she added another point, which was required of all her followers, viz: That of *forming a chain*. To perfect this chain required a man and woman to make the link. The way it was formed was on this wise: Each were sewed up in separate sacks, with their head out, arms tied close against the body, and feet tied together; they were then put to bed by the old lady. In the morning they were brought before the old woman as Inspector-General, and if they stated that they had *slept innocently together*, they became a link in the chain of the Rhodianite church. Tradition tells us that many husbands were separated from their wives to form a link in the Rhodianite church.

After this sect arose a new sect, called New Lights, who made converts from the ranks of both the Halyconites and the Rhodianites by scores. They believed in immersion as the true mode of baptism, and that the Saviour was not equal to God, the Father, and was not from everlasting. They also believed in washing each other's feet at their communion. They would strip off their feet, get a basin of water and a towel, and go amongst all the brethren and sisters and wash their feet. These New Lights increased rapidly for a few years on the borders of Washington and Greene County, Marshall County, Virginia, and the adjoining counties of Ohio. They held both camp and bush-meetings.

In connection with this subject we might say that "Mormonism" had its origin in Amity, in the township of Amwell, whose history we have given under that township. Thus have we finished the history of superstition, which exerts so baneful an influence upon the human mind.

School-House.

Alexander Frazer, Esq., of this place, informs me that the first school taught in the western part of Finley township commenced in the spring of 1799 and continued for one year. The teacher's name was McDonald, who could read, write, and cipher to the double rule of three. The books used were Dilworth's spelling book, the Old and New Testament, and the Shorter Catechism.

1801. A young man by the name of Carroll, of Finley township, with another by the name of Richmond, went out early in the morning to hunt wild turkeys. The experienced hunter can give the turkey call so exact that the turkeys themselves are deceived by it. This unfortunately was the result of this case. These hunters became separated, and after a time Carroll, who was hid in the bushes, gave the turkey call. Richmond being a long distance off, hearing the call and seeing something dark moving in the brush, shot, and the ball passed through the head of his companion. Richmond, at the accident, became almost frantic, took up Carroll's gun, shot it off and laid it across his body and went home. He revealed the secret to his sister, who advised him to keep the secret, fearing he might be apprehended for murder, they being ignorant of the law. Richmond and his sister went that night and watched the corpse lest the wolves might devour it. The next day Carroll was missing, search was made, the body found, and the opinion was he had shot himself. This remained a profound secret until Richmond, on his death-bed, revealed the secret.

East Finley Township

Was formed from the eastern part of Finley township, on the 24th day of December, 1828. Its boundaries are—Donegal and Buffalo on the north, Franklin and Morris on the east, Greene County on the south, and Donegal and West Finley on the west. It is centrally distant from Washington, southwest, fifteen miles. It is drained by the branches of Wheeling Creek. In 1860 its population was 1261. It has eight schools, employing five male and three female teachers, the former receiving $35.80, the latter $33.50 per month, with 300 scholars (180 males and 120 females). Cost of tuition per month $1.07 cents. Total amount of taxes levied for school purposes $1557.04, from the State appropriation $108.42. It has five stores. There are four churches in this township, a Baptist church near Pleasant Grove in the eastern end, a Methodist Episcopal church near school-house No. 4, on Mr. Enslow's farm, in the centre, a Presbyterian church near Mrs. Jordan's in the west, and a United Presbyterian church in the southeast on Lockhart's Run near Dr. Simpson's. East Finley has several valuable steam grist and sawmills. Its greatest length is nine miles, breadth four miles.

The Baptist church called Pleasant Grove, in this township, was constituted November 14, 1840, by Elders Isaac Pettet, Simeon Siegfred, and Levi Griffith, with fifty-three members who had been members of Mount Herman church, the old Tenmile Baptist church. Those who have officiated as pastors are, Elder Levi Griffith from its organization to October, 1847. Rev. Isaac Winn supplied the pulpit for six months, when Rev. Eli C. Town was elected and served to April, 1848. Rev. A. J. Davis served six months, when Rev. John Thomas became the pastor and served until April, 1857. His successor was Elder John Scott, who preached until July, 1857. The church had occasional supplies until February, 1858, when Rev. Job Rossel was chosen pastor and served until 1861, when Rev. John B. Linsked was elected and served until April, 1866. His successor and present pastor was elected May 5, 1866.

The following persons have been *Deacons* of this church at various times since its organization: Messrs. John Tilton, Samuel Kelly, Elliott Patterson, Daniel Tilton, Thomas McKahan, J. Y. Holmes, Josiah Patterson, William McCleary, Joseph Ryan, and Manson Trussel.

Church Clerks from organization, Edward O. Town, Ezra Town, Thomas McKahan, and Robert Kerr. The following persons have been licensed to preach the gospel at official meetings held in this church, viz: Eli C. Town in 1847, Hugh R. Craig and Wm. Scott in 1854, and J. Y. Holmes in 1861. This church has been instrumental in establishing churches at Buffalotown and North Wheeling, West Finley township.

WHEELING U. P. CHURCH was organized August, 1836. Rev. Joseph Shaw was pastor from June 20, 1843, to April 20, 1852. Rev. James C. Murch from September, 1853, to 1859. Rev. James A. McKee from August, 1860, until the present time, with a membership of 75.

WEST FINLEY TOWNSHIP

Was organized the same time as East Finley, on the 24th of December, 1828. Its boundaries are Donegal on the north, East Finley on the east, Greene County on the south, and West Virginia on the east. This township is centrally distant southwest of Washington 17 miles. It is chiefly drained by Templeton's and Robinson's forks of Wheeling Creek. The population in 1860 was 1453, of which 33 are colored, with four stores. It has ten school-houses employing five male and five female teachers, the former receiving $27.19 and the latter $23 03 per month, with 468 scholars, 251 males and 217 females, the tuition costing per month 65 cents; taxes for school purposes $1468.70, and its State appropriation $146.25; levied for building purposes $587.48.

Its towns are Good Intent and Burnsville.
Burnsville is in the southern part.
Good Intent and Burnsville are small thriving villages.

The greatest length of this township is 9 miles, breadth 4½ miles. There is a Presbyterian church on the northwest of Burnsville, and Disciple church north of the same town.

In this township the United Presbyterian congregation is under the care of Rev. J. A. McKee.

Morris Township

Was formed by an order of the Court of Quarter Sessions, March 13, 1788. Its original boundaries were Amwell on the north, Bethlehem on the east, Franklin on the south, and Donegal on the west. It is at present bounded by East Finley, Franklin, and Amwell on the north, Amwell on the east, Greene County on the south, and East Finley on the west. Centrally distant from the borough of Washington 9 miles southwest. Greatest length 6½ miles; breadth 4 miles. It is drained by the north fork of Tenmile Creek and its branches. The population in 1860 was 1148, of which one is colored. It has three stores, seven schools, employing four males and three female teachers, the former receiving $35.25, and the latter $31 per month, with 288 scholars, 176 males and 112 females; the cost of tuition is 94 cents per month; amount of taxes raised for school purposes $1664.67; from the State appropriation $95.94.

Its towns are Sparta, Prosperity, and Lindley's Mills.

Sparta and Lindley's Mills are small villages, but Prosperity has twenty-two dwelling-houses, two stores, grist-mill, and several departments of the mechanical arts, and is ten miles from Washington.

Two miles west of Prosperity is a Methodist Episcopal church, called Mount Zion, near Robert S. Andrew's farm.

Upper Tenmile Presbyterian Church

Is located in Morris township. It was organized August 15, 1781, at the house of Jacob Cook, with 25 members, Rev. Thaddeus Dodd being elected and ordained its first pastor. It is worthy of remark that he was the second minister who settled west of the Monongahela River, the Rev. John McMillen having preceded him. Through his instrumentality and the Upper Tenmile church, the FIRST classical school west of the Alleghenies was established as early as 1782, of which he was its first principal. Rev. T. Dodd occupied the pulpit of both Upper and Lower Tenmile congregations; the Upper was at Lindley's settlement, and the Lower at Cook's settlement. The site of the Upper Tenmile church was given by Demas Lindley, upon which they built a meeting-house of hewn logs, while in 1785 was erected the same kind of a church for the people of Lower Tenmile. The Rev. Thaddeus Dodd taught a classical school in the log court-house in Washington about 1788 or 1789. Rev. Thaddeus Dodd died in 1793, and was succeeded by Rev. Thomas Moore, who labored until 1803. On the 14th of December, 1803, Rev. Cephas Dodd (son of Rev. Thaddeus Dodd), was ordained as the minister of both Upper and Lower Tenmile churches, like his predecessors, but in 1817 they separated, each having a minister, session, &c., Rev. Cephas Dodd remaining with the Lower Tenmile church.

In 1817, or immediately after the separation, Rev. Thomas Hoge served this congregation as a stated supply for three years, and during his labors the frame meeting-house was erected. From 1819 to 1821 the pulpit was filled by Rev. Andrew Wylie, D. D., President of Washington College, as a stated supply. In 1821 and 22, Rev. Boyd Mercer was the pastor. Rev. L. Robbins preached for one year. After this the church was vacant for several years, only filled by supplies from Presbytery. However, in December 1827, the Rev. Cornelius Laughran was elected and installed and served for eighteen months. The church was again without a pastor until 1830, when Rev. Jacob Lindley became the stated supply. From 1832 to 1838 this congregation had the occasional labors of Rev. David Elliott, Rev. John Stockton, and Rev. John McCluskey. In 1838 the Rev. James M. Smith was ordained and served until 1841. From 1841 to 1846 the church was supplied by appointments of Presbytery, viz: Rev. Alfred Paull, Rev. J. Miller, and Rev. John R. Dundas, but in the spring of 1846 Rev. Nicholas Murray (a Professor in Washington College) accepted a call as the stated supply; he labored until 1853, when he "fell asleep in Jesus." His successor was Rev. Cyrus Braddock for one year. After him was the Rev. E. C. Wines, D. D., who took charge of the church in 1855, and resigned in 1859.

The successor to the pastorate of the church after Rev. Dr. Wines had resigned was the Rev. N. B. Lyon, who faithfully and zealously discharged his ministerial duties, and in the very manhood of his ministry was called away to his eternal rest, to receive the crown for his labors of love on earth. His remains are buried in the beautiful Cemetery at Washington, Washington County. Rev. N. B. Lyon, deceased, was succeeded by Rev. Henry Wood, the present pastor, Professor of Ancient Languages in Washington and Jefferson College, and is doing noble and efficient service in the cause of his Divine Master.

There is a Sabbath school connected with the church, which was organized in 1825, having fifteen teachers, one hundred and twenty scholars, and near four hundred volumes in their library.

In the year 1854 the congregation erected their *third* place of worship. The present one occupies the same site where its two predecessors stood.

In connection with the Upper Tenmile Church we will add the history of the

LOWER TENMILE PRESBYTERIAN CHURCH.

It is true this church is located in Amity, Amwell township, and its history properly belonged to that township, but as we could not well separate their history, we delayed it until it could be more appropriately and understandingly given, for it must be remembered that both "Upper and Lower Tenmile Congregations" were but one ecclesiastical organization, with the same pastor and session, from their organization in 1781 until 1817, when they became two distinct bodies.

The ministers who officiated from 1781 to the division of the church were Rev. Thaddeus Dodd, Rev. Thomas Moore, Rev. Cephas Dodd (who at the separation remained with the Lower Tenmile Church), Rev. James W. McKennan, Rev. W. P. Harvison, and Rev. J. W. Hamilton, its present esteemed pastor. Several years while the church was without a pastor, it had the services as stated supplies of such ministers as the Rev. James Black, D. D., and Rev. W. J. Brugh.

The original church was of hewn logs, and the present neat and chaste edifice is in close proximity to the former, while in the rear is the rural cemetery of Amity, in which repose the honored remains of many loved ones, loved in life and honored in death. There is a Sabbath school connected with the church, which was organized in 1826, having eleven teachers, eighty scholars, and three hundred and twenty volumes in the library.

CHARTIERS TOWNSHIP

Was formed out of Cecil on March 23, 1790. Its original boundaries were Robinson on the north, Strabane on the east and south, and Cecil on the west. Its present boundaries are Mount Pleasant and Cecil on the north, Cecil north and south, Strabane on the east, South Strabane and Canton on the south, and Mount Pleasant and Canton on the west. It is centrally distant north of the borough of Washington six miles; its greatest length, seven miles; breadth, five miles. October 6, 1831, the line of this township was changed and part given to Mount Pleasant township, and at the August term of Court, 1863, the boundary lines between Chartiers and Canton townships were altered and confirmed by the court.

Chartiers Creek flows on the southern boundary.

Population in 1860 was 1795, of which 211 are colored.

Within the township limits are two stores, eight schools, employing one male and seven female teachers, their monthly pay being $29.37 each. The schools contain 337 scholars, of which 163 are males, and 174 are females, the tuition for each costing 84 cents per month; amount levied for school purposes, $1620; and the fund received from the State $141.57.

TOWNS.

Its towns are Canonsburg and McConnellsville, the former being a borough; its history will be given in connection with and after the township history.

McConnellsville is a small village near the centre of the township, with thirty dwelling-houses and a population of about one hundred and forty.

INCIDENT.

In connection with the early history of this township we mention the following incident from the Pittsburg *Gazette* of May 15, 1790, speaking of the navigation of Chartiers' Creek:—

"About five or six days since a number of men to the amount of thirteen left Canonsburg, on Chartiers' Creek, and, with the advantage of a rising flood, conducted two boats from thence in about twelve hours into the Ohio River. One was large and heavy, built for the purpose of carrying flour to New Orleans, forty-seven feet in length and twelve in breadth; a small part of the cargo to the amount of forty barrels on board. The other, a barge 25 feet in length, built for the genteel reception of passengers. The amazing facility with which these boats passed down the creek to the mouth, their safe crossing of two mill-dams, one of which was about twelve feet high, with the rudeness of the creek in its natural state, especially at the falls, sufficiently show what immense advantage might arise to thousands of people in the county of Washington were the legislature to attend to the improvement of its navigation. From Canonsburg and nearer Washington the charge of carriage to Pittsburg, on account of hills and deep roads, is not less than three shillings and ninepence per barrel for flour; yet were attention paid to the cultivation of this excellent stream of water, one boat of the afore-mentioned size would, in all probability, carry two hundred barrels to the Ohio without detriment thereto or a farthing of expense."

We learn from old residents of Canonsburg that Col. Canon headed this flotilla, while about the same time a load of flour was also sent from Bradford's mill, afterwards owned by Dr. Robert R. Reed, and now owned by Mr. Wilson. There can be no doubt of the truthfulness of these facts, because, in addition to the evidence, we have legislative action on the subject, wherein, on April 8, 1793, Chartiers' Creek from its mouth to David Bradford's mill was declared to be a public highway for boats and rafts, and all natural and artificial obstructions were required to be removed

CHURCHES.

On December 26, 1797, John Canon conveyed to Nicholas Little, Samuel Agnew, Thomas Menary, David Reed, John Hays, John White, and Jeremiah Simpson, Trustees of the Associate Congregation of Chartiers township, four acres, two rods, and fifteen perches of land for $45. This church is situated about one mile southwest of Canonsburg, and is generally known as Rev. Dr. Ramsay's Church, from his long, faithful, and efficient services. His successors were Rev. John B. Clarke and Rev. David Huston French. The old church has been torn down, and the congregation has in process of erection in the borough a beautiful brick edifice.

Chartiers Cross Road Church.

This is situated on the Hickory road, and south of McConnellsville. The following ministers have successively filled the pulpit as regular pastors: Rev. Dr. Finley, Rev. Mr. Graham, Rev. David Ferguson, Rev. A. McCahan, Rev. Thomas L. Spears, Rev. Joseph Andrews, Rev. J. C. Herron, from June 19, 1860, to April 1, 1867. This church has a membership of 140; it belongs to the United Presbyterian denomination, and is built of brick.

Spears' Spring Church

Is on the bank of Chartiers' Creek, one-half mile northwest of Canonsburg, and belongs to the United Presbyterians, and is a plain, substantial brick edifice. It has a rural and beautiful cemetery.

Its ordained ministers have been Rev. Alexander McCahan, Rev. Thomas Callohan, Rev. William Wallace, Rev. David Paull, Rev. Wm. H. Andrew, Rev. John W. Bane, and Rev. James G. Carson. This church has a membership of 214.

Chartiers U. P. Church has been removed during this year, 1869, from its original site to near the borough limits. It was organized about 1780. Rev. Matthew Henderson was ordained in 1781, and officiated until October 2, 1795, when Rev. — Smith was elected pastor; his successor was Rev. James Ramsey, D. D., who served from September 4, 1805, to June 12, 1849; Rev. John B. Clark, D. D., from May 12, 1853, to June 9, 1860; Rev. D. H. French, from May 2, 1861, to June 20, 1866; Rev. H. A. McDonald was ordained pastor October 14, 1869. It has a membership of 175.

Canonsburg.

Canonsburg was laid out by Col. John Canon, of Chartiers township, on the 15th of April, 1788. It is situated on Chartiers' Creek, 17 miles from Pittsburg, 7 miles from Washington, and 40 miles from Wheeling. The country around it is elevated, beautiful, and fertile. A daily line of stages pass through it, and on the route of the Chartiers Valley Railroad. By reference to the recorder's office I fine a plot of the town recorded in volume P., page 441, on January 24, 1800. This plot has twenty-eight lots, with the names of the purchasers, viz: Dr. Thompson, Daniel McCoy, James Morrison, David Garret, Andrew Munroe, John Todd, Robert Bowland, Craig Ritchie, Col. Matthew Ritchie, William Marshall, and Abraham De Haven. This plot contains the conditions of purchase, viz: To those who have as well as those who may become purchasers Col. Canon conveys to them, their heirs and assigns, their respective lots of ground in which their names are inserted. The inhabitants of the town to have the privilege of cutting and using underwood, and taking coal for their own use forever, gratis. The purchaser to pay the said Canon three pounds purchase money, and one dollar annually forever afterwards; and to build, a stone, frame, or hewed log house, at least twenty feet in front, with a stone or brick chimney, within two years from the date of their purchase. A convenient road to be allowed to the coal near John Laughlin's; the road to be only as laid off on the plot, and the bank as described on the same.

This plot also designated the following roads: to Mr. McMillan's meeting-house, to Washington, to Mr. Smith's meeting-house on Buffalo, to Mr. Henderson's meeting-house, *to the coal bank*, to Gamble's mill, to Wells's mill, and to Devore's ferry.

This town became a borough on the 22d of February, 1802, and is the oldest borough in the county. In 1860 it had a resident population of 975, but the number of students attending Jefferson College increased it about one-third. It has one hundred and ninety-five dwelling-houses, fifteen retail stores, two confectioneries, one saving fund society, one furniture manufactory, one woollen manufactory, one broker. It has four schools, employing one male and three female teachers, the former receiving $52.03, and the latter $31.28, per month; having 314 scholars, 171 males and 143 females; cost of tuition per month, 60 cts.; amount levied for school purposes, $1271.70; from State appropriation, $112.76. One female Seminary and Jefferson College. In 1829 the Associate body or Seceders established a Theological Seminary at this place, and erected the requisite buildings; but a few years since it was removed to Xenia, Ohio.

Jefferson College.

This college was originally chartered by the legislature, under the name of the "Academy and Library Company of Canonsburg," in 1794, although its origin may be dated to July, 1791, when David Johnston became the first teacher. As soon as a convenient house was built the Rev. Mr. McMillan transferred a Latin school, which he had been teaching at his own house for six or seven years, to the chartered academy. This building was erected on a lot given by Col. Canon as a present to the academy.

In October, 1791, the Redstone Presbytery approved of the action of the Synod of Virginia, to appropriate funds to the Canonsburg Academy as a Presbyterian institution, and appointed Dr. McMillan to receive contributions for that purpose, the Presbytery having previously determined that Canonsburg should be the seat of learning; and, in 1793, we find that the Presbytery passed a resolution that if the wants of the church demanded another institution they would not oppose it.

Col. Canon erected a stone building on the lot presented by him for college purposes, for which the trustees were to reimburse him, and on December 1, 1796, he and his wife made a deed to the trustees of the Academy, for the lot, on the payment of three hundred and seventy pounds, the balance in full for the building. This lot contained two acres and thirty-two perches; he reserved, however, one half acre of said lot for the use of an English school, with a free access of fifteen feet wide from Main Street to the English school lot.

In the Pittsburg *Gazette* of 1792, it is mentioned that a grammar school was in successful operation at Canonsburg, under Mr. David Johnston, while Mr. Miller was employed as professor in the mathematical sciences.

In this year, 1796, the trustees petitioned the legislature that in case a college was established west of the Allegheny Mountains, to make Canonsburg its site, as their Academy was a perfect success, dispensing its benefits throughout this section of county. The trustees employed David Johnston and James Mountain as teachers, for one year, at the end of which Mr. Johnston became engaged in other business, but Mr. Mountain continued teaching until April, 1797.

These teachers were succeeded by Mr. Jas. Canahan and Joseph Stockton, who taught until November, 1797, when John Watson was employed for one year, with authority to engage the services of an usher. In 1798, for the eminent services rendered to the Academy by Dr. McMillan, he was elected president, as an honorary office. In 1800, the Academy received a grant of one thousand dollars from the legislature, which enabled the trustees to pay off all outstanding debts, and in October of this year, the trustees made a movement to convert the Academy into a college, which event was not consummated until January 15, 1802, when the State legislature granted a charter for Jefferson College.

The trustees named in the charter met on the 27th of April, 1802, and were organized by Judge Edgar, who administered to each trustee an oath to execute the duties of his office. Dr. McMillan was elected President of the Board, and Craig Ritchie, Clerk. At this meeting they arranged the number of professors and classes, as well as the studies appertaining to each class. They elected Rev. John Watson President of the College, and Professor of Moral Philosophy and the Languages; Rev. Dr. John McMillan Professor of Divinity; Samuel Miller Professor of Mathematics, Natural Philosophy, and Geography. On November 30, 1802, the Rev John Watson, the *first* President of the College, died.

In the spring of 1803, the Rev. James Dunlap was elected President, and he was empowered to engage his own tutors. To the duties of President, he added the Pastorate of Miller's Run church, five miles from Canonsburg. In 1805, Rev. Dr. John McMillan was elected Vice-President of Jefferson College. In this year the college received a second donation from the State legislature of $3000, while in 1807 Gen. Hamilton, who was the representative of this district in Congress, through his personal exertion, received from his friends two hundred and ten dollars, to be applied to the building of a college edifice.

In September, 1807, the trustees of Jefferson College received a communication from the trustees of Washington College, asking the appointment of a committee to devise a plan for the union of the two colleges, both being in Washington County, and but seven miles apart. This communication was referred to a committee, who, in April, 1808, reported that the committees could agree on no terms, yet regretting that it could not be accomplished on liberal and equitable principles.

On 25th of April, 1811, Rev. Dr. Dunlap resigned the Presidency of the College, and the duties of the office devolved upon Dr. McMillan the Vice-President, who was authorized to employ the necessary professors.

In April, 1812, Rev. Dr. Andrew Wylie was elected President, with authority to select his assistants. The College prospering, by the accession of students, the trustees deemed it expedient, in 1815, to appoint a committee to make preparations for the erection of a new college edifice, but while this committee was maturing a plan, the trustees, in September of this year, received a communication from the trustees of Washington College, respecting a union of the two colleges. The committee from Washington College trustees were Rev. John Anderson, Rev. Wm. Spear, Alexander Murdoch, and Parker Campbell, Esqs.; those from Jefferson College were Rev. Dr. McMillan, James Kerr, Mr. McDonald, and Samuel Murdoch, Esqs. These committees met on the 25th of October, when the committee from Washington College proposed that they would place at the disposal of the united Board all the present funds with $5000, provided that Washington was made the permanent site of the united college; this proposition the committee of Jefferson College declined, as they could not consent that the college should be removed from Canonsburg, unless that the hand of Providence should be clearly discernible in such measure, either by casting lots or leaving it to the decision of the legislature. They reported their action, however, to the trustees of Jefferson College, who passed a resolution stating that if the trustees of Washington College would not recede from their position claiming the site of the college at Washington, but would give $5000 in addition to their funds, half the trustees, and the casting vote in the choice of the faculty, the Board of Trustees of Jefferson College will unite in petitioning the legislature to effect the object in view. Final action was postponed until the professors, who were deeply interested in the movement, should be consulted. President Wylie and Prof. Miller replied that if the trustees of Jefferson College did not accede to the proposition from Washington College, they would continue as professors, and render the institution respectable; but if these proposals should give the Board and Faculty of Jefferson College the preponderancy and priority they should accede to the proposition. The trustees, after hearing these views, were prepared to vote on the question; the question being taken there was a tie vote, the President not voting. On 4th of January, 1816, an adjourned meeting of the trustees was held, and the President voted affirmatively, but the students remonstrated, and the trustees passed another resolution that the union recommended could not be confirmed and ratified. This brought on a bitter and angry discussion, which resulted in the two colleges remaining separate as rival institutions.

In the spring of 1816, the trustees bought the grounds upon which the present college buildings are erected from Mrs. Canon, and appointed a committee to sell the old stone college and lot.

On September 24, 1817, the Rev. Dr. Andrew Wylie resigned the office of President, and Rev. Dr. McMillan was chosen President. In April, 1818, Rev. Abraham Anderson was chosen Professor of Languages. The trustees resumed the subject of building a new college edifice, and in the spring of 1819 Dr. McMillan had permission to travel for two months and receive contributions for this purpose.

In 1820 the legislature made a *third* appropriation of $1000 to the college. In September of this year Prof. Anderson resigned, and Rev. Wm. Smith was elected Professor of Languages.

In August, 1822, Rev. Dr. McMillan resigned, and Rev. Wm. Smith was elected President *pro tem.*, but on the 24th of September, 1822, Rev. Matthew Brown, D. D. was elected President.

In June, 1826, the Jefferson Medical College of Philadelphia was attached as a portion of Jefferson College and placed under its charter, the legislature authorizing the election of ten additional trustees to reside in Philadelphia. This act provided that the medical school was not to have any claims on the funds of Jefferson College.

In 1827 the State legislature granted a *fourth* appropriation of $1000 for three successive years, and in 1833 a *fifth* for $2000.

In 1829 the President, Dr. Brown, was appointed to raise the necessary funds for the erecting of new buildings, and so pre-eminently successful was Dr. Brown, that the trustees held a meeting in the new college building on the 27th of March, 1833, and from this circumstance the building was named PROVIDENCE HALL. It is sixty by ninety feet, in which commencements and contests are held, and the Presbyterian church of Canonsburg statedly worship therein.

In 1830 the trustees purchased a farm adjoining the town to incorporate with the college the manual labor system, but the enterprise failed without loss to the college.

After a long and prosperous Presidency, Dr. Brown resigned in 1845, who was the instrument in raising Jefferson College to a state of unparalleled prosperity. His successor was Rev. Dr. R. J. Brackenridge, who filled the office until 1847, but not with the success of his predecessor. He was succeeded by Rev. Dr. A. B. Brown, who filled the office acceptably both to the trustees, and the people, and the students, and had health been spared him, would have rivalled his honored father both in his literary attainments and his superior executive and administrative abilities, but ill health compelled him to resign in 1857, when Rev. Dr. Alden was elected

President, and a permanent endowment fund of sixty thousand dollars was raised.

In March, 1854, it was proposed to place Jefferson College under the care of the Synod of Pittsburg, but the Board of Trustees of the college declined the proposed ecclesiastical connection for the following reasons: 1. That it had received money and lands from the State. 2. That other religious denominations were alike interested in its prosperity. 3. That the present prosperity did not call for the change. 4. That the funds of the college could be as well used for a "more sanctified education" in the present arrangement than by making it an ecclesiastical college. The college quietly proceeded to accomplish the intention of its founders, until the union took place with Washington College, for the history of which see Washington College, page 153.

With this history I shall add a list of the Principals and Professors of the Jefferson College from its organization.

1802, April 27.—Rev. JOHN WATSON was elected PRESIDENT and Professor of Languages and Moral Philosophy. He died November 30, 1802.
1802, April 27.—Rev. John McMillan was elected Professor of Divinity.
1802, April 27.—Samuel Miller, A. M., was elected Professor of Mathematics and Natural Philosophy. Resigned September, 1830. Died in 1831.
1803, April 27.—Rev. JAMES DUNLAP, A. M., was elected PRESIDENT and Professor of Languages and Moral Philosophy. Resigned April 25, 1811.
1805, April 27.—Rev. John McMillan, D. D., was elected Vice President. Died November 16, 1833.
1812, April 29.—Rev. ANDREW WYLIE, D. D., was elected PRESIDENT. Resigned April 24, 1816.
1817, September 24.—Rev. WILLIAM MCMILLAN, A. M., was elected PRESIDENT. Resigned August 14, 1822.
1818, September 24.—Rev. Abraham Anderson, A. M., was elected Professor of Languages. Resigned September, 1821.
1821, September 24.—Rev. William Smith, A. M., was elected Professor of Languages
1822, September 25.—Rev. MATTHEW BROWN, D. D., LL. D., was elected PRESIDENT. Resigned September 27, 1845.
1824, April.—Rev. James Ramsey, D. D., was elected Professor of Hebrew.
1826, April.—Rev. Richard Campbell, A. M., was elected Professor of Languages and Mathematics. Resigned 1827.
1827, February.—Alexander T. McGill, A. B., was elected Tutor.
1829, March.—Jacob Coon, A. B., was elected Tutor.
1830, February.—Rev. John H. Kennedy, A. M., was elected Professor of Mathematics. Died December 15, 1840.
1832, March.—Jacob Green, M. D., was elected Professor of Chemistry, Mineralogy, and Natural History. Died February, 1841.
1834, March.—C. J. Hadermann, Esq., was elected Professor of Mathematics and Modern Languages. Resigned in 1836.
1836, September.—Washington McCartney, Esq., A. M., was elected Professor of Mathematics and Modern Languages. Resigned September, 1837.

1837, September.—Rev. Charles S. Dodd, A. M., was elected Professor of Mathematics and Modern Languages. Resigned September, 1839.

1838, March.—William Darby, Esq., A. M., was elected Professor of History, Geography, and Astronomy. Resigned 1839.

1841, February.—Richard S. McCulloh, Esq., A. M., was elected Professor of Mathematics, Natural Philosophy, and Chemistry. Resigned September, 1843.

1841, February.—Rev. A. B. Brown, A. M., was elected Professor of Belles-Lettres and Adjunct Professor of Languages. Resigned October, 1847.

1841, March.—Henry Snyder, A. M., was elected Adjunct Professor of Mathematics.

1841, July.—Charles Martin was elected Tutor.

1843, July.—Rev. Henry Snyder, A. M., was elected Professor of Mathematics.

1843, September.—S. R. Williams, Esq., A. M., was elected Professor of Natural Philosophy and Chemistry.

1844, September.—Rev. Robert W. Orr, A. M., was elected Professor of Civil Engineering and Natural History.

1845, January 2.—Rev. ROBERT J. BRACKENRIDGE, D. D., LL. D., was elected PRESIDENT. He resigned June 9, 1847.

1845, December.—Rev. A. B. Brown was elected Professor of Belles-Letters, Rhetoric, Logic, and History.

1845, December.—Rev. Robert W. Orr was elected Professor of Latin Language and Literature.

1846, March.—Rev. Thomas Beveridge, D. D., was elected Professor Extraordinary of Evidences of Natural and Revealed Religion.

1846, March.—John D. Vowell, M. D., was elected Professor Extraordinary of Physiology and Comparative Anatomy.

1847, October 14.—Rev. A. B. BROWN, D. D., was elected PRESIDENT. Resigned July 31, 1855. Died September 8, 1863.

1848, June.—Rev. Robert M. White, A. M., was elected Professor Extraordinary of Rhetoric. Died December, 1848.

1849, July.—Rev. Joseph R. Wilson, A. M., was elected Professor Extraordinary of Rhetoric.

1849, July.—W. W. West, A. B., was elected Principal of the Classical Department.

1850, August.—Robert Patterson was elected Professor of Mathematics. Resigned November, 1854.

1850, August.—Rev. William Wallace was elected Professor of Moral Science. Died January, 1851.

1852.—Rev. Wm. Ewing, A. M., was elected Professor Extraordinary of History and Languages.

1852.—Rev. Samuel R. Williams, A. M., was elected Professor Extraordinary of Natural Sciences. Resigned 1854.

1852, September.—Samuel Jones, A. M., was elected Professor of Natural Philosophy and Chemistry.

1852, December.—Rev. Aaron Williams, D. D., was elected Professor of Latin Language and Literature. Resigned August 2, 1859.

1852, December.—Rev. Abm. Anderson, D. D., was elected Professor Extraordinary of Hebrew. Died May, 1855.

1855, February.—John Frazer, A. M., was elected Professor of Mathematics. Resigned April, 1865.

1855, February.—John B. Stilley, A. M., was elected Professor of Civil Engineering.

1855, July.—Rev. John B. Clark was elected Professor Extraordinary of Hebrew.
1857, January 7.—Rev. JOSEPH ALDEN, D. D., LL. D., was elected PRESIDENT, and inaugurated March 25, 1857. Resigned November 4, 1862.
1857, March.—Rev. Alexander B. Brown, D. D., was elected Professor Extraordinary of History and Political Economy. Resigned August 4, 1857.
1857, August.—Rev. Alexander B. Brown, D. D., was elected Professor Extraordinary of English Literature. Resigned July 31, 1860. Died September 8, 1863.
1857, August.—Alonzo Linn, A. M., was elected Professor of History and Political Economy.
1857, August.—M. B. Riddle, A. M., was elected Adjunct Professor of the Greek Language.
1860, March.—Rev. Isaac N. McKinney, A. M., was elected Professor of the Latin Language. Resigned January 2, 1861. Died November 20, 1864.
1861, February.—C. M. Dodd, A. M., was elected Professor of the Latin Language. Resigned April, 1865.
1861, March.—I. V. Herriott, A. M., M. D., was elected Professor of Anatomy and Physiology.
1861, August.—Alonzo Linn was elected Professor of the Greek Language.
1862, November 4.—Rev. DAVID H. RIDDLE, D. D., LL. D., was elected PRESIDENT and Professor of Intellectual and Moral Philosophy, inaugurated March 25, 1863. Resigned April, 1864. Rev. Riddle was President at the union of Washington and Jefferson Colleges.
1864, August.—W. G. Barnett, A. M., M. D., was elected Professor of Anatomy and Physiology.
1866, March 6.—Rev. Jonathan Edwards inaugurated President April 4, 1866.

For list of Professors under act of March 4, 1865, see WASHINGTON AND JEFFERSON COLLEGE, under title of WASHINGTON BOROUGH. See page 170.

Jefferson College has a college library of 10,000 volumes, and philosophical and astronomical apparatus. In connection with Jefferson College are two Societies, viz : The PHILO LITERARY SOCIETY and the FRANKLIN LITERARY SOCIETY, each of which has a valuable library connected therewith of 3800 volumes.

The Philo Literary Society was founded August 23, 1797. Its founders were the Rev. *John Watson* (first President of the College), Rev. *Samuel Tate*, Rev. *Robert Johnston*, Rev. *James Satterfield*, Rev. *John M. Lain*, Rev. *Elisha McCurdy*, *William Fowler*, Rev. *John Boggs*, Rev. *Robert Lee*, Rev. *W. Moorehead*, Rev. *William W. Millan*, D. D., and *Joseph Smith*. It has a library of 3700 volumes.

The Franklin Literary Society was founded November 14, 1797, by *James Carnahan*, *Cephas Dodd*, *James Galbraith*, *Thomas Hughes*, *David Imbrie*, *Jacob Lindly*, *Stephen Lindly*, *William Wood*, and *William Wick*.

The object of these societies is, mental and moral improvement, and mutual friendship. The Christian Association has about 1200 volumes.

228   HISTORY OF WASHINGTON COUNTY.

November 3, 1817, a female academy was opened in Canonsburg, under the superintendence of Rev. Matthew Brown and J. Williams.
December 29, 1817, first Sabbath school established in Canonsburg.
This township in 1789 had *fourteen* distilleries, in 1790 *ten*, and in 1791 *sixteen*, but this year (1869) none are in operation.
The Methodist Episcopal Church of Canonsburg was organized in 1842. Its *first* class was composed of but three members, viz: John Ramsey, H. N. Capron, and Henry Yerty. By perseverance and zeal they were enabled to purchase a lot and erect a brick building thereon in 1845, forty by sixty feet. Its first pastor was Rev. I. Sutton; his successors have been Rev. I. Callender, Rev. H. Snyder, Rev. D. A. McCready, Rev. R. A. Cunningham, Rev. A. Jackson, Rev. R. L. Miller, Rev. Latshaw McGuire, Rev. J. F. Jones, Rev. Sylvester Jones, Rev. Robert Miller, Rev. Alexander Scott, Rev. D. A. Pierce, Rev. H. Neff, Rev. I. C. Cassel, Rev. Mr. Huddleston.

There is a Sunday school connected with this church, having twelve teachers and one hundred and seventy scholars, with a library of 900 volumes.

PRESBYTERIAN CHURCH.

The Presbyterian Church of Canonsburg was organized October 25, 1830. Most of its original members were previously connected with the Chartiers congregation. Presbytery for some time hesitated about organizing a church at Canonsburg. At first Chartiers and Canonsburg churches formed one pastoral charge. The congregation since their organization have used Providence Hall in the new college building as a place of worship. Rev. Matthew Brown, D. D., was its first pastor. On the 12th of December, 1845, the Rev. Robert J. Brackenridge, D. D., was installed; he resigned the pastorate June 20, 1847. Rev. Alexander Brown, D. D., was elected pastor December 23, 1847; installed in February, 1848; and continued to serve the congregation until April 7, 1857. Rev. Aaron Williams, D. D., was chosen co-pastor with Rev. Dr. A. Brown September 30, 1853; he served about six years. On April 7, 1857, Rev. Dr. Joseph Alden, President of Jefferson College, was invited to take part with Dr. Williams in the ministerial labors of the congregation. At the resignation of Dr. Williams, Dr. Alden was followed by Rev. D. H. Riddle, D. D., who was installed January, 1863; he resigned April 10, 1868.

His immediate successor was Rev. Dr. Jonathan Edwards, President of Washington and Jefferson College. He became the stated supply and served until April, 1869. In March, 1870, Rev. Wm. F. Brown, of the Presbytery of Ohio, received a call, and is now laboring among the people; his ordination will take place June 21, 1870.

There is a Sabbath school connected with the church of one hundred and twenty members.

Reception of James Monroe, President of the United States, at Canonsburg, September 7, 1817.

A committee on behalf of the citizens of Canonsburg, and Capt. Miller's company of light infantry, met the President and conducted him to Mr. Emory's inn, where the Principal of Jefferson College, Dr. Matthew Brown, presented him the address of the Committee in behalf of the Corporation and College.

SIR: The Faculty of Jefferson College, together with the citizens of this borough, rejoice in the opportunity of presenting their respectful salutations to the Chief Magistrate of the nation. We, with our fellow citizens in other sections of the Union, view your tour through the different States as a favorable indication of your devoted attachment to the real interests of the people over whom you preside. Under your auspices we anticipate the rising splendor of our literary institutions, and of all those establishments which contribute to the independence, wealth, and general prosperity of our country.

We therefore hail you, sir, upon your arrival at the original seat of literature in the West, with sentiments of the greatest cordiality and respect. This was the consecrated spot which first gave birth to science in this western region. This institution as a college was founded in honor of your illustrious predecessor, Mr. Jefferson, in 1802, and has since been the principal nursery of literature in the western country.

Besides the common elementary course of literature, it has been the constant aim in this institution to inspire the minds of youth with those principles of piety and virtue—with those ennobling sentiments, and that sincere love of truth and duty, which are the greatest ornaments of human character, and which are best calculated to form the man and the citizen.

It has been the object of this seminary, according to the most enlightened views of human nature and the interests of society that we could obtain, to preserve in close alliance the interests of religion and learning, of piety and virtue, as essential to the energy and effect of our political institutions, and as greatly subservient to public order, harmony, and liberty. We have ever viewed sound morality and intelligence as the great supports of free government, and the principal guarantee of our rights and privileges, both civil and religious.

In this representation of our views of the general object of public education, and the influence of sound morality and science in supporting our republican institutions, we are persuaded they accord with your own sentiments, and refer to objects which you judge worthy of high consideration.

We present to your view, sir, that portion of the youth of our country which now attend this institution, and we are happy that we can bear testimony of their regard to the interesting objects of literary pursuit, and to those attainments on which their future usefulness depends. We, indeed, exhibit an emblem of the simplicity of republican manners, which, to a man of your discernment and intelligence, cannot operate as a disparagement, provided we endeavor to cherish those generous affections, and aid at those solid acquirements which shall bind us to our country, and render us instrumental in promoting its interests, and strengthening and protecting its precious institutions.

Permit us, with our fellow citizens, to congratulate you, sir, upon the auspicious circumstances which attend the commencement of your administration—circumstances which cannot fail to unite you and the people together, and impress the public mind with the belief of your devoted attachment to the best interests of our common country. Accept our earnest wishes and prayers for its prosperous course and happy issue, and indulge us with expressing the desire that when you are engaged in the appropriate functions of your high station, you may enjoy the favor and blessing of heaven, and that it may be our privilege, by fidelity and perseverance in our respective spheres, under the smiles of the same beneficent Providence, to coöperate in the work of patriotism by diffusing the light of knowledge and the saving influence of religion and morals.

CRAIG RITCHIE,   SAMUEL MILLER,
WM. MCMILLAN,   JAS. P. MILLER.
WM. GIBSON,

PRESIDENT MONROE'S ANSWER.

I thank you, Sir, and this committee, for the respect and friendship with which I have been received on my arrival here. It is with sincere gratification that I received your address. Be assured, sir, that I am deeply affected with it.

When I first meditated this tour, which was some time before I left the seat of government, I thought it would be practicable, and it was my desire to perform it in the character of a private citizen. But finding my fellow citizens wished otherwise, and everywhere met me with expressions of respect and attachment, I yielded to their wishes, and have met them with the same feelings. In these expressions of public regard, which my humble services could not inspire, I see the fixed attachment of the people to the principles of our free government.

I am happy in meeting with this Faculty, and these young men. The views of the nature and object of public education contained in your address, agree with my own. During my tour through an extensive continent I have met with many similar institutions, all entertaining nearly the same sentiments respecting the instruction of youth. And I ask you, sir, in what more noble principles could they be instructed than those of virtue and our holy religion ? These are the most solid basis on which our free government can rest, and that they should be instilled into the rising youth of our country, to whom its destinies are soon to be consigned, is of high importance. The aged pass away in rapid succession, and give place to the younger. Those who are now the hope of their country will soon become its pride. Educated in these principles, we can with confidence repose our free government, and the interests of our beloved country, in their care, assured that they will preserve, protect, and cherish them, and will fill the place of those who have gone before them with equal honor and advantage. I was led into this subject on which I have dwelt, because it is pleasing to me by the observations contained in your address.

With respect to the objects of my tour, you do me justice. You all know how necessary it is that a person in my station should be acquainted with the circumstances and situation of the country over which he presides. To acquire this knowledge I have visited our marine coasts and inland frontiers, parts most exposed to invasion. Having accomplished the objects of my tour to the full extent I at first contemplated, to me, sir, it is peculiarly gratifying, now on my return to the seat of government, to be hailed with the sentiments of approbation contained in your address.

To me it is a source of high satisfaction that, in all the places which I have visited in this tour, I have found the people so generally united, and so strongly attached to the principles of our excellent Constitution. In the union of the people our Government is sufficiently strong, and on this union I confidently rely. Our Government has proved its strength. We have terminated with honor a war carried on against a powerful nation, and that nation peculiarly favored by fortunate circumstances. Our army gained glory—our navy acquired renown—and all classes of citizens, as opportunity offered, and where the pressure was greatest, acquitted themselves with honor.

This nation is now respectable for numbers, and more respectable as an enlightened people. That its future auspices and glory may answer to its present prosperity, is my sincere desire.

Be assured, sir, that I shall always take a deep interest in the prosperity of this institution. It is known at a distance among scientific men. You have chosen for it a name not unknown abroad to science, and which to me is peculiarly interesting. I avail myself of this opportunity of bearing my testimony to the talents, learning, and great public services of that venerable statesman and philosopher whose name you have prefixed to your institution.

Accept, gentlemen, my grateful acknowledgments for the kindness with which I have been received, and my sincere wishes for your individual happiness and prosperity.

Cross Creek Township.

On the 23d day of March, 1790, the Court of Quarter Sessions erected this township out of Hopewell. Its boundaries are Smith and Jefferson on the north, Mount Pleasant and Smith on the east, Independence and Hopewell on the south, and Jefferson on the west. This township is fifteen miles northwest of Washington. The creek, which gives the name to the township, rises on the borders of Hopewell and Mount Pleasant, and runs northwest to the Ohio River. Harman's Creek pursues the same course to the same river. Several grist and saw-mills are located on these waters. Its population in 1860 was 1110, of which 81 are colored. It has three stores, ten schools, with five male and five female teachers, the former receiving $32 and the latter $28.58 per month, having two hundred and ninety-six scholars, of which one hundred and fifty-three are males and one hundred and forty-three females, tuition costing per month $1.28. Amount levied for school purposes, $1916.10, and receiving from the State appropriation $101.40.

Its town is Cross Creek village, having fifty-eight dwelling-houses, a Presbyterian church, a Methodist Episcopal church, a cemetery, an Academy, stores, boot and shoe establishments, harness-maker, &c. &c.

1787, Mr. Park, a brother of Mrs. Marquis, was tomahawked and scalped near his own dwelling-house, near where Cross Creek village now stands.

1795, September 5, Mary Patterson, of Cross Creek township, directed her executors to pay into the hands of the treasurer of the fund for the education of pious youths for the gospel ministry, the sum of £5, under the direction of the Ohio Presbytery.

1795, November 30, Henry Graham and Mary his wife, conveyed

to Samuel Fleming, Aaron Lyle, and John Wilkins, trustees of the Cross Creek congregation, in consideration of £6, and now under the care of the Rev. Thomas Marquis, a member of the Ohio Presbytery and Synod of Virginia, both under the care of the General Assembly of the Presbyterian church, and to the only use of said congregation for ever, the said congregation holding to Calvinistic principles, the lot to contain six and one-fourth acres and thirty-four and a half perches.

This congregation has erected successively *five* houses of worship, viz: In 1779, of unhewed logs, twenty-six by twenty-two feet; the second in 1784, of hewed logs, sixty by thirty feet, to this, some years afterwards, was added a gallery; the third in 1803, of stone, fifty-six by fifty-six feet; the fourth in 1830, of brick, seventy-six by fifty-six feet, with a gallery on three sides, and the fifth in 1864, of brick, eighty-two by forty-two feet. Their *first* pastor was the Rev. Joseph Smith, who received a call on June 21, 1779, who was succeeded by Rev. Thomas Marquis, whose election bears date October 18, 1793. The third and present pastor is the Rev. John Stockton, D. D., who accepted a call in April, 1827. Thus for ninety years has this church been signally blessed by having but three stated ministers, whose labors were acceptable to the people and blessed by the Lord.

ORIGINAL SETTLERS.

From James Simpson, Esq., I learn that the following persons were the original settlers in Cross Creek township: Samuel Johnson, John Tenell, Alexander Wells, William Patterson, Ephraim Hart, Jacob Buxton, Thomas Beatty, William Renolds, David Renolds, Thomas Bay, Henry Graham, James Jackson, William Calvin, Col. James Marshall, George Marquis, David Vance, Thomas Crawford, Col. John Marshall, John Marquis, William McCombs.

FORTS.

Wilson's Fort was at Wells' (now Fullerton's) mill; it was a regular stockade fort.

There was a blockhouse on the farm now owned by William M. Lee, Esq., called Renolds' Fort, from the owner of the land, Wm. Renolds, Esq. Another blockhouse, called Marshall's Fort (after Col. James Marshall), on the property now owned by Thomas McCorkle, Esq. Col. Marshall was the *first* sheriff of the county.

CANTON TOWNSHIP.

On the 23d of April, 1792, Canton township was formed by a decree of the court, bounded on the north by Chartiers, on the east by Chartiers, Washington, and Amwell, on the south by Amwell, and on the west by Hopewell.

HISTORY OF WASHINGTON COUNTY.   233

Its present boundaries are Mount Pleasant and Chartiers on the north, Chartiers, South Strabane, and Washington on the east, Franklin and Washington on the south, Hopewell and Buffalo on the west. The National turnpike and Hempfield railroad passes westerly through this township. It is drained by Chartiers' Creek and its tributaries. It adjoins the borough of Washington. The population, in 1860, was 587, of which 39 were colored. It has five schools employing two male and three female teachers, the former receiving $30 and the latter $29.29 per month, with 198 scholars, 108 males and 90 females, the tuition costing 71 cents per month. Amount raised for school purposes by taxation $875.20, from the State appropriation $63.98. The National pike and Hempfield railroad passes through this township. It contains one fulling mill, one woollen factory, one flouring mill, one grist-mill, and four saw-mills. Greatest length of this township is 6 miles, breadth 3 miles.

The boundary lines between this and Chartiers changed August term, 1863.

PIKE RUN TOWNSHIP

Was formed by a decree of the court April 23, 1792. Its boundaries were Fallowfield and Somerset on the north, the Monongahela River on the east, Bethlehem township on the south and west.

On the 9th day of March, 1839, it was divided into East and West Pike Run. Pike Run and Little Pike Run rise in the township and flow east to the Monongahela River.

1797, December 26, John Samms conveyed to David Grave, Jacob Griffith, John Head, John Almund, Joseph Pennock, and Alexander Peden, trustees on behalf of the people called Quakers, appointed by the Westland monthly meeting for this special purpose, four and one-fourth acres of land, for the purpose of a meeting-house called "Pike Run Meeting." Upon this ground was erected a meeting-house, but subsequently a division was created, one party being called the orthodox and the other Hicksite church. Both churches have been abandoned, and a Methodist Episcopal church erected within one hundred yards in West Pike Run township. This church was built about ten years since, and is called Clover Hill M. E. church, and on the circuit under the charge of Rev. J. B. Yarnall.

EAST PIKE RUN

Constituted the eastern portion of Pike Run township, but by a decree of the court it was divided into two townships, East and West Pike Run. The boundaries of East Pike Run are Fallowfield township on the north, Allen and the Monongahela River on the east, E. Bethlehem and the Monongahela River on the south, W. Pike Run and E. Bethlehem on the west. It is centrally distant from Washington 18 miles southeast. Greatest length 6 miles, breadth 3 miles. The population in 1860 was 1221. It has five schools with three male and two female teachers, the former receiving $45, and the latter $40 per month, with 197 scholars, 113 males and 84 females; cost of tuition per month being $1.47; amount levied for school and building purposes being $1276.54, from the State $83.46.

August 29, 1850, the township lines between East and West Pike Run changed and confirmed by the court. February 1, 1857, the lines between East and West Pike Run and Fallowfield were changed by a decree of the court. Its towns are *West Brownsville, Greenfield, California,* and *Granville,* the three former of which being boroughs, their respective history will be inserted after that of Granville.

Granville is on the forks of Pike Run. It contains 25 dwelling-houses, a population of 130, and has an extensive pottery and a woollen factory. In the township is one woollen factory, one distillery, two grist-mills, and a saw-mill. There are also two excellent shipping coal works in this township.

WEST BROWNSVILLE

Was erected into a borough April 2, 1852.

This town was laid out by Ephraim L. Blaine, Esq., in 1831, but Mr. J. Bowman added the addition to it west of the run. The land originally belonged to Neal Gillespie, deceased. The original town consists of 103 lots, 60 feet front, and ranging from 93 to 270 feet, on account of the abruptness of the river hill. The streets are 60 feet wide; Water, Middle, and Main streets run parallel with the Monongahela River; Bridge, Broadway, and Liberty cross these streets at right angles.

In Bowman's addition there are 61 lots, 60 feet in front and 151 feet deep, with two streets, viz., Pennsylvania and Vine streets.

This place is connected with Brownsville, Fayette County, by a bridge over the Monongahela River, 630 feet long, which cost $50,000, and was erected in 1832.

West Brownsville has a population of 540; three schools, three teachers, one male and two female, the former at $45 and the latter at $26.50 per month; 187 scholars, 97 males and 90 females, cost of tuition being 65 cts. per month; amount levied for school purposes, $342.00; for building purposes, $400.00; received from State appropriation, $60.45. It contains ten stores, two confectioneries, and four distilleries, one stoneware manufactory, two hotels, blacksmith shop, &c., two boat yards, one owned by John S. Pringle, Esq., which employs 200 hands, the other by the Messrs. Cocks. From these yards have been launched the best boats on the Ohio and Mississippi rivers. Planing mills and sash factory are in successful operation by Messrs. Aubrey, Cromlow & Coon.

West Brownsville has a town hall, which is used for a church, although the people generally have pews in the different churches in Brownsville. The national road passes through this place, and it is distant from Washington 23 miles. The town is supplied with coal from a vein seven feet in thickness. There are the remains of an old Indian graveyard in West Brownsville, immediately above the Monongahela River.

GREENFIELD.

It was laid out as a town at the confluence of Pike Run with the Monongahela River, in 1819, by Robert Jackman, and was afterwards erected into a borough by the State legislature on the 9th day of April, 1834.

It contains 82 dwelling-houses, eight stores, one confectionery, two churches, the usual number of mechanical branches, with a population of 465, and is twenty-two miles distant from Washington.

There are two churches in this borough, one under the control of the Methodist Episcopal denomination, and the other, the Cumberland Presbyterians. The Methodist church was erected in 1838, but in a few years afterwards was enlarged. The pulpit is supplied by Rev. D. A. Pierce.

The Cumberland Presbyterian church is a new edifice, although the first was built about 1839. It has also a large school-house, containing two schools, employing two female teachers, at $30 per month, with 107 scholars, 63 males and 44 females; the price of tuition per month being 72 cents; amount levied for school purposes being $242.45, and received from the State, $46.48.

As a portion of the local history of the town of Greenfield we may state that on the 18th of July, 1814, an association was formed called the *Farmers' and Mechanics' Commercial* Store of Greenfield, for the purpose of raising a fund to establish a store, and connect thereby a speedy market for their surplus produce. Capital stock, $20,000, in shares of $10 each, to be under the control of a president and nine directors, who were authorized to erect a storehouse, and purchase keel-boats to carry the produce to Pittsburg.

CALIFORNIA,

Situate in East Pike Run township, on the Monongahela River, became a borough on the 26th day of November, 1853. It was laid out on the 1st day of May, 1849, when four hundred lots were offered for sale by the proprietors, Job Johnston, Abraham Fry, W. W. Jackman, George W. Hornbeck, John Wood, and Samuel Ashmead, who purchased the farm upon which it is laid out from John Ringland. This town is 55 miles from Pittsburg, 23 from Washington, and 7 miles from Brownsville. The ground upon which the borough is located is celebrated in the annals of Youghiogheny County history, when Virginia claimed this portion of our State. It was at this point the Indians met in 1767, when the Rev. Dr. Steele, of Carlisle, was sent out to persuade the white men not to invade the hunting grounds of the Indians. This land was known as belonging to "Indian Peter," who transferred it to Samuel Young, who afterwards sold it to Robert Jackman, but in 1784 Mr. Jackman obtained a patent for the same.

The town is beautifully laid out upon the river bank, with streets crossing each other at right angles, 60 feet wide, alleys 20 feet, and lots are 50 by 150 feet, with a resident population of 640. It is separated from the borough of Greenfield by Pike Run, which empties into the Monongahela River.

It contains 88 dwelling houses; the Southwestern Normal College of the tenth district, which comprises the counties of Washington, Fayette, Greene, and Somerset; one large hotel conducted on temperance principles, built in the modern style; one boat-yard employing about sixty hands, which was established July 4, 1851; one steam tannery, one sash and door factory, five stores, one confectionery, and one drug store, with the usual number of mechanical branches, two grist-mills, a saw-mill, and two churches.

SOUTHWESTERN NORMAL COLLEGE.

A high school which had been established when the town was laid out, was the nucleus of the Normal College. In its infancy so prosperous was the high school that in about ten years it became an academy, and the perseverance and zeal which had characterized the professors, trustees, and the citizens in their laudable efforts to promote the educational interests of our State was crowned with triumphant success by the academy being changed into the Normal College on the 16th of March, 1865.

The college grounds contain ten acres. The building has a chapel, lecture-rooms, recitation-rooms, society hall, dining-room, dormitories. The object of this Normal College is to prepare teachers for the promotion and dissemination of the great cause of education, and thereby elevating the profession to that high standard of moral and mental culture which the interests of our State demand.

The faculty consists of—

J. C. GILCHRIST, Principal and Professor of Didactics, Mental and Moral Science, and Languages.

J. G. Good, Professor of Higher Mathematics and Natural Science.

G. G. Hertzog, Professor of Arithmetic and Book-Keeping.

Mrs. H. C. Gilchrist, Professor of English Grammar and Literature and History.

Miss Annie M. Hurfort, Professor of the English Branches, Elocution, and Penmanship.

Mrs. S. C. Hays and Miss H. N. Riggs, teachers of Model School.

Miss Minnie Beacom, teacher of Instrumental Music.

METHODIST EPISCOPAL CHURCH

Of this borough is under the care of Rev. D. A. Pierce. It is a large fine brick edifice, and erected near the centre of the town.

The Disciples also have a church organization.

There are literary societies connected with the college, while the town sustains Lodge 491 of Independent Order of Odd Fellows, the Temple of Honor No. 11, and the Social Temple No. 22, these two latter being temperance organizations.

Bituminous coal abounds throughout the whole region of country. California has four schools employing one male and three female teachers, the former receiving $60 and the latter $33 per month, with 202 scholars, 108 males and 94 females, tuition costing per month 71 cents; amount levied for school purposes $427.15, received from the State appropriation $70.98.

WEST PIKE RUN

Was formed into a separate township on the 9th day of March, 1839. Its boundaries are Fallowfield township on the north; E. Pike Run on the east; E. Bethlehem on the south; Somerset and W. Bethlehem on the west. Greatest length six miles, breadth four miles. This township is centrally distant from the borough of Washington 14 miles. Its population in 1860, was 869, of which 73 are colored.

It has three stores, seven schools, with three male and four female teachers employed, the former at $31.19, the latter at $30, with 322 scholars, 167 males, 155 females, tuition costing per month 85 cents; tax levied for school purposes $1044.32, appropriation from the State $90.00.

At the February term, 1858, the township lines between West Pike Run and Fallowfield were altered and confirmed by the court.

Centreville and *Beallsville* are on the National pike, which divides East Bethlehem and West Pike Run, as also the two towns. We have placed Centreville in this township, but Beallsville being a borough, its history will be given at its appropriate place.

On the farm of Mr. West stands an Episcopal church called St. Thomas', which was erected in 1777, when this territory belonged to Youghiogheny County, Virginia. Its first minister was Rev. Mr. Ayres; his successors Rev. Mr. Davis, Rev. Mr. Peiffer, Rev. Mr. Boston, Rev. Mr. Freeman, Rev. Mr. Temple, Rev. Mr. Tenbrooke, and others. It is on the Brownsville and Pittsburg road, 7 miles from Brownsville, 26 miles from Pittsburg, 3½ miles from Greenfield. It is built of logs, and weather-boarded, 30 feet square, two stories, with a gallery around it. It is the oldest church in the county.

At the time of the whiskey insurrection, and during the ministry of Rev. Mr. Ayres, and while the insurgents were marching towards Parkinson's Ferry, they stopped at this church, in which Rev. Mr. Ayres was then preaching, and for his supposed disloyal sentiments, he advocating the duty of the citizen towards the government, these insurgents took him from the pulpit, determined to shoot him, but by a Providental interference the wrath of man was restrained, and he returned to the church and finished his sermon.

Among the papers of Rev. Joseph Dodridge, I find the following memorandum:—

"At a convention held at St. Thomas' Church, in Washington County, Pa., September 25, 1803, present, Rev. Robert Ayres, Rev. Joseph Dod ridge, Rev. Francis Reno, and Rev. Mr. Seaton. After divine service Rev. R. Ayres was appointed chairman, and Stephen John Francis secretary, when the following resolution was adopted:—

Resolved, That application for supplies shall be made to the convention in writing, with the names annexed of those who wish the supply, and that they shall become responsible to the minister for a sum not less than four dollars.

This convention passed another resolution that an adjourned meeting thereof should be held in six months, at the church near Gen. Neville's old place, on Chartiers' Creek; Rev. R. Ayres to preach the opening sermon."

In 1810, a meeting of the Protestant Episcopal clergymen was held in Washington, when it was resolved that the Rev. Jos. Dodridge open a correspondence with the Rt. Rev. Bishop White, for the purpose of obtaining, through him, permission from the General Convention to form a diocese in the western country embracing the western counties of Pennsylvania, Western Virginia, and the State of Ohio, and to elect a bishop.

There is a Methodist Episcopal church in Centreville; also two miles from this place is a brick church called Taylor's M. E. church, both under the care of Rev. J. C. McIntire.

The township contains two grist-mills, four steam saw-mills, two sorghum manufactories, one vineyard, which manufactures about 600 gallons of wine annually, and one distillery.

Centreville is three miles east of Beallsville on the National pike, and was laid out by Samuel Rogers in 1819. It derives its name from being midway between Hillsboro and Brownsville. It contains fifty dwellings, four stores, and the usual number of the mechanical professions, with a population of 263. It is distant from Washington eighteen miles. There is an Odd Fellows' Lodge in this place.

BEALLSVILLE

Was erected into a borough February 16, 1852. This town was laid out by Zephaniah Bealle, George Jackson, Christian Kreider, and S. W. Blake, on the 23d of August, 1819, on the National pike. The lots (60 by 180 feet) were sold on the 12th of September following. It is eight miles from Brownsville, and fifteen from Washington, on the boundary line between Pike Run and E. Bethlehem, containing seventy-eight dwelling houses, two hotels, four stores, two groceries, two tailors, saddle and harness maker, blacksmith, wagon-maker, a marble manufactory, shoe makers, &c. &c., a Methodist Episcopal church, a Masonic hall, and one school-house, with a population of 410.

The Presbyterian denomination some time since had an organization and a brick church, but it has been sold to the Free Masons.

It has two schools with two teachers, one male at $55 and one female at $30 per month, having 95 scholars, 48 males, 47 females; cost of tuition per month 98 cents; amount of tax levied, $219.68; received from the State appropriation $39.78.

Main Street, on the National road, is the principal street, although Gay Street crosses it nearly at right angles. This street is on the State road leading from Pittsburg to Morgantown. The lots are 60 by 180 feet.

There is a Baptist church west of Beallsville, near the township line of West Bethlehem, and a Methodist Protestant church near J. Baker, Esq., in the centre of the township.

RICH HILL TOWNSHIP.

The Supreme Executive Council, on March 13, 1793, upon the application of the court of Washington County, established this township, assigning as its boundaries Finley township on the north, Franklin and Greene on the east, Mason and Dixon's line on the south, and Virginia on the west. By the act of the legislature of February 9, 1796, this township, with Franklin, Greene, Morgan, and Cumberland townships, comprised Greene County.

BUFFALO TOWNSHIP

Was organized by a decree of the Court of Quarter Sessions, on 8th May, 1799. It was bounded on the north by Hopewell, on the east by Canton, on the south by Morris and Finley, and on the west by Donegal.

Its present boundaries are Hopewell and Independence townships on the north, Canton and Franklin on the east, East Finley and Franklin on the south, and Donegal on the west. Greatest length eight miles, breadth seven miles. It is centrally distant from Washington borough, seven miles. It is drained by Buffalo Creek and its branches, which flow northwest into the Ohio River. Upon this creek are many grist and saw-mills. In 1860 its population was 1578, of which 2 were colored. At the February term of the court, 1866, the lines between Buffalo and Franklin townships were confirmed.

It has two stores, one distillery, and eight schools, employing three male and five female teachers, the former at $36.66, the latter at $35, with three hundred and twenty scholars, one hundred and ninety males, one hundred and forty females ; cost of tuition, $1.51 per month ; amount of taxes for school purposes, $1484.63, and building purposes, $1487.63 ; State appropriation, $127.92.

Its towns are Taylorstown and Buffalo village. Originally Taylorstown was called New Brunswick, and in 1808 elections were held at this place by law. Afterwards it became changed to its present name. It is situate on Buffalo Creek, eight miles west of Washington, containing forty-two dwelling houses and a population of two hundred and sixty-five.

Buffalo village is on a fork of Buffalo Creek, seven miles southwest of Washington.

Presbyterian Church

Is situated in this township, on the head-waters of the east fork of Buffalo Creek, one-half mile south of the National road.

This church was built about 1830, and has had the ministerial labors of Rev. W. P. Alrich until 1864, when he resigned. His immediate successor was Rev. Mr. Alexander, who has since died. The present incumbent is the Rev. R. W. Morton. There is a Sabbath school connected with this church.

There are also the following churches in this township, viz : A M. E. church, near Roney's Point, in the northern part, a Baptist church, southwest of the Railroad depot, near Mr. Caldwell's, and two United Presbyterian churches.

North Buffalo U. P. church was organized about 1780. Rev. Matthew Henderson was pastor from 1781 until October 2, 1795; Rev. Robert Laing from 1796 until 1805 ; Rev. David French from July 2, 1811, until June 14, 1853; Rev. W. M. C. Gibson from November 29, 1855, until November 12, 1861 ; Rev. R. C. Welch from May 14, 1867, to December 22, 1868, with a membership of one hundred and seventeen.

South Buffalo U. P. church was organized in 1810. Rev. David French was pastor from July 2, 1811, until November 22, 1852; Rev. James G. Carson from November 13, 1856, until April 30, 1867, with a membership of eighty-one.

Mount Pleasant Township.

This township, by a decree of the court, was erected 12th May, 1806.

Its original boundaries were Cecil township on the northeast, Chartiers on the southeast, Canton and Hopewell on the south, Cross Creek on the west, and Smith on the northwest: greatest length 9 miles, breadth 5½ miles.

Its boundaries are Smith and Robinson townships on the north; Cecil and Chartiers on the east; Chartiers, Canton, and Hopewell on the south; and Smith, Cross Creek, and Hopewell on the west. It is centrally distant from Washington, northwest, 10 miles. In 1860 its population was 1348, of which 20 were colored. It is drained north by Racoon Creek, south and east by Chartiers' Creek and branches of that stream, and west by the middle fork of Cross Creek.

It has four stores, ten schools, employing three male and seven female teachers, the former receiving $32.26 and the latter $30.57 monthly, with 366 scholars, 175 males and 191 females, the cost of tuition being $1.04 per month ; amount levied for school purposes, $1620.63 ; State appropriation, $129.48.

Hickory is its chief town, and, from its position in the township, roads to all parts radiate from it. It contains 52 dwellings—fair grounds, beautifully located—a population of 280, and the necessary number of stores and mechanical branches.

Adjoining the town is *Mount Pleasant U. P. church*, a handsome brick building. It was organized about 1809. Its pulpit has been filled by Rev. W. C. Brownlee, D. D., from May 3, 1809, to September 1, 1812; Rev. Alexander Donan from July 6, 1819, to April 20, 1852; Rev. Joseph R. Thompson from April 28, 1853, to December 16, 1861; Rev. W. A. McConnel from July 4, 1865, to the present time, with a membership of 160.

This congregation is occupying the third house of worship; the present was erected in 1868, at a cost of $12,000, built of brick, 60 by 80 feet, handsomely frescoed, and finished in modern style. The Sabbath school has one hundred scholars under competent teachers, with an excellent library.

One mile west of Hickory is Mount Prospect Presbyterian church, which was organized in the year 1826. This congregation has had two church edifices, the first of frame, built immediately upon its organization, the second of brick, built two years since.

The ministers who have officiated as pastors since its organization were: 1, Rev. David Hervey; 2, Rev. John Moore; 3, Rev. David R. Campbell; 4, Rev. W. B. Keeling; 5, Rev. J. C. Caldwell; 6, Rev. R. T. Price, the present faithful incumbent. There is a Sabbath school connected with the church.

Carroll Township

Was formed on September 30, 1834, from Nottingham and Fallowfield. It was originally named by the viewers Knox township, but the court changed it to Carroll.

Its boundaries are the Monongahela River and Union township on the north, the Monongahela River on the east, Fallowfield and Monongahela River on the south, and Nottingham and Fallowfield on the west. It is centrally distant from Washington nineteen miles. In 1860 its population was 1907, of which 74 were colored. It has five stores, one confectionery, nine schools, with two male and seven female teachers, their pay being $35 per month, with 486 scholars, 267 males and 219 females, cost of tuition per month being 79 cents; amount levied for school tax purposes, $1480.92; State appropriation, $132.60; greatest length eight miles, breadth three miles.

Its towns are Monongahela City (formerly Parkinson's Ferry, but subsequently called Williamsport); Columbia, population 200, on the Monongahela River. Monongahela City being a borough, its history will be given after the villages.

September 12, 1814. Charles DeHass laid out the town of *Columbia* this day, on the farm of Mr. Hoover, four miles above Williamsport. The proprietor, to induce people to purchase lots, says, it is in contemplation to form a new county, and from its being so very central in the contemplated county, he has laid off the town with large lots, and wide streets and alleys, with public grounds for a church, academy, burying-ground, public buildings, &c. Columbia is in a deep bend of the river, twenty-one miles distant from Washington.

There are the remains of an old Presbyterian church on the farm of William Crawford, now owned by John Wilson, Esq. It was built about 1785, and additions were made to it until it had sixteen corners; the Rev. Mr. Ralston occupied the pulpit. The burying ground is used by the old citizens. The remains of this church are three miles from Monongahela City, and close to the township line which separates Carrol and Fallowfield.

The Horseshoe Baptist Church is two miles from Monongahela City, erected in 1790. The first church was built of logs, but the present one is brick. Rev. Mr. Hargrave is the present pastor.

This township contains two grist-mills, one paper mill, and five collieries.

Ginger Hill Lutheran Church was erected in 1847; built of brick; of modern style; Rev. Mr. Waters, Rev. Mr. Emory, Rev. Mr. Melhom, Rev. A. Wylie, Rev. Mr. Ryder were the pastors.

There is an United Brethren Church near the tollgate, in which the different denominations occasionally preach, with no settled pastor.

Union Township.

This township was organized March 31, 1836, from Peters and Nottingham townships. On September 1, 1846, the boundary lines between Union and Peters were confirmed by the court, and another change and confirmation took place at the November term 1862.

Its boundaries are Allegheny County on the north, Allegheny County and the Monongahela River on the east, Carroll township on the south, and Peters and Nottingham on the west. It is centrally distant from Washington 14 miles. In 1860 its population was 1452, of which 10 are colored. Greatest length 6 miles, breadth 3 miles. It has nine stores, seven schools, employing four male and three female teachers, at $40 per month, with 435 scholars, 229 males 196 females; the cost of tuition being 75 cents per month; taxes levied for school purposes $1776.11; State appropriation $141.96.

Its towns are Limetown and Finleyville.

Finleyville is on the road from Washington to Pittsburg, 12 miles northeast of Washington. It was laid out by a sea-captain who purchased the land and named the place Rogue Alley, after the name of his ship. He sold it to James Finley and Mr. Mellinger, about 1790, from which time it bears the name of Finleyville. It has a population of about eighty, and also an Odd Fellows' hall.

Limetown is on the left bank of the Monongahela River. The town is chiefly composed of miners, there being many large and extensive collieries in the immediate vicinity of the place. The town may be said to extend about four miles, the houses being built upon lots, on the narrow strip of land between the Monongahela River and the abrupt hills, under which lie immense strata of bituminous coal.

There are about 650 inhabitants. Several extensive stores are doing a successful business.

In connection with the original history of this township, we may state that John Wright, father of Enoch Wright, Esq., N. Powers, and another man started with produce to New Orleans, and below Wheeling were attacked by the Indians in ambuscade; after wounding several Indians, Wright and Pomeroy were captured, Powers being wounded was killed, but Wright was burned at the stake after being taken to Sandusky.

Near Findleyville is a Seceder church which was organized about 1832; the last minister was Rev. Thomas Callohan.

The Presbyterian church of Mingo was organized in the year 1786. It is two miles south of Findleyville on a branch of Mingo Creek. From the records of the Redstone Presbytery, I find that Mingo Creek, Horseshoebottom, and Pike Run churches applied to Presbytery for a minister on August, 15, 1786. Rev. Samuel Ralston, D.D., was its first regular pastor. He was ordained and installed November 30, 1796, and took charge of this congregation and the one at Monongahela City, formerly Parkinson's Ferry, although he afterwards resigned its charge in 1836. He officiated in Mingo Creek for forty years. His successors were Rev. Mr. Shotwell, Rev. James M. Smith, Rev. John R. Dunlap, Rev. Mr. Rockwell, Rev. Mr. Greenough, and Rev. J. J. Beacom. At present they have no settled pastor.

In 1828 a Sabbath-school was organized. In 1864 it had thirteen teachers and eighty-four scholars, with a library of three hundred and eighty-two volumes.

In February, 1794, the Mingo Creek Society was organized; it consisted of Col. Hamilton's battalion, and was governed by a president and council. The electors were those subject to military duty of eighteen years of age and upwards, who elected their respective captains in certain districts, and these captains elected the council, who by the constitution were required to be not less than twenty-five years of age. One councilman was chosen for each district. It met monthly at Mingo Creek meeting-house on the first Friday of each month.

This society had power to hear and determine all matters in variance and dispute between parties, encourage teachers of schools, introduce the Bible and other religious books into schools, encourage the industrious and men of merit. No money could be expended unless by vote of the society.

Monongahela City.

On July 25th, 1796, Joseph Parkinson laid out on the western banks of the Monongahela River and below the mouth of Pigeon Creek at Parkinson's Ferry, a town which he named Williamsport, but it generally took the name of Parkinson's Ferry, because the post-office was so called. In 1833 the name of the post-office was changed to Williamsport, and on April 1, 1837, it was changed from Williamsport to Monongahela City.

The town was situated on the main road leading from Philadelphia to Washington, being twenty miles distant from this latter place. It is well to be remembered that Mr. Parkinson reserved the Ferry for himself and his heirs, but sold the lots in three equal annual payments, donating, however, one lot for a market-house and another for a meeting-house. All lots were sixty by two hundred feet with the necessary number of streets (sixty feet wide), and alleys (twenty feet wide).

An addition to the original plan of the town was made by Adam Wickerham, who laid out the lots west of Capt. Harvey's hotel, and named it Georgetown, but when the act of incorporation was procured for Monongahela City, the charter embraced both Williamsport, Georgetown, and some additional outlots.

This place has a world-wide fame as Parkinson's Ferry, as it was the rallying point during the whiskey insurrection, full particulars of which will be found in the Appendix, Chapter IV.

We shall mention the public buildings and works as they were kindly pointed to us by several of the citizens.

Horseshoebottom Presbyterian Church.

Rev. Dr. Samuel Ralston, D. D., received a call from this and Mingo Creek congregations in November, 1796, which he accepted and was therefore ordained. In the latter church he labored forty years, and in the former thirty-five years. This Horseshoebottom congregation was originally established three and one-half miles from Parkinson's Ferry, on the ridge road leading from this place to Brownsville on Simon Wilson's farm. It was a log church, had a graveyard connected with it, and part of the foundation is still visible. (See p. 240).

Dr. Ralston preached in this church until 1807, when it was removed to (Williamsport) Monongahela City. Mr. Moore, says: Dr. Ralston preached his first sermon in a little school-house near the present church building, preaching two years in the winter time in this school-house, and in the summer time in a tent in a sugar grove below town. Mr. Lamb and his wife were the first two persons who joined the church in Williamsport. The first communion was held in August, 1816, when Dr. Ralston was assisted by Rev. Matthew Brown, D. D. The whole number of communicants at that time were forty-five.

The church is located on Chess Street, a neat, substantial brick building; its pulpit has been filled by Rev. Dr. Ralston until 1835. His successors have been Rev. George D. Porter, from 1835 to 1838, Rev. J. W. Kerr from 1839 to 1861, Rev. S. G. Dunlap from 1862 to 1867, Rev. J. S. Sutchell from 1867 to the present time, but I learn he has sent in nis resignation.

The following persons have been ordained ruling elders since the pastorate of Dr. Ralston, viz: James Hair, James McGrew, Jesse Martin, Robert McFarland, Aaron Kerr, Isaac Vanvoorhis, James Gordon, Henry Fulton, Joseph Kiddoo, John Power, James Dickey, James Curry, E. W. Tower, John Wright, Francis J. Gardner, David Moore, David D. Yohe, Samuel Hindman, three of whom have passed into the spirit land, each upwards of eighty years of age, to receive a crown of righteousness.

There is a Sabbath school connected with the church, which by the last report numbers 17 teachers, 250 scholars, and has a library of about fifteen hundred volumes. Its organization is placed at various dates, but the Rev. Mr. Dunlap thinks it was established in the year 1822.

CUMBERLAND PRESBYTERIAN CHURCH.

Rev. John Morgan and Rev. Alfred Bryan as missionaries instituted the Cumberland Presbyterian church on the 31st of Jan. 1833, in this place. A church was erected and ready for occupancy by September 1, 1833. The following ministers were ordained as pastors: 1833, Rev. Samuel M. Sparks; 1834, Rev. Alexander Robinson; 1835, Rev. S. M. Sparks; 1836, Rev. John Carey; 1837, Rev. Saml. E. Hudson; 1840, Rev. Mr. Dunlap; 1841, Rev. B. Miller; 1842, Rev. Mr. Brice. The books show a membership of one hundred and four members, but for the last twenty years there has been no regular meetings held, the members having joined other denominations.

METHODIST EPISCOPAL CHURCH

Was organized about the year 1812. Two local preachers by the name of Riggs (who were brothers) held the first meeting on the farm of Mrs. Baxter, now owned by Ira Butler. In 1813 the *first* class-meeting was held in the house which stood at the corner of Race Street and Cherry Alley, which was owned by Wm. Wickerham. The *first* Methodist preaching was held in the log schoolhouse, on the same lot on which the Presbyterian church now stands. In 1833, Rev. Dr. Charles Cook being stationed preacher, applied himself diligently to the work, and the substantial brick edifice on the corner of Race and Chess streets was erected, at a cost of twenty-five hundred dollars, Wm. Imsen having presented the lot. The congregation worshipped in this edifice until 1868, when they erected a new building on Main Street, which cost forty-five thousand dollars, a magnificent structure, and does honor to that denomination. Rev. Hiram Miller is the present officiating clergyman. We regret exceedingly our inability to procure the records of a church which in a little more than half a century held their first meeting in a log school-house, and now boasts of the finest architectural church in Monongahela City.

There is a Sabbath school connected with the church, organized

January 1, 1820, of which Thomas Collins, Esq., was chosen first superintendent. It has twenty teachers, and a library of three hundred volumes.

WESLEYAN METHODIST CHURCH.

This denomination has an organization in Monongahela City.

PROTESTANT EPISCOPAL CHURCH.

The parish of St. Paul's Episcopal Church was organized by Rev. Bishop Alonzo Potter, at Monongahela City, November, 18, 1863, the following persons being elected vestrymen : William Manown, John S. Markle, R. T. Robinson, R. M. Gee, Francis Nelson, James P. Shepler, and E. W. Crittenden.

The corner-stone of their beautiful church was laid in 1866. It being a Gothic stone building of fifty by ninety feet, with a tower attached, at a cost of fifteen thousand dollars. December 4, 1863, Rev. H. Mackay took charge as the first rector. He served until March 1870, when Rev. J. B. Linskea was elected.

It has a Sabbath school with eight teachers and eighty scholars. It was organized in the spring of 1862, by Rev. Mr. Ten Broeck, who preached as a missionary one year before the church was established.

CHURCH OF THE TRANSFIGURATION

Have a church, which was organized as early as 1816, and has received the services of such eminent divines as father McGuire, O'Conner, &c. The Catholic church is named the church of the Transfiguration. It was built in 1865, and is situated in the west end of the city; its erection cost six thousand dollars. The building was commenced under the Rev. Dennis Kearney. He was succeeded by Rev. John O. G. Scanlon, who was followed by the Rev. William F. Hayes, the present pastor.

There are one hundred and seventeen families connected with the church.

LUTHERAN CHURCH.

This congregation has recently purchased the Methodist Episcopal church edifice, on the corner of Race and Chess Streets, having paid for the same thirty-seven hundred dollars. It is under the pastoral care of Rev. Mr. Rider, who, by his zeal in his master's cause, bids fair to add another auxiliary to the propagation of the religion of Christ.

FIRST BAPTIST CHURCH

Was organized in 1860. Rev. R. R. Sutton was the first minister; his successor is Rev. Mr. Hardgrave. The congregation are erecting a church thirty-seven by fifty feet. It was incorporated in 1869. There is a Sabbath-school attached.

AFRICAN METHODIST EPISCOPAL CHURCH

Was founded in 1833. The ministers who have officiated as regular pastors comprise the following persons: 1833, Rev. Samuel Clingman; 1835, Thomas Lawrence; 1836, Rev. S. Clingman; 1838, Rev. Wm. Newman; 1840, Rev. Fayette Davis; 1842, Rev. James Coleman; 1844, Rev. George Coleman; 1846, Rev. Augustus R. Greer; 1848, Rev. Wm. Morgan; 1849, Rev. James Coleman; 1850, Rev. Nelson Carter; 1853, Rev. Levan Gross; 1855, Rev. John W. Jones; 1856, Rev. Shugart T. Jones; 1858, Rev. Levan Gross; 1860, Rev. S. T. Jones; 1861, Rev. Levan Gross; 1863, Rev. A. Harwell; 1864, Rev. A. Harwell; 1865, Rev. L. Gross; 1866, Rev. Charles Greene; 1867, Rev. Alfred Newman; 1868, Rev. L. Gross; 1869, Rev. W. C. West; 1870, Rev. W. H. Thomas.

The congregation rented different houses to worship in, until 1842, when it made arrangements to build a suitable house. In 1849 the basement was finished, in which religious services were held, but the church was finally finished in 1858. The church has a membership of, ninety-five, and a Sabbath-school connected, with the usual number of teachers and scholars.

MONONGAHELA CEMETERY.

This beautiful city of the dead attracts universal admiration, not only for its situation, but the manner in which it is laid out. Here the sorrowing son and daughter of sighing humanity can quietly, peacefully, and with Christian resignation, commit the remains of their loved ones, buoyed up by the message of our Saviour, who whispers to each disconsolate heart, "What I do thou knowest not now, but thou shalt know hereafter."

This company was established in 1863, and immediately after its organization purchased thirty-two acres for the purposes contemplated by the charter. The improvements are estimated at sixty thousand dollars. Its officers are James Stockdale, Esq., President, William J. Alexander, Esq., Treasurer, and Dr. R. C. King, Secretary.

UNION SCHOOL-HOUSE

Is a beautiful, substantial, and plain three-story edifice, built in modern style, to promote the educational interests of the pupils.

Monongahela City has eight schools, employing two male and six female teachers, the former receiving $55 and the latter $40 per month, with four hundred and thirty nine scholars (224 males and 215 females). Cost of tuition per month, ninety-three cents for each scholar. Amount of tax levied for school purposes, $2903.88, and receiving from the State appropriation, $181.74.

It would be invidious were we to enter into a full account of the iron foundries, glass works, planing-mills, saw-mills, and others of private enterprise, but we believe in doing justice to the banking-house of Alexander & Co., and Union Paper Mills.

BANKING HOUSE

Was established in 1861, by Alexander & Co. The firm has now in process of erection a magnificent banking house on Main Street, with the private residence of W. J. Alexander, Esq., attached. The building is ornamented with a Mansard roof. Every possible precaution has been taken to make the banking departments not only fire but burglar proof. The establishment of this house, the gentlemanly and courteous manner, and obliging disposition of those who regulate it, have secured the entire approbation of the whole community.

UNION PAPER-MILLS

Were originally erected by S. D. Culbertson. They are now owned by his son, Albert Culbertson, Esq. They employ thirty hands, and manufacture monthly one hundred and twenty-five tons of paper straw boards, using two steam engines, one forty horse power and one twelve horse power.

A description of the Odd Fellows' Hall we will reserve for Chapter VIII., as it more appropriately belongs there.

ALLEN TOWNSHIP

Was erected on the 14th day of June, 1853.

It is bounded on the north and west by Fallowfield township, on the east and south by the Monongahela River. Its greatest length 4 miles, its breadth 3 miles.

The lines of Allen township were changed by the court, May, 1859, by which the lands of T. C. Huggins, H. S. Chalfant, and Lucinda Chalfant were transferred to East Pike Run township.

Independence, the only village in this township, is opposite Cookstown. The post-office is named Bellzane.

There are two Methodist Episcopal churches in this township. Howe's Methodist Episcopal Church is one-half mile from Greenfield, on the road from Greenfield to Belle Vernon. The land was deeded to the church by Mr. Howe in the year 1818.

The other church is called Mount Tabor M. E. Church. The land was formerly owned by the Quakers, who use the burying ground. It is situate half way between Cookstown and Greenfield. Its pastor is Rev. C. H. Edwards.

Speers' Baptist Church is on the banks of the Monongahela River, at Speers' Ferry. The church was organized in 1795. Its first preacher was Rev. Mr. Speers. His successors were Rev. Mr. Winnet, Rev. Mr. Whitlack.

This township contains four extensive collieries, two stores, and two grist-mills. Baldwin's water-mill, turned by water power, was among the oldest mills in the county, to which persons came for many miles. In 1860 it had a population of 635, of which 14 were colored. At this time it has four schools, employing two male and two female teachers, the former at $37.50, the latter at $36.25, with 185 scholars, 93 males and 92 females, the cost of tuition monthly being 99 cents; tax levied for school purposes, $587.52; amount received from State appropriation, $66.69.

JEFFERSON TOWNSHIP

Was erected out of Hopewell township on the 16th day of June, 1853.

It is bounded north by Hanover, east by Smith and Cross Creek, south by Independence and Cross Creek, and west by West Virginia. Greatest length 7½ miles, breadth 4 miles.

Eldersville is the only town in the township in its northern part, containing 40 dwellings and a Methodist Protestant church, with a population of 218. It is 19 miles from Washington.

The township has four stores, six schools, employing three male and three female teachers, at $30 per month, with 303 scholars, 159 males and 144 females, tuition costing per month 77 cents; tax levied for school purposes, $767.33; for building purposes $767.33, and receiving from the State appropriation $90.48.

There is a Methodist Episcopal church near Mr. Gillespie's farm, on the road leading from Eldersville to Wellsburg, and a Presbyterian church near Mr. Weaver's; also, several grist and saw-mills.

The Pittsburg and Steubenville Railroad passes through the northern part of this township.

The township in 1860 had a population of 984, of which 8 were colored.

INDEPENDENCE TOWNSHIP

Was formed May 18, 1853, from Cross Creek township.

It is bounded north by Hanover, east by Smith and Cross Creek, south by Independence and Cross Creek, and west by West Virginia. Greatest length 7 miles, breadth 4 miles.

The only town is called *Independence*, 16 miles from Washington, and 7 miles from Wellsburg, West Virginia, in the western part of the township, containing 40 dwellings, a Presbyterian church, under the care of Rev. J. Fleming, a Methodist Episcopal church, and a United Presbyterian church.

This township contains five stores, six schools, employing three male and three female teachers, at $45 per month, with 295 scholars, 166 males and 129 females, tuition costing $131 per month; tax levied for school purposes, $1852 97; receiving from the State appropriation, $91.33; had a population in 1860 of 1078, of which 97 were colored.

Mount Hope U. P. Church was organized as early as 1800. The Rev. Thomas Allison was pastor from February 4, 1802, to November 28, 1837; Rev. David Thompson from September 12, 1838, to June 15, 1847; Rev. John T. Brownlee from June 12, 1851, until the present time, with a membership of 100.

FRANKLIN TOWNSHIP

Was erected out of parts of Canton and Morris, August 13, 1855.

It is bounded on the north by Buffalo, Canton, Washington, and S. Strabane; on the east by S. Strabane, Amwell, and Washington; on the south by Morris, and on the west by E. Finley and Buffalo. Greatest length 7½ miles, breadth 4½ miles.

This township has seven schools, employing three male and four female teachers, at $35 dollars per month, with 252 scholars, 137 males and 115 females, tuition costing $1.25 per month; amount levied for school purposes, $918.09; for building purposes, $688.54, and receiving from State appropriation $102.57.

Bethel Church is located near Van Buren, under the Cumberland Presbyterians.

Concord Church is connected with the same denomination, and is situated on the farm of Elias Day.

CHAPTER VI.

ELECTED OFFICERS OF WASHINGTON COUNTY FROM 1790.

Members of Congress—Senators and Representatives—President Judges—Associate Judges and Deputy Attorney-Generals—Attorneys-at-Law—Prothonotaries—Registers—Recorders—Clerk of the Courts—Sheriffs—Coroners—Commissioners—Clerks to Commissioners—Treasurers—Auditors—Notary Public—Directors of the Poor—Deputy Surveyor-Generals—Justices of the Peace.

MEMBERS OF CONGRESS

Under the Constitution of September 2, 1790.

1.—October, 1790. Hon. Thomas Scott, for Washington County.
2.— " 1797. " Albert Gallatin and John Woods, for Washington and Allegheny.
3.— " 1798. " Albert Gallatin, for Washington, Allegheny, and Greene.
4.— " 1801. " William Hoge, for Washington, Allegheny, Greene, and Crawford.

HISTORY OF WASHINGTON COUNTY. 251

5.—October,	1808.	Hon.	Aaron Lyle.
6.	" 1816.	"	Thomas Patterson.
7.	" 1824.	"	Joseph Lawrence.
8.	" 1828.	"	William McCreary.
9.	" 1830.	"	Thomas M. T. McKennan, for Washington.
10.	" 1838.	"	Isaac Leet, for Washington.
11.	" 1840.	"	Joseph Lawrence (died April 17, 1842) for Washington.
12.—May,	1842.	"	Thomas M. T. McKennan, for Washington.
13.—October,	1843.	"	John Dickey, for Washington and Beaver.
14.	" 1844.	"	John H. Ewing, for Washington and Beaver.
15.	" 1846.	"	John Dickey, " " " "
16.	" 1848.	"	Robert R. Reed, M. D., for Washington and Beaver.
17.	" 1850.	"	Thomas J. Power, for Washington and Beaver.
18.	" 1852.	"	John L. Dawson, for Washington, Fayette, and Greene.
19.	" 1854.	"	Jonathan Knight, for Washington, Fayette, and Greene.
20.	" 1856.	"	William Montgomery, for Washington, Fayette, and Greene.
21.	" 1860.	"	Jesse Lazear, for Washington, Fayette, and Greene.
22.	" 1864.	"	George V. Lawrence, for Washington, Greene, Beaver, and Lawrence.
23.	" 1868.	"	J. B. Donnelly, for Washington, Greene, Beaver, and Lawrence.

SENATORS

Who have been elected and served the period of their election, under the Constitution of 1790 and 1838.

1.—1790, October. Hon. John Hoge, for Washington and Fayette counties.
2.—1792, " " John Hoge and John Smilie, for Washington and Fayette counties.
3.—1794,* " " Thomas Stokely and Absalom Baird, for Washington and Allegheny.
4.—1796, " " John Hamilton and Thomas Moreton, for Washington and Allegheny.
5.—1800, " " John Hamilton and John Woods, for Washington, Allegheny and Greene.
6.—1806, " " Isaac Weaver and James Stevenson, for Washington and Greene.
7.—1810, " " Abel McFarland, for Washington and Greene.
8.—1812, " " Isaac Weaver, " " " "
9.—1814, " " Abel McFarland " " " "
10.—1816, " " Isaac Weaver, " " " "
11.—1818, " " Thomas McCall, " " " "

---

* The Senate declared the election held in October, 1794, as unconstitutional on account of the four western counties being in a state of insurrection, and ordered a special election in February, 1795, when the same Senators were re-elected. See History of Whiskey Insurrection (Appendix, Chapter 4), for full particulars.

252   HISTORY OF WASHINGTON COUNTY.

12.—1820, October, Hon. Isaac Weaver, for Washington and Greene.
13.—1822, " " Joshua Dickerson, " " " "
14.—1824, " " Jonathan Knight and Wm. G. Hawkins, for Washington and Greene.
15.—1828, " " Thomas Ringland and Wm. G. Hawkins, for Washington and Greene.
16.—1834, " " Isaac Leet, for Washington.
17.—1838, " " John H. Ewing, for Washington.
18.—1842, " " Walter Craig, " "
19.—1845, " " E. G. Creacraft, " "
20.—1848, " " Geo. V. Lawrence, for Washington.
21.—1851, " " M. McCaslin, for Washington and Greene.
22.—1854, " " John C. Flenniken, for Washington and Greene.
23.—1857, " " George W. Miller, " " " "
24.—1860, " " George V. Lawrence, for Washington and Greene.
25.—1863, " " William Hopkins, for Washington and Greene.
26.—1866, " " A. W. Taylor, for Washington and Beaver.
27.—1869, " " James S. Rutan, " " "

REPRESENTATIVES TO THE SUPREME EXECUTIVE COUNCIL.

1781, November 30.—Hon. James Edgar and John Canon.
1782, December 4.— " Matthew Ritchie and William McCleary.
1783, November 10.— " Matthew Ritchie and John Stephenson.
1784, November 1.— " Matthew Ritchie and John Stephenson.

REPRESENTATIVES ELECTED TO THE HOUSE OF REPRESENTATIVES.

Under the Constitution of 1790 and 1838.

1790, October.—Hon. Thomas Ryerson.
1791, " " John Minor, Thomas Scott, Daniel Leet, and Thomas Stokely.
1792, " " Thomas Stokely, Daniel Leet, John Canon, and David Bradford.
1793, " " Thomas Stokely, Craig Ritchie, John Minor, and Benjamin White.
1794,* " " James Brice, William Wallace, Benjamin White, and Craig Ritchie.
1795, " " John Minor, William Wallace, David Acheson, and Craig Ritchie.
1796, " " David Johnson, William Wallace, David Acheson, and William Hoge.
1797, " " William Hoge, William Wallace, David Acheson, and David Johnson.
1798, " " John McDowell, Absalom Baird, and Aaron Lyle.
1799, " " John McDowell, Samuel Urie, and Aaron Lyle.
1800, " " John McDowell, Samuel Urie, and Aaron Lyle.
1801, " " John McDowell, Samuel Urie, Aaron Lyle, and James Kerr.

---

* January 5, 1795. These members, with those of Westmoreland, Fayette, and Allegheny counties, were declared unconstitutionally elected, on account of the Whiskey Insurrection, and, at a special election held in February, 1795, were re-elected.

1802, October.—Hon. Samuel Agnew, Joseph Vance, John Marshall, and James Kerr.
1803, " " Samuel Agnew, Joseph Vance, John Marshall, and James Kerr.
1804, " " Samuel Agnew, David Acheson, John Marshall, and James Stephenson.
1805, " " Samuel Agnew, Aaron Lyle, John Marshall, and James Stephenson.
1806, " " James Kerr, Abel McFarland, Ebenezer Jennings, and James Stephenson.
1807, " " James Kerr, Abel McFarland, Ebenezer Jennings, and James Stephenson.
1808, " " Abel McFarland, John Colmery, Thomas McCall, and Robert Mahon.
1809, " " James Kerr, John Colmery, Thomas McCall, and Andrew Sutton.
1810, " " Thomas Hopkins, John Colmery, Joshua Dickerson, and Andrew Sutton.
1811, " " Thomas McCall, Richard Donaldson, Robert Anderson, and Joshua Dickerson.
1812, " " Thomas McCall, James Kerr, Robert Anderson, and Joshua Dickerson.
1813, " " Thomas McCall, James Kerr, James Stephenson, and Joshua Dickerson.
1814, " " Thomas Morgan, Andrew Sutton, James Stephenson, and Joshua Dickerson.
1815, " " Thomas Morgan, John Hamilton, James Stephenson, and William Vance.
1816, " " Joshua Dickerson, Jacob Weirich, James Kerr, and William Vance.
1817, " " Joshua Dickerson, Jacob Weirich, James Kerr, and John Reed.
1818, " " Joseph Lawrence, Walter Craig, James Keys, and John Reed.
1819, " " Joseph Lawrence, Walter Craig, James Keys, and John Reed.
1820, " " Joseph Lawrence, Thomas McCall, Dickerson Roberts, and John Reed.
1821, " " Joseph Lawrence, Thomas McCall, Joseph Ritner, and John Reed.
1822, " " Joseph Lawrence, Jonathan Knight, Joseph Ritner, and James Keys.
1823, " " Joseph Lawrence, Jonathan Knight, Joseph Ritner, and James Keys.
1824, " " William McCreary, Aaron Kerr, Joseph Ritner, and James Keys.
1825, " " William McCreary, Aaron Kerr, Joseph Ritner, and Thomas Ringland.
1826, " " William McCreary, Aaron Kerr, Thomas Ringland, and Joseph Ritner.
1827, " " William McCreary, Aaron Kerr, Samuel Workman, and Thomas Ringland.
1828, " " William Waugh, Aaron Kerr, Samuel Workman, and William Patterson.
1829, " " William Waugh, Samuel Workman, and William Patterson.

1830, October.—Hon. William Waugh, Wallace McWilliams, and William Patterson.
1831, " " William Waugh, Wallace McWilliams, and William Patterson.
1832, " " William Waugh, Robert Love, and Joseph Henderson.
1833, " " William McCreary, Robert Love, and William Patterson.
1834, " " William Hopkins, Joseph Lawrence, and David Frazier.
1835, " " John H. Ewing, Joseph Lawrence, and Edward McDonald.
1836, Feb'y 18.— " Thomas McGiffin elected at a special election in place of Jos. Lawrence, elected State Treasurer.
1836, October.— " Robert Love, William Hopkins, and John Parke.
1837, " " Robert Love, William Hopkins, and John Parke.
1838, " " Robert Love, William Hopkins, and John Parke.
1839, " " Robert Love, William Hopkins, and John Parke.
1840, " " Jonathan Leatherman, Samuel Livingston, and Aaron Kerr.
1841, " " Wallace McWilliams, James McFarren, and Jesse Martin.
1842, " " Samuel Livingston, William McDaniel, and John Storer.
1843, " " O. B. McFadden and George V. Lawrence.
1844, " " Daniel Rider and John Meloy.
1845, " " Daniel Rider and Richard Donaldson.
1846, " " George V. Lawrence and Richard Donaldson.
1847, " " Thomas Watson and Jacob Cort.
1848, " " John McKee and Jacob Cort.
1849, " " Jonathan D. Leet and Thomas Watson.
1850, " " Jonathan D. Leet and David Riddle.
1851, " " Hugh Craig and John Meloy.
1852, " " John N. McDonald and J. W. Alexander.
1853, " " Matthew Linn and Jehu Jackman.
1854, " " Samuel J. Krepps and James McCulloch.
1855, " " John W. Miller and David Riddle.
1856, " " John C. Sloan and J. S. Vanvoorhis.
1857, " " John N. McDonald and James Donehoo.
1858, " " George V. Lawrence and William Graham.
1859, " " George V. Lawrence and William Graham.
1860, " " John A. Happer and Robert Anderson.
1861, " " John A. Happer and William Hopkins.
1862, " " William Glenn and William Hopkins.
1863, " " Robert R. Reed and J. R. Kelley.
1864, " " Robert R. Reed, J. R. Kelley, and M. S. Quay, Washington and Beaver.
1865, " " Joseph Welsh, J. R. Kelley, and M. S. Quay, Washington and Beaver.
1866, " " John Ewing, J. R. Day, and M. S. Quay, Washington and Beaver.
1867, " " John Ewing, J. R. Day, and Thomas Nicholson, Washington and Beaver.
1868, " " A. J. Buffington, H. J. Vankirk, and Thomas Nicholson, Washington and Beaver.

1869, October.—Hon. A. J. Buffington, H. J. Vankirk, and W. Davidson, Washington and Beaver.

President Judges

Of the Court of Common Pleas, Orphans' Court, Quarter Sessions, and Oyer and Terminer since 1781.

1781, Oct. 2. Hon. Henry Taylor.   1788, Sept. 30. Hon. Henry Taylor.
1783, Oct. 31. Hon. Dorsey Pentecost.

These were Presiding Judges of the County Court, composed of Justices of the Peace, who held office under the Constitution of Pennsylvania adopted September 28, 1776.

1791, Sept. 22. Hon. Alexander Addison for Washington, Fayette, Westmoreland, and Allegheny counties.
1803, June 2. Hon. Samuel Roberts for Washington, Fayette, Greene, and Beaver counties.
1818, Oct. 19. Hon. Thomas H. Baird for Washington, Fayette, Greene, and Somerset counties.
1838, Feb. 28. Hon. Nathaniel Ewing for Washington, Fayette, and Greene counties.

These presided over the various courts of the district under the Constitution of September 2, 1790.*

Under the Constitution of 1838

the following persons distinguished for their legal abilities have been elected in this district:—

1848, Feb. 28. Hon. Samuel A. Gilmore, Washington, Fayette, and Greene counties.
1851, Oct. 11. Hon. Samuel A. Gilmore, Washington, Fayette, and Greene counties.
1861, Oct. 11. Hon. James Lindsey, Washington, Fayette, and Greene counties.
1865, Jan. 9. Hon. J. Kennedy Ewing, Washington, Fayette, and Greene counties.
1866, Feb. 19. Hon. B. B. Chamberlin, Washington and Beaver counties.
1866, Nov. 15. Hon. Alexander W. Acheson, Washington and Beaver counties.

Associate Judges

were first appointed under the Constitution of 1790 during good behavior. The law of March 21, 1806, provided that no vacancy in the office of Associate Judge could be supplied in any county unless the number of Associates shall be reduced to less than two,

---

* The Constitution of 1838 provided that one half of the commissions of those Judges who held office for ten years or more at its adoption, should expire February 27, 1839; and the commissions of the other half on the 27th of February, 1842; and the commissions of the remaining Judges, who had not held office for ten years, should expire on the 26th of February next after the end of ten years from the date of their commission; under this provision Judge Ewing held his office until February, 1848.

when that number shall be completed. In 1838 by the Constitution the life tenure of office was abolished and Associate Judges were elected.

1791, April 16. Hon. Henry Taylor.
1791, April 16. Hon. James Edgar.
1791, April 16. Hon. James Allison.
1791, April 16. Hon. Matthew Ritchie.
1798, April 6. William Hoge.
1802, May 31. John McDowell.
1802, May 31. John Hamilton.
1806, Jan. 1. Rev. Boyd Mercer.

When the Constitution of 1838 went into operation, Hon. John Hamilton and Rev. Boyd Mercer were on the bench, and the following persons were elected:—*

1838, Oct. Hon. Boyd Mercer.
1838, Oct. Hon. Thomas McKeever.
1840, Mar. 26. Hon. Samuel Hill.
1843, Mar. 18. Hon. John Grayson.
1845, Mar. 8. Hon. James Gordon.
1849, Feb. 19. Hon. Isaac Hodgens.
1851, Mar. 12. Hon. William Vankirk.
1851, Oct. 16. Hon. Abraham Wotring.
1851, Oct. 16. Hon. John Freeman.
1856, Oct. 12. Hon. James G. Hart.
1856, Oct. 12. Hon. Jacob Slagle.
1861, Oct. 23. Hon. James G. Hart.
1861, Oct. 23. Hon. Wm. Vankirk. (his election declared illegal and his opponent was sworn in.)
1862, June 3. Hon. Thomas McCarrol.
1866, Oct. 9. Hon. James C. Chambers.
1866, Oct. 9. Hon. John Farrar.

PROTHONOTARIES

Under the Supreme Executive Council.

1.—1781, April 2. Thomas Scott. | 2.—1789, Mar. 28. Alexander Scott.

Under the Constitution of September 2, 1790.

3.—1791, Aug. 14. David Reddick.
4.—1803, Jan. 11. Wm. McKennan.
5.—1811, Dec. 17. Alexander Murdoch.
6.—1819, May 6. William Sample.
7.—1821, Feb. 12. Thos. Morgan.
8.—1823, Dec. 30. William Sample.
9.—1830, Feb. 10. Thomas Officer.
10.—1836, Jan. 8. George W. Acheson.
11.—1837, Oct. 25. John Urie.
12.—1839, Feb. 5. John Grayson, Sr.

Under the Constitution of 1838, elected by the people for three years.

13.—1839, Oct. 14. John Grayson, Sr.
14.—1842, Oct. 12. Eph. L. Blaine.
15.—1845, Oct. 17. O. B. McFadden.
16.—1848, Oct. 5. James Brown.
17.—1851, Oct. 22. James Brown.
18.—1854, Oct. 14. Wm. S. Moore.
19.—1857, Oct. 11. James B. Ruple.
20.—1860, Oct. 10. James B. Ruple.
21.—1863, Oct. 9. John E. Bell.
22.—1866, Oct. 9. John L. Gow.
23.—1869, Oct. 12. D. M. Donehoo.

---

* By the Constitution the Associate Judges were thus classified; they were divided into four classes by the legislature. The commission of the first class expired February 27, 1840; the 2d class on February 27, 1841; the 3d class, February 27, 1843. Their commissions were arranged according to seniority.

Registers

Under the Supreme Executive Council.

1.—1781, April 4. James Marshal. | 2.—1784, Sept. 30. Thos. Stokely.

Under the Constitution of September 2, 1790.

3.—1791, Aug. 17, James Marshall.
4.—1795, March 6. Samuel Clarke.
5.—1800, Jan. 15. John Israel.
6.—1806, Dec. 24. Isaac Kerr.
7.—1819, May 21. Robert Colmery.
8.—1821, Feb. 22. Samuel Lyon.
9.—1824, Jan. 27. Robert Colmery.
10.—1830, Mar. 19. John Grayson, Sr.
11.—1836, Jan. 20. Sam'l Cunningham.
12.—1839, Mar. 3. James Gordon.

Under the Constitution of 1838.

13.—1839, Oct. 14. Geo. Morrison.
14.—1842, Oct. 12. James Sprigg.
15.—1845, Oct. 17. Wm. Workman.
16.—1848, Oct. 5. Odel Squier.
17.—1851, Oct. 22. John Grayson, Jr.
18.—1854, Oct. 14. John Meloy.
19.—1857, Oct. 11. Harvey J. Vankirk.
20.—1860, Oct. 10. Wm. A. Mickey.
21.—1863, Oct. 9. Wm. A. Mickey.
22.—1866, Oct. 9. Geo. Buchanan.
23.—1869, Oct. 12. I. Y. Hamilton.

Recorder of Deeds

Under the Supreme Executive Council.

1.—1781, April 4. James Marshall.

Under the Constitution of 1790.

2.—1791, Aug. 17. Jas. Marshall.
3.—1795, Mar. 6. Samuel Clark.
4.—1800, Jan. 15. John Israel.
5.—1806, Dec. 1. Isaac Kerr.
6.—1819, May 9. Robt. Colmery.
7.—1821, Feb. 12. Samuel Lyon.
8.—1823, Dec. 30. Robert Colmery.
9.—1830, Feb. 19. William Hoge.
10.—1836, Jan. 8. William H. Cornwall.
12.—1839, Feb. 5. James Brown.

Under the Constitution of 1838.

13.—1839, Nov. 14. James Brown.
14.—1842, " 12, James Brown.
15.—1845, " 17, James Brown.
16.—1848, " 5. F. Cooper Morrison.
17.—1851, " 22, F. Cooper Morrison.
18.—1854, Nov. 14. Cyrus Underwood
19.—1857, Nov, 13. Freeman Brady Jr.
20.—1860, " 23. Wm. H. Horn.
21.—1863, Dec. 1. Alvin King.
22.—1866, " 3. M. L. A. McCracken.
23.—1869, Oct. 12. John P. Charlton.

Clerk of the Quarter Sessions, Orphans' Court, Oyer and Terminer, &c. &c.

Under the Supreme Executive Council.

1.—1781, April 2. Thomas Scott.
2.—1789, March 28. Alexander Scott.

HISTORY OF WASHINGTON COUNTY.

Under the Constitution of 1790.

3.—1792, Sept. 2. David Reddick.
4.—1803, Jan. 11. Wm. McKennan.
5.—1811, Dec. 17. Alexander Murdoch.
6.—1819, May 6. Wm. Sample.
7.—1821, Feb. 12. Robt. Colmery.
8.—1823, Dec. 30. Jos. Henderson.
9.—1830, Feb. 19. James Ruple.
10.—1836, Jan. 8. James Blaine.
11.—1839, Feb. 5. James Ruple.

Under the Constitution of 1838.

12.—1839, Nov. 14. James Ruple.
13.—1842, " 12. Alex. G. Marshman.
14.—1845, " 17. William Hays.
15.—1848, " 5. Robt. F. Cooper.
16.—1851, " 22. Geo. Passmore.
17.—1854, Nov. 14. David Aiken.
18.—1857, " 13. David Aiken.
19.—1860, " 23. David Aiken.
20.—1863, Dec. 3. Wm. A. Kidd.
21.—1869, " 5. Samuel Ruth.

The offices of Prothonotary and Clerks of the court were combined until 1821, and those of Register and Recorder until 1830; at these dates they became separated as they now exist.

SHERIFFS

Under the Supreme Executive Council.

1.—Nov. 30, 1781. Van Swearingen.
2.—Nov. 1, 1784. James Marshall.
3.—Oct. 26, 1787. David Williamson.
4.—Nov. 9, 1790. William Wallace.

Under the Constitution of 1790, elected Second Tuesday of October every Third Year.

5.—1793, Oct. 22. John Hamilton.
6.—1796, Nov. 2. Thos. Hamilton.
7.—1799. " 2. Absalom Baird.
8.—1802, " 6. Geo. Hamilton.
9.—1805, Oct. 21. John McCluney.
10.—1808, " Rob't Anderson.
11.—1811, " George Baird.
12.—1814, " Thomas Officer.
13.—1817, " Dickerson Roberts.
14.—1820, Oct. 21. Robert Officer.
15.—1823, " Sam'l Workman.
16.—1826, " Robert McClelland.
17.—1829, " Jos. Henderson.
18.—1832, " Samuel Cunningham.
19.—1835, " John Marshall.
20.—1836, " John Wilson.*
21.—1837, " James Spriggs.

Under Constitution of 1838.

22.—1840, Oct. Sheshbazzar Bentley, Jr.
23.—1843, " Jehu Jackman.
24.—1846, " Alex. G. Marshman.
25.—1849, " Peter Wolfe.
26.—1852, " Jno. McAllister.
27.—1855, Oct. Andrew Bruce.
28.—1858, " Norton McGiffin.
29.—1861, " James M. Byers.
30.—1864, " Edward R. Smith.
31.—1867, " Hugh Keys.

CORONERS

Under Supreme Executive Council.

1.—1781, Nov. 30. Wm. McFarland.
2.—1784, " 1. Wm. McCombs.
3.—1787, Oct. 26. Robert Benham.
4.—1789, Nov. 6. Samuel Clarke.

---

* Succeeded as coroner.

HISTORY OF WASHINGTON COUNTY.

Under Constitution of 1790.

5.—1790, Samuel Clark.	12.—1817, Oct.	James Ruple.
6.—1794, Feb. 16. James Marshall.	13.—1820, "	John Johnston.
7.—1799, Nov. 18. Wm. Slemens.	14.—1823, "	George Sowers.
8.—1802, " 6. Dorsey Pentecost.	15.—1826, "	Alex. Gordon.
	16.—1829, "	Moses Linn.
9.—1805, Oct. 21. Thos. Hutchinson.	17.—1832, "	Jas. McCadden.
10.—1811, " Wm. Marshall.	18.—1835, "	John Wilson.
11.—1814, " William Carter.	19.—1837, "	John R. Griffith.

Under Constitution of 1838.

20.—1840, Oct. William Tweed, Jr.	26.—1858, Oct.	Jonathan Martin.
21.—1843, " Wm. J. Wilson.	27.—1861, "	John E. Black.
22.—1846, " Oliver Lindsey.	28.—1864, "	Isaac Vance.
23.—1849, " James D. Best.	29.—1867, "	Chas. W. McDaniel.
24.—1852, " William B. Cundall.	30.—1868, "	Lewis Barker.
25.—1855, " Moses Little.		

COMMISSIONERS.

The Board of County Commissioners is composed of three electors, one of whom is elected at the annual October election; consequently to ascertain who constitutes the Board, it will only be necessary to compute any three successive years and the Board can be easily ascertained.

1. { 1781. George Vallandigham.
    1781. Thomas Crooks.
    1781. John McDowell.
2.—1782. George McCormick.
3.—1783. Demas Lindley.
4.—1784. James Allison.
5.—1785. James McCready.
6.—1786. James Bradford.
7.—1787. Thomas Marquis.
8.—1788. Henry Vanmetre.
9.—1789. James McCready.
10.—1790. William Meetkirke.
11.—1791. James Brice.
12.—1792. Zachariah Gapen.
13.—1793. Isaac Leet, Jr.
14.—1794. Samuel Clarke.
15.—1795. William Seaton.
16.—1796. John Colton.
17.—1797. Robert McCready.
18.—1798. James Brice.
19.—1799. William Campbell.
20.—1800. Joshua Anderson.
21.—1801. Isaac Leet, Jr.
22.—1802. Robert Mahon.
23.—1803. John Lyle.
24.—1804. Thomas Hopkins.
25.—1805. Edward Todd.
26.—1806. Joseph Alexander.
27.—1807. Aaron Lyle.
28.—1808. Joseph Alexander.
29.—1809. William Marshall.
30.—1810. Moses McWhirter.
31.—1811. Isaac Leet, Jr.
32.—1812. Daniel Kehr.
33.—1813. William Vance.
34.—1814. John Brownlee.
35.—1815. John Reed.
36.—1816. Walter Craig.*
37. } 1817. Jonathan Knight.
37. }   Moses Lyle.
38.—1818. John Lacock.
39.—1819. Alexander Scott.
40.—1820. Matthias Luse.
41.—1821. William McCreary.
42.—1822. John Urie.
43.—1823. John Macoy.
44.—1824. Robert Moore.
45.—1825. Robert Patterson.

---

* Walter Craig resigned and two Commissioners elected in 1817, James Gordon appointed to serve until the following October, 1818.

46.—1826. Wallace McWilliams.
47.—1827. Robert Love.
48.—1828. Thomas Axtell.
49.—1829. Isaac Hodgens.
50.—1830. Samuel Cunningham.
51.—1831. James McBurney.
52.—1832. { Jesse Cooper. 2 years.
           { James Miller. 3 years.
53.—1833. William McElroy.
54.—1834. James Lee.
55.—1835. S. Bentley. Jr.*
56.—1836. { B. Anderson. 1 year.
           { J. Jackman. 3 years.
57.—
58.—1837. Matthew Linn.
59.—1838. Andrew Shearer.
60.—1839. James Pollock.
61.—1840. Samuel Linton.
62.—1841. Hugh Craig.
63.—1842. Thomas Byers.
64.—1843. George Passmore.
65.—1844. James Donehoo.
66. { 1845. Alexander Frazier.
     { 1846. Dutton Shannon.
67.—1847. John McAlister.
68.—1848. John Birch.
69.—1849. Andrew Bruce.
70.—1850. Samuel Becket.
71.—1851. Isaac Thompson.
72.—1852. Thomas McCarrol.
73.—1853. Daniel Swickard.
74.—1854. John Stewart.
75.—1855. John N. Walker.
76.—1856. Nathan Cleaver.
77.—1857. Joseph Vankirk.
78.—1858. O. P. Cook.
79.—1859. George Taylor.
80.—1860. James S. Elliott.
81.—1861. Abel M. Evans.
82.—1862. Frank Neilson.
83.—1863. Joseph W. Cowan.
84.—1864. T. J. Bell.
85.—1865. James Walker.
86.—1866. Samuel K. Weirich.
87.—1867. H. B. McLean.
88.—1868. James Kerr.
89.—1869. S. P. Riddle.

Clerks to the Commissioners.

1.—1782. Thomas Byers.
2.—1783. James McCready.
3.—1793. Thomas Swearingen.
4.—1796. John Colerick.
5.—1800. Isaac Kerr.
6.—1801. Robert Moore.
7.—1803. John Gilmore.
8.—1804. David McKeehan.
9.—1805. Alexander Blair.
10.—1808. William Baird.
11.—1814. John Baird.
12.—1819. Robert Jackson.
13.—1822. Thomas Good.
14.—1834. James Palmer.
15.—1841. William Hughes.
16.—1843. William R. Oliver.
17.—1845. Adam Silvey.
18.—1853. David P. Lowary.
19.—1854. John Gamble.
20.—1857. Elias McClelland.
21.—1858. Samuel Linton.
22.—1864. Isaac H. Longdon.
23.—1869. Joseph A. McKee.
24.—1870. John Grayson, Jr.

Deputy Attorney-Generals.

1.—1781. David Sample.
2.—1783. David Bradford.
3.—1790. John Purviance.
4.—1796. Parker Campbell.
5.—1805. James Ashbrook.
6.—1809. Thomas H. Baird.
7.—1829. William Baird.
8.—1824. William Waugh.
9.—1830. Isaac Leet.
10.—1835. Alex. W. Acheson.
11.—1836. R. H. Lee.
12.—1837. William McKennan.
13.—1839. Alex. W. Acheson.
14.—1845. William Montgomery.
15.—1846. Alex. W. Acheson.
16.—1847. George S. Hart.
17.—1848. Robert H. Koontz.
18.—1850. George S. Hart.
19.—1853. William Lynn.
20.—1856. Alexander Wilson.
21.—1862. James R. Ruth.
22.—1865. Boyd Crumrine.
23.—1868. Ianthus Bentley.

---

* S. Bentley resigned October 25. W. V. Leet appointed August 31, in place of S. Cunningham.

HISTORY OF WASHINGTON COUNTY. 261

List of Attorneys

Who were admitted to practise law in the courts of Washington County, from its organization to the present time, with the term in which they were admitted. Those marked thus † were resident attorneys.

Name	Term	Name	Term
†Acheson, Hon. Alexander W.	June, 1832.	†Bradford, David	April, 1782.
Acheson, George	May, 1843.	†Brady Freeman, Jr.	May, 1860.
†Acheson, George W.	Dec., 1830.	Brady Jasper E.	Feb., 1857.
†Acheson Marcus	Dec., 1868.	†Brady, John S.	June, 1817.
Acheson Marcus W.	May, 1852.	Brown, D. W.	Aug., 1869.
†Addison, Hon. Alex.	Mar., 1787.	Buchanan, Andrew	July, 1811.
†Addison, Alexander	Dec., 1820.	Buchanan, J. A. J.	Aug., 1848.
†Aiken, John	Dec., 1869.	Buckingham, S.	May, 1863.
Alden, T. J. Fox	May, 1838.	Caldwell, Alexander	June, 1817.
Allison, Alexander	Sept., 1835.	Caldwell, George W.	Aug., 1862.
Allison, William	Dec., 1838.	Callender, Robert	Aug., 1799.
†Alter, Solomon	May, 1843.	Campbell, Charles	Nov., 1823.
Andrews, A.	June, 1819.	Campbell, Francis C.	June., 1830.
Appleton, George	Aug., 1846.	Campbell, Henry M.	June, 1818.
†Ashbrook, James	Nov., 1798.	Campbell, James	Mar., 1830.
Avery, P. J.	Mar., 1838.	†Campbell, Parker	June, 1794.
Ayres, William	Nov., 1798.	Carson, John	Mar., 1786.
		Chapline, John H.	July, 1810.
Bailey, Isaac	Aug., 1862.	†Clarke, J. Murray	Nov., 1861.
†Baird, Hon. Th. H.	Mar., 1808.	Cleavinger, Samuel	Oct., 1832.
†Baird, Thomas H., Jr.	Feb., 1846.	Cloyd, John	Aug., 1798.
†Baird, William	June, 1812.	Cochran, A. G.	Feb., 1868.
Baird, William	Aug., 1849.	Cochran, George R.	May, 1868.
Baldwin, Henry	June, 1815.	Cochran, S. N.	May, 1855.
Baldwin, Henry	Mar., 1838.	Cole, Samuel, Jr.	May, 1855.
Barr, S. Gailey	Aug., 1865.	Coleman, Charles	June, 1826.
†Beall, Thomas B.	Oct., 1834.	Collins, Thomas	Mar., 1796.
Beckett, J. B.	Dec., 1812.	†Cooper, R. F.	May, 1842.
Beebe, Walter B.	Oct., 1818.	Craft, James S.	Oct., 1818.
Bell, D. B.	May, 1852.	Craig, David	Feb., 1848.
†Bell, Solomon	Dec., 1867.	Craig, I. H.	May, 1856.
†Bentley, Ianthus	Feb., 1866.	Crawford, David	Feb., 1862.
Biddle, Richard	Mar., 1824.	†Creacraft, E. G.	Aug., 1846.
Bigham, T. J.	June, 1837.	†Creigh, Samuel	Dec., 1829.
Black, Ross	Feb., 1841.	Creigh, Thomas	July, 1796.
Black, J. L.	Aug., 1869.	†Crumrine, Bishop	Aug., 1867.
Blair, David	June, 1838.	†Crumrine, Boyd	Aug., 1861.
Boice, Ebenezer	Aug., 1844.	Cunningham, Thomas	June, 1812.
Bowman, John	June, 1837.		
Bowman, J. L.	Jan., 1817.	Dawson, John	June, 1819.
Bowman, William	Nov., 1852.	Denny, Harmar	Oct., 1818.
†Boyd, Thomas	" 1861.	Dodridge, Philip	July, 1811.
Brackenridge, Alex.	Mar., 1818.	†Donehoo, John R.	May, 1858.
Brackenridge, H. H.	Oct., 1814.	†Donnan, John W.	Aug., 1867.
Brackenridge, H. M.	" 1781.	Donaldson, John W.	Dec., 1867.
†Braden, John D.	Feb., 1851.	Douglass, John	Aug., 1805.

	Term.		Term.
†Dugan, Henry M.	May, 1869.	†Hopkins, Andrew	Nov., 1847.
Duncan, Hon. Thomas	Dec., 1782.	Howell, Alfred	Feb., 1850.
		Howell, Joshua B.	June, 1831.
Edgington, Jesse	Oct., 1810.	Huffnagle, William	Dec. 1783.
Ege, Peter F.	Aug., 1840.	Humbrickhouse, T. S.	Oct., 1832.
Ellmaker, Ellis E.	Feb., 1805.	†Hurd, Seth T.	May, 1841.
Espy, David	Jan., 1782.		
†Ewing, John H.	June, 1818.	Ingall, R. C.	Feb., 1846.
Ewing, Hon. Nathaniel	June, 1816.	Irwin, Samuel	Oct., 1781.
Ewing, Thomas L.	Feb., 1858.	Israel, Charles H.	Nov., 1824.
Fanning, N. D.	Aug., 1858.	Jennings, David	June, 1812.
Ferero, E.	Nov., 1855.	Jennings, Obadiah	Nov., 1801.
Fetterman, N. P.	Jan., 1831.	Johnston, B. W.	Nov., 1849.
Fetterman, W. W.	Mar., 1824.	†Johnston, Job	Feb., 1845.
Fitzhugh, S. H.	Sept., 1819.	Johnston, F. W.	Aug., 1843.
Fitzwilliams, F. P.	Aug., 1858.	†Johnston, Thomas G.	Nov., 1798.
Flenniken, John C.	Aug., 1849.	†Judson, J. Lawrence	Aug., 1851.
Flenniken, R. P.	Nov., 1842.		
Forrest, Joshua R.	May, 1869.	Kane, Daniel	Aug., 1849.
Forward, Walter	Dec., 1812.	†Kelso, Charles W.	Oct., 1832.
Foster, W. Alexander	Feb., 1802.	†Keppelle, George H.	Sept., 1795.
Frew, Samuel	Mar., 1839.	Kennedy, Hon. John	Aug., 1799.
		Kerr, Isaac	Aug., 1800.
Galbraith, Robert	April, 1782.	King, Sampson, S.	Feb., 1802.
Gantz, Henry	May, 1865.	†King, W. W.	Jan., 1825.
Gapen, W. A.	Feb., 1859.	Kingston, J.	Aug., 1841.
Garret, John S.	Dec., 1820.	Koote, Ephraim	Sept., 1819.
Gazzam, Edward D.	Mar., 1827.	†Koontz, Robert H.	Aug., 1840.
†Gibson, R. M.	Aug., 1853.	Krepps, John B.	Aug., 1853.
Gilmore, John	Aug., 1800.	Kurtz, Wm. K.	Jan., 1815.
Glenn, John	June, 1829.		
Goodenow, John M.	June, 1817.	Lacey, B. W.	Nov., 1854.
Gormley, Samuel	June, 1830.	Lacock, Ira J.	Aug., 1858.
Gow, Alexander M.	Feb., 1857.	Lane, Richard Carr	July, 1810.
Gow, George L.	May, 1867.	†Lee, R. H.	Oct., 1834.
†Gow, John L.	June, 1824.	†Leet, Isaac	June, 1826.
†Gow, John L., Jr.	Feb., 1866.	Leet, Daniel W.	May, 1839.
Grayson. William	Aug., 1846.	†Leet, Jonathan, D.	Nov., 1843.
Gregg, Ellis	Nov., 1850.	Lewis, R. P.	Feb., 1859.
		Lindsey, Hon. James	Nov., 1859.
Hadden, Thomas	Oct., 1796.	Lindsey, William C.	May, 1862.
†Hamilton, Isaac Y.	May, 1861.	†Little, Le Roy Woods	May, 1861.
Hamilton, John	Mar., 1785.	†Lynn, William	May, 1850.
†Hart, George S.	Aug., 1846.	Lyon, John	July, 1797.
Harvey, William	Sept., 1819.	Lyon, Samuel	Oct., 1814.
Hawkins, William G.	Mar., 1821.		
Hasbrouck, Cicero	May, 1869.	Mahon, Samuel S.	Oct., 1796.
Hays, Charles McClure	Aug., 1860.	Marsh, Roswell	Nov., 1823.
Hays, Joseph	Nov., 1865.	Marshall, John	Feb., 1807.
†Hazzard, T. R.	Nov., 1840.	Massey, M. B.	May, 1861.
Heaton, Hiram	Sept., 1819.	Meason, Thomas	Aug., 1798.
†Henderson, Joseph	May, 1839.	Meredith, William	Nov., 1841.
Hoffman, R. C.	Feb., 1868.	†Messinger, John	Aug., 1853.

HISTORY OF WASHINGTON COUNTY. 263

	TERM.		TERM.
Miller, Alexander	May, 1845.	Oliver, Addison	Feb., 1857.
†Miller, George W.	Feb., 1851.	Oliver, George M.	Nov., 1848.
Milligan, I. M.	Feb., 1866.	Owens, William, Jr.	May, 1867.
Mills, William	Aug., 1855.		
Montgomery, James	Oct., 1796.	Pane, George A.	Nov., 1853.
†Montgomery, William	Nov., 1841.	†Patterson, David F.	May, 1865.
Moody, R. S.	May, 1848.	Patterson, R. B.	Dec., 1867.
Moore, Robert	Aug., 1800.	Patton, Hon. Benjamin	Mar., 1833.
Moore, J.	Mar., 1809.	Patton, William J.	Nov., 1861.
†Moore, William S.	Nov., 1848.	Paul, George	May, 1805.
Moreland, W. C.	Aug., 1867.	Paxton, Wilson N.	" 1860.
Morrison, A. P.	Nov., 1853.	Penny, John P.	Nov., 1846.
Morrison, James	Sept., 1795	Pentecost, Dorsey B.	July, 1823.
Morrison, Joseph S.	Nov., 1847.	†Pentecost, Joseph	Sept., 1792.
Morrison, R. L.	Feb., 1868.	Pentecost, J. Ross	Nov., 1823.
†Morgan, Thomas	Mar., 1813.	Pepper, Samuel G.	" 1850.
Morgan, Thomas Gibbs	June, 1821.	Pierson, Hon. John J.	May, 1848.
Moss, J. W.	Nov., 1858.	Pollock, H. C.	Aug., 1867.
Mountain, A. S.	Mar., 1823.	Porter, John	" 1805.
Mountain, James	Nov., 1801.	Purman, Andrew A.	Feb., 1860.
†Murdoch, Alexander	Aug., 1843.	†Purviance, John	Mar., 1790.
		Purviance, John, Jr.	Feb., 1805.
McBride, Archibald	Aug., 1859.		
McCarrel, L.	Aug., 1869.	Quail, Huston	Feb., 1850.
McComb, John H.	May, 1843.		
McConnell, R. A.	Feb., 1862.	Ralph, John	June, 1790.
McCook, George W.	May, 1867.	Rutan, J. S.	Feb., 1863.
†McCracken, M. L. A.	May, 1867.	†Reddick, David	Dec., 1782.
McDonald, John	Dec., 1807.	Reddick, Jonathan	Nov., 1803.
†McDonald, Wm. K.	June, 1831.	Reed, David	May, 1846.
McDowell, J. W.	Aug., 1869.	Roberts, Lewis	Feb., 1840.
McEddington, Daniel	Mar., 1839.	Rodgers, H. Gould	Nov., 1860.
†McFadden, O. B.	Feb., 1843.	Rodgers, Thomas L.	June, 1824.
†McFarlane, Samuel	Dec., 1827.	Ross, Hugh	Sept., 1792.
McGiffin, George W.	Nov., 1846.	Ross, James	Oct., 1781.
†McGiffin, Thomas, Sr.	Feb., 1807.	†Ruple, Charles M.	May, 1866.
†McGiffin, Thomas, Jr.	" 1841.	†Ruple, John G.	April, 1861.
McIlvaine, G. W.	Aug., 1844.	†Ruth, James R.	May, 1861.
†McIlvaine, John A.	" 1867.	Runyan, Hill	Feb., 1805.
McIlvaine, R. F.	" 1844.		
McMahon, Peter B.	May, 1855.	Sample, Cunningham	Nov., 1798.
McKee, John	Nov., 1847.	Sample, David	Oct, 1781.
McKeehan, David	Dec., 1792.	Sampson, John P. C.	June, 1815.
†McKennan, James W.	June, 1825.	Sayer, James P.	Dec., 1869.
†McKennan, Th. T. M.	Oct., 1814.	†Scott, Thomas	Sept., 1791.
†McKennan, William	June, 1837.	Selden, George	June, 1825.
†McWilliams, John W.	Dec., 1867.	Seney, Joshua	" 1822.
		Shaler, Charles, Hon.	Mar., 1817.
Nesbitt, Thomas	July, 1797.	Shannon, John	Oct., 1808.
Neville, Morgan	Dec., 1806.	Shields, Thomas L.	" 1831.
Nicholls, John	May, 1854.	Shiras, George, Jr.	June, 1867.
Nickerson, Wm.	Aug., 1868.	Simison, James C.	Jan., 1824.
		Smith, David S.	Aug., 1865.
Oliphant, Ethelbert P.	Dec., 1829.	†Smith, Jonathan B.	Nov., 1823.

	Term.		Term.		Term.
Smith, Thomas	Jan., 1782.	†Watson, James	Oct., 1831.		
Slagle, Jacob, Jr.	Nov., 1852.	Watson, John	Aug., 1841.		
St. Clair, Arthur	Sept., 1794.	†Waugh, John H.	Sept., 1820.		
St. Clair, David	" 1789.	†Waugh, William	June, 1818.		
Stewart, J.	June, 1819.	Weigley, Joseph	Oct., 1810.		
†Stewart, Benjamin S.	" 1829.	Weills, John S. C.	May, 1866.		
Stockdale, John	May, 1851.	White, John	" 1806.		
Stokely, Samuel	Oct., 1816.	†White, J. W. F.	" 1844.		
Stokes, Will. A.	May, 1858.	White, S. F.	" 1864.		
Swartzwelder, Marshal	Feb., 1865.	Whitehill, Robert	Oct., 1797.		
Sweitzer, Bowman	Nov., 1845.	Wiley, John Wishart	Aug., 1867.		
		Wilkins, William	Mar., 1808.		
Tarr, John	Oct., 1808.	Williams, E., Jr.	May, 1867.		
Taylor, James	Sept., 1806.	Wilson, Alexander	June, 1826.		
Taylor, Samuel O.	Aug., 1863.	†Wilson, Alexander	Nov., 1852.		
†Templeton, William F.	May, 1860.	†Wilson, A. Wiley	Aug., 1863.		
†Todd, Alexander M.	" 1868.	†Wilson, David Shields	" 1849.		
Todd, James	June, 1824.	Winge, Isaiah	Sept., 1820.		
Tomlinson, W. F.	May, 1860.	†Wise, Uriah W.	Feb., 1844.		
		Withey, Griffith, Jr.	June, 1830.		
Vallandigham, George	April, 1786.	†Wolf, Westley	Aug., 1863.		
†Vankirk, Harvey J.	Feb., 1851.	Woods, Henry	June, 1794.		
Veech, James	Jan., 1834.	Woods, John	Dec., 1783.		
		Woods, J. G.	Aug., 1867.		
Walker, Stephen D.	June, 1819.	Woods, Robert	" 1840.		
Walker, David	Dec., 1832.	Wright, John C.	Mar., 1813.		
†Watson, David T.	July, 1866.				
Watson, George	Jan., 1842.	Young, John	Nov., 1789.		

Treasurers.

1.—1783. Feb. Andrew Swearingen.
2.—1795. June. David Reddick.
3.—1801. " Isaac Kerr.
4.—1806. " Daniel Kehr.
5.—1811. Aug. Robert Colmery.
6.—1815. " William Baird.
7.—1817. " Thomas Good.
8.—1822. " Samuel Workman.
9.—1823. Nov. James Dougherty.
10.—1824. Jan. James Allison.
11.—1826. " Isaac Leet.
12.—1829. " Samuel McFarland.
13.—1832. " Samuel Marshall.
14.—1833. " Benj. S. Stewart.
15.—1834. " Samuel Marshall.
16.—1835. Feb. Henry Langley.
17.—1838. Jan. Zachariah Reynolds.
18.—1841. Oct. William Workman.
19.—1843. " William Hughes.
20.—1845. " James D. McGugin.
21.—1847. " Robert K. Todd.
22.—1849. " Norton McGiffin.
23.—1851. " John Hall.
24.—1853. " Thaddeus Stanton.
25.—1855. " H. B. Elliott.
26.—1857. " Thomas Martindale.
27.—1859. " John E. Bell.
28.—1861. " James Pollock.
29.—1862. Feb. William S. Moore.
30.—1863. Oct. J. W. Douds.
31.—1865. " A. W. Pollock.
32.—1867. " James P. Hart.
33.—1869. " James B. Gibson.

Auditors.

On the 10th of March, 1809, an act of the General Assembly was passed, authorizing the election of Auditors at the general election as a more effectual mode of settling the public accounts of the Commissioners and Treasurer. Prior to this time the courts appointed

1809. Thomas Acheson.
1809. Isaac Kerr.
1809. Joshua Dickinson.
1810. Eleazer Jenkins.
1811. Isaac Kerr, 3 years.
1811. Thomas Patterson, 1 year.
1812. John Colmery.
1813. Dickinson Roberts, 3 years.
1813. Samuel Scott, 1 year.
1814. Isaac Kerr, 3 years.
1814. Jacob Crabbs, 2 years.
1815. James McQuown.
1816. John Wilson.
1817. William Sample.
1818. Richard Crooks.
1819. Isaac Kerr.
1820. William Colmery.
1821. Robert Bowland.
1822. Joseph Henderson.
1823. Joseph Patton.
1824. William Welsh.
1825. James Gordon.
1826. James Orr.
1827. Robert Officer.
1828. Samuel Hill.
1829. Stephen Wood.
1830. Robert Officer.
1831. William Hopkins.
1832. James Pollock.
1833. Thomas Enlow.
1834. Benjamin Bubbett, 3 years.
1834. Jehu Jackman, 2 years.
1835. Joseph Henderson.
1836. James McClelland.
1837. H. J. Rauhauser.
1838. Henry Langley, 3 years.

1838. R. Donaldson, 2 years.
1839. Dickinson Roberts.
1840. John K. Wilson.
1841. Thomas Watson.
1842. John Macoy.
1843. E. B. Marsh.
1844. Abraham Wotring.
1845. Jacob Morgan.
1846. John K. Wilson.
1847. John McCullough.
1848. Joseph W. Cowan.
1849. John Stephenson.
1850. Adam Winnett.
1851. Jehu P. Smith, 1 year.
1851. J. E. Black, 3 years.
1852. James Taggart.
1853. Isaac J. Newkirk.
1854. Robert C. Burns.
1855. W. C King (appointed).
1855. J. D. Irwin, 3 years.
1855. J. B. Ringland, 1 year.
1856. Joseph W. Douds.
1857. Isaac Newkirk.
1857. John Murphy, Jr.
1858. John L. Phillips.
1859. Samuel Scott.
1860. David Bradford.
1861. James Ely.
1862. Thomas D. Ohara.
1863. James P. McCord.
1864. D. M. Leatherman.
1865. George Buchanan.
1866. Grier McIlvaine, Jr.
1867. Joseph Linton.
1868. A. E. Walker.
1869. G. W. Morrison.

DIRECTORS OF THE POOR.

The act of incorporation to provide for the erection of a house for the employment and support of the poor in the county of Washington, was approved by Governor George Wolf on the sixth day of April, 1830.

The commissioners appointed by the said act to determine upon and purchase a site or farm, on which suitable buildings should be erected, were James Lee, of Cross Creek; Alexander Reed, of Washington; Joseph Barr, of Nottingham; Wallace McWilliams, of Buffalo; Zephaniah Beall, of West Bethlehem; William Patterson, of Tenmile; and David Eckert, Esqs., of Washington.

After diligent inquiry, both as to its situation and locality, they purchased one hundred and seventy-two acres of land in Chartiers township, one mile and a half north of Washington, from Robert Colmery and Maria his wife, for two thousand seven hundred and fifty-two dollars, being sixteen dollars per acre.

On the 26th April, 1865, John Burns, John L. Cooke, and William Davis, constituting the Board of Directors, purchased from John Melone and Mary his wife, six acres of land, contiguous to the poor-house farm, for six hundred dollars.

On April 1, 1867, William Davis, William Dinsmore, and William Wylie, Esqs., the Board of Directors, purchased from John L. Cooke and Catharine D. his wife, twenty-eight acres and one hundred and fifty-one perches, at one hundred dollars per acre. This farm now contains, by recent survey, two hundred and nine acres.

So faithful, so diligent, so devoted to the interests of the unfortunate poor who become tenants of the county farm, that the office of superintendent has been filled during this entire period by but three persons, viz : Dr. John Logan, who was elected the first superintendent in 1832, and continued as such until September, 1851, a period of nineteen years ; his successor was Major William W. Wilson, who served seven years, or until April 1, 1858, when the present incumbent, John Gamble, Esq., assumed its onerous duties, and for the last eleven years has been discharging his duties satisfactorily to the inmates, the directors, and the citizens of this county.

It will be interesting to remark that during the first twenty years of its existence the entire cost of the purchase of land, erection of buildings, support of the inmates, and all other expenses pertaining to the institution, amounted to one hundred and seven thousand one hundred and four dollars, averaging per year $5289. During the next seven years the cost was fifty-two thousand nine hundred and ninety-five dollars and twenty-eight cents, averaging per year $7570.15 ; during the last eleven years the entire cost was sixty-four thousand five hundred and eighty-three dollars and nineteen cents, averaging per year $5871.19. This last item includes the purchase of two parcels of land, amounting to thirty-five hundred dollars.

1830. John Watson.
" William Hunter.
" Stephen Woods.
1831. Enoch Wright.
1832. Lewis Hewitt.
1833. John Cooke.
1834. Robert Moore.
1835. William Wylie.
1836. John Brownlee.
1837. John Morgan.
1838. John Horn.
1839. John Bower.
1840. William Lindley.
1841. John Johnson.
1842. Joseph Vanewan.
1843. James McClaskey.
1844. Joseph Wise.
1845. John Kenna.
1846. Daniel Darragh.
1847. Joseph Wier.
1848. Aaron Miller.
1849. John Holland.
1850. Joseph Vankirk.
1851. Benjamin Anderson.
1852. James Fife.
1853. John Sampson.
1854. James Brown.
1855. Thomas Buchanan.

HISTORY OF WASHINGTON COUNTY. 267

1856. James Stroud.
1857. William Wylie.
1858. Alexander Sprowls.
1859. A. B. Scott.
1860. William Wylie.
1861. William Davis.
1862. John Burns.

1863. John L. Cooke.
1864. William Davis.
1865. William Dinsmore.
1866. William Wylie.
1867. William Davis.
1868. J. Miller Day.
1869. Workman Hughes.

DEPUTY SURVEYOR-GENERALS.

1.—July 15, 1769. Jas. Hendricks.
2.—April 17, 1776. Daniel Leet.
3.—March 27, 1780. Thos. Stokely.
4.—March 8, 1784. John Hoge.
5.—Dec. 7, 1784. David Reddick.
6.—Aug. 12, 1785. Pressly Neville.
7.— "   "   " MatthewRitchie.
8.— "   "   " Alex. McClean.
9.—June 5, 1801. Jonathan Leet.
10.—Feb. 2, 1810. Wm. Hawkins.
11.—Sept. 10, 1811. Jonathan Mendenhall.
12.—Dec. 15, 1817. James Reed.

13.—April 12, 1822. Wm. V. Leet.
14.—Feb. 8, 1825. Stephen Woods.
15.—May 10, 1836. James McQuowen.
16.—Aug. 27, 1839. E. G. Creacraft.
17.—March 19, 1846. T. C. Noble.
18.—March 17, 1851. H. J. Vankirk.
19.—Dec. 10, 1854. T. C. Noble.
20.—Dec. 13, 1858. Thos. J. Boyd.
21.—Oct. 28, 1862. Francis Reader.
22.—Dec. 1, 1865. Demas Bennington.
23.—Oct. 1869. Jacob Gayman.

JUSTICES OF THE PEACE.

The organic law provided that the trustees should divide the county into the necessary number of townships, in each of which justices should be elected. Accordingly, on the 15th July, the electors of the thirteen townships met in their respective election districts, and elected these officers. The justices of the peace were also commissioned to be justices of the Court of Common Pleas, and of the Orphans' Court. But by the constitution of 1790 the judiciary system was changed, and their powers as judges of the court ceased February, 1792. This constitution provided for the appointment of justices of the peace by the governor with limited powers.* In 1838 justices were elected by the new constitution, and have continued so until the present time.

In the following table the Roman numerals refer to the number of terms to which the individual was elected.

NAME.   DATE.   DISTRICT.
Adams, Alexander. Nov. 18, 1811. Cross Creek and Hopewell.
Ailes, Isaac; II. April 14, 1839. East Pike Run.
Allen, Thomas G. April 15, 1845. Hopewell.

---

* By an act of legislature of May 4, 1803, the commissioners divided Washington County into eleven districts for the appointment of justices. 1st district, Washington and Strabane townships; 2d, Buffalo and Canton; 3d, Hopewell and Cross Creek; 4th, Smith, Hanover, and Robinson; 5th, Cecil and Chartiers; 6th, Peters and Nottingham; 7th, Pike Run and Fallowfield; 8th, Somerset; 9th, East and West Bethlehem; 10th, Morris and Amwell; 11th, Finley and Donegal. At the same session of the legislature the Court of Quarter Session was authorized to lay off, alter, and divide townships by appointing three impartial men, if necessary, to inquire into the propriety of granting the petition; and it shall be their duty to make a plot or draught of the townships proposed to be divided.

NAME.	DATE.	DISTRICT.

Alexander, Andrew J.   April 10, 1849.   East Bethlehem.
Alexander, Henry.   Dec. 10, 1817.   E. Bethlehem.
Alexander, Joseph.   Feb. 9, 1799.   Donegal.
Alexander, Joseph.   March 26, 1817.   Donegal and Finley.
Alexander, William S.   May 19, 1857.   Donegal.
Allison, Adam.   Jan. 7, 1805.   Canton and Buffalo.
Allison, Patrick.   April 16, 1792.
Ammons, Joshua M.   April 12, 1859.   Millsborough.
Archer, David T.   Dec. 8, 1823.   Cross Creek, Hopewell, Mt. Pleasant.
Archer, Ebenezer.   Aug. 6, 1845.   Peters.
Archer, James.   April 6, 1790.   Franklin.
Armstrong, Hugh.   Oct. 29, 1829.   Finley and Donegal.

Bailey, Eli.   April 21, 1794.   Cumberland.
Baird, Absalom ; II.   March 3, 1789.   Washington.
Baird, George.   April 11, 1848.   Washington.
Barnett, Samuel.   May 13, 1858.   West Bethlehem.
Baker, Lewis F.   April 10, 1860.   West Pike Run.
Barr, John.   April 10, 1849.   Somerset.
Barr, John A.   April 13, 1869.   Somerset.
Beall, Zephaniah ; II.   Aug. 24, 1790.   Bethlehem.
Bean, Isaac.   April 16, 1792.
Bearley, Nicholas ; III.   April 14, 1839.   Claysville.
Bebout, Ira C.   April 9, 1850.   North Strabane.
Bell, James.   Jan. 11, 1790.   Morgan.
Bentley, Shazbazzar, Sr.   Feb. 8, 1819.   Somerset.
Bentley, Shazbazzar, Jr. Feb. 18, 1830.   Peters, Nottingham, Mt. Pleasant.
Bentley, Shazbazzar, Jr.   April 10, 1860.   Monongahela City.
Bennington, Moses ; II.   Oct. 17, 1836.   Pike Run and Fallowfield.
Berry, William.   Dec. 13, 1815.   Chartiers and Cecil.
Bigger, Thomas.   June 12, 1822.   Smith, Hanover, and Robinson.
Birch, John ; II.   April 15, 1845.   Claysville.
Blaine, James ; III.   Jan. 1, 1817.   Washington.
Blaine, Eph. L.; II.   April 12, 1827.   East and West Bethlehem.
Blackeny, Gabriel.   Feb. 26, 1793.   Washington.
Boggs, Andrew.   Feb. 17, 1797.   Fallowfield.
Bowers, John ; II.   Jan. 16, 1819.   Peters and Nottingham.
Bowers, John, Jr.   April 14, 1854.   Hanover.
Bowers, Andrew ; II.   Aug. 13, 1836.   East and West Bethlehem.
Bower, George.   April 10, 1849.   Peters.
Bower, Benj. F.   April 10, 1860.   East Bethlehem.
Botkins, G. W.   March 9, 1861.   Claysville.
Boyd, John.   Nov. 17, 1837.   Cross Creek, Hopewell, Mt. Pleasant, and West Middleton.
Boyd, John ; III.   April 14, 1840.   West Middletown.
Boyd, Geo. W.   April 15, 1845.   Canton.
Brackenridge, John.   June 18, 1800.   Peters.
Bramley, William.   April 10, 1849.   Millsborough.
Brenton, Joseph.   April 11, 1854.   East Pike Run.
Brice, George W.; IV.   April 14, 1839.   Washington.
Brice, Henry.   April 14, 1840.   Buffalo.
Brownlee, James.   July 24, 1821.   Canton and Buffalo.
Brownlee, John.   April 14, 1840.   Canton.
Brownlee, John ; III.   April 16, 1856.   Franklin.

| NAME. | DATE. | DISTRICT. |

Brown, Joseph; II. April 9, 1850. Canonsburg.
Brown, David. April 14, 1857. Hopewell.
Buchanan, David. April 18, 1870. Independence.
Buchanan, John. Dec. 9, 1799. Hopewell.
Buchanan, John. Dec. 13, 1824. Smith, Hanover, Robinson, and Mount Pleasant.
Buchanan, James S. Nov. 6, 1869. Mount Pleasant.
Buchanan, Walter; III. April 11, 1848. Hanover.
Buck, Thomas. April 10, 1860. Buffalo.
Bubbet, Benjamin T. Dec. 8, 1823. Smith, Hanover, Robinson, and Mount Pleasant.
Buffington, Seth, Jan. 23, 1819. Pike Run and Fallowfield.
Burgan, Daniel. April 14, 1839. Somerset.
Bumgarner, Jesse. Jan. 3, 1816. East and West Bethlehem.
Bumgarner, David. April 9, 1850. Millsboro'.
Burns, John; IV. April 14, 1839. West Finley.
Burns, Alexander. June 23, 1845. West Middletown.
Butler, Ira R.; IV. April 15, 1845. Carroll.
Butz, David. April 21, 1862. Beallsville.
Baker, D. G. C. April 11, 1865. California.
Boyd, D. M.; II. April 11, 1865. Hopewell.
Baker, L. F. April 11, 1865. West Pike Run.
Baker, L. J. April 17, 1866. Greenfield.
Boyd, Thomas. April 14, 1868. Independence.

Caesber, Jonathan. April 11, 1865. Nottingham.
Caldwell, John; II. April 14, 1839. Somerset.
Caldwell, Robert. April 9, 1850. Peters.
Campbell, John. Feb. 8, 1799. Peters.
Campbell, John. April 14, 1840. Smith.
Canon, John; III. Oct. 6, 1784. Chartiers.
Carrol, William; II. April 11, 1854. California.
Carson, Thomas. Jan. 1, 1806. Pike Run and Fallowfield.
Carson, Washington. April 11, 1865. Fallowfield.
Carter, John. Dec. 8, 1823. Amwell and Morris.
Castner, Daniel. April 11, 1865. Carroll.
Chalfant, H. S. April 12, 1859. Greenfield.
Chalfant, H. S. April 11, 1865. East Pike Run.
Chester, Morrison. April 15, 1845. East Pike Run.
Clark, David. July 15, 1781. Smith.
Clark, David. July 15, 1781. Strabane.
Clarke, Andrew; IV. August 25, 1845. Nottingham.
Clarke, Harvey H. April 10, 1849. Canton.
Clarke, William. April 3, 1799. Chartiers.
Clarke, J. Murray. April 15, 1851. Robinson.
Cleaver, Isaac N.; III. April 9, 1850. East Bethlehem.
Clemens, William. Feb. 5, 1801. Donegal and Buffalo.
Clemens, John. March 28, 1836. Peters, Nottingham, and Carrol.
Clemens, John; V. April 14, 1839. Monongahela City.
Clemens, John; II. April 10, 1860. Buffalo.
Cloakey, John S. April 14, 1839. Carroll.
Cloakey, John S. April 13, 1847. Canton.
Cole, John; II. April 15, 1845. Cross Creek.
Colmery, John. April 1, 1811. Washington and Strabane.

270 HISTORY OF WASHINGTON COUNTY.

NAME. DATE. DISTRICT.

Colmery, William. Jan. 5, 1825. Chartiers, Cecil, and Mount Pleasant.
Colmery, Robert. April 14, 1840. South Strabane.
Collins, Thomas; v. April 14, 1839. Carroll.
Conklin, William; II. March 9, 1860. Morris.
Cook, Zeba. April 2, 1802. Amwell.
Conn, Jacob; II. April 17, 1864. Millsboro'.
Cooper, Jesse. April 20, 1829. East and West Bethlehem.
Cooper, Robert F. April 10, 1860. Monongahela City.
Cowen, Joseph W. April 9, 1844. West Bethlehem.
Cox, Andrew; III. Jan. 18, 1838. East and West Bethlehem.
Crabs, Jacob. June 5, 1801. Fallowfield.
Craig, John. July 15, 1781. Amwell.
Craig, John. July 15, 1781. Strabane.
Craig, William. Oct. 24, 1807. Amwell and Morris.
Craig, Hugh; III. April 14, 1839. Buffalo.
Craighead, George. Jan. 19, 1799. Strabane.
Crawford, William. Nov. 12, 1838. Pike Run and Fallowfield.
Creacraft, William; II. April 14, 1839. Morris.
Creighton, Edward; III. April 9, 1850. Fallowfield.
Crooks, Thomas. July 15, 1781. Bethlehem.
Crooks, Thomas. Nov. 21, 1781. Bethlehem.
Crouch, George. April 14, 1840. Nottingham.
Crow, Benjamin. April 10, 1860. Fallowfield.
Crow, Azariah; III. April 10, 1855. Allen.
Curry, Milton B. April 11, 1865. Amwell.

Darragh, Daniel; II. March 6, 1823. Peters, Nottingham, and Mount Pleasant.
Day, Luther. April 15, 1836. Amwell and Morris.
De France, Hugh. April 13, 1853.
De Pue, Daniel. March 12, 1793. Fallowfield.
Devore, Samuel. April 14, 1839. Monongahela City.
Dolby, Thomas. April 11, 1848. Millsboro'.
Donaldson, James. April 14, 1839. Greenfield.
Donaldson, Richard. April 2, 1803. Robinson.
Donaldson, Richard; II. April 14, 1840. Robinson.
Donahoo, James; v. April 14, 1839. Cross Creek.
Donnell, Henry; III. April 15, 1845. Cecil.
Dowler, Thos. H. April 13, 1853.
Douglass, John. July 15, 1781. Peters.
Douglass, John. March 3, 1789. Washington.
Dugan, Robert. April 11, 1848. West Bethlehem.
Duncan, John S. April 12, 1859. Cross Creek.

Eddie, Alexander. July 15, 1781. Strabane.
Edgar, James; II. July 15, 1781. Smith.
Elliott, George; II. Nov. 18, 1830. Cross Creek, Hopewell, West Middletown, and Mount Pleasant.
Elliott, James S. April 10, 1866. Cecil.
Elrod, Johnston. April 16, 1866. Monongahela City.
Enlow, Henry. Dec. 10, 1816. Finley and Donegal.
England, Samuel. Oct. 24, 1807. Canton and Buffalo.
Ervins, James. July 15, 1781. Robinson.
Evans, Abel M. April 10, 1867. Amwell.

HISTORY OF WASHINGTON COUNTY. 271

NAME.   DATE.   DISTRICT.
Evans, David J. April 10, 1840. Amwell.
Ewart, John; III. April 10, 1850. Beallsville.

Farley, John. April 9, 1850. South Strabane.
Fee, William; II. April 14, 1840. Chartiers.
Fergus, Hugh; II. April 9, 1850. Chartiers.
Ferguson, John; III. April 15, 1845. Smith.
Finley, Henry B. April 12, 1842. Union.
Finley, Levi. March 1, 1836. Peters, Nottingham, and Union.
Fleming, Samuel. Feb. 9, 1799. Hanover.
Fleming, Robert W. Sept. 24, 1818. Pike Run and Fallowfield.
Frazier, Alexander; IV. April 14, 1839. West Finley.
Frazier, David. Dec. 10, 1816. Finley and Donegal.
Frazier, Thomas; II. May 22, 1856. West Finley.
Freeman, John; II. April 14, 1839. E. Bethlehem

Galbraith, William. April 15, 1845. Smith.
Gardner, David. April 17, 1864. Jefferson.
Garret, Robert. May 25, 1815. Cross Creek and Hopewell.
Garret, Samuel. April 17, 1866. West Bethlehem.
Gaston, Joseph S.; IV. April 11, 1843. Union
Gaston, W. R. April 14, 1868. Union.
Gaston, Joseph S. April 13, 1869. Union.
Gillespie, James. June 5, 1801. Hopewell.
Gilmore, James. Jan. 1, 1807. Canton and Buffalo.
Glassgow, Samuel. May 6, 1788. Hanover.
Goble, Ebenezer. Feb. 29, 1793. Morris.
Gordon, James. April 9, 1850. Monongahela City.
Graham Henry. Aug. 24, 1790. Cross Creek.
Gray, David. April, 1792. Rich Hill.
Grayson, John, Jr.; III. April 14, 1863. Washington.
Gregg, Andrew; IV. April 20, 1829. Pike Run and Fallowfield.
Gregg, A. T. April 10, 1855. Carroll.
Gregg, Henry. Feb. 27, 1796. Fallowfield.
Griffith, Elisha. April 28, 1858. West Brownsville.
Guthrey, John. April, 1792.
Guy, Shepherd L. May 19, 1857. Donegal.

Howell, John. July 15, 1781. Amwell.
Hair, John. July 4, 1806. Peters and Nottingham.
Hall, John. July 15, 1781. Fallowfield.
Hallam, William. Dec. 23, 1818. Amwell and Morris.
Hamilton, David. Feb. 29, 1792. Nottingham.
Hanna, Thomas; II. April 16, 1856. Morris.
Hart, David. June 10, 1822. Somerset.
Hart, James G. April 15, 1845. East Bethlehem.
Harvey, D. W. C. April 10, 1855. West Brownsville.
Hawthorne, W. W.; VI. April 13, 1841. Millsborough.
Hay, John; III. April 14, 1840. Chartiers.
Hays, John B. April 10, 1860. Smith.
Hays, William. April 3, 1799. Chartiers.
Hazzard, T. R. April 15, 1845. Monongahela City.
Hedge, William; II. May 18, 1858. West Bethlehem.
Henderson, Joseph. Jan. 7, 1805. Finley and Donegal.

NAME.	DATE.	DISTRICT.
Henderson, John.	April 10, 1855.	Chartiers.
Henkins, Abm.; II.	April 9, 1850.	Morris.
Hermill, John.	April 10, 1855.	East Bethlehem.
Hervey, John C.	April 10, 1860.	Donegal.
Hill, Joseph.	May 26, 1795.	Bethlehem.
Hill, Stephen.	April 6, 1827.	Pike Run and Fallowfield.
Hill, Stephen.	April 10, 1849.	West Bethlehem.
Hilliard, John Wilkes.	Feb. 24, 1798.	Chartiers.
Hipple, George.	May 30, 1831.	Somerset.
Hodgens, Isaac.	April 12, 1842.	Buffalo.
Hodgens, John; II.	April 10, 1860.	Chartiers.
Hoge, John.	Nov. 21, 1786.	Washington.
Hootman, David, Jr.	May 5, 1866.	Nottingham.
Hopkins, William.	April 12, 1827.	Pike Run and Fallowfield.
Hopkins, White F.; II.	April 14, 1840.	West Pike Run.
Hornish, William; II.	April 24, 1857.	Canonsburg.
Hornish, William.	April, 1868.	Washington.
Howe, John.	April 10, 1860.	East Finley.
Howell, Abner.	July 15, 1781.	Amwell.
Howell, John W.; II.	May 16, 1862.	Chartiers.
Hughes, Ellis.	March 7, 1825.	Amwell and Morris.
Hughes, James; V.	April 14, 1840.	Mount Pleasant.
Hughes, Remembrance.	July 31, 1840.	Millsborough.
Hughes, Samuel L.; VI.	April 14, 1839.	Amwell.
Hughes Thomas.	July 14, 1792.	Cumberland.
Hughes, William.	April 13, 1858.	Washington.
Hughes, Workman.	April 10, 1860.	South Strabane.
Hunter, Archibald.	Feb. 4, 1825.	Smith, Hanover, Robinson, and Mount Pleasant.
Hyde, Saml.	April, 1792.	

Irons, Joseph.	April 2, 1803.	Canton.
Irwin, Thomas S.	June 9, 1856.	Claysville.
Irwin, William.	June 5, 1801.	Fallowfield.

Jackman, Simeon.	April 14, 1839.	East Pike Run.
Jackson, George.	Dec. 8, 1823.	Pike Run and Fallowfield.
Jamison, John.	April 11, 1865.	Donegal.
Jeffry, John.	April 10, 1860.	Independence.
Jenkins, Eleazer.	Feb. 28, 1789.	Bethlehem.
Jenkinson, Isaac.	May 26, 1795.	East Bethlehem.
Johnston, Job; II.	April 10, 1860.	California.
Johnston, Richard.	March 22, 1819.	Washington and Strabane.
Johnston, Samuel.	July 15, 1781.	Smith.
Johnston, William.	Feb. 6, 1786.	Donegal.
Judson, J. Lawrence; III.	April 13, 1853.	Washington.

Karrod, Levi.	July 15, 1781.	Morgan.
Kennedy, John; III.	April 14, 1839.	Union.
Kennedy, John.	June 1, 1836.	Peters, Nottingham, Union, and Carrol.
Kerr, James; III.	April 12, 1859.	N. Strabane.
Kerr, Willison.	April 13, 1869.	Bentleysville.
Kerr, Wilson.	June 2, 1857.	Union.
Keys, James.	May 16, 1818.	Smith, Hanover, and Robinson.

NAME.	DATE.	DISTRICT.

Keys, David. April 16, 1856. N. Strabane.
Kidd, Alexander. April 14, 1840. Smith.
Kidd, William. April 12, 1859. Jefferson.

Leech, James. Dec. 5, 1818. Smith, Hanover, and Robinson.
Leet, Daniel. July 15, 1781. Strabane.
Leet, Jonathan. Jan. 12, 1802. Canton.
Leffler, Jacob. Jan. 7, 1805. Finley and Donegal.
Leonard, Isaac. April 2, 1802. Somerset.
Little, Nicholas. July 15, 1781. Strabane.
Lindley, William; IV. March 4, 1824. Amwell and Morris.
Lindley, James E.; III. April 10, 1849. Hopewell and W. Middletown.
Linn, James. April 13, 1841. S. Strabane.
Linn, Matthew; V. April 15, 1845. N. Strabane.
Linnville, George. April 10, 1855. Hopewell.
Logan, James. Dec. 31, 1838. Canton and Buffalo.
Lytle, Alexander. April 6, 1805. Washington and Strabane.
Lyttle, Isaac. April 15, 1862. Union.

Mahon, Robert. Jan. 23, 1801. Somerset.
Marshall, John. July 15, 1781. Fallowfield.
Marshall, John. May 20, 1822. Washington and Strabane.
Marshman, A. G. April 14 1868.
Martin, Jonathan; II. April 14, 1846. S. Strabane.
Mason, Samuel. July 15, 1781. Donegal.
Mayes, Isaac. April 14, 1839. Donegal.
Mayes, Joseph T.; II. April 21, 1862. Donegal.
Meetkirke, William. Feb. 26, 1793. Washington.
Melchie, E. M. April 9, 1850. W. Brownsville.
Melchie, E. M. April 9, 1867. California.
Meloy, John. April 12, 1842. Buffalo.
Mickey, William A.; II. April 9, 1850. W. Pike Run.
Miller, David. March 4, 1824. Smith, Hanover, and Robinson.
Miller, John; II. April 15, 1845. Donegal.
Miller, Thomas. April 4, 1822. Finley and Donegal.
Minor, John. July 15, 1781. Cumberland.
Minor, John; II. April 15, 1782. Cumberland.
Minton, Mathias. April 14, 1868. Morris.
Mitchell, David. April 13, 1847. Carroll.
Mitchell, David, Jr. April 13, 1869. Bentleysville.
Mitchell, James. July 28, 1790. Peters.
Mitchell, March; II. April 15, 1845. Fallowfield.
Moffitt, James, Jr.; III. April 11, 1843. E. Bethlehem.
Moffitt, James. April 13, 1858. W. Brownsville.
Moore, Andrew. April 10, 1855. Nottingham.
Moore, James. April 14, 1819. Chartiers and Cecil.
Moore, John. April 11, 1848. Buffalo.
Moore, W. W. June 7, 1836. Smith, Hanover, Robinson, and Mt. Pleasant.
Monroe, Andrew. April 6, 1798. Chartiers.
Monroe, Joshua. March 12, 1819. Washington and Strabane.
Montgomery, William; II. April 11, 1854. E. Finley.
Morehead, John. April 14, 1840. Cecil.

| NAME. | DATE. | DISTRICT. |

Morgan, John.   Oct. 25, 1832.   Chartiers, Cecil, Mt. Pleasant, and Canonsburg.
Morgan, Thomas.   Dec. 3, 1823.   Washington and Strabane.
Morrison, J. L.   July 21, 1839.   Pike Run and Fallowfield.
Morrison, Samuel.   April 15, 1845.   Nottingham.
Murdoch, Alexander.   April 2, 1804.   Chartiers and Cecil.
Murphey, John, Jr.   July 12, 1860.   Canonsburg.

McAfee, Henry.   April 10, 1860.   Canonsburg.
McAllister, James.   April 10, 1855.   Monongahela City.
McBurney, Ebenezer.   April 11, 1854.   S. Strabane.
McBurney, James.   April 3, 1799.   Cecil.
McBurney, Robert.   April 14, 1846.   Robinson.
McCalmont, James; II.   April 11, 1854.   Robinson.
McCarrol, Thomas; II.   April 10, 1860.   Mt. Pleasant.
McClain, William.   May 18, 1818.   Cross Creek and Hopewell.
McClaskey, Hugh.   April 9, 1850.   Claysville.
McClaskey, James.   April 13, 1853.   Mt. Pleasant.
McCleary, Alex.   April 17, 1866.   W. Finley.
McClees, Alexander; III.   April 15, 1845.   Buffalo.
McClure, R. B.; II.   June 17, 1864.   W. Middletown.
McClelland, Hugh.   April 15, 1845.   E. Finley.
McClelland, James.   March 15, 1836.   Chartiers, Cecil, Canonsburg, and Mt. Pleasant.
McClelland, James; IV.   April 14, 1837.   Canonsburg.
McConaughy, James K.   May 13, 1858.   Independence.
McConaughy, R.   April 14, 1863.   Independence.
McConnell, Matthew.   July 15, 1781.   Cecil.
McConnell, Matthew.   July 15, 1781.   Smith.
McCord, John A.; III.   April 9, 1850.   Cecil.
McCoy, O. H. P.   April 13, 1869.   Buffalo.
McCreary, William.   Dec. 10, 1816.   Smith, Hanover, and Robinson.
McCullough, James.   April 14, 1839.   Canonsburg.
McCullough, John; V.   April 15, 1845.   Hanover.
McCullough, Patrick.   July 15, 1781.   Fallowfield.
McCullough, Patrick.   July 15, 1781.   Fallowfield.
McDonald, Edward.   Aug. 15, 1822.   Smith, Hanover, Robinson, and Mt. Pleasant.
McDonough, Henry; V.   Feb. 23, 1801.   Somerset.
McDowell, James.   May 19, 1830.   Washington and Strabane.
McElroy, James.   April 10, 1860.   Chartiers.
McFadden, James.   April 14, 1840.   West Middletown.
McFadden, O. B.   June 21, 1839.   E. and W. Bethlehem.
McFadden, Thomas.   May 25, 1857.   West Middletown.
McFarland, William.   Sept. 30, 1788.   Amwell.
McFarren, James.   Aug. 29, 1821.   Pike Run and Fallowfield.
McGibbony, George.   April 14, 1839.   Nottingham.
McGaugh, Samuel.   April 13, 1869.   Jefferson.
McGuire, John B.; II.   April 10, 1860.   W. Finley.
McIlvaine, R. F.   April 15, 1845.   Greenfield.
McIlvaine, S. B.   April 13, 1869.   Somerset.
McJunkin, John.   May 30, 1857.   Beallsville.
McKee, Robert.   April 9, 1850.   Hopewell.
McKeen, Matthew.   June 3, 1865.   Finley.

HISTORY OF WASHINGTON COUNTY. 275

NAME. DATE. DISTRICT.
McKennan, William. Jan. 2, 1804. Washington.
McKeever, A. B. April 9, 1850. Mt. Pleasant.
McKeever, Thomas. July 2, 1824. Cross Creek, Hopewell, Mt. Pleasant, and W. Middletown.
McKinley, Robert; II. April 14, 1863. W. Brownsville.
McLoney, John. April 14, 1839. Peters.
McMannis, John. June 3, 1865. Buffalo.
McNall, Joseph. June 3, 1865. Robinson.
McNary, James; III. April 9, 1850. Nottingham.
McNary, Matthew. Dec. 4. 1820. Washington and Strabane.
McNary, Matthew; II. April 14, 1840. N. Strabane.
McNary, Thomas. Feb. 1, 1799. Strabane.
McLean, H. B. April 17, 1866. W. Pike Run.
McPherson, Samuel; II. April 14, 1839. Cecil.
McVay, Jacob. August 10, 1827. Finley and Donegal.

Nailor, Wm. April, 1792.
Nelson, Francis. April 14, 1864. Carroll.
Nesbitt, John; II. April 5, 1845. S. Strabane.
Neely, Robert; II. April 14, 1863. Hanover.
Nicholls, Atkinson. April 19, 1851.
Nicholls, James. April 9, 1850. E. Finley.
Noble, James; II. February 18, 1837. Finley and Donegal.
Noble, James; IV. April 14, 1839. Claysville.

Palmer, Daniel. May 7, 1819. Washington and Strabane.
Parker, John. July 15, 1781. Fallowfield.
Parker, Silas; III. April 11, 1848. Amwell.
Parker, William. April 3, 1782. Somerset.
Parkinson, Benjamin. July 15, 1781. Nottingham.
Parkinson, Joseph. July 15, 1781. Nottingham.
Parkinson, Washington. December 13, 1820.
Parsons, Abraham. April 13, 1853. W. Pike Run.
Patterson, Robert. December 5, 1818. Smith, Hanover, and Robinons.
Patterson, Thomas M. April 10, 1860. Cross Creek.
Patterson, James L. June 3, 1865. Smith.
Passmore, George. April 14, 1837. Fallowfield.
Peden, David. April 14, 1840. E. Finley.
Pees, James B. April 10, 1849. N. Strabane.
Phillips, David; II. April 10, 1855. Peters.
Plummer, Geo. June 13, 1822. Cross Creek, Hopewell, and Mt. Pleasant.
Plummer, George. April 14, 1837. Hopewell.
Pollock, James, Jr. December 26, 1822. Peters and Nottingham.
Pollock, James; V. April 14, 1840. Robinson.
Powell, James. April 10, 1792.
Proudfit, John L. April 10, 1855. Smith.

Quail, David; II. January 31, 1822. Washington and N. Strabane.
Quail, Robert; II. March 6, 1823. E. and W. Bethlehem.
Quail, J. W. July 12, 1865. E. Bethlehem.

Ramsey, John. October 29, 1829. Cross Creek, Hopewell, Mt. Pleasant and W. Middletown.
Rankin, James. April 14, 1868. Mt. Pleasant.

| NAME. | DATE. | DISTRICT. |

Ray, William. March 24, 1823. Cross Creek, Hopewell, and Mt. Pleasant.
Reader, Francis. April 14, 1839. Union.
Reader, F. Francis; v. June 11, 1844. Greenfield.
Reed, John. July 15, 1781. Smith.
Reed, John. November 8, 1788. Cecil.
Reed, John; IV. April 14, 1800. Mt. Pleasant.
Reed, Joseph. April 10, 1855. Cecil
Reed, Dr. Robert R. April 15, 1845. Canton.
Reed, Thomas R.; III. Jan. 26, 1853. Allen.
Reynolds, D. L. April 10, 1866. S. Strabane.
Riddle, John. March 4, 1796. Smith.
Riddle, Hugh. April 15, 1845. Canonsburg.
Riddle, Samuel P.; II. April 10, 1860. Smith.
Rider, John. April 15, 1845. Fallowfield.
Richardson, Richard. April 16, 1856. Fallowfield.
Ritchie, Andrew S. April 10, 1860. West Middletown.
Ritchie, Craig. Nov. 14, 1784. Chartiers.
Ritchie, Matthew. October 6, 1784. Strabane.
Robb, Ebenezer. March 28, 1837. South Hanover, Robinson, and Mt. Pleasant.
Robb, William L. April 14, 1839. Hanover.
Roberts, Dickinson. April 14, 1839. South Strabane.
Ross, Timothy. March 9, 1861. Morris.
Ryerson, Thomas. April 8, 1789. Greene.

Samuels, John. Nov. 1, 1836. Peters, Nottingham, Union, Carroll, and Mt. Pleasant.
Sanders, Michael. April 10, 1855. Union.
Sanders, William. June 23, 1856. Morris.
Schmidt, Charles. April 9, 1867. South Strabane.
Scott, Hugh. Nov. 8, 1788. Nottingham.
Scott, A. D.; III. January 11, 1852. Beallsville.
Scott, John; III. April 11, 1854. Somerset.
Scott, Joseph. Sept. 25, 1787. Robinson.
Scott, Josiah N. April 10, 1855. Jefferson.
Scott, Parker. May 28, 1819. Pike Run and Fallowfield.
Scott, Samuel. Feb. 8, 1799. Robinson.
Scott, Thomas. Nov. 21, 1786. Washington.
Scott, William. July 15, 1781. Hopewell.
Sedgwick, Thomas. April, 1792.
Shannon, Samuel. May 26, 1795. Washington.
Sharp, Isaac. April 11, 1854.
Simpson, R. L. May 10, 1861. Buffalo.
Slemens, William. Nov. 1, 1799. Hopewell and Canton.
Smiley, William. Nov. 10, 1788. Hopewell.
Smith, George E.; III. May 13, 1858. Peters.
Smith, Henry. Jan. 18, 1838. Cross Creek, Hopewell, Mt. Pleasant, and W. Middletown.
Smith, James. April 3, 1821. Canton and Buffalo.
Smith, James. Dec. 13, 1820. Somerset.
Smith, John. Dec. 7, 1836. Hanover, Robinson, and Mt. Pleasant.
Smith, John H.; III. April 14, 1839. Hopewell.
Smith, Lewis E.; II. April 9, 1850. Greenfield.
Smith, Robert. April 11, 1854.

HISTORY OF WASHINGTON COUNTY. 277

| NAME. | DATE. | DISTRICT. |

Smith, Samuel. March 4, 1796. Cross Creek.
Smith, William. Dec. 21, 1789. Finley.
Springer, C. J.; II. April 21, 1862. East Pike Run.
St. Clair, Jesse. August 13, 1827. Finley and Donegal.
Stephenson, Moses. March 12, 1822. Smith, Hanover, and Robinson.
Stevenson, John. July 15, 1781. Fallowfield.
Stevenson, John. April 3, 1783. Somerset.
Stevenson, John. March 12, 1793. Donegal.
Stevenson, John. April 9, 1860. Smith.
Stevenson, Robert. April 2, 1803. Finley.
Stockdale, Robert. April 14, 1866. Amwell.
Stokely, Thomas. Sept. 3, 1787. Washington.
Stewart, James A.; II. April 10, 1860. Jefferson.
'Stroud, James; II. April 14, 1839. Fallowfield.
Sutherland, John; III. April 11, 1843. Donegal.
Swabe, Samuel. April 10th, 1855. Fallowfield.
Swearingen, Andrew. April 3, 1789. Chartiers.

Talbert, Richard. April, 1792.
Taylor, George; III. April 13, 1853. W. Bethlehem.
Taylor, Henry; II. July 15, 1781. Strabane.
Taylor, Samuel. August 29, 1797. Donegal.
Templeton, Wm. H. April 11, 1854. Cross Creek.
Thompson, Robert. July 15, 1781. Peters.
Townsend, Elijah. December 3, 1823. Peters and Nottingham.
Townsend, Elijah. April 14, 1840. Peters.

Urie, Samuel. April 21, 1794. Hopewell.

Vance, Isaac. April 10, 1860. S. Strabane.
Vaneman, Jos. April 19, 1838. Chartiers, Mt. Pleasant, and Canonsburg.
Vanmetre, Henry. April 3, 1782. Cumberland.
Vansbinder, John. April 10, 1855. Hopewell.
Vanvoorhis, Abm. March 6, 1823. Amwell and Morris.
Vernon, Persifor F. April 15, 1845. Millsboro'.
Vore, Isaac W. April 15, 1851. W. Pike Run.

Walker, Alexander E. April 13, 1869. Cross Creek.
Wallace, Oliver M. April 10, 1855. Buffalo.
Wallace, William. June 30, 1788. Somerset.
Wallace, William. October 14, 1807. Somerset.
Wells, Jefferson. April 16, 1856. Independence.
Wells, William. April 13, 1841. Greenfield.
Welsh, William. December 10, 1816. E. and W. Bethlehem.
Welsh, Joseph B. April 13, 1869. East Bethlehem.
Weirich, Samuel K. April 15, 1845. Canton.
Wherry, James. April, 1792.
White, Alexander. April 13, 1853. Claysville.
White, Benjamin. April 9. 1850. W. Pike Run.
White, John. July 15, 1781. Strabane.
White, John. July 1, 1817. E. and W. Bethlehem.
White, John. January 23, 1819. Chartiers and Cecil.
White, James. April 14, 1839. Canton.

NAME.	DATE.	DISTRICT.
Wilkins, John.	April 2, 1803.	Smith.
Williams, Abraham; II.	April 9, 1850.	Buffalo.
Williamson, Samuel.	July 15, 1781.	Donegal.
Wilson, John; II.	February 1, 1799.	Washington.
Wilson, John V.	April 10, 1860.	Franklin.
Winter, David.	September 20, 1819.	Finley and Donegal.
Wise, Freeman.	April 10, 1867.	W. Brownville.
Wolfe, Jacob.	June 7, 1793.	Donegal.
Wood, Israel.	April 10, 1855.	E. Finley.
Worth, John.	November 1, 1786.	Fallowfield.
Wotring, Abraham; III.	April 14, 1857.	Hopewell.
Wright, Alexander.	July 15, 1781.	Robinson.
Yoke, Daniel; IV.	April 9, 1850.	Carroll.
Young, Abraham; II.	April 15, 1845.	E. and W. Bethlehem.
Zediker, John.	April 10, 1855.	S. Strabane.

CHAPTER VII.

MILITARY HISTORY OF WASHINGTON COUNTY.

Brig.-Gen. Clark's expedition in 1781—Col. David Williamson's expedition in 1782—Col. William Crawford's expedition in 1782—Whiskey Insurrection in 1791-4—Outrage on the Chesapeake Frigate, 1807—War of 1812—Texas Revolution, in 1836—Mexican War in 1846—Southern Rebellion in 1861.

BRIG. GEN. GEORGE CLARK'S HISTORY AND EXPEDITIONS.

BRIG.-GENERAL CLARK (formerly Col. Clark) was raised to the office of Brigadier-General by the State of Virginia for his meritorious services against the Indians. Col. Daniel Brodhead, under date of Fort Pitt, Sept. 5, 1780, to President Reed, of Supreme Executive Council of Pennsylvania, says: "I am informed that Col. Clark had destroyed two of the Shawnee towns, killed six men and one woman, and is returned to the Falls of Ohio." On 25th February, 1781, Col. Clark was ordered to proceed from Fort Pitt (to which place he had returned) to the Falls of Ohio, and from thence to Wabash. His instructions were from General Washington, the Commander-in-Chief, because he exercised unbounded influence over the inhabitants of the western country by his military skill and indomitable energy. On March 10th of the same year we find him busily engaged in purchasing large quantities of flour and Indian corn to carry on an expedition against the Indians. Thomas Jefferson, Governor of Virginia, writes to Col. Brodhead, February 13, 1781: "Gen. Washington's letter, transmitted by you to Gen. Clark, will no doubt have satisfied you how earnestly he espouses the service on which that gentleman is ordered, and that it is his desire he should receive from you every aid of men and necessaries which you can help him to. I rely, for your cordial execution of this desire, on your zeal for the common cause, as well as your respect for the wishes of the Commander-in-Chief."

On the 23d March, 1781, Gen. Clark addressed a letter to President Reed, in which he says: "I am ordered to the command of the greatest consequence to the frontiers of Pennsylvania and Virginia, if our resources should not be such as to enable us to remain in the Indian country during the fair season. I am in hopes that they will be sufficient to visit the Shawnees, Delaware, and Sandusky towns. Defeating the enemy and laying those countries waste would give great ease to the frontiers of both States, whom I think equally interested. I am confident from the nature of the intended expedition you would wish to give it every aid in your power. I hope, sir, that you will inform the inhabitants on this side of the mountain that such are your sentiments. I hope that you will honor me with an immediate answer per express, as it is of the greatest consequence to us, and that the fate of the Indians at present appears to depend on the resolutions you may take."

President Reed replied on the 23d of March, that "the enterprise you refer to has never been officially communicated to us, but from common report we learn that an expedition under your command is destined against Detroit. We are very sensible of its importance to this State, as well as Virginia, and there is no gentleman in whose abilities and good conduct we have more confidence on such an occasion. After this it seems unnecessary to add that it will give us great satisfaction if the inhabitants of this State cheerfully concur in it, and we authorize you to declare that so far from giving offence to their government we shall consider their service with you as highly meritorious. At the same time we must add that, from the exhausted state of our treasury, we are in no condition to answer any demands of a pecuniary kind, and therefore do not mean by anything we have said to raise an expectation we cannot answer."

The position thus taken for an expedition was, therefore, not only approved by President Reed, but urged by other letters to Col. Brodhead and Governor Thomas Jefferson, the necessity of immediate and energetic action.

Gen. Clark, under these influences, on the 3d June, 1781 addressed the officers of Westmoreland and Washington counties to raise an expedition against the Shawnees, Delawares, and Sandusky towns. The people assembled on the 18th of June, 1781, and adopted the following preamble and resolutions:—

WHEREAS, There was a number of the principal people met on said day, and unanimously chose John Proctor, John Pomroy, Charles Campbell, Samuel Moorhead, James Barr, Charles Foreman, Isaac Meason, James Smith, and Hugh Martin a committee to enter into resolves for the defence of our frontiers, as they were informed by Christ. Hays, Esq., that their proceedings would be approved of by the council—

1. *Resolved*, That a campaign be carried on with Gen. Clark.
2. *Resolved*, That Gen. Clark be furnished with 300 men out of Pomroy's, Beard's, and Davis's battalions.
3. *Resolved*, That Col. Archd. Lochry give orders to said Colonels to raise their quota by volunteer or draft.
4. *Resolved*, That £6 be advanced to every volunteer that marches under the command of Gen. Clark on the proposed campaign.
5. And for the further encouragement of volunteers, that grain be raised by subscription by the different companies.
6. That Col. Lochry counsel with the officers of Virginia respecting the manner of drafting those that associate in that State and others.
7. *Resolved*, That Col. Lochry meet Gen. Clark and other officers, and Col. Crawford, on the 23d inst., to confer with them concerning the day of rendezvous.

On the 5th of June a council of the militia officers was held at the court-house of Youghiogheny County, and the fifth part of the militia of said county was drafted for Gen. Clark's expedition ; but the people, generally believing that the territory of Youghiogheny County belonged to Pennsylvania, denied their authority, and refused to submit until the State line was finally determined. In this state of affairs Col. Hays gave public notice to the inhabitants of Washington and Westmoreland counties that he had money placed in his hands, by the Supreme Executive Council, for the purpose of protecting the frontiers. The people, therefore, resolved to raise the requisite number of men to assist Gen. Clark to conquer the Delawares, Shawnees, and Wyandott Indians, especially the Sandusky towns. The militia composing Gen Clark's command was made up of drafted men of the counties of Youghiogheny, Monongahela, and Ohio County of Virginia, although parts of each were claimed as Washington County by Pennsylvania. This expedition was sanctioned by the Supreme Executive Council of Pennsylvania. President Reed sanctions Gen. Clark's cause, being well satisfied that if the people will sustain him he would give effectual relief to the frontiers, and expect very shortly to congratulate the country on Gen. Clark's success. President Reed also wrote to Col. Lochry advising him to encourage the people to assist in the expedition, as some aid and support would give effectual relief to the frontiers from the distresses they have so long and so seriously suffered. The influence which was brought about by the Supreme Executive Council had the desired effect. Companies and battalions were organized and went into camp, as will appear from the following letter from Dorsey Pentecost, Esq., to President Reed, dated *Washington County*, July 27, 1781.

"I am now in Gen. Clark's camp, about three miles below Fort Pitt, and am about to leave this county on the expedition under that gentleman's command."

Dorsey Pentecost was Lieutenant of Washington County, and through his zeal and exertion furnished the quota of the county and marched the militia into camp. Notwithstanding the efforts of many patriotic men to protect the frontiers, yet such men as Thomas Scott, Esq., thought the expedition would be injurious to the interests of Pennsylvania, and oppressive on some who were steadfast friends of the government. Gen. Clark condemned all such would-be patriots in a letter to President Reed, and rebuked such as unworthy of private or public confidence.

On the 4th of August, 1781, Col. Lochry wrote to President Reed that he had left Westmoreland County with Capt. Stokely's company of Rangers, and about fifty volunteers, to join Gen. Clark at Fort Henry, on the Ohio River, where his army had been in rendezvous for some weeks. The very fact of these men going into camp and placing themselves under Gen. Clark's command, caused new difficulties in Washington County. James Marshall had been appointed Lieutenant of the county, and was opposed to the expedition. Many statements have been made by the enemies of Gen. Clark, charging upon him and his friends cruel treatment by apprehending those who were drafted and did not obey. But the prominent inhabitants of Washington County addressed a letter to President Reed on the 15th August, 1781, stating that as Gen. Clark had an expedition carrying on for the salvation of the country, it was improper for an election to be held the same day, and the result of which was that men who lived 'in comparative security were elected to office, which caused more dissatisfaction than the drafting of the militia. President Reed having learned all the questions at issue, wrote to the people of Washington County that he could not help fearing that too many, in consequence of the unsettled state of boundaries, avail themselves of a pretence to withhold their services from the public at a time they are most wanted. "We cannot," he says, "help also observing that by letters received from the principal gentlemen in Westmoreland, it seems evident they approve of Gen. Clark's expedition, and that the lieutenants of both counties united on the plan of raising three hundred men for that service, and even now I am at a loss to account for the different opinions entertained on the point by the people of Westmoreland and Washington counties."

It appears from a letter of Hon. Christ. Hays to President Reed, dated August 25, 1781, that every obstacle was placed in the way of Gen. Clark's success—feelings engendered by jealousy—as the letter of Mr. Hays will abundantly show.

"There have been divers meetings for devising the best mode for the protection of this country, and there has been a majority of a small number of men at said meetings, who fell on a plan of joining Gen. Clark with a number of troops from this county, as has been represented to you, which I by no means could consent or agree to, and yet has been forced by Col. Lochry, contrary to the will and pleasure of the major part of the inhabitants of this county, and to the great disadvantage of the distressed frontiers and for the benefit of the State of Virginia alone, as has, since Gen. Clark's departure, been made known to me by Col. Gibson and several other Virginia officers, which obliged Col. D. Brodhead, with the assistance of the militia of this and Washington County, to carry on a campaign by the 5th of September against the same towns that Gen. Clark and Col. Lochry purposed to go to. Fifty-eight good men, belonging to Captain Stokely's and Captain Shearer's companies (in a manner naked), besides a number of volunteers, have been sent with Gen. Clark for the protection of the frontiers of Virginia.

"I would have represented all matters in a clear light to you, concerning this affair, before Gen. Clark's departure from Washington County, could I have had the benefit of the last express that has been sent to you from this county, which, perhaps, might have altered the whole of the above mentioned proceedings, but, contrary to all promises, it was sent unknown to me."

President Reed replied that Gen. Clark had no other authority than to take such volunteers as might offer, and to purchase provisions. At the same time, he says, we must observe that at a general meeting of the principal inhabitants, both of Virginia and Pennsylvania, the expedition appeared so beneficial to the latter that the lieutenants of both joined to promote it, and agreed that three hundred men should be furnished. We apprehend that parties have taken too deep root, and that there are too many who avail themselves of the dispute of State boundary to withhold their services from the public, a disposition which ought to have no countenance whatever. To this letter I would add that in a subsequent letter of President Reed to Mr. Hays he throws the whole weight of responsibility upon the latter gentleman, and asserts that his approbation of furnishing Gen. Clark with men, was founded upon representations made by himself and other gentlemen, which, he presumes, was free and voluntary.

While a war of words was progressing, Gen. Clark and his officers and soldiers were busily engaged in preparing for conquering the Indians; but on the 24th of August his command was defeated, as the following letter from Gen. Irvine, dated Fort Pitt, Dec. 3, 1781, will show:—

"I am sorry to inform your excellency that this county has got a severe stroke by the loss of Col. Lochry and about one hundred of the best men of Westmoreland County, including Captain Stokely and his company of Rangers. They were going down the Ohio on Gen. Clark's expedition. Many accounts agree that they were all killed or taken at the mouth of the Miami River, I believe chiefly killed; the misfortune added to the failure of Gen. Clark's expedition has filled the people with great dismay. Many talk of retiring to the east side of the mountain early in the spring."

Col. Lochry, at the time of his death, held the office of Prothonotary and of Lieutenant of Westmoreland County. On the fact being made known to the Executive Council, Michael Huffnagle was appointed to the former and Edward Cook to the latter office in December, 1781.

On the 3d day of July, 1782, President Moore received the following memorial from the prisoners, taken captives by the Indians:—

"We the subscribers, inhabitants of the county of Westmoreland, beg leave to represent to your excellency and the council, that we had the misfortune to be made prisoners of by the Indians on the 24th of August last, and carried to Montreal, and there kept in close confinement until the 25th of May, 1782, when we were so fortunate as to make our escape, and after a long and fatiguing march through the wilderness, we got to this city (Philadelphia) yesterday at 3 o'clock. As we are at present destitute of both money and clothes, without which we cannot go home, we pray your excellency and council to take our case into consideration and order us pay from the time we were made prisoners to this.

"We were under the command of Col. Lochry when taken, and have a list of all those, both officers and privates, who are now prisoners of this party, which together with such information as is in our power we are ready to give for the satisfaction of your excellency and council.

"We have the honor to be your excellency's humble servants,
ISAAC ANDERSON.
Lieutenant Capt. Sherer's Company Rangers.
RICHARD WALLACE,
Late Quarter-Master to Col. Lochry."

The Council immediately granted nine pounds seven shillings and sixpence specie to Lieut. Anderson, and seven pounds seventeen shillings and sixpence specie to Richard Wallace, to bear their expenses from Philadelphia to Westmoreland County.

On January 6, 1783, a representation was read to Council signed by John Boyd, Captain of the Rangers, and Thomas Stokely, Captain of the Second Company of Rangers, representing the situations of Henry Dugan, Sergeant of Captain Boyd's company, and Robert Watson, John Marus, and Michael Hare, of Capt. Stokely's company, now returned from captivity among the Indians; whereupon the Council ordered two months' pay to be advanced to each soldier, and that each also be furnished with a hat, two shirts, a waistcoat, a pair of overalls, a pair of stockings, a pair of shoes, and cloth and trimmings for a coat.

COL. DAVID WILLIAMSON'S EXPEDITIONS.

In the fall of 1781 the militia of the frontier counties of Pennsylvania resolved to break up the Moravian towns on the Muskingum, because it was very truthfully stated that it was half way between this county and the Wyandotte tribe of Indians. Through fear these Moravian settlements sheltered, protected, and procured for these hostile Indians provisions to carry on excursions into the settlements; hence it was that the *first* campaign was undertaken. Col. Williamson marched his forces, found but few Indians there, the greater part having gone to Sandusky, and took them as hostages to Fort Pitt and delivered them to General Irvine. After their liberation, Dodridge says they crossed the river and killed or made prisoners of a family of the name of Monteur, on Monteur's Island, seven miles below Pittsburg. This island at that time was a part of Washington County. Also it was said that a family had been killed on Buffalo Creek, and it was by one of them, who, after being made prisoner, made his escape, and that the leader of the party was a Moravian. Such were the reports prevalent in that day, and upon these reports Colonel Williamson's character suffered severely for not killing the Indians instead of sending them to Fort Pitt.

This gave rise to the *second* expedition under the command of Colonel Williamson, who marched out with his command in March, 1782, his soldiers being composed of the frontier settlers, whose hatred to the Indian was both implacable and irreconcilable. On their way they passed through the settlement of the Moravian Indians, who had the reputation of being both peaceable and Christian in character, but it is said that these soldiers found among the Moravian Indians many memorials of their families, trinkets, the gifts of love, clothing still bloody, and worn by their own wives and daughters, who had been tomahawked and killed. Without reflection, and believing that this tribe of Indians were also guilty (being in possession of these articles), they, without the consent of their commander, whose orders they disregarded, massacred the Indians indiscriminately, because revenge, the worst passion of the human heart, had taken possession of every soldier. In this paroxysm of revenge, human nature forgot itself, and the blood of those who were near and dear to them seemed to call for retaliation, and the dying agonies of their own innocent ones all seemed to urge them on to complete the work of destruction.

After their desires had been gratified, and reason had resumed her throne, Col. Williamson determined to go no further after witnessing this act of insubordination. He returned to Washington County with his men, having resolved to submit the massacre of the Moravian Indians to a decision of his fellow-citizens. Hence, at the October election in 1887, he offered himself as a candidate for Sheriff, and for his acknowledged bravery, and devotion to their interests, he was triumphantly elected; nor did the people ever hold him accountable for the insubordination which prevailed, and which no human power could prevent. His election thereupon to that important office is a complete refutation of the charge made against him by the historian Loskiel, who charges him with perpetrating the most infamous act of border warfare, viz: the destruction of the peaceable Moravian Christian Indians. Rev. Jos. Dodridge says:

'In justice to the memory of Col. Williamson, I have to say that although at that time very young, I was personally acquainted with him, and I say with confidence that he was a brave man, but not cruel. He would meet an enemy in battle and fight like a soldier, but not murder a prisoner. His only fault was that of too easy a compliance with popular opinion and popular prejudice. On this account his memory has been loaded with unmerited reproach." It is eminently due, after passion and prejudice have passed away, and the third generation of men can view history from a different standpoint, that the memory of Col. Williamson should be vindicated, and the fame of the brave and meritorious not blackened with unfounded charges. He has gone to accomplish his destiny, and we leave Col. Williamson in the hands of that God who in this case will "judge righteous judgment."

In order to place this affair of the massacre of the Moravian Indians in its true light, I shall now give the official facts and the testimony of Dorsey Pentecost, Esq., who corroborates the position I have taken.

In March, 1782, Col. Williamson set out upon his expedition, the result of which I have already stated, but in a letter of L. Weiss, to Charles Thompson, Secretary of Congress, dated April 7, 1782, he says: "I received this afternoon a letter from Rev. Nathaniel, Bishop of the united churches of the brethren residing at Bethlehem. He informs me that the same day a melancholy report was brought to him by one Mr. Leinbach, relative to a murder committed by white men upon a number of Christian Indians, at a place called Muskingum."

It appears, however, that Mr. Leinbach himself was not at the scene of action, but he received it from two of his neighbors living near Easton, who had returned from a visit to their friends at the Monongahela River. The statement made was—

"That some time in February, preceding, one hundred and sixty men, living upon Monongahela, set off on horseback to the Muskingum, in order to destroy three Indian settlements of which they seemed to be sure of being the towns of some enemy Indians. After coming nigh to one of the towns, they discovered some Indians on both sides of the river Muskingum. They then concluded to divide themselves into two parties, the one to cross the river and the other to attack those Indians on this side. When the party got over the river they saw one of the Indians coming up towards them. They laid themselves flat on the ground waiting till the Indian was nigh enough, then one of them shot the Indian and broke his arm, then three of the militia ran towards him with tomahawks. When they were yet a little distance from him, he asked them why they fired at him; he was minister Shebosh's (John Bull's) son, but they took no notice of what he said, but killed him on the spot. They then surrounded the field and took all the other Indians as prisoners. The Indians told them that they were Christians, and made no resistance. When the militia gave them to understand that they must bring them as prisoners to Fort Pitt, they seemed to be very glad. They were ordered to prepare themselves for the journey, and to take all their effects along with them. Accordingly, they did so. They were asked how it came they had no cattle. They answered that the small stock that was left them had been sent to Sandusky.

In the evening the militia held a council, when the commander of the militia told his men that he would leave it to their choice either to carry the Indians to Fort Pitt as prisoners or to kill them, when they agreed that they should be killed. Of this resolution of the council they gave notice to the Indians by two messengers, who told them that, as they had said they were Christians, they would give them this night to prepare themselves accordingly. Whereupon the women met together and sung hymns and psalms all night, and so did likewise the men, and kept on singing as long as there were three alive.

In the morning the militia chose two houses, which they called the slaughter-houses, and then fetched the Indians, two or three at a time, with ropes about their necks, and dragged them into the slaughter-houses where they knocked them down. They then set these two houses on fire, as likewise all the other houses. This done, they went to the other towns and set fire to the houses, took their plunder and returned to the Monongahela, where they kept a vendue among themselves. Before these informants came away it was agreed that six hundred men should meet on the 18th of March, 1782, to go to Sandusky, which is about one hundred miles from the Muskingum.

John Etwine, of Litiz, under date of March 31st of the same year, says: "It is reported from Lancaster that one hundred militiamen from the Ohio have destroyed two Delaware Indian towns, and have killed ninety-five Indians."

George Niser, of York, under date of April 2, says: "I have seen a letter written by a woman at Fort Pitt, dated March 21, 1782, which contains these particulars, viz: The militia have killed ninety-nine of the Moravian Indians, viz: thirty-three men and sixty-six women and children."

In another letter by the same person, but dated April 5, he writes: "The Moravian Indian congregation at Sandusky is butchered, as it is reported by the Scotch. They came and told them they must prepare directly for death. The Indians requested but an hour's time for this purpose, which was granted. They went to their meeting-house to join in prayers to the Lord. After the hour had passed they fell upon them and butchered all of them in cold blood in the meeting-house and then set fire to the house."

These various rumors, somewhat contradictory in their facts, reached the Supreme Executive Council, who directed Gen. Wm. Irvine, then stationed at Fort Pitt, by letter dated April 13, 1782, to inquire if a party of militia had killed a number of Indians at or near Muskingum, and also if a Mr. Bull was killed at the same time, and to transmit the facts relative thereto, authenticated in the clearest manner. To this charge Col. Williamson and Col. Marshall both replied, and by order of the Supreme Executive Council was laid before Congress.

The following letter of Dorsey Pentecost, dated at Fort Pitt, May 8, 1782, throws much light upon this question. He says:—

"I arrived at home last Thursday; yesterday I came to this place and had long conferences with Gen. Irvine and Col. Gibson respecting the excursion to Muskingum. That affair is a subject of great speculation here, some condemning, others applauding the measure, but the accounts are so various that it is not only difficult, but almost, indeed utterly impossible to ascertain the REAL TRUTH. No person can give intelligence but those that were along, notwithstanding there seems to have been some differences amongst themselves about that business, yet they will say nothing.

"I hear there is great preparation making for a descent on Sandusky, to set out the 20th of this month, which will be conducted by a gentleman of experience and veracity." The writer speaks of Col. Crawford's expedition. He then adds: "It is said here, and *I believe with truth*, that sundry articles were found amongst the Indians that were taken from the inhabitants of Washington County, and that the Indians confessed themselves, that when they set out from Sandusky ten warriors came with them who had gone into the settlements, and that four of them were then in the towns who had returned. If those Indians that were killed were really friends, they must have been very imprudent to return to settle at a place they knew the white people had been at and would go to again, without giving us notice, and besides to bring warriors with them who had come into the settlements and after murdering would return to their towns, and of course draw people after them filled with revenge, indignation, and sorrow for the loss of their friends their wives and their children." He also writes that "the people are greatly divided in sentiment about it (the Moravian affair), and an investigation may produce serious effects, and at least leave us as ignorant as when we began, and instead of rendering a service may produce confusion and ill-will amongst the people."

He recommends to the Supreme Council to forbid that, in future excursions, women, children, and infirm persons should be killed, being contrary to the laws of man as well as Christianity.

Thus terminated the campaign under Col. Williamson.

COL. WILLIAM CRAWFORD'S EXPEDITION.

In the summer of 1782 a third expedition was commenced after the return of Col. Williamson, by a regiment of four hundred and eighty-two men, who were principally from east of the Monongahela River, in Fayette County, except one company from the Tenmile settlement, in Washington County. Hence we give an account of this expedition.

On the 20th of May, 1782, the regiment left Beesontown (now Uniontown) under the temporary command of Col. William Crawford, whose residence was at the forks of Youghiogheny, near Connellsville. On May 22, they reached Catfish (now Washington), where they were joined by a company from Tenmile, in this county. On the 26th of May they encamped at old Indian Mingo town, where an election was held for Colonel, the candidates being Col. William Crawford and Col. David Williamson. The election resulted in favor of Col. Crawford. The regiment on that day took up the line of march by the same Indian trail which Col. Williamson had passed over, and on the 4th of June they encamped on the Sandusky plains. The battle was fought on the 5th and 6th of June, 1782.

From the most authentic accounts we learn that the Indians were apprised of the approach of Col. Crawford, and were prepared for his regiment by being concealed in ambush. At a preconcerted signal the Indians commenced firing, which was returned by the regiment. Both parties fought with great fury until dark (of June 5th), when the Indians retreated and the soldiers encamped upon the battle-ground, sleeping upon their arms.

The next day (June 6th) skirmishing began and fighting ensued. Col. Crawford discovered that the Indian forces through the night had been greatly increased. A council of officers was held, and they determined that prudence would dictate a retreat, because many valuable lives were lost (about one hundred soldiers being killed), and that their ammunition and provisions were nearly exhausted. A little before midnight the remaining members of the regiment were arranged in order, and the retreat began, having left their camp-fires burning so as to deceive the Indians.* They had not proceeded far when shots were fired by the Indians, which necessarily caused great confusion and disorder, as the officers and soldiers believed that their movements had been discovered by their wily foe. Each man, therefore, determined to seek his own safety in flight; but the savage Indians, thirsting for revenge for the death of the Moravian Indians, and with that sagacity which belongs to their race, overtook most of the soldiers, and they fell victims to the tomahawk. The massacre was terrible.

Among the captives were Col. Crawford and his nephew, Dr. Knight. These they retained for a sadder and more terrible death. The Indians, failing to secure Col. Williamson, visited upon Col. Crawford the death of the Moravian Indians, although he had not in any of his Indian expeditions harmed a Moravian Indian. Here I may add that Wingenund, an old Indian chief who had known Col. Crawford for many years, and had even visited his (Crawford's) house, said to him, after they had painted him black (a symbol of the horrible death he was to undergo): "Had we Williamson in your place, there might be some hope for you; but as it is, there is not." From the intimacy which always existed between this old chief and Col. Crawford, he said to him: "Col. Crawford, your fate is fixed. Meet it as a soldier should. Farewell. They are coming, and I will retire where I cannot see you." These two brave men, representing entirely different interests, parted, each shedding tears.

On the arrival of the band of Indians who were to take charge of Col. Crawford, their hellish work began. While Dr. Knight, his nephew, was seated close by as a witness of the torments which Col. Crawford was to endure. On the 11th of June, 1782, Col. Crawford was led to a stake driven in the ground, at Sandusky Plains, with

---

* The retreat of Col. Crawford's men was conducted by Major Daniel Leet, who was the intimate friend of Col. Crawford. Their intimacy arose from the fact that Gen. Washington had selected them to survey and locate lands in Virginia and Kentucky, hence he was selected to take command of the right wing of the army, in which was the company of the Tenmile settlement of this county.

his hands secured firmly behind his back by means of strong thongs. A rope was then fastened to these between the wrists, and the other end to the bottom of the stake. The rope was long enough to allow him to walk backward and forward several times, while around the stake, and within the circle which the rope would allow him to pass over, were heaped dry and combustible fagots. When these were ignited the tortures commenced. The Colonel had previously been stripped naked, and after an Indian speech, about seventy loads of powder were discharged upon his naked body. His ears were cut off, and burning brands and fagots applied to his body ; he was scalped, and squaws threw burning coals and hot embers upon his head and body. Col. Crawford, having committed himself to the Almighty, bore all his torments with manly fortitude. It seemed as if God in mercy and in answer to his prayer had so benumbed his nerves that he felt no pain. Dr. Knight, who was witness of it, and afterwards made his escape, said that he seemed unconscious of the presence of his tormentors, and was exclusively engaged in close communion with his Saviour. It is said by those who have visited the spot, about half a mile from Little Sandusky, that nothing will grow within the circuit which Col. Crawford made when tied to the stake, and God, as a memorial of the wickedness of the crime, thus marks the spot where an innocent man suffered a cruel death.

It may be well to remark that Col. Crawford emigrated from Berkeley County, Virginia, in 1768, to near Connellsville, Fayette County, Pennsylvania. He served as captain in Forbes's expedition in 1758. He was the intimate friend of Gen. Washington, who had been an inmate of his humble dwelling during his visit to this county to locate lands. At the commencement of the American Revolution he raised a regiment by his own exertions, and held a commission of Colonel in the Continental army. Thus perished, at the age of fifty years, Col. William Crawford, who held many positions of honor and profit under both Virginia and Pennsylvania, especially when Washington County was considered as belonging to Virginia by the name of Youghiogheny County. Pennsylvania has honored his memory by naming one of the northwestern counties after him, to perpetuate his fame and his deeds.

Since writing the above, my friend, J. T. F. Wright, sent me the narrative of Col. James Paul, who was with Crawford at his defeat. Col. Paul died in 1841, aged 84 years. Col. Paul corrects an error into which some writers have fallen, as to the motives of Col. Crawford and his noble band of volunteers in going to Upper Sandusky, which object was in reality to conquer the Wyandottes and bands of hostile Indians, and to burn their town, and not, as erroneously reported, to complete the slaughter of the remainder of the peaceable Christian Moravian Indians. This narrative further states that a scheme was formed and put on foot, the object of which was to check the Sandusky Indians, principally that of the Wyandotte tribe, which tribe was at that time the most bold, daring, and ferocious of any of the other hostile tribes, whose depredations on the frontier settlers had grown hard to be borne. A further object of this scheme was the destruction of the Indian town at Upper Sandusky, and thus to check and put a stop, if possible, to the scalping, murdering, and plundering which were continually committed on the defenceless frontiers of Western Pennsylvania and Virginia. Col. Paul thus nobly repels the charge made by Weems and some few others, who have misstated the object of these brave, noble-hearted volunteers who risked their lives in an enemy's country.

To preserve the history of that memorable event with which Washington County is so intimately connected, I shall add letters written at the time by our own citizens.

Dorsey Pentecost, Esq., under date of June 17, 1782, to President Moore, says:—

"I have just time to tell you that on the 25th of May four hundred and seventy-eight (some say four hundred and eighty-eight) soldiers, mounted on horseback, set out, under the command of Col. Crawford, for St. Duskie. They were discovered at the Muskingum and from there all the way out spies were kept on them. The St. Duskie people collected the Shawnees and the light dragoons from the British posts between St. Duskie and the post at Detroit, they attacked our people in the plains of St. Duskie, near the St. Duskie River, on Tuesday was a week last. The battle continued two days, the first day was very close and hot work, the second day was at long shot only. On the night of the second day our people retreated, and the Indians broke in on them in the retreat and routed them. However, about two hundred stuck together and brought off all the wounded except three, which were left on the ground. The next day the Indians attacked our people in the rear, but were repulsed with considerable loss on their side. They then pursued their retreat with success and unmolested.

"There are about twenty wounded (a few dangerous) and about half that number killed. There are a good many missing, amongst which is Colonel Crawford and a number of other valuable men, but as the scattered parties are coming in daily, I have hopes of them. As the people were much confused when I met them (at the Mingo bottom), I could not get the information requisite. What little I got was from Major Ross, Aide-de-camp to Gen. Irvine, and who went aid to Col. Crawford, and I hope the General (Irvine) will give you a particular account, as he will receive it from the Major. I am told that the Indians were much superior to our people, and that in the engagement they suffered greatly, and also that Col. Crawford strongly recommended to return before they got to the town, alleging that our people were too weak, as the Indians had early intelligence of their coming, but he was overruled by the rest of the officers."

July 5, 1782, Gen. Irvine writes from Fort Pitt, stating that

"Dr. Knight has this moment arrived—the Surgeon I sent with the volunteers to Sandusky; he was several days in the hands of the Indians, but fortunately made his escape from his keeper, who was conducting him to another settlement to be burned. He brings the disagreeable account that Col. Crawford and all the rest (about twelve to the doctor's knowledge) who fell into their hands, were burned to death in a most shocking manner. The unfortunate Colonel in particular was upwards of four hours burning. The reason they assign for this uncommon barbarity is retaliation for the

Moravian affair. (I have given an account of this affair under Col. Williamson's expedition.) The doctor adds that he understood those people had laid aside their religious principles and have gone to war, that he himself saw two of them bring in scalps whom he formerly knew."

WHISKEY INSURRECTION.

This was the FOURTH important military movement in this county, and which extended itself to Westmoreland, Fayette, Allegheny, and Bedford counties, and that part of Western Virginia on the Ohio River and borders of Pennsylvania. To subdue this rebellion, which began July 27, 1791, and was ended in 1794, by an amnesty proclamation and an oath of allegiance subscribed by the people, it cost the government *six hundred and sixty-nine thousand nine hundred and ninety-two dollars* and *thirty-four cents*. I have given full particulars of this insurrection in the Appendix to this work in Chapter IV., on the Whiskey Insurrection, to which I would refer my readers.

OUTRAGE ON THE CHESAPEAKE FRIGATE.

The people of Washington County, on the 18th of July, 1807, jealous of their rights, their liberties, and their military fame, called a meeting to take measures with regard to the outrages committed on the Chesapeake frigate by a British ship-of-war. We may name this as the *fifth* military movement. Col. William McKennan was chosen Chairman, and Gen. John Morgan Secretary. The proceedings of citizens of Norfolk, Hampton, Philadelphia, and other cities, were read, and Parker Campbell, Gen. John Morgan, Thomas Acheson, Edward Todd, and John Simonson, Esqs., were appointed a committee to report resolutions, who reported that the people of Washington County sensibly feel the outrageous conduct of the tyrants of the ocean, and pledged themselves, by all the ties most sacred among men, to support, by every exertion and all the means in their power, all measures of defence or retaliation best adapted to prevent a repetition of such outrages, and enforce proper concessions for the past.

The meeting also tendered their services to government, and promised to repair to the posts assigned to them at the first call, approving and applauding the executive prohibition of the entrance of British ships-of-war into the ports and harbors of the United States, and of all intercourse with them. They also wisely resolved that hospitality under such circumstances ceases to be a duty, and the honor and independence of our country forbid a continuance of it, and they also urge the necessity of a prompt attention to arms, equipments, &c., to defend an injured country.

On the 10th of February, 1809, Col. Thomas Acheson issued the following military address in connection with this subject, to the 23d Regiment, in Washington County:—

"Fellow Soldiers: It will be remembered that in consequence of the outrageous attack and cowardly murder of our fellow-citizens on board the Chesapeake by the slaves of Britain in the month of June, 1807, that the President ordered ten thousand militia of the United States to be held in readiness for actual service. That on the 10th of August of the same year you were called together for the same purpose of furnishing the proper quota of men from this regiment, when three hundred and five patriots tendered their services to the President to march at a moment's warning to any part of the Union or elsewhere. But the law under which that tender was made having expired, you once more have an opportunity of renewing that tender.

"It appears that no kind of satisfaction was ever offered by the British government for the murder of our fellow-citizens on board the Chesapeake, but that notwithstanding the forbearance of our general government, insult was added to injury, hence the blood of your brethren still cries aloud for vengeance. While we are informed that the yeomanry of enslaved Europe are fighting for their task-masters, and thereby riveting their own chains, shall the free and independent citizens of this happy country shrink from the defence of our homes? I trust not, but that all those young patriots who voluntarily tendered their services on the former occasion will now be first to renew that tender, and evince to the world that the honor, dignity, and independence of this injured country, so dearly purchased by their father's blood, is nearer to them than life, and that they will rally around the standard of liberty, and defend and support the government of their choice against insidious and domestic traitors."

War between the United States and Great Britain.

The SIXTH military event in the history of Washington County was the interest she evinced in the war of 1812, commonly called the Second War for Independence. It will be remembered that war was declared by the United States on the 19th day of June, 1812, because England claimed the right to search all neutral vessels for British seamen, and all were claimed as such who could not exhibit official papers of their birth and regular shipment under a neutral government; hence native born citizens of America were taken from under our flag and impressed into service, the consequences of which was the war of 1812. The difficulties were hastened by the attack on the Chesapeake. On the 22d of June following, a public meeting of the citizens of this county was held to ascertain the public sentiment with respect to the measures of the general government, of which David Morris, Esq., was chairman. A committee consisting of Thomas Acheson, Robert Anderson, Alexander Murdoch, Thomas H. Baird, and Parker Campbell, were appointed to prepare an address to be submitted to the people, at an adjourned county meeting, on the 27th of June, at which meeting Rev. Thomas L. Birch, William Hoge, and Parker Campbell, Esqs., made patriotic addresses.

On the 24th of August, 1812, Gen. Thomas Acheson, as chairman of the Committee, issued an address, in the following words, to the people of Washington County:—

"They owe it to the brave volunteers to make known to the world that the spirit of the Washington County militia is the spirit of liberty, of patriotism, and of humanity, and that when any emergency requires their exertions, no consideration of personal danger or inconvenience can prevent them from rushing to the scene of apprehended attack."

On Wednesday, the 26th of July, news arrived in Washington, by express from Gen. Wadsworth, that Gen. Hull and his army had been captured, and that a body of five thousand British and Indians were advancing with barbarous ferocity upon our defenceless frontiers. This information was confirmed by several other express messengers, who arrived in Pittsburg with the alarming intelligence that they had in fact marched within nine miles of Cleveland, Ohio.

A Committee of Safety and Arrangement was formed, who were directed to appeal to their fellow-citizens in Washington County, and to open a communication so as to secure a co-operation in their plans and organizations. They appealed, and they appealed not in vain. In forty-eight hours from the first call a company of young men from the town of Washington and its vicinity, of light infantry, under the command of Captain William Sample, volunteered themselves to march to the scene of savage slaughter and devastation. By the amiable and spirited assistance of the LADIES of Washington, they were completely uniformed and equipped.

Another company was also formed within the bounds of the Washington regiment, and the " Rifle Rangers," under the command of Capt. (afterwards Governor) Joseph Ritner, volunteered their services as a body. A troop of horse from Col. Dickerson's regiment, under Capt. Lawrence, turned out with alacrity. A company of infantry, under Capt. Buchanan, of Middletown, also offered their services. Two hundred and fifty brave volunteers, under the command of Col. Dickerson, informed Gen. Acheson that they were ready to march at a moment's warning. Capt. Cartey and part of his troop, and the troop of Capt. Shouse, from Williamsport (now Monongahela City) were also ready to march. The Williamsport Rangers, and Capt. Thomas's infantry held themselves subject to orders. From this brigade there were not less than seven hundred men, exclusive of two hundred and fifty men from Burgettstown, under the command of Col. Thos. Patterson, Major John Vance, and Capt. McCready.

By the liberal contributions of spirited individuals, *six hundred dollars* were subscribed in Washington in a few minutes; between *three and four hundred dollars* in Middletown; *four hundred dollars* in Burgettstown, with considerable sums from other places, for the purpose of defraying the expenses of the detachment.

A letter from Burgettstown, dated August 28th, 1812, says:—

"I will inform you of the movement at this place for the last ten days. On Monday evening an express came who brought the news of the loss of Gen. Hull's army, and that the enemy were advancing by rapid marches towards Cleveland.* Expresses were despatched in all quarters, and on Tuesday evening the greater part of the 23d regiment, of Washington County, met at this place. About two hundred volunteers volunteered to repel the enemy. On Wednesday evening all was bustle. A committee of arrangement was appointed to provide wagons, provisions, &c. The females, young and old, were employed in making knapsacks and hunting shirts. Children of ten years were engaged in scraping lint for the medicine chest. All were busily engaged in some necessary work; blacksmiths making tomahawks and knives, carpenters handling them, &c. Yesterday Col. Patterson's detachment marched, consisting of about three hundred men, part of which were cavalry, and encamped nine miles from this place. The detachment is furnished with five baggage wagons and eighteen bullocks, and supplied with everything for comfort and accommodation."

From our aged and honored friend James McFarren, Esq., now deceased, we received the following letter on the same subject:—

"In the month of August, 1812, an express arrived in the northwest part of Washington County from Gen. Beal, of Wooster, Ohio, stating that the British and Indians had landed in large numbers at the mouth of Huron River, and were marching on Pittsburg. A number of riders set out and alarmed the inhabitants of the surrounding townships. On the second day a large meeting was held in Burgettstown; a battalion formed of about three hundred volunteers. Ladies sat up the whole night making knapsacks, tents, &c. This battalion was composed of four companies commanded respectively by Capt. Thomas Patterson, Capt. Wm. Vance, Capt. Samuel Rankin, and Capt. Robert Withrew's light dragoons, who rendezvoused at the *Briceland Cross Roads.* After all were in readiness, the first day they marched to the edge of Beaver County, the second day they held an election, and John Vance was elected major. The battalion on the third day took up the line of march, crossed the Ohio River at Georgetown, and encamped on the bottom at the mouth of Dry Run. On the fourth day, being Saturday, they arrived at New Lisbon a little before sunset. During this day's march they met a number of Gen. Hull's soldiers, and among the rest Gen. Lucas, who was afterwards Governor of Ohio, who informed us that Hull had surrendered his army at Detroit; that the men were taken to Malden, U. C., where they were dismissed on parole and sent to the mouth of Huron River, and it was from this fact that the false alarm had arisen.

"Major Vance's battalion, however, pitched their tents half a mile east of Lisbon, remained until Monday morning, when they struck their tents and took up their line of march for home."

"On September 7, 1812, the citizens of Washington County assembled for the purpose of raising a fund for the support of the families of such volunteers as should require aid, and also pledged themselves to use their influence with the legislature to procure the passage of a law to pay each volunteer a stipulated sum in addition to the pay allowed by the United States.

"September 14, 1812, Gen. Acheson received additional orders to furnish a further quota of two hundred men, to assemble at Washington on the 28th and march to Pittsburg, where two thousand men are to rendezvous on

---

* Gen. Hull surrendered on 16th July, 1812, fourteen hundred men to three hundred English soldiers, four hundred Canadian militia, and a band of Indian allies, for which disgraceful conduct he was tried for treason and cowardice by a court-martial, convicted of the latter charge, and sentenced to be shot, but pardoned by the President.

HISTORY OF WASHINGTON COUNTY.

Friday, October 2, 1812. From thence they will be required to march and join the army assembling in Ohio, for the defence of the western frontiers.

"December 28, 1812, Capt. W. Sample returned from Buffalo, N. Y., the six months volunteers having been furloughed or dismissed. He states that all are on their road home except Lieut. James Ruple, who was left at Buffalo, but is now convalescent.

"February 15, 1813, Captain William Patterson, who had command of the Tenmile Rangers, unitedly and unconditionally volunteered their services, and marched to the beach several times for the purpose of embarking for Canada, but was ordered back by the commanding general. We need but add that the campaign of 1812 closed unsuccessfully, and the soldiers returned home Feb. 22, 1813. The officers of the Washington Infantry composed of Capt. William Sample, Lieut. James Ruple, and Lieut. George Taylor, on behelf of the company, tendered their sincere thanks to Major James Herriott, for his conduct after their organization at Buffalo in December last, and in providing for the men on their way home."

After the disgraceful surrender of Hull, the citizen soldier felt the necessity of retrieving the honor of the nation, by prosecuting the war. Volunteer companies were raised in Ohio, Kentucky, Tennessee, Virginia, and Western Pennsylvania furnished her quota under Gen. Richard Crooks, who had been elected brigadier-general of the detachment rendezvousing at Pittsburg. The command of the army was given to Gen. W. H. Harrison, who established his headquarters in January, 1813, at Franklinton, to recover Detroit and the Michigan territory. Of the victories of the American arms at Fort Meigs, Fort Stevenson, Lake Erie, and the Thames, under the command of Gen. Harrison, over the combined British and Indian armies under Gen. Proctor and Tecumseh, it is unnecessary for me to speak; suffice it to say that Western Pennsylvania, and especially the soldiers of Washington County, fought valiantly in these battles, and after a twelve months' tour were discharged about the middle of September, 1813.

In July, 1814, Admiral Cochrane's British fleet arrived for the supposed purpose of destroying the American flotilla which had been chased some weeks before up the Patuxent, but in August this British squadron landed a small army at Benedict, on the river Patuxent, under General Ross, to make an attack on Washington City, which it accomplished on the 24th of August, 1814, by the destruction of all the public buildings, library of Congress, &c., which vandal act so roused the spirit of the nation that the citizen soldiers volunteered their services to retrieve the honor of the nation.

Emboldened by this vandal act, General Ross determined with his five thousand British soldiers to make his winter quarters in Baltimore; was met on September 12, 1814, by the American forces, when he was killed, with forty-six others, two hundred wounded, and many taken prisoners.

While Major James Dunlap was on his march with his quota of soldiers from Washington County on November 24, 1814, to join the encampment at that place, his detachment was disbanded, Gov.

Simon Snyder having notified him that the services of the four thousand Pennsylvania militia were for the present dispensed with. The Governor added his high sense of the honorable feeling and patriotic spirit manifested by those who were ready to march and willing to subject themselves at this inclement season to the privations and hardships always inseparable from military service, in defence of their beloved country, and to avert the dangers with which it was threatened.

The soldiers having returned, the patriotic citizens of Washington still believed that the duty of preparing for war was essentially necessary, and to provide, should a new danger occur, for the supply of any force which may be required, kept up military organizations.

The Hon. Alexander W. Acheson handed me the following paper, which throws much light upon the foregoing fact, and is worthy of being recorded, being indorsed in these words: *Subscription of the citizens of Washington to equip a company of volunteers, to enable them to meet the enemy.*

We, the subscribers, do promise to pay the sums annexed to our respective names for the purpose of equipping such of the volunteers now about to march on a tour of duty as are unprepared for the expedition. Witness our hands at Washington, October 31st, 1814.

Thomas and David Acheson, $50; Alexander Murdoch, $20; Thomas H. Baird, $20; John Wishart, $5; H. Hagarty, $5; James Dougherty, $5; R. Anderson, $5; Thomas McGiffin, $5; David Morris, $5; William Hunter, $3; James Marshall, $2; George Jackson, $1.50; James Orr, $1.50; Thomas Officer, $5; F. Julius Lemoyne, $5; James Dunlap, $5; John Kuntz, $5; Parker Campbell, $10; John Barrington, $10; Isaac Kerr, 10; John Johnson, $5; John Gregg, $7; Hugh Wylie, $5; Robert Hazlett, $5; George Baird, $5; Alexander Reed, $10; John Neal, $5; James Blaine, $5; Richard Donaldson, $5; J. Patton, $1.50; James Reed, $3; William Baird, $6; James Cummins, $4; Col. Scott, $5; Thomas Ramsey, $4. Amounting to $253.50.

On the 8th of January, 1815, under General Andrew Jackson, the last battle was fought with the English nation at New Orleans, by which a victory of the most unparalleled brilliancy and importance was achieved. It is unnecessary to enlarge upon its consequences; suffice it to say, however, that the most important commercial portal of our country was preserved from the rude grasp of a foreign power, and the fruits of the industry of the soil preserved to its owners by the American eagle, the ensign of liberty triumphing over the British lion.

Time would fail me, as well as the patience of my readers would become exhausted, were I to recount and recapitulate the battles in which the officers and soldiers of Washington County have been engaged since the organization of this county; I shall, therefore, leave this interesting question to the student of history to consult other general historical works, and give the names and present ages of the survivors of the war of 1812 residing in Washington County in 1870.

John Conlin, 90 years; George Howe, 89 years; James McClelland, 86 years; Hon. John Grayson, 87 years; John Urie, 86 years; Amos Pratt, 84 years; James Edgar, 83 years; James White, 83 years; Benjamin Bennett, 83 years; Jonathan Hixon, 83 years; Jacob Jordan, 83 years; Allen Thompson, 80 years; Alexander McConnell, 80 years; John McCombs, 80 years; Joseph Miller, 79 years; Samuel Cole, 78 years; George Spence, 78 years; James Boon, 78 years; John Fitzwilliams, 76 years; Horatio Molden, 76 years; James McDermot, 75 years; John Ritter, 75 years; Jacob Dimit, 74 years; Joseph Henderson, 72 years.

There are but six widows in Washington County drawing pensions for the services of their husbands in the war of 1812, viz: Mrs. Catharine A. Wilson, Mrs. Nancy J. Wolf, Mrs. Hannah Day, Mrs. Elizabeth Porter, Mrs. Mary Fowler, and Mrs. Margaret Black.

TEXAS.

The SEVENTH military event in which this county was engaged took place on September 6th, 1836, when Texas struggled to be free and become a component part of the United States. The address, written on the occasion by Thomas Jefferson Morgan, Esq., of this place, and editor of a paper called "Our Country," speaks for itself, giving all the reasons why we should assist Texas to gain her independence. It is in these words:—

To ALL PATRIOTIC AND ENTERPRISING MEN.
EMIGRANTS FOR TEXAS.
To Rendezvous at Washington, Pa., on 6th September, 1836.

THE DESCENDANTS OF THE REVOLUTIONARY HEROES too well appreciate the blessings of FREEDOM to fail in sympathizing with nations struggling for INDEPENDENCE. Greece asserted her rights, and the sons and daughters of our happy republic vied with one another in sustaining the cause of liberty upon the classic soil of Athens and of Sparta. Bleeding Poland sought to disenthral herself from the servile grasp of Russia's autocrat, and whilst France and England calmly gazed upon the scene of slaughter, permitting interest to subvert the heaven-born principles of justice and humanity, the people of the United States were again found actively engaged in contributing to the aid and succoring the cause of the chivalric and patriotic Pole. The plains upon which Sobieski fought and Kosciusko bled, are yet the haunts of the oppressor; but do not their exiled heroes, their matrons, and their virgins, supplicate at the throne of the Great Eternal for the preservation of the liberties of our beloved Columbia?

FREEDOM'S call once more summons us to action. Humanity beckons, philanthropy beseeches, duty commands us to hasten to the rescue of our fellow countrymen! Not to go beyond seas; not to rally around the standard of strangers in a distant land, but we are called upon by all that is honorable, all that is sacred, all that is noble, to fly to the succor of our fellow-citizens and avenge the slaughter of our butchered brethren.

The causes which produced the present Texan struggle for independence are too familiar to the citizens of the United States to require a recapitulation. Suffice it to say that the people of this country were invited to colonize certain districts of land in the Republic of Mexico. Our citizens were promised laws and a constitution similar to our own. This invitation, upon the part of the Mexican government being accepted, thousands of emigrants from the United States poured into Texas. The Mexicans, becoming jealous of their rapidly increasing strength, sought to circumscribe the energies of the Texans by the enaction of tyrannical and unwarrantable laws, equally incompatible with liberty, justice, and humanity. The Texans, upon demanding a redress of their grievances, were treated with insult, and their commissioners cast into a dungeon. But it is unnecessary to follow the course of events which have enkindled the spark of freedom in the bosoms of the colonists, and lit the flame of revolution upon the hills and upon the plains of Texas. The damning treachery and demoniac thirst for blood exhibited by Santa Anna and his coadjutors in deeds of hellish cruelty, are ample evidence of their utter destitution of all those qualifications which should be the characteristics of the governors of a *free people*.

The Texans are emphatically "blood of our blood and bone of our bone;" they confidently cast their eyes to the United States for assistance in their struggle for independence. Shall they be disappointed? Shall the blood of Fannin, Travis, Bowie, Crockett, and a host of other martyrs in the cause of freedom have been shed in vain? Look to yon fearful pile upon which are stretched the yet struggling forms of those victims of Mexican duplicity and worse than savage barbarity! See, the torch is applied, and now the awful deafening shriek ensues. Anon, the curling smoke ascends towards heaven, and bones and ashes are the sad remnants of our countrymen! Who does not cry aloud for vengeance? Who does not burn with impatience to chastise these Mexican bloodhounds? If there be any one, let him eschew the appellation of American citizen! Let him flee the land where liberty dwells, and seek a more congenial asylum within the walls of Constantinople or St. Petersburg.

Countrymen! I know full well it is unnecessary to mention any other inducement which is extended to volunteers, than that of a desire to establish free and liberal principles upon the ruins of tyranny, fanaticism, and bloodshed, but for the sake of information I shall subjoin

The Terms upon which Volunteers enter the Army of Texas.

1st. Each volunteer serving three months shall receive 320 acres of land.
2d. Each volunteer serving for six months shall receive 640 acres of land.
3d. Each volunteer serving during the war and establishing himself in the country, shall receive 2110 acres of land if a single man, and if a married man he shall receive 5240 acres of land.

In addition to these munificent bounties in land, emigrants serving in the army, both privates and officers, shall receive the same pay, rations, and clothing allowed by the United States.

History does not furnish so wide and fertile a field for enterprise as ever having been presented to the view of any people. Those individuals who have no other aim in this life than the mere accumulation of riches, where will *they* have so favorable an opportunity to realize their hopes as is now offered upon the plains of Texas? If *wealth* then *be your sole desire*, go to Texas, *the fairest of a thousand lands.*

Countrymen! well do I realize the motives which alone will impel you to vigorous and speedy action. Well do I know that the men whom I address set a higher value upon one moment of virtuous liberty than upon the massive piles of Persia's fabled treasure.

The undersigned has been authorized to recruit 280 volunteers, and in accordance with this authority I now call upon the freemen of Western Pennsylvania, and of the surrounding districts of Ohio and Virginia, and upon all patriots wherever may be their habitation to join me in my undertaking. It is my desire that all volunteers should rendezvous at Washington upon the 6th of September, or as speedily afterwards as practicable. Each individual should be well supplied with necessary clothing of a *substantial* character, particularly *socks* and *shoes or boots* with *heavy soles*. No one need be under the least apprehension of danger owing to the change of climate, the season of the year at which we shall reach Texas, will be peculiarly favorable to emigrants. Any further information upon the subject can be obtained by addressing the subscriber (post paid), at this place.

Rally! fellow-countrymen, rally! Thousands of our citizens from the south and from the west are pouring into Texas; some of our greatest and best men are to be found among the number; will *you* be backward when the cause of Freedom is at hazard? No! I know you better! You will prove true to your ancestors, true to yourselves, and true to posterity! Come on, come on! Liberty calls you to her standard, the spirits of our departed heroes beckon you onward! Come on, come on! Riches, honor, happiness await you! On! on!! The free of every clime will pour forth to the god of battles their fervent supplications for your success, and unborn millions will bless your memories! T. JEFFERSON MORGAN.
Washington, Pa., Aug. 18, 1836.

Meetings were held through different parts of Washington County, and committees appointed to solicit contributions in aid of the Texan emigrants. On the 19th of Sept., the Morgan riflemen of Pennsylvania took up the line of march, under the command of Thomas Jefferson Morgan, who left Washington with thirty men, but was augmented at Wheeling. I shall add the list of names who composed the "Morgan Rifle Company."

OFFICERS.—T. Jefferson Morgan, Captain, Pennsylvania; John L. Gilder, 1st Lieutenant, Philadelphia; John W. Brown, 2d Lieutenant, Upper Canada.

NON-COMMISSIONED OFFICERS.—Harrison Gregg, 1st Sergeant, Pennsylvania; Lewis F. Shuster, 2d Sergeant, France; Thomas Ralston, 3d Sergeant, Pennsylvania; Melancthon Locke, 4th Sergeant, New York; Isaac B. Noble, 1st Corporal, New York; Wm. Richardson, 2d Corporal, Virginia; J. A. Henderson, 3d Corporal, Pennsylvania; Jackson Proctor, 4th Corporal, Virginia.

PRIVATES.—John Adams, Pennsylvania; J. W. Alexander, Kentucky; W. Baker, Pennsylvania; H. Bundhart, Germany; George Barry, Pennsylvania; John Breckle, Germany; Jacob Buchanan, Germany; J. H. Bauer, France; John Blair, Tennessee; John Collier, Maryland; John Curtz, Germany; Fred. Drehler, Germany; Francis Glenner, New York; Chs. Garner. Germany; W. C. Haymond, Virginia; George Huff, Pennsylvania; Theodore Hamar, France; Joseph Hiller, Germany; Joshua Hudson, Pennsylvania; James Hamilton, Pennsylvania; George Hamilton, Pennsylvania; Fred. Happel, Germany; J. Holt, Virginia; G. S. Haas, Germany; Alex. Hunter, Pennsylvania; Chs. Johnston, New York; John Kelsey, Louisiana; Peter Knole, Germany; Samuel Lint, Pennsylvania; George Meyer, Germany; Henry Miller, Germany; Anthony Miller, Germany; W. F. Nicholson, Pennsylvania; C. G. W. Naffee, New Jersey; John Rahn, Switzerland; Egelbert Reihl, Germany; J. Sappington, Pennsylvania; David Stoelzle, Germany; Henry Smith, Germany; Lewis Stuntzner, Pennsylvania; Thomas Sharpe, Pennsylvania; Louis Thiner, Germany; R. M, Williams, Maryland; Anthony Weiss, France; Henry B. Ward, Kentucky; David Wyand, New York; F. Walbold, Pennsylvania.

June 21, 1837, Capt. Thomas J. Morgan, promoted to the office of Brigadier General, with the rank and emolution of a major of cavalry.

George W. Morgan was promoted from 2d Lieutenant to 1st Lieutenant of Artillery.

THE MEXICAN, OR EIGHTH WAR
in which Washington County was engaged.

It is an established fact that the Mexican war was brought on by the annexation of Texas to the United States, as its minister at that time protested against it as an act of aggression, and as despoiling her of a considerable portion of her territory. The minister on presenting his protest demanded his passport.

In March, 1846, President Polk directed Gen. Z. Taylor to concentrate his forces on the left bank of the Del Norte, which formed the southwestern boundary of Texas, and was therefore an exposed frontier. The Mexican general, on hearing of the arrival of our army, held a conference with the United States officers, which resulted in our officers refusing to abandon the country and their position. The Mexican General issued an appeal to the American army to abandon the standard of their country, and not fight in so inglorious a cause. The appeal had no effect either upon the officers or soldiers, and from this time we may date the commencement of hostilities. The first cause happened on April 21, 1846, when the body of Col. Cross was found, having been robbed and murdered by Mexican soldiers.

History speaks in glowing terms of the battles of Palo Alto—of the surrender of Monterey, of Buena Vista; the siege of Vera Cruz, Cerro Gordo, Contreras, Cherubusco, Molino del Rey, Chepultepec, Tampico, and finally the surrender of the city of Mexico to Gen. Winfield Scott and his soldiers, on September 14, 1846.

Although Washington County, like many other counties, did not participate largely by sending companies, battalions, or regiments; yet the name of Col. Norton McGiffin, who left his mother's home to risk life, fame, and fortune by doing a soldier's duty, will be ever held in remembrance by our citizens. He volunteered his services, was accepted, and proved himself worthy of the position tendered to and accepted by him.

Col. McGiffin served both as captain and lieut.-colonel of the 12th regiment in the rebellion of 1861.

James Phillips, of Washington, went to the Mexican war, and proved himself a brave and gallant soldier, as also did James Mackey, Henry Woods, and Jack Lowrey, who were the only immediate representatives of Washington County.

THE REBELLION OF 1861, OR NINTH WAR
in which Washington County was engaged.

The soldiers of Washington County, emulating the patriotic deeds of their fathers, resolved to battle against the gigantic rebellion which attempted to destroy the best of governments. The history of their prowess on the battle-field is fresh in the hearts of the living, while memory sheds a tear to the brave ones who fell in defence of the Constitution. To preserve, therefore, the names of the living and the dead—soldiers of Washington County—who fought, bled, and died, I shall not only give their names, but the company in which they marched, as well as the casualties which happened to each on the battle-field.

Before proceeding to this personal interesting history, it were well to remark that thirteen Southern States declared themselves absolved from the government of the United States by each passing ordinances of secession. They severally proclaimed themselves as free and independent, with the right to levy war, conclude peace, negotiate treaties, and to do all acts whatever, that rightly appertain to free and independent States. These ordinances of secession were passed by the several States in the following order :—

1. *South Carolina*, on December 20, 1860, by a unanimous vote of one hundred and sixty-nine members. On April 3, 1861, the State Convention ratified the Confederate Constitution by a vote of one hundred and fourteen to sixteen.

2. *Mississippi*, on January 9, 1861, passed the ordinance with fifteen dissenting votes, and on March 30, 1861, ratified the Confederate Constitution by a vote of seventy-eight to seven.

3. *Florida*, on January 12, 1861, by a vote of sixty-two to seven.

4. *Alabama*, on January 11, 1861, by a vote of sixty-one to thirty-nine.

5. *Georgia*, on January 19, 1861, by a vote of two hundred and eight to eighty-nine.

6. *Louisiana*, on January 26, 1861, by a vote of one hundred and thirteen to seventeen.

The vote of the people was, for secession, 20,448, against 17,296.

7. *Texas*, on February 1, 1861, subject to a vote of the people, to be held on 23d day of February, and to take effect on March 4, 1861, if approved.

8. *Virginia*, on April 17, 1861, by a vote of sixty to fifty-three, repealed the ratification of the Constitution of the United States, subject to a vote of the people in the following May, and on the 6th of May Virginia was admitted as a member of the Southern Confederacy.

9. *Arkansas*, on May 6, 1861, by a vote of sixty-nine to one, and was admitted to the Southern Confederacy May 18, 1861.

10. *Tennessee*, on February 19, 1861, voted against secession, but on May 6, 1861, it was proclaimed out of the Union by the legislature, which, however, gave the people the liberty to vote on the 24th of June following; the vote stood for separation from the Government of the United States, 104,913; against, 47,238.

11. *North Carolina*, on May 20, 1861, passed an ordinance of secession, also ratifying the Constitution of the Confederate States.

12. *Missouri*, on August 5, 1861, through Gov. C. F. Jackson, published a Declaration of Independence, and on the 21st of the same

month this State was admitted into the Southern Confederacy on certain conditions, but a convention emanating from the people was held on July 31st, and Hamilton R. Gamble was inaugurated as Governor on August 1, 1861. In his position as Governor he was promised the aid and co-operation of the General Government.

13. *Kentucky*, on November 20, 1861, adopted a Declaration of Independence and ordinance of separation, and on December 14, 1861, elected, by its legislative council, delegates to the Southern Confederacy, and on December 16, 1861, the Senators from Kentucky were sworn in, the State having been admitted. Kentucky was entitled to twelve representatives.

The following seven States, by their representatives, held a convention at Montgomery, Alabama, on February 4, 1861, and adopted a constitution for the Confederate States of America, viz., Alabama, Florida, Georgia, Louisiana, Mississippi, North Carolina, and South Carolina. On February 9, Jefferson Davis was elected President, and Alexander H. Stephens Vice-President, who were inaugurated on February 18th. This Congress continued in session until May 21, and adjourned to meet at Richmond July 20. At the July session Virginia sent thirteen delegates, who were admitted. The meeting of the *first* session under its constitution was held February 18, 1862, the following States being represented: Alabama, Arkansas, Florida, Georgia, Kentucky, Louisiana, Mississippi, Missouri, North Carolina, South Carolina, Tennessee, Texas, Virginia.

In connection with the Virginia question I may add that on June 17, 1861, the convention emanating from the people of Western Virginia unanimously voted that by the action of the State of Virginia they were independent of and declared themselves as the State of West Virginia. On June 20, the people elected a governor, and on June 26 the President of the United States recognized the State of West Virginia.

With these preliminary remarks we shall proceed to the history of the rebellion. The firing of the first gun was on April 12, 1861, at 4.30 A. M., when an attack was made upon Fort Sumter from Fort Moultrie, the batteries on Mount Pleasant, Cummings' Point, and the floating batteries, numbering seventeen mortars and thirty large guns for shot, mostly columbiads. April 13, 1861, at 12.55 P. M., the flag of Fort Sumter was hauled down and the fort was surrendered on honorable terms by Major Robert Anderson, although he did not evacuate it until the 15th. President Lincoln on this day called for 75,000 men to serve for three months to suppress the rebellion, of which soldiers Pennsylvania's quota was fourteen regiments, each regiment to consist of seven hundred and eighty officers and men; yet Pennsylvania increased her quota to twenty-five regiments, and so patriotic were the feelings of the people that thirty additional regiments were refused. These twenty-five regiments, consisting of twenty-nine thousand, nine hundred and seventy-nine soldiers, after honorably serving their full term, were mustered out of service.

HISTORY OF WASHINGTON COUNTY.   303

Under this call Washington County responded by two companies marching to Pittsburg and organizing the 12th Regiment, under the supervision of General James S. Negely.

On the 25th of April, 1861, these two companies, with eight others, elected their field officers—David Campbell, of Pittsburg, Colonel; Norton McGiffin, of Washington, Lieutenant-Colonel; Alexander Hays, of Pittsburg, Major. This regiment fulfilled its mission, and the term of enlistment, three months, having expired, it was mustered out of service at Harrisburg, August 5, 1861.*

COMPANY E was composed of the following officers and men, and was recruited in Washington, Pennsylvania, and mustered into service April 25, 1861:—

OFFICERS.—Norton McGiffin, Captain; W. F. Templeton, 1st Lieutenant; Samuel T. Griffith, 2d Lieutenant.

NON-COMMISSIONED OFFICERS.—Oliver R. McNary, 1st Sergeant; David Brady, 2d Sergeant; John Q. A. Boyd, 3d Sergeant; David Acheson, 4th Sergeant; John D. McKahan, 1st Corporal; Henry Brown, 2d Corporal; Robert B. Elliott, 3d Corporal; George B. Caldwell, 4th Corporal.

MUSICIANS.—William A. McCoy and Simon W. Lewis.

PRIVATES.—John W. Acheson, Henry H. Alter, James Barr, Edwin W. Bausman, Peter Blonberg, Hugh P. Boon, John V. Brobst, John A. Byers, John L. Cooke, Henry M. Dougan, Horace B. Durant, Tertius A. Durant, Henry Erdman, Hardman Gantz, John L. Gettys, James Grier, John M. Griffith, Charles Hallam, Wm. T. Hamilton, Alexander C. Hamilton, Wm. Hart, Eli Hess, Wm. H. Horn, J. W. Hughes, Robert P. Hughes, Andrew J. Hyde, James B. Kennedy, John Kendall, Philip P. Kuntz, John Lawton, Joseph J. Lane, Matthew P. Linn, Chas. L. Linton, John Loughman, John Laughlin, Taylor McFarland, Thomas M. McKeever, John McKeever, Caleb J. McNulty, James Munford, Wm. M. Morris, Henry C. Odenbaugh, George A. Perret, Rollin O. Phillips, Henry A. Purviance, Alexander Rankin, George B. Reed, Samuel B. Rickey, John B. Ritner, Alexander W. Scott, Cephas D. Sharp, David Shepherd, Jas. Stocking, Andrew J. Swartz, John R. Sweeney, Samuel M. Templeton, Joseph H. Templeton, Robert Thompson, Robert L. Thompson, Wm. H. Underwood, Isaac Vance, Geo. J. Walker, Andrew W. Wilson, Jas. B. Wilson, Robert T. Wishart, Wesley Wolf.

After Capt. Norton McGiffin was elected Lieut.-Col. Capt. James Armstrong, of Washington, Pa., was elected and served as Captain.

COMPANY G recruited at Monongahela City, Washington County, and mustered into service April 25, 1861.

OFFICERS.—Robert F. Cooper, Captain; John S. McBride, 1st Lieutenant; Jesse C. Taylor, 2d Lieutenant.

NON-COMMISSIONED OFFICERS.—Wm. W. Thompson, 1st Sergeant; John Myers, 2d Sergeant; Owen Bullard, 3d Sergeant; John S. Slanger, 4th

---

* This regiment, although impatient to be in the advance, yet were required to remain to the end of their service preserving and protecting the Northern Central Railroad, which runs from Baltimore to Harrisburg, it being on the main line of communication with Washington City. They became proficient in military drill.

Sergeant; Rees Boyd, 1st Corporal; Benjamin F. Scott, 2d Corporal; John H. Woodward, 3d Corporal; A. O. D. O'Donavan, 4th Corporal.

MUSICIANS.—Frederick Layman and James S. Scott.

PRIVATES.—Francis Allen, Isaac R. Beazell, Harrison Bennington, John Boyd, Wm. B. Brooks, John Bellas, Wm. Baxter, Jr., Samuel Beazell, Michael Barry, Patrick Collins, Sylvester Collins, Wm. S. Cooper, Benjamin G. Dickey, John C. Dougherty, Andrew Elliott, W. H. H. Eberhart, Andrew Grant, Alexander Gregg, John M. Gibbs, Jos. D. V. Hazard, S. Bentley Howe, Wm. H. Howe, James S. Harris, W. H. Heath, Wm. J. Hoffman, Alexander Haney, David Kearney, H. B. King, Wm. G. Kennedy, James Long, Andrew Louderbeck, Ellis N. Lilly, George C. Leighty, David Moreton, James Mehaffey, Charles McCain, Wm. T. Meredith, Thomas Morgan, Thomas Mack, Wm. Mack, Daniel Mockbee, Jacob S. Miller, Augustus J. Miller, Hillery Miller, John Merrick, Wm. Ong, Charles Oliver, William Oliver, George W. Potts, Samuel B. Paxton, Samuel Pritchard, Joseph G. Reager, John Rinard, Reuben Sutton, Geo. Stewart, Alfred M. Sickman, Jefferson G. Vangilder, Theophilus Vankirk, Robt. S. Wilson, Wm. Woodward, W. H. H. Wickersham, James S. White, Samuel Young, Daniel D. Yates.

On April 30, 1861, the legislature of Pennsylvania convened, and passed an act on the 15th of May following, to organize fifteen regiments for the defence of the State, which should be called the Reserve Volunteer Corps of Pennsylvania, and whose term of service should continue for three years. These fifteen regiments were composed of thirteen regiments of infantry, one of cavalry, and one of artillery. This Reserve Corps was called into the service of the United States on the 23d of July, 1861, the day succeeding the disaster at Bull Run. The whole force of this corps comprised fifteen thousand eight hundred and fifty-six officers and men.

It will be our province at this time to speak particularly of the 37th Regiment (numerically numbered) or usually called the EIGHTH Reserve, because Company K of this regiment was recruited in Washington. This regiment numbered eight hundred and ninety men, well equipped and well drilled, its Colonel being Geo. S. Hays, of Allegheny County.

37TH REGIMENT, 8TH RESERVE CORPS.

Roll of Company K, commanded by Capt. A. Wishart, of Washington, Pennsylvania, was called into service June 28, 1861, to serve for three years, and mustered out 24th of May, 1864.

The battles in which this company was engaged were Dranesville, Mechanicsville, Gaines' Mill, New Market Cross Roads, Malvern Hill, Bull Run, South Mountain, Antietam, Fredericksburg, Wilderness, Spottsylvania Court House, Gettysburg, Briscoe Station, Mine Run, North Anna, and Bethesda Church.

This company was called the "Hopkins Infantry," after our esteemed fellow-citizen Col. William Hopkins, who was tendered the command; but on account of physical inability to endure camp life declined, yet at all times he was untiring in his efforts to promote its interests.

HISTORY OF WASHINGTON COUNTY. 305

The regiment was first under the command of Col. Geo. S. Hays, elected Feb. 25, 1862. He resigned July 6, 1862. Col. Silas M. Bailey was elected Sept. 14, 1862.

Explanation of Small Capital Letters.—W. Wounded. R. Resigned. P. Promoted. DIS. Discharged by surgeon's certificate for physical disability. D. Died. K. Killed. T. Transferred to another regiment to fill up their time.

OFFICERS.—Alexander Wishart, Captain, W. R.; Samuel S. Bulford, 1st Lieutenant, P.; Thos. Foster, 2d Lieutenant, T.

NON-COMMISSIONED OFFICERS.—Peter Kennedy, 1st Sergeant, DIS.; Geo. W. Silvey, 2d Sergeant; John McIlvaine, 3d Sergeant, W. DIS.; Alexander Hart, 4th Sergeant, P.; James S. Dennison, 5th Sergeant; Boyce Irvin McClure, 1st Corporal, W.; And. S. Eagleson, 2d Corporal, P.; M. L. A. McCracken, 3d Corporal; Hugh Moore, 4th Corporal, DIS.; A. J. Luellan, 5th Corporal, D.; L. E. Ozenbaugh, 6th Corporal, K.; Theodore J. Dye, 7th Corporal, K.; Hugh Gettiens, 8th Corporal.

MUSICIANS.—Francis W. Orr and Joseph W. Christy.

PRIVATES.—Alfred W. Anderson, D.; Dennis Butler, K.; David Bamburger, W.; James D. Brownlee, W. DIS.; James L. Boardman, DIS.; Geo. W. Brice, by order of C. M.; William Burke, DIS.; Michael Bell, John L. Butts, Wm. H. Barnet, K.; Wm. Burns, T.; William Conley, Ezekiel Clark, Amos P. Cline, K.; Geo. W. Dye, D.; Geo. M. Davis, T.; Samuel A. Davis, DIS.; Andrew Daily, DIS.; Sylvester S. Durbin, K.; Daniel Day, DIS.; James M. Evans, DIS.; Samuel Eckles, D.; Geo. W. Freeby, D.; And. D. French, K.; David Gilmore, W. DIS.; John W. Greer, Hugh Gettiens, John M. Griffith, T. 191st, W.; Henry Henderson, William Hart, DIS.; Andrew Harshman, Christian Hornish, DIS.; Henry A. Herrick, DIS.; William Immel, D.; Wm. R. King, William Loafman, D.; W. H. Harrison Link, T.; Joseph M. Lennom, T.; George Mallum, D.; George V. Miller, DIS.; Antonio Moriles, Wm. M. Middleton, DIS. D.; George Martin, Thomas H. Marshal, K.; William Miles, Edward A. Myers, James D. McMillen, K.; Robert. McMillen, W. DIS.; Nelson R. McNeil, James McVehil, DIS.; Joseph McCreary, DIS.'; M. Taylor McFarland, T.; Peter McCreary, J. Warren Oliver, DIS.; John M. Oliver, James Plymire, Robert M. Poland, DIS.; Cephas A. Ryan, D.; Michael Rush, DIS.; Randolph Rush, D.; Robert M. Scott, T.; Leander Sinclair, D.; James C. Spriggs, Arthur W. Sprouls, W. DIS.; Thomas M. Steep, Griffith D. Taylor, K.; H. H. B. Thompson, DIS.; Francis L. Wheatley, T.; Theodore S. Webb, John B. Wolf, Geo. W. C. Wilkins, T.; William Wiles, W.

The loss the Company sustained in battle was partially filled by the following recruits :—

Ephraim Allen, T.; John M. Bane, William Barnes, T.; John Brotherton, T.; John Bulford, T.; Samuel Cowen, Samuel Dickerson, T.; James Eckles, K.; Caleb H. Golden, Lieut. Alexander Hart, W.; F. A. Heisley, T.; Peter Hess, Charles W. Hoffman, T.; Elias B. Polk, T.; George A. Porter, T.; George A. Quinn, T.; Henry Pethel, Henry Sleighter, Francis J. L. Steep, T.; Henry Taylor.

This company when mustered out had but 24 men—26 discharged, 19 transferred to 191st Regiment, 22 died and killed in action, and 7 deserters.

The 8th Regiment had a regimental band attached, part of the same being from Washington County, whose names I add :—

William H. Stoy, Leader; Alexander Rankin, W. H. Boardman, James S. Seaman, and George A. Perrett.

The band was discharged by General Order issued Aug. 8, 1862.

We now take up the history of the 10TH RESERVE CORPS (39th Regiment) so far as Washington County is concerned.

The companies composing this regiment rendezvoused at Camp Wilkins, near Pittsburg, and were organized June 30, 1861, by the election of John S. McCalmont as colonel, James T. Kirk, of Washington County, lieut.-colonel, and Harrison Allen major. On the 9th of May, 1862, Col. McCalmont resigned, and Lieut.-Col. Kirk was promoted to the colonelcy. Col. Kirk afterwards resigned, and Col. A. J. Warner was elected October 18, 1862: he resigned November 23, 1863.

JEFFERSON LIGHT GUARDS,

Or company D of the 10th Reserve Corps, was recruited at Canonsburg, and tendered their services through their captain, William S. Callohan, to Governor Curtin, which were accepted; but the quota being filled the Light Guards, under the command of Captain James T. Kirk, marched to Pittsburg on May 6, 1861, and enlisted for three years or during the war. Capt. Kirk resigned June 19, 1861, on his promotion to lieut.-colonel, and Charles W. McDaniel was elected captain July 1, 1868. After Lieut. Coleman resigned, Charles Davis was elected 2d lieut. August 1, 1862. The battles in which Company D was engaged were at Dranesville, Mechanicsville, Gaines' Mill, Charles City Cross Roads, Bull Run, South Mountain, Antietam, Fredericksburg, Gettysburg, Bristoe Station, Spottsylvania Court House, and Bethesda Church. On the 11th of June, 1864, the regiment was mustered out of service, but many of this regiment re-enlisted as veterans, and formed part of the 190th and 191st regiments.

Roll of the Jefferson Guards:—

OFFICERS.—Charles W. McDaniel, Captain; John H. M'Nary, 1st Lieutenant; Frank Coleman, 2d Lieutenant, R.

NON-COMMISSIONED OFFICERS.—C. Frank Ritchie, Orderly Sergeant; Charles Davis, 1st Sergeant, P.; Robert Brady, 2d Sergeant, W.; John Gundy, 3d Sergeant, K.; S. Beck, 4th Sergeant, DIS.; B. L. Anderson, 1st Corporal, W.; William S. Houston, 2d Corporal, W.; Samuel G. Hodgens, 3d Corporal, W. DIS.; W. P. M'Nary, 4th Corporal; William Glass, 5th Corporal, K.; James S. Hughes, 6th Corporal, D.; Thomas Paxton, 7th Corporal, K.; William Maggs, 8th Corporal.

MUSICIANS.—Josiah R. Chambers, T., and James C. Merriman, DIS.

PRIVATES.—Alfred Ackey, DIS.; Samuel Anderson, W. L. Atlee, T.; James L. Black, W.; Samuel Brown, DIS.; Garland Briceland, T. J. Black, W.; Joshua Brady, T.; George Cain, DIS; David Crum, D.; William Cain, Wilson Cochran, Hugh Cochran, DIS.; William S. Caldwell, John V. H. Cook, John S. Chambers, DIS.: J. W. Cowan, DIS. W.; J. Z. Culver, DIS. P.; Samuel Cook, K.; J. R. Chambers, William Devall, DIS.; J. B. Duff, T.; Nathaniel E. Dickey, William Donaldson, T.; Benjamin Evans, Frank B.

Eaton, w.; Luther C. Furst, T.; Thomas Ford, K.; F. W. Fleming, James Ferguson, w. T.; P. M. Foreman, G. S. Graham, w.; Mathew H. Greer, D.; William J. Hunter, DIS.; M. M. Havlin, DIS.; Daniel Hallas Hammond, D.; Charles Horn, Alexander Houston, w. T.; George Hallas, w. T.; William Hallas, T.; William Havlin, T.; George Hayden, T.; William Hollingshead, Daniel Hallas, T.; William Harsha, T.; George Hiles, T.; A. Inghram, Joseph Jackson, T.; William Jackson, DIS.; John W. Jackson, John Jeffers, K.; Thomas Jackson, w. T.; R. N. Lang, D.; J. E. Lang, George Lewellyn, Samuel Mackey, w.; James L. Mackey, Alexander M. Musser, w.; J. McPeak, R. N. McPeak, K.; J. O. McPeak, J. H. McPeak, w.; J. McCullough, William McWilliams, James McCahan, w.; John P. McCord, DIS.; John McClosky, T.; James McFadden, H. McJames, W. Pollock McNary, DIS.; James Perry, James R. Patton, T.; Henry H. Petitt, Alexander Prowitt, William P. Pennell, J. F. Phillips, DIS; James Quail, DIS.; William Roberts, J. H. Rhinehart, w.; B. F. Ryan, DIS.; A. J. Strosnider, John Storment, John Sutton, DIS. w.; W. Wallace Scott, T.; James M. Scott, w. T.; John Sarver, H. H. Sheaff, w.; Brown Scott, DIS.; George Tibby, J. H. Thompson, w. T.; Robert Wilson, w.; J. E. Wilson, Joseph Wallace, DIS.; William Williams, K.; Anthony Williams, T.; James Young.

Lieut. Charles Davis was promoted to Lieut., and also Lieut. R. N. McPeak. Both were killed.

First Pennsylvania Cavalry (15th P. R. R. C.)

This is also numerically called the 44th Regiment. It was composed of twelve companies. Company I was recruited in Washington County, and Company K in Washington and Allegheny counties. These two companies, with Company H, of Fayette County, were mustered into the State service during the month of August, and soon after joined the regiment.

Companies I and K participated in the battle at Dranesville, Harrisonburg, Cross Keys, Cedar Mountain, Gainesville, Bull Run, Fredericksburg, Brandy Station, Aldie, Gettysburg, Shepherdstown, Culpepper, Auburn, Mine Run, Todd's Tavern, Fortifications of Richmond, Hawes' Shop, Coal Harbor, Trenham Station, St. Mary's Church, Beam's Station, Bellefield.

The campaign of 1863 was soon ended, and the army withdrew across the Rappahannock. Col. Geo. D. Bayard commanded the First Pennsylvania Cavalry, Jacob Higgins, Lieutenant-Colonel. and Thos. S. Richards, Major, when originally organized.

Roll of Company I, recruited in Washington County, and was mustered into service September 6, 1861:—

OFFICERS.—W. W. McNulty, Captain, R. P.; Francis S. Morgan, 1st Lieutenant, P.; George W. Seigrist, 2d Lieutenant, R.

NON-COMMISSIONED OFFICERS.—Samuel C. Work, 1st Sergeant, P. W. M.; Samuel W. McKee, 2d Major-Sergeant, w.; P. H. McNulty, Commissary-Sergeant, w. M.; A. B. Wythe, Sergeant, DIS.; Jno. G. Wells, Sergeant, D.; Jno. Richmond, Sergeant, DIS.; Wm. Denniston, Sergeant. DIS.; Jas. D. Scott, Sergeant, M.; Jno. L. Mustard, Sergeant, w.; R. D. Wilkin, Sergeant, M.; D. Pollock, Sergeant, M.; A. C. Elliott, Sergeant, w. T. M.; Thos. R. Starer, Corporal, P.; Jno. H. Gaston, Corporal, P. DIS.; Wm. C. Richey, Corporal, DIS.; David Ackleson, Corporal, K.; Moses Hastings,

308   HISTORY OF WASHINGTON COUNTY.

Corporal, K.; Eli Lescallett, Corporal, K.; James Barry, Corporal, K.; S. McConkey, Corporal, K.; Thos. Richmond, Corporal, K.; Hilleary Wilson, Corporal, M.; John McKinley, Corporal, P.; David McGugin, Corporal, W. M.; Louis Kramer, Corporal, P. M.; Thos. H. Cowan, Corporal, P. M.; W. J. Rippey, Corporal, P. M.
MUSICIANS.—Wm. H. Rose, DIS.; Chester P. Murray, M.
PRIVATES.—Samuel F. Bitts, M.; George Becroft, M.; John Becroft, DIS.; Alexander Berwick, DIS.; Frank Berwick, T.; John A. Bingham, W. T.; Wm. Crider, M.; John Clyde, M.; Andrew Crouch, DIS.; William A. Curtis, T.; Thos. H. Conan, DIS.; John Chester, T.; Thomas Dunkle, DIS.; Thomas J. Dowling; Robert C. Elliott, T.; Rudolph Essick, T.; John F. Foust, DIS.; Samuel A. Garret, M.; John H. Groff, M.; Moses F. Gaumer; John Gibson, T.; George W. Gist, D.; Jacob George, D.; Joshua J. Hunter, DIS.; Walter Johnson, M.; John B. Loughead, T. M.; George J. Labarre, T.; William J. Lowry, M.; William McElroy, M.; William McCall, M.; W. S. McCormick, M.; H..C. McGregor, P.; William McCarrel, M.; Peter Mulligan, M.; And. F. McClure, DIS.; James Miller, Jr., D.; James Miller, Sr., DIS.; Isaac McConkey, T.; Charles Morrow, T.; James W. McKee, K.; Hugh McGowan, M.; Arch. Newell, M.; Wm. F. Patton, DIS.; Wm. P. Patton, M.; Thos. Parkes, D.; Wm. M. Porter, D.; Thomas Patterson, D.; Elmore Powelson; Lewis W. Quilland, DIS.; David Richmond, M.; J. B. Richie, P.; A. B. Rosenberger, M.; Lorenzo A. Rice, DIS.; J. L. Robertson, T.; James Smiley, M.; Jno. G. Sauppe, M.; Wm. F. Smith, DIS.; John G. Wells, D.; A. L. Williams, T.; Grafton Wells, T.; Jacob Wolf, P.

REMARKS.

Capt. W. W. MCNULTY was mustered into service September 6, 1861; he resigned same day to accept promotion.

JOHN ROSS was promoted from 1st Lieutenant to the Captaincy, September 24, 1861, and resigned November 23, 1861.

GEORGE T. WORK, promoted from 1st Lieutenant November 23, 1861, and resigned June 21, 1862.

JAMES M. GASTON, promoted to 2d Lieutenant August 24, 1861, to 1st Lieutenant November 23, 1861; to Captain July 12, 1862; to Major March 1, 1863, and honorably discharged August 1, 1864.

T. C. MCGREGOR, promoted to 2d Lieutenant May 10, 1862; to 1st Lieutenant July 12, 1862; to Captain March 1, 1863; transferred to battalion September 1, 1864, and mustered out by consolidation June 20, 1865.

JOSEPH B. RICHIE was elected 2d Lieutenant July 12, 1862, and discharged February 18, 1863.

GEO. W. LYON, elected 2d Lieutenant February 25, 1863, and killed September 6, 1863.

COMPANY K, RECRUITED IN WASHINGTON AND ALLEGHENY COUNTIES.

This company's history is connected with the foregoing in their marches and battles.

Captain Wm. Boyce mustered into service September 6, 1861, resigned December 27, 1861; he was succeeded by Joseph H. Williams, who was elected January 1, 1862. The company was transferred to a battalion September 1, 1864, composed of five companies; mustered out September 27, 1864.

OFFICERS.—Wm. A. Kennedy, 1st Lieutenant, mustered into service September 6, 1861, wounded at Hawes' Shop, Va., and mustered out September 9, 1864; Samuel W. Morgan, 2d Lieutenant, entered service September 6, 1861, wounded and mustered out September 9, 1864.

NON-COMMISSIONED OFFICERS.—William J. McEwen, 1st Sergeant, DIS.; John T. Kennedy, Sergeant, D.; Arch. D. Darragh, Sergeant, P. M.; D. W. Boyce, Sergeant; John A. Lattimer, Sergeant, M.; Wm. M. Foster, Sergeant, P.; Joseph Wright, Sergeant, DIS.; John W. Gault, Sergeant, D.; Robert Boyce, Sergeant, P. M.; John W. Boyce, Sergeant, P. M.; John Patterson, Sergeant, P. M.; B. Morgan, Sergeant, P. M.; Jacob Hanna, Sergeant, P. M.; Joseph Boyce, Corporal, DIS.; Andrew G. Happer, Corporal, T.; Saml. Morton, Corporal, DIS.; Thomas Conner, Corporal, DIS.; John M. Boyce, Corporal, M.; Samuel N. Ralston, Corporal, P. M.; Joshua Connelly, Corporal, P.M.; Thomas Westerman, Corporal, P. M.; Samuel R. Patton, Corporal, P. M.

MUSICIANS.—Samuel Brown, DIS.; John C. Keifer, K.

PRIVATES.—John A. Anderson, M.; James Beumont, DIS.; Thomas D. Boyce, T. D.; Isaac N. Boyce, Robert Cain, DIS.; Edward Curran, T.; Chas. A. Calligan, T.; Abraham Cox, T.; Geo. W. Coup, T.; Jacob Coup, T. D.; W. F. Coup, W. D.; John Douglass, DIS.; John M. Duncan, T.; Charles P. Dilks, John Dimler, Jas. F. Dodd, T.; Wm. Ewing, DIS.; James Ewing, D.; Hugh Flanigan, Joseph B. Fitterer, T.; Joseph Feather, William Gordon, T.; John Herriott, M.; Wilson Herrill, M.; Samuel Hopper, T.; Hamilton Ingram, DIS.; John Jamison, Thomas Jones, M.; Joseph M. Kennedy, T.; Samuel Keifer, K.; Richard Lesnett, M.; John H. Morgan, M.; H. R. Morrison, M.; John L. McAlister, M.; Mathew McCombs, M.; Jacob C. McDowell, M.; John McDonald, M.; William McDonald, M.; George McFeely, M.; Jas. M. G. Mouck, DIS.; Thomas McCoombs, T.; John Meredith, T.; M. McBride, T.; William McMurray, T.; William H. Meanor, T.; Joseph Morrison, D.; Joseph McClanahan, K.; William J. McClure, S. C. Obony, DIS.; John C. Phillips, T.; Frederick Quigg, M.; John M. Reignaman, DIS.; William Roberts, DIS.; George W. Reed, T.; David Schaffer, M.; William Stewart, DIS.; Joseph M. Sample, DIS.; B. F. Shield, DIS.; Joseph M. Shaffer, D.; John Trimble, M.; George Thompson, Sr., DIS.; George Thompson, Jr., DIS.; Henry Vance, T.; J. H. Westerman, M.; Samuel Wallace, DIS.; James Williams, T.; W. S. Wilson.

62D REGIMENT, COL. S. W. BLACK.

Originally Co. B, now Co. K.

Al. King, 1st Lieutenant, W.

Corporals—T. R. Scott, G. T. Deems, G. M. Coulter.

PRIVATES.—M. Arthur, J. B. Baker, H. Koontz, H. S. Koontz, E. Crall, Josiah Fox, K.; Wm. Gibbs, Charles Gibbs, K.; M. Hayward, W.; Wm. Henning, James Heines, J. Maloy, J. P. Mouk, K.; T. McKean, Wm. McCormick, Thomas McElroy, James McGrew, G. W. McKinley, Jefferson McClain, J. T. McMillan, T. Patterson, R. Simpkins, K; W. H. Stoops, W. C. Todd, K.; R. Whittaker, K.; R. Wilby, K.; S. Workman, K.; M. Workman, Silas Wright, John Young.

Co. G, George Watson Buchanan, D.

COMPANY D,

Of the 79th Regiment Pennsylvania Volunteers, was organized at Lancaster September 19, 1861; its term of service was three years, and re-enlisted as a veteran organization. It was mustered out of service July 12, 1865, near Alexandria, Virginia. H. A. Hambright was the Colonel. Major Wm. S. Mellinger was elected Major October 18, 1861, and resigned November 8, 1862. Captain John S. McBride, of Company D, was elected Major December 20, 1864, and mustered out with Company D as Captain July 12, 1865. Dr. Thomas H. Phillips was appointed Assistant Surgeon January 10, 1865, and remained until mustered out. Captain John S. McBride elected September 21, 1861, and promoted to Major; his successor was Joseph D. V. Hazzard, elected December 20, 1864, and mustered out with Company as 1st Lieutenant July 12, 1865.

Brisben Wall, 1st Lieutenant, elected September 21, 1861, resigned April 25, 1862; J. D. V. Hazzard, 1st Lieutenant, elected May 1, 1862, and promoted to Captain; Luke P. Beazell, 1st Lieutenant, elected December 20, 1864, and mustered out as 2d Lieutenant July 12, 1865; J. D. V. Hazzard, 2d Lieutenant, elected September 21, 1861, promoted to 1st Lieutenant; Samuel P. Keller, 2d Lieutenant, elected May 1, 1862, resigned February 17, 1863; Alexander D. O. Donavan, 2d Lieutenant, elected March 29, 1863, honorably discharged October 14, 1863; Luke P. Beazell, 2d Lieutenant, elected April 1, 1865, and promoted to 1st Lieutenant.

This company was called the Mellenger Guards, Co. B, and was organized in Monongahela City, September 16, 1861.

NON-COMMISSIONED OFFICERS.— —— Keller, 1st Sergeant; —— Myers, 2d Sergeant; A. O. Donavan, 3d Sergeant; —— Watson, 4th Sergeant; Ianthus Bentley, 5th Sergeant; M. Berry, 1st Corporal; H. B. Hart, 2d Corporal, w.; A. Frye, 3d Corporal; W. Woodward, 4th Corporal, w.; J. W. Downer, 5th Corporal; W. Brooks, 6th Corporal; J. Gibbs, 7th Corporal; J. S. Miller, 8th Corporal, w.; H. D. Cooper, Commissary, w.

MUSICIANS.—F. Layman and Amzi Eckles.

WAGONER.—Wm. Galbraith.

PRIVATES.—Geo. Allhouse, Chr. Anderson, K.; John Anderson, D.; Robert Boyd, D.; George Barringer, John Barringer, Wm. Barringer, D. C. Bitting, K.; Fr. Burgan, K.; V. Brooks, w.; W. Butler, w.; Wm. Brown, Michael Bramin, B. Brubaker, K.; W. Bennington, K.; Luke Beazle, L. Chester, E. Craven, W. S. Cooper, w.; S. Collins, K.; J. Cusworth, Lafayette Culbertston, W. Devlin, K.; James Dutton, w.; M. Dougherty, w.; Alfred Eckles, Simon Fry, D.; Thomas Fry, D.; J. Flowers, K.; M. Ferguson, K.; Charles Galloway, w.; W. Graham, D.; J. Gundy, K.; G. Gibson, w.; J. Gilmer, W. P. Gilmer, S. Hendrickson, w.; J. Hodge, D. Hobaugh, S. Jester, w.; A. Johnson, w.; H. Kelly, W. S. Mellinger, J. Merrick, J. H. Miller, w.; W. Miller, W. H. Mortimer, H. McCain, H. McGrew, w.; P. McGreery, J. McLeod, J. Ostrander, w.; I. Purcil, G. W. Potts, I. Parkinson, H. Pace, w.; T. Pritchard, w.; J. Reynerd, J. Rose, B. Rollison.

W. Shield, w.; J. D. Stewart, W. T. Smith, w.; G. Swenger, W. Wallace, J. W. Wolf, w.; John Warren, K.; J. Wood, J. A. Watson, w.; J. H. Watson, Wm. Young, J. M. Yohe.

85TH REGIMENT INFANTRY

Was organized at Uniontown, Pa., Oct. 16, 1861, to serve three years, and mustered out of service, except veterans and recruits, Nov. 22, 1864. The veterans and recruits were transferred to the 188th regiment. As Washington County soldiers were attached to nearly every company, we shall give the names of the officers of these companies, and the full companies from Washington County; as we have no means of designating the individual soldiers from this county, which we deeply regret.

This regiment was under the command of the following officers:—

Joshua B. Howell, Colonel, Fayette County; Norton McGiffin, Lieut. Colonel, Washington County; Absalom Guiler, Major, Fayette County; John Murphy, Jr., Quartermaster, Washington County; Boyd Crumrine, Q. M. Sergeant, Washington County; Andrew Stewart, Jr., Adjutant, Fayette County; James Lindsay, Sergeant-Major, Greene County; John Laidley, Surgeon, Greene County; John C. Levis, Assistant Surgeon, Beaver County; Rev. John N. Peirce, Chaplain, Greene County; Rev. J. P. Caldwell, appointed Chaplain Oct. 21, 1862, and resigned May 1, 1863; D. Ewing Hook, Drum Major, Fayette County; Wm. Beall, Com. Sergeant, Somerset County; F. H. Anderson, Sutler, Alleghany County; Joseph Reager, Color Sergeant, Fayette County.

Mountain Rifles.—Hagan Z. Ludington, Captain, Fayette County; Reason Smurr, 1st Lieutenant, Fayette County; Stephen K. Brown, 2d Lieutenant, Fayette County.

Howell Fencibles.—John R. Weltner, Captain, Fayette County; E. H. Oliphant, 1st Lieutenant, Fayette County; Houston Devan, 2d Lieutenant, Fayette County.

Redstone Blues.—John C. Wilkinson, Captain, Fayette County; Isaac R. Beazell, 1st Lieutenant, Westmoreland County; George J. Vangilder, 2d Lieutenant, Washington County.

Monongahela Guards.—Isaac M. Abraham, Captain, Fayette County; John A. Gordon, 1st Lieutenant, Greene County; John M. Crawford, 2d Lieutenant Greene County.

Washington Guards.—Henry A. Purviance, Captain, Washington County; Lewis Watkins, 1st Lieutenant, Washington County; Richard W. Dawson, 2d Lieutenant, Fayette County.

Union Guards.—Harvey J. Vankirk, Captain, Washington County; William W. Kerr, 1st Lieutenant, Washington County; John Rowley, 2d Lieutenant, Washington County.

Lafayette Guards.—William H. Horn, Captain, Washington County; Rolla O. Phillips, 1st Lieutenant, Greene County; John E. Michener, 2d Lieutenant, Washington County.

Ellsworth Cadets.—Morgan W. Zollars, Captain, Washington County; Robert P. Hughes, 1st Lieutenant, Washington County; George H. Hooker, 2d Lieutenant, Brooke County, Va.

Tenmile Grays.—John Morris, Captain, Greene County; Edward Campbell, 1st Lieutenant, Fayette County; John Remley, 2d Lieutenant, Fayette County.

Independent Blues.—James B. Tredwell, Captain, Somerset County; Jas. Hamilton, 1st Lieutenant, Somerset County; Milton O. Black, 2d Lieutenant, Somerset County.

Company A Union Guards.

OFFICERS.—H. J. Vankirk, Captain; W. W. Kerr, 1st Lieutenant; John Rowley, 2d Lieutenant; S. L. McHenry, 1st Sergeant; S. McGregor, 2d Sergeant; J. M. Welch, 3d Sergeant; A. W. Pollock, 4th Sergeant; R. T. Wishart, 5th Sergeant; R. W. Criswell, 1st Corporal; Greer Hair, 2d Corporal; J. M. S. Crafty, 3d Corporal; M. Templeton, 4th Corporal; H. T. Reynolds, 5th Corporal; J. N. Morrison, 6th Corporal; J. N. Brown, 7th Corporal; W. D. Shaw, 8th Corporal.

PRIVATES.—James Allison, James W. Andrew, J. L. Bebout. S. M. H. Bebout, Robert H. Byers, J. B. Bell, David Baldwin, Thomas Briggs, Ariel Brownlee, Thomas J. Barr, Collin W. Barr, John S. Butterfass, Jonathan Beatty, William Crasson, William H. Cheeks, Samuel L. Coulter, James Carothers, Joseph Campsey, James S. Craig, Charles Caldwell, Samuel R. Caldwell, Robert Caldwell, John Carothers, John Curren, Nathan A. Day, Walter Donnel, Frank Dillon, Dennis Farrell, Hugh D. Furgus, Thomas H. Fulton, A. Gilkisod, Cyrus Grieves, Thomas Griffith, Robert Greer, W. H. Hines, Greer Hair, Samuel Hendrickson, Franklin Henderson, James Higby, James Hardy, Andrew J. Hutchinson, John W. Ingles, Adam Johnston, Patterson Jobes, D. from wounds, Joseph Kerr, John R. Kline, Hamilton Lyon, Oscar F. Lyon, Andrew A. Lovejoy, Matthew Lynn, John Low, John M. Moore, James H. McCune, John A. McMillin, Joseph E. McCabe, William Milligan, Philip Martin, Jr., William Morrison, John A. Mansfield, Henry W. Nickerson, John Neil, Walter O'Donnel, D.; David G. Pascal, John Patterson, James A. Proudfit, John Park, Joseph Palmer, A. M. Ross, W. H. Randolph, Jacob Richison, Matthew Ross, Jr., Moses Ross, Henry T. Reynolds, William Sires, Joseph Schell, Joseph Shaw, William Scott, Thomas H. Sawhill, R. B. Thompson, Jacob L. Thompson, Thomas Thompson, Andrew Thompson, Alexander H. Vance, John Waible, William Waible, Joseph Welch, W. J. Wilson, Wm. Weibley.

Captain H. J. Vankirk elected September 13, 1861, resigned November 7, 1862, when 1st Lieutenant William W. Kerr was elected Captain November 8, 1862, and served until mustered out November 22, 1864.

1st Lieutenant W. W. Kerr elected September 23, 1861, was promoted to Captain, and S. M. McGregor elected November 8, 1862, and mustered out with the company.

2d Lieutenant John Rowley elected November 8, 1861, honorably discharged April 7, 1862, at which time John W. Acheson was elected 2d Lieutenant; he was transferred and promoted to 1st Lieutenant of Company C, and Robert T. Wishart was elected August 2, 1862; he resigned November 20, 1862, when James M. Welch was elected and served until August 14, 1863.

Company B, or Ellsworth Cadets.

Captain Morgan W. Zellars elected September 23, 1861, and resigned May 19, 1864; he was succeeded by Captain Geo. H. Hooker, who was honorably discharged November 20, 1864

HISTORY OF WASHINGTON COUNTY. 313

First Lieutenant Robert P. Hughes elected September 23, 1861, afterwards elected Captain of Company C, or Independent Blues, May 19, 1862, and transferred to 199th Regiment, Pennsylvania Volunteers. These were the only officers in this company from Washington County.

CORPORALS.—Jackson Crumrine, w.; McCullough, w.
PRIVATES.—J. W. Smith, w.; W. H. Butler, John Watson.

COMPANY C, OR, INDEPENDENT BLUES,

Was composed of soldiers from Washington and Somerset counties. It was originally organized by Captain James B. Treadwell, of Somerset, October 1, 1861, but he being promoted to Major June 3, 1863, Lieutenant Robert P. Hughes, of Company B, was elected Captain, and transferred to 199th Regiment as Lieutenant-Colonel; appointed Brevet Colonel April 2, 1865, and mustered out with regiment June 28, 1865.

John W. Acheson, 1st Lieutenant, was elected August 2, 1862, from Company A, and promoted to Captain and Assistant Adjutant-General February 29, 1864.

Wm. R. Davis, 1st Lieutenant, elected April 13, 1864, and mustered out with company.

D. H. Lancaster, 2d Lieutenant, was elected July 1, 1862, and resigned March 6, 1863.

CORPORAL.—John Wood, w.
PRIVATES.—Lewis Laclerc, w.; G. Blackly, w.

COMPANY D, LAFAYETTE GUARDS,

Was organized September 20, 1861; it was commanded by Captain Wm. H. Horn, of Washington County, who was elected at that time and resigned July 6, 1862; he was succeeded by 1st Lieutenant Rollo O. Phillips, of Greene County, elected July 6, 1862, and mustered out November 22, 1864.

1st Lieutenant John E. Michener elected July 6, 1862, and transferred to the Mountain Rangers, Company K. Lieut. Michener had entered the service as 2d Lieutenant September 21, 1861; he was elected 1st Lieutenant Dec. 3, 1863, and afterwards its Captain; he was succeeded by Lieut. Wm. H. Myers, on July 6, 1862, and honorably discharged April 29, 1864. His successor was George S. Fulmer, elected June 20, 1864, and mustered out with Company.

In connection with these facts we give one or two items, however. Prior to their departure from Uniontown, each member of Captain Horn's company received from the Pigeon Creek Presbyterian Church (Rev. Dr. Sloan, pastor) a neatly-bound copy of the New Testament. These books were received by Captain Horn in a neat and appropriate address. J. E. Michener, Second Lieutenant of the company, was presented with an elegant sword by the citizens of

21

Centerville, the present being accompanied by a highly complimentary address, by Colonel Howell. The Lieutenant responded in a felicitous manner. The company, as will be seen by the roll, numbers eighty-five men.

OFFICERS.—William H. Horn, Captain ; R. O. Phillips, 1st Lieutenant, J. E. Michener, 2d, Lieutenant.

NON-COMMISSIONED OFFICERS.—W. H. Myers, 1st Sergeant, Howard Caar, Sergeant; John Horn, Sergeant; George McGiffin, Sergeant; John N. Donaghho, Sergeant; H. S. Spohn, Corporal; A. C. Morgan, Corporal; H. S. Myers, Corporal; Thomas M. Harford, Corporal ; Jacob B. Speers, Corporal ; W. W. Garber, Corporal; G. S. Fulmer, Corporal; S. O. Thomas, Corporal.

MUSICIANS.—James I. Wells, Isaiah Jordon.

WAGONER.—William A. Rider.

PRIVATES.—George Aimes, Joseph Aimes, Wm. Allman, Enoch Brooks, Henry Bush, Joseph Burson, William A. Bell, Josias Bratton, John Bratton, James W. Burgan, S. Clendaniel, D. W. Crumrine, Hiram Crouch, Harvey Cox, Israel Cumson, M. D. Donaghho, Henry G. Dales, Geo. Dales, Abraham Finley, William H. Fulmer, George W. Fisher, George W. Garber, T. J. Gage, Hezekiah Horn, Elias Horn, Jonas Horn, B. F. Hathway, Richard Hathway, T. J. Hathway, Alexander Hathway, Hiram Haver, Jacob Haver, Barnet Johnson, L. F. Jones, W. H. Jackman, George Ketchim, William B. Lash, A. R. Luker, James Meeks, Jesse S. Moore, John Milliken, Jasper Morgan, Oliver McVay, Abraham Miller, W. H. McGiffin, Milton McJunkin, Alexander McKay, John McIlvaine, Benjamin Marshall, Wilson Pryor, Robert Pryor, James M. Roach, Edward Roberts, Boon Reese, John Reese, J. Sunedecker, Eli Smith, Adam Staub, William Stull, W. H. Virgin, Ames Walton, Henry Walton, Theophilus Wilson, Henry C. Yorty.

It is due to the friends of Captain Horn, to state that he commanded the brigade pickets as senior captain at the battle of Fair Oaks, and held his position until compelled to retreat by the superior forces of Gen. Stonewall Jackson.

COMPANY E, WASHINGTON GUARDS,

Was organized in Washington, October 15, 1861, and elected H. A. Purviance, Captain, who was afterwards promoted to Lieut.-Colonel, May 15, 1862, and killed Aug. 31, 1863. His successor was First Lieutenant Edward Campbell, of Fayette County, who had previously filled the office of Second Lieutenant. Capt. Campbell was promoted to Major, and First Lieutenant Lewis Watkins was elected Captain, Sept. 6, 1864. He died Sept. 28, 1864, from wounds received in battle. His successor was Lieut. Jacob Davis, who was elected Sept. 28, 1864. He had filled the offices of both First and Second Lieutenant, and was mustered out of service with the company, Nov. 22, 1864. Thomas S. Purviance was elected Second Lieutenant May 15, 1862, and killed at the battle of Fair Oaks, May 31, 1862. His successor was Robert G. Taylor, elected May 31, 1862, and resigned January 28, 1863.

HISTORY OF WASHINGTON COUNTY. 315

OFFICERS.—H. A. Purviance, Captain ; Lewis Watkins, 1st Lieutenant; Edward Campbell, 2d Lieutenant.
NON-COMMISSIONED OFFICERS.—Oliver P. Henderson, 1st Sergeant; Jacob D. Moore, 2d Sergeant; Thompson S. Purviance, 3d Sergeant; Moses McKeag, 4th Sergeant; John D. Heckard, 5th Sergeant; Robert G. Taylor, 1st Corporal; Jacob Hanna, 2d Corporal; James Peters, 3d Corporal; William J. Graham, 4th Corporal; James Watkins, 5th Corporal; Martin Pope, 6th Corporal; Samuel Marshall, 7th Corporal; Davis Kimmegar, 8th Corporal.
MUSICIANS.—Samuel Wood and Henry J. Rigdon.
TEAMSTER.—Eli Huston.
PRIVATES.—John Adams, Joseph Andrews, Matthew Axton, Thomas Byers, Elbridge Collins, Greenbury Crosland, Clark Chew, Josiah W. Crawford, William G. Crow, John Clark, Joseph Chase, Newton Chase, Andrew Devore, John Dean, Jacob Davis, John Dougan, George Downer, Jeremiah Dawson, w.; Jacob Desellam, Charles Eckels, Milton Edingfield, John Flinder, John Fordyce, John Finnegan, Isaac Fisher, George Fisher, Henry Garrett, Jacob Grover, Benjamin Gill, William Hartman, William McC. Hill, James W. Huff, Andrew J. Huff, William B. Hayes, Henry M. Hanna, w.; William Hanna, Jeremiah Hartzell, Milton S. Hall, Edward M. Hall, Thomas Henesy, Adolphus J. Inks, Thomas J. Jenkins, w.; B. Jenkins, w.; Michael Keenan, Gideon Knight, Frederick Lowry, William Lynn, w.; John Lynn, Mordecai Lincoln, Jefferson Lowe, David McKeag, John Means, Hugh B. McNeill, John F. McCoy, John McLean, Stephen McDowell, Benjamin McAllister, Henry J. McAllister, William McCoon, James Mayhorn, George Miller, William Mehaffy, Robert Mitchell, Joseph Neely, David R. Parker, George C. Rocky, Elijah Rockwell, Jacob Rockwell, William Rimmell, Rudolph Smith, Henry Smith, Cyrus Sprowls, Henry M. Taylor, Charles Varndell, John Woodward, Christy Welsh, John White.

100TH REGIMENT INFANTRY, PENNA. VOLUNTEERS, CALLED THE ROUND HEAD REGIMENT.

This name was given to this regiment by Hon. Simon Cameron, Secretary of War, in 1861, and for six months after its organization was known by no other name. It was organized at Pittsburg, Aug. 31, 1861, the term of service being three years. It re-enlisted as a veteran organization at Blaine's Cross Roads, Tennessee, Dec. 28, 1863, and was mustered out of service July 24, 1865, at Harrisburg. It participated in the following engagements, viz : Port Royal Ferry, S. C., Port Royal, S. C., James Island, S. C., Bull Run, Chantilly, South Mountain, Antietam, Fredericksburg, siege of Vicksburg, Jackson, Blue Springs, Campbell Station, siege of Knoxville, Wilderness, Spottsylvania C. H., North Anna River, Coal Harbor, Petersburg, Mine Explosion, Weldon Railroad, Poplar Grove Church, and Hatcher's Run, Fort Steadman, and final assault on Petersburg, Va. It joined the expedition under Gen. W. T. Sherman, returned to Virginia and joined Gen. Burnside's forces. It was originally commanded by Col. Daniel Leasure, of Lawrence, and subsequently by Lieut. Col. N. J. Maxwell, of Mercer.

The following field and staff officers with company A, belonged to Washington County—

Lieut. Col. James Armstrong, elected October 9, 1861, resigned July 12, 1682.

Lieut. Col. Joseph H. Pentecost, elected August 15, 1864, appointed brevet Colonel March 25, 1865. He died from wounds received in battle.

Major James Armstrong, elected July 12, 1862, and promoted to Lieut. Col.

Adjutant H. M. Dougan, appointed August 1, 1864, and mustered out with the regiment.

Assistant Surgeon H. B. Durant, appointed March 23, 1864, and honorably discharged March 17, 1865.

Roll of Company A.

Capt. James Armstrong elected August 26, 1861, and promoted to Major and afterwards to Lieut.-Col. He was succeeded by Capt. W. F. Templeton, Sept. 11, 1861, and killed at Bull Run, Va., Aug. 29, 1862. Joseph H. Pentecost, elected September 8, 1862, and promoted to Lieut.-Col. Both his successors were from Alleghany County.

1st Lieut. William F. Templeton was elected August 26, 1861, and promoted to captain, his successors residing in Washington County, were Joseph H. Pentecost, elected September 15, 1861, and promoted to captain. Lieut. James H. Montford, who was elected September 8, 1862, and resigned September 3, 1864. Lieut. James S. Stocking elected August 15, 1864, and resigned January 10, 1865, and William H. Billings, elected March 6, 1865, and mustered out with the company.

The 2d Lieutenants of this company residing in Washington County were, Lieut. Joseph H. Pentecost, elected August 26, 1861, and promoted to 1st Lieut. Lieut. William Oker, elected Sept. 16, 1861, and resigned November 26, 1862. Lieut. E. W. Bausman, elected November 28, 1862, and resigned March 16, 1864. Lieut. James S. Stocking, elected September 22, 1864, and promoted to 1st Lieut. Lieut. W. H. Billings, elected February 22, 1865, and promoted to 1st Lieut. Lieut. George Metzner, elected May 12, 1865.

Sergeants—John Cooke, Robert B. Elliott, Eleven Alvey, William A. Gabby, Joseph H, Templeton, w.; Monterville D. Dewire.

Corporals—John B. Brobst, Morris B. McKeever, Horace B. Durant, George B. Caldwell, W. H. Horn, Alexander Adams, w.; James McIlvaine, w.; David A. Templeton, John C. Ralston, John W. Kerr, William Claffey, w.; Isaac H. Richmond.

Musicians—William H. Walker, D.; and James P. Hays.

Wagoner—Daniel B. Mowry.

PRIVATES.—Joseph M. Aiken, w. ; Thomas Acton, DIS. ; James Aiken, Charles Aberly, Nelson F. Baker, James Barr, w. ; Stephen Billings, Peter A. Blomberg, D.; Thomas F. Boon, John G. Brice, DIS.; Martin Burke, Benj. U. Best, w.; James Brown, w.; Thomas Baty, Augustus Bupp, John Blake, Moses M. Bell, Castle Brookins, Cyrus J. Barker, K. ; David J. Boynton,

John C. Caldwell, Charles D. Chase, DIS.; John Clemens, K.; John Clarke, W.; Thomas Couboy, W.; Michael Curran, W.; Patrick Collins, H. M. Dougan, DIS.; Tertius A. Durant, William Durant, DIS.; Samuel M. Decker, Thomas Donley, D.; Michael Daguin, Patrick Danford, James Dalton, Andrew Davidson, James C. Eckles, Samuel P. Ewing, D.; Samuel M. Fowler, W.; Sylvestus G. Fowler, John D. France, W.; Leonidas A. Fowler, William J. Fennerty, Isaac R. W. Garretson, K.; William Gray, K.; Thomas Greer, William Greer, W.; Robert Gordon, W.; Lewis Haager, W.; Daniel Hall, W.; James Hart, DIS.; Jacob Hartstein, D.; Charles Heer, K.; Alexander Howell, D.; Thomas Hutcheson, DIS.; H. T. Hamilton, D.; Jeremiah L. Hannen, W.; John Hanney, W.; Lemuel Harris, W.; James Higgins, John S. Johnson, DIS.; Robert D. Jobs, D.; George O. Jones, W.; John S. Jeffrey, W.; Alexander Kerns, W.; Ferdinand Kleives, DIS.; John Klotzbarker, DIS.; John W. Koontz, DIS.; John B. Kendall, W.; William Lange, DIS.; John W. Langfitt, W.; Elijah Linsley, DIS.; James W. Lowry, D.; Simon W. Lewis, K.; William H. Lewis, C. C. Lobinger, DIS.; Henry H. Linley, D.; John W. Lanery, W.; George Leasure, DIS.; Addison Liggett, George W. McClelland, DIS.; Chas. B. McCollum, DIS.; Jacob L. McCullough, K.; John L. McCullough, W.; Nathaniel McCullough, W.; Joseph E. McCullough, W.; Samuel McCullough, Joseph McGill, W.; W. T. McGill, W.; John B. McKeever, D.; Thomas McKeever, D. drowned; Alexander C. McKeever, T.; Andrew McPeak, DIS.; Julius P. Miller, DIS.; John Moloney, DIS.; Josiah Mullen, W.; John Marsh, K.; John R. McClure, DIS.; Samuel J. Melvin, George W. McFarlane, Benjamin F. McClure, W.; Maxwell McCausland, W.; Ebenezer McElroy, Enoch Mountz, W.; Martin Moore, W.; Samuel Mishner, Thomas Miller, W. B. McGarvy, Daniel McCann, DIS.; Henry C. Obenbaugh, K.; Thomas Orr, Jacob C. Pry, W.; Samuel Potter, Perry Phillips, W.; John Pier, Curtus R. Potter, Frederick Rau, DIS.; Franklin A. Rose, Simon S. Russel, W.; James Reardon, George Robertson, D.; Thomas Russel, W.; Theodore Robertson, Simon H. Reed, Thomas Reichter, D.; Edward Riley, W.; David Shephard, DIS.; William S. Simcox, D.; George W. Smith, Isaac N. Stranger, John E. Stephenson, DIS.; George N. Stephenson, DIS.; Wm. Saunders, K.; Henry Sloppy, Joseph E. Shaffer, Wm. Stork, Robert J. Taggart, DIS.; Aaron Templeton, K.; James B. Thompson. D.; Andrew Thompson, D.; Samuel F. Thompson, W.; George W. Thompson, Thomas B. Templeton, D.; John S. Weirich, D.; John Wherry, K.; Jackson Wimer, John Wonder, Lorenzo D. Wilgus, Henry Young, James Young.

COMPANY M.

Jesse C. Taylor, 1st Lieutenant.
John Merrick, 2d Sergeant, K.
B. F. Taylor, Corporal.
PRIVATES.—J. W. Cocaine, Sam'l Grist, J. B. Haley, G. W. Haley, J. Housen, Isaac Housen, M. Lape, H. Lennox, J. R. Moss, George Rudge, Wm. Rothrick, Solomon Stroop, R. H. Sickles, Samuel Throp, Wm. Waddington, John West, John C. White.

140th REGIMENT INFANTRY

Was organized at Harrisburg, from August 26 to September 2, 1862; term of service for three years. It was mustered out of service May 28, 1865, at Washington city, except new recruits, which were transferred to the 57th Volunteers.

This regiment participated in the following engagements, viz:

Fredericksburg, Chancellorsville, Gettysburg, Antietam, Kelly's Ford, Mine Run, Wilderness, Spottsylvania, North Anna, Talopotonecy, Coal Harbor, Petersburg, Strawberry Plains, Deep Bottom, Bristow Station, Poplar Spring Church, and Boydton Road. Five companies of this regiment were from Washington County. Its first field officers were, Colonel, Richard P. Roberts, of Beaver, elected September 8, 1862, killed at Gettysburg July 2, 1863; Lieut.-Colonel, John Fraser, of Washington County, at date of service; he was elected Lieutenant-Colonel September 8, 1862, and promoted to Colonel July 4, 1863, afterwards Brigadier-General, and honorably discharged; Major, Thomas B. Rodgers, of Mercer, elected September 8, 1862, and promoted to Lieutenant-Colonel July 4, 1863; Adjutant, John M. Ray, appointed October 20, 1864; Quarter-Master, Samuel B. Bentley, appointed September 12, 1862; Surgeon, Dr. John Wilson Wishart, September 12, 1862; Assistant Surgeons, Dr. W. W. Sharpe, September 12, 1862, Dr. B. F. Hill, November 5, 1862; these officers belonged to Washington County.

Roll of Company C, or Brady Artillery.

Captain David Acheson organized the company, and was elected August 22, 1852, and killed at the battle of Gettysburg July 2, 1863. His successor was Captain Isaac N. Vance, elected September 14, 1863, and honorably discharged January 12, 1864; he lost his left hand at Gettysburg July 2, 1863. He was succeeded by Captain Alexander W. Acheson January 16, 1864, who was honorably discharged December 3, 1864. Lieut. John Milton Ray was elected Captain January 30, 1864, and mustered out with the company May 31, 1865. Isaac N. Vance, 1st Lieutenant, elected August 22, 1862, and was promoted to Captain; Alexander W. Acheson, 1st Lieutenant, elected September 14, 1863, and promoted to Captain; John M. Ray, 1st Lieutenant, elected January 30, 1864, and appointed Adjutant; W. J. Cunningham, elected December 4, 1864, and killed April 7, 1865; Charles L. Linton, 2d Lieutenant, elected August 22, 1862, and promoted to Captain in Company D. Robert R. Reed, Jr., 2d Lieutenant, elected May 22, 1862, died July 19, 1863; Alexander W. Acheson, 2d Lieutenant, elected August 16, 1863; to 1st Lieutenant; John M. Ray, 2d Lieutenant, elected August 20, 1863, to 1st Lieutenant; John W. Wiley, 2d Lieutenant, elected December 18, 1864, transferred to 53d Regiment May 30, 1865.

Non-Commissioned Officers.—Robert R. Reed, Jr., O. Sergeant; Jas. D. Campbell, 2d Sergeant; H. J. Boatman, 3d Sergeant; J. Milton Ray, 4th Sergeant; W. J. Cunningham, 5th Sergeant; John Cully, 1st Corporal; James Blake, 2d Corporal; E. H. Linton, 3d Corporal; James P. Sayer, 4th Corporal; John D. Wishart, 5th Corporal, transferred to Battery B, 1st R. I. artillery; J. M. Dye, 6th Corporal, transferred to same artillery; Thomas Hardesty, 7th Corporal, also transferred to same; John S. Martin, 8th Corporal.

PRIVATES.—Sandie Acheson, w.; Wm. Amon, K; Wm. Armstrong, D.; Jas. Baird, trans. to Battery B, R. I. artillery; Sam'l Baird, John Billick, J. K. Bishop, DIS., w.; Julius Black, w.; John Blair, w.; Jas. Blake, Henry J. Boatman, Ephraim C. Brown, K.; Samuel Bunnell, w.; J. D. Campbell, Lewis M. Cleaver, w.; Isaac J. Cleaver, David W. Cleaver, James B. Clemins, Ellis J. Cole, K.; Philip A. Cooper, John P. Cully, J. W. Cunningham, Samuel Curry, N. D. Cutten, w.; Benton Devore, w., D.; John A. Dickey, w.; David Dowling, J. W. Dowling, D.; A. S. Duncan, J. W. Duncan, J. M. Dye, transferred to Battery B, R. I. artillery; Jas. Eckert, w.; Samuel Fergus, w.; Nehemiah Gilbert, w.; Aaron Gunn, w.; Mason Hart, A. F. Hartford, Thomas Hardesty, Robert Henderson, Lewis Henry, w. and D.; William Horton, K.; William Howard, DESERTED; Clarke Irey, w.; Richard Jones, w.; Thomas Jones, K.; John J. Jordan, w.; David Jones, D. L. Keeney, K.; James S. Kelley, K.; Frederick Kesner, Robert Lindsey, D.; Thomas Long, w.; John Lowe, Thomas B. Lucas, K.; James L. Martin, w., DIS.; John S. Martin, Daniel McClain, John McConn, w. and D.; Hugh B. McNeil, David McCoy, John E. McCullough, Thomas McCune, w.; James H. McFarland, w.; Frank B. McNear, w.; Samuel Mills, Richard Miller, K.; John Moore, Tellinghast Mourie, w.; Anthony Mull, K.; Alvin Newman, D.; George Norris, w.; Hugh Needham, w.; Robert Patterson, DESERTED; John Pattison, Albertus Pattison, MISSING; Andrew Plants, William Pollock, William H. Pollock, Esau Powell, John W. Penney, William B. Post, w.; Jackson Praul, K.; Charles Quail, William J. Radcliffe, J. M. Ray, Robert R. Reed, Jr., Charles Rentz, Sam'l Rettig, Henry Richards, w.; M. Austin Richards, Alexander Robinson, w.; Sam'l Roop, w.; Gales S. Rose, w.; David Ruble, w.; Silas A. Sanders, James Sayers, Presley H. Shipley, K.; John Smalley, w.; Wm. Stockwell, K.; James Stockwell, w.; John Stockwell, Jonathan Tucker, Simeon Vankirk, Wm. Vankirk, Isaac Wall, Colin Waltz, w.; James Wise, K.; Samuel Wise, J. D. Wishart, T. to Battery B, R. I. artillery; Jefferson Younkin.

Recapitulation.—Commissioned officers, 3; enlisted men, 99—102. Killed, 11; died, 5; transferred, 7; discharged, 3; deserted, 2—28.

COMPANY D, TENMILE INFANTRY.

Captain Silas Parker, elected Aug. 22, 1862, and was honorably discharged, April 16, 1863. He died June, 1863, and was buried at Amity, in this county. He was succeeded by Charles L. Linton, who served until May 1, 1865, when he was honorably discharged.

First Lieutenant James Mannon, elected August 22, 1862, honorably discharged January 16, 1863. His successor was Matthias Minton, elected January 16, 1863, and served until August 19, 1863, when he was honorably discharged. On the 25th August James B. Van Dyke was elected, and honorably discharged May 31, 1864. His successor was J. Fulton Bell, elected January 16, 1863, who was mustered out with the company, May 31, 1865.

Second Lieutenant Matthias Minton, elected August 22, 1862, afterwards promoted to 1st Lieutenant. Second Lieutenant James B. Van Dyke, elected January 16, 1863, afterwards promoted to 1st Lieutenant.

NON-COMMISSIONED OFFICERS.—James B. Van Dyke, 1st Sergeant; Henry C. Swart, 2d Sergeant; Moses McCollum, 3d Sergeant; Cephas D. Sharp,

4th Sergeant; Leicester Bebout, 5th Sergeant; John A. Black, 1st Corporal; Calvin Ramsey, 2d Corporal; Leroy W. Day, 3d Corporal; Beden Bebout, 4th Corporal; Isaac Sharp, 5th Corporal; James A. Bebout, 6th Corporal; James M. Hughes, 7th Corporal; Fulton Bell, 8th Corporal; Alpheus Cunningham, Drummer; John B. McDonald, Commissary.

PRIVATES.—Abner Birch, Samuel Johnson, L. W. Day, A. J. Swart, Beden Behout, Amos Kenstwick, Thomas Doty, H. C. Swart, Enoch Baker, John Kelly, Wilson Doty, Cephas D. Sharp, Fulton J. Bell, Cyrus Lindley, Lewis Dille, Emmor Smalley, Hazlett M. Bell, Milton Lindley, Abner Enoch, Isaac Sharp, Ira Baldwin, John W. Lewis, Joseph Evans, John Sibert, John A. Black, John Loafman, Nathan P. Evans, John W. Sanders, James A. Bebout, William Loyd, Enoch French, Joseph Sherrick, John L. Brannon, Isaac Lacock, Jacob Frazee, James Sibert, Lester Bebout, George Moore, Charles Guttery, William H. Teagarden, Milton Blachly, James Montgomery, James Hathaway, George W. Teagarden, Robert Birch, John B. McDonald, John L. Hathaway, Jacob McAfee, Sample F. Bell, James Van Dyke, James Hilton, Joseph Meeks, William Bebout, William S. Watson, Jacob Hatfield, James Miles, Zachariah Baker, Henry Watson, Jonathan W. Hughes, Moses McCollum, Andrew Curry, Jacob Yodes, James M. Hughes, Winder McKinney, Alpheus Cunningham, Andrew J. Vankirk, Albert G. Parker, Calvin Ramsey, Charles Cunningham, Christopher C. Welsh, Hamilton Parker, Daniel W. Sowers, Charles H. Cane, George Redd, Philo Paul, Hiram Tharp, John W. Cooper, Isaac Tucker, Harvey Pope, James Birch, Milton Clutter, James M. Miller, Judson W. Paden, Joseph Swihart, Levi Curry, Joseph Brannon, Peter Phillips, James Stansberry, Franklin Ijams, Simeon S. Sanders, William Rutan, Samuel Evans, James A. Jackson, Thomas Glenn, Amos Swart, W. H. Williams, John Closser.

James Montgomery D, from wounds.

Killed.—Emmor Smalley, Judson W. Paden, James Birch, Amos Swart, Philo Paul, John L. Brannon.

Wounded.—Andrew J. Vankirk, H. C. Swart, James McAfee, Samuel Evans, Z. Baker, Abner Birch, James Hathaway, Robert Hatfield, James Miller, Wm. Teagarden, Christopher C. Welsh, Jacob Yoders, Joseph Sherrick, Charles Guttery, Capt. C. L. Linton, Ira Lewis, Frank. Ijams.

COMPANY E

Was organized Aug. 22, 1862. Its first captain was Aaron T. Gregg, elected at its organization, and honorably discharged June 5, 1863. His successor, Iram F. Sansom, was elected June 5, 1863, and discharged July 26, 1864. Capt. Jesse T. Power was elected December 14, 1864, and mustered out with company May 31, 1865.

1st Lieut. Thomas A. Stone, elected Aug. 22, 1862, honorably discharged June 5, 1863; Iram F. Sansom was elected his successor Feb. 6, 1863, and afterwards promoted to Captain. John F. Wilson, elected July 4, 1863, and promoted to Captain of Company G. James A. Russel, elected Sept. 28, 1863, and discharged April 13, 1864. William B. Lank, elected Dec. 14, 1864, and killed at Sailor's Creek April 6, 1865.

2d Lieut. Iram F. Sansom, elected Aug. 22, 1862, and promoted to 1st Lieut.; his successor was Francis R. Stover, elected Feb. 6, 1863, and honorably discharged Dec. 14, 1863.

COMPANY G—BROWN INFANTRY,

Was recruited at Canonsburg by Capt. John Fraser, Professor of Mathematics at Jefferson College. Under his command the following families sent forty-seven sons to the army: John Gaston, 4; Thomas Jackson, 4; James Ryan, 4; Harmon M. Peck, 4; Samuel L. Hughes, 3; Samuel Stewart, 3; Rev. Wm. Smith, 3; John Paxton, 3; Dr. Stewart, 3; Mrs. Hallas, 3; James Coleman, 3; John Brady, 2; Hugh Huston, 2; Samuel R. Cook, 2; W. H. McNary, 2; Wm. Black, 2.

Capt. John Fraser was elected Aug. 22, 1864; promoted to Lieut.-Col. July 4, 1863. He was succeeded by Capt. W. H. H. Bingham the same day, who was promoted to Major of U. S. Volunteers Aug. 1, 1864. His successor was Capt. John F. Wilson, elected Oct. 10, 1864, and died April 14, 1865, of wounds received in battle. Capt Wilson N. Paxton was elected April 16, 1865, and honorably discharged as 1st Lieut. May 15, 1865, and he was succeeded by Capt. John R. Paxton May 16, 1865, who was mustered out with the company May 31, 1865.

1st Lieut. W. H. H. Bingham, elected May 22, 1864, and promoted to Captain.

1st Lieutenant Wilson N. Paxton, elected Aug. 22, 1864, and promoted to Captain.

1st Lieut. John R. Paxton, elected April 16, 1865, and promoted to Captain.

2d Lieutenant Wilson N. Paxton, elected Aug. 22, 1862, and promoted to 1st Lieut.

2d Lieut. Jos. W. McEwen, elected Aug. 22, 1862, killed at Chancellorsville May 3, 1863.

2d Lieut. Alex. M. Wilson, elected March 4, 1863, killed at Gettysburg July 2, 1863.

2d Lieut. John R. Paxton, elected Oct. 14, 1864, and promoted to 1st Lieut.

NON-COMMISSIONED OFFICERS.—Alex. M. Wilson, 1st Sergeant; Jasper E. Brady, Jr., 2d Sergeant; T. J. Weaver, 3d Sergeant; Benjamin Black, 4th Sergeant; James Voltenburg, 5th Sergeant, K.; James M. Patton, 1st Corporal; David L. Taggart, 2d Corporal; E. H. Martin, 3d Corporal; John R. Mitchell, 4th Corporal; Dunning Hart, 5th Corporal; G. Harold McGinnis, 6th Corporal; John F. Wilson, 7th Corporal; Bankhead B. Barr, 8th Corporal.

PRIVATES.—James Allison, Wm. Armstrong, James Armstrong, John Arnold, Simon Arnold, Boyd E. Atkinson, John Barr, James L. Berry, w.; John M. Berry, David Berry, David W. Boyd, David Boyce, Josiah Carroll, Stephen Champ, A. A. Coleman, Eli Crawford, James M. Crawford, Vincent Crawford, James S. Daggs, John C. Davis, George Davis, Charles R. Donaldson, Wm. G. Donaldson, E. G. Emery, Alexander Gaston, K.; John Gilkeson, John L. Gow, Levi Griffith, w.; James W. Griffith, Wm. I. Greer, George Grier, James Hamilton,* D.; David Havelin, Wm. A.

---

* Died of typhoid fever, September 23d.

HISTORY OF WASHINGTON COUNTY.

Helt, Joseph Hemphill, James Himmeger, John W. Hogdens, Frank Ijams, J. B. Johnson, Wm. H. Jackson, James B. Jackson, Robert S. Jackson, Cornelius D. B. Kirk, James P. Kerr, Wm. A. Kerr, Joseph Lawson, Wm. H. Lanum, James Lynn, James S. McGlumphey, w.; Samuel B. McBride, G. W. McGibbony, Robert R. McJunkin, John W. McMeans, T. M. McNary, John McNutt, John R. Mitchell, Joseph L. Moore, George R. Murray, Robert B. Parkinson, John R. Paxton, Wm. J. P. Patton, Thomas A. Perrine, David B. Phillips, Wayne J. Phillips, James W. Pollock, William Pollock, James S. Rankin, James G. Sloan, William Sheets, John Speer, Robert L. Speer, R. L. Stewart, John M. Stewart, Wm. B. Stewart, John T. Sumney, David Sumney, James Thomas, Cyrus Townsend, John M. Watson, James P. Weaver, Joshua Weaver, Thomas Weaver, Joseph Wilson, Hugh Wier, David White, James Young.

Company G returned to Canonsburg, June 8, 1865, and was received at the college chapel by an address from Rev. Dr. Riddle W. McDaniel, Esq., and Rev. F. Collier. The original roll was called by ———— Pollock, O. S., and as the roll-calling proceeded the absent one was accounted for; but of the one hundred and three men all did their duty nobly, save one who deserted. They afterwards adjourned to Briceland's hotel, and partook of supper, and also were refreshed at Capt. Paxton's house.

COMPANY K.

Capt. William A. F. Stockton was elected Aug. 22, 1862, appointed Brigade Major April 9, 1865, and mustered out with company May 31, 1865.

First Lieutenant Alexander Sweeney, Jr., elected April 22, 1862, and served until mustered out.

Second Lieutenant William B. Cook, elected August 22, 1862, and honorably discharged May 17, 1865.

PRIVATES.—Edward Alexander, Jas. B. Allison, Abraham Andres, Peter Andres, James Arthrus, Jas. S. Berryhill, Milton R. Boyd, Benjamin B. Buchanan, D. J. Butterfoss, Lazarus Briggs, George W. Carter, Jesse Carter, Thomas J. Carter, Andrew Chester, w.; Isaac W. Chrisholm, Silas Cooke, James Cochran, Joseph Corbin, David W. Corbin, Ezra Conway, Benjamin H. Cummins, Andrew B. Davis, Michael Daugherty, John Day, Henry Dickson, Isaac Donaldson, Robert B. Dungan, Benjamin F. Earnest, John Fulton, James H. Fordyce, Joseph C. Frazier, John F. Gardner, William M. Geary, J. Smith Graham, Martin Grim, Joseph Guess, George A. Hanlin, William Hanlin, Benjamin F. Hawthorn, Thomas C. Hays, John Henderson, Robert W. Hull, George W. Johnston, Robert Lyle, James C. Lyle, James K. P. Magill, John Makeown, John Marshall, John Marshall, D.; John D. McCabe, John A. McCalmot, Robert McClurg, James K. McCurdy, Benjamin McCullough, Harrison McConnell, Owen McElfish, Robert A. Meldoon, John Meloy, Norris Metcalfe, William H. Miller, Isaac Miller, J. J. Morris, George Morrow, Enoch Mountz, John W. Nickerson, Colin R. Nickerson, James L. Noah, Thomas L. Noble, William Porter, Wm. R. H. Powelson, Benjamin F. Powelson, William Lewis Pry, Robert A. Pry, David McC. Pry, George Ralston, William M. Rea, William Ruffner, William Scott, Henderson Scott, Nathaniel Seese, Samuel K. Shindles,

George Sprowls, Jesse M. Sprowls, Oliver Staley, George Star, William Stollard, John Toppin, Robert Virtue, Ulysses Wheeler, Thomas Wilkin, James Worstell, Marshall Wright.

152D REGIMENT—3D PENNSYLVANIA ARTILLERY,

Was organized at Harrisburg and Philadelphia for three years' service, October 8, 1862, and was mustered out July 11, 1865.

In Company K of this regiment were J. P. Charlton, Samuel C. Wolf, Edward Mouck, and Robert F. Cooper, of Washington County. R. F. Cooper was commissioned 2d Lieutenant, but died shortly afterwards.

159TH REGIMENT, COMPANY H—14TH PENNSYLVANIA CAVALRY,

Was organized by Capt. John J. Shutterly, of Canonsburg, who was elected Captain Nov. 24, 1862, and resigned Oct. 2, 1863.

Henry McMurray, of Washington County, was elected 1st Lieutenant June 5, 1865, and honorably discharged Oct. 27, 1865; he had previously been elected 2d Lieutenant Oct. 2, 1863. His successor as 2d Lieutenant was James B. Johnson, who was honorably discharged July 31, 1865.

NON-COMMISSIONED OFFICERS.—Henry McMurray, O. S.; Benj. F. Craig, Quartermaster; Samuel Ruth, Commissary; Colton Donavan, 1st Duty; Alfred W. Murray, 3d; James Chaney, 4th; James Barker, 5th; James B. Johnston, 3d Corporal; David Orr, 4th Corporal; James McAdoo, 7th Corporal.

PRIVATES.—John Brown, James Campsey, Simon Donovan, Frank C. Forbes, Jonathan Fox, John Gilmore, Edward McGlaughlin, Thomas J. McPeak, Wilson McMurray, Sylvester McElfish, Sylvanus McAdoo, Andrew McPeak, Thomas Odey, George Ryan, James Sims, James Sees, George W. Trussel, Jonathan R. Wilson, William Wilson, Thomas White, James White.

The above were from Washington County; the remaining officers and soldiers from other counties and Virginia. The regiment was under the command of Col. James M. Schoonmaker.

This regiment was in the following battles: Winchester, Cedar Creek, Fisher's Hill, Lynchburg.

154TH REGIMENT PENNSYLVANIA DRAFTED MILITIA COMPANY.

This company was drafted for nine months' service October 16, 1862, and was composed of one hundred and nine men. We give a list of the officers and non-commissioned officers and privates who resided in Washington County. The non-commissioned officers were appointed December 1, 1862.

OFFICERS.—John B. Hays, Captain; Samuel T. Griffith, 1st Lieutenant; Jos. S. McBribe, 2d Lieutenant.

NON-COMMISSIONED OFFICERS.—James Blythe, Orderly Sergeant; John T. Roberts, 2d Sergeant; John Park, 3d Sergeant; Benjamin K. Kennedy, 4th Sergeant; Samuel M. Decker, 5th Sergeant; Andrew M. Welch, 1st

Corporal; Cyrus A. Foster, 2d Corporal; Samuel Davidson, 3d Corporal; Wm. Boon, 4th Corporal; John Bell, 5th Corporal; James P. Young, 6th Corporal; Joel England, 7th Corporal; Hagan H. Arnold, 8th Corporal.

PRIVATES.—Benjamin A. Ayres, Thomas Baldwin, James Caldwell, James Cavanaugh, Isaac B. Coates, Freegrift C. Cole, Samuel T. Decker, Nelson Ely, Henry A. Foster, Simon R. Hixenbaugh, William Hurley, Frank Kenner, F. Kalterlee, David Martin, John B. Miller, Carson Malone, Gilbert C. Marshall, Jonathan Morris, Hugh B. McKinley, Edward Mellon, Hugh McCoy, Davis Olds, Tyre Robinson, Thomas W. Ross, Robert C. Sheplar, J. Taylor Simpson, Thomas M. Stewart, F. Scriber, Thomas Shanafeet, James P. Young.

COMPANY K OF THE 161ST REGIMENT (16TH CAVALRY).

This company we referred to when giving the history of Captain Work's company.

It was organized under the command of Captain R. W. Parkinson, October 25, 1862; he resigned April 12, 1863, and was succeeded by Lieutenant Jonathan R. Day, April 30, 1863, Lt. Day having filled the office of 1st Lieutenant from its organization. Upon the promotion of Lieutenant Day, Henry Granville was elected November 20, 1862, who served until February 20, 1863, when Edmund Dunn was elected 1st Lieutenant February 21, 1863, and served until the company was mustered out August 11, 1869. 2d Lieutenant Alexander A. Gunn served as such from its organization until February 27, 1863, when he resigned, when Luther Day was elected; but he being killed in action December 1, 1864, J. Newton Minton was elected December 2, 1864, and regularly mustered out August 11, 1865. Lieutenant Jonathan R. Day was appointed Adjutant of this regiment October 18, 1862; Francis J. Lemoyne, M. D., Surgeon.

This regiment participated in the following engagements: Kellysford, Middleburg, Ashby's Gap, Gettysburg, Shepherdstown, Sulphur Springs, Bristoe's Station, Mine Run, Todd's Tavern, Hawes' Shop, Fortifications of Richmond, Trevillian Station, St. Mary's Church, Deep Bottom, Ream's Station, Boydton Road, and Stony Creek Station.

OFFICERS.—R. W. Parkinson, Captain; J. R. Day, 1st Lieutenant; A. A. Gunn, 2d Lieutenant.

NON-COMMISSIONED OFFICERS.—E. Dunn, Orderly Sergeant; L. Day, 1st Sergeant; C. H. McVay, 2d Sergeant; A. H. Miller, 3d Sergeant; M. Woods, 4th Sergeant; W. S. Craft, 5th Sergeant; S. D. Waddie, Commissary Sergeant; N. D. Chutter, Quarter-Master Sergeant; J. N. Minton, 1st Corporal; G. F. Simpson, 2d Corporal; T. J. Penn, 3d Sergeant; G. W. McDavid, 4th Corporal; G. W. Conger, 5th Corporal; O. L. Garrett, 6th Corporal; J. Dunn, 7th Corporal; J. England, 8th Corporal; Wm. D. Carroll, 1st Bugler; S. Saunders, 2d Bugler.

PRIVATES.—D. Archer, J. Ackley, J. Brooks, S. Birch, G. Baldwin, J. Baldwin, O. G. Boord, W. Chester, R. Chester, N. Cheese, D. Cooper, J. Craft, H. Cranville, J. Caldwell, O. Conklin, J. Cracraft, S. Carter, J. Carter, A. Clutter, G. W. Clutter, J. Dailey, H. P. Day, S. Denny, J. Denny,

J. M. Dilley, J. Dickson, H. Dickson, J. Dewbery, J. Dougherty, A. Frazier, B. Fry, A. H. Hewit, J. Hazlett, H. Howell, J. Hanna, M. Jones, E. Lowery, W. Lewis, H. Little, N. Little, William Lyon, w.; G. W. Hays, Louis Kendall, N. Lightner, S. Lindley, E. Mattox, J. W. Miller, B. Marshman, R. Marshman, T. J. Marshal, S. McDaniel, M. McMahon, Wm. Mendlen, C. Mears, I. Milligan J. W. Milligan, J. Milligan, S. Pipes, S. Potter, W. Potter, M. Patterson, S. Porter, J. Post, J. Roney, J. Z. Riley, J. Riley, A. Stillwell, J. Saunders, J. B. Sheets, J. P. K. Smith, w.; J. Stewart, J. Throgmorten, A. Teagarden, S. Winget, F. Winget, J. Wright, J. Walker, J. Wilson, S. Wilson.

185TH REGIMENT, 22D CAVALRY REGIMENT,

Was organized at Cumberland, Md., February 22, 1864; its history fully given after the roll of this company.

RINGGOLD CAVALRY.

Roll of Ringgold Cavalry, Company A, of the Ringgold Cavalry Battalion of Washington County.—This company was commanded by Captain John Keys, and takes rank from June 6, 1861. Its term of service was three years, and assigned to the 22d Regiment Pennsylvania Cavalry, organized February 25, 1864.

Captain John Keys, mustered into service October 2, 1861, died November 10, 1863. 1st Lieutenant Henry A. Myers was elected October 2, 1861, and promoted to Captain November 12, 1863, and afterwards to Major 1st Lieutenant James P. Hart was promoted November 12, 1863, and on March 27, 1864, elected Captain and mustered out with Company A, 3d Prov. Cavalry October 31, 1865. 1st Lieutenant Henry Anisansel, who resigned and was commissioned by Gov. Pierrepont, of Virginia, to raise a regiment of cavalry, of which he served as Colonel. Captain Farrabees' company was in this regiment. 2d Lieutenant James P. Hart was elected October 2, 1861, and promoted to 1st Lieutenant. 2d Lieutenant John Holland was elected November 12, 1863; March 17, 1864, elected 1st Lieutenant, and mustered out August 23, 1864. 2d Lieutenant Geo. Gass was elected March 17, 1864, and 1st Lieutenant August 24, 1864. 2d Lieutenant Thomas Nutt was elected August 24, 1864.

NON-COMMISSIONED OFFICERS.—Samuel B. Holland, Quarter-Master Sergeant; Joseph E. Abell, Company Commissary Sergeant; John Holland, 1st Sergeant; Geo. Gass, 2d Sergeant; Adam Wickersham, 3d Sergeant; Thomas Nutt, 4th Sergeant; Hopkins Moffitt, 5th Sergeant; Wm. Parshall, 1st Corporal; Joseph Householder, 2d Corporal; Stephen P. Beatty, 3d Corporal; Isaac P. Dawson, 4th Corporal; Hugh P. Hedge, 5th Corporal; Chauncey R. Dover, 6th Corporal; James Robinson, 7th Corporal, John Streiner, 8th Corporal.

MUSICIANS.—Napoleon B. Rigden and William M. Morrison.
BLACKSMITH.—Jacob Dickson.
WAGONER.—William Harford.
PRIVATES.—Alexander Artist, Joseph E. Abell, John L. Abell, Lewis Arthur, Thomas C. Buckingham, George W. Brevard, Madison Blackburn,

George Baumgarner, Samuel D. Bane, Sample S. Bane, William A. Bane, Patrick Bane, William Charlton, Samuel Conditt, John S. Corbitt, John Crouch, James Crouch, Michael H. Core, James A. Dudgeon, Angier Dobbs, Andrew J. Davis, Chancey R. Dever, John Z. Davis, Jas. Dorsey, John W. Elwood, Andrew S. Frazer, William H. French, Andrew J. Floyd, David W. French, Franklin Fitzsimmons, John Gregg, K.; Ivin Gregg, K.; James Gray, John W. Gray, Andrew B. Grant, L. Geo. Grant, Antuban Hill, John Hunter, Jacob Hoover, Michael Hemler, David A. Huston, Francis M. Hirst, David Hart, W. W. Holland, Wm. Hartranft, K.; James A. Harrison, Thomas Kerns, Samuel Kerns, Christian Kinder, Christian Krepps, T.; John S. Lever, Harrison Linn, Thomas M. Linn, John Linn, Jas. H. Lever, Joseph Lever, William Lafferty, Thompson McKinley, John McGovern, Andrew J. Manning, John D. Manning, John A. Meeks, Henry Mitchell, William Mason, Joseph B. Morton, James McDow, Thomas P. Morton, James McBride, John M. Myers, Henry C. McJenkin, Lewis Noel, Ben. S. Province, George E. Parshall, James Patterson, Jacob L. Pierce, James S. Parshall, Amos Queen, Daniel Rhorer, James Robinson, Leonard A. Roberts, Thomas Reeves, T.; A. B. Richardson, W.; James Robinson, K.; John M. Sinclair, Christian Snyder, K.; George W. Snyder, K.; Herman Sherholtz, Frank Smith, Elliot, F. Weaver, Francis M. White, David D. Williams, L. Williams, Thos. Williams, Israel Youmans, Harvey H. Young.

In connection with this and the six succeeding cavalry companies we will state that the Ringgold Battalion, under the command of Major John Keys, was comprised of seven companies, viz: Ringgold Cavalry, commanded by Captain John Keys; Keystone Cavalry, commanded by Captain George T. Work; Washington Cavalry, by Captain A. J. Greenfield; Beallsville Cavalry, by Captain H. H. Young; Patton Cavalry, by Captain A. J. Barr; La Fayette Cavalry, by Captain A. V. Smith; and Independent Cavalry, by Captain M. W. Mitchener. These companies were a part of the 185th Regiment (22d Pennsylvania Cavalry Regiment), which was organized February 25, 1864, with the following officers: Jacob Higgins, Colonel; A. J. Greenfield, Lieutenant-Colonel; Geo. T. Work, Elias S. Troxall, Henry A. Myers, Majors; J. G. Isenberg, Adjutant; W. E. Bailey, Quartermaster; S. Webster French, Acting Commissary Sergeant; W. C. Phelps, Surgeon; W. R. Lynch and S. M. Finley, Assistant Surgeons.

On June 19, 1865, the Beallsville Cavalry, at that time commanded by Captain Hugh Keys, and the Independent Cavalry, by Captain James Y. Chessround, were mustered out of service at New Creek, Virginia; the remaining companies consolidated with the 163d Regiment (18th Pennsylvania Cavalry) June 24, 1865, and designated the 3d Regiment Pennsylvania Provisional Cavalry, and were finally mustered out of service at Cumberland, Maryland, October 31, 1865.

The companies in the 185th Regiment were numbered as follows: Capt Keys, A; Captain Greenfield, B; Captain Work, C; Captain Young, D; Captain Chessround, E; Captain Barr, F; Captain Smith, G.

Non-Commissioned Staff Officers.—Robert A. Laird, Sergeant-Major; Samuel T. Dodd, Hospital Steward; John Reynolds, Assistant; David Hoyt, Quarter-Master Sergeant, Levi Scott, Chief Bugler; Wm. Ritchey, R. B.; Dr. Z. B. Kent, Veterinary Surgeon; John W. Cook, R. S.

WASHINGTON CAVALRY COMPANY

Was mustered into the service of the United States Aug. 19, 1861, and assigned to the 22d Regiment, Pennsylvania Cavalry, which was organized March, 1864, its term of service being three years. It was Company B in this regiment.

Officers.—A. J. Greenfield, Captain; John Dabinett, 1st Lieut.; G. W. Jenkins, 2d Lieut.

Non-Commissioned Officers.—James M. Weaver, Q. M. Sergeant; W. Brown, Orderly Sergeant; Armour Thompson, 1st Sergeant; Joseph W. Hill, 2d Sergeant; Theodore Day, 3d Sergeant; Samuel Sinclair, 4th Sergeant; Ross Adams, 1st Corporal; Eli Moffit, 2d Corporal; Hardman Gantz, 3d Corporal; Wm. Worcester, 4th Corporal; Wm. Shaffer, 5th Corporal; Harvey Kinder, 6th Corporal; Hiram Sargent, 7th Corporal; Thomas Sargent, 8th Corporal.

Privates.—Andrew Axten, John Ashman, Albert Allen, Harrison Bennington, W. F. Booth, D. M. Barnett, Frederick Branner, James P. Brock, David Claffey, Theodore Dwyer, Samuel Drumm, Silas Drumm, Stephen A. Day, Harrison Deems, John A. Dage, James S. French, Benj. Fitzenburg, Patrick Grace, Peter Hickman, Hugh H. Horn, J. W. Hendricks, Jacob Horn, Henry Haler, Thomas Jackson, Joseph Knight, Jacob Klinefelter, George Lap, Geo. H. Murray, Nicholas Miller, Thomas Mason, Samuel Moore, Henry Myers, Clark Newcomer, J. A. Nichols, W. H. Plymire, Samuel Potter, Charles Rogers, Samuel J. Rogers, Andrew Smith, Henry Storer, John H. Smith, Amos Smith, James B. Sinclair, Charles Sinclair, W. H. Statters, Demas S. Snyder, Edmund Stone, Lewis Upperman, Abraham Vanvoorhis, Wm. H. Watkins, William Wright, James White, Thomas Welsh, John West, James M. Weaver, w.

Capt. Greenfield, being promoted to Lieut.-Colonel of the 185th Regiment, was succeeded by 2d Lieut. Geo. W. Jenkins, who was elected Feb. 28, 1864, and mustered out with the company Oct. 7, 1864.

Lieut. Dabinett remained with Company B from its organization to its mustering out.

Lieut. Jenkins being promoted to the captaincy Feb. 25, 1864, Lieut. Wm. Brown was elected 2d lieut., and mustered out Oct. 7, 1864.

On November 26, 1864, the Washington Cavalry was reorganized by the election of the following officers: Captain, W. E. Griffith; 1st Lieut., J. B. Henderson; 2d Lieut., Joshua B. Deems. The officers served until mustered out, October 31, 1865.

WINFIELD HUSSARS, AFTERWARDS CALLED KEYSTONE CAVALRY.

On the 25th July, 1862, Capt. George T. Work was authorized by Governor Curtin to raise a company of cavalry for the United

States' service. Capt. Work applied himself diligently to the recruiting of men, and on the 10th of August following so successful was he in the undertaking that he divided the company by giving Capt. Parkinson fifty of his recruits, and again filled up his company to the requisite number; and on the 6th of September was mustered into service by Capt. Ludington, at Washington.

This company was attached to the 22d Regiment, Pennsylvania Cavalry (term of service for three years), which regiment was organized March, 1864, under Col. Geo. D. Bayard, of McCall's division. It was Company I in this regiment. When the Ringgold Battalion was organized it became Company C.

OFFICERS.—George T. Work, Captain; C. J. McNulty, 1st Lieutenant; Robert C. Welch, 2d Lieutenant.

NON-COMMISSIONED OFFICERS.—Joseph J. Lane, 1st Sergeant; Joseph Porter, Quartermaster; Joseph C. Hunter, C. S.; S. W. French, 1st Duty Sergeant, Wm. R. Galbreath, 2d Duty Sergeant; Wm. L. Oliver, 3d Duty Sergeant; Wm. Jamison, 4th Duty Sergeant; David Scott, 5th Duty Sergeant; Thomas Stewart, 1st Corporal; Samuel S. Armstrong, 2d Corporal; Samuel C. Brownlee, 3d Corporal; Abraham H. Wilkin, 4th Corporal; James C. Smith, 5th Corporal; Milton S. Davis, 6th Corporal; Samuel Donaldson, 7th Corporal; Robert G. Rush, 8th Corporal; Samuel C. Forester, Blacksmith; John S. Thornburg, Farrier; Levi Scott, 1st Bugler; C. B. McKeever, 2d Bugler; Edward Linton, Wagoner.

PRIVATES.—Samuel C. Adams, Thomas Algeo, Joseph Armstrong, Absalom Ashbrook, D.; Stephen P. Bane, John F. Bell, Charles Black, Francis M. Bolles, Robert Boon, Joseph W. Brownlee, Wm. Burke, DIS.; William Barnett, Thomas Campsey, George R. Chambers, John S. Clark. Daniel L. Crider, P.; Thomas B. Craig, Wm. H. Cowan, Charles C. Colee, John L. Cummins, David S. Cummins, Wm. Delaney, Thomas E. Dowler, Hawthorn Dunkle, Michael Essick, Richard Fisher, Joseph Fuller, Benjamin Fuller, John Gardner, David Griffith, Joseph Guinea, Robert Henderson, William Hair, George Hardee, Hiram Headley, Peter Hoy, John W. Huston, J. Joshua Hunter, Henry Johnston, Samuel F. Kelly, Frederick Kitsner, Lemuel Laggett, Edward P. Linn, Jacob Loughman, Robert Loughman, William McCarty, Alex. W. McConnel, Archibald McClelland, James McFait, Ebenezer McGuffin, John McEwen, George W. Mitchell, John F. Milligan, Andrew Means, Edward C. Miller, Richard Mountz, John H. Murray, Robert D. Nesbit, Thomas B. O'Donald, Warren Joseph Oliver, John Patterson, Henry Pense, Hugh Porter, Robert G. Rush, Wm. H. Rose, David H. Ralston, George W. Ramsey, David Rizer, Washington Ritchey, Wm. C. Richards, Wm. Sears, James Stewart, James B. Semult, Richard P. Shipley, John G. Stewart, Joseph Starr, James Smith, K.; Adam A. Thornburg, Samuel Turner, Thomas J. White, Wm. T. White, Daniel H. Wilson, Samuel Williamson, Wm. Woodburn, James R. Woodburn.

Capt. G. T. Work, promoted to Major September 6, 1862; his successor, Lieut. C. J. McNulty, elected Feb. 25, 1864, and honorably discharged June 1, 1865; his successor, Lieut. Robert C. Welch, elected March 3, 1865, and honorably discharged May 18, 1865.

Lieut. McNulty having been elected captain, Lieut Welch was

elected 1st Lieut. Feb. 25, 1864, and his successor was Joseph J. Lane, elected Nov. 26, 1864; he was succeeded by Lieut. Wm. R. Galbraith March 3, 1865, and mustered out with company Oct. 31, 1865.

Lieut. Welch being promoted Joseph J. Lane succeeded him as 2d Lieut. Feb. 25, 1864, and served until Dec. 25, 1869, when Wm. R. Galbraith was elected.

BEALLSVILLE CAVALRY

Was organized in Washington, September 2, 1862. John H. Buchanan promoted to 2d Lieutenant and took charge of a military school in Philadelphia, and subsequently officered in South Carolina and Florida. It was mustered into the service of the United States September 6, 1862, under the command of Captain Harvey H. Young. From 1862 to the organization of the 185th Regiment (22d Pennsylvania Cavalry), they were known as the Ringgold Cavalry Battalion.

We give the names of the officers and men of Company D.

OFFICERS.—H. H. Young, Captain; Hugh Keys, 1st Lieutenant; Felix H. Crago, 2d Lieutenant.

NON-COMMISSIONED OFFICERS.—Isaac M. Regester, 1st Sergeant; Gideon H. Hawkins, Quartermaster, D.; David M. Snyder, Commissary; Robert Galbraith, 1st duty Sergeant; Wm. H. Wickersham, 2d duty Sergeant John N. Horn, 3d duty Sergeant; Emmer H. Hill, 4th duty Sergeant; James M. Quivey, 5th duty Sergeant, P.; James A. S. White, 1st Corporal; Thomas W. Lynch, 2d Corporal; Joseph Jennings, 3d Corporal; Alexander C. Powell, 4th Corporal; John L. Cock, 5th Corporal; Cyrus Hoffman, 6th Corporal; Benjamin F. Floyd, 7th Corporal; Ellis B. Gregg, 8th Corporal; George W. Dougherty, 1st Bugler, D.; Wm. H. Crago, 2d Bugler; William Sheets and Christopher Long, Farriers; Adah Crough, Wagoner.

PRIVATES.—Isaac H. Allfree, Alexander R. Armstrong, Jessie A. Armstrong, James Armstrong, Joseph E. Bane, Cyrus Baxter, K.; Lawrence W. Bower, Jonathan D. Burk, D.; George R. Bower, D.; Alfred Burkhart, Alonzo Brightwell, Jesse Benner, Francis M. Clark, Simon S. Condit, Wm. C. Condit, w.; Daniel W. Condit, Jaboz Condit, Philip D. Campbell, William H. Cragg, DIS.; Thomas J. Crago, Henry C. Crago, Joseph F. Craven, Richard Crawford, Samuel R. Crawford, Jas. M. Crawford, Henry Dague, James N. David, Kennedy Davis, George W. Eagy, P.; George Eicher, Sebastian B. Elliott, Elias A. Fleniken, Lewis Fry, Wm. Gardner, John T. Gass, D.; James B. Groomes, Jacob Guseman, Joseph Hamilton, Andrew Hamilton, Jonah Harris, D.; John W. Hawkins, Isaac Hill, Andrew H. Holmes, P.; Levi Horn, Wm. H. Horner, Wm. S. Hutchinson, D. ; John C. Jennings, Joseph S. John, John Kann, Geo. Keihl, Freeman Kelly, P.; George Kerr, Huston Kerr, Wm. Lee, Francis I. Luellen, P. ; Charles Luellen, Peter Malone, Jacob R. Maxwell, P.; Wm. McClellan, Jas. McCloud, Samuel B. McLane, P.; Thomas H. McLane, Emmor H. Miller, D.; Isaac I. Mitchell, D.; Adam S. Morton, K.; Wm. H. Mosier, Jacob Nedrow, D.; Thos. Neff, DIS.; Wm. C. Nimon, Stewart Patterson, Albert G. Powell, Taylor Pyle, Jas. M. Phillips, P.; John S. Reeves, John R. Regester, K.; Stephen C. Richardson, Joseph H. Rogers, Robert E. Ross, John B. Shallenberger, Wm. Sheets, D.; Wm. Shively, John Smith, D.; George Sample, Henry Snyder, Wm. B. Sutton, P.; Griffith Taylor, John B Taylor, Benj. L. Taylor, P.; Wm. H. White, David A. White, Sam'l H. White, Wm. P. White, James N. Wheeler, James S. Wickersham, Cephas Wiley, K.; John M. Young.

Captain Young served until February 25, 1864, when Lieutenant Hugh Keys was elected March 1, 1864, and remained with the company until it was mustered out of service October 31, 1865.

Felix H. Crago was promoted to 1st Lieutenant, and Isaac M. Regester to 2d Lieutenant March 1, 1864.

Independent Cavalry, Company E,

Was mustered into service at Wheeling, Virginia, October 13, 1862, in the 185th Regiment (22d Pennsylvania Cavalry), under the command of Captain Milton W. Mitchenor. He served until April 1, 1864, when he was honorably discharged, and James Y. Chessround was elected Captain, who served until March 19, 1865, when Felix Boyle was elected.

1st Lieutenant J. Y. Chessround was elected at the organization and afterwards promoted to the captaincy; his successor was Felix Boyle, elected February 12, 1863, and upon his promotion Lieutenant Jas. Gibson was elected 1st Lieutenant.

2d Lieutenant R. S. H. Keys was elected 2d Lieutenant at the company's organization; he was honorably discharged February 12, 1863, and Felix Boyle elected February 12, 1863; his successor was Lieutenant James Gibson, who was afterwards promoted to the first Lieutenancy. Clinton Teeple was elected March 19, 1865. The company was mustered out July 19, 1865.

Non-Commissioned Officers.—Clinton Teeple, Orderly Sergeant; J. M. Teeple, Quarter-Master; D. H. Williams, Commissary; George Robson, 1st Sergeant; John McCracken, 2d Sergeant, w.; John Behanna, 3d Sergeant, w.; John E. Rail, 4th Sergeant; Robert White, 5th Sergeant, w.; Peter Stacker, 1st Corporal; John S. Yohe, 2d Corporal; Samuel Wright, 3d Corporal, w.; W. W. Hess, 4th Corporal; C. Z. Koechline, 5th Corporal; And. McDonell, 6th Corporal; Hiram Myers, 7th Corporal; James Kearney, 8th Corporal; Chs. F. Troesher and H. Robson, Buglers; Joseph A. Scott, Saddler; John Lutes and George Lutes, Blacksmiths.

Privates.—Andrew Amos, Vincent Amos, Abraham Anderson, John Atcheson, Samuel Atcheson, w.; Francis Allen, Jacob Baker, Jacob W. Beck, Alexander Behanna, Samuel Behanna, Charles Behanna, John Behanna, Jr., Samuel Black, John Boyle, Jr., Richard Burns, David Byers, James Boyd, James W. Baxter, George W. Brown, K.; B. F. Bowen, David Behanna, Jerome Byers, Samuel Caldwell, David Clarke, D.; John W. Craven, Abner J. Craven, John Crouch, James Craven, John Dolen, Hiram Degarmo, D.; W. H. H. Degarmo, Holliday Donaldson, Thomas Flanagan, Noah Henry, James F. Henry, Franklin Hendrickson, w.; Willis Hendrickson, Edward Hendrickson, Henry Hillman, B. F. Helmick, John Hamilton, Robert Jones, John P. Jordan, Cardena Jordon, John M. Kiehl, James Kerns, Andrew Kimble, John Leyda, Henry Leaver, K.; B. F. Leonard,

Marcus Mellinger, John S. Mareown, Samuel Marker, Robert Molden, Jacob Molden, William Mitchell, Samuel A. Munn, Jeremiah Myers, Thos. H. Moffit, Eli W. Mancha, w.; Eli A. Miller, Joseph A. McClure, George W. McClair, Thomas McAllister, Joseph Marker, Alexander McKee, Henry Minks, Enoch J. Newkirk, George W. Owen, Elymas Pettit, Vear R. Porter, Clark Preston, DIS.; Marshall Robinson, George W. Robb, w.; Charles E. Rose, D.; John M. Sutman, Aaron Sutman, Samuel Sullivan, John Snyder, Frederick Surg, w.; John Stacker, W. P. Starr, K.; John Saunders, K.; James B. Smith, K.; Boyd E. Summey, D.; Thomas W. Teeple, J. C. Thompson, John Trussler, w.; James M. Williams, William White, K.; Peter Young.

The battles and skirmishes in which this regiment were engaged were Stumps' Mills, Moorfield, Winchester, Pergetsville, N. Mountain Depot, Petersburg, Williamsport, Burlington, Romney, Lost River Gap, Piedmont, Rockfish Gap, Lynchburg, Lexington, Salem, Dorcasville, Pleasant Valley, Monterey, Taylorstown, Snicker's Gap, Ashley's Gap, Kearnstown, Martinsburg, Opequan Creek, Berryville, Charlestown, Martinsburg, Stephenson Depot, Bunker Hill, Strasburg, Fisher's Hill, Mount Jackson, Brown's Gap, Mount Vernon Forge, Cedar Creek.

PATTON CAVALRY COMPANY

Was mustered into the service of the United States October 14, 1862. This company was raised under the name of the PATTON CAVALRY, term of service three years, and assigned to the 22d Regiment, Pennsylvania Cavalry, and subsequently organized in the Ringgold Battalion of Volunteer Cavalry as Company F.

Captain Barr served until February 25, 1864, when Lieutenant Benjamin W. Denny was elected, and mustered out of service July 19, 1865. Lieutenant Denny had served as 1st Lieutenant from the organization of the company. David Wishart was elected 1st Lieutenant May 11, 1864, and honorably discharged May 16, 1865. He was succeeded by Lieutenant Benjamin F. Hasson, May 17, 1865, and remained with the company until mustered out.

Lieutenant George T. Hammond served until November 29, 1864, when he was honorably discharged, and was succeeded by Lieut. B. F. Hasson, who served until his promotion to first Lieutenancy, May 17, 1865, when William Hedge was elected second Lieutenant, and mustered out with the company.

OFFICERS.—A. J. Barr, Captain; B. W. Denny, 1st Lieutenant; George T. Hammond, 2d Lieutenant.

PRIVATES.—John A. Arnold, David Braden, Samuel Barr, William Burk, James Bradley, Sol. S. Bane, Samuel B. Barnard, Lindsey Baker, John N. Braddock, John B. Buckingham, Silas Cowen, David Campbell, Alexander Crumrine, Peter Deems, Samuel H. Doak, Sylvester F. Dodd, Samuel T. Dodd, Zoliver Dotts, Harvey H. Eller, Andrew Elliott, Thomas C. Enochs, Martin V. Frazer, John Flowers, Terrance Farmer, Samuel Gayman, Stephen J. Guinea, Christian Garrett, Benj. Harden, Charles Hallam, Samuel S. Hallam, Benj. F. Hasson, William Hedge, W. P. Hayner, George T.

Hammond, Jr., Hiram A. Holmes, George Johnston, William Jenkins, George Kauffman, Dallas Link, Atlas Lacock, Nathan B. Marsh, Michael Moore, Abel Moore, Leet S. Moore, James S. Margerum, George W. Moninger, Martin Murphy, John W. Manning, James A. McDonald, Levi H. Pope, Thomas Patterson, John A. Prall, John N. Prall, Henry Prall, John W. Penny, Joseph R. Province, John H. Reynolds, Josephus Ross, Wm. T. Rigg, Joseph Ritman, Thomas Slusher, Henry Slusher, Andrew J. Sowers, Andrew Scott, Samuel Simons, Eberhardt Teagarden, Hiram Tharp, Robert Thompson, Samuel Trusler, Jacob Ulery, William Vankirk, Samuel Wilson, Samuel J. Wilson, David Wishart, Samuel K. West, Jacob L. Wise, James Watson, Richard White.

LA FAYETTE CAVALRY

Was mustered into the service of the United States October 23, 1862. Its term of service was three years, and served with the Ringold battalion until the organization of the 22d regiment of Pennsylvania cavalry, organized March, 1864. This company ranked in the regiment as Company G.

Captain Alexander V. Smith was elected its first Captain and served until September 5, 1863, when he was honorably discharged, and his successor was Captain William F. Spear, who was promoted from 2d Lieut., and who with the company was mustered out October 31, 1865.

1st Lieut. Frank B. Smith served from the organization until December 21, 1864, when, being honorably discharged on account of a severe wound, received at Charleston, W. V., he was succeeded by Lieut. J. G. Van Gilder, who had previously filled the office of 2d Lieut. from September 6, 1863. Lieut. James C. Hubbs, who was elected December 22, 1864, succeeded 2d Lieut. J. G. Van Gilder; his successor was Lieut. W. H. Frost, elected May 31, 1865, and mustered out with the company.

McKENNAN INFANTRY

Was organized April 27, 1861, in Washington County. This company tendered their services to the general government but were not accepted, the quota being full. They were invited to West Virginia, marched to Wheeling, and on July 10, 1861, were received by authority of Governor Pierpont, and elected officers who were duly commissioned by him.

Captain Smith was taken prisoner at Cattell's Station on the Manassas railroad, and after his parole and exchange November 23, 1862, resigned, and Lieut. N. W. Truxal was elected November 24, 1862.

OFFICERS.—Lewis E. Smith, Captain; A. A. Devore, 1st Lieut.; N. W. Truxal, 2d. Lieut.

NON-COMMISSIONED OFFICERS.—J. K. Billingsly, Sergeant; Thos. Young, Sergeant; Jacob Kent, Sergeant, P.; J. B. Montgomery, Sergeant; Jacob Qualk, Sergeant; A. Ledbeater, Corporal; J. Hornbake, Corporal, P.; G. Underwood, Corporal, P.; John Lopp, Corporal; Samuel Kent, Corporal,

HISTORY OF WASHINGTON COUNTY. 333

P.; S. Amalong, Corporal; J. Weaver, Corporal, P.; Robert Jobes, Corporal.
PRIVATES.—J. F. Ailes, K.; Jesse Ammon, Henry Barnhart, Jas. F. Bigelow, P.; Jac. D. Billingsly, Thos. Bee, Geo. D. Boyd, Wm. Bunton, Nathaniel Balding, James W. Blair, Sidney J. Benedict, Wm. H. H. Billingsly, N. Baldwin, D. O. Carpenter, Geo. W. Clendennel, John Cunnard, Jefferson Clendennel, John N. Crow, Augustus Clark, Joseph W. Chester, Marion Crumrine, Theophilus V. Devore, P.; Henry E. Devore, Jehu Dehaven, Michael Dowling, James R. Dowling, John C. Evans, Hamilton Fitzsimmons, Lewis M. Freeman, D.; William Geho, DeWitt Clinton Graham, Jas. M. H. Gordon, Wm. Garton, P.; Andrew J. Harris, Wm. J. Harris, Wm. H. Hornbake, Osmond Hutchison, P.; Charles S. Hixenbaugh, Robert Herron, Noble Houdon, Samuel J. Howe, Daniel Howe, K.; Lemuel B. Howe, Ewd. Jones, Samuel Jobes, Andrew N. Jobes, Jos. Jobes, Wm. W. Jobes, Robt. Jobes, Joseph Johnson, Jas. M. Johnson, Alex. S. Latta, P.; Hugh Lancaster, Elijah Lichteberger, P.; Wm. L. Latta, Allen Moore, Robt. McDonald, Robt. Mayhorn, P.; Jos. Mayhorn, Wm. McCoy, Robt. McCoy, Geo. Marker, Sanson Miller, James P. McCain, Isaac S. McCain, John McLaughlin, William Norcross, Nathaniel Patterson, David R. Phillips, Hiram Qualk, Frank S. Reader, Jas. Reader, Jr., John Rimmel, Frederick Rimmel, Felix Russell, Augustus Shaffer, Cuthbert Soulsby, D.; Wm. Showalters; Nehemiah Sikes, Philip Thomas, John W. Truxal, Foster H. Truxal, D.; Elihu Underwood, Hiram Wells, Alfred D. Wolf, Wm. Worrell, Wm. Wilkin, Stephen Ward, Finley Wise, Thos. Walker, Abraham Weaver, John Weaver, J. R. Williams, Stephen H. Ward, P.; Robt. Young, Nathaniel Young.

November 24, 1862, Lieut. N. W. Truxal was elected Captain. Charles H. Day elected 1st Lieut. December 3, 1863. James R. Billingsly elected 2d Lieut. January 11, 1862, and promoted from 2d Lieut. to Captain March 5, 1863. James B. Montgomery elected 2d Lieut. December 3, 1863. Lieut. A. A. Devore resigned October 10, 1861.

This company participated in the following battles, viz: Allegheny Mountain, Huntersville, Monterey, McDowell, Cross Keys, Cedar Mountain, Kelley's Ford, Warterloo Bridge, Gainsville, Sulphur Springs, Bull Run, Beverly, Rocky Gap, and Drop Mountain. It was mustered out of service July 28, 1864, at Wheeling, Va.

6TH REGIMENT, PENNSYLVANIA MILITIA.

This regiment was organized September 15, 1862, at Harrisburg, by the election of Capt. James Armstrong as Colonel. It marched to Camp McClure, two miles west of Chambersburg, and mustered out September 28, 1862. David Aiken was appointed Quartermaster Sept. 15, 1862; James E. Smiley, Assistant Quartermaster; Boyd Crumrine, Quartermaster's Clerk; Rev. Wm. P. Alrich, Chaplain; Ordinance Sergeant, William Hart.

The Wayne Infantry left Washington Sept. 13, 1862, under the command of Capt. James Armstrong, numbering one hundred and forty men, but by the authority of the Adjutant-General it was divided into two companies, Capt. Armstrong being re-elected captain of the Wayne Infantry, and Capt. Norton McGiffin of the McGiffin Riflemen.

Roll of Company A.

OFFICERS.—Norton McGiffin, Captain; S. M. Templeton, 1st Lieut.; H. H. Alter, 2d Lieut.

NON-COMMISSIONED OFFICERS.—J. B. Wilson, 1st Sergeant; H. B. McCollum, 2d Sergeant; David Brady, 3d Sergeant; Wesley Wolf, 4th Sergeant; J. C. Acheson, 5th Sergeant; J. M. Spriggs, 1st Corporal; H B. McCollum, 2d Corporal; J. F. Steck, 3d Corporal; John Wylie, 4th Corporal; T. G. Wolf, 5th Corporal; J. Ross Thompson, 6th Corporal; H. M. Aiken, 7th Corporal; J. W. Dinsmore, 8th Corporal.

MUSICIAN.—Charles White.

PRIVATES.—H. H. Arnold, J. C. Alrich, Wm. Allen, Norton Braddock, J. N. Bane, Wm. Burk, Wm. T. Beatty, Samuel Cook, J. L. Cooke, S. A. Clark, G. W. Driver, G. L. Gow, Wm. Greer, Charles Glum, John Hainer, J. N. Hainer, George Hammond, John Hallams, G. O. Jones, T. C. Kerr, J. C. Kieser, A. H. Little, George Lindsay, Gust Lonkert, Wm. McClaine, James McCreary, J. E. McCullough, J. B. McKennan, Jerry Marshel, G. W. Murphy, Wm. Paull, S. H. Rial, J. G. Ruple, J. G. Rode, J. P. Reimond, A. D. Rickey, James Seaman, J. W. Seaman, R. F. Strain, J. H. Scott, A. M. Todd, Theodore Turner, R. L. Thompson, F. P. Varro, Wm. M. Vance, D. C. Valentine, T. M. Wylie, J. W. Wylie, F. J. L. Wylie, J. C. S. Wiles, W. M. L. Wiles, J. G. Winsworth, Samuel Weirich, J. S. Wolf, F. R. Wotring, David Watson.

Commissioned Officers, 3; Non-Commissioned Officers, 13; Musician, 1; Privates, 56; total, 73.

Roll of Company F, 6th Regiment Pa. Volunteer Militia.

OFFICERS.—John H. Ewing, Capt.; Alfred Creigh, 1st Lieut.; Samuel O. Williams, 2d Lieut.

NON-COMMISSIONED OFFICERS.—James M. Byers, 1st Sergeant; Thomas D. O'Hara, 2d Sergeant; Wm. Hart, 3d Sergeant; Geo. Reed, 4th Sergeant; Wm. T. Fleming, 5th Sergeant; Samuel T. Griffith, 1st Corporal; James Brown, 2d Corporal; R. B. Patterson, 3d Corporal; Jas. R. Ruth, 4th Corporal; Mathew Linn, 5th Corporal; Wm. Phillips, 6th Corporal; Wm. W. Smith, 7th Corporal; F. Gabby, 8th Corporal.

MUSICIAN.—Moses T. Scott.

PRIVATES.—Rev. Wm. Alrich, David Aiken, Wm. Amon, Agnew, Alexander, R. M. Andrews, A. J. Buffington, N. B. Brobst, John Baird, Dr. M. H. Clark, Boyd Crumrine, John R. Donehoo, Richard R. Forest, Samuel Foster, Henry Foster, Charles Grier, David Guinea, I. J. Guinea, John H. Gregg, Wm. P. Hart, Joseph Henderson, Joseph Holmes, Samuel Hazlett, Jr., George S. Hart, Samuel Hutson, Joseph Jones, J. E. Lucas, John Linn, John Lowe, Wm. J. Mathews, Jacob Metzler, Thomas McKennan, Thomas McKean, George Mitchell, John McElroy, J. A. Marchand, Wm. Post, Collin M. Reed, Thomas Stewart, Samuel Shealer, Rev. Jacob Schaffer, Rev. John W. Scott, Sample Sweeney John Sweeney, James E. Smiley, Scheffer Thompson, John Wilson, Edward Wilkins, William Wylie, Wright Tappan Wylie, John A. Wills, John P. Westley, J. S. Young.

Commissioned Officers, 3; Non-Commissioned Officers, 13; Musician, 1; Privates, 52; total, 69.

Capt. Armstrong being re-elected Colonel, John H. Ewing was elected Captain.

HISTORY OF WASHINGTON COUNTY. 335

1ST BATTALION, 100 DAYS' ARTILLERY, PENNSYLVANIA VOLUNTEERS,

Under command of Major Joseph M. Knapp, organized June, 1864, and mustered out the following September.

David Watson, Lieutenant.
R. T. Hall, Joseph McK. Acheson, Sandy Clark, James Martin, William McMeillin, John Monniger, Privates.

9TH RESERVE, CO. A.

C. F. Jackson, Colonel.
W. K. Bailey, M. R. Taggart, M. P. Morrison (Serg.-Maj.) w.

6TH HEAVY ARTILLERY, 212th REGIMENT, Co. E.

J. W. Downer, 2d Jun. Lieut., William Woodward, O. S., Abraham Van-Voorhis, 1st Sergeant.
PRIVATES.—G. L. Bayhe, James Behanna, Ebert Newbold, James Flannigan, D.; James Quigg, J. Rufner, John Ray.

PROVOST GUARD.

By general orders, No. 172, of the War Department, dated June 9, 1863, this State was divided into two military departments: 1st, the department of the Monongahela; and 2d, the department of the Susquehanna. In the department of the Monongahela, besides the 54th, 55th, 56th, 57th, and 58th Regiments of ninety days militia, there was one unattached company of artillery, and one of cavalry.

There was also organized, August 8, 1864, in this department, for the six months United States service, the Provost Guard, stationed at Pittsburg, under the command of the following officers: Capt. Samuel T. Griffith, 1st Lieut. Samuel M. Decker, 2d Lieut. William R. Jamison.

The following non-commissioned officers and privates were from Washington County.

NON-COMMISSIONED OFFICERS.—Benjamin K. Kennedy, Orderly Sergeant; Henry H. Arnold, 2d Sergeant; Thomas H. Stewart, 3d Sergeant; Samuel T. Decker, 4th Sergeant.
Corporals.—Hugh B. McKinley, Robert C. Shepler, Charles Boyd, Theodore M. Turner, Wm. T. Decker.
PRIVATES.—Wm. T. Creigh, Joseph Day, Theodore Eaches, John W. Frank, James S. Harter, Joseph A. Jones, Frank L. Oliver, Thaddeus Ryan, Samuel S. Stewart, J. Taylor Simpson, William Zelt.

The number of men on the company-roll, including non-commissioned officers, was 103; all except the above were from adjoining counties. The company was discharged on the expiration of term of enlistment, January 29, 1864.

Frank L. Oliver was discharged, by writ of habeas corpus, Aug. 10, 1863.

LIST OF OFFICERS FROM WASHINGTON COUNTY

Who have been connected with other regiments than those specified, with the rank of each :—

Wm. S. Mellinger, Major 13th Regiment, elected April 25, 1861. Mustered out August 6, 1861.
" " Major 79th Regiment, elected October 18, 1861. Resigned November 8, 1862.
A. G. Happer, 2d Lieutenant 11th Regiment, Company I, elected March 21, 1864. Honorably discharged October 20, 1865.
J. W. Alexander, Assistant Surgeon 26th Regiment, appointed January 16, 1862.
" " Surgeon 85th Regiment, appointed June 10, 1862. Mustered out October 13, 1862.
" " Surgeon 160th Regiment, appointed October 20, 1862. Mustered out June 21, 1865.
Thomas B. Reed, Surgeon 31st Regiment, appointed June 6, 1861. Transferred to U. S. volunteers April 20, 1862.
Rev. Wm. Aiken, Chaplain 37th Regiment, appointed June 24, 1861. Mustered out May 24, 1864.
Rev. Thomas Patterson, Chaplain, 22d Regiment, Company D, appointed February, 1864. Mustered out.
S. B. Bennington, Captain 37th Regiment, Company D, elected December 28, 1862. Resigned December 25, 1863.
Thomas McGee, 1st Lieutenant 37th Regiment, Company D, elected December 14, 1862. Mustered out May 24, 1864.
Solomon G. Krepps, 2d Lieutenant, 37th Regiment, Company D, elected October 1, 1861. Transferred to 4th U. S. Infantry May 1, 1862.
Frank J. Le Moyne, Assistant Surgeon 38th Regiment, appointed March 14, 1863.
" " Surgeon 161st Regiment, appointed January 9, 1864. Mustered out July 24, 1865.
Chill W. Hazard, 1st and 2d Lieutenant 41st Regiment, Company F, elected September 10, 1861. Transferred to Company I.
" " Captain 41st Regiment, Company I, elected August 1, 1862. Mustered out June 11, 1864; appointed brevet Major.
J. B. McDonough, Assistant Surgeon 46th Regiment, appointed January 21, 1863. Mustered out July 16, 1865.
S. J. McFarren, 1st Lieutenant 60th Regiment, Company I, elected February 14, 1865. Mustered out August 7, 1865.
Alvin King, 1st Lieutenant 62d Regiment, Company K, elected July 4, 1861. Honorably discharged March 19, 1863.
Josiah P. Morrell, 2d Lieutenant 62d Regiment, Company K, elected December 17, 1862. Killed at Gettysburg July 2, 1863.
Joshua C. Prall, 2d Lieutenant 64th Regiment, Company I, elected December 24, 1861. Resigned December 25, 1862.
Thomas H. Phillips, Assistant Surgeon 79th Regiment, appointed January 10, 1865. Mustered out July 12, 1865. Dr. P. served as Assistant Surgeon in the 196th Regiment, being appointed July 26, 1864, and mustered out November 17, 1864.

Jonathan Wotring, Assistant Surgeon 83d Regiment, appointed March 14, 1863. Resigned May 13, 1863.
T. C. M. Stockton, Assistant Surgeon 83d Regiment, appointed April 26, 1864. Mustered out June 28, 1865.
Rev. J. P. Caldwell, Chaplain 85th Regiment, appointed October 21, 1862. Resigned May 1, 1863.
S. J. Van Gilder, 2d Lieutenant 85th Regiment, Company H, elected September 23, 1861. Resigned July 31, 1862.
J. E. Michener, 1st Lieutenant 85th Regiment, Company D, elected July 6, 1862. Transferred to Company K.
" " Captain 85th Regiment, Company K, elected December 3, 1863. Term expired November 22, 1864.
Samuel L. McHenry, 1st Lieutenant 85th Regiment, Company K, elected July 21, 1862. Appointed Adjutant and Assistant Adjutant General of Brigade June 1, 1863.
Samuel S. Bulford, Lieutenant-Colonel 87th Regiment, elected June 15, 1865. Mustered out as Captain of Company H, June, 29, 1865. Colonel Bulford ranked as Captain of Company H from March 15, 1865.
Jesse C. Taylor, 1st Lieutenant 100th Regiment, Company M, elected August 26, 1861. Discharged March 8, 1862.
Robert F. Cooper, Adjutant 101st Regiment, appointed Adjutant October 15, 1861. Resigned June 21, 1862.
M. P. Morrison, Assistant Surgeon 102d Regiment, appointed August 6, 1861. Promoted to Surgeon September 15, 1862.
George S. Ringland, Captain 108th Regiment (11th Cavalry), Company A, elected October 1, 1862. Served as 1st Lieutenant from August 15, 1861. Mustered out at expiration of term October 4, 1864.
George W. Bassett, 1st Lieutenant 108th Regiment, Company A, October 1, 1862. 2d Lieutenant August 15, 1861.
Thomas Moreley, 1st Lieutenant 113th Regiment (12th Cavalry), Company G, July 22, 1863. 2d Lieutenant June 26, 1862. He was promoted to Captain of Company I, January 20, 1865, and honorably discharged April 8, 1865.
Robert J. Taggart, Major 116th Regiment, elected June 4, 1865, and mustered out as Captain of Company I July 14, 1865, having been elected Captain May 13, 1865, and 1st Lieutenant February 18, 1865.
Wm. P. McNary, Adjutant 123d Regiment, November 28, 1862. Mustered out with Regiment May 13, 1863.
" " Lieutenant-Colonel 58th Regiment, July 10, 1863. Mustered out August 15, 1863.
Rev. Thomas Storer, Chaplain 133d Regiment, August 20, 1862. Mustered out with regiment May 26, 1863.
Jas. R. Patten, Assistant Surgeon 139th Regiment, April 13, 1863. Mustered out with regiment June 21, 1865.
Selden L. Wilson, 2d Lieutenant 160th Regiment, May 29, 1865. Mustered out with regiment June 21, 1865.
James K. McCurdy, Assistant Surgeon 163d Regiment, December 29, 1864. Mustered out with regiment July 21, 1865.
Wm. A. Young, 1st Lieutenant 163d Regiment, Company F, October 3, 1864 (2d Lieutenant June 25, 1863). Mustered out October 31, 1865, as 2d Lieutenant of Company E, 3d Prov. Cavalry, October 31, 1865.

Vincent Colvin, 2d Lieutenant 163d Regiment, Company F, March 30, 1863. Died June 24, 1863.
John Murphy, Lieutenant-Colonel 168th Regiment, December 4, 1862. Mustered out July 25, 1863.
Alexander M. Rea, Assistant Surgeon 168th Regiment, May 14, 1863. Mustered out July 25, 1863.
Rev. John L. Staples, Chaplain 168th Regiment, March 12, 1863. Mustered out July 25, 1863.
R. P. Hughes, Lieutenant-Colonel 199th Regiment, November 28, 1864; appointed brevet Colonel April 2, 1865. Mustered out June 28, 1865.
James R. Clark, 2d Lieutenant 204th Regiment (5th artillery), September 16, 1864. Mustered out June 30, 1865.
A. R. Wyeth, Assistant-Surgeon 208th Regiment, September 12, 1864. Honorably discharged March 3, 1865.
J. L. Rea, Assistant Surgeon 212th Regiment (6th artillery), September 13, 1864. Mustered out June 13, 1865.
James L. Downer, 2d Lieutenant 212th Regiment, Company E, November 1, 1864. Mustered out June 13, 1865.
Fra. Eichelberger, 1st Lieutenant Battery C, Pennsylvania artillery, October 11, 1864. Resigned June 17, 1865. He had served as 2d Lieutenant from June 30, 1864, to his promotion as 1st Lieutenant.

Militia Mustered into State Service, 90 days.

H. J. Vankirk, Major 58th Regiment, July 10, 1863. Mustered out August 15, 1863.
Mat. Templeton, Captain,
Z. A. White, 1st Lieutenant, } 58th Regiment, Company B, July 10, 1860. Mustered out August 14, 1863.
Thomas Foster, 2d Lieutenant,
Wm. J. Carey, 2d Lieutenant 58th Regiment, Company D, July 4, 1863. Mustered out August 14, 1863.
S. S. Rogers, Surgeon 10th Regiment, September 16, 1862. Mustered out with regiment.
Wm. S. Calohan, Captain,
J. M. McWilliams, 1st Lieutenant, } 14th Regiment, Company E, Sept. 16, 1862. Discharged with company.
John W. Havelin, 2d Lieutenant,
John C. Brown, Major 18th Regiment, September 12, 1862. Discharged with regiment.
W. J. Alexander, Captain,
Irwin C. Stump, 1st Lieutenant, } 18th Regiment, Company G, Sept. 12, 1862. Discharged with company.
Wm. H. Wilson, 2d Lieutenant,
John Weaver, Captain,
Wm. Quail, 1st Lieutenant, } 18th Regiment Company H, September 17, 1862. Discharged with company.
Wm. McMillan, 2d Lieutenant,

We close this chapter of the military history of Washington County by stating that the legislature passed an act authorizing the commissioners of each county to assess a tax for the relief of those families who volunteered in the service of their country. Accordingly, on May 20, 1861, Messrs. Cook, Taylor, and Elliott, the commissioners, assessed one mill on the dollar, which was directed to be added to the duplicates in the hands of the treasurer

On the subsequent day the commissioners and associate judges, Jacob Slagle and James G. Hart, Esqs., met as a Board of Relief and appointed Job Johnston, of California, T. R. Hazzard, of Monongahela City, Wm. McDaniel, of Canonsburg, Andrew S. Ritchie, of West Middletown, and Andrew Brady, of Washington, to ascertain the families of such persons as are entitled to relief, and report the circumstances of each, to enable the Board to give the necessary relief."

On June 3, 1861, disbursing agents were appointed to carry out the provisions of the law in the several localities where there are persons needing relief. The Board adopted, as a general rule, to give two dollars per week to the wife and fifty cents per week for each child, to be computed from the time the soldier entered the service.

September 25th the Board reduced the appropriation to ten dollars per month, as the maximum for each family, and allowed discrimination below that according to circumstances.

October 14th the appropriation was reduced to eight dollars per month, except in extreme cases.

Thus the Board of Relief acted promptly and energetically in the discharge of their duties, to the satisfaction of the citizens of the county and the soldier and his family.

THE SOLDIER'S MONUMENT.

The undersigned have been appointed a committee to decide upon a plan for carrying out the purpose of the contributors. This enterprise has been delayed for the want of adequate funds. The money heretofore collected was invested securely, and the accumulated fund, together with uncollected subscriptions deemed good, now amount to from five to six thousand dollars. In fulfilment of the wishes of the contributors it is now proposed to go forward and expend the money to the best advantage. The committee have two designs before them for their consideration.

First: A *Marble Monument* of as large dimensions as the sum will warrant. It was originally proposed to inscribe on this monument the name of every soldier of Washington County who had died in the service from disease or wounds during the war. On account of the large number (over eight hundred) this may be impracticable, but some other method in connection with the monument, like that hereafter suggested, might be resorted to for perpetuating their memory.

Second: A *Memorial Chapel,* built out of our common red sandstone, of sufficient dimensions to allow the insertion of marble tablets in the wall, and between the openings, on which the soldiers' names from each township and borough would be inscribed, together with any private memorial which the friends of any particular soldier might desire to place on the walls, busts of distinguished military characters, and relics and trophies of the war. This design contemplates an indestructible book containing a brief historical account of each soldier, to be kept within the chapel, open to the inspection of visitors.

These are the two plans under consideration. To accomplish either of them satisfactorily, and in such manner as to do credit to Washington County, would require larger means than we have at command.

The Washington Cemetery is to be the location. Its central position, easiness of access and marvellous development rendering it the largest, as it is certainly the most attractive and beautiful burial place in the county, point it out as the most suitable site for the monument or memorial chapel.

The committee desire to obtain the following information at as early a day as possible:—

1. The name, company, and regiment of each soldier who volunteered, enlisted as a substitute, or was drafted into the service of the United States during the late war, and who afterwards died in the service, or after his discharge, from wounds received, or disease contracted whilst in the service, accompanied with a statement of his birth, age, and place of residence when he entered the service.

2. The cause of death, and if from wounds, the place or engagement where received.

3. The exact date of death, giving the day of the month and year.

4. The place of death.

It is proper to say that as there is a call for the completion of the undertaking, all that the committee can do is to adopt some plan within the compass of the means furnished. Beyond that they cannot go, and the inadequacy of the fund is the great source of perplexity and embarrassment. If the soldiers' memorial should not suit the public expectation, while it would be a source of regret to the committee, they would feel that they had performed their duty. But before final action is taken, we would solicit immediate voluntary and individual subscription, by direct communication with the committee, from every citizen who feels an interest in the enterprise, and desires the soldiers' monument to be worthy of the patriotic dead who in the late war so nobly represented Washington County.

A. W. ACHESON,
BOYD CRUMRINE,
THOS. MCKENNAN,
Committee.

CHAPTER VIII.

HISTORY OF ASSOCIATIONS, AND EVENTS WHICH TRANSPIRED IN WASHINGTON COUNTY.

FREE MASONRY.

LODGE 54.

THE oldest organization outside of the church, of which we have any knowledge, is the Masonic Order.

Although Bassetville, or, subsequently, Washington, was laid out in 1781, yet nine years afterwards we find its prominent citizens taking the necessary steps to organize a Masonic lodge. Six of the original settlers of the town made the necessary application to the R. W. Grand Lodge, and a charter was granted to Brother Jas. Chambers as Worshipful Master, Brother Absalom Baird as Senior Warden, Brother Cyrus Beckwith as Junior Warden, Brother Alex. Roney as Treasurer, Brother James Whiteside as Secretary, and Brother James Farchar as Tyler. The lodge was constituted by Brother Matthew Ritchie, D. D. G. M., June 25, 1792, and was numbered 54. It continued in existence until 1812, when the labors of masonry were temporarily interrupted by the representatives of the people declaring war against Great Britain.

From its organization until 1802, it met in several places, but afterwards in their own hall, which stood in the rear of the lot now occupied by Brother John Grayson.

During the term of its existence eight brethren presided as Worshipful Masters, viz: John Chambers, Dr. Absalom Baird, John Hoge, George H. Keppelle, David Cooke, Samuel Clark, John Wilson, and Alexander Reed.

It is worthy of remark that the written records of this lodge, under date of January 6, 1800, show the fact that the members were required to wear a scarf on their left arm, and a black rose on their apron for one year as a memorial of the death of their brother Gen. George Washington.

WASHINGTON LODGE, 164.

This lodge was chartered upon the petition of the members of No. 54, which had been in abeyance since the war. It was constituted March 1, 1819, by Hon. John H. Walker, D. D. G. M., and met in the hall of No. 54 until 1825, when it erected a hall on Maiden St. (second house west of the Round Corner). This lodge continued in successful operation until 1832, when it suspended labor until the officers should again summon the craftsmen to work. They suspended their labor on account of the wicked and persecuting spirit of anti-Masonry, which blighted church and State, and even separated families. So full of evil was this destroying spirit that good men shuddered at its wicked and iniquitous demands. But the fury of the storm soon passed over; ten years of anti-Masonic darkness, from the year 1826 to 1836, was sufficient to convince the people of its malignant designs, and the persecutors of the order were universally consigned to the tomb of oblivion.

On the 14th of April, 1845, the W. M. Brother George Baird summoned the craft to labor, and during the thirteen years of its suspension; death had not robbed the Masonic Temple of either officers or members, but all were present and participated in erecting an altar to God, and placing thereon its first great light. Since 1845, the progress of this lodge has been *onward*, her membership discharging their entire duty, beloved and respected both as citizens and as Masons.

From its organization to the present time the following persons have filled the office of Worshipful Masters, viz : George Jackson, Thomas H. Baird, George Baird, Alfred Creigh, William Wolf, William Smith, H. H. Frisbie, William Boardman, W. Hart, Alexander Wishart, James C. Acheson, James M. Byers, James M. House, David Aiken, and Frederick Whittlesey, its present Worshipful Master.

HIRAM LODGE, No. 170,

Was instituted at Monongahela City, December 6, 1819, and continued in existence until 1827. Its only Worshipful Master was Dr. Pollock.

HILLSBORO UNION LODGE, No. 209,

Was chartered April 17, 1827, and located at Hillsboro, but its charter was vacated March 16, 1837. Its Past Masters were Brother John M. Davis, Hugh Keys, and George Morrison.

CHANDLER LODGE, No. 237,

Was located in Washington, and chartered March 5, 1849. It was subsequently removed to *Beallsville* in this county.

Its Past Masters are Brother James T. Dagg, James B. Ruple, J. B. Musser, Samuel Thompson, George Passmore, J. McDonough, Isaac Register, J. Madison Miller, John Ewart, and Ahira Jones, its present Master.

CHARTIERS LODGE, No. 297,

Was chartered May 15, 1856, and constituted in Canonsburg. The following brethren have filled the office of Worshipful Master, viz :

John J. Shutterly, John Murphy, Jr., John Brown, William Hornish, J. B. Musser, Henry Sheaff, Adam Harbison, Jr., and Dr. J. W. Alexander, its present Master.

H. M. PHILLIPS LODGE, 337,

Was chartered March 5, 1860, and located in Monongahela City. The following brethren have filled the office of Worshipful Master, viz: John Witherow, W. L. S. Wilson, S. Bentley, Jr., Joel Grable, R. S. H. Keys, D. K. Stevenson, Edward Creighton, and John Holland.

TENMILE LODGE, 356,

Is situated in Tenmile village, and was chartered March 1, 1865. Its Worshipful Masters are Dr. J. C. Milliken, William H. Horn, Washington L. Dunn, and Jacob L. Bricker.

CLAYSVILLE LODGE, 447,

Was chartered by the R. W. Grand Lodge, September 1869, and located in Claysville. Its Worshipful Master is Isaac Teal, and was constituted October 4, 1869.

RICHARD VAUX LODGE, 454,

Is located in Burgettstown, and received a charter from the R. W. Grand Lodge, December 5, 1869, and was constitued January 21, 1870. Its Worshipful Master is George T. McCord.

MONONGAHELA VALLEY LODGE, 461,

Was chartered by the Grand Lodge of Pennsylvania, March 2, 1870, and constituted at Greenfield, April 17, 1870. Its Worshipful Master is N. S. Veatch.

ROYAL ARCH MASONRY.

WASHINGTON CHAPTER 150.

In addition to these lodges, Washington Chapter claims an existence under her present charter since February 4, 1828, although the Royal Arch Degree was conferred under the charter of Lodge 164, as early as 1821. The companions who have been honored with the office of High Priest, were David Acheson, George Baird, John Best, Alfred Creigh, William Broadman, H. H. Frisbie, William Wolf, William Smith, J. B. Musser, William Hart, James M. Byers, Alexander Wishart, James C. Acheson, and James M. House.

CRYPTIC MASONRY.

WASHINGTON COUNCIL, No. 1,

Of Royal Super-Excellent and Select Masters was instituted by the R. P. Grand Council, November 16, 1847. The following illustrious companions have presided as Thrice Illustrious Grand Masters, viz: Alfred Creigh, Andrew Hopkins, William Wolf, William Broadman, J. B. Musser, H. H. Frisbie, William Hart, Alexander Wishart, J. C. Acheson, J. M. Byers, and J. M. House.

CHIVALRIC ORDER OF MASONRY.

JACQUES DE MOLAY COMMANDERY, No. 3.

The Masonic fraternity of Washington County, desirous of having within her border all the various grades of Masonry, made application for a dispensation to open a Commandery. This was granted by Sir W. B. Hubbard, G. G. M. of Grand Encampment of the United States, September 12, 1849. Numerically it was numbered TWO, but after the union with the Grand Encampment of Philadelphia, it became No. 3.

The following Sir Knights have filled the office of Eminent Commander, viz: Alfred Creigh, J. B. Musser, William Wolf, Alexander Wishart, James M. Byers, John Hall, Boyd Crumrine, and John C. McCoy.

ODD FELLOWSHIP.

Washington County has nine lodges of this benevolent society within her limits. We give the location of each and the names of the Past Grands, those who have honorably filled the chair to the satisfaction of the brethren, and for their efficient services are esteemed by the craft. Bro. G. L. Bayhe, of Lodge 377, was appointed D. D. G. Master, May, 1869, and from his zeal in the cause and devotion to the principles of Odd Fellowship, ranks among the first District Deputy Grand Masters in the State.

NATIONAL LODGE, No. 81,

Was established in Washington, February 13, 1843, by Joseph Browne, Grand Master of the Grand Lodge of I. O. O. F. The lodge held its first meetings two lots south of the corner of Main and Maiden streets. In three years it was removed to the "Round Corner." Subsequently to Beau Street, on the property of William Smith, and in 1870 it has secured a permanent hall in J. S. Young's extensive buildings adjoining the public square.

The following brethren from its organization have filled the office of Noble Grand, and are now ranked as Past Grands. The list is made out as they each presided.

1. Geo. Morrison; 2. James W. Smith; 3. Wm. K. Shannon; 4. Thos. S. McKinley; 5. Thos. Logan; 6. Jas. M. Hutchinson; 7. Alfred Creigh; 8. Jas. McKinley; 9. Wm. Wolf; 10. Philip Kuhn; 11. David Orr; 12. Jonathan D. Leet; 13. John Davis; 14. Wm. J. Wilson; 15. Hugh H. Reynolds; 16. Wm. Harter; 17. Thomas Walker; 18. Peter Griffin; 19. O. B. McFadden; 20. Alfred McGowen; 21. Morgan Hays; 22. John Thompson; 23. Thos. M. Hall; 24. John Allen; 25. James F. Sarrat; 26. John Wilson; 27. Marshal H. Hays; 28. Saml. M. Decker; 29. Wm. R. Terry; 30. C. Z. Koechline; 31. Mathew Griffin; 32. George T. Hammond; 33. Freeman Brady, Jr.; 34. H. B. McCollum; 35. Frank Fitzwilliams; 36. David Aiken; 37. John Brady; 38. Jos. M. Spriggs; 39. Chas. Post; 40. Thos. L. Birch; 41. Jacob Goldsmith; 42. J. Nick Hainer; 43. George W. Driver; 44. Thomas D. Ohara; 45. Robert McElheny; 46. Wm. Allen; 47. Henry Schoenthal; 48. John Low; 49. Chas. H. Ruple.

PETERS' CREEK LODGE, 248,

Was instituted at Findleyville, May 17, 1847. The following brethren have presided as N. G. since its organization:—

William Gaston, W. B. Lank, Wm. Gist, Isaac Lytle, James Angus, James Morrison, Joseph M. Curry, Samuel Atcheson, R. R. Bell, James McAlister, W. M. Mouck, John Huston, William Feree, Michael Sanders. Joseph Conlin, John Barclay, Frederick Snell, A. P. Heath, Isaiah Brown, John Stoeful, Thos. Snee, A. V. Crouch, Josiah Estep, Abel Buckingham, Louis Welch, Geo. W. Lyons, E. N. Wright, Samuel P. Hutchinson, R. Campbell, Robert Cowen, Samuel Messner, Geo. Gibson, Frank R. Storer, J. M. Snee.

NUCLEUS LODGE, 377,

Was organized at Monongahela City on the 14th day of September, 1849. The following is a list of its Past Grands.

Robert Coulter, Raphael Coulter, J. W. Carmac, Peter S. Griffin, C. Beach, A. T. Gregg, Shed. Hiser, T. R. Hazzard, W. S. Mellinger, D. J. Hamilton, Munson Clark, R. H. Young, J. W. Downer, F. M. Myers, Isaac Lowman, R. M. Gee, John Gilfillan, M. G. Gibson, Mark Boreland, David Lackey, Michael Bowman, George Callohan, J. B. Williams, Thos. Wilson, G. M. Groves, G. W. Frana, Thomas Coatsworth, J. L. Gee, Joseph Coatsworth, M. Sanders, G. L. Bayne, and H. C. Underwood.

The Odd Fellows have a convenient and elegant hall under the control of *Nucleus Association*, worth seventeen thousand dollars, situate on Main Street. It has all the necessary rooms handsomely furnished, also a room for public meetings, while the Odd Fellows' Mutual Co-operative Association has a large and extensive store on the first floor. The trustees of the Nucleus Association are, J. S. Crall, President; T. R. Hazzard, Secretary; R. M. Gee, J. B. Finley, A. C. Sampson, and A. T. Gregg, trustees.

The *Odd Fellows' Mutual Co-operative Association* has a capital of forty thousand dollars, and was organized April 6, 1867. Its trustees are J. L. Gee, President; R. M. Gee, J. B. Finley, Jas.

Louted, H. A. Warran, J. W. Downer. Clerks in the store—T. Wilson and L. Shreckongost.

REBECCA DEGREE.

Nucleus Lodge has attached Priscilla Lodge for the benefit of females whose fathers, husbands, and brothers belong to the lodge. Bro. A. T. Gregg is the presiding officer, and Mrs. J. S. Crall is secretary. It was organized March 21, 1870.

PIKE RUN LODGE, No. 491,

Is located in California, Washington County. Its Past Grands are

John S. Van Horn, James S. Lewellen, Jacob G. Huggins, G. Dowler, Jacob Hornbake, Samuel Lewis, John Clendaniel, Joseph S. Wilkins, John W. Paxton, D. H. Jacobs, James L. Long, James Herron, G. G. Hertzog, and James M. Berkinsha.

TENMILE LODGE, No. 552,

Was chartered May 19, 1859, and is located at Amity. Its Past Grands are

H. C. Swartz, S. M. Walton, James A. Bebout, Dr. W. W. Sharp, M. McCollum, A. J. McCollum, J. D. Huston, John McAfee, J. W. Denman, J. B. Vandyke, Isaac Sharp, Wm. Kelly, F. F. Ijams, W. C. Condit, J. B. McAfee, A. J. Swartz.

CEDAR LODGE, No. 633,

Was chartered August 1, 1868, and is located in Centreville, East Bethlehem township. Its Past Grands are

W. N. Hoskinson, E. S. Yeho, and E. H. Griffith.

LONE PINE LODGE, No. 693,

Is located at Pin Hook, and was organized March 26, 1870, by D. D. G. M., G. L. Bayhe. Its Past Grands are

J. D. Houston and John Closser.

VESTA LODGE, No. 696,

Was established at Greenfield, March 3, 1870, by Geo. L. Bayhe. Its Past Grand is Thomas Young.

JOHN F. LOGAN LODGE, No. 697,

Was instituted at Coal Bluffs, by G. L. Bayhe, D. D. G. M., January 28, 1870. Its Past Grands are

Wm. Wilson, H. McKinney, R. McMasters, J. Barclay, A. Fuller, S. Messner, and James Craig.

ENCAMPMENTS OF I. O. O. F.

SHAKSPEARE ENCAMPMENT, No. 20,

Was chartered November 4, 1845. Its founders were James B. Ruple, William Smith, William Garrity, Thomas S. McKinley, S. B. Hayes, and William Gaston. It is located in Washington, Pa.

The following persons have presided as Chief Patriarchs in the order given :—

1. James B. Ruple; 2. James M. Hutchison; 3. John T. Port; 4. John Davis; 5. William Wolf; 6. Thomas Logan; 7. Peter Griffin; 8. William Harter; 9. Thomas Walker; 10. William J. Wilson; 11. Wm. Hamilton; 12. Morgan Hayes; 13. James F. Sarratt; 14. Jacob Goldsmith; 15. Michael G. Kuntz; 16. George F. Hammond.

On February 24, 1863, it suspended meetings on account of the rebellion, but was revived February 25, 1870, its presiding officer, #17th, is Marshal H. Hayes.

PARKINSON'S FERRY ENCAMPMENT, No. 175.

Was instituted March 6, 1869, in Monongahela City. Its Past Chief Patriarchs are

R. M. Gee, T. R. Hazzard, and J. L. Gee.

EVENTS AND INCIDENTS.

We shall advert to a few events and incidents which will interest the reader.

1782. March 27. Jacob Cook, Jr., bequeathed to the trustees of the Presbyterian congregation of the middle fork of Tenmile Creek, fifty pounds for the use and benefit of the congregation.

WOOD RANGERS.

1788. April 16. The court ordered that William Campbell, Andrew McFarlane, Isaac Leet, Henry Dickson, and Henry Van Metre be licensed wood rangers for Washington County, and established the following fees: For entering each horse in the township book, 2s. 6d.; advertising in three public places, 5s.; for each search if found 1s. 6d.; if not found 9d.; for an order to the owner to take his horse out of the custody of him who has him in keeping, 1s. For casual and necessary expenses a reasonable allowance was made.

U. S. SENATOR.

James Ross, of Washington, elected United States Senator.

LOCUSTS.

1795. The summer of this year was remarkable for swarms of locusts which came up out of the earth until it was fairly covered. They remained about six weeks. Locusts have also made their appearance in 1812, 1829, 1846, and 1863.

THEATRICAL.

1796. February 9. A tragedy called *The Revenge* was performed at the hotel of Mr. Fisher (in the house formerly occupied by James Ross, Esq.,) composed of a company of young gentlemen of Washington. The proceeds were devoted to benevolent purposes. These exhibitions were continued to 1810.

ROYAL FAMILY.

1797. June 20. The three sons of the late Duke of Orleans passed through Washington Borough on their way to Philadelphia, having explored a great part of the western country.

TAVERN SIGNS.

In early times tavern signs were more significant than at present. I shall enumerate some: The Harp and the Crown; The Swan; The Indian Queen; The Globe; The Green Tree; The Cross Keys; General Washington; General Wayne; The Buck. But the most conspicuous and which attracted most attention was the picture of a colored boy standing in a tub of water and a white boy endeavoring to scrub him white with a brush. The motto above the painting was "Labor in vain."

FAIRS.

1798. Cattle fairs were held at Morganza in May and October of this year by Dennis Pursell. He advertised to supply a *cold cut* for 6d.; a warm meal at 1s. 10d.

MAY POLE.

1798. A May pole was put up in Washington upon which was placed the French flag. It was ordered to be cut down by the authorities of the town, as it excited in the minds of some fears that it might be metamorphosed into a liberty tree. The following lines written on the occasion explain themselves :—

>   1. The pole stood firm with flying flag,
>   And stripes sixteen in number,
>   Columbia's boast and all her brag
>   Red round with stripes of umber.
>
>   2. But Dignity, whose eyes were foggy,
>   Thought this the flag of France,
>   Around which those who were so groggy
>   Began to hop and dance.
>
>   3. Up thro' the town he bent his course
>   To hunt some honest soul,
>   Who would by smiles, if not by force,
>   Cut down the pretty pole.

Snow.

1799. In the winter of 1799 the greatest snow fell at one time ever known in this county. It commenced snowing on Friday evening and continued to snow until the next Monday morning. The snow was three feet deep. It was almost impossible for cattle and horses to go to their watering places. One woman in Finley township (her husband being absent) went to a neighbor's house for fire (for in those days there were no matches), and to return home she was required to borrow a horse. Deer and other wild animals died from starvation.

Phenomenon.

1801. January 12. On Wednesday evening last about eight o'clock, the atmosphere being cloudy and the night very dark, an extraordinary glare of light arose near the southern horizon and illuminated the whole atmosphere for about five seconds, and in about four minutes and a half was succeeded by an explosion similar to a discharge of a large cannon at a distance, which considerably shook the houses in Washington and kept the windows and door-latches in continual trepidation for the space of about twenty seconds

New County.

On the 14th of September, 1799, a number of the inhabitants of Washington and the adjoining counties met at Parkinson's Ferry (now Monongahela city), with the view of taking the necessary steps towards the formation of a new county, the principal portion of the territory to be taken off Washington County. Joseph Beckett was chosen Chairman and John Hoge, Secretary.

The following resolutions were unanimously adopted:—

1. That it is the opinion of this meeting that a *new county* ought to be established by the following lines, viz: Beginning on the Monongahela River, at the mouth of Peters' Creek, thence up the said creek to that branch thereof which runs from the Rev. David Phillips' farm, thence by a direct line to include the place on which James Mitchell, Esq., now lives, thence by a like line to include the place on which George Myers, Sen., now lives, thence to Bentley's upper mill on Pigeon Creek, thence to the Monongahela River opposite to the mouth of Little Redstone Creek, thence by a direct line to the mouth of Washington's Run on the Youghiogheny River, thence down the same to F. Moses' place, and thence by a direct line to the place of beginning.

2. That in the opinion of this meeting the seat of justice for the new county should be established at Parkinson's Ferry on the Monongahela River.

3. That John Hoge, Major Devore, and Captain Royall be appointed a committee to draft a petition to the next legislature praying for the establishment of a new county.

This measure was defeated by a remonstrance. The same question was successively renewed in 1820, 1822, and 1835, when it was proposed to make the county twenty miles square—1837 and in 1838—but the attempt to divide or diminish the present limits of Washington County meets with a prompt rejection by the people.

BURNERS.

About the year 1794, and immediately after the Whiskey Insurrection, Washington County was thrown into consternation by anonymous notices stuck up in the night time on the houses and highways, calling upon certain individuals to pay certain sums of money by a certain day or their houses and barns would be burned. Those who refused to satisfy the demand suffered the threatened penalty. Many meetings were held at Finleyville and other points, to detect the villains engaged in this nefarious plot, but these failed. At length Robert James took a determined stand, after having lost his barn, haystacks, outhouses, cattle, &c. &c., and prosecuted a man whom he suspected as the ring-leader. Before his apprehension he fled the country, and the burning operations ceased and peace and tranquillity reigned.

My friend, Dr. W. B. Lank, of Finleyville, has furnished me one of the original notices, given to him by Samuel Gaston, Esq., who lived in those troublesome times. The letter is directed to John Finley, Henry Hulee, James Cildoo, with this notice: *Jacobus Curkindale, if you don't carry this to John Finley your barn will be burnt.* The letter reads thus:—

John Finley, ...	30 dollars.
James Cildoo, ...	30 "
Henry Hulee, ...	30 "
	90 dollars.

My friend, if you don't pay this demand five days after sight, I will fall to burning your property, such as haystacks, barns, mills, and still-houses. If you pay this demand no more will be asked of you—fail not, for the sake of your property. The undertakers of this plot are sure but slow. You may pay it to Thomas McMuhn. Nothing will put a stop to this business but the detection of the authors.

In this manner farmers and others were blackmailed, and suffered severely if they did not comply with the notice.

NEWSPAPERS

Published in Washington County, with the date of their publication.

Western Telegraph and Washington Advertiser, August 22, 1795, by Messrs. Colerick, Hunter & Beaumont. On August 16, 1797, John Colerick sold out his interest to his partners.
Herald of Liberty, May 21, 1798, by John Israel.
Western Missionary Magazine, from 1803 to 1806.
Washington Reporter, August 15, 1808, by B. Brown and Wm. Sample.
" " February 12, 1810, by William Sample.
" " May 31, 1819, by Samuel Workman.

HISTORY OF WASHINGTON COUNTY. 351

Washington Reporter, May 28, 1821, by William Sample.
" " 1833, by B. S. Stewart and Geo. W. Acheson.
" " 1835, by John Ramsey and S. B. Robinson.
" " 1837, by Uriah W. Wise.
" " November 9, 1839, by John Bausman.
" " April 22, 1848, by John Bausman and J. W. F. White.
" " February 16, 1852, by John Bausman.
" " February 16, 1856, by Jas. G. and R. F. Strean.
" " *and Commonwealth*, April 1, 1858, by Jas. G. and R. F. Strean.
" " *and Tribune*, April 1, 1860, by Wm. S. Moore, H. A. Purviance, and Jas. Armstrong.
" " " " August 30, 1863, by Wm. S. Moore and Jas. Armstrong.
" " " " November 20, 1867, by Wm. S. Moore and J. W. McWilliams.
" " " " February 11, 1869, by Wm. S. Moore and Jas. W. Kelly.
Democratic Eagle, August 25, 1828, by Thomas Morgan.
Western Register, February 3, 1837, by Robert Fee.
Washington Examiner, May 28, 1817, by John Grayson.
" " 1833, by John Grayson and ―――― Jack.
" " John and T. W. Grayson.
" " June 10, 1840, by T. W. Grayson and C. C. Kaine.
" " November 9, 1844, T. W. Grayson and Jas. B. Ruple.
" " November 16, 1846, by T. W. Grayson and Andrew Hopkins.
" " May 12, 1853, by T. W. Grayson and George S. Hart.
" " 1858, by T. W. Grayson and A. H. Ecker.
" " A. H. Ecker and John R. Donehoo.
" " A. H. Ecker and D. F. Patterson.
" " *and Review*, A. H. Ecker and Wm. Swan.
The *Phœnix* in *Monongahela City*, May 7, 1821, by B. Brown.
The *Pennsylvanian*, " " June 25, 1828, by John Bausmon.
Our Country (Washington), June 5, 1835, by Thomas Jefferson Morgan.
Washington Review, by Wm. Swan.
The *Commonwealth*, 1848, by Seth T. Hurd.
The *Patriot*, 1843, by Russel Erret.
Students' Enterprise (Canonsburg), 1849, by Wm. S. Hamill.
The *Florence Enterprise*, 1850, by James Robb.
The *Collegian*, 1852, by B. W. Lacey.
American Union, 1855, by J. B. Musser.
Monongahela Valley Republican, July 7, 1848, established by Solomon Alter; in 1851 it was purchased by David Ramaley and P. H. Rhienhardt; in 1855 they sold to T. R. Hazzard and Chill Hazzard.
The *Tribune*, 1856, by John Bausman.
Valley Spirit (California), by G. W. Hillier.
Colleaguer, 1859, by J. W. Moss.

EDUCATION.

1795, September 8, Charles Visiner opened a school in Washington, to teach the French language, at $4 per quarter.

1809, February 16, Mrs. Good opened a school to teach young ladies tambouring, embroidery, open work, painting, and drawing, together with plain sewing and reading.

1812, November 12, Mrs. Baker's young ladies' seminary held its semi-annual exhibition at Washington. Premiums were presented in the first class to Miss Collins, of Pittsburg; Miss Clark, of Clarksville; Miss Buchanan, of Canonsburg; and Miss McKennan, of Washington. In the second class, to Miss Campbell, Miss Cooke, and Miss Neal, of Washington. In the third class, to Miss Cust, of Greensburg, and Miss Acheson, of Washington. Miss Scott, of Gettysburg, on presenting the premiums delivered an appropriate address, to which Miss Collins, of Pittsburg, replied. The exhibition concluded with a ballet dance, exhibiting in the rural style the young ladies, with branches of roses and honeysuckles in their hands during the dance.

1825, October 17, Rev. O. Jennings, assisted by Samuel Marshall, opened a French school.

1834, November 4, in pursuance of an act of the legislature, to establish the common school system, a joint meeting of the county commissioners, and one delegate from the twenty-three boards of directors, into which number the county was divided, met at the court-house, and determined by a vote of twenty-one to five to establish the system, and levied a tax of four thousand eight hundred dollars. In 1835 the common school convention appropriated six thousand dollars. In 1836, twelve thousand dollars. The first tax levied for the education of children in Washington County was in 1805; and in the years 1805–6–7–8 respectively it was one hundred dollars; in 1809, eight hundred dollars; 1810–11–12–13–14 it was two hundred dollars in each of these years; in 1815–16 it was three hundred dollars each; in 1817–18 it was five hundred dollars each; in 1819 it was one thousand dollars; in 1820, five hundred dollars; in 1821, one thousand dollars; in 1822–23–24–25 it was fifteen hundred dollars in each year; in 1826, twelve hundred dollars; in 1827, one thousand dollars; in 1828, twelve hundred dollars; in 1829, sixteen hundred dollars; in 1830–31, fifteen hundred dollars in each year; in 1832–33, twenty-five hundred dollars each. The amount of taxes paid from 1805 to 1836 inclusive, in Washington County, is fifty-one thousand three hundred and fifty dollars. Since 1836 the laws have been changed. In 1849 they were all collected and passed in one act, and in 1857 the normal school was adopted.

The first bill providing for a common school system was approved by George Wolf, April 1, 1834.

WASHINGTON MECHANICAL SOCIETY.

Was organized May 12, 1792, with Jonathan Morris as president, and David Reddick as secretary. The object was to create a fund, and loan money, not exceeding three months, for charitable, political, and generous purposes, at six per cent.

March 1, 1794, the society resolved to adopt measures to procure an accurate account of the various machines in use in this western country, the prices of labor in the different mechanical employments in use, the amount of moneys expended for public buildings, the obstruction in the navigation of our creeks and rivers, and the mode of transporting our produce to market, with all other information connected with mechanics which may be useful in forming the history of the early settlements of this county.

In 1795 the secretary was directed to open a correspondence with the Philadelphia Mechanical Society for the purpose of encouraging foreign mechanics to emigrate to this country.

Hon. David Reddick delivered the annual oration on St. Tammany's Day.

In 1798 a committee, consisting of Robert Hamilton, Samuel Clarke, and D. Cook, was appointed to report the best mode of procuring tin for a tin manufactory. The mode and manner were approved, and a quantity brought to Washington to be placed and made up.

In 1800 Parker Campbell delivered the annual oration.

These minutes close in 1801, and are very interesting. The names of the old citizens of this town show that they were members of this society.

MONONGAHELA AND WILLIAMSPORT MANUFACTURING COMPANY.

1814, January 17, articles of association for a bank, to be entitled the Monongahela and Williamsport Manufacturing Company, was formed in Williamsport (now Monongahela City) with a capital of one hundred and twenty-five thousand dollars, in shares of fifty dollars each; Samuel Black was president. Its charter was to extend for twenty years.

EXTENSIVE CARRIAGE MANUFACTORY.

In the fall of the year 1841 Sheldon B., Charles, and Morgan Hays erected a carriage manufactory in the rear of the court-house, and on the southern part of the lot now owned by Robert Boyd, Esq. The factory was of frame, thirty by fifty feet, two stories high. The business of the firm was conducted under the name of S. B. Hays & Co. The wood-work, trimming, painting, and smith-work were all conducted in this building, the demand for carriages and buggies not being so great as at present.

The first buggy body was made by Morgan Hays, the trimming and painting by Wm. Garrety (one of the founders of Lodge 81 of

I. O. O. F. of Washington), the smith-work by **J. Clark**, of Kinderhook, N. Y., and the first paint furnished by Dr. Alfred Creigh. The first apprentice was Henry Layton, whom we all remember for his steadfast devotion to his Sunday school and church, and which he ever exemplified through his Christian life.

Business increasing, a brick building was added, with horse-power attached to do the sawing and turning; yet increased business required a four-horse engine, and three days in each week of the engine however being sufficient to do the necessary amount of labor to occupy the hands one week. About this time Morgan Hays sold out to his partners, and he became the foreman. Messrs. S. B. & C. Hays added another story to the main building, and also an additional room of thirty feet to the first floor.

On November 8th, 1851, the entire factory, with nearly all its contents, was destroyed by fire, which occurred on Saturday. On the Monday following, Messrs. S. B. and C. Hays purchased from John H. Ewing, James G. Strean, Thomas McKean, T. M. T. McKennan, Alexander W. Acheson, and Collin M. Reed, Trustees of the Presbyterian church, their church edifice, with two lots situate on First and Maiden streets, and extending to Strawberry Alley, the congregation having removed to their new edifice, corner of Second and Belle streets. On the following Tuesday, the day after the purchase, the seats were taken out and all hands busily engaged in the manufactory, as if no fire had ever taken place.

To this brick carriage factory (formerly the church) they added a brick smithshop thirty by seventy feet. In 1852 they erected a machine shop with an engine of sufficient power for sawing, turning, making wheels, &c. &c. The machinery, shafting, &c., was put up by Martin Luther, Esq., of Worcester, Massachusetts, and, from his practical knowledge of machinery as well as of business, he has become a partner in the establishment.

To these improvements a planing machine, and all the necessary machinery for planing, manufacturing flooring boards, making doors, sash, shutters, &c., have been added, with a seventy-horse power engine, while to the buildings have been added a boarding-house, a carriage repository, with two rooms thirty by sixty feet each, used expressly for sales room.

January 1, 1867, the establishment was changed to S. B. and C. W. Hays & Co., consisting of Sheldon B. Hays, Charles W. Hays, Martin Luther, and Morgan Hays. Thirty-three hands are employed in the manufactory.

To this establishment has been added an extensive lumber yard.

House's Carriage Manufactory.

On the first of January, 1868, James M. House and Robert R. Forrest established a carriage factory on East Belle Street, the buildings being brick, two stories high fronting on Belle Street sixty by thirty feet. To this has been added another brick building of the same height, ninety by twenty-three feet, costing six thousand dollars. The annual sales amount to twelve thousand dollars. Fourteen hands are employed, but no engine is used.

On December 4, 1868, James M. House became sole proprietor, having purchased the interest of R. R. Forrest.

MANUFACTORIES.

1807. Several wool-carding establishments and other useful manufactories were established this year in this county. In 1808 David and Thomas Acheson, in their advertisement, said: "Conceiving it to be our duty to lend all our aid in order to promote the interest of this western country, and to encourage manufacturing, whereby we may become truly independent of foreign nations, assert that the western part of Pennsylvania, being well adapted for the raising of flax and the manufacturing of linen, propose to purchase any quantity of *flax and tow linen*, if wove forty-two inches wide, so as to measure forty and one-half inches when bleached, for which we will pay from four to six cents per yard extra above the common price."

1815, August 15. The wool growers of Washington County were invited to meet in Washington to consider the propriety of establishing a woollen manufactory to be erected by stock.

HOON & MCCLAIN'S WOOLLEN FACTORY.

In 1867 John Hoon established on the west end of Belle Street a woollen factory in a large two-story extensive brick building; but on April 16th, 1869, he received as a partner John McClain. The estimated value of the establishment is eight thousand dollars. A twenty-horse power engine is used. The establishment manufactures thirty thousand pounds of wool by spinning it into yarn, carding and weaving it. They manufacture two thousand five hundred yards of blankets and sixteen hundred yards of flannel annually, employing five hands.

CAMPBELL'S WOOLLEN FACTORY.

This is the oldest woollen factory in and about Washington, having been established by Philip Buckley as early as 1843, who carried it on very successfully to his death. In 1853 it passed into the hands of David Campbell, and since his death, who died in the Rebellion in defence of the Constitution of his adopted country, it is now carried on by his widow, Mrs. Amelia Campbell. It is situated on West Beau Street and West Alley, has all the necessary improvements, and a fifteen-horse power engine. It manufactures annually from fifteen to twenty thousand pounds of wool, and about twelve hundred yards of flannel and blankets. The whole property is estimated to be worth six thousand dollars.

Steam Tannery.

When the steam tannery, which is situated on the west end on Belle Street, was established, the partners were Thomas J. Hodgens, John M. Wilson, and John McElroy, but in 1862 Mr. Wilson sold out to Messrs. Hodgens and McElroy, since which time it has been under their control. The tannery is built of brick, two stories high, with a twelve-horse power engine. The estimated value of the establishment is ten thousand dollars.

They manufacture annually four thousand sides of leather, and fifteen hundred calf and kip skins, using three hundred cords of oak bark, and employing eight hands.

Steam Planing Factory.

In 1867 Thomas Walker and William Fitzwilliams purchased the lot of ground on West Belle Street, which formerly belonged to the United Presbyterian congregation, and upon which was erected a brick church, in which the congregation worshipped from 1834 until they removed to their present edifice. The church being torn down, Messrs. Walker and Fitzwilliams erected a two-story frame building fifty by twenty-six feet, two stories high, as a planing manufactory. It contains a thirty-horse power engine, employing from six to eight hands. The cost of machinery in the establishment was six thousand dollars. Being practical carpenters and builders (which business they carry on in connection with the factory), they manufacture for sale everything in connection with the finishing of buildings, such as flooring boards, doors, sash, shutters, brackets, &c.

Steam Grist and Flour Mill.

In 1844 Samuel Hazlett and Daniel Dye erected on the west end of Belle Street a four story mill, forty by sixty feet, the carpenter work being performed by Messrs. John Prigg and Daniel Dye. Afterwards Daniel Dye purchased the interest of Samuel Hazlett. After the death of Daniel Dye the mill was sold to John McElroy in 1850. About the year 1858 John McElroy sold to A. J. Caton. On February 15, 1865, Messrs. Wilson and George M. and W. W. Warrick became the purchasers. The estimated value of the property is seven thousand dollars; a thirty-horse power engine is used. The mill manufactures annually seven thousand five hundred barrels of flour; grinds five thousand bushels of corn and rye; has two pair of wheat burrs and one pair of choppers, and employs three hands.

The capacity of the mill on wheat is three barrels per hour; the cost of toll, three cents per barrel of flour.

INVENTIONS.

1812, December 14. Colonel John G. Chambers, of Amwell township has invented a gun which he can charge in such a manner that by a single operation on the trigger it will discharge six or eight loads in succession with space between each sufficient to take another aim. The gun has but one barrel, and does not exceed a common gun in size. On the 15th of January, 1815, the Senate of Pennsylvania appointed a committee to examine the utility of Colonel Chambers gun, and at three o'clock P. M., of January 22, 1815, an experiment was made of its utility on the State-house hill, in the presence of the legislature and other citizens. The gun was considered a very extraordinary piece of machinery, and a powerful instrument in the destruction of an enemy.

Freeman Brady, Jr., of Washington, and John Noble, of Claysville, patented a repeating or magazine gun. It fires about twenty effective and forty random shots in a minute, equalling in range and far excelling in faculty of loading and rapidity of firing any gun of modern improvement.

Dr. George W. Moffit has invented a self car coupler, intended to couple cars without any preliminary preparations, and with the common link and pin now in use. Both for coupling and uncoupling it is perfect, because by the very act of uncoupling itself it is prepared for coupling.

James S. Wolf, of Washington, has made an important discovery in charging bomb shells. Upon exploding it unites and burns a strong flame, setting fire to any combustible material; thus it will be seen it combines not only the terrible explosive power of a shell, but the firing power of a hot shot. It will light up any battery or fort into which it is thrown.

MEDICAL SOCIETY.

1813, June 10. The Washington County Medical Society was organized by adopting a Constitution and electing the following officers: Dr. Joseph Dodridge, President; Dr. D. G. Mitchell, Secretary. Its members were, Drs. John Wishart, John Warring, John Julius Le Moyne, Robert Glenn, Wm. Warnock, John Byers, Wm. Hamilton, Benjamin Carroll, James Mitchell, Wm. Quigley, H. H. Blachley, John Smith, M. L. Todd, Thomas McGarrough, James Hayden, James Patterson, David Staunton, John Baird, Alexander Crawford, Thomas Hersey, M. Adams, Shipley Homes, John Mulliken, Samuel Murdoch.

Dr. Joseph Dodridge delivered a eulogium upon the character of Dr. Benjamin Rush.

1835, November 26. Washington and Allegheny Counties established a Medical Society.

The *third* County Medical Society was organized April 2, 1855. Its officers were, Dr. John Wishart, President; Dr. James Stevens and Dr. Boyd Emery, Vice-Presidents; Dr. J. R. Wilson, Recording Secretary; Dr. I. S. Van Voorhis, Corresponding Secretary; and Dr. Wray Grayson, Treasurer.

Its present officers are, Dr. S. L. Blachley, President; Dr. J. H. Little, Vice President; Dr. G. A. Dougherty, Secretary; Dr. M. H. Clark, Treasurer. The following are the list of members scattered throughout Washington County: J. W. Alexander, J. W. Acheson, D. Anderson, S. L. Blachley, E. Carey, H. S. Chalfant, M. H. Clark, J. G. Dickson, Thaddeus Dodd, G. A. Dougherty, E. F. Dodd, D. S. Eagleson, Boyd Emery, H. D. Enoch, W. Gillfillen, S. E. Hill, W. King, J. H. Little, George A. Linn, I. McDonough, A. S. McElree, Thomas McKennan, W. Mitchell, M. P. Morrison, T. H. Phillips, W. W. Sharp, T. R. Storer, S. S. Strous, W. R. Thompson, J. R. Wilson, A. M. Rea, David Shaner.

Washington Library Association

Was organized December 22, 1867. It has one thousand volumes and one hundred and eighty-six subscribers, who each pay three dollars per annum for the use of the books. Rev. Dr. W. A. Davidson is President; **Rev.** Henry Wood, Secretary; Miss Martha Grayson, Librarian.

Benevolent Society.

1814, February 14. The citizens of Washington formed a humane and benevolent society to see that the poor laws were promptly administered by the Overseers of the Poor, and also to establish a *Sunday-school* for the education of indigent children, to discourage the use of spirituous liquors, and the suppression of vice and immorality.

Rev. Dr. M. Brown, Obadiah Jennings, Esq., and Dr. John Wishart reported a constitution for its government.

Bible Society.

1814, September 2. The Washington Bible Society was formed to supply the destitute with a copy of the Holy Scriptures. This society was organized in the Presbyterian Church, and was governed by the following persons as its officers: Rev. John Anderson, President; Rev. M. Brown, Secretary; Gen. Thomas Acheson, Treasurer; Parker Campbell, Alexander Murdock, Geo. Baird, Thomas Officer, Rev. Joseph Stephenson, Rev. Andrew Gwin, Rev. Cephas Dodd, Rev. Henry Kurtz, Obadiah Jennings, Thomas Hoge, Alex. Reed, Rev. James Brice, and John Carmichael were Directors.

June 1, 1815, Rev. John Anderson preached the first annual sermon.

From its formation to January 16, 1817, the Society had expended $859.54, in the purchase of Bibles. In one township fifty-nine families were found destitute of the word of life. The Rev. Joseph Stephenson was appointed the agent of the Society.

MORAL SOCIETY.

1815, April 4. The Washington Moral Society was established to discountenance and suppress those vices and immoralities which are cognizable by the laws of the commonwealth. Each member was required to report to the proper officer any person guilty of profane swearing, Sabbath-breaking, intoxication, unlawful gaming, keeping a disorderly public house or any other immoral act.

Alexander Reed was President, Thomas H. Baird, Secretary; John Neal, Treasurer, and Obadiah Jennings, Councillor.

The Rev. Thomas Hoge delivered an address on the objects of the Society at its organization. The dockets of the justices of the peace at the time, abundantly show its good effects by the prosecution and fining of offenders.

1816, June 24. The moral societies of the various townships met in Washington and consolidated into a general one for the county.

1815, November 24. Washington Female Mite Society organized in the court-house.

LIBRARY COMPANY.

February 19, 1816. The Washington Library Company was established. It was held by stockholders, yet the public had access to the books by paying a small pecuniary recompense. Matthew Sample was appointed librarian.

October 5, 1818. Washington Museum opened.

October 26, 1821. Washington County Agricultural Society organized.

January 15, 1829. The Mingo Creek Literary Society was established with a library attached. Samuel Morrison, President; Jas. Love, Secretary, and Edward Webb, David Barr, and David Moore were elected trustees.

STEAM MILL.

1814, January 17. David Shields, secretary of the Washington Steam Mill and Manufacturing Company, issued proposals for the erection of a mill house 47 by 50 feet, four stories high. He also notified stockholders to pay their instalments monthly, commencing on February 1st. This company was incorporated January 31, 1814.

COLD DAY.

January 19, 1810, was the coldest day in the recollection of the oldest inhabitant. Many cattle were frozen to death.

TEMPERANCE SOCIETY.

1835, September 28. Washington County Temperance Society organized, and the county divided into districts in which addresses should be delivered. Alexander Read, president; Samuel McFarland, secretary.

1836, May 20. Independent Blues organized as an infantry company.

1836, May 23. Washington Rifle Company.

GENERAL JACKSON.

1836, September 24. A public meeting held to make arrangements to receive Gen. Andrew Jackson. He was received with appropriate honors, March 14, 1837.

COMMODORE ELLIOTT.

1838, October 23. The trustees of Washington College returned thanks to Commodore Elliott for a choice selection of ancient coins collected in Greece, Italy, and Palestine.

HON. ISAAC LEET.

1840, May 6. Introduced resolutions in the Senate on the improvement of the Monongahela River, which bounds Washington County on the east, near forty miles.

POST OFFICES IN WASHINGTON COUNTY IN 1870, WITH THE NAMES OF POSTMASTERS.

Amity, Mrs. E. J. Bebout.
Atchison, Miss S. A. Johnson.
Bavington, James McBride.
Beallsville, Arthur Oddbert.
Beck's Mill, Harvey Lyon.
Bellzane, John Fields.
Bentleysville, O. T. McElheny.
Bower Hill, John Bower.
Brush Run, Samuel Merchant.
Buffalo, John H. Smith.
Burgettstown, Samuel Wilson.
Bulger, James Bussell.
California, David H. Lancaster.
Candor, H. J. Cook.
Canonsburg (money order), Mrs. Elizabeth A. McGinnis.
Cardville, Mr. Galbreath.
Cherry Valley, Ebenezer Smith.
Claysville, W. H. Adams.
Clokeysville, Samuel Clokey.
Coal Bluffs, James K. Logan.
Commettsburg, Wm. Gilliland.
Coon Island, George Chaney.
Cross Creek Village, A. McFarland.
Dinsmore, John M. Smith.
Donley, Samuel Snodgrass.
Dunningsville, John T. Sumney.
Dunsport,
East Bethlehen, Emmor H. Griffith.
East Finley, John S. Knox.
Eldersville, Robert C. Osburn.
Finleyville, Frank R. Storer.
Florence, Samuel Livingston.
Fredericktown, S. G. Hill.
Ginger Hill, Andrew Clark.
Good Intent, Isaac S. Blair.
Hanlin Station, Charles Hanlin.
Havelock, James Euwer.
Herriottsville, James P. Young.
Hickory, J. M. Campbell.
Independence, J. K. McConaughy.
Kerr's Station, Wm. Kerr.
Lindley's Mill, S. McVey.
Lock No. 4, John Lomas.
Locust Hill, Wm. A. Hill
Long Pine, J. Huston.
Meloy, Miss Catharine McWreath.
Midway, John Kennedy.
Millsboro, Jesse Phillips.
Monongahela City (money order), C. Hazzard.
Mount Airy, Thos. Richardson.
Muntown, Joseph Barkley.
Murdocksville, Joseph McClaren.

HISTORY OF WASHINGTON COUNTY. 361

Paris, Martha Bedoute.
Patterson's Mill, J. J. Elliott.
Pike Run, John Barker.
Prosperity, Arvida Day.
Raccoon, C. H. Bolek.
Scenery Hill, Rachel Standley.
Simpson's Store, John Fitzpatrick.
Sparta, Milton Andrew.
Strabane, N. Buchanan.
Taylorstown, Oliver M. Wallace.
Tenmile, Joseph W. Little.
Thompsonville, A. Wilson Pollock.
Van Buren, Stephen Pipes.
Vanceville, L. Vaneman.
Venice, Joseph L. Scott.
Washington (money order), Wm. C. Wiley.
West Alexander, Miss E. A. Ray.
West Brownsville, John W. Ward.
West Finley, Saml. Grum.
West Middleton, G. McFadden.
Woodrow, John Morgan.
Yortysville, Mrs. J. Yorty.
Zollarsville, Ed. R. Smith.

1833, April 8. The theological seminary of the Associate Presbyterian Church at Canonsburg was incorporated; and on April 13, 1853, an act was passed to give it perpetual succession. It was afterwards removed to Xenia, Ohio.

1854, April 29. Canonsburg Saving Fund was incorporated.

AGRICULTURAL SOCIETIES.

In 1869 there were four agricultural societies, viz:—
1. Washington Agricultural Society, established in Washington. James F. Gabby, president.
2. Union Agricultural Association, at Burgettstown. John B. Hays, of Smith township, president.
3. Mt. Pleasant Equitable Agricultural Association, at Hickory. Organized in 1859.
4. Monongahela Valley Association.

FIRE DEPARTMENT.

The first authentic account of a fire company can be traced to May 18, 1801, when the Washington Fire Company was organized, which was placed during a fire under the control of four managers. These managers placed the engine under two directors and sixteen men, the ladder party, with one director and six men, the water company with two directors and the remaining members of the company. At that date we find the roll of members to consist of eighty-two members.

February 26, 1820, a fire company was organized and a new engine was purchased.

February 22, 1822, funds were appropriated to purchase another engine and make cisterns for water.

September 7, 1831, two hundred and fifty feet of hose ordered to be purchased, with suitable carriage for the same, and the engines to be kept in different parts of the borough.

February 11, 1837, the Hope and Good Intent fire companies were reorganized.

December 4, 1844, Good Intent Fire Company made application for the erection of an engine-house, and house erected on Pine

24

Alley (Mrs. Gregg's lot). December 12, 1845, a reel and hose carriage ordered for the same company.

July 5, 1847, Eagle Engine purchased for eight hundred dollars.

October 9, 1848, engine and council-house ordered to be erected.

September 17, 1859, the suction engine purchased.

SEMI-CENTENNIAL VOTERS.

At the October election in Washington, in 1869, the following eleven persons, who had voted in the year 1819, deposited their ballots for the fiftieth time, viz: Samuel Cunningham, John H. Ewing, John Grayson, John R. Griffith, John Harter, Joseph Henderson, Samuel Hornish, George Kuntz, Dr. F. J. Lemoyne, Jacob Slagle, and Simon Wolf. In 1819 there were three hundred and five voters, but in 1869 six hundred and ninety.

SLAVERY.

On this question we shall mention a few facts connected with the history of this county.

1781, April 30, the estate of Alexander McCandless sold a negro girl for sixty pounds.

1781, May 16, Jacob Johnston bequeaths unto his wife Mary Johnson, a negro woman slave named Suke; to his daughter Elizabeth Pierce, a negro girl named Zelph, and her future increase; to his daughter Eleanor Decker, the first child, male or female, of Suke; to his daughter Esther Johnson, at the death of her mother, the above-named slave Suke. Should the said Suke have no childen, one hundred pounds, in the hands of John Buchanan, is to be divided equally between his daughters; but if children are born to the slave Suke, the money is to be divided among his five children.

1795, June 3, Reason Pumphrey sells his slaves at the following prices: *Lot*, aged 18 years, for seventy pounds; Ben, aged 14 years, for one hundred pounds; Dinah, aged 10 years, for seventy-five pounds.

1795, March 20, John Moore manumitted two slaves named Abraham and Jonas.

In the *Reporter* of March 8, 1813, is the following advertisement: For sale, a negro boy who has thirteen years to serve; he is stout and healthy. Apply at the office of the *Reporter*.

1823, December 29, the first meeting of the citizens of Washington County was held to form a society for the abolition of slavery. The society organized January 26, 1824, at the court-house.

1834, July 4, Washington County Anti-slavery Society organized.

1835, October 2, the citizens of this county met to express their disapprobation of the cause of the abolitionists, and presided over by Judge Baird. Messrs. R. H. Lee, Rev. Thomas Hoge, Alexander Reed, W. K. McDonald, and Dr. John Wishart were appointed the committee to report resolutions. One of the resolutions states that any combination of citizens of one State organized for the purpose of disturbing the civil institutions of another State, is a violation of the spirit of the Union and of the enactments of the Federal Constitution, and must tend to dissolve the Union. This, with other resolutions of the same spirit, was unanimously adopted.

1836, June 23, a town meeting was held, presided over by John R. Griffith, Chief Burgess, to make arrangements to prevent abolitionists from holding meetings, as the citizens of this place deem it unwise and highly inexpedient for abolitionists to intrude upon the people of this county and borough the peculiar and offensive doctrines maintained and urged by the agents of the Abolition Society.

1836, June 27, a meeting was held at West Middletown denouncing and disapproving of the meeting at Washington on the 23d, as proscriptive in their nature and disorderly in their tendency.

Of the changes which have taken place on this subject since this period, I need not explain; they are patent to all men; the unknown future must determine this question, involving not only the future destiny of our own nation, but the peculiar relation which the negro race shall maintain.

Turnpikes.

1817, June 16, books were opened for the sale of stock in the Washington and Pittsburg turnpike.

1819, August 16, D. H. Blaine and James Kincaid established a line of coaches over this pike, to run tri-weekly.

National Road.

1818, August 1, the U. S. mail stage commenced running from Washington City to Wheeling, over the national road. This road was located by Col. Eli Williams (who died in the 73d year of his age, January 29, 1822). The road west of the Monongahela River through Washington County was given, per contract, to John Kincaid, James Beck, Gabriel Evans, John Kennedy and John Miller, at the rate of $6400 per mile.

This road, passing through the counties of Somerset, Fayette, and Washington, was transferred by the general government to the States through which it passed, but the Governor was required to appoint a commissioner to report to the court of each county annually its condition. Subsequently the court appointed the commissioner. The following gentlemen have filled this important office: Robert Quail, Benj. Leonard, Col. William Hopkins, William Seawright, Joseph Doak, William Cleary, J. D. Roberts, Mark Mitchell, Samuel Beatty, Alexander Frazer, Geo. W. Botkins, John Long.

1835, June 8, mail stages established tri-weekly by John Irons from Washington to Lake Erie, connecting with the National Road Stage Company to Baltimore and Philadelphia.

WASHINGTON AND WELLSBURG.

1819, June 12, Jonathan Knight, Moses Lyle and James Leacock were appointed commissioners to lay out a pike from Washington to Wellsburg.

1817, June 23, Washington and Williamsport Turnpike Company incorporated.

RAILROADS.

1837, January 18, a bill was presented to Senate to incorporate the *Washington Railroad* Company from a point at or near Allison's Run to Washington, with power to extend it north to Canonsburg. Shares of stock $50 each. The commissioners were Daniel Moore, William Hunter, Alexander Reed, James Ruple, John K. Wilson, John H. Ewing, John Cooke, John N. Dagg, and Samuel Hazlett.

HEMPFIELD RAILROAD.

1852, March 23, the Commissioners of Washington County subscribed for four thousand shares of stock in the Hempfield Railroad Company, shares valued at $50 each. Act passed Feb. 24, 1852.

1852, May 14, the Burgesses and Council subscribed for one thousand shares of stock in the Hempfield Railroad.

CHARTIERS VALLEY RAILROAD.

1854, January, the borough of Washington subscribed for five hundred shares of stock in the Chartiers Valley Railroad, amounting to twenty five thousand dollars. Chartiers Valley Railroad made application to the court for a subscription of one hundred thousand dollars.

UPPER TENMILE PLANK ROAD.

1853, June 21, the Town Council of the borough of Washington, subscribed for two hundred shares of stock at twenty-five dollars per share, to the Upper Tenmile Plank Road, leading from Washington to Prosperity, which subscription was referred to a vote of the people and carried.

TOWN CLOCK.

1852, April 26, town clock placed on cupola of court-house, it having been purchased from John B. McFadden, of Pittsburg, for the sum of four hundred dollars.

D. B. COOPER.

One of the most remarkable cases which ever transpired in the annals of jurisprudence, happened in Washington County, in which personal identity was lost, and the father and his neighbors were unable to recognize the features of the son and friend. Yet we shall not venture an opinion, but submit the facts, because there is too much mystery involved in the case, upon which hung the life or death of an innocent man.

On the 8th of January, 1840, D. B. Cooper, who, a short time previous, had resided with his father, Sylvanus Cooper, in Morris township in this county, but at that time residing in Lowell, Ohio, resolved to visit his home and former friends. He was accompanied as far as Wheeling in a jumper by William Long, and put up at a hotel in that city. Mr. Cooper left the hotel they were stopping at, and Mr. Long was unable to find him; accordingly Mr. Long took Mr. Cooper's horse and jumper to his father's house, Sylvanus Cooper, although, before doing so, he remained several days in the neighborhood, using the property of D. B. Cooper, and without delivering the same to Sylvanus Cooper. Suspicions arose against Mr. Long, and a warrant was issued by Justice Blaine, of Washington; he was arrested, and so great was the excitement against him, that he could not procure bail, and was remanded to prison for thirty days unless sooner demanded by the Governor of Virginia.

Time rolls on slowly to an innocent man incarcerated in a felon's cell. Fuel is added to the flame when the intelligence reaches Washington that on Jan. 10th, 1840, a dead body is found below Wheeling, supposed to be that of D. B. Cooper. The father and his friends make immediate arrangements to visit the place of interment of the dead body, while the innocent man is buoyed up with the consciousness that his own innocency will be proclaimed in due time. But not so—the father of D. B. Cooper and his friends sign and publish the following card in "Our Country," a paper published in Washington.

We, the undersigned, having seen a notice in the Wheeling Gazette of the 10th of January, of an account given by the postmaster of Granville Island, giving the description of the body of a person being found in the river at that place, and supposing from the description that it was the body of D. B. Cooper (who was missing in Wheeling on the morning of the 8th of January last), we repaired to the place and opened the grave, and from a PARTICULAR EXAMINATION OF HIS PERSON and clothing, are *convinced* beyond a doubt that it was the *identical body* of the said D. B. Cooper.

SYLVANUS COOPER, JOSEPH BRYANT, EZRA DILLE,
JOHN A. DILLE, SAMUEL DAY

To this was added the annexed statement:—

The description of clothing given by the above-named persons are the same that my brother had on when he left me at Lowell, in Washington County, Ohio. ZEBULON COOPER.

On the 21st January, 1840, William Long was brought before Justice Blaine for the murder of D. B. Cooper in or about Wheeling. The testimony elicited on that occasion was principally the honest confession of the prisoner to every witness, viz: that they had travelled from Lowell to Wheeling; had put up at a hotel on the 7th of January; ate supper together; that Cooper went out and attended to some business; that afterwards both parties met at a barber shop; that they returned, slept together in the same bed, and in the morning before breakfast both walked to the market, and while they examined a sled with bear and deer meat upon it, Cooper passed on.

Sylvanus Cooper, the father, stated that he had made the affidavit on the influence of the report that the body of his son had been found and other circumstances; that he went to Wheeling and inquired of the landlord, who stated that both had left his house in the morning to go to market about 7 o'clock; that Long returned without Cooper and wanted his breakfast for Cooper, but showed no signs of uneasiness about the matter, and that Long remained in the house until 12 o'clock before he left, and then left the next day.

John Morrow testified to the same statements of Long, with the addition that Stuart, a tobacconist, said it was curious that Cooper had gone off and left his horse, that likely he had got on a sled and went out to his father's, Sylvanus Cooper.

Andrew Means testified that a man by the name of Saunders told him that Long said that when they stopped at Fish Creek, Cooper went to pay his bill and pulled out a roll of money, but did not know how much there was.

James Stuart testified that he told Long that Cooper might have gone home with Saunders (the man who had the bear and deer meat), who was from Cooper's neighborhood, and that Long told him to tell Cooper that he had gone home to his father's with the horse and jumper.

We now return to Mr. D. B. Cooper, whom we had lost in Wheeling. Having considerable money with him and without giving his friend any notice of his intentions, and hearing of the many speculations which were transpiring in Illinois, he set out for that country; two months rolled away, and poor Long is still incarcerated, yet his father Sylvanus Cooper knew that he was still alive, but on account of the certificate he had given, a copy of which has been given above, his conscience, or some other unknown cause, operated upon his mind, he resolved to keep the location of his son a profound secret, until the secret was revealed by a friend of Cooper's to whom it had been communicated. Public indignation burst forth against Sylvanus Cooper. Long was liberated, and it was said money was paid to recompense Long for his incarceration. The causes which impelled Sylvanus Cooper to take so iniquitous a course is so mysterious, that the final day of accounts will only reveal its truthfulness. We give the case therefore, as among the most extraordinary instances of personal identity and of human depravity which can be anywhere found.

EXECUTIONS.

The first person executed was Thomas Richardson, on October 2, 1784. He was tried for burglary in the court, where it was held on the lot now owned by James G. Strean, on the corner of Main

Street and Strawberry Alley. The following letter from the commissioners of the county (viz: Van Swearingen, James Marshall, and Thomas Scott), dated Washington, June 28, 1784, explains itself:—

To his Excellency President Dickinson:
Sir: This county, as well as Fayette, has for some time past been greatly infested by a troop of robbers from the lower parts of the State, namely, Doanes and others, who, by frequent burglaries and robberies, under the countenance and protection of divers evil disposed persons amongst ourselves, have reduced us to the necessity of calling out parties of militia and making general search for the burglars and their accomplices, whereupon the said burglars, with numbers of horses, negroes, and other valuable property, of which they had robbed the inhabitants (in the most daring and insolent manner), set off for Detroit, our party pursued about one hundred miles from this place before they overtook them. However, we have now got of the said party lodged in the gaol of this county, the following persons, viz.: Abraham Doane, one who calls himself *Thomas Richason*, and two women who profess themselves wives to some of the party, the remainder having escaped our most vigilant pursuit, although we have recovered the greatest part of the property. We have also divers others in confinement and under recognizance as accomplices, and expect yet to make further discoveries, but our gaol being insufficient, and this same Abraham Doane having been rescued from it once before by an armed party, we are obliged to keep a strong guard constantly over them, and not having seen a supplement to the act for apprehending these villians (which we are informed exists), are at a loss what to do with them, therefore prays the direction of the council in the premises.

Eph. Douglass, under date of Uniontown, May 29, 1784, says:—

The banditti have established themselves in some part of this country, not certainly known, but thought to be in the deserted part of Washington County, whence they make frequent incursions into the settlements under cover of the night, terrify the inhabitants, sometimes beat them unmercifully, and always rob them of such property as they think proper, and then retire to their lurking places..

The court of Washington proceeded to the trial of Thomas Richardson for burglary, and he was convicted and a full copy of the record forwarded to the Supreme Executive Council, and from the records of said council, under date of September 10, 1784, we make the following extract:—

The record of the conviction of Thomas Richardson of burglary in the county of Washington, was read and considered, upon which it was

Ordered, That execution of the sentence of the court be made and done upon him, the said Thomas Richardson, on Saturday, the 2d day of October next, between the hours of ten of the clock in the forenoon and two of the clock in the afternoon of the same day, at the most proper and public place within the said day.

Richardson was taken from the jail in a cart to *Gallows Hill* (and it is from this circumstance that that locality derives its name). Arriving at the gallows, Sheriff Van Swearingen mounted the ladder and fixed the rope secure, and afterwards around the neck of the culprit, when the cart was driven off and the prisoner launched into eternity.

Second Execution—Wm. Crawford.

Thirty-nine years had almost elapsed before a similar scene was enacted on *Gallows Hill.*

WILLIAM CRAWFORD, an aged man, was tried for the murder of his own son before the Court of Oyer and Terminer of Washington, which assembled on November 20, 1822, before the Hon. Thomas H. Baird, President Judge, and his associates, Boyd Mercer and John Hamilton, Esqs.

A true bill was found by the grand jury, to which the prisoner plead, *not guilty.* By direction of the court a jury was empanelled of the prisoner's own selecting, consisting of Nathan Pyle, Benjamin Linton, James Ruple, Robert Gregg, Sr., William Clark, Samuel McDowell, Ebenezer Martin, Caleb Leonard, Thomas Jones, Ephraim Estep, Russel Moore, and Ezra Dille, who, being sworn and hearing the testimony, pleadings, and the charge of the court, rendered a verdict of *guilty of murder in the first degree.*

November 23, 1822, Judge Baird pronounced the following sentence upon the prisoner: "That you be taken from hence to the jail of the county of Washington, from whence you came, and from thence to the place of execution, and there be hanged by the neck until you are dead."

On the 25th November, 1822, exceptions were filed by his attorneys in arrest of judgment, but were overruled by the court, and the prisoner was executed on the 21st day of February, 1823, on Gallows Hill, south of the borough.

William Baird (Deputy Prosecuting Attorney) and J. Pentecost, represented the commonwealth; and James Ross, Parker Campbell, John Kennedy, and T. M. T. McKennan, were the counsel for the prisoner; Robert Officer, Esq., being high sheriff of the county.

Third Execution—Christopher Sharp.

On the 26th day of March, 1828, a court of oyer and terminer was held in Washington, presided over by Hon. Thomas H. Baird, and Boyd Mercer and John Hamilton, Esqs., his associates. A colored man (a slave) by the name of CHRISTIAN SHARP (commonly called "Kit") was tried for the murder of his master, Robert Carlisle, of Woodford, Kentucky. A true bill was found. The prisoner was brought into court on the 27th March, and asked a continuance of his case until the next term of court.

June 25, 1828, the prisoner was brought into court for trial, and the following persons sworn in as jurors, viz: David Clark, Robert Grant, David Hootman, John McLoney, Reed Doake, Samuel Boreland, John Bell, Adam Wier, Richard B. Chaplan, John

McCoy, Sr., Parker Scott, and Cyrus Huston. After hearing the testimony, the argument of counsel, and the charge of the court, the jury found the said Sharp *guilty of murder in the first degree.* On the 28th of June, 1828, his Honor Judge Baird sentenced the prisoner to be taken to the jail, from thence to the place of execution on Gallows Hill, and there hanged by the neck until he be dead.

He was executed by Robert McClelland, Esq., sheriff of the county, on the 22d day of November, 1828, on Gallows Hill. William Waugh, Esq. (Deputy Prosecuting Attorney), counsel on behalf of the commonwealth, assisted by John S. Brady, Esq. Counsel for the prisoner were Samuel McFarland, William Baird, and John Kennedy, Esqs.

FOURTH EXECUTION—ROBERT FOGLER.

On December 4, 1866, Robert W. Dinsmore, of Hopewell township, was murdered about ten o'clock at night by Robert Fogler. The county court being in session, the commissioners of the county by direction of Judge Acheson, offered a reward of one thousand dollars for the apprehension of the murderer. On the following day Robert Fogler was arrested, one remarkable circumstance clearly and conclusively pointing to his guilt. In the scuffle which ensued between Mr. Dinsmore and the prisoner, the heel of Fogler's boot was knocked off, and after his arrest Sheriff Smith, having procured the boots Fogler wore, found the heel missing, and thereby circumstantially pointing to the murderer. The prisoner was asked to explain the circumstance, when he made a full confession.

On the 20th February, 1867, the Court of Oyer and Terminer of Washington County was held, Judge Acheson on the bench, his associates Hon. John C. Chambers and John Farrer. Fogler was arraigned for the murder, the grand jury having previously found a true bill. The prisoner was defended by Messrs. James R. Ruth, I. Y. Hamilton, and L. R. Woods Little, Esqs., while the commonwealth was represented by Boyd Crumrine, Esq., District Attorney, assisted by H. J. Vankirk, of this county, and N. P. Fetterman, Esq., of Pittsburg.

The jurors who were empanelled to try the case, were Alex. B. Duval, David Bigler, W. V. McFarland, James B. Wilson, John Baker, Alexander McCalmant, John S. Barr, W. R. Sutherland, George T. Work, Lewis E. Smith, Edward R. McCready, James V. Dorsey. The trial commenced on Thursday morning and the case went to the jury at half-past four o'clock on Saturday, February 23d, and at six o'clock a verdict was rendered of murder in the first degree.

On Thursday afternoon, February 28, Robert Fogler was brought into court and Judge Acheson pronounced the death sentence upon the prisoner. The death warrant was issued April 4, 1867, for his execution, which took place May 15, 1867, inside of the jail yard, about seventy persons having received tickets of admission from the sheriff.

WASHINGTON COUNTY MUTUAL INSURANCE COMPANY.

This company was incorporated April 1, 1837, for the purpose of insuring dwelling-houses, stores, shops, and other buildings and property against loss or damage by fire. The number of policies which it has issued for five years amounts to twenty-eight hundred. The present efficient directors are William J. Matthews, President; Samuel Hazlett, John Wylie, John McElroy, A. C. Morrow, Alexander Murdoch, George W. Warrick, V. Harding, David Aiken, John Hastings, Lewis Barker, John D. Boyle, and Thomas Hodgens; L. M. Marsh, Secretary.

It is worthy of remark that during the whole existence of this company, the directors have never been compelled to make an assessment on their deposit notes. We add their financial condition:—

Cash on deposit with Samuel Hazlett,	$3,600
Interest unpaid,	3,400
Bills receivable,	750
Deposit notes,	130,000
	$137,750.

GENERAL INSURANCE AGENCY.

Under this title of Fire Insurance Agency, we may add that David Aiken, Esq., many years since established a General Insurance Agency, in which capital to the amount of $17,693,055.87 is represented by cash assets in the following companies:—

Home, of New York,	$4,516,368.46
Ætna, of Hartford, Connecticut,	5,549,504.97
Insurance Company of North America, Phila.,	2,783,580.96
Franklin, of Philadelphia,	2,825,731.67
Security, of New York,	2,017,889.81

In these companies no premium notes are taken, and consequently no assessments can be made on their policies. Dwellings and other property insured for five years. David Aiken, Esq , has appointed as solicitors for these companies, R. H. Morris and Joseph A. McKee. Mr. Aiken is also special agent for the Home Insurance Company, of New York, for the State of Pennsylvania.

CORRESPONDENCE BETWEEN HON. DAVID REDDICK AND THOMAS JEFFERSON, PRESIDENT OF THE UNITED STATES.

The following correspondence, which was originally intended for no other person than Mr. Reddick, was handed me by a particular friend, to insert in the History of Washington County if I deemed it of important interest. I have done so, because it places Mr. Jefferson, with regard to his religious opinions, in his true position, although his memory has been the subject of much criticism. I may state that Mr. Reddick was not only a member of the Supreme Executive Council of Pennsylvania, from Washington County, but held many important offices of honor and trust, and was also elected an honorary member of the American Philosophical Society on January 16, 1789, his diploma bearing the signatures of Benj. Franklin, President; Rev. Dr. Ewing, Bishop White, Vice-Presidents, and other distinguished gentlemen. The letter referred to reads thus:—

Washington, Penna., June 10, 1802.

SIR: About three weeks ago I received a letter from a respectable gentleman, who resides amongst the Indians, concerned in the missionary affairs of the United Brethren of Bethlehem. In this letter he has stated respecting you in the following words: "One act, however, if true, may operate in the decree of heaven much against him in the long run, viz: That he should have told the Indian chiefs, who lately visited him, that he stood in no need of being taught in Christianity, that they were a separate nation and people from the whites, and that their mode of living (without the religion of the whites) was perfectly right and conformable to the intention of their Creator, who had given them a different skin, different ideas, and a different way of maintaining themselves, and for that, reason placed them on a separate island by themselves." This is reported by Capt. George Whiteeyes, one of the Indian chiefs. He has it from the mouth of those it was spoken to by Mr. Jefferson, through a French interpreter at a private conference; however, please mention not my name in relating the story.

In my answer, I mentioned my disbelief of the story, that it was no doubt propagated by political enemies to injure you, and thought little more about it for some time, until I heard that a letter to the same purpose had been read in Presbytery in the State of Kentucky, upon which I began to fear that the story, if uncontradicted, might have mischievous effects. It appear alarmed, and it is pretty plain from the letter in my hand, the Moravians were likewise so. The story, after a continued currency, may gain credit enough to be used by the Indians, who may be averse to cultivation of their people, and at the same time operate unfavorably to yourself and your friends and country. Under this idea, I consulted Mr. Edgar and Mr. McDowell of this county on the subject, who, with me, were much uneasy about it and of opinion that you ought to be informed before the mischief might become rooted. As I am not at liberty to name the gentleman who writes me this story, I assure you he has to my knowledge given evidence of his high regard for your character at a time not long past. I am, with due respect, yours, DAVID REDDICK.

To which Thomas Jefferson replies:—

Washington, June 19, 1802.

SIR: Your letter of the 10th inst. has been received, and I am duly sensible of the favor of your attention to the *calumny* which was the subject of it, seeing the impossibility that special vindications should ever keep pace with the endless falsehoods invented and disseminated against me. I came at once to a resolution to rest on the justice and good sense of my fellow citizens, to consider from my general character and conduct through life, not unknown to them, whether these calumnies were probable, and I have made it an invariable rule never to enter the lists of the public papers with the propagators of them. In private communications with my friends, I have contradicted them without reserve. In this light you will be pleased to consider the present letter as meant for your own satisfaction, and to assure you that the falsehoods may be contradicted with safety by yourself or any others, but not that this letter should get into the public papers, or itself or any copy of it go out of your hands.

I know not to what party of Indians the calumny is meant to allude, as there were several parties on visits here last summer, but *it is false as to every party*. I never uttered the sentiments there stated, nor anything equivalent or like to them to any Indian, or, to any other person here or anywhere else. I had but one private conversation the last summer with any Indian, that was with the Little Turtle in the presence of Capt. Wells, his interpreter. I remember asking from him the opinions of the Indians with respect to a Supreme Being, the worship of Him, and a future state. He answered me frankly, but I carefully avoided the impropriety of either controverting or concurring in these opinions, or of saying one syllable on the comparative merits of any religious opinion. The story, therefore, is a mere fabrication, false in its substance and in all its circumstances. I readily conjecture the missionary who wrote to you on the subject, and know his worth and candor too well not to wish that his mind should be set to rights on this subject. I will ask, if you please, that addition to your favors, and pray you to accept my esteem and best wishes.   THOMAS JEFFERSON.

DAVID REDDICK, ESQ.

WASHINGTON COUNTY SABBATH SCHOOL CONVENTION.

Several of our citizens met March 29, 1862, at the house of Thomas McKean, Esq., to confer about the propriety of organizing a County Sabbath School Convention, and after an interchange of opinion they decided unanimously that it was both right and expedient, and designated the 21st and 22d days of April as the time, and the Presbyterian church of Washington as the place.

Each Sabbath school appointed two representatives, who met and issued a call for the convention, addressed to all the pastors, superintendents, and friends of Sabbath schools in Washington County, and also appointed a committee to superintend and direct the comfort of delegates.

On April 21, 1862, the convention assembled in the Presbyterian church, and elected James Donehoo as president; Peter Camp and Wm McCleary, as vice-presidents; and Thomas McKean, D. M. Leatherman, and I. N. Hainer as secretaries.

Delegates from the following Sabbath schools were admitted:—

From the *Methodist Episcopal Churches* of Canonsburg, Monongahela City, Providence Chapel, Hanover, and Washington.

From the *United Presbyterian Churches* of North Buffalo, West Alexander, Canonsburg, Chartiers, Pigeon Creek, Washington, Chartiers Cross Roads, and West Middleton.

From the *Presbyterian Churches* of Canonsburg, Lower Tenmile, Mount Prospect, Claysville, Florence, Pigeon Creek, East Buffalo, Cross Creek, Upper Tenmile, Racoon, Chartiers, Upper Buffalo,

Monongahela City, Burgettstown, Independence, Pine Grove, and Washington.
From the *Protestant Episcopal Church* of Washington
From the *Union Sabbath School* of South Pigeon Creek.
From the *Lutheran Congregation* of West Bethlehem, Carroll, Hillsborough, and Washington.
From the *Cumberland Presbyterian Churches* of Washington, Windy Gap, and Concord (at Sparta).
From the *Baptist Churches* of Pleasant Grove and Washington.
From the *Methodist Protestant Churches* of Washington and Amity.
From the *Disciples Churches* of Williamsburg, West Middleton, Washington, and Pleasant Valley.
A constitution was adopted, and under its provisions an executive committee appointed.

May 19, 1863.

The *second* annual Washington County Sabbath School convened in the Presbyterian church; Wm. McDaniel, of Canonsburg, president, with the constitutional officers. In addition to the Sabbath schools reported last year the following additional ones became members, viz:—

Methodist Episcopal Churches of Bentleysville, Pigeon Creek, Beallsville, Taylor's Church, Centreville, Prospect, Clover Hill, and Zollarsville.

United Presbyterian Churches of Peters Creek, Mount Hope, and South Buffalo.

Presbyterian Churches of Fairview, Centre, and West Alexander.

Baptist Churches of Mount Hermon and Pigeon Creek.

Methodist Protestant Church of Eldersville.

Wesleyan Methodist Church of West Middleton.

Protestant Episcopal Church of West Brownsville and Monongahela City.

Union Sabbath Schools of Windy Gap, Ridge (East Pike Run), South Strabane Valley Missionary School.

Lutheran Churches of Bethel and Mount Zion.

Cumberland Presbyterian Churches of Pleasant Hill, Bethel (at Vanburen), Millsborough, and Greenfield.

Disciples—Peters Creek, California, Burnsville, Pigeon Creek, Buffalo (the five last not represented).

May 24, 1864.

The *third* annual Sabbath School County Convention assembled in the college chapel, and was presided over by Gen. James Lee, of Cross Creek, with the customary officers. Fifty-four delegates in attendance, representing the Sabbath schools of the county.

June 14, 1865.

The *fourth* annual Sabbath School County Convention met in the Presbyterian church of Monongahela City, and was presided over by Rev. Wm. Ewing, of Canonsburg, and other officers. Fifty-six delegates in attendance.

The questions for discussion which were usually discussed by the conventions were the relation of pastor to the Sabbath school, the plan to produce the best results, the requisite qualifications of superintendents and teachers, the relation of the Sabbath school to family religion, the best method of teaching, the influence of Sabbath schools upon the church, how to retain the older scholars, the best mode of distributing books, and is the Sabbath school an indispensable auxiliary to the church. These and similar questions, all tending to promote Sabbath school instruction, and the co-operation of Christians in promoting the welfare of our common country and enlarging the Redeemer's kingdom, were discussed with the happiest effects.

From the records of the County Sabbath School Conventions I learn the following interesting facts, giving each denomination the maximum in the several years reported:—

Name.	No. of Schools.	Scholars.	Teachers.	Vols. in Library.
Presbyterian	17	2114	226	8487
Methodist Episcopal	13	1380	147	3554
United Presbyterian	9	719	82	2415
Cumberland Presbyterian	6	493	60	1025
Lutheran	4	299	34	1325
Protestant Episcopal	4	375	43	1042
Baptist	4	202	29	775
Disciples	4	180	25	250
Union Schools	3	245	38	775
Methodist Protestant	3	310	26	900
Wesleyan Methodist	1	80	12	250
Mission School	1	75	14	
Methodist Episcopal (Colored)	1	115	14	246
	70	6587	750	21,044

Golden Wedding.

We deem it of sufficient importance to place upon record, from the minutes of the town council of Washington, the occurrence of a golden wedding which was celebrated in this borough on Monday evening, April 18, 1870.

The council adopted the following preamble and resolutions:—

WHEREAS, Joseph Henderson, Esq., and his wife celebrate the 50th anniversary of their marriage this evening, and friends and acquaintances have assembled with them to return thanks to God that their lives have been spared for the enjoyment of fifty years of connubial felicity.

AND WHEREAS, This is the first occasion of the kind which has transpired since the foundation of our town eighty years since; the burgesses and council of the borough of Washington feel it to be their duty as well as their individual inclination to express their sentiments on so interesting an occasion, believing that by so doing they are representing the united opinion of every citizen of your ancient borough ; therefore,

Resolved, That we congratulate Joseph Henderson, Esq., and his wife, upon the return of their 50th marriage anniversary—an anniversary which reminds them of their early love—of their placing upon the altar of Hymen two willing, devoted hearts, united by solemn vows—of their preëminent attachment to each other, and their devotion.to each other's interest, and governed during their entire matrimonial life by the principles of the Christian religion.

Resolved, That the days of the years of their existence having been preeminently crowned by Him who divinely ordained the marriage institution, it is our heartfelt wish that the same protecting being who is the God of all the families of the earth, will sustain, support, and keep them during the remainder of their earthly existence, giving them kind friends, obliging neighbors, and devoted citizens, and when life shall terminate, and their souls pass into the spirit-land, may a reunion take place, which shall be measured, not by the years of time, but as eternal as the existence of God.

The preamble and resolutions were prepared by Alfred Creigh, signed by all the members of the council, with the seal attached, and presented by John D. Boyle, Chief Burgess.

ADDENDA.

Additional list of Attorneys who practice at the Washington county bar.

Coyle, John,
Downey, R. W.,
Ewing, Hon. J. Kennedy,
Hopkins, James H.,
Johnston, W. F.,
Minor, L.,

M'Neill, J.,
Sayres, Ezra,
Strean, Robt. F.,
Shutterly, Lewis,
Wills, John A.

APPENDIX

TO

HISTORY OF WASHINGTON COUNTY.

BY

DR. ALFRED CREIGH,
OF WASHINGTON.

APPENDIX.

CHAPTER I.

THE VIRGINIA AND PENNSYLVANIA CONTROVERSY, FROM 1752 TO 1783.

The date of the earliest settlements by Virginians and Pennsylvanians—The difficulties between the Governors of both States arising from these settlements—The names of the first settlers—The various acts of Captain Connolly as the representative of Virginia in claiming Fort Duquesne (Pittsburg) as within Virginia—His treason—Commissioners appointed by both States to run a temporary line until the Revolutionary War would terminate—The action of both States approving of the same, and the necessity of erecting Washington County.

THE earliest account of any permanent settlement having been made west of the Allegheny Mountains may be traced to the spring of 1765. In the month of April of that year a letter is on record in the Pennsylvania archives, dated at Williamsburg, Virginia, stating that the frontier inhabitants of the colony of Virginia, as well as Maryland, are removing fast over the Allegheny Mountains, in order to settle and live there.

It is also true that in addition to this information it was asserted that it was wrong for settlements to be made west of the mountains, because a controversy between Virginia and Pennsylvania about their respective boundary lines, had been commenced as early as 1752; the *former* relying upon the charter of James the First, while the *latter* claimed under Charles the Second, in 1681, which assigns the Delaware River as the eastern boundary, to extend five degrees in longitude, to be computed from said eastern bounds. The Penns contended that Pennsylvania extended several miles beyond Fort Duquesne (Pittsburg), while, on the other hand, the Virginia claim may be more satisfactorily exhibited in the language of B. Mayer, Esq., in an address before the Maryland Historical Society, in 1851.

It was only a few years after Pontiac's war that small settlements of whites had crept westward through the defiles of the Alleghenies and along the principal paths, the northernmost of which converged at old Fort Duquesne (Pittsburg). A town was laid out on the east bank of the Monongahela, within two hundred yards of Fort

Pitt, and for seventy miles above it a route had been cut through the wilderness to Redstone old Fort, near the mouth of Dunlap's Creek, now the site of Brownsville.

About the year 1774, Virginia still claimed, by virtue of her charter, all the territory between the parallels of 36° 30′ and 39° 40′ north latitude, from the margin of the Atlantic due west to the Mississippi, and thus inclosed within her assumed limit, not only the region which at present is comprised in Kentucky, but also the northern half of Illinois, one-third of Ohio, and an extensive part of Western Pennsylvania. Settlements had been planted upon most of the *eastern* branches of the Monongahela, the Youghiogheny, and on the small eastern tributaries of the upper Ohio, for 120 miles below Pittsburg, as well as on the sources of the Greenbrier, the Little Kanawha, and Elk River, west of the mountains, embracing in these districts, the northwestern counties of Virginia, and the southwestern of Pennsylvania, as at present defined. Pittsburg was claimed as a frontier town of Virginia, while the southern settlements on the tributaries of the Monongahela were held to belong to the same province.

After this digression we again return to demonstrate the fact of the early settlement of the lands west of the Allegheny Mountains, notwithstanding the claim of Virginia. On the 24th of October, 1765, His Majesty, King George II., gives the following instruction to John Penn, Lieutenant-Governor of Pennsylvania: WHEREAS, it hath been represented unto us that several persons from Pennsylvania and the back settlements of Virginia have immigrated to the westward of the Allegheny Mountains, and there have seated themselves on lands contiguous to the river Ohio, in express disobedience to our royal proclamation of October 7, 1763, it is, therefore, our will and pleasure, and you are enjoined and required to put a stop to all these, and all other the like encroachments for the future, by causing all persons who have irregularly seated themselves on lands to the westward of the Allegheny Mountains, immediately to evacuate these premises.

On December 11, 1766, Francis Fauquier, Lieutenant-Governor of Virginia, addressed a letter to John Penn, Governor of Pennsylvania, in which he says: "No regard is paid to the proclamations of 7th October, 1763, and 10th of April, 1766 (by you). But the commander-in-chief has taken a more effectual method to remove them, by giving orders to an officer and party to summon the settlers on Red Sandstone Creek, to warn them to quit these illegal settlements, and in case of refusal to threaten military execution."

On this subject General Gage, under date of July 2, 1766, writes to Governor Penn: If you will please to take proper and legal methods, as I presume Redstone Creek (at Brownsville) is within your government, the garrison of Fort Pitt shall assist to drive away the settlers.

The chiefs of the Six Nations at a council held at Fort Pitt, May

24, 1766, said that as soon as the peace was made in 1765, contrary to our engagements with them, a number of white people came over the great mountain and settled at Redstone Creek and upon the Monongahela.

George Croghan, Esq., the Indian agent, in addressing General Gage, said : If some effectual measures are not speedily taken to remove those people settled on Redstone Creek, till a boundary can be properly settled as proposed, and the governors pursue vigorous measures, the consequences may be dreadful, and we be involved in all the calamities of another general war.

In consequence, therefore, of all the difficulties surrounding the case, and to religiously perform every engagement entered into by Governor Penn with the Indians, Alexander Mackay, commanding a part of the 42d regiment issued the following proclamation, by authority of the commander-in-chief, and dated at Redstone Creek, June 22, 1766. This proclamation was addressed: To all people now inhabiting to the westward of the Allegheny Mountains: In consequence of several complaints made by the savages against the people who have presumed to inhabit some parts of the country west of the Allegheny Mountains, which, by treaty, belong to them, and had never been purchased, and which is contrary to his majesty's royal proclamation. His excellency, the commander-in-chief, out of compassion to your ignorance, before he proceeds to extremity, have been pleased to order me, with a detachment from the garrison at Fort Pitt, to come here and collect you together, to inform you of the lawless and licentious manner in which you behave, and to order you also to return to your several provinces without delay, which I am to do in the presence of some Indian chiefs now along with me. I, therefore, desire you will all come to this place along with the bearer, who I have sent on purpose to collect you together.

His excellency, the commander-in-chief, has ordered, in case you should remain after this notice, to seize and make prize of all goods and merchandise brought on this side the Allegheny Mountains or exposed to sale to Indians, at any place except at his majesty's garrison ; that goods thus seized will be a lawful prize and become the property of the captors. The Indians will be encouraged in this way of doing themselves justice, and if accidents should happen, you lawless people must look upon yourselves as the cause of whatever may be the consequence hurtful to your persons and estates, and if this should not be sufficient to make you return to your several provinces, his excellency, the commander-in-chief, will order an armed force to drive you from the lands you have taken possession of to the westward of the Allegheny Mountains, *the property of the Indians*, till such time as his Majesty may be pleased to fix a further boundary.

Such people as won't come to this place are to send their names and the province they belong to, and what they are to do, by the bearer, that his excellency, the commander-in-chief, may be acquainted with their intentions.

On the 31st of July, 1766, Governor Fauquier issued his proclamation to those people of Virginia who had seated themselves on these lands west of the Alleghany Mountains and contiguous to the river Cheat, in disobedience of the proclamations of 1763 and 1766, requiring all persons immediately to evacuate the same, which, if they failed to do, they must expect no protection or mercy from the government, and be exposed to the revenge of the exasperated Indians.

The General Assembly of Pennsylvania also feeling the necessity of immediate action with regard to these settlements west of the Allegheny Mountains, addressed a message to Governor Penn on the 12th of September, 1766, in which Joseph Fox, Speaker of the House, said: "But as we apprehend many of these rash people have gone from Virginia, between which province and this the boundary has not been exactly ascertained, nor is it distinctly known on which side of the supposed boundary these people are settled, we beg leave to recommend it to your honor to take the earliest opportunity to communicate to Governor Fauquier the necessity of his uniting with you in taking the most expeditious, as well as effectual steps to remove those intruders on the lands to the westward of the Allegheny Mountains, agreeably to his majesty's proclamations."

One month afterwards Governor Penn addressed Governor Fauquier on this subject, in which he stated that without any authority whatever from Pennsylvania, settlements had been made near Redstone Creek and the Monongahela, and he presumed also without the consent of the government of Virginia, and in violation of the rights of the nations. Governor Penn desired Governor Fauquier to unite with him in removing the settlers from the Monongahela lands, and if necessary promises a military force to effect the object.

To which Governor Fauquier replied, that he had already issued three proclamations to these settlers, but that the commander-in-chief had taken a more effectual method to remove them, by ordering an officer and detachment of soldiers to summon the settlers on Redstone Creek, the Monongahela Valley, and other parts westward of the Allegheny Mountains, to quit these illegal settlements, and in case of a refusal, to threaten military execution. This proclamation it seems had the desired effect with some few, but a large majority of families remained.

Governor Penn wisely said that as the boundary line between Virginia and Pennsylvania near their western limits, where these settlements were chiefly made, had not been made, and even added that the settlers no doubt would shelter themselves under a disputed jurisdiction, which subsequent events fairly demonstrated. In his address, however, to the General Assembly on the 5th of January, 1768, he said: "I must inform you that those settlements upon the Indian lands to the westward of the Allegheny Mountains, now appear by the line lately run between Pennsylvania and Maryland, *to be within the bounds of this province.*"

HISTORY OF WASHINGTON COUNTY. 7

The Assembly, through the advice of the Governor, passed a law on the subject of the removal of all settlers on the Indian lands, but deemed it most prudent to issue a proclamation on this important and exciting subject. And to carry the purpose of the Assembly into full effect, they commissioned Rev. John Steele (of the Presbyterian church of Carlisle), John Allison, Christopher Lemes, and Capt. James Potter, of Cumberland County, to visit the Monongahela, Youghiogheny, and other places west of the Allegheny Mountains, where any settlements were made in Pennsylvania, to read and explain the proclamation and the law, and induce them to pay due obedience thereto. Sixty pounds in cash were appropriated to each commissioner to defray his expenses. The proclamation is so very important, that I add it at this point in the history.

By the honorable John Penn, Esq., Lieutenant-Governor of Pennsylvania—

WHEREAS, By an act of the General Assembly of this Province, passed in the present year, it is among other things provided, that if any person or persons settle upon any lands within the boundaries of this Province not purchased of the Indians by the proprietors thereof, shall neglect or refuse to remove themselves and families off and from the said land, within the space of thirty days after he or they shall be required so to do, either by such persons as the Governor of this Province shall appoint for that purpose, or by his proclamation to be set up in the most public places of the settlements on such unpurchased lands, or if any person or persons being so removed shall afterwards return to his or their settlements, or the settlement of any other person with his or their family, or without any family, to remain and settle on any such lands, or if any person shall, after the said notice to be given as aforesaid, reside and settle on such lands, every such person or persons so neglecting or refusing to move with his or their family, or returning to settle as aforesaid, or that shall settle on any such lands after the requisition or notice aforesaid, being thereof legally convicted, by their own confessions or the verdict of a jury *shall suffer death without the benefit of clergy.*

Provided always, nevertheless, That nothing herein contained shall be deemed or construed to extend to any person or persons who now are, or hereafter may be settled on the main roads or communications leading through this Province to Fort Pitt, under the approbation and permission of the commander-in-chief of his majesty's forces in North America, or of the chief officer commanding in the western district to the Ohio, for the time being, for the more convenient accommodation of the soldiers and others, or to such person or persons as are or shall be settled in the neighborhood of Fort Pitt, under the approbation and permission, or to a settlement made by Geo. Croghan, Deputy Superintendent of Indian affairs under Sir William Johnston, on the Ohio River above said fort, anything herein contained to the contrary notwithstanding.

In pursuance thereof of the said act, I have thought proper by the advice of the council, to issue this my proclamation, hereby giving notice to all persons to remove themselves and families off and from said lands on or before the first day of May, 1768. And I do hereby strictly charge and command such person or persons, under the pains and penalties of the said act imposed, that they do not on any pretence whatever remain or continue on the said lands *longer than thirty days after the first day of May next.*

Governor Penn, in addition to this proclamation, instructed the commissioners whom I have mentioned, to collect together as many people of each of the settlements as they could, to read the proclamation, explain its nature, expostulate with them on the folly and injustice of their settling upon the Indian lands, the dangerous tendency of such a rash step both to themselves and other settlers upon the frontiers, the necessity and use of civil government, the obligations we owe to law and good governments and the consequences of disobedience. The commissioners were also instructed to procure the names of all the settlers and report the same to the governor.

The commissioners reached Redstone settlement on the 23d of March, 1768, having left Carlisle on the 2d of March. The people met on the 24th and heard the proclamation read and the law expounded, after which the business was postponed until the 27th. This being Sunday, a considerable number of the people attended, and after a sermon by the Rev. John Steele the meeting was reorganized. Immediately after its reorganization, word was received that a number of Indians had arrived at Indian Peters (this was a point on the west side of the Monongahela and directly opposite Redstone's old fort), and the commissioners sent for them. After their arrival and the business fully stated, the Indians and settlers agreed that nothing would be done until the treaty between George Croghan and the Indians was concluded. These Indians were principally from the Mingo towns. The settlers concluded that as the Indians evinced no hostile disposition they would remain and wait the issue of the treaty, while some, however, declared their intention to remove to their former province.

The commissioners, pursuant to their instructions, sent notice to the people on Cheat River and to Stewart's Crossing of Youghiogheny, to meet them at Guesses', the most central place, and also to a place called Turkeyfoot.

The names of the persons who settled near REDSTONE were John Wiseman, Henry Swartz, Henry Prisser, Joseph McClean, William Linn, Jesse Martin, William Colvin, Adam Hatton, John Vervalson, Sr., John Vervalson, Jr., Abraham Tygard, James Waller, Thomas Brown, Thomas Douter, Richard Rodgers, Captain Coburn, John Delong, Michael Hooter, Peter Young, Andrew Linn, George Martin, Gabriel Conn, Thomas Down, John Martin, Andrew Gudgeon, Hans Cack, Philip Sute, Daniel McCay, James Crawford, and Josias Crawford.

Names at Guesses' place.—John Bloomfield, Richard Harrison, James Lynn, Ezekiel Johnston, J. Johnston, Thomas Guesse, Henry Burken, Charles Lindsey, Lawrence Harrison, James Wallace, and Ralph Hickenbottom.

Names at Turkeyfoot.—Henry Abrahams, Ezekiel Heckman, Ezekiel Dewitt, John Enslow, James Spencer, Henry Enslow, Benjamin Jennings, Benjamin Pursley, and John Cooper.

Rev. Mr. Steele gave it as his opinion to the Governor that, from the best information he could obtain, there were only about one hundred and fifty families in the different settlements of Redstone, Youghiogheny, and Cheat River.

We have referred to the treaty of George Croghan, John Allen, and Joseph Shippen, who were appointed commissioners to meet the chief and principal warriors of the Six Nations, which met at Pittsburg, May 9, 1768. The result of the conference was that two messengers, viz., John Frazer and John Thompson, should visit the people settled at Redstone, Youghiogheny, and Monongahela, and signify to them the great displeasure of the Six Nations at their taking possession of their lands and making settlements on them, and that it is expected they will, with their families, remove without further notice. These two deputies were to be accompanied by the white Mingo and the three deputies sent from the Six Nation country; but when the time of their departure arrived they refused to go, saying that their instructions were only to attend to making a treaty, and that the driving the white people away from these settlements was a matter which no Indian could with any satisfaction be concerned in, and they thought it most proper for the English themselves to compel their own people to remove them from the Indian lands.

The commissioners, finding all efforts fruitless to gain over the Indian deputies, determined to return to Philadelphia, and, while making their arrangements, they were visited at their lodgings by one of the principal warriors of the Six Nations, who stated that he regretted the state of affairs, only fearing the ill-will of the white people, yet pledging his Indian faith and Indian honor that the Six Nations had good hearts to all their English brethren. Thus ended this treaty at Fort Pitt.

From this period, or until the year 1773, the country west of the Allegheny Mountains began to fill up with a growing population, the inhabitants feeling that they were well protected by the military forces at Fort Pitt in case of an Indian attack. Richard Penn, then Governor of Pennsylvania, urged the Assembly to have a sufficient number of soldiers at that post, but the Assembly differed from the Governor, believing that, if the fort was heavily garrisoned, the Indians would naturally become alarmed at such warlike preparations, and the worst consequences might be the result—although the Assembly pledged itself that whenever called upon by the exigencies of the time, they would afford every kind of protection to the western inhabitants.

The boundary question was one which involved not only the extent of Pennsylvania, but the title of lands. James Hendricks, a surveyor of Cumberland County, being written to on the subject in September, 1769, replied that he could not tell precisely where the western boundary crossed the Monongahela, but he inclined to the belief that Chartiers' Creek must be in the province of Pennsylvania, as its junction with the Ohio is but four miles from Fort Pitt, about northwest, and on going to Redstone old fort (Brownsville) you cross it several times, and Redstone old fort is several degrees to the westward of south from Fort Pitt.

Col. William Crawford, on the 9th of August, 1771, in writing on the same subject, says, it was the opinion of some of the best judges that the line of the province would not extend so far (as that of Mr. Hendricks) as it would be settled at *forty-eight miles* to a degree of longitude, which was the distance of a degree of longitude allowed at the time the charter was granted to William Penn.

Among the persons who were prominent in creating disturbances with regard to the boundary question was Michael Cressap, who declared that the province of Pennsylvania did not extend beyond the Allegheny Mountains, but *that all westward of it was the king's land*. This assertion easily gained credence among those who settled on the disputed lands, while Mr. Croghan, in a letter to Arthur St. Clair, dated June 4, 1772, asserted that it was not a great number of years since the Assembly refused to build a trading house or fort, alleging it to be out of Mr. Penn's grant, and that even afterwards the same Assembly refused granting money for the king's use, to assist in the reduction of Fort Duquesne (Pittsburg). In the same letter he says the people are fools if they do not keep their money until they are fully satisfied that their property is sure, and that they are under the jurisdiction of Pennsylvania.

The fact need not be disguised that the proprietaries of Pennsylvania not only claimed all the country about Pittsburg, but the settlers themselves acquiesced in that claim until January 1, 1774. Up to this period the records of Cumberland, Bedford, and Westmoreland counties all establish this fact. Whether it was legally made was a question which concerned the king, and not the Earl of Dunmore, then Governor of Virginia. The charters of Virginia and Pennsylvania were derived from a common origin, and the crown alone could settle the dispute. In the midst of all this perplexity—and to add additional fuel to the burning embers, Dr. John Connolly, a citizen of Virginia (but formerly a native of Lancaster County, Pennsylvania), appeared, and posted up the following significant notice:—

WHEREAS his Excellency John, Earl of Dunmore, Governor of the colony of Virginia, has been pleased to nominate and appoint me Captain Commandant of the militia of Pittsburg and its dependencies, with instructions to assure his majesty's subjects settled on the western waters that, having the greatest regard to their prosperity and interest—and convinced from the reported memorials of the grievances of which they complain—that he purposes recommending to the house of Burgesses the necessity of erecting a new county to include Pittsburg, for the redress of your grievances, and to take every other step that may tend to afford you that justice which you solicit. In order to facilitate this desirable circumstance, I (John Connolly) hereby require and command all persons in the dependency of Pittsburg to assemble themselves there as militia on the 25th inst., at which time I shall communicate other matters for the promotion of public utility.

As soon as Governor Penn had learned of the above circular, and ascertained the wishes of the western people, he sent an express informing them that he had forwarded a letter to Governor Dunmore demanding an explanation of his strange and unaccountable conduct through his agent Dr. Connolly. At the same time, he urged and required the magistrates to assert the right of Pennsylvania and protect the people in every part within its own limits, adding that Fort Pitt was most certainly within the Province of Pennsylvania. The Governor also directed the magistrates to apprehend Dr. Connolly and some of his partisans and magistrates, at the expense of government.

In pursuance of these directions, Captain Connolly was arrested and committed to gaol on refusing to find securities for his good behavior till next court. It seems, however, that the captain prevailed with the sheriff, and obtained his leave of absence for a few days, and, instead of returning to gaol (which was then at Hannahstown, Westmoreland County), he went to the Redstone settlement, and from thence to Virginia, being guarded by his associates.

While Captain Connolly was returning to Virginia, Governor Dunmore sent the following spicy letter to Governor Penn, dated at Williamsburg, March 3, 1774 :—

SIR: I have been favored with your letter of the 31st of January. From the opinion of his majesty's council, I must inform you that I cannot possibly, in compliance with your request, either revoke the commissions and appointments already made, or defer the appointing of such other officers as I may find necessary for the good government of that part of the country which we cannot but consider to be within the dominion of Virginia, until his majesty shall declare the contrary. And I flatter myself I can rely so far on the prudence and discretion of the officers whom I have appointed, that the measure which I have pursued may have no tendency to raise disturbances in your province, as you seem to apprehend, and if any should ensue, I cannot but believe they will be occasioned, on the contrary, by the violent proceedings of your officers, in which opinion I am justified by what has already taken place, in the irregular committment of Captain John Connolly for acting under my authority, which, however, as I must suppose, was entirely without your participation. I conclude he is before this time released, but, nevertheless, the act being of so outrageous a nature, and of a tendency so detrimental to both colonies that, with the advice of his majesty's council, I do insist upon the most ample reparation being made for so great an insult on the authority of his majesty's government of Virginia, and no less can possibly be admitted than the dismission of the clerk (Arthur St. Clair) of Westmoreland County, who had the au-

dacity, without any authority, to commit a magistrate acting in the legal discharge of his trust, unless he (St. Clair) can prevail, on proper submission. on Mr. Connolly to demand his pardon of me. I am yours,
DUNMORE.

Governor Penn being highly displeased with Dunmore's letter, and unwilling that so valuable an officer as St. Clair should either be dismissed or make an apology, immediately forwarded his reply, couched in the following language, dated at Philadelphia on the 31st March, 1774:—

MY LORD: am truly concerned that you should think the commitment of Mr. Connolly so great an insult on the authority of the government of Virginia, as nothing less than Mr. St. Clair's dismissal from his office can repair. The lands in the neighborhood were surveyed for the Proprietaries of Pennsylvania early in the year 1769, and a very rapid settlement under this government soon took place, and magistrates were appointed by this government to act there in the beginning of 1771, who have ever since administered justice without any interposition of the government of Virginia, till the present affair. It could not, therefore, fail of being both surprising and alarming that Mr. Connolly should appear to act on that stage, under a commission from Virginia, before any intimation of claim or right was ever notified to this government. The proclamation of Mr. Connolly had a strong tendency to raise disturbances and occasion a breach of the public peace in a part of the country where the jurisdiction of Pennsylvania hath been exercised without objection, and, therefore, Mr. St. Clair thought himself bound, as a good magistrate, to take legal notice of Mr. Connolly. You must excuse my not complying with your lordship's requisition of stripping him on this occasion of his office and livelihood, which you will allow me to think not only *unreasonable but somewhat dictatorial.*

I should be extremely concerned that any misunderstanding should take place between this government and that of Virginia. I shall carefully avoid every occasion of it, and shall be always ready to join with you in the proper measures to prevent so disagreeable an incident, yet I cannot prevail on myself to accede in the manner you require, to a claim which I esteem, and which I think must appear to everybody else to be altogether groundless. I am your lordship's obd't serv't,
JOHN PENN.

Mr. Connolly, finding himself supported in his measures by Lord Dunmore, returned to Pittsburg, and had himself surrounded constantly with an armed body of men to do his bidding in defence of Virginia laws. Whenever the courts of Pennsylvania would issue a process—or even a magistrate—Mr. Connolly, under his authority from Lord Dunmore, would obstruct its execution. It appears that he was determined to overawe the court of Westmoreland County with his measures, and addressed them by a written communication in the following language:—

GENTLEMEN: I am come here to be the occasion of no disturbances, but to prevent them. As I am countenanced by my government, whatever you may say or conceive, some of the justices of this bench are the cause of this appearance, and not me. I have done this to prevent myself from being illegally taken to Philadelphia. My orders from the government of

Virginia not being explicit, but claiming the country about Pittsburg, I have raised the militia to support the civil authority of that colony vested in me.

I am come here to free myself of a promise made to Captain Proctor, but have not conceived myself amenable to the court of Westmoreland County by any authority from Pennsylvania, upon which account I cannot apprehend that you have any right to remain here as justices of the peace, constituting a court under that province. But, in order to prevent confusion, I agree that you may continue to act in that capacity in all such matters as may be submitted to your determination by the acquiescence of the people, until I may have instructions to the contrary from Virginia, or until his majesty's pleasure shall be further known on the subject.

The Justices of Westmoreland County Court *immediately* returned the following reply :—

The jurisdiction of the court and the officers of the County of Westmoreland rests on the legislative authority of the Province of Pennsylvania, confirmed by his majesty in council. That jurisdiction has been regularly exercised, and the court and officers will continue to exercise it in the same regular manner. It is far from their intention to occasion or foment disturbances, and they apprehend that no such intentions can, with propriety, be inferred from any part of their conduct. On the contrary, they wish and will do all in their power to preserve the public tranquillity. In order to contribute to this salutary purpose, they give information that every step will be taken on the part of the Province of Pennsylvania to accommodate any differences that have arisen between and the colony of Virginia, by fixing a temporary line between them.

The effect which this communication had, was that Devereaux Smith, Aeneas Mackay, and Andrew McFarland, magistrates, as they were returning from court, on the 9th of April, 1774, were arrested by the king's warrant by order of Captain Connolly, and refusing to give bail, under the Virginia laws, arrangements were made to send them off to Staunton, Virginia, for trial. On their way to Staunton, Justice Mackay called at Williamsburg to visit Lord Dunmore in person and make a statement of the facts of the case, but he replied that Captain Connolly was authorized by him to prosecute the claim of the colony of Virginia to Pittsburg and its dependencies. These justices, however, after their arrival at Staunton, gave security and returned to their homes.

Col. William Crawford, however, President of the Court, immediately sent an express to Governor Penn at Philadelphia, giving the facts in detail and at the same time stating that Captain Connolly a few weeks before went to Staunton and was sworn in as a justice of the peace for Augusta County, in which it is pretended that the country about Pittsburg is included, that under that authority he is constantly surrounded by an armed body of about one hundred and eighty militia, and that he obstructs the execution of every legal process, whether emanating from the court or a single magistrate.

The Provincial Council, then holding its deliberations in Philadelphia, and to whom the communication had been sent, after deliberating on the subject, sent two letters under date of April 22, 1774, one to the justices arrested by Captain Connolly, and the other to Colonel Crawford, the president of the court. In the former Governor Penn assures the justices under confinement that he will send commissioners with all possible expedition to Lord Dunmore, applying for their discharge and give instructions to procure for them any security or credit they may stand in need of, so as to make their disagreeable situation as comfortable as may be. But to Col. Crawford, Governor Penn wrote deprecating the present alarming situation of affairs, promising that the commissioners should expostulate with Lord Dunmore upon the behavior of the officers acting under his authority, yet at the same time assuring Col. Crawford that as Virginia had the power to raise a much larger military force than Pennsylvania, prudence would dictate the propriety of not attempting to contend with them by way of force, neither would he advise the magistracy of Westmoreland County to proceed by way of criminal prosecution against them for exercising the laws of the dominion of Virginia.

The commissioners who were sent to Lord Dunmore were James Tilghman and Andrew Allen, Esquires, who were instructed to negotiate with the Governor of Virginia on the disturbances of Westmoreland County—then embracing all the territory of Pennsylvania west of the mountains—the question of jurisdiction and such other matters as would quiet the minds of the inhabitants near the borders of the two colonies. These commissioners proceeded on their mission May 12, 1774, and arrived at Williamsburg, and immediately called upon Lord Dunmore in his official capacity as Governor. They informed him that they, as the representatives of Pennsylvania, wished to settle upon some line of jurisdiction to remedy the inconveniences of the present clashing jurisdiction between the colonies of Virginia and Pennsylvania, and also to apply to the crown to fix the boundaries of Pennsylvania. Lord Dunmore partially and verbally consented to the propositions, but insisted upon *retaining the jurisdiction of Fort Pitt* or the lands to the eastward of the Monongahela River. In his letter to the commissioners after reconsidering the subject, he uses the following emphatic language: Your proposals, amounting in reality to nothing, could not possibly be complied with, and your resolution with regard to Fort Pitt, the jurisdiction over which I must tell you at all events will not be relinquished by this government without his majesty's order, puts an entire stop to further treaty. The commissioners replied by regretting his determination to hold Fort Pitt, and thereby continuing the inconveniences arising from a clashing and disputed jurisdiction. Their mission being accomplished, however unsatisfactory to them, they left for Philadelphia.

The commissioners having departed, Lord Dunmore, as Governor of Virginia, immediately issued the following proclamation, on the 25th of May, 1774:—

WHEREAS, I have reason to apprehend that the government of Pennsylvania, in prosecution of their claim to Pittsburg and its dependencies, will endeavor to obstruct his majesty's government thereof under my administration by illegal and unwarrantable commitment of the officers I have appointed for that purpose, and that that settlement is in some danger of annoyance from the Indians also, and it being necessary to support the dignity of his majesty's government and protect his subjects in the quiet and peaceable enjoyment of their rights, I have therefore thought proper, by and with the consent of his majesty's council, by this proclamation in his majesty's name, to order and require the officers of the militia in that district to embody a sufficient number of men to repel any insult whatever, and all his majesty's liege subjects within this colony are hereby strictly required to be aiding and assisting therein, as they shall answer the contrary at their peril. And I do further enjoin and require the several inhabitants of the territory aforesaid to pay his majesty's quitrents and all public dues to such officers as are or shall be appointed to collect the same within this dominion, until his majesty's pleasure shall be known.

The Indians, now discovering the hostility which prevailed between the Virginians and Pennsylvanians, and considering that their own rights had been trampled upon by both colonies taking from them their hunting grounds, and these lands held more sacred to them by containing the bones of their ancestors, resolved to avenge themselves on the whites. The result was, that as soon as this fact became known, a great part of the settlers fled from their habitations, and the fear was that there would be a total desertion of the whole country and a general Indian war.

To meet this emergency, Governor Penn convened an Assembly in May, 1774, at Philadelphia, and informed them that in the month of April previous, eleven Delaware and Shawnee Indians had been barbarously murdered on the Ohio River, below Pittsburg, by two parties of white men, said to be Virginians; that the Indians in revenge had murdered a number of Virginians, settled to the westward of the Monongahela River; that although the Indian nations are at peace with the Colony of Pennsylvania, yet that Captain Connolly, appointed by the Virginia government at Pittsburg, and who has lately taken possession of that place under pretence of its being out of the Province of Pennsylvania within the Colony of Virginia, with his party has actually attacked the Indians, and that the inference may be justly arrived at that this Assembly must provide for the security of the frontier settlements in case of a war with the Indians.

Governor Penn sent a message to the chiefs and warriors of the Shawnese Indians, in which he says to them that if any of the wicked people of Virginia have murdered any of your people, you should make complaint to the Governor, and he will have them punished. You should not in such case take revenge upon innocent people who have never injured you. A similar message was sent to the Delawares, and in these messages Governor Penn assures them that he will write to the Governor of Virginia on the subject. In pursuance of these messages, and the friendship exhibited by Governor Penn, the Indians held a council at Pittsburg, June 29, 1774, and all the unhappy differences were satisfactorily settled, the Indians having determined, in their own language, "to hold fast the chain of friendship, and make their young men sit quiet."

Captain Connolly, it appears, was not satisfied with this peaceful termination of affairs, for in the month of July following, in writing to Arthur St. Clair, he says: "The people of the frontiers want nothing but the countenance of government to execute every desirable purpose, and your province (Pennsylvania) appearing backward at this critical juncture, it will most indubitably be highly displeasing to all the western settlers. I am determined no longer to be a dupe to their amiable professions, but, on the contrary, shall pursue every measure to offend them (the Indians), whether I may have the friendly assistance or not of the neighboring country."

While Captain Connolly was acting in this domineering manner, a letter arrived from the Earl of Dartmouth, dated at Whitehall, September 8, 1774, and addressed to Lord Dunmore, in which he says:—

"My intelligence through a variety of other channels adds further, that this Captain Connolly, using your Lordship's name, and pleading your authority, has presumed to re-establish the fort at Pittsburg, which was demolished by the king's express orders. The duty I owe the king, and the regard I entertain for your lordship, induce me to take the earliest opportunity of acquainting your lordship with this information, to the end that the facts asserted, if not true, may be contradicted by your lordship's authority; but if otherwise, which I cannot suppose to be the case, such steps may be taken as the king's dignity and justice shall dictate."

Governor Penn justly considering that neither Virginia nor the Indians would give his province any further trouble, either with regard to the boundary question, or an incursion by the Indians, was surprised to find that the question of jurisdiction was again to be thrust upon him by a new proclamation issued by Lord Dunmore. Upon its appearance, Governor Penn issued the following proclamation on October 12, 1774.

WHEREAS, I have received information that his excellency, the Earl of Dunmore, governor-general in and over his majesty's colony of Virginia, hath lately issued a very extraordinary proclamation, setting forth "that the rapid settlement made on the west of the Allegheny Mountains by his majesty's subjects, within the course of these few years, had become an object of real concern to his majesty's interest in that quarter, that the Province of Pennsylvania had unduly laid claim to a very valuable and extensive quantity of his majesty's territory, and the executive part of that government, in consequence thereof, had most arbitrarily and unwarrantably proceeded to abuse the laudable adventurers in that part of his majesty's dominions, by many oppressive and illegal measures, in discharge of their imaginary authority, and that the ancient claim laid to that country by the Colony of Virginia, *founded in reason by pre-occupancy, and the general acquiescence of all persons,* together with the instructions he had lately received from his majesty's servants, ordering him to take that country under his administration; and as the evident injustice manifestly offered to his majesty by the immoderate strides taken by the proprietaries of Pennsylvania, in prosecution of their wild claim to country, demand an immediate remedy, he (Lord Dunmore) did thereby, in his majesty's name, require and command all his majesty's subjects west of the Laurel Hill to pay a due respect to his said proclamation, thereby strictly prohibiting the execution of any act of authority on behalf of the Province of Pennsylvania, at their peril, in that country; but, on the contrary, that a due regard and obedience to the laws of his majesty's Colony of Virginia, under his administration, should be observed, to the end that regularity might ensue, and a just regard to the interest of his majesty in that quarter, as well as to his majesty's subjects, might be the consequence."

AND WHEREAS, although the western limits of the Province of Pennsylvania have not been settled by any authority from the crown, yet it has been sufficiently demonstrated by lines accurately run by the most skilful artists, that not only a great tract of country west of the Laurel Hill, but Fort Pitt also, are comprehended within the charter bounds of this province, a great part of which country has been actually settled, and is now held under grants from the Proprietaries of Pennsylvania, and the jurisdiction of this government has been peaceably exercised in that quarter of the country till the late strange claim set up by the Earl of Dunmore, in behalf of his majesty's Colony of Virginia, founded, as his lordship is above pleased to say, " in *reason, pre-occupancy*, and the general acquiescence of all persons," which claims to lands within the said charter limits must appear still the more extraordinary, as his most gracious majesty, in an act passed the very last session of Parliament, " for making more effectual provision for the government of the Province of Quebec," has been pleased in the fullest manner to recognize the charter of the Province of Pennsylvania, by expressly referring to the same, and binding the said Province of Quebec by the northern and western bounds thereof. Wherefore there is the greatest reason to conclude that any instructions the Governor of Virginia may have received from his majesty's servants, to take that country under his administration, must be founded on some misrepresentation to them respecting the western extent of this province. In justice, therefore, to the proprietaries of the Province of Pennsylvania, who are only desirous to secure their own undoubted property from the encroachment of others, I have thought fit, with the advice of the Council, to issue this, my proclamation, hereby requiring all persons west of the Laurel Hill to retain their settlements, as aforesaid, made under this province, and to pay due obedience to the laws of this government; and all magistrates and other officers who hold commissions or office under this government, to proceed as usual in the administration of justice, without paying the least regard to the said recited proclamation (of Lord Dunmore) until his majesty's pleasure (King George) shall be known in the premises, at the same time strictly charging and enjoining the said inhabitants and magistrates to use their utmost endeavors to preserve peace and good order.

This proclamation had the desired effect of calming the public mind for some months; but in February, 1775, the conflicting jurisdiction of the provinces of Virginia and Pennsylvania broke out afresh, and the magistrates acting under Pennsylvania laws were threatened with imprisonment if they continued to officiate as magistrates. Even Virginians, who were incarcerated in jails under the Pennsylvania laws, were turned loose by an armed mob pretending

B

to act under the authority of Virginia laws. Confusion reigned in the territory west of the Laurel Hill, lands already occupied were given to friends and favorites by Virginia officers, the courts of justice under Pennsylvania laws were obstructed, and land offices were even opened by direction of the government of Virginia.

These outrages being certified to by the justices, Governor Penn, on the 1st of March, 1775, dispatched an express to Lord Dunmore, in which he stated that the justice due to himself, and the protection he owes to the people, "who have taken up lands in this province, and settled them long before your lordship thought fit to disturb its peace by extending the government of Virginia within our chartered limits, obliges me to apply to your lordship to know if these violent proceedings are the effect of your orders, or have your countenance, that, in case they have, I may take the proper measures, or, if they have not, that they may receive your discouragement. Your lordship well knows that a petition is depending before the crown for settling the bounds and running the lines of this province, which, when done, will put an end to the unhappy disputes between the two governments. You will consider that the country which is the seat of the present disturbances was *first* settled under this province, and that our jurisdiction was extended there in the term of your predecessor, Lord Botetourt, and recognized by his lordship in his sending hither for trial a person who had committed a murder at Stewart's Crossings, which is westward of the Laurel Hill."

This murder happened in 1770. John Ingman, a slave of Col. Crawford's, killed an Indian named Stephen, and was sent by Lieut. Inglis to Governor Penn, with the necessary depositions, proving his guilt, and also his confession.

While such was the state of feeling in the western part of the province of Pennsylvania, the court of the district of West Augusta was also engaged in promoting the interests of Virginia, as the following facts will abundantly show:—

At a justices' court held at Fort Dunmore (Pittsburg), *February* 21, 1776, the case of William Elliott was called up, for disturbing the minds of his Majesty's good people by demanding in an arbitrary and illegal manner of sundry persons what personal estate they are possessed of, that the same may be taxed according to the laws of Pennsylvania. He appeared, and, on hearing the argument of the attorneys, the court are of opinion that he be committed to the gaol of the county, there to remain until he enter into recognizance for his good behavior, whereupon John Hervie and Charles Sims became his securities.

February 22, 1775. James Caveat was also arraigned before the court for malevolently upbraiding the authority of his Majesty's officers of the government of Virginia at sundry times, and for riotously opposing the legal establishment of his Majesty's laws. He offered as a plea the want of jurisdiction of the court, which was overruled, and he was required to give security for one year and a day, and desist from acknowledging as a magistrate within the colony of Virginia any authority derived from the province of Pennsylvania.

May 1, 1775. Thomas Scott was also bound over for acting and doing business as a justice of the peace under Pennsylvania laws, in contempt of the Earl of Dunmore's proclamation, and also other misdemeanors, and was required to desist from acting as a magistrate within the colony of Virginia.

September 20, 1775. George Wilson, gentleman, was bound over for aiding, advising, and abetting certain disorderly persons, who, on the morning of the 22d of June last, violently seized and carried away Captain John Connolly from Fort Dunmore, and also advising others not to aid the officers of justice when called upon to apprehend the aforesaid disturbers of the peace. He not appearing, his recognizance was forfeited.

In addition to these illegal arrests, Robert Hanna, Æneas Mackay, James Smith, and others were tried by the court held at Fort Dunmore, Pittsburg, and sent to the gaol of the county, through the instrumentality of Captain John Connolly. The patience of the people at length became exhausted by the best of their citizens being wantonly cast into prison, and they determined to redress their own insupportable grievances. The Pennsylvanians seized Capt. Connolly, the cause of all their troubles, and took him to Philadelphia, while the Virginia court directed that Col. George Wilson, Devereaux Smith, and Joseph Spear should be kept as hostages for the safe return of Captain Connolly; and to provide against any contingency of these hostages being rescued from their power, they were sent off immediately in a flat boat to Wheeling, to be detained there until future events would secure their liberty, which was afterwards accomplished.

The people of the colonies at this date (1775), on account of the encroachments which the king and parliament were making upon all the colonies, felt the necessity of casting aside all minor differences, and of organizing themselves for the defence of their lives, their liberties, and their property. Every thought, every feeling, every aspiration was brought to bear upon the all-absorbing question of the freedom of America. Conventions were called in every colony, provincial councils were dissolved, committees of safety were substituted, courts of justice were reorganized, new oaths taken, political offenders were pardoned, and all united in the heaven-born design of liberty and union.

From this time forward Captain Connolly became the enemy of his country, although a native-born citizen of Lancaster County, Pennsylvania. In November, 1775 (after his reprieve), he was arrested in Fredericktown, Maryland, being engaged in treasonable projects, and was ordered to be kept in close and safe custody until the orders of Congress should be known. He was afterwards removed to the gaol of Philadelphia, and remained there until April 2, 1777, when the Supreme Executive Council directed his conditional release by permitting him to retire to the plantation of James Ewing, Esq., giving security himself in £2000, and two freeholders in £1000 each, for his good behavior, and that he will not write to, speak, or correspond with any person employed under the authority of the king or parliament, nor any person unfriendly to the United States of America, or employ or procure any person to take up arms, or aid and assist the enemies of the said States in any sort whatever, and shall appear before the Council whenever called for. He complied with these requirements; but what was his after fate—how he lived and how he died—we cannot ascertain. However, such was the character of the man who created all the disturbances in the western portion of the province of Pennsylvania, to gratify the jealousy of Lord Dunmore and his own selfish passions.

One year after the States had become "free and independent" (or on July 5, 1777), the Supreme Executive Council of Pennsylvania conceived it to be their duty to have the boundary line between themselves and the State of Virginia peacefully and quietly settled, as questions of vital importance would necessarily arise, in which both States would be interested, especially in waging a war for a common cause. The Supreme Council therefore directed Thomas Wharton, Jr., their President, to forward a letter to the delegates of the State of Virginia, then in Congress. The following is a copy of the letter dated,

IN COUNCIL. *Philadelphia*, July 5, 1777.
GENTLEMEN: Being authorized by the Commonwealth of Pennsylvania to propose to the Commonwealth of Virginia, a final settlement of the disputed boundary line between the two States, I think myself happy to have the opportunity of doing it through you. The proposals on our side, taken together, will, I conceive, appear so reasonable, that I flatter myself they lay a foundation for a happy adjustment of all differences. You have them in the enclosed extract from the minutes of Assembly, to which I beg leave to refer you.   Being, sir, your very humble servant,
THOMAS WHARTON, Jr., President.

On December 10, 1777, Francis Lightfoot Lee informed the Executive Council of Pennsylvania, that the delegates from Virginia desired another copy of the proposals, as they feared the copy to their Assembly had miscarried. Affairs remained in this situation until February 6, 1779, when Thomas Adams, Merriweather Smith, and Cyrus Griffin, delegates in Congress from Virginia, wrote a letter to Joseph Reed, President of the Executive Council, communicating the resolutions of the Assembly of Virginia, which were directed to be sent to the Assembly of Pennsylvania.

Patrick Henry, Governor of Virginia, on May 22, 1779, communicated to President Reed that the resolutions of the General Assembly fully expresses their sense on the subject of negotiating the boundary line between Pennsylvania and Virginia, which was afterwards adopted in council, on the following 5th of June.

The correspondence of the General Assembly of Pennsylvania and

Virginia, through their respective officers, Patrick Henry, Governor of the latter, and Joseph Reed of the former State, resulted in the appointment of George Bryan, Rev. Dr. John Ewing, and David Rittenhouse, commissioners on behalf of Pennsylvania, and James Madison (Bishop), and Robert Andrew, on behalf of Virginia, who met at Baltimore on the 31st day of August, 1779, and entered into the following agreement after four days' negotiation. That the line commonly called Mason and Dixon's line, be extended due west five degrees of longitude, to be computed from the river Delaware for the southern boundary of Pennsylvania, and that a meridian drawn from the western extremity thereof, to the Northern limits of the said States respectively, be the western boundary forever, on condition that the private property and rights of all persons acquired under, founded on, or recognized by the laws of either country, previous to the date hereof, be saved and confirmed to them, although they should be found to fall within the other, and that in decision of disputes thereon, preference shall be given to the elder or prior right, whichever of the said States the same shall have been acquired under, such persons paying, within whose boundary their land shall be included, the same purchase or consideration money which would have been due from them to the State under which they claimed the rights, and where any such purchase or consideration money hath since the Declaration of American Independence been received by either State, for lands, which according to the before recited agreement, shall fall within the territory of the other, the same shall be reciprocally refunded and repaid, and that the inhabitants of the disputed territory now ceded to the State of Pennsylvania, shall not, before the 1st day of December in the present year, be subject to the payment of any tax, nor at any time to the payment of arrears of taxes or impositions heretofore laid by either State.

This agreement, with conditions annexed, was adopted by resolution of the legislature of Pennsylvania, September 23, 1780, and transmitted to the State of Virginia for their confirmation.

While the negotiations were pending, Congress passed the following preamble and resolution, on December 27, 1779.

WHEREAS, It appears to Congress from the representation of the delegates from the State of Pennsylvania, that disputes had arisen between the States of Pennsylvania and Virginia, relative to the extent of their boundaries, which may probably be productive of serious evils to both States, and tend to lesson their exertions in the common defence, therefore

Resolved, That it be recommended to the contending parties not to grant any part of the disputed lands or to disturb the possession of any person living thereon, and to avoid every appearance of force, until the dispute can be amicably adjusted by both States, or brought to a just decision by the intervention of Congress. That possessions forcibly taken be restored to the original possessors, and things be placed in the situation in which they were at the commencement of the present war, without prejudice to the claims of either party.

In March, 1780, the Supreme Executive Council of Pennsylvania addressed Congress on the disputed line between Virginia and itself, complimented Congress upon the foregoing recommendatory resolutions, but claimed that Virginia still harasses the innocent and unfortunate settlers of Pennsylvania ; that as the representatives of the people they will not consent to see their State insulted, and that if Pennsylvania must arm for her internal defence, she must necessarily withdraw her forces from the continental line, and trust they shall stand acquitted before them and the world.

This earnest protest to Congress had a salutary effect upon the State of Virginia, for on the 7th day of August, 1784, a letter was received from Patrick Henry, Governor of said State, inclosing a resolution confirming the line agreed upon by the commissioners in August, 1779, as above recited.

The General Assembly of Pennsylvania, on the 23d of September, 1780, authorized the President and Executive Council to appoint two commissioners on the part of this State, in conjunction with the commissioners of Virginia, to extend the line commonly called Mason and Dixon's line, five degrees of longitude from the Delaware River, and from the western termination of the line so extended to run and mark, as soon as may be, a meridian line to the Ohio river, the remainder of the line to be run as soon as the council, taking into consideration the disposition of the Indians, shall think it prudent.

February 21, 1781, Alexander McClean, of Pennsylvania, and Jos. Neville, of Youghiogheny County, Virginia, were appointed by their respective States to run a temporary line. They met on the 10th of May following and proceeded with their business, to mark a temporary boundary line between Pennsylvania and Virginia, according to the agreement of the commissioners at Baltimore on the 31st of August, 1780. The commissioners in marking the line were instructed to have cleared out at least fifteen feet in width, and on large trees, or other suitable objects, cause the letters P and V to be marked on the different sides. Each commissioner was allowed twenty shillings per day, exclusive of all necessary contingent expenses.

President Reed writes to Colonel James Marshall, Lieutenant of Washington County, in 1781 :—

It was much our wish, and equally our intention, to run the line this spring, but the State of Virginia being invaded, and the affairs of the Government in great confusion, there has not been the time or opportunity for that purpose which was necessary. Besides that, upon inquiry, we found the season was too far advanced for those astronomical observations which were necessary to run the line with exactness. We have therefore POSTPONED THE GRAND OPERATION to next spring. But as we knew it was highly necessary to have a partition of territory and jurisdiction, we proposed to Virginia to run a TEMPORARY LINE, beginning at the end of Mason and Dixon's line, and measuring twenty-three miles, what is by common computation the five degrees of longitude called for in the charter of King Charles II. This has been agreed to, and the State of Virginia has sent orders to the Surveyor of Youghiogheny County to join with one to be appointed by us. We have appointed Alexander McClean, Esq. Should he have occasion for a guard, or any other assistance from you, we make no doubt he will receive it. As soon as they have run the line and reported their proceedings, we shall send up proclamations calling upon all those who fall into this State to conform to its laws and government.

The temporary boundary line run by Alexander McClean, of Pennsylvania, and Joseph Neville, of Virginia, was to be recognized as such until the end of the Revolutionary war, or until the States might be in more tranquillity. A resolution was unanimously adopted by the legislature of Pennsylvania, on the 22d of March, 1783, approving of the line lately run between Virginia and Pennsylvania, and the resolution directed to be sent to the legislature of Virginia. This being accomplished, it only became necessary for the President of the Supreme Executive Council to issue a proclamation, to quiet the minds of the people, which he did, in the following language:—

WHEREAS, The General Assembly of this Commonwealth, by their resolution of the twenty-second day of the present month, did approve and confirm the line lately run by Messrs. McClean and Neville as the boundary between this State and that of Virginia, until the final settlement thereof be obtained, we have thought fit to make known the same, and we do hereby charge, enjoin, and require all persons whatsoever, residing within that tract of country situate between the meridian line run by Messrs. Sinclair and McClean, and that lately run by Messrs. Neville and McClean, bounded southward by the extension of Mason and Dixon's line, and northward by the Ohio River, and also all others residing eastward of the said line run by Messrs. Sinclair and McClean, who heretofore may have supposed themselves to be there settled within the State of Virginia, to take notice of the proceedings aforesaid, and to pay due obedience to the laws of this Commonwealth.

Given in Council at Philadelphia, this 26th day of March, 1783.

JOHN DICKINSON, *President*

Attest: JOHN ARMSTRONG, JR., *Secretary.*

Thus was temporarily settled the boundary line between these two States, which was afterwards finally and fully adjusted by the adoption, extension, and approval of the Mason and Dixon's line, a history of which we reserve for another chapter. But the student of history cannot fail to observe that when Virginia ceded this part of Pennsylvania, formerly claimed by it, to the State of Pennsylvania, there was a necessity for erecting a new county, hence *Washington County* was erected in 1781, comprising all the State west of the Monongahela, and southwest of the Ohio.

CHAPTER II.

THE MASON AND DIXON'S LINE.

Its full history—the line run by Charles Mason and Jeremiah Dixon—the claim of Pennsylvania—the claim of Lord Baltimore—the appointment of commissioners—the labors of Mason and Dixon ended in 1767—new commissioners appointed in 1783 by the States of Virginia and Pennsylvania—letter from Joseph Reed on the scientific apparatus to be used—report of the joint-commissioners—report of the Pennsylvania commissioners—cost of running the line—the western line of Pennsylvania run by commissioners appointed by both States, and the report of the commissioners thereupon—the origin of the Pan Handle in West Virginia.

IN tracing the history of the Virginia and Pennsylvania controversy in the preceding chapter, we were necessarily required to advert to the Mason and Dixon's line, which was extended twenty-three miles, and finally adjusted by the commissioners of the two States. We propose in the present chapter to give a history of this celebrated line, which is the southern boundary of our State, and for want of which there was so much trouble, perplexity, and controversial discussions, until its final adjustment and the erection of Washington County, Pennsylvania.

This line was fixed by the distinguished mathematicians and astronomers, CHARLES MASON and JEREMIAH DIXON, during the years 1763–4–5–6–7, and afterwards extended, by authority and consent of the States of Virginia and Pennsylvania, temporarily, but finally adjusted in 1784. We may add, the line properly begins at the northeast corner of Maryland, and runs due west. The Indians (as we will show) were troublesome to the surveyors, but by treaties they permitted them to proceed as far west as the old war path, within thirty-six miles of the whole distance to be run, when the Indian escort informed them that it was the will of the Six Nations the surveyors should cease their labors; there was no alternative. The surveyors stopped, and hence arose the difficulties which we have narrated in our preceding chapter.

By reference to the charter granted by King Charles II. to William Penn, his heirs and assigns, on the 4th of March, 1681, we find the following described land: "All that tract or part of land in America, with all the islands therein contained, as the same is bounded on the east by Delaware River, from twelve miles distant northwards of New Castletown unto the three and fortieth degree of northern latitude, if the said river doth extend so far northward; but if the said river shall not extend so far northward, then by the said river so far as it doth extend; and from the head of the said river the eastern bounds are to be determined by a meridian line to be drawn from the head of the said river unto the said three and fortieth degree. The said land to extend westwards five degrees in longitude to be computed from the said eastern bounds; and the said lands to be bounded on the north by the beginning of the three and fortieth degree of northern latitude, and on the south by a circle drawn at twelve miles distance from New Castle northwards, and westwards unto the beginning of the fortieth degree of northern latitude, and then by a straight line westwards to the limits of longitude above mentioned."

It is evident that Penn's grant of land from King Charles was to lie west of the Delaware River, and north of Maryland, because the charter by Lord Baltimore for Maryland included all the land to the Delaware Bay, "which lieth under the fortieth degree of north latitude, where New England terminates;" hence the only mode by which the form and extent of Pennsylvania could be determined was by the two natural landmarks, viz., New Castletown and the River Delaware. This river being her eastern boundary, New Castle was to be used as the centre of a circle of twelve miles radius, whose northwestern segment was to connect the river with the beginning of the fortieth degree, while the province was to extend westward five degrees in longitude, to be computed from said eastern bounds.

The Penns claimed for the western boundary a line beginning at thirty-nine degrees, at the distance of five degrees of longitude from the Delaware; thence at the same distance from that river in every point to north latitude forty-two degrees, which would take into the province of Pennsylvania some fifty miles square of Northwestern Virginia, west of the west line of Maryland. Lord Dunmore, however, scouted this claim, and insisted that it would be difficult to ascertain such a line with mathematical exactness, and that the western boundary of Pennsylvania should be a meridian line run south from the end of five degrees of longitude from the Delaware, on the line of forty-two degrees. This claim, on the other hand, would have thrown the western line of Pennsylvania fifty miles east of Pittsburg.

The foundation of the Mason and Dixon's line was based upon an agreement entered into on the 4th of July, 1760, between Lord Baltimore, of the province of Maryland, and Thomas and Richard Penn, of the province of Pennsylvania, and the three lower counties of Newcastle, Kent, and Sussex on the Delaware—on account of the very long litigations and contests which had subsisted between these provinces from the year 1683. These parties mutually agreed among other things to appoint a sufficient number of discreet and proper persons, not more than seven on each side, to be their respective commissioners, with full power to the said seven persons, or any three or more of them, for the actual running, marking, and laying out the said part of the circle (as mentioned in the charter from Charles II. to William Penn), and the said before-mentioned lines. The commissioners were to fix upon their time of commencing said line not later than the following October, and proceed with all fairness, candor, and dispatch ; marking said line with stones and posts on both sides, and complete the same before the 25th of December, 1763, so that no disputes may hereafter arise concerning the same.

James Hamilton (Governor), Richard Peters, Rev. Dr. John Ewing, William Allen (Chief Justice), William Coleman, Thomas Willing, and Benjamin Chew were appointed commissioners on the part of the Penns.

Horatio Sharpe (Governor), J. Ridout, John Leeds, John Barclay, George Stewart, Dan of St. Thomas Jenifer, and J. Beale Boardley on behalf of Lord Baltimore.

The Board of Commissioners met at New Castle, in November, 1760, and each province selected its own surveyors. The Pennsylvania surveyors were John Lukens and Archibald McClain. Those of Maryland were John F. A. Priggs and Jonathan Hall.

The commissioners and surveyors agreed that the peninsular lines from Henlopen to the Chesapeake, made under a decree of Lord Hardwicke in 1750, was correct, hence they fixed the court-house at New Castle as the centre of the circle, and the surveyors proceeded on this data to measure and mark the lines. James Veech, Esq., in his history of Mason and Dixon's line, says:—

"Three years were diligently devoted to finding the bearing of the western line of Delaware, so as to make it a tangent to the circle, at the end of a twelve mile radius. The instruments and appliances employed seem to have been those commonly used by surveyors. The proprietors residing in or near London, grew weary of this slow progress, which perhaps they set down to the incompetency of the artists. To this groundless suspicion we owe their supersedure and the introduction of the men *Mason* and *Dixon*, who have immortalized their memory in the name of the principal line which had yet to be run."

In August, 1763, Charles Mason and Jeremiah Dixon, of London, England, were selected by Lord Baltimore and the Penns, to complete their lines, as per agreement, made on the fourth of July, 1760, and arrived at Philadelphia in November, for that purpose, furnished, says Mr. Veech, with instructions and the most approved instruments, among them a four foot zenith sector. They go to work at once, erect an observatory on Cedar Street, Philadelphia, to facilitate the ascertainment of its latitude, which building they use by January, 1764, and it has been pronounced the first building erected in America for astronomical observations. They then go to New Castle, adopt the radius as measured by their predecessors, and after numerous tracings of the tangent line, adopt also their tangent point, from which they say they could not make the tangent line pass one inch to the eastward or westward. They therefore cause that line and point to be marked, and adjourn to Philadelphia to find its southern limit on Cedar or South Street. This they make to be 39° 56' 29", while the latitude of the State has been marked as 39° 56' 29". They then proceed to extend that latitude sufficiently far to the west to be due north of the tangent point. Thence they measure down south fifteen miles to the latitude of the great due west line, and run its parallel for a short distance. Then they go to the tangent point and run due north to that latitude, and at the point of intersection, in a deep ravine, near a spring, they cause to be planted the corner-stone, at which begins the celebrated "Mason and Dixon's line."

We shall continue the graphic description of our learned friend James Veech, Esq. Having ascertained the latitude of this line to be 39° 43' 32" (although more accurate observations make it 39° 43' 26".8, consequently it is a little over nineteen miles south of 40° as now located) they, under instructions, run its parallel to the Susquehanna, twenty-three miles; and having verified the latitude there, they return to the tangent point, from which they run the due north line to the fifteen mile corner and that part of the circle which it cuts off to the west, and which by agreement was to go to New Castle County. (This little bow or arc is about a mile and a half long and its middle width one hundred and sixteen feet. From its upper end where the three States join, to the fifteen mile point where the great Mason and Dixon's line begins, is a little over three and a half miles, and from the fifteen mile corner due east to the circle is a little over three-quarters of a mile. This was the only part of the circle which Mason and Dixon run, Lord Baltimore having no concern in the residue; Penn, however, had it run and marked with "four good notches" by Isaac Taylor and Thomas Pierson in 1700-1.) Where it cuts the circle is the corner of three dominions, an important point, and therefore they cause it to be well ascertained and well marked. This brings them to the end of 1764.

They resume their labors in June, 1765. If to extend this parallel did not require so great skill as did the nice adjustments of the other lines and intersections, it summoned its performers to greater endurance. A tented army penetrates the forest, but their purposes are peaceful and they move merrily. Besides the surveyors and their assistants, there were chain bearers, rod men, axe men, commissioners, cooks, and baggage carriers, with numerous servants and laborers. By the 27th of October, they come to the North (Cove or Kittatinny) Mountain, ninety-five miles from the Susquehanna, and where the temporary line of 1739 terminated. After taking Captain Shelby with them to its summit *to show them the course of the Potomac,* and point out the Allegheny Mountain, the surveyors and their attendants return to the settlements to pass the winter and to get their appointment renewed.

Early in 1766 they are again at their posts, and by the 4th of June they are on the top of the little Allegheny Mountain; the first west of Wills' Creek. They have now carried the line about one hundred and sixty miles from its beginning. The Indians into whose ungranted territory they had deeply penetrated, grow restive and threatening. They forbid any further advance, and they had to be obeyed. The agents of the proprietors now find that there are other lords of the soil whose favor must be propitiated. The six Indian nations were the lords paramount of the territory yet to be traversed. To obtain their consent to the consummation of the line, the Governors of Pennsylvania and Maryland, in the winter of 1766-7, at an expense of more than £500, procured, under the agency of Sir William Johnston, a grand convocation of the tribes of that powerful confederacy. The application was successful, and early in June, 1767, an escort of fourteen warriors, with an interpreter and chief, deputed by the Iroquois council, met the surveyors and their camp at the summit of the great Allegheny to escort them down into the valley of the Ohio, whose tributaries they were soon to cross.

Safety being thus secured, the extension of the line was pushed on vigorously in the summer of 1767. Soon the host of red and white men led by the London surveyors, came to the western limit of Maryland, "the meridian of the first fountain of the Potomac," and why they did not stop there is a mystery, for there their functions terminated. But they pass by it unheeded, because unknown, resolved to reach the utmost limit of Penn's "five degrees of longitude" from the Delaware, for so were they instructed. By the 24th of August they came to the crossing of Braddock's road. The escort now became restless. The Mohawk chief and his nephew leave. The Shawnese and Delaware, tenants of the hunting grounds, begin to grow terrific. On the 27th of September, when encamped on the Monongahela River, two hundred and thirty-three miles from the Delaware River, twenty-six of the laborers desert, and but fifteen axe-men are left. Being so near the goal, the surveyors (for none of the commissioners were with them) evince their courage by coolly sending back to Fort Cumberland for aid, and in the mean time they push on. At length they came to where the line crosses the Warrior branch of the old Catawba war path, at the second crossing of Dunkard Creek, a little west of Mount Morris, in Greene County, and there the Indian escort say to them, "*that they were instructed by their chiefs in council, not to let the line be run westward of that path.*" Their commands are peremptory, and there for fifteen years MASON AND DIXON'S LINE IS STAYED.

Mason and Dixon, with their pack-horse train and attendants, return to the east without molestation and report to the commissioners, who approved their conduct, and on the 27th of December, 1767, grant to them an honorable discharge, and agreed to pay them an additional price for a map or plan of their work.

The commissioners caused stones to be erected upon the lines and at the corners and intersections around and near the three counties of Delaware. On the 9th day of November, 1768, they made their final report to the proprietors.

It would be well to remark that along the line and at the end of every fifth mile, a stone was planted on which were graven the arms of the proprietors on the side facing their possessions respectively, while the intermediate miles were noted by a stone bearing the initials of the respective State thereon. The line opened was of the breadth of twenty-four feet, made by felling all the large trees, which were left to rot upon the ground ; the stones were erected along the middle of this pathway.

The instruments used by Mason and Dixon were an ordinary surveyor's compass to find their bearings generally, a quadrant, and the four feet zenith sector, for absolute accuracy, and which enabled them to be guided by the unerring luminaries of the heavens.

The measurements were made with a four pole chain of one hundred links each, except that on hills and mountains, one of two poles and sometimes a one pole measure was used. These were frequently tested by a statute chain carried along for that purpose. Great care was enjoined as to the plumbings on uneven ground, and so far as they have been since tested, the measurements seem to have been very true.

The width of a degree of longitude varies according to the latitude it traverses, expanding towards the equator, and contracting towards the pole. In the latitude of our line, Mason and Dixon computed it at fifty-three miles and one hundred and sixty-seven and one-tenth perches. They consequently made Penn's five degrees of longitude from the Delaware, to be two hundred and sixty-seven miles and one hundred and ninety-five and one-sixteenth perches. To their stopping place at the war-path on Dunkard, they say was two hundred and forty-four miles, one hundred and thirteen perches and seven and one fourth feet. Hence they left, as they computed it, *twenty-three miles and eighty-three perches* to be run. It was subsequently ascertained that this was about a mile and a half too much, as the surveyors of 1784 made it two hundred and sixty-six miles, ninety-nine and one-fifth perches.

After a long controversy with Virginia, which we have narrated in the preceding chapter, and up to September 4, 1783, and after the erection of Washington County, Pennsylvania, the General Assembly resolved that as many of the objections which have hitherto prevented the determination of the boundary line are now removed, it becomes necessary to close that business with all possible accuracy and dispatch, whereupon Pennsylvania and Virginia therefore appointed the Rev. Dr. John Ewing, David Rittenhouse, John Lukens, and Thomas Hutchins, on behalf of Pennsylvania, while Virginia appointed Right Reverend James Madison, Bishop of Virginia, Rev. Robert Andrews, John Page, and Andrew Elliott, of Maryland, their respective commissioners, to provide the necessary instruments and make all necessary preparations for running the line.

At this point of our history, it will be interesting to our scientific readers to introduce an official letter written by Joseph Reed, President of the Supreme Executive Council of Pennsylvania, to Thomas Jefferson, Governor of Virginia. The original is in the archives of the city of Richmond.

IN COUNCIL. *Philadelphia*, May 14, 1781.

DEAR SIR: Since I had the honor of addressing your Excellency on the 6th inst., we have conferred with the commissioners, who settled the agreement entered into at Baltimore in August, 1779, and we fully concur in the method proposed by your Excellency of settling the extent of the five degrees of longitude by astronomical observation, not only as determining the present question with more certainty, but as it tends to solve a problem both useful and curious to the learned world. But we are sorry to find that it is the opinion of our gentlemen of science that the season will be too far advanced before the observations can be commenced, and more especially as the principal astronomical instruments in this city are so scattered and out of repair as to require a considerable time to put them in order.

For these reasons, though with great reluctance, we have thought it best, after expressing our full acquiescence in the mode suggested by your Excellency, to propose the 1st of May next to run the line by astronomical observations. But in the mean time, for the sake of settling the minds of the people, and preventing disputes among the borderers, to have a temporary line run by common surveyors from the termination of Mason and Dixon's line to the Ohio; or if that should not be agreeable, to extend it twenty-three miles from the end of Mason and Dixon's line, that being the extent of five degrees, according to common computation. In this case we only propose to mark the trees, avoiding as much as possible unnecessary expense. We hope this last proposition, in which we have no other intentions than to quiet the minds of the people and compel militia services, will be acceptable to your Excellency as the best and indeed the only expedient which can now be adopted.

I am, with great consideration and respect, your Excellency's obedient servant, JOSEPH REED, *President*.

James Veech, Esq., very justly observes that the commissioners undertook the task from an anxious desire to gratify the astronomical world in the performance of a problem which has never yet been attempted in any country, and to prevent the State of Pennsylvania from the chance of losing many hundred thousands of acres secured to it by the agreement at Baltimore. To solve the novel problem, two of the artists of each State, provided with the proper astronomical instruments and a good timepiece, repaired to Wilmington, Delaware, nearly on the line, where they erected an observatory. The other four in like manner furnished, and with commissary, soldiers, and servants, proceeded to the west end of the *temporary line*, near to which, on one of the highest of the Fish Creek hills, they also erected a rude observatory. At these stations each party, during six long weeks of days and nights, preceding the autumnal equinox of 1784, continued to make observations of the eclipses of Jupiter's moons, and other celestial phenomena, for the purpose of determining their respective meridians and latitude, and adjusting their timepieces. This done, two of each party come together, and they find their stations were apart *twenty minutes and one and an eighth seconds.* The Wilmington station was one hundred and fourteen (four poles) chains and thirteen links west of the Delaware. Knowing that twenty minutes of time were equal to five degrees of longitude, they make allowance for said one hundred and fourteen chains and thirteen links, and for the said one and an eighth seconds (equal, they say, to nineteen chains and ninety-six links), and upon these data they shorten back on the line to twenty minutes from the Delaware, and fix the southwest corner of the State by setting up a square unlettered white oak post, around which they rear a conical pyramid of stones, "and they are there unto this day."

As but very few persons can have access to the original reports of the commissioners, we insert them for future reference.

Joint Report of Commissioners on Boundary between Pennsylvania and Virginia.

Agreeably to the commission given by the State of Virginia to James Madison, Robert Andrews, John Page, and Andrew Elliott, and by the State of Pennsylvania to John Ewing, David Rittenhouse, John Lukens, and Thomas Hutchins, to determine by astronomical observations the extent of five degrees of longitude west from the river Delaware in the latitude of Mason and Dixon's line, and to run and mark the boundaries which are common to both States, according to an agreement entered into by commissioners from the said two States at Baltimore in 1779 and afterwards ratified by their respective Assemblies, we, the underwritten commissioners, together with the gentlemen with whom we are joined in commission, have, by corresponding astronomical observations, made near the Delaware and in the western country, ascertained the extent of the said five degrees of longitude; and the underwritten commissioners have continued Mason and Dixon's line to the termination of the said five degrees of longitude, by which work the southern boundary of Pennsylvania is completed. The continuation we have marked by opening vistas over the most remarkable heights which lie in its course, and by planting on many of these heights, in the parallel of latitude, the true boundary, posts marked with the letters P. and V., each letter facing the State of which it is the initial. At the extremity of this line, which is the southwest corner of the State of Pennsylvania, we have planted a squared unlettered white oak post, around whose base we have raised a pile of stones. The corner is in the last vista we cut, on the east side of a hill, one hundred and thirty-four chains and nine links east of the meridian of the western observatory, and two chains and fifty-four links west of a deep narrow valley, through which the said last vista is cut. At the distance of fifty-one links, and bearing from it north twenty-three degrees east, stands a white oak marked on the south side with three notches, and bearing south twelve degrees west, and at the distance of twenty-nine links, stands a black oak on the north side with four notches. The advanced season of the year, and the inclemency of the weather, have obliged us to suspend our operations, but we have agreed to meet again at the southwest corner of Pennsylvania on the 16th day of May next to complete the object of our commission.

Given under our hands and seals, in the County of Washington, in Pennsylvania, this 18th day of November, 1784.

     Robert Andrews, ☐ Andrew Elliott, ☐
     John Ewing, ☐   David Rittenhouse, ☐
        Tho. Hutchins. ☐

To this report I add the report of the Pennsylvania Commissioners on the boundary with Virginia, which was received by the Supreme Executive Council December 23, 1784.

To his Excellency John Dickinson, Esq., President of the State, and to the Honorable the Supreme Executive Council of the Commonwealth of Pennsylvania :—

The commissioners appointed for ascertaining the length of five degrees of longitude, and for determining and fixing the boundary lines between this State and Virginia by astronomical observations, beg leave to report

That after procuring the necessary instruments, according to the directions of council in the preceding spring, we set off for our respective places of observation about the beginning of June, Messrs. Rittenhouse and Lukens to Wilmington, and Ewing and Hutchins to the southwest corner of the State.

The observers at Wilmington completed their observatory and furnished it with the necessary instruments, so as to begin their astronomical operations in conjunction with Messrs. Page and Andrews, commissioners from Virginia, about the beginning of July, where they continued observing the eclipses of Jupiter's satellites till the 20th of September, that they might have a sufficient number of them, both before and after his opposition to the sun ; and although the summer proved very unfavorable for astronomical purposes, they were fortunate enough to make, amongst them, near sixty observations of these eclipses, besides many other observations of the other heavenly bodies for the regulation of their clock and fixing their meridian line, so that they were well ascertained of their time to a single second.

In the mean time, the other observers, setting out from Philadelphia, pursued their rout to the southwestern extremity of the State, where they arrived about the middle of July, having been greatly retarded by the badness of the roads through that mountainous country. There they met with Messrs. Madison and Elliott, the commissioners from the State of Virginia, who had arrived about the same time. With all possible dispatch they erected their observatory on a very high hill at the place where the continuation of Messrs. Mason and Dixon's line, by Messrs. Neville and McClean, ended, supposing that this place would prove to be near to the western extremity of five degrees of longitude from the river Delaware. After erecting their instruments, which had not sustained the least damage by the carriage through so long a journey, and the most unfavorable roads, they began their astronomical observations about the middle of July, and they continued them night and day till the 20th of September following. Although they were frequently interrupted and disappointed by an uncommon quantity of rain and foggy weather, which seems peculiar to that hilly country, yet by their attention to the business of their mission, they made between forty and fifty observations of the eclipses of Jupiter's satellites, many of which were correspondent with the observations made by the other astronomers at Wilmington, besides innumerable observations of the sun and stars for the regulation of their timepieces and the marking of their meridian with the greatest precision.

In this part of their work, situated nearly thirty miles beyond any of the inhabitants, the commissioners were greatly assisted by the diligence and indefatigable activity of Col. Porter, their commissary, to whose industry in providing everything necessary, and prudence in managing the business in his department with the utmost economy, the State is greatly indebted.

The astronomical observations being completed on the 20th of September, the eastern astronomers set out to meet the other commissioners in the west, in order to compare them together. Messrs. Rittenhouse and Andrews carried with them the observations made at Wilmington, while Messrs. Lukens and Page returned home, not being able to endure the fatigues of so long a journey, nor the subsequent labor of running and marking the boundary line. Mr. Madison continued with the western astronomers till the arrival of Messrs. Rittenhouse and Andrews, when the affairs of his family and public station obliged him to relinquish the business at this stage and return home, after concurring with the other commissioners as to the principles on which the matter was fully determined.

Upon comparison of the observations made at both extremities of our southern boundary, your commissioners have the pleasure of assuring you that no discouragements, arising from the unfavorable state of the weather or the unavoidable fatigues of constant application by day and frequent watchings by night, have prevented them from embracing every opportunity and making a sufficient number of astronomical observations, to determine the length of five degrees of longitude with greater precision than could be attained by terrestrial measures of a degree of latitude in different places of the earth; and further, that they have completed their observations with so much accuracy and certainty as to remove from their minds every degree of doubt concerning their final determination of the southwestern corner of the State.

In the result of the calculations they found that their observatories were distant from each other twenty minutes and one second and an eighth part of a second of time. But as the observatory at Wilmington was fixed at *one hundred and fourteen chains and thirteen links* west of the intersection of the boundary line of this State with the river Delaware; and as twenty minutes of time are equivalent to five degrees of longitude, they made the necessary correction for the said *one hundred and fourteen chains and thirteen links*, and also for the said one second and one-eighth part of a second, which is equal to *nineteen chains and ninety-six links*, and accordingly fixed and marked the southwestern corner of the State in the manner mentioned in the joint agreement and report of the commissioners of both States under their hands and seals, which we have the honor of laying before the council.

After these calculations were made, the commissioners proceeded with all convenient dispatch to the place where Mason and Dixon formerly were interrupted by the Indian nation in running the southern boundary of this State, in order to extend the said boundary westward to the length of five degrees from the river Delaware. Being prevented by rainy weather for near a week from making any astronomical observations in order to ascertain the direction of the parallel of latitude, which we were to extend, we concluded, to save time and expense, that it would be eligible to take the last direction of Mason and Dixon's line and to correct it, if necessary, when we should have an opportunity of a serene sky. Upon extending the line in this manner *one hundred and ninety-five chains* from the place where they ended their work, we found, by astronomical observation, that we were *thirty-two feet and five inches* north of the true parallel, and we accordingly made the necessary correction here and marked a tree with the

C

letters P on the north side and V on the south. From thence we assumed a new direction, which we again corrected in like manner at the distance of *five hundred and seventy-five chains*, where we found our line to be *seventy-three feet and six inches* north of the parallel of latitude. We made the offset accordingly and planted a large post in the true parallel marked as above. From thence we found another direction by calculation, which, beginning at the said post, should, at the distance of eight miles from it, intersect the said parallel, making offsets at convenient distances and planting posts in the true parallel. This direction being continued *thirty-three chains* farther than the eight miles above mentioned, fell *twenty-three inches* south of the parallel, where we also planted a post in the true boundary, marked as before, and from thence to the southwest corner of the State we assumed a new direction which, being continued, fell *two feet and eight inches* south of the said corner. This correction, therefore, being made, we planted a squared white oak post in the said point and marked its bearing from different objects, as mentioned in our joint report. Besides the marking of this boundary line by the posts and stones above mentioned, your commissioners took good care to have a vista of *twenty or thirty feet* wide cut over all the most remarkable ridges which were in the direction of the parallels.

For a more full description of this part of our work we beg leave to refer to the annexed plan (this plan has never yet been found among the State papers) and sketch of the country through which the line passes. The season being now far advanced, we were obliged to desist from any further prosecution of the work, and agreed with the Virginia commissioners to meet them at the southwestern corner of our State on the 17th of May next, to proceed in running and marking the WESTERN boundary of this State.

Agreeably to our commission we were required to report the situation of the country and the best means of preserving the communication and connection between the eastern and western parts of the State. We beg leave to observe that the natural obstructions to so desirable a purpose may be in a great measure removed by a few easy instances of attention, paid by the legislature of this State to the situation and exhausted condition of the western citizens. Their public roads are numerous, extensive, and in bad order; while the citizens being few in number, scattered at a distance from each other, and being harassed and exhausted by an Indian war, are unable to repair their roads or to open them through more easy and convenient passes, over the hills and mountains. A few hundred pounds, not exceeding one thousand, judiciously and frugally applied, would, in our opinion, make a tolerable good wagon road from York County to the Monongahela; and thereby facilitate the exportation of goods from this city to that western country and secure their trade with us, especially if the ferry over the Susquehanna was made free to all the citizens of the State. It appears probable to us that otherwise the exertions of Maryland and Virginia to repair their roads to that country will frustrate the expectation which we are entitled to entertain of enjoying the advantages of the trade with the western parts of our own State. We beg leave further to observe that the natural attachment of the western citizens to this State might be increased and fixed by an indulgence to their distressed situation in the price of their lands and the terms of payment; and particularly in the remission of the interest due on the purchase money during the time they have been obliged to evacuate their possessions by the savages and fly to forts for the security of their lives and families. JOHN EWING, DAVID RITTTENHOUSE, JOHN LUKENS, THOMAS HUTCHINS.

The twenty-three miles from the war path to the southwest corner cost the State £1455 specie, equivalent to about four thousand dollars, besides six dollars per day to each of the astronomers. From the accounts of the commissary, Col. Andrew Porter—the father of ex-Governor Porter—we copy the following bill, to show how well the commissioners lived; yet it must be borne in mind there was a necessity for procuring a great variety of articles, as they were laboring about thirty miles from the settlements. The bill calls for

120 gallons of spirits, 40 gallons of brandy, 80 gallons of Madeira wine, 200 pounds of loaf sugar, a small keg of lemon juice, 6 pounds of tea, 100 pounds of coffee, 60 pounds of chocolate, and 40 pounds of Scotch barley, pepper, 6 bushels of salt, 4 tin mugs, 1 coffee-mill, 1 pewter teapot, 1 tin coffee-pot, 1 frying pan, 1 gridiron, 6 boiling kettles, 1 Dutch oven, 1 tea-kettle, 2 pair of snuffers, 4 candlesticks, 2 funnels, 100 lbs. candles, 2 hand saws, 1 cross-cut saw, 6 files, 2 hammers, 12 gimlets, 50 lbs. nails, 1 set of knives and forks, teacups, saucers, glasses, tumblers, bowls, dishes, plates, tin spoons, and basins, 6 large camp stools and six small ones, 2 marquees or 4 horsemen's tents, 60 felling axes, 100 lbs. steel, 6 shovels, 6 pickaxes, 6 spades, 12 pair of H L hinges, 3 four-horse wagons and one light wagon with 4 horses, 20 fathom of half-inch rope, 2 crowbars, 2 planes, 2 augers, 4 mattresses, 4 blankets, 4 pillows, 1 frower, 2 mauls and rings, 2 wedges, 1 broadaxe, 2 drawing knives, ½ box of window glass, 1 ream of paper, 100 quills, 6 sticks of wax, 2 doz. pencils, 1 box wafers, 2 inkstands, 2 large camp tables, 1 doz. memorandum books, cheese, 2 doz. hams, 1 doz. kegs white biscuit.

Thus ends the history of all the difficulties which are embraced in this and the preceding chapter, and including the rise, progress, and settlement of the celebrated Mason and Dixon's line, from the year 1752 to the 23d of December, 1784, when the commissioners made their final report, which was adopted by the State of Pennsylvania through her legally constituted representatives.

Western Line of Pennsylvania.

In connection with this subject and for the benefit of our readers, we add that on the 9th of April, 1785, the Supreme Executive Council appointed David Rittenhouse and Andrew Porter, Esqs., on behalf of this State, to meet Joseph Neville and Andrew Elliott, who had been appointed by the Governor of Virginia, to run and mark the boundary lines from the southern corner to the northwest corner of the State, between Pennsylvania and Virginia. The Pennsylvania commissioners were instructed to act in conjunction with the commissioners on the part of the State of Virginia, as far as they may choose to proceed. The reason assigned for this was that the Virginia pretensions ended at a given point by reason of her cession of the northwest territory to the United States in 1784. Our commissioners were also instructed that if any commissioners on behalf of the United States should appear to join with them, to co-operate with them cheerfully.

On the 29th of July, 1785, President Dickinson wrote a letter to the commissioners urging the prosecution of the important business intrusted to them with the utmost diligence and with all the dispatch that is compatible with accuracy in their proceedings. About one month afterwards the commissioners finished their labors, as we find from the following report:—

We, the subscribers, commissioners appointed by the States of Pennsylvania and Virginia, to ascertain the boundary between the said States—

Do certify that we have carried on a meridian line from the southwest corner of Pennsylvania northward to the river Ohio, and marked it by cutting a wide vista over all the principal hills intersected by the said line, and by falling or deadening a line of trees generally through all the lower grounds, and we have likewise placed stones marked on the east side P, and on the west side V, on most of the principal hills and where the line strikes the Ohio, which stones are accurately placed in the true meridian bounding the States as aforesaid. Witness our hands and seals this 23d day of August, 1785.   David Rittenhouse, ☐   Andrew Porter, ☐
    Andew Elliott,   ☐   Joseph Neville, ☐

The Supreme Executive Council appointed Andrew Porter and Alexander McClean on the 19th of June, 1786, to extend the line of the western boundary of the State, and on the 4th of October, 1786, they made the following report:—

We, the commissioners appointed to ascertain and complete the line of the western boundary of the State of Pennsylvania, beg leave to report that we have ascertained and completed said line by astronomical observations as far as Lake Erie, having opened a vista and planted stones in the proper direction, marked on the east side P, and that said line extends some distance in the lake.   Andrew Porter.
    Alexander McClean.

We may add that the length of this line is about one hundred and fifty-eight miles.

Pan-Handle of West Virginia.

From the date of the report of Rev. Dr. Madison and Robert Andrews, Esq., of Virginia, to the legislature of that State made on the 8th day of October, 1785, may be considered as the legal existence of what is now known as the Pan-Handle.

J. G. Jacob, Esq., in his life of Patrick Gass, thus describes the Pan-Handle previous to October 8, 1785: Ohio County had, been formed from Youghiogheny, by the line of Cross Creek, and says the record, on the settlement of the boundary question in 1789, that portion of Youghiogheny lying north of this creek was added to Ohio, being too small for a separate county, and the county of Youghiogheny became thereupon extinct. (See page 15 for history of Youghiogheny County.) Hancock, then and so much of Brooke as lies north of Cross Creek was the last of the ancient Youghiogheny.

Tradition, in accounting for the strip of land driven in wedge-like between Ohio and Pennsylvania, constituting what is called the Pan-handle, states that it was owing to an error in reckoning that the five degrees of west longitude reached so far to the west, and that much dissatisfaction was excited when the result was definitely settled; as great importance was attached to the command of the Ohio River by the authorities of either State.

When the State of Ohio was formed, in 1802, the Pan-handle first showed its beautiful proportions on the map of the United States. It received its name in legislative debate, from Hon. John McMillan, delegate from Brooke County, to match the Accomac projection, which he dubbed the Spoon-handle.

New State.

On October 19, 1782, Brigadier-General Irvine, then stationed at Fort Pitt, officially informed the Supreme Executive Council of Pennsylvania, that many deluded men, governed by ambition, seriously contemplated the formation of a new State on the frontiers of this State; whereupon the Council, on the 19th of November following, adopted a resolution appointing the Rev. James Finley, of Chester County, to travel through the counties of Washington and Westmoreland, and by moral persuasion endeavor to bring over the deluded citizens to a proper sense of their duty. Rev. Finley was specially selected because he was not only well acquainted with the people generally, but because he had preached amongst them.

On the 28th of April, 1783, Rev. James Finley reported to Hon. John Dickinson, President of Council, that as the honorable council had appointed him to fulfil the intentions of the legislature, by endeavoring to bring these deluded citizens in the western counties to a proper sense of their duty, who seemed disposed to separate from the Commonwealth of Pennsylvania, and erect a new and independent State and to act as prudence might dictate, he therefore would give the following account of his commission:—

Immediately upon the receipt of the appointment and the instructions, he set off to gain all the knowledge he could of the sentiments of the people in the different parts of the settlement. He found that the inhabitants on the east side of Youghiogheny River were mostly opposed to a new State, that a considerable number of people between the Youghiogheny and the Monongahela River, and a great part of Washington County was in favor of it, being misled by a few aspiring and ill-designing men, or men who had not thoroughly considered the whole matter, which latter was the case of some of the clergy.

Rev. Finley also reported that he found that the act to prevent the erecting any new and independent State, and likewise the act for the sale of certain lands therein mentioned, of December 3, 1782, quite intimidated and discouraged the populace, who had been buoyed up with the hopes of easily obtaining, and prospects of great advantage of, a new State; he therefore called upon a number of the ministers and other gentlemen, conversed with some and wrote to others, as well as cautioned the people, after sermon, against the formation of a new State.

Rev. Finley resided six weeks among and visiting the people, and wrote a letter upon the subject of the formation of a new State, in which he used the following arguments : That its formation would be premature and unjust and dangerous to the settlement, that the expenses incurred in its formation and support would be greater than the people could bear; that Pennsylvania has a clear title to all the lands within her boundary; that Congress treated an application for a new State with the greatest displeasure; that as Christians it becomes the people to be honest, peaceful, and submissive, and that they should pay their taxes and quietly submit to the laws of the State.

Rev. Finley, at the termination of his labors, assured the Supreme Executive Council that he was satisfied in his own mind that the new State affair was finally and forever settled, which proved to be the case, and the act of the Council, passed in December, 1782, declaring it *treason* to attempt the formation of a new State, assisted the well-disposed citizens to urge upon all immediate and unconditional submission, and the abandonment of so wicked a project.

The contemplated limits of the new State, says James Veech, Esq., was to include Western Pennsylvania, Ohio east of the Muskingum, and Virginia northeast of the Kanawha, with PITTSBURG as the seat of empire.

CHAPTER III.

INDIAN HISTORY OF WESTERN PENNSYLVANIA AND VIRGINIA.

Names of all the tribes of North America in 1764—Those inhabiting Western Pennsylvania and adjoining territory—Letters on the Indian wrongs from 1765 to 1780—Rice's fort—Letters from Dr. J. C. Hupp on Miller's blockhouse—Captivity and escape of Jacob Miller, and the cruel murder of five of Miller's friends—Vance's fort—Wells's fort—Lindley's fort.

IN 1764, John Stuart, Esq., Superintendent of Indian Affairs, received from his majesty a plan for the future management of Indian affairs in America. This plan was submitted on the 10th of July, 1764, by the commissioners of trade, consisting of Lord Hillsborough, George Rice, B. Gascoygne, and J. Dyson, and approved by his majesty. This plan consists of forty-three articles, regulating all matters connected with the several tribes of Indians. The second article divides the whole British dominion into two districts, making the river Ohio the boundary line, but shortly afterwards these same commissioners, finding that several of the northern nations had not only claims and interest, but possibly actual possession and residence to the south of some parts of the Ohio River, they had recourse to distinguishing each district by naming the several tribes to be comprehended within each. It will also be observed that the Piankishaws, Wawiaghtonos, and other tribes which resided upon the Wabash and other rivers to the north of the confluence of the Ohio with the Mississippi, they placed in the northern district.

I shall enumerate *first the names of the tribes of the northern district of North America*, in alphabetical order—

Arundacks, Algonkins, Abinaquis, Arsigunticooks, Cayugas, Conoys, Caghnawagas, Canassadagas, Chippewaghs (or Missisagais), Delawares, Folsavoins, Foxes, Hurons, Illinois, Keskesias, Kickapous, Mohocks, Meynomenis, Masconteus, Mickmacks, Nanticokes, Norwidgewalks, Oneidas, Onondagas, Oswegatchies, Ottawas, Pawtiwatamais, Puano, Piankashaws, Penobscots, Senecas, Saponeys, Skaghquanoghronos, Shawnese, Saxes, Sioux, St. Johns, Tuscaroras, Tuteeres, Twightiveas, Wawiaghtonos, Wyandotts, amounting to 42.

Second, the Indian tribes in the southern district—

Attacapas, Bayuglas, Beluxis, Cherokees, Creeks, Chickasaws, Chactaws, Catawabas, Humas, Ofulgas, Peluches, Querphas, Tunicas, amounting to 13.

Before writing of the Indian wars which took place in Western Pennsylvania and the territory adjoining, it will be well to state the residence of some of these tribes for the benefit of the general reader, who desires to investigate the subject and read Indian history understandingly.

Those tribes of Indians who inhabited Pennsylvania and the adjoining colonies, were the " Six Nations," known originally as the Five Nations, called by the French, Iroquois. These five tribes consisted of the MOHAWKS and ONEIDAS (which were the oldest), SENECAS, ONONDAGOS, and CAYUGAS. In 1712, the Tuscaroras, who had resided in North Carolina, were driven off from their hunting grounds in the southern district, and became the SIXTH of this powerful Indian confederacy. They were called the Six Indian Nations, because they all spoke the same language.

In describing the settlement of these Six Nations, it cannot be done in more appropriate language than in the words of an Oneida Chief, at a conference with the Indians held in 1762. In addressing the Governor, James Hamilton, he says :—

" It was we of the Mohawks, Oneidas, Senecas, Onondagos, Cayugas, and Tuscaroras, that first brought about the good work of peace. The Mohawks and Oneidas are the eldest of the Six Nations, both of a height. I will let you know the Mohawks are the eldest, yet they are the furthest off to the eastward. When they hear anything, they pass through the Oneidas to the Onondagos, where the council fire burns. Likewise when the Senecas hear anything, they come to the Cayugas, because they are next to the Onondago council, so that whenever they hear anything to the east or west, it is carried to the Onondago council."

In other words, there are only two doors to the Onondago council fire, either through the Mohocks in the east, or the Senecas in the west. This Indian confederacy of the Six Nations embraced what now comprises the States of Western New York, Northwestern Pennsylvania, West Virginia, Ohio, and their influence was felt even to the Mississippi, and in fact all the Indian tribes of the northern jurisdiction, more particularly the six western Indian tribes called the Delawares, Shawnese, Twightees, Wiwaghtamies, Kickapoes, and Tuscaroras. The remains of these Six Indian Nations still exist, but in very small numbers, by reservations secured to them by the States of New York and Pennsylvania. On the 25th of January, 1866, the legislature of Pennsylvania directed a monument to be erected to the memory of CORNPLANTER, of the Seneca tribe, and a principal chief of the Six Nations, for his distinguished services in behalf of the Revolutionary war. The monument was erected at Jennesadaga, Warren County, Pa., and dedicated with appropriate honors. Leaving Gy-ant-wa-chia, or Cornplanter, the last chief of the Senecas and of the Iroquois or Six Nations, buried in his last home, the old homestead in which he lived and died at the age of one hundred years, we trace our steps to speak of Indian war, Indian cruelty, and Indian barbarity, made upon the early pioneers of the land upon which we dwell.

The first Indian war with which we as a county are immediately interested, was that of 1763, when all the Indian nations of the western country united against the frontier settlements of Pennsylvania and Virginia and other colonies. We have already, in our first chapter, exhibited the authority of the colonies of Pennsylvania and Virginia to restrain their citizens from making settlements west of the Allegheny Mountains, because the lands were claimed by the Indians. The indomitable courage of our people was neither daunted by government or fear, but gradually they made settlement after settlement, erected forts and block-houses, until the Indians resolved to take up arms in their own defence. They therefore resolved on a general massacre of all the white people not only in the western country, but along the Susquehanna, where many of their tribes were settled.

History tells us that their first attack was against the English traders settled at different points, and out of about one hundred and twenty, but two or three escaped; that the garrisons of Presque Isle, St. Joseph, and Michilimakinac, were taken and a general slaughter ensued, and that it was with great difficulty that the forts at Bedford, Ligonier, Niagara, Detroit, and Pittsburg, were preserved. Fort Pitt being far from the settlements, the Indians resolved to reduce it by famine, but failed in the attempt.

That the Indians were exasperated to this course of conduct, we can readily imagine from the tenor of the following letters :—

WINCHESTER, 30th April, 1765.

The frontier inhabitants of this colony (Virginia) and Maryland are removing fast over the Allegheny Mountains in order to settle and live there. The two hunters who killed the two Indians near Pittsburg, some time ago, are so audacious as to boast of the fact and show the scalps publicly— what may not such proceedings produce? One of these hunters lives in Maryland, the other, named Walker, lives in Augusta County, Virginia.

Extract of a Letter from Carlisle, 1765.

A number of men from this settlement went up to Shamokin (Fort Augusta) to kill the Indians there, which caused them all to fly from that place.

Extract of a Letter from Fort Loudon, 1768.

The last news we have had here, and which is very certain, is the killing of nine Shawnese Indians, in Augusta County, Virginia, who were passing this way to the Cherokee nation, to war against them, and *had obtained a pass* from one Col. Lewis of that county. Yet, notwithstanding, a number of the county people met them a few miles from Col Lewis' and killed nine of them, there being but ten in the company.

From Lord Botetourt, Governor of Virginia, 1770.

I have the honor to inclose two depositions, together with an answer to a letter wrote by the Attorney-General, and have sent to your Excellency, by Lieutenant Inglis, the body of John Ingman, he having confessed himself concerned in the murder of Indian Stephen, which was committed on ground claimed by your government. You will find that there never was an act of villany more unprovoked or more deliberately undertaken. It is therefore extremely my wish that the laws may enable you to do justice, and appease, by rigid punishment, a nation of offended Indians. Mr. Wm. Crawford, who is master of John Ingham, has engaged to do his utmost to procure any evidence which you may think material to examine.

Letter from Charles Edmonstone, Fort Pitt, 1771.

I take the liberty to inclose for your perusal the copy of an affidavit taken here, relative to the murder of two Seneca Indians. I have the supposed perpetrator of the crime in custody, and intend sending him to Bedford jail. I have had several meetings with the chiefs of the different tribes, who seem all pleased with the steps taken in this affair.

Letter from Arthur St. Clair, 1774 (Ligonier).

The murder of a Delaware Indian chief was perpetrated eighteen miles from this place. It is the most astonishing thing in the world, the disposition of the common people of this county; actuated by the most savage cruelty, they wantonly perpetrate crimes that are a disgrace to humanity, and seem at the same time to be under a kind of religious enthusiasm, whilst they want the daring spirit that usually inspires. * * * The Delawares are still friendly and it may perhaps prevent a general war if they can be kept in temper (by making them presents or to cover his bones as they express it). I shall go to Fort Pitt and will consider well of it.

Extract from a Letter of Alexander McKea, Fort Pitt, 1774.

You must ere this be acquainted with the critical situation of this country, the unhappy disturbances which have lately rose between the Virginians and the natives, the event of which still continues doubtful whether matters will be brought to a general rupture or accommodation. Hostilities, however, have been committed on both sides, but at present there seems to be a cessation. Some wise interposition of government is truly necessary, and would undoubtedly restore peace; without it, impossible, and thousands of the inhabitants must be involved in misery and distress. But to do the Indians justice, they have given more proof of their pacific disposition and have acted with more moderation than those who ought to have been more rational, a few Mingoes and Shawnese excepted, who have long been refractory. There are more effectual means of chastising them for their insolence and perjury than by involving the defenceless country in a war, which there is too much reason to fear at this time will become general, and which must inevitably be the destruction of this country.

Extract of a Letter from D. Smith, Pittsburg, 1774.

The Indians were surprised to see a number of armed men at this place with their colors at different times, making a warlike appearance, and said that some of the militia fired on them at their camps near the mouth of the Sawmill Run.

Letter from Aeneas Mackay, 1774, Pittsburg.

We don't know what day or hour we will be attacked by our savage and provoked enemy, the Indians, who have already massacred sixteen persons to our certain knowledge, about and in the neighborhood of Tenmile Creek. A party of the militia, consisting of Captain McClure, Lieutenant Kincaid, and forty privates, were on their march to join Connolly at the mouth of Wheeling, where he intended to erect a stockade fort, when on a sudden they were attacked by only four Indians, who killed the captain on the spot, wounded the lieutenant, and made their escape.

On the 14th June, 1774, a petition was signed at Pittsburg by the prominent citizens of Westmoreland County (which then embraced Washington County), representing to Governor Penn that there is the greatest reason to apprehend that this part of the county will be immediately involved in all the horrors of an Indian war; that in the midst of these scenes of desolation and ruin, next to the Almighty, they look up to his honor for protection and relief.

Extract of a Letter from John Montgomery, 1774, Carlisle.

The Shawnees seem well disposed and inclinable for peace, and will continue so unless provoked by the Virginians. The Delawares are all for peace. Logan's party had returned and had thirteen scalps and one prisoner. Logan says he is now satisfied for the loss of his relatives, and will sit still unless he hears what the Long Knife (the Virginians) will say. I am in hopes the storm will blow over, and that peace and tranquillity will be restored to the back inhabitants.

Extract from Richard Butler's Letter of 1774, Pittsburg.

* * * These facts (as above enumerated) were sufficient to bring on a war with a Christian instead of a savage people, and I declare it as my opinion that the Shawnese did not intend a war this season, let their future intentions be what they might. I likewise declare, that I am afraid from the proceedings of the chiefs of the white people here, that they will bring on a general war, as there is so little pains taken to restrain the common people, whose prejudices lead them to greater lengths than ought to be shown by civilized people; and their superiors take too little, if any pains, and I do really think are much to blame themselves in the whole affair.

The Council of the Colony of Virginia met on the 12th of March, 1777, to consider the situation of Indian affairs; appointed George Morgan, agent for Indian affairs at Pittsburg, and John Neville, Esqs., to confer with the chiefs of the Delaware and Shawnee Indians, and procure their good will and favor in chastising those tribes who have been annoying their citizens; and in case of their refusal, a battalion of three hundred men, with the necessary officers, was ordered to be raised to make the contemplated expedition to Pluggystown, and punish that tribe for their unprovoked cruelties committed on the inhabitants of Virginia.

Col. David Shephard, of Ohio County, was appointed Commander-in-Chief of the expedition; Major Henry Taylor, of Youghiogheny (now Washington) County, to be Major; and the other officers were appointed from the counties of Monongahela, Youghiogheny, and Ohio, of which I have spoken in a preceding chapter.

In consequence of these preparations the friendly Indians (the Delawares and Shawnese) exercised their influence to prevent a war, and I find from a letter of Samuel Mason to Brigadier-General Hand, dated June 8, 1777, at Fort Henry, in which he says: "I set off at eight this morning and flatter myself that you will not disapprove our proceeding, but call on me, if any occasion should require, and as I may not return to the ensuing council at CATFISH (Washington), I take this opportunity of returning to you the strength of my company, which consists of fifty men, furnished for going on any emergency.

The distressed situation of the frontier inhabitants at this time required active and energetic measures, and the people erected two stockade forts at Ligonier and Hannahstown, Westmoreland County. I find Thomas Scott (whose name, subsequently, appears as the first Prothonotary of Washington County), under date of August 1, 1778, writes: "The Indians have made several breaches on the inhabitants, of late, in different parts of this country. Captain Miller, of the 8th Pennsylvania Regiment, with a party of nine men, chiefly continental soldiers, were bringing grain from the neighborhood to a fort called Fort Hand, about fourteen miles north of Hannahstown, and on their return were surprised by a party of Indians, who killed the captain and seven others."

On account of this sad state of affairs, Congress deemed it advisable to appoint commissioners to hold a treaty with the Delaware, Shawnese, and other Indians, and appointed Fort Pitt as the place of meeting, two commissioners to be appointed from Pennsylvania and one from Virginia. Col. Lewis, from Virginia, attended, but the record does not give the names of the Pennsylvania commissioners.

Gen. McIntosh writes under date of January 29, 1779, from Fort Pitt, that Capt. Clark, of the 8th Pennsylvania Regiment, as he was returning from Fort Lawrence with a sergeant and fourteen men, on three miles of this side of that fort he was attacked by Simon Girty and a party of Mingoes, who killed two of our men, wounded four, and took one prisoner. This is the same Girty who took the oath of allegiance at Pittsburg and was afterwards engaged in the murderous treatment of Col. William Crawford, in 1782.

On 24th June, 1779, Col. Broadhead writes from Pittsburg that the Indians proceeded to the Sewickley settlement, where they killed a woman and her four children and took two children prisoners. These children were afterwards recovered; one resided in Westmoreland County and the other in Butler.

March 18, 1780, at a sugar camp on Racoon Creek, near Fort Pitt, five men were killed and three boys and three girls taken prisoners. This murder was committed by the Wyandotts.

April 17, 1780, Northumberland County was authorized by the Supreme Executive Council to offer the following premiums for every male prisoner, whether white or Indian (if the former is acting with the latter), *fifteen hundred* dollars, and *one thousand dollars* for every Indian scalp. The Council were actuated to this course because they believed it more effectual than any sort of defensive operations.

September 5, 1780, the Indians killed two men on Robinson's Run, in what is called Youghiogheny County.

Washington County, April 5, 1783, the Indians took one Mrs. Walker prisoner on the 27th, on Buffalo Creek, but she made her escape. The 1st of April they took Boice and family, consisting of eight persons, and a man was killed the day following near Washington County court-house.

May 12, 1784, two men killed at or near Cross Creek by the Indians.

The above history and extracts from letters contain all the Indian murders which were committed in this part of the country, whether known as Westmoreland, Youghiogheny, Monongahela, and Ohio counties, or, since Virginia relinquished her claim, in Washington County, Pennsylvania. Since its erection as a county, in 1781, no Indian murders have been perpetrated, yet it would be proper to state that all the Indian campaigns, commencing with Pontiac's war, in 1763, Lord Dunmore's war of 1774, Gen. McIntosh's campaign in 1778, the Coshocton campaign in 1780, the Moravian campaign, in 1782, had an influence and effect upon the settlement and prospects of Washington County, because farms could not be cultivated and the people were in constant dread of an Indian attack, and hence forts were erected here and there, to which, in case of danger, the people fled for protection. While the farmer was cultivating his ground he had his trusty rifle by his side for defence.

Of these forts I now speak. It appears that RICE'S Fort furnishes the most satisfactory history of those times, which I have been able to procure.

RICE'S FORT.

This fort is situated on Buffalo Creek, about twelve miles from its junction with the Ohio River.

Rev. Dr. Dodridge gives the following description of a fort, which is worthy of being inserted as tending to throw much light upon the distinctions which should be borne in mind by the reader.

The *fort* consisted of CABINS, BLOCK-HOUSES, and STOCKADES. A range of *cabins* commonly formed one side, at least, of the fort. Divisions or partitions of logs separated the cabins from each other. The walls on the outside were ten or twelve feet high, the slope of the roof being turned wholly inward. A very few of these cabins had puncheon floors, the greater part were earthen. The *block-houses* were built at the angles of the fort. They projected about two feet beyond the outer walls of the cabin and stockade. Their upper stories were about eighteen inches every way larger in dimension than the under one, leaving an opening at the commencement of the second story to prevent the enemy from making a lodgment under their walls. In some forts, instead of block-houses, the angles of the fort were furnished with *bastions*. A large folding gate, made of thick slabs, nearest the spring, closed the fort. The stockades, bastions, cabins, and block-house walls, were furnished with portholes at proper heights and distances. The whole of the outside was made completely bullet-proof. In some places less exposed, a single block-house, with a cabin or two, constituted the whole fort. These forts answered the purpose for what they were intended, as the Indians had no artillery; they seldom attacked and scarcely ever took one of them.

The Indians, being defeated at Wheeling, resolved to strike a severe blow in the country, and hence about one hundred warriors marched to Rice's Fort, but the inhabitants being made aware of their approach, each ran to his cabin for his gun, and all took refuge in the block-house or fort. Although they intended to take it by assault, yet they failed, as the sequel will show, and they continued their depredations, destroying barns, fences, cattle, &c., but finally retreated. Rev. Dr. Dodridge, in his account of this fort, says:—

This place was defended by a Spartan band of men, against one hundred chosen warriors, exasperated to madness by their failure at Wheeling Fort. Their names shall be inscribed in the list of the heroes of our early times. They were Jacob Miller, George Leffer, Peter Fullenweider, Daniel Rice, George Felebaum, and Jacob Leffer, Jr. George Felebaum was shot in the forehead through a porthole at the second fire of the Indians, and instantly expired, so that in reality the defence of the place was made by only five men. Four of the Indians were killed. The next morning sixty men collected and pursued the Indians, but discovered they had separated into small parties, and the pursuit was given up.

Miller's Block-House.

After I had consented to write the history of Washington County, I learned that my friend John C. Hupp, M. D., of Wheeling, Virginia, had in his possession notes of the attack on Miller's blockhouse; also of the capture, escape, and trials of Captain Jacob Miller in 1781, as well as the murder of five of Miller's friends, which he procured from the lips of his aged and venerable father. I accordingly addressed Dr. Hupp a letter, and he kindly furnished to me the following communication on the subject of Miller's blockhouse.

Wheeling, Va., March 31, 1861

Dr. Alfred Creigh :—

Dear Sir: I have, at your request, elicited the following facts in relation to the siege of Miller's block-house, from the lips of my aged father. He received them from those who, on this day seventy-nine years ago, were its courageous and heroic defenders.

They are are as follows: In the spring of 1782 Indian hostilities commenced much earlier than usual along the western frontier. As early as the month of March hordes of savages were ascertained to have crossed the Ohio, and were making their way into the settlements.

The settlers thus threatened with the massacres, plunderings, burnings, and captivities, with which they had already become so familiar, were filled with spirit-stirring excitement, commingled with alarm.

In this predicament of apprehension and danger, the settlers along the Buffalo Valley betook themselves with their families to the forts and blockhouses.

About three miles northeast of West Alexandria, on the right bank of the "Dutch Fork of Buffalo," is a peninsula formed by the meandering creek on the one side and "Miller's Run" on the other. The isthmus next to the run is skirted by a narrow strip of bottom land, which expands to many acres towards the creek and its confluence with the run. The side of the isthmus washed by the creek has a bold and precipitous bluff. On this isthmus was located "Miller's block-house,"* which was besieged by a party of about seventy Shawanese on Easter Sunday, 1782.

With their characteristic cunning and caution, the savages arrived in the vicinity the night previous, distributing themselves in ambush around the block-house and along the paths leading thereto. Thus lying concealed among the bushes or "pea vines," behind trees or fallen timber, they awaited the operation of circumstances.

The most of the men were absent from the block-house on this occasion, some of them being at Rice's Fort, which was about two miles further down the creek. Of this fact the Indians most likely were apprised, and on this account the attack on the block-house is supposed to have been deferred, and the ambush protracted, in order to destroy the men on their return to the block-house.

Of those who were in this rude shelter on that fatal Sabbath morning were John Hupp, Sr., wife and four children, Margaret, Mary, John, and Eliza-

---

* The block-house was located about midway between William Miller's spring and the graveyard—from this limpid fount the block-house received its supply of water.

beth; Jacob Miller, Sr., and several of his family; the family of Edward Gaither, and an old man named Matthias Ault.

The sun had appeared above the eastern hills, tinging with his feeble rays the summits of the lofty trees of the dense forest that surrounded this primitive place of defence. The quietude of the woods was undisturbed save by the ocasional chirp of the wooded songster, carolling his morning anthem.

One of the matrons of the block-house had fearful forebodings that some awful calamity was about to befall her husband, and followed him to the door, entreating him not to carry into execution his determination to accompany his friend on that morning in search of a colt that had estrayed. The night previous she had dreamed that a "coppersnake" struck its fangs into the palm of her husband's hand, and that all her efforts to detach the venomous reptile were unavailing. This vision she interpreted as ominous of evil to her husband. But despite the entreaties and importunities of his wife, John Hupp, Sr., set out in company with his friend, Jacob Miller, Sr., in search of the estray.

They entered the path leading across the run and through the woods in a northeasterly direction from the block-house, and were soon out of view. Soon the quietude of the woods was disturbed by the crack of a rifle, quickly followed by a savage warwhoop issuing from that portion of the forest into which Hupp and Miller had just entered.

This alarm filled the minds of the women with consternation and apprehensions as to their fate. But Hupp being in the prime and vigor of manhood, fleet and athletic (if not merely overpowered with numbers), his quick return to the block-house was confidently expected by the inmates. But he had fallen a victim to the foe that lay concealed patiently awaiting the approach of some ill-fated person.

The two unsuspecting men had been allowed to follow the ambushed path as far as the second little ravine on land, now owned by William Miller. Here, from his concealment behind fallen timber, a savage fired upon Hupp, wounding him mortally; he, however, after he was shot, ran some sixty or seventy yards and sank to rise no more. Miller, being an elderly man, was boldly rushed upon by the merciless wretches, with loud and exultant yells, and tomahawked on the spot.

Flushed with success, the savages now left their hapless victims, scalped and pilfered of all clothing, to join in the beleaguerment of the block-house.

While this tragic scene was being enacted, the wild excitement and confusion among the women and children at the block-house, with no male defender but the old man Ault, can be better imagined than described.

But at this trying moment Providence panoplied a female hero with a courage sufficiently unfaltering for the dire emergency, in the person of Ann Hupp. Having now realized the dread forebodings of her vision, and shaking off the shackles of despondency, she now turned to calm the moral whirlwind that was raging amongst the frantic women and children—to inspire them with hope, and to rally the only and infirm male defender.

She in the mean time had deputed Frederick Miller, an active lad aged about eleven years, as messenger to Rice's fort for aid. But in this strategy she was foiled; for the lad had gone willingly and heroically only a few hundred yards down the peninsula on his dangerous embassy, when he was intercepted by the Indians. Retracing his steps, he was pursued by two savages with hideous yells and uplifted tomahawks. This frightful race for life was witnessed from the block-house with anxiety the most intense. Every moment it seemed as though the lad would certainly fall beneath the deadly stroke of one of the two bloodthirsty pursuers, each vieing with the other which should strike the first and fatal blow.

A fence was to be scaled by the boy without a blunder, or death—certain, instant death—was his doom. Summoning all his boyhood and failing strength he leaped the barrier fence, touching it merely with his hand as the foremost Indian's tomahawk struck the rail, accompanied with a yell of disappointment, when both savages fired at him.

In his struggle to escape, his arm being flexed, one of the balls took effect, passing through his flexed arm both above the elbow and between that joint and the wrist, whirling him around several times.

Now subdued shrieks, commingled with joy and terror, were heard in the block-house as the female hero who sent out the boy ambassador received him in her arms as he bounded to the door exhausted from the race and loss of blood.

At this moment the Indians, leaping from their concealment, appeared in every direction around the block-house, and a hot and continuous firing commenced. The female band, with Ault as their counsellor, in despair and anguish were forced to the conclusion that the block-house would now soon be taken by storm, or envelop them in its flames, and with no hope of a successful resistance were about to "give up."

Again, in this crisis of terrible trial, Ann Hupp proved equal to the emergency. Encouraging the trembling Ault and the weeping women with the consoling language of hope—nerving her arm and steeling her heart to the severe duties of the moment, she, with true Spartanism, snatching up a rifle *fired at the approaching savages*, and then "ran from porthole to porthole," protruding its muzzle in different directions—to convey the idea of great forces in the house—at each presentation causing the savages to cower behind trees or other objects for protection. This happily conceived and promptly executed strategy of this pioneer heroine, without doubt, saved the inmates from what was otherwise inevitable—an immediate and horrible death.

A number of Indians had taken shelter behind a stable that stood not far from the block-house; emboldened by their firing not being promptly returned from the block-house, one of them would occasionally step out to view, holding up before himself as a shield a "clap-board," and then quickly retreat again to his shelter. He at length stepped out boldly into an open space, defiantly stretching his savage frame high in air, at which Ault was prevailed upon to fire; but palpably without doing any harm. This exasperated the savages, causing the assault to become still more terrible.

At this stage of the siege the women saw and recognized three of their men approaching in great haste from the direction of Rice's Fort, when they commenced screaming at the top of their voices, and beckoning the men in the direction they supposed to be the safest point to pass the Indians in gaining the block-house.

While the Indians stood in confusion and wonderment, not comprehending the meaning of the screams, the men rushed forward, passing very near to where some of the savages stood, and before the Indians sufficiently recovered from their surprise to fire upon them, they, with faces red and turgid from the race, bounded into the block-house unscathed.

The names of these three daring spirits, who thus perilled their lives to save their helpless mothers, brothers, and sisters from savage fury, or perish with them, were Jacob Rowe, Jacob Miller, Jr., and Philip Hupp. One of these, Jacob Rowe, being about ten years old, in the fall of 1776, when in company with his mother and three brothers, and his father, Adam-Rowe, on their way to Kentucky, made a hair-breadth escape from the In dians at a point not far from the mouth of Grave Creek. Here the little caravan was attacked by a party of marauding savages, who killed Mrs. Rowe and her oldest son, and took captive Daniel, the youngest child, aged about seven years. Jacob escaped by running into a thicket of willows near at hand, when closely pursued by a large muscular Indian, who had his little brother Daniel a captive on his back, and this is the last account ever heard of the captive boy. After his escape Jacob, trembling with fear, travelled all the day stealthily through the wild and dense woods, along the deep and dark hollows and over the precipitous hills lying in his way, back to Buffalo, and when nightfall overtook him with all its hideousness, in the midst of the deep woods, he, overcome with fright, fatigue, and hunger, nestled himself down amongst the leaves at the root of a fallen tree for the night. (He died with a throat affection which doubtless was founded on that, to him, cold, dread, and dreary November night.) The next day he arrived at Buffalo and was received into the arms of his sister, Ann Hupp, to whom the weeping lad related the tragic scenes he had witnessed on the previous morning.

Adam Rowe and his son Adam also returned to the neighborhood and afterwards went to Kentucky; but Jacob remained with his sister, and was her survivor some three or four years.

After the arrival of these men in the block-house, the fury and boldness of the savages somewhat abated, and during the rest of the day the firing was less frequent and finally ceased.

Evidently filled with chagrin and disappointment, they skulked about the neighborhood till nightfall, and nothing more was heard of them, they, no doubt, fearing a reinforcement, left during the night, bearing away with them only the scalps of Hupp and Miller. After the loss of her husband, Mrs. Hupp and her children, in accordance with her own wish, were taken by her brother-in-law, P. Hupp, to his cabin, near where the village of Millsborough now stands, where they remained four years, and again returned to Buffalo, where, subsequently, she married John May, whom she survived several years, and on the 23d day of June, 1823, died in the sixty-sixth year of her age. Two of her children, John Hupp and Elizabeth Rodgers, still survive, and are living on Buffalo Creek, having seen the pioneer heroes and heroines of their youth one by one gathered to their fathers, *they* now stand the last of a race who learned from their lips those thrilling incidents of pioneer life.

The loss of these two men to the neighborhood was severely felt at a time when men were so much needed; but all hearts in that block-house were overflowing with thanks and gratitude to a kind and merciful Preserver for vouchsafing to them his aid and protection when their great and terror-filling peril was impending, and for saving them from the ruthless hands of the merciless savages.

About noon on Monday the men ventured out from the block-house, going sadly and cautiously in search of Hupp and Miller, with the purpose of performing for them the last sad rites of the dear departed. About three hundred yards from the block-house they found the body of Miller, lying near the bloody path, and following the traces of blood on the leaves and other objects over which Hupp had run, his body was promptly discovered.

Their mutilated and frozen bodies were borne to the peninsula and laid side by side a few yards from the block-house, in the same grave, with "puncheons" for their coffin, and to-day are lying clustered around the grave of these two pioneers the remains of Jacob Rowe, Jacob Miller, Jr. (Capt.), Frederick Miller, the heroine Ann Hupp, and her daughter Margaret Titus. When living, the cement and panoply of affection and good

D

will bound them together at once in the tender natal, social, and moral ties of domestic kindness, friendship, and love, and the union for defence, and when dead they are not separated.

Frederick and Capt. Jacob were sons of the unfortunate Jacob Miller, Sr. Frederick died on the 27th day of March, 1814, aged forty-three years, and Captain Jacob Miller died August 20, 1830, aged nearly sixty-eight years.

Obediently and truly yours,
John C. Hupp, M. D.

Wheeling, Va., December 20, 1862.

Dr. Alfred Creigh :—

Dear Sir: I have at length been able to comply with the wish expressed in your last letter.

I give substantially the statement of one of the captains,* as received of him by my father,† namely :—

At the dawn of a fine September morning, in the year 1781, Jacob Miller, Frank Hupp, and Jacob Fisher set out from Miller's block-house, on Buffalo Creek, with the double purpose of performing the dangerous duties of spies and looking after estray horses. Each had with him his trusty rifle, and equipments well supplied with powder and ball.

With alert and vigorous steps they pursued a westerly course, which soon led them beyond the reach of the most distant view of their homes and into the nearly unbroken forest lying between "The Three Ridges" (now West Alexander) and the Ohio.

Having spent the day in unsuccessful search and scouting, returning, they were overtaken by nightfall near the cabin‡ of Jonathan Link, on Middle Wheeling Creek.

Here they turned in and were greeted with that hearty kind of welcome peculiar to backwoodsmen.

They were cordially invited to share the comforts of his fireside for the night, which was cheerfully accepted. What, in these perilous times, were their subjects of conversation during the evening, need no exercise of fancy to conjecture.

Having made their supper on Indian Johnny cake and water, with some "jerked venison," which happened to be in the cabin, they retired to their beds on the loft.

It was a bright starlight night, and all nature seemed propitious for security and repose, and had it not been for the fierce barking of their dogs, no danger would have been apprehended. The men conjectured that the disturbance kept up by the dogs augured more than merely the proximity of wolves, or the hooting of owls, which could be heard occasionally in different parts of the deep woods that surrounded the cabin.

Link, in his anxiety to render his guests contented in the enjoyment of

---

* Capt. Jacob Miller, who, in 1782, distinguished himself at the sieges of Rice's fort and Miller's block-house.

† John Hupp, who, when about two years of age, was in Miller's block-house during its siege.

‡ About three miles south of West Alexander, on the right bank of Middle Wheeling Creek, and on land now owned by Robert Erskine, Esq., was the site of Link's cabin. We were recently piloted, by S. M. Bell, Esq., and the venerable William Porter, Sr., to the spot where, eighty-one years ago, this rude cabin stood. Traces of its ruins are still to be seen. It stood just a few feet east of the West Virginia line

his hospitality, affected indifference, hoping to allay their apprehensions of danger.

But notwithstanding one or other of the party seemed to employ his time alternately in disturbed rest, and then, with anxious solicitude for their safety, casting watchful glances around the cabin, or gazing around the opening, and on the warlike masses of forest which loomed up dimly against the skylight, seeming to inclose it in far-stretching mountain ramparts. But no visible danger could be discovered.

At length the chirping of the wood birds and the peculiar chill and ruffling of the air, which are always the precursors of approaching day, announced that the dawn was close at hand. The hooting of the owls had ceased, and the dogs lay in slumber curled down near the cabin door.

During the night a band of savages had crept cautiously and inaudibly to places of concealment near the cabin. Here they lay, ambushing the door and the path leading to the spring near by.

The men arose from their restless beds, each cheerfully acknowledging to the other that his fears of danger had been unfounded. But, alas! how versatile and fleeting are human hopes and joys.

Hupp and Fisher, unsuspectedly opening the door, stepped down to the limpid, gurgling spring, which was but a few paces below, for the purpose of performing their morning ablutions.

Immediately a discharge of rifles issued from the covert of weeds and bushes near by, killing Fisher and mortally wounding Hupp, who ran into the cabin and up on to the loft, and while exhorting his companions not to give up, sank down into the embrace of death.

The bloodthirsty savages now rushed frantically into the cabin, demanding of the men to surrender immediately and hand down their guns, or they would fire the house and envelop them in flames.

In this awful crisis of trepidation and alarm, being overpowered by numbers, Miller and Link had no alternative but unconditional compliance.

While their hands and arms were being firmly bound, Hupp was precipitated from the loft, dragged beyond the threshold, and scalped.

Pickets having been detached, the front Indians of the file facing a northeasterly direction, the noiseless march commenced, leaving the mutilated remains of their victims to the mercy of the wild beasts.

The prisoners, with painful anxiety for their relatives and friends, now knew with certainty that the Dutch Fork settlement was doomed to speedy scalpings, captivities, and murders. A rapid march was thus continued, in profound silence, till they arrived at the summit of the ridge, now owned by Charles Rodgers, Esq., and immediately east of his present residence.

Here they were met by the returning pickets, and a halt ensued. At this place leaving a guard with the prisoners, the march was promptly resumed.

The grand object now was to make a descent on the cabin of Presley Peak, which stratagetic move was carried into successful operation, and resulted in the capture of Peak, a man by the name of Burnet, and William Hawkins. As the relentless savages rushed with exultant yells around the cabin, Peak essayed to make his escape through a hemp patch in the rear of his cabin, amid a shower of bullets, which literally mowed down the hemp stalks around him in his speedy flight. But bounding over the rude fence unharmed by the leaden missiles, and alighting amongst the bushes that fringed the dense woods, he was intercepted and surrounded by the ubiquitous savage warriors at that moment springing from their covert, and he was a captive.

These three prisoners, having been securely bound, were left in charge of a guard, when a detachment of Indians started forthwith down the creek, while another party hastened to the cabin* of William Hawkins, which was about half a mile further up the creek.

Here they captured Miss Elizabeth Hawkins. She being sick at the time prevented her from making good her escape with the rest of the family, who had fled and concealed themselves in the surrounding woods.

Mrs. Hawkins lay concealed amongst the leaves and branches of a fallen tree with an infant † in her arms, which she gagged well nigh to strangulation with her apron, lest its cries should betray her, whilst the bloodthirsty captors of her husband and daughter passed within a few feet of where she lay, undiscovered, in agonizing terror and trepidation.

And what is a remarkable fact, her little dog that had followed her to her place of concealment, crouched quietly quivering by her side while the Indians were passing !

The party going down the creek were less successful in their predatory incursion upon the cabin of Edward Gaither, which stood at the forks of the creek, near the spot where now stands the residence of John Cain, Esq.

With their accustomed caution, they approached the cabin in all directions, with an apparent certainty of again having an opportunity of carrying into successful execution their murderous and marauding purposes; but in this instance they were foiled.

At the moment of the attack on Peak and his comrades, it being less than a mile up the bottom from the confluence of the streams and in hearing of the guns, the Gaither's family was about to be seated for dinner when, alarmed by the rapid firing, they immediately betook themselves to the Miller block-house.

The Indians, however, did ample justice to the untouched and still smoking edibles left on the table, which to them was an acceptable and bounteous repast. And having pillaged the house of such articles as they wished to carry along with them, set fire to it, and hastened with their plunder to the rendezvous on the ridge, where they were soon joined by the other party and its prisoners.

The feelings of the prisoners, father, daughter, and neighbors, brought thus in their distressing helplessness face to face, in the deep and wild woods under such trying circumstances of terror and apprehension, can be much more readily imagined than described.

Some of the exultant savages gave vent to their feelings by grotesque contortions of countenance and gyrations of body. They whooped, and danced, and sung—now chiming the warwhoop in concert, and then uttering yells of triumph. Whilst others gave evidence of hatred and malignity of purpose, by derisive looks and gestures towards some of the prisoners, and by jerking from their roots the hairs of their heads.

Hawkins and Burnett were the special sufferers from these demonstrations, the former having red hair and the latter having a superabundance of hair about his person, which characteristics are notoriously repulsive to savage taste.

These demonstrations were interpreted by the prisoners as the precursors of untold horrors yet in reservation.

Contrary to savage custom as to the treatment of the generality of pri-

---

* Hawkins' cabin stood a few feet south of where the National Road is now located, near the foot of what is known as "Hawkins' Hill," on land now owned by John Conner, Esq. The stable on the north of the road, here, was constructed of the logs from the ancient cabin.

† This infant was William Hawkins, who was County Surveyor of Washington County about the year 1820.

soners in such an emergency, though being faint and feeble from fright and sickness, and unable to keep pace with the Indians in their hurried march, the fair Miss Hawkins was retained a prisoner and treated with the utmost indulgence and decorum. Such was her feebleness and trepidation for the moment, that she fell from the horse on which the Indians had seated her; but with their characteristic indulgence and decorous forbearance, with which "they are universally seen to treat captive women," she was kindly reseated on the animal, and hurried forward far in advance of the other prisoners.

An Indian council was held. The scene which quickly followed, and which was the consummation of the purposes of the council, was sufficient to chill the heart's blood of even savage barbarity.

The five prisoners, firmly bound, sat side by side on the trunk of a fallen tree. They were approached from the rear by five large and powerful Indians, each with uplifted tomahawk in hand, three of whom dealt simultaneous blows, and Hawkins, Peak, and Burnett lay with cloven skulls, weltering in their life's blood.

The other two savages seemed to recoil from the work of atrocity that had been assigned them; but each stood with uplifted tomahawk over the head of his intended victim.

In this awful moment of suspense, Miller and Link, fortunately for themselves, gave no evidence of terror or trepidation.

At that moment a warbling songster of the wood struck up its mournful song from the pendent branches of an ancient monarch of the forest overhanging the scene of this awful tragedy.

Two of the intended executioners, immediately cowering back from their intrepid and indomitably courageous prisoners, quickly returned their tomahawks to their belts; and the whole of the savages, palpably overwhelmed with consternation and dismay, hastened to form in line with the front Indians of the file facing toward the Ohio. Miller and Link led, like dogs, by long strips of raw-hide, had a place assigned to them about the middle of the file.

Thus with light, silent, and cat-like tread they advanced on their retreat rapidly till they neared the banks of Big Wheeling Creek, where, nightfall coming on, a halt was made, a fire was kindled some distance away from the place selected for an encampment, which was quickly extinguished as soon as it had served the purpose of cooking their scanty evening meal.

Here, for the first time since a few minutes before the enactment of the tragic scenes first related, was Miss Hawkins cheered with the sight of any of the other prisoners.

In agonizing filial apprehensions she strained her eyes in anxious search along the approaching file for a sight of her father; but when she saw only Miller and Link she instinctively divined what had happened.

Being now composed, reason and judgment were measurably under her control, and her familiarity with the Indian character and peculiarities, admonished her that she should not betray to the keen perceptions of the savages the real state of her feelings. With a resolute endurance and a heroism befitting the occasion, she succeeded in stifling the better feelings of her nature; and, affecting indifference to what had transpired within the last fifteen hours, she partook with apparent cheerfulness of the parsimonious and frugal entertainment which the Indians served up to her and the other prisoners.

From the indistinguishable jabbering among the Indians, it was evident they were arranging to get that sleep of which they had been so long deprived, and to make a judicious and safe disposition of the prisoners for the night.

At length they stretched themselves out upon the ground, with such an arrangement, that on either side of each prisoner was an Indian. As a further precaution to security, the end of the thong by which each prisoner had been led in the march was securely fastened around the body of an Indian. Doubly bound, as they were, the prisoners gave up all hope of escape.

The Indians soon fell asleep. Their minds were too busy, their nerves too excited, and their torture from their bonds too intense, to allow the prisoners any inclination to close their eyes.

Pinioned and distributed as they were among the Indians, they were precluded the possibility of any communication with one another, by word, or even gesture.

Miller, notwithstanding his anxiety of mind and distress of body, had matured a plan for his escape: which was to sunder, by means of his teeth, the tough thongs which served to bind him so securely.

He "impatiently waited for midnight, when the sleep of the Indians would be most likely to be profound." Time passed away, and at last even Link* and Miss Hawkins† sank into a fitful slumber.

Miller, imploring divine assistance, embraced this as the auspicious moment to begin the difficult and dangerous work he had in contemplation.

With an unconquerable will and unfaltering determination, he labored for some time, accomplishing but little.

Though having a set of good teeth, he at times almost despaired of success, on account of the toughness of the material on which he was operating.

But at length one of the sundered fetters dropped slowly from its deep track, where it was imbedded in the muscles of his arms. One of the savages turned in his sleep. Miller lay in the semblance of sleep. Ten minutes elapsed, and, no further movement being observed, he resumed his efforts to unfetter himself.

At length his success was complete. He stole forth cautiously from the circle of his captors, and was soon on his way back to Buffalo, where he arrived about the break of day.

As soon as he entered the block-house alone, and without his gun, the inmates knew that some awful calamity had befallen himself and his companions.

When inquired of as to Hupp and Fisher, the great deep of his manly soul was broken up, and the awfully harrowing scenes of the last twenty-four hours rushing through his mind, rendered him speechless.

And his only response was to point to the deep and purple marks still

---

* Link was not so successful as Miller in his endeavors to escape. He was dragged along with the Indians to their villages beyond the Ohio. And tradition says, that some two weeks after his capture he was brought back into the neighborhood, and taken up on the hill north of his own cabin and in full view of it, where he was set up as a target and shot at by the Indians. He, no doubt, was buried by the side of Hupp and Fisher, about midway between his cabin and the creek. The cut through the bank for the county road has disturbed the sepulchre of these prisoner martyrs. Here, at the road-side, the venerable William Porter, Sr., has frequently picked portions of human bones out of the crumbling bank.

† Miss Hawkins was carried by the Indians to their villages in the interior of Ohio. Here she was led in triumph to the wigwam, and with due form and ceremony adopted into the tribe. She soon learned to reciprocate that disinterested tenderness with which she was so affectionately loved by the mother of her adoption. Many years after she had been wedded to a Shawnee Chief she returned to the neighborhood on a visit to her pale-faced relatives. But she soon returned to her wild Indian home, the dull monotony of civilized life having no charms for her.

remaining in his arms, and amid the emotional throbbings of his heart and the heaving of his herculean chest, burst into a flood of unbidden tears.

The abundant tribute of tears, from those collecting around him, convinced Miller that true sympathy is natural to the human heart.

The sad events of the day previous having been learned, it was desirable to extend the rite of sepulture to those who had fallen.

Amongst those who shouldered their rifles* and set out, headed by Capt. Miller, to perform these last sad rites, were John Miller, Andrew Deeds, and Jacob Rowe.

In after years Miller seldom related this, to him, painful narrative; and when he did, it was always with tears streaming down his manly cheeks.

I am, dear sir, obediently yours.

JOHN C. HUPP.

Scattered throughout Youghiogheny, but now Washington County, were many forts, some of which we shall particularize: VANCE's fort, one mile north of Cross Creek village, situate on Cross Creek, which empties into the Ohio River, and now in the possession of Allison Vance, a lineal descendant of Major William Vance. WELLS's fort, five miles west of Cross Creek village. The Rev. Dr. John Stockton, of Cross Creek, says:—

"In these forts, social and afterwards public worship was kept up for seven years, especially in summer and autumn, the seasons when the Indians were wont to make their raids; and it was a common thing for men to go to these meetings armed with their trusty rifles, and to stand guard during the services. The first gospel sermon ever preached in that region was under an oak tree, just outside *the gate of Vance's fort*, on the 18th September, 1778, by the Rev. James Powers."

LINDLEY's fort, near the present village of Prosperity, was one of the strongest forts in the western country, because it was the most exposed to the hostile incursions of the savage inhabitants.

Beeman's block-house was situated on Beeman's Run, which empties into the north fork of Wheeling Creek. In front of this blockhouse was a long, narrow field, on which horses were pastured. At the extremity of the field the fence was down, and two boys passed through into the woods in search of the horses which had strayed off. The Indians had thrown down the fence as a ruse, and taken the horses into the woods, and thither the boys ignorantly went. The Indians seized them and carried them off. That night the boys were tomahawked, scalped, and left for dead. In the morning, on awakening, one of the boys found the Indians had left and his brother dead, went to the river and pursued its course until evening, when he arrived at Wheeling.

WOLFE's fort, or block-house and stockade,. stood about five miles west of *Catfish* and inclosed Jacob Wolfe's house. The National road now passes over the ground occupied by the fort. William Darby thus describes the situation of affairs:—

---

* The rifle and the *remnants* of the equipments carried by Jacob Rowe on this occasion are now in the possession of the writer of this letter.

"We remained in Mr. Wolfe's house until February, 1782, while my father was preparing his cabin, into which we finally entered, but not to rest. In fifteen or twenty days after entrance into our log cabin, Martin Jolly came running breathless to tell us that a savage murder had been committed but ten miles distant. In two hours we were in Wolfe's fort. From the fort my parents removed to *Catfish* (Washington), and spent the residue of 1782 and to April, 1783, on the farm of Alexander Reynolds, recently owned by Dr. F. J. Lemoyne. On this farm we were living when the Moravian Indians were massacred, and when the militia army were defeated under Col. William Crawford, and he captured and burned by a slow torture to death. James and Hugh Workman were both in that expedition, and I fancy I see the two women now, when James Reynolds came running to my mother exclaiming, 'Jamy Workman is killed!' James Workman, who was a married man, was not killed, but returned to his family and lived many years afterwards. A like report came in regard to Hugh, and happily proved untrue, to the great joy of his betrothed wife, Peggy Bryson, living then with her brother-in-law, Thomas Nichol. John Campbell, of Pigeon Creek, was killed in the action. The fate of William Huston, son of John Huston, William Johnston, and William Nimmons, was never accounted for. The two latter were both married men, and left children."

FROMAN'S fort was on Chartiers' Creek.

There was a block-house in Mount Pleasant township on Wilson's farm, which is now owned by Andrew Russel, Esq.

BECKET'S fort was near the Monongahela River.

There was also a fort in West Bethlehem township, at the village of Zollarsville, and directly in the rear of the dwelling-house and store of Edward R. Smith, Esq., on the high bluff which overlooks the creek.

Another at Taylorstown; this place, however, was originally called New Brunswick.

JACKSON'S fort was near Waynesburg.

FINLEY TOWNSHIP.

The following interesting facts I received from our esteemed fellow citizen, Alexander Frazier, Esq., concerning the first settlement of the western part of Washington County, known as Finley township.

The first settlement in this township was about 1785—the first fort was Roney's block-house. In this year a man by the name of McIntosh, with his wife and eight children, settled on what is now called the Blockhouse Run (from the fact that Campbell's blockhouse was erected there). Some time in August, as the McIntoshes were engaged in stacking hay, they were fired upon by the Indians; he himself was shot off the stack, while his wife, who was pitching hay, fled towards the house, but was overtaken, tomahawked, and scalped, while the children were treated in the same manner. The Indians, before they left the house, placed one of the dead boys before the door, with a knife in one hand and a corn-stalk in the other, while in the house they took the infant out of the cradle, and, after scalping it, beat its brains out against the wall, holding it by its heels.

The neighbors found one of the girls fifty yards from the house, scalped, while the eldest made her escape and rode to Roney's fort and communicated the sad intelligence. Hercules Roney, with a party of men from the fort, repaired to the scene of action, prepared a grave, and deposited all the bodies therein.

The Indians, after this cruel murder, remained quiet until about 1790, when they again broke out and continued troublesome until Wayne's treaty. In the year 1792 they killed an old lady, Mrs. Nancy Ross, near where West Alexander now stands. She went out of her cabin to look for her cow, when she was overtaken by Indians who lay in ambush, tomahawked, and scalped. The Indians then went to *Beekman's Run*, in West Finley township, where they captured two boys by the name of Beekman, who were in the woods hunting their horses. They took them some distance with the horses, when they halted and put them under the care of one of the Indians, while the other two went to seek a camping ground. It appears a dog had been following the boys, which, when the Indians discovered, they took alarm—fearing they were pursued—tomahawked and scalped the boys, and left them for dead. The elder boy received a gash on the forehead above his left eye, which did not penetrate the skull, but glanced into the eye, cutting the eyeball. As soon as they came to, the elder boy put his brother on the horse, but he was too weak to ride. He himself mounted the horse and started for home, but, after riding some distance, became weak and faint from the loss of blood, dismounted, hitched the horse, went some distance down into a gully at the head of the run, and crept under a rock to rest. Fortunately the colt, which had followed, chewed the bridle, and let the mare go. In a short time the Indians came on the trail of the horses. He saw them from his hiding place pass by, and, after waiting some considerable time, he set off, and by a different route reached home. I have seen this boy when grown up to manhood, with his scalp off and his eye closed up, with a large scar above it.

About this time two young girls on Wheeling Creek, by the name of Crow, were in the woods hunting their cows. They were captured by some Indians, and, after some consultation, the elder was tomahawked and scalped; but the younger being twelve years of age, they reserved her for another death, but providentially they were doomed to disappointment. They stripped her of her clothing, gave her some yards start, and a young Indian larger than herself was ordered to pursue, tomahawk, and scalp her. In running the chase for life or death the foot of the Indian was caught by the root of a tree and he fell. Before he recovered himself she was too far off to be taken, notwithstanding the Indians fired their rifles after her.

The lands in West Finley township were chiefly owned by Messrs. Shields and Hollingsworth, of Philadelphia, part of which was purchased from them in 1790 by Scotch Presbyterian emigrants direct from Scotland—hence it was often known by the name of the "Scotch Settlement." On this land they built *Campbell's block-house* in the summer of that year. It was situate about one mile and a half west of the village of Good Intent. These settlers had exceedingly hard times. During part of the summer months they were shut up in the block-house, and it was with the greatest difficulty and peril they could raise corn sufficient for their families and their stock. Another great inconvenience was, they had no mill within fifteen or twenty miles, hence they had to manufacture their corn for family use; and, as necessity is the mother of invention, they made graters upon which to rub the corn, which answered for meal. They also pounded it in a mortar, with a pestle made about three feet long, with an iron wedge made fast to one end. They would pound awhile, then sift the fine part out, with which they would make their bread, as also their mush. The coarser part they would make into hominy. Some, however, made hand-mills, while an ingenious man by the name of Elliott invented a kind of hand-mill with some gearing attached, which two men could work with a windlass, similar to a draw-well. Some years afterwards the same man erected a horse mill, and by perseverance and patience became a self-made practical millwright.

While on this subject we may add that Peter Wolf erected a small mill on Robinson's fork of Wheeling Creek. In a year or two afterwards John Richmond built another mill where Good Intent village now stands.

William Bailey's Captivity.

In early times there resided near Candor, Washington County (then Westmoreland County), four brothers by the name of Bailey. It was harvest time, and they were in the harvest field, assisted by Josiah Scott and others. When Scott had finished his row he mounted the fence to rest himself until the remainder of the reapers would come up. When Scott was seated on the fence he was shot by the Indians, who were in ambush, and William Bailey was captured, while the rest made their escape, and he was tied fast with a rope. Word was immediately sent to Fort McIntosh (Beaver) and to Pittsburg, and soldiers were sent out to intercept them. When the officers and soldiers discovered the Indians they lay in ambush to surprise and capture the whole party, but one of their number, being very much excited, fired his gun, which defeated the desired object. However, the Indian who had Mr. Bailey in a bark canoe with him was killed, and the boat turned upside down, while the other Indians who were in the bark canoes made their escape. Mr. Bailey not being an experienced swimmer, with the assistance of the soldiers was brought to the shore perfectly exhausted. After recovery he was sent to Pittsburg, and afterwards reached home in safety.

Rev. John Corbley

Was an eminent Baptist preacher who had settled at Muddy Creek (Washington), now Greene County. He details his sufferings, and those of his family, in a letter to Rev. Dr. Rogers, of Philadelphia, in the following language:—

Muddy Creek, Washington County, July 8, 1788.

On the second Sabbath of May, 1782, being by appointment at one of my meeting-houses, about a mile from my dwelling-house, I set out with my dear wife and five children for public worship. Not suspecting any danger, I walked behind two hundred yards, with my Bible in my hand, meditating; as I was thus employed, all on a sudden I was greatly alarmed with the frightful shrieks of my dear family before me. I immediately ran with all the speed I could, vainly hunting a club as I ran, till I got within forty yards of them. My poor wife seeing me, cried to me to make my escape. An Indian ran up to shoot me. I then fled, and, by so doing, outran him. My wife had a sucking child in her arms. This little infant they killed and scalped. They then struck my wife several times, but, not getting her down, the Indian who aimed to shoot me ran to her, shot her through the body, and scalped her. My little boy, an only son about six years old, they sunk the hatchet into his brains, and thus despatched him. A daughter, besides the infant, they also killed and scalped. My eldest daughter, who is yet alive, was hid in a tree about twenty yards from the place where the rest were killed, and saw the whole proceedings. She, seeing the Indians all go off, as she thought, got up and deliberately crept out of the hollow trunk; but one of them espying her, ran hastily up, knocked her down, and scalped her, also her only sister, on whose head they did not leave more than an inch round either of flesh or of skin, besides taking a piece of her skull. They still retain their senses, notwithstanding the painful operations they have already, and must yet pass through.

CHAPTER IV.

WHISKEY INSURRECTION.

Washington County was settled by pioneers from Cumberland Valley and Virginia, after the close of the war with Pontiac, which occurred on the 30th day of October, 1763. The settlements were made along the Monongahela. It is an historical fact, however, that on the 27th of January, 1750, the Assembly of the Province of Pennsylvania erected the county of Cumberland by an act of that date, which necessarily embraced all the counties west of the Susquehanna. The act referred to recites the boundaries as follows: "That all and singular the land lying within the Province of Pennsylvania, to the westward of the Susquehanna, and northward and westward of the county of York, be erected into a county to be called Cumberland, bounded northward and westward with the line of the Province;

eastward, partly with the river Susquehanna and partly with the said county of York, and southward in part by the said county of York, and part by the line dividing the said Province from that of Maryland."

The seat of justice being located at Carlisle, the people were required to travel hundreds of miles on account of the extensive limits of the county, at great expense and loss of time. To remedy this evil, the boundaries of Cumberland County were reduced by the erection of new counties, some of which I shall enumerate, as they constitute a part of the present history.

BEDFORD COUNTY was erected into a county March 9, 1771; WESTMORELAND COUNTY, February 26, 1773; WASHINGTON COUNTY, March 28, 1781; FAYETTE COUNTY, September 26, 1783, and ALLEGHENY COUNTY, September 24, 1788. Cumberland County having brought into civil existence these and other counties, has always been known politically and otherwise as *"Mother Cumberland,"* and the *sobriquet* has been as justly bestowed and as equally merited.

From the census table of 1790, we learn that these *five* counties, which then composed *Western* Pennsylvania, had a population of 76,642 inhabitants, which were distributed as follows: Bedford County had a population of 13,124; Westmoreland County, 16,018; Washington County, 23,866; Fayette County, 13,325, and Allegheny County, 10,309, while in 1800 the population had increased in these five counties to the number of 98,304, showing an increase of 21,162 in ten years. Taking these statistical tables as a correct data, we are safe in asserting that at the period when the whiskey insurrection was at its zenith, the population was not less than 87,473.

This population was composed of men who devoted their time chiefly to agricultural pursuits, and the virgin soil yielded its fruits prolifically as a reward to the husbandman. So productive were the cereals, that there was neither market nor purchasers for the surplus quantity, the only mode of consequence being to send the products of the soil across the mountains on pack-horses, and in return bring salt, iron, groceries, &c. &c. This remarkably slow mode of sending their articles to market, and the necessity of receiving in return the comforts of life, caused deep thought and anxious solicitude among a population of upwards of 87,000 people. The question, therefore, was discussed among the people how their crops could be made more available. Many plans were devised, suggested, and discussed, but, as *necessity is the mother of invention*, the idea was happily conceived that the grain could be converted into *distilled liquor*, and instead of a horse carrying but *four bushels* of rye over the mountains, it could transport the product of twenty-four bushels manufactured into whiskey, hence whiskey became the medium of exchange between the east and the west; the "old Monongahela" became renowned for its purity, and the agriculturists bent all the energies of their mind to increase the cereal products of the earth, because *a new way* was opened up, which promised to the frugal and industrious, the rewards consequent upon well-bestowed labor.

In the midst of this unexampled prosperity, the people were reminded that the Assembly of the Province of Pennsylvania, as early as 1756, had passed an EXCISE LAW by which a tax was placed upon every article supposed not to be necessary, or, in other words, on the luxuries of life. This law, however, had always been imperative, and as no tax was ever collected under *that* excise law in any of the counties east of the mountains, the people of Western Pennsylvania regarded it as merely nominal so far as related to *domestic distilled liquors.*

But the *first* Congress in January, 1791, on the report of Alex. Hamilton, then Secretary of the Treasury, passed an excise law imposing a tax of from ten to twenty-five cents payable upon every gallon of domestic distilled liquor, which he calculated would yield $826,000 to meet the charges growing out of the assumption of State debts, and in connection therewith, placed a tax upon *stills*, according to their capacity, with which it was manufactured. The people of Western Pennsylvania felt that this law was wrong and unjust and an encroachment on their rights and privileges, and all agreed upon the principle enunciated by the Congress of 1774, that an excise law "was the horror of all free States." They felt, too, that this law would operate peculiarly severe upon the inhabitants of Western Pennsylvania from the fact that they had no direct communication with the east, except by transporting their productions in the form of distilled liquor upon pack-horses, and that the blow would, if carried out, prostrate their trade, their business, and their future prospects, and they boldly contended that the fact need not be disguised or concealed, that nowhere in the United States could a population of 87,000 persons be found where there were as many stills, and consequently as much domestic liquor distilled as in Western Pennsylvania. But the reason was self-evident. There were neither large distilleries nor commission warehouses to purchase the grain, and had such been the case, there was no mode of transportation, except upon pack-horses, each horse carrying but four bushels of grain. Hence in every neighborhood some farmer became a distiller *from necessity*, and he not only manufactured his own grain into whiskey, but that of five or six of his immediate neighbors. Upon a fair calculation, therefore, every sixth man became a distiller, but all equally bound to resist the excise law, which would fall heavily upon every farmer, as the money which they would procure in the east from the sale of their liquor would, on their return, be demanded by the excise officer, to keep up the expenses of the government.

The excise law provided for the erection of inspection districts, in each of which an inspector was appointed whose duty it was to examine all distilleries, the capacity of the stills, gauge their barrels, brand their casks, and note in his book the result, and to crown the iniquity of the law with its most odious feature—the "duty imposed on each was required to be paid on the liquors before they were even removed from the distilleries." Yet notwithstanding the appointment of collectors, the people held meetings and passed resolutions condemning every man who would accept the office in the following words:—

That whereas, Some men may be found among us, so far lost to every sense of virtue and all feeling for the distresses of their country as to accept the office of collector, therefore,

Resolved, That in future we shall consider such persons as unworthy of our friendship, have no intercourse or dealing with them, withdraw from them every assistance, withhold all the comforts of life which depend upon those duties that as men and fellow-citizens we owe to each other, and upon all occasions treat them with that contempt they deserve, and that it be and it is hereby most earnestly recommended to the people at large to follow the same line of conduct towards them.

The men composing the counties of Western Pennsylvania were generally from the north of Ireland, or were the immediate descendents of Scotch-Irish. They personally, or by tradition, remembered the scenes of their fatherland, and the requirements which the officers of the crown demanded. They contemplated the Stamp Act, and the principle involved in the *tea* question—acts and principles which gave birth to American liberty—and while contemplating these things, they resolved *peaceably* to memorialize Congress to repeal this unjust and iniquitous act. Public meetings were held throughout the western counties of the State with the same objects in view, but with no effect. At length, in 1791, a meeting was held in Washington, and Mr. Gallatin says "that the persons assembled not only agreed to remonstrate, but they expressed a determination to hold no communication with, and to treat with contempt such inhabitants of the western country as would accept offices under the law; and they recommended the same line of conduct to the people at large," as the following statement will show:—

Pittsburg Resolutions.

Delegates convened in the city of Pittsburg on the 7th day of September, 1791, from the following counties, viz:—

Westmoreland County was represented by Nehemiah Stokely and John Young; Washington County by Col. James Marshall, Rev. David Phillips, and David Bradford; Fayette County by Edward Cook, Nathaniel Bradley, and John Oliphant, and Allegheny County by Thomas Morton, John Woods, and William Plumer.

Edward Cook was elected Chairman, and John Young appointed Secretary.

At this meeting the following resolutions were passed—

Resolved, That having considered the laws of the late Congress, it is our opinion that in a very short time hasty strides have been made to all that is unjust and oppressive. We note particularly the exorbitant salaries of officers, the unreasonable interest of the public debt, and the making no discrimination between the original holders of public securities and the transferees, contrary to the ideas of natural justice in sanctioning an advantage which was not in the contemplation of the party himself to receive, and contrary to the municipal law of most nations and ours particularly; the carrying into effect an unconscionable bargain where an undue advantage has been taken of the ignorance or necessities of another, and also contrary to the interest and happiness of these States, being subversive of interest by common means, where men seem to make fortunes by the fortuitous concurrence of circumstances, rather than by economic, virtuous, and useful employment. What is an evil still greater, the constituting a capital of nearly eighty millions of dollars in the hands of a few persons who may influence those occasionally in power to evade the constitution. As an instance of this has already taken place, we note the act establishing a national bank on the doctrine of implication, but more especially we bear testimony to what is a base offspring of the funding system, the excise law of Congress, entitled "An act laying duties upon distilled spirits in the United States," passed the 3d day of March, 1791.

Resolved, That the said law is deservedly obnoxious to the feelings and interests of the people in general as being attended with infringements on liberty, partial in its operations, attended with great expense in the collection, and liable to much abuse. It operates on a domestic manufacture, a manufacture not equal throughout the States. It is insulting to the feelings of the people to have their vessels marked, houses painted and ransacked, to be subject to informers gaining by the occasional delinquency of others. It is a bad precedent, tending to introduce the excise laws of Great Britain and of countries where the liberty, property, and even the morals of the people are sported with to gratify particular men in their ambitious and interested measures.

Resolved, That in the opinion of the committee the duties imposed by the said act on spirits distilled from the produce of the soil of the United States, will eventually discourage agriculture and a manufacture highly beneficial in the present state of the country. That those duties will fall heavily especially upon the western parts of the United States, which are for the most part newly settled and where the aggregate of the citizens is of the laborious and poorer class, who have not the means of procuring the wines, spirituous liquors, etc., imported from foreign countries.

Resolved, That there appears to be no substantial difference between a duty on what is manufactured from the produce of a country and the produce in its natural state, except, perhaps, that in the first instance the article is more deserving of the encouragement of wise legislation, as promotive of industry, the population, and strength of the country at large. The excise on homemade spirituous liquors affects particularly the raising of grain, especially rye, and there can be no solid reason for taxing it more than any other article of the growth of the United States.

Resolved, That the foregoing representations be presented to the legislature of the United States.

Resolved, That the following remonstrance be presented to the legislature of Pennsylvania.

Resolved, That the following address, together with the whole proceedings of this committee, which were *unanimously* adopted, be printed in the *Pittsburg Gazette*.

Other places held meetings and reiterated the same sentiments, and this hardy race of men, inured to hardships and privations, without preconcerted action, conceived that they were necessitated to defend their inalienable rights, Congress having refused to grant their petitions. The result was that on the 6th of September, 1791, Robert Johnson, Collector for Washington and Allegheny counties, was waylaid near Pigeon Creek, in Washington County, and was *tarred and feathered and his hair cut off, and required to promise not to show his face again west of the mountains.* He resigned his office July 20, 1794. The persons engaged in this bold and unlawful act were not punished, because the whole community, from a common interest, while they pitied the officer, despised the law; while it was generally believed that the Governor of the State would not insist upon the collection of the excise tax, as he considered it onerous and unjust.

On the 8th of May, 1792, material modifications were made in the law by lightening the duty and allowing monthly payments.

The President issued a proclamation September 15th, 1792, enjoining all persons to submit to the law—Government determined to prosecute delinquents, to seize unexcised spirits on their way to market, and to make no purchases for the army except of such spirits as had paid duty.

Rev. Dr. James Carnahan, in his address before the New Jersey Historical Society, in 1853, in referring to the subject of the treatment of deputy inspectors, says :—

"I shall mention one which fell under my notice about the last of June or first of July, 1794. John Lynn, a deputy inspector, residing in Canonsburg, Washington County, was taken from his bed, carried into the woods, and received a coat of tar and feathers, and he was left tied to a tree so loosely that he could easily extricate himself. He returned to his house, and after undergoing an ablution with grease and soap and sand and water, he exhibited himself to the boys in the academy (afterwards Jefferson College) and others, and laughed and made sport of the whole matter."

It is true there were a few law abiding men who registered their stills, gave the amount of gallons distilled, and had their casks gauged and branded, but even these were required to succumb to public opinion, as a neglect or refusal was followed by not only the destruction of the stills, but sometimes their real estate. The magistrates at that time truthfully asserted *that the laws could not be executed so as to afford protection, owing to the too general combination of the people in Western Pennsylvania to oppose the revenue laws.*

This "*combination of the people*" to which the magistrates referred, related to a powerful, secret, and indiscoverable organization, which had unlimited control and universal influence over every man—*secret*, except the name of the pretended leader—*powerful* to avenge and punish imaginary wrongs—and *indiscoverable*, because an investigation as to the place of meeting only mystified, embarrassed, and bewildered, and the investigator suffered by the loss of his property.

In April, 1793, the house of Benj. Wells, of Connelsville, Fayette, was broken open, himself and family threatened, terrified, and abused. Warrants were issued, but the sheriff refused to serve them. On the 22d of November, 1793, the house of Wells was again broken open—he was compelled to surrender his commission and books, and resign his office.

In January, 1794, Robert Strawhan had his barn burned, James Kiddoo his stills injured, and Wm. Conghbran his still and grist-mill damaged. In June, 1794, John Wells, collector of Westmoreland, opened an office at the house of P. Regan. They burnt the barn of Regan and the house of Wells.

The name of the leader of this combination was called TOM THE TINKER, and whenever he gave notice of his intention to strike a blow it was always followed with the worst consequences. Through the instrumentality of Tom the Tinker's boys, the whiskey insurrection was brought into existence, and by which it was fostered and cherished, until the strong arm of the law crushed out this first rebellion against government. The *modus operandi* of Tom the Tinker was to place a letter on the house of a suspected person, and if he did not publish the letter in a Pittsburg paper and attend the meetings of the combination, the threatened consequences were visited upon the person notified.

We give two of the letters which accidentally came into our possession, and which fully explain themselves.

ADVERTISEMENT.

In taking a survey of the troops under my direction in the late expedition against that insolent excise man, John Neville, I find there were a great many delinquents even among those who carry on distilling ; it will therefore be observed that I, TOM THE TINKER, will not suffer any certain class or set of men to be excluded from the service of this my district when notified to attend, on any expedition carried on in order to obstruct the execution of the excise law and obtain a repeal thereof.

And I do declare on my solemn word, that if such delinquents do not come forth at the next alarm with equipments and to their assistance as much as in them lies, in opposing the execution and obtaining a repeal of the excise law, he or they shall be deemed as enemies and stand opposed to virtuous principles of republican liberty, and shall receive punishment according to the nature of the offence.

AND WHEREAS, A certain John Reed, now resident in Washington, and being at his place near Pittsburg, called Reedsburgh, and having a set of stills employed at said Reedsburgh, entered on the excise docket contrary to the will and good pleasure of his fellow-citizens, and came not forth to assist in the suppression of the execution of the said law by aiding and assisting in the expedition, has, by delinquency, manifested his approbation to the execution of the aforesaid law, is hereby charged *forthwith* to cause the contents of this notice, without adding or diminishing, to be published in the *Pittsburg Gazette* the ensuing week, under the no less penalty than the consumation of his distillery. Given under my hand this 19th day of July, 1794. TOM THE TINKER.

Accordingly in the *Pittsburg Gazette* of July 23, 1794, it appeared as an advertisement with the following note :—

MR. SCULL: I am under the necessity of requesting you to publish the following in your next paper. It was found pasted on a tree near my distillery.   JOHN REED.
Feb. 23, 1794.

From Pittsburg Gazette, Aug. 31, 1794.

To JOHN GASTON—

Sir: You will have this printed in the Pittsburg paper this week, or you may abide by the consequence.

Poor Tom takes this opportunity to inform his friends throughout all the country that he is obliged to take up his commission once more though disagreeable to his inclination. I thought when I laid down my commission before, that we had got the country so well united that there would have been no more for me in that line, but my friends see more need for me now than ever—they chose a set of men whom they thought they could confide in, but find themselves much mistaken, for the majority of them has proved traitors. Four or five big men below has scared a great many, but few is killed yet, but I hope none of those are any that ever pretended to be a friend to Poor Tom, so I would have all my friends keep up their spirits and stand to their integrity for their rights and liberty, and you will find Poor Tom to be your friend. This is fair warning. Traitors! take care, for my hammer is up and my ladle is hot, I cannot travel the country for nothing. From your old friend,   TOM THE TINKER.

Judge Lobingier, in an address before the Mount Pleasant (Westmoreland County) Temperance Society, gives his recollections and impressions of the whiskey insurrection, and among other things in speaking of *Tom the Tinker* he says:—

"This Tom the Tinker was a new god added to mythology at this time, and was supposed to preside over whiskey-stills and still-houses. Whoever hurrahed stoutly for Tom the Tinker was of unquestionable loyalty with the whiskey boys, while those who would not were branded as traitors to this new deity and their country."

The effect and influence of these inflammatory letters or handbills prevented some from complying with the law through fear of loss of property and probably life, while it emboldened others to deeds of daring and unflinching hardihood. The excitement consequent upon this open rebellion was of such a magnitude that it required the presence of the United States Marshal to visit officially the delinquent distillers in Washington and other counties, and serve warrants upon them to appear before the United States Court east of the mountain. This official visit of the U. S. Marshal was made in consequence of the following notice which had been published in the newspapers.

PUBLIC NOTICE.

WHEREAS, A number of distillers have not entered their stills according to law, those who are distillers or dealers in spirits will take notice that suits will be brought and seizures made against those who do not comply therewith.   ROBERT JOHNSON.
Dec. 6, 1793.   *Collector for Washington and Allegheny Counties.*

The same notice was also published in the remaining three counties by Benjamin Wells, Collector of Westmoreland and Fayette counties, and John Webster, Collector of Bedford County.

Offices of inspection were opened to receive entries of stills, at the house of Benjamin Wells, in Fayette County; at Philip Regan's, in Westmoreland County; at Robert Johnston's, in Allegheny County; at John Lynn's, in Washington County; and John Webster's, in Bedford County, while Gen. John Neville was Chief Inspector of the 4th survey district of Pennsylvania. Here I may remark that subsequently in the 4th district, Washington County was the only county in which no office of inspection existed, which was occasioned by the tarring and feathering of John Lynn, of Canonsburg, whose case I have narrated, and the attending circumstances.

In the service of these writs for not complying with the law, after receiving the public notice, the U. S. Marshal was surprised as he passed from distiller to distiller to find that no opposition was made, but the sequel of the affair revealed a different state of affairs. Thos. McKean, Chief Justice of Pennsylvania, and Gen. Wm. Irvine, who were appointed commissioners by the Governor of Pennsylvania to confer with the inhabitants of the western counties, in their official report say:—

Pittsburg, Aug. 22, 1794.

The marshal for the district of Pennsylvania had processes to serve upon divers persons residing in the counties of Fayette and Allegheny, and had executed them all (above thirty) without molestation or difficulty, excepting one, which was against a Mr. Miller; he, or some other person, went to the place where Doctor Absalom Baird, the Brigade Inspector of Washington County, was hearing appeals made by some of the militia of a battalion, who had been called upon for a proportion of the quota of this State of the eighty thousand men to be in readiness agreeably to an act of Congress. There were upwards of fifty men there with their fire-arms, to whom it was related that the FEDERAL SHERIFF, as they styled the marshal, had been serving writs in Allegheny County, and carrying the people to Philadelphia, for not complying with the excise laws, and that he was at Gen. Neville's house."

The United States Marshal called upon Gen. Neville, as Chief Inspector of the Revenue, to accompany him to the dwelling of Mr. Miller, one of his neighbors near Peters Creek to serve the last writ. This occurrence took place on the 15th of July, 1794, the day previous to the military training before mentioned.* As soon as the fact was communicated, between thirty and forty of "Tom the Tinker's boys" flew to arms and marched that night towards Gen. Neville's, the distance being about seven miles, where they appeared early in the morning of the 16th. This party demanded from Gen. Neville his commission as Inspector of Revenue and all his offi dcialocuments and

---

* Mr. Miller, upon whom the writ was served, afterwards told Mr. Brackenridge that he was mad with passion, when he reflected that being obliged to pay $250 and the expense of going to Philadelphia would ruin him, and his blood boiled at seeing Gen. Neville along, to pilot the officer to his very door.

papers. These were as peremptorily refused—the door was shut—the firing commenced, and five or six of the insurgents were wounded by Neville and his friends, who had anticipated an attack and had thereupon prepared themselves for the emergency.

The military meeting at Mingo Creek meeting-house to which I have referred, hearing of the sad occurrence and that blood had been shed, an immediate call was made upon every man who valued life, liberty, and happiness, *forthwith* to march and avenge the outrage.

At that meeting, the Rev. Mr. Clarke, near eighty years of age, besought and counselled the people not to proceed in such an unholy and unlawful business, but the worst passion of the human heart triumphed, REVENGE WAS THEIR BATTLE CRY. The military force raised at Mingo Creek meeting-house marched under the command of Major James McFarland, who had served as an officer of the Revolutionary war.

On the 17th of July, the forces under Major James McFarland, when they came within half a mile of Gen. Neville's house, halted, and those who had arms advanced and demanded the surrender of Gen. Neville. They were informed by Major Abraham Kirkpatrick (who had also served in the Revolutionary war) that Gen. Neville had left the house, and that he was there with a detachment of United States soldiers to defend it. Gen. Neville's commission and official papers were demanded, but again refused. The women and children were notified to leave the house under a white flag, which they accordingly did, when an attack was made, and after a continuous fire of one hour, the house (estimated to be worth ten thousand dollars) was set on fire and consumed to ashes, and Major Kirkpatrick and his soldiers surrendered themselves as prisoners, and were permitted to leave uninjured, while the marshal was required to promise not to serve another writ under penalty of death.

During the attack Major McFarland was killed and several wounded, but the insurgents temporarily triumphed and the popular frenzy was at its height. Before them lay their military leader in the repose of death, who fell battling for their rights; but what had been gained? A meeting was proposed should take place at Mingo Creek meeting-house, and that there the death of Major McFarland would speak in unmistakable accents to the halting and wavering, while tears of sorrow and sympathy would flow at his funeral, and these united would prove the germ of their principles, and would awaken in every man's breast those latent and inestimable principles of civil liberty for which they and their fathers had fought, bled, and died.*

---

* In the graveyard at Mingo Creek meeting-house repose the remains of Major James McFarland. The epitaph on his tombstone tells the cause of his death:—

"Here lies the body of Capt. James McFarland, of Washington County, Pa., who departed this life the 17th July, 1794, aged 43 years.

"He served during the war with undaunted courage, in defence of American independence, against the lawless and despotic encroachments of Great Britain. He fell

At this period there resided in the town of Washington David Bradford, Esq., a lawyer, and who had been a member of the legislature of Virginia, when parts of Washington and Fayette counties were considered as belonging to Virginia. His residence was on Main Street, having erected the two-story stone house a few doors north of the property of Adam C. Morrow, on the corner of Main and Maiden streets. Col. Marshall also resided in this place—was the intimate and confidential friend of David Bradford—and had not only filled the office of sheriff of this county, but several other important offices. These men, on account of their commanding influence, were sent for to attend the Mingo Creek meeting, and after the messenger had used all his arguments they consented to attend the meeting, heard the facts of the case, and through the impetuosity of their feelings they avowed their determination, at all hazards, to resist the tyranny of the government.

This meeting was organized at Mingo Creek on the 23d July, 1794. Inflammatory speeches were made and the meeting resolved to call another general meeting on the 14th of August, at Parkinson's Ferry, now Monongahela City. Prior to this meeting the principal actors were busily engaged not only in issuing incendiary documents and making exciting speeches to the people, because they felt that if the steps taken would prove abortive, the death penalty would be inflicted, hence their determination to involve the whole western country in one common fate—either for weal or for woe. Accordingly, orders were issued by the Council of Safety (which the meeting had appointed), consisting of Col. John Marshall, John Canon, L. Lockny, T. Spears, B. Parkinson, D. Bradford, and A. Fulton, to issue an order to all the colonels commanding regiments in the counties of Washington, Westmoreland, Fayette, and Allegheny, to march with their respective commands to Braddock's Field on the 1st of August, 1794, with four days' rations, to deliberate upon the unhappy crisis of their affairs.

The letter or circular which was dispatched to the colonels of the various regiments read thus :—

July 28, 1794.

SIR : Having had suspicions that the Pittsburg post would carry with him the sentiments of some of the people of the county respecting our present situation, and the letters by the post being now in our possession, *by which certain secrets are discovered*, hostile to our interests, it is, therefore, now come to that crisis that every citizen must express his sentiments, not by his word, but by his actions. You are then called upon, as a citizen of the western country, to render your personal service, with as many volunteers as you can raise, to rendezvous at your usual place of meeting on Wednesday next, and thence you will march to the usual places of rendezvous at Braddock's Field, on the Monongahela, on Friday,

---

at last by the hands of an unprincipled villain, in the support of what he supposed to be the rights of his country, much lamented by a numerous and respectable circle of acquaintances."

the 1st day of August next, to be there at two o'clock in the afternoon, with arms and accoutrements in good order. If any volunteers shall want arms and ammunition, bring them forward and they shall be supplied as well as possible. Here, sir, is an expedition proposed in which you will have an opportunity of displaying your military talents and of rendering services to your country. Four days' provisions will be wanted—let the men be thus supplied.

JOHN CANON, T. SPEARS, B. PARKINSON,
L. LOCKNY, D. BRADFORD, J. MARSHALL,
A. FULTON.

The letters taken from the mail were addressed to Gen. Morgan by Col. Neville; to the Governor of Pennsylvania by Gen. John Gibson; also one by James Brison to the Secretary of the Treasury by Edward Day; and to the Secretary of War by Major Butler.

Among the number of regiments which were ordered to the place of rendezvous was one commanded by Col. John Hamilton, then Sheriff of Washington County, who resided at Mingo Creek. Upon the reception of the order he immediately rode to Washington to endeavor to prevail on Col. Marshall to countermand the orders, requiring his regiment to march to Braddock's Field. But it was useless; Col. Marshall was firm in his purpose, and the officers and men of Col. Hamilton had participated in the riots, and he concluded he would go to prevent ultra measures.

While these measures were progressing, and the eyes of the insurgents were directed to the contemplated meeting at Braddock's Field, a delegation from Washington visited Pittsburg, and the following proceedings of a town meeting give all the particulars, which proceedings are prefixed by the

Affidavit of Wm. Meetkirke, one of the Delegates from Washington to the town of Pittsburg.

We accordingly went to Pittsburg. When we arrived there a number of people came to the house where we put up to inquire of us if we knew what object the people had in view that were to assemble at Braddock's Field. We informed them that it was in consequence of letters that had been found in the mail, written by several persons in that place to government, misstating their conduct (as they termed it), and that the people conceived them to be very obnoxious characters, particularly Major Kirkpatrick, Mr. Brison, and Mr. Day. And it was our opinion that if some of those who had written the letters did not leave the town, that it was in danger of being destroyed from the apparent rage of the people. The same evening there was a town meeting of the inhabitants of the place, as we understood, to take into consideration what was best to be done for their own safety.

On hearing that we had come to town, they appointed a committee, consisting of Mr. Breckenridge, Gen. Wilkins, and Judge Wallace, to confer with us and to have our opinion on the subject. We produced to them the letters that had been taken out of the mail, viz: Major Butler to Gen. Knox, Gen. Gibson to Gov. Mifflin, Mr. Brison, to the same, Col. Neville to Gen. Morgan, and one without signature to the Secretary of the Treasury, in the handwriting of Edward Day, which were read in their presence. They asked us what we thought were the intentions of the people that were to assemble at Braddock's Field the next day. We gave it as our opinion that the town was in imminent danger of being destroyed if some of the obnoxious characters were not sent away, for that we ourselves had been insulted on the road coming there by some people, when they understood we were going to Pittsburg, for they said we were going there as spies, to tell the people to get out of the way, and that we ought to be taken prisoners. And they actually raised a party to follow us for that purpose, as we were afterwards informed, after which they returned to the meeting and gave the information from us, in consequence of which they entered into resolutions to expel certain persons, and which was afterwards published in handbills.

Resolutions of the Town Meeting of Pittsburg.

At a meeting of the inhabitants of Pittsburg, on Thursday evening, July 31, 1794, to take into consideration the present situation of affairs and declare their sentiments on this delicate crisis, Gen. John Gibson in the chair and Matthew Ernest secretary, a great majority, almost the whole of the inhabitants of the town assembled. It being announced to the meeting that certain gentlemen from the town of Washington (viz. A. Baird, Wm. Meetkirke, Henry Purviance, Col. Blakeny) had arrived and had signified that they were intrusted with a message to the inhabitants of the town relative to present affairs, a committee of three persons was appointed to confer with them and report the message to the meeting. The persons appointed were George Wallace, H. H. Brackenridge, and John Wilkins, Jr. These gentlemen made a report to the meeting, to wit, that in consequence of certain letters sent by the last mail, certain persons were discovered as advocates of the excise law and enemies to the interest of the country, and that a certain Edward Day, James Brison, and Abraham Kirkpatrick were particularly obnoxious, and that it was expected by the country that they should be dismissed without delay; whereupon, it was resolved it should be so done, and a committee of twenty-one was appointed to see this resolution carried into effect.

Also, that whereas it is a part of the message from the gentlemen of Washington, that a great body of the people of the county will meet to-morrow at Braddock's Field, in order to carry into effect measures that may seem to them advisable, with respect to the excise law and the advocates of it.

Resolved, That the above committee shall, at an early hour, wait upon the people on the ground, and assure the people that the above resolution, with respect to the proscribed persons, has been carried into effect.

Resolved, also, That the inhabitants of the town shall march out and join the people on Braddock's Field, as brethren, to carry into effect with them, any measures that may seem to them advisable for the common cause.

Resolved, also, That we shall be watchful among ourselves of all characters that by word or act may be unfriendly to the common cause, and when discovered, will not suffer them to live amongst us, but they shall instantly depart the town.

Resolved, That the above committee shall exist as a committee of information and correspondence, as an organ of our sentiments, until our next town meeting. And that whereas, a general meeting of delegates from the townships of the county on the west of the mountains will be held at Parkinson's Ferry, on the Monongahela, on the 14th of August next.

Resolved, That the delegates shall be appointed to that meeting, and that the 9th of August next be appointed for a town meeting to elect such delegates.

Resolved also, That a number of handbills be struck off at the expense of the committee and distributed among the inhabitants of the town, that they may conduct themselves accordingly.

The committee of *twenty-one* above referred to, was composed of George Robinson, H. H. Brackenridge, Peter Audrain, John Scull, John McMasters, John Wilkins, Andrew McIntyre, George Wallace, John Irwin, Andrew Watson, George Adams, David Evans, Josiah Tannehill, Matthew Ernest, William Earl, Andrew McNickle, Col. John Irwin, James Clow, William Gormley, and Nathaniel Irish.

Not less than from 1500 to 2000 men were assembled on Braddock's Field, which is about nine miles from Pittsburg and immediately on the north bank of the Monongahela River in Allegheny County. It is the celebrated battle-ground famed for the destruction of an army intended to capture Fort Duquesne (now Pittsburg). Here Braddock fell, and Washington displayed his first military genius, and here too the insurgents met to devise some plan by which they would free themselves from imaginary wrongs. Many plans were suggested, but no *definite action* taken upon any of the proposed measures, except to visit Pittsburg with a military parade under the command of Maj.-Gen. David Bradford and Edward Cook as Marshal, and Col. Blakeney, as officer of the day, in order to exhibit their strength and power and control public feeling. On their arrival, fear caused the people of Pittsburg to receive this army of Bradford's as the guests of the city. Prior to their march, however, David Bradford issued the following circular:—

To the Inhabitants of Monongahela, Virginia:—

Washington, Aug. 6, 1794.

GENTLEMEN: I presume you have heard of the spirited opposition given to the excise law in this State. Matters have been so brought to pass here, that all are under the necessity of bringing their minds to a final conclusion. This has been the question amongst us some days: "Shall we disapprove of the conduct of those engaged against Neville, the excise officer, or approve?" Or in other words, "Shall we suffer them to fall a sacrifice to federal prosecution, or shall we support them?" On the result of this business we have fully deliberated, and have determined with *head, heart, hand,* and *voice,* that we will support the opposition to the excise law. The crisis is now come, *submission or opposition;* we are determined in the opposition. We are determined in future to act agreeably to system; to form arrangements guided by *reason, prudence, fortitude, and spirited conduct.* We have proposed a general meeting of the four counties of Pennsylvania, and have invited our brethren in the neighboring counties in Virginia to come forward and join us in council and deliberation on this important crisis, and conclude upon measures interesting to the western counties of Pennsylvania and Virginia. A notification of this kind may be seen in the Pittsburg paper. Parkinson's Ferry is *the place* proposed as the most central, and the 14th of August *the time.*

We solicit you by all the ties that an union of interests can suggest to come forward and join us in our deliberations. The cause is common to us all—we invite you to come even should you differ with us in opinion. We wish you to hear our reasons influencing our conduct.

Yours with esteem, DAVID BRADFORD.

Before this meeting at Braddock's Field dispersed, however, the barn of Major Abrabam Kirkpatrick was burned, the grain and hay of the tenant consumed, and unsuccessful attempts were made to set fire to his house to avenge the death of Major McFarland. Some of that army, however, disclaimed the course pursued, and published the following card:—

We, the undersigned, on behalf of ourselves and the great body of the column that marched from Braddock's Field on the 3d of Aug. 1794, think it necessary to express our disapprobation of the disorderly proceeding of those of the troops who were concerned in setting fire to the house of Abraham Kirkpatrick, on the hill opposite the town of Pittsburg, also of the attempt made by others of burning his house in the town, as these acts was not within the sentence of the committee of volunteers in Braddock's Field, and therefore there could be no authority for carrying them into effect.

We consider it as a blemish on the good order of the march of the column through the town of Pittsburg, and their cantonment in the neighborhood of it. It has been endeavored to be removed as much as possible by repaying the tenant of Kirkpatrick his damages.

EDWARD COOK, FRANCIS MCFARLAND, THOMAS STOKELEY.
DIXON HUSTON, JAMES TERRY, THOMAS SEDGWICK.
HAMILTON HUSTON, WM. MCCLURE, DAVID HAMILTON,
WM. MEETKIRKE, WM. NAILOR, JOHN HAMILTON,
JAMES MARSHALL, JOHN HUGHES, ABSALOM BAIRD.

From this period to the 14th of August, *Tom the Tinker's boys* were busily engaged in erecting liberty poles, and had flags floating therefrom with the significant words, "LIBERTY; NO EXCISE; DEATH TO TRAITORS." Any man who refused to assist in erecting a liberty pole was deemed an enemy to the common cause, and Tom the Tinker gave him the significant notice.

The eventful 14th of August arrived, and the first movement was to erect a liberty pole with the following inscription thereon: "EQUAL TAXATION AND NO EXCISE; NO ASYLUM FOR TRAITORS AND COWARDS." After the meeting was organized by appointing Col. Edward Cook, chairman, and Albert Gallatin, secretary, two hundred and twenty-six delegates were accredited as representatives from the various townships, besides a large concourse of spectators. Speeches were made by Bradford, Marshall, Brackenridge, Edgar, Gallatin, Parkinson, and Husband, upon the following resolutions proposed by Col. John Marshal.

1. *Resolved,* That taking citizens of the United States from their respective abodes or vicinage, to be tried for real or supposed offences, is a violation of the rights of the citizens; is a forced and dangerous construction of the constitution, and ought not under any pretence whatever to be exercised by the judicial authority.

2. *Resolved,* That a standing committee be appointed to consist of members from each county, to be denominated a committee of public safety, whose duty it shall be to call forth the resources of the western country, to repel any hostile attempts that may be made against the rights of the citizens or of the body of the people.

3. *Resolved,* That a committee of   members be appointed to draft a remonstrance to Congress praying a repeal of the excise law, and that a more equal and less odious tax may be laid, and at the same time giving assurance to the representatives of the people that such tax will be cheerfully paid by the people of these counties, and that the said remonstrance be signed by the chairman of this meeting in behalf of the people whom we represent.

4. WHEREAS, The motives by which the people of the western country have been actuated in the late unhappy disturbances at Neville's house, and in the great and general rendezvous of the people at Braddock's Field, &c. &c., are liable to be misconstrued, as well by our fellow-citizens throughout the United States, as by their and our public servants, to whom is consigned the administration of the Federal Government, therefore,

Resolved, That a committee of   be appointed to make a fair and candid statement of the whole transaction to the President of the United States, and to the Governors of Pennsylvania and Virginia, and if it should become necessary that the said committee do publish to the world a manifest or declaration, whereby the true motives and principles in this country shall be fairly and fully stated.

5. That we will, with the rest of our fellow-citizens, support the laws and government of the respective States in which we live, and the laws and government of the United States (the excise law and the taking citizens out of their respective counties only excepted), and therefore we will aid and assist all civil officers in the execution of their respective functions, and endeavor by every proper means in our power to bring to justice all offenders in the premises.

These resolutions were amended by the meeting, and adopted after much discussion in the following words, which we trust every reader will carefully compare. To the *first* resolution there was no objection, but the remaining resolutions adopted read as follows:—

2. *Resolved,* That a standing committee to consist of one member from each township be appointed for the purposes hereinafter mentioned, viz:—

To draft a remonstrance to Congress praying a repeal of the excise law, at the same time requesting that a more equal and less odious tax may be laid, and giving assurances to the representatives of the people that such tax will be cheerfully paid by the people of these counties.

To make and publish a statement of the transactions which have lately taken place in this country relative to the excise law, and of the causes which gave rise thereto, and to make a representation to the President on the subject.

To have power to call together a meeting either of a new representation of the people, or of the deputies here convened, for the purpose of taking such further measures as the future situation of affairs may require, and in case of any sudden emergency, to take such temporary measures as they may think necessary.

3. *Resolved,* That we will exert ourselves, and that it be earnestly recommended to our fellow-citizens to exert themselves, in support of the munici-

pal laws of the respective States, and especially in preventing any violence or outrage against the property and person of any individual.

4. *Resolved*, That a committee to consist of three members from each county be appointed to meet any commissioners that have or may be appointed by the Government, and to report the result of this conference to the standing committee.

The standing committee under the 2d resolution consisted of sixty members, while that under the 4th resolution was composed of fifteen members.

The standing committee of sixty met and appointed the 2d day of September, 1794, and designated Brownsville as the place of meeting. *They* chose the *Committee of Conference* of *twelve*, *three* from each county, and these fixed their meeting at Pittsburg, on the 20th of August. This committee consisted of twelve delegates from the four western counties of Pennsylvania, and three from Virginia. Their names were John Kirkpatrick, George Smith, and John Powers, for Westmoreland County; David Bradford, Jas. Marshall, and James Edgar, for Washington County; Edward Cook Albert Gallatin, and James Lang, for Fayette County; Thos. Morton, John B. C. Lucas, and H. H. Brackenridge, for Allegheny County; and Robert Stevenson, Wm. McKinley, and Wm. Southerland, for Ohio County, Virginia. Col. Cook chosen chairman.

The delegates from Virginia did not participate in the deliberations of the Committee of Conference, hence the number was reduced to twelve commissioners.

While this meeting of the 14th of August was in session at Parkinson's Ferry, it was notified of the approach of three commissioners on the part of the United States, and two on behalf of the State of Pennsylvania. Wm. Bradford, Attorney-General of the United States, and Jasper Yates, and James Ross, represented the United States; and Thomas McKean and General William Irvine, the State of Pennsylvania.

The twelve commissioners under the 4th resolution met the National and State commissioners on the 20th of August in the city of Pittsburg. The prominent actors on that committee were Messrs. Marshall, Bradford, Brackenridge, Cook, and Gallatin, who were all favorable to acceding to the propositions of the commissioners except Mr. Bradford. The propositions were an unconditional submission to the laws of the United States by all the citizens, to abstain from all violence towards the officers in the execution of the laws, not to injure or allow others to injure the personal or real estate of any citizen, and that in case of compliance therewith, full and free pardon was offered to all.

The committee of twelve who had met consented to these terms, but they had no authority to act further than to report the result of their conference to the standing committee appointed under the second resolution, which was composed of sixty persons. To this committee was delegated the power to call together a meeting either of a new representative of the people or of the deputies here convened for the purpose of taking such further measures as the future situation of affairs may require, and in case of any sudden emergency to take such temporary measures as they may think necessary. Under these delegated instructions, the committee of fifteen called a meeting of the standing committee of sixty to meet at old Fort Redstone, (Brownsville) on the 2d day of September.

The National and State commissioners from their intercourse with the citizens and the excitement prevailing, believed that the interests of the people themselves as well as the government demanded *immediate action,* they, therefore, had the meeting changed to the 28th of August, five days sooner than the time appointed. This fact aroused Bradford and his associates, and the charge of bribery and corruption was publicly made against not only the commissioners, but the committee themselves, and Tom the Tinker, by his inflammatory bills, overawed the people and those who desired to submit. From this time to the meeting the wildest excitement prevailed; some proposed the formation of *a new state,* others, *resistance to government,* while another class favored *reconciliation.* In the midst of this anarchy and confusion throughout the rebellious counties, the day of the appointed meeting had arrived (the 28th of August). Gallatin in speaking of that meeting says:—

"Fifty-seven members attended, *twenty-three* of whom were sent by the county of Washington alone, and *thirty* by the three counties of Westmoreland, Fayette, and Allegheny; *one* came from Bedford County, and three from the county of Ohio, in Virginia. All that could be obtained was a resolve that, in the opinion of the committee, it was the interest of the people of this country to accede to the proposals made by the commissioners on the part of the United States; the question upon it being taken by ballot, *thirty-four* voting for the resolution and *twenty-three* against it. Bradford, as soon as he heard the vote, retired in disgust."

This meeting, however, appointed another committee of conference, to obtain further time from the National and State commissioners, in order that the people might have time for reflection. The commissioners and the committee agreed that instead of any further action by the committee, that the people themselves should vote directly on the question of submission, and the 11th of September was designated. The following is the result of that election:—

"In the county of Fayette, which contains two thousand and eight hundred taxable inhabitants, eight hundred and sixty attended, five hundred and eighty of whom voted for submission and two hundred and eighty against it. In the counties of Washington, Westmoreland, and Allegheny, which contains eleven thousand taxable inhabitants, two thousand seven hundred signed the declarations of submission."—*Gallatin.*

These facts convinced the commissioners that there was no general submission, and they returned to the seat of government, and reported their proceedings, as well as those of the rebellious counties to President Washington.

The following deposition, explanatory of the committee meeting at old Fort Redstone, by Judge Alexander Addison, will throw much light upon the subject.

UNITED STATES—PENNSYLVANIA DISTRICT, ss.

Before me, Richard Peters, Judge of the District Court in the United States, in the Pennsylvania District, appeared Alexander Addison, of the town of Washington, in the State of Pennsylvania, and made oath that he was present at Brownsville, or Redstone old fort, in the county of Fayette and State of Pennsylvania, on the 28th and 29th of August last, when what was called the Standing Committee met to receive the report of the committee appointed to confer with the commissioners on the part of government—that the minds of all men appeared to be strongly impressed with a sense of the critical situation of this country and the minds of almost all with a fear of opposing the current of the popular opinion; and this deponent believes these impressions were greatly increased by the appearance of a body of armed men assembled there from Muddy Creek, in Washington County, to punish Samuel Jackson as an enemy to what they called their cause.

This deponent further made oath that, on the 29th, Mr. Gallatin opened the business of the meeting by proposing a resolution that in the opinion of that committee it was the interest of this country to accept of the terms offered by the commissioners, and, by a speech of great length, stating the impolicy and danger of force in resistance of law, the incompetency of these western counties to contend with the United States, and the necessity of submission. That Mr. Brackenridge followed him also at great length and to the same effect.

This deponent further made oath that then Mr. Bradford rose and answered and opposed the various arguments used by Mr. Brackenridge and Mr. Gallatin, alluded to the revolutions in America and in France as models of imitation, and inducements to hope of success in the opposition of these counties to government; stated the capacity of these western counties, from their situation as separated from the eastern country by mountains and from other circumstances, to maintain a successful war against the United States, and in a state of separation to attain and secure all the essential objects and protection, safety, and trade.

This deponent cannot undertake to repeat the expressions of Mr. Bradford, but is certain that he has stated the ideas which they communicated to him, and his whole speech seemed manifestly calculated to keep up the opposition to government and prevent the adoption of the resolutions proposed by Mr. Gallatin.

This deponent further made oath that Mr. Bradford, in a conversation with this deponent on the 27th of September last, told this deponent that he made the speech before alluded to with a view to maintain his influence with the people under an opinion that unless some show of resistance was made to the terms of accommodation, the people would reject them and consider themselves as betrayed.

Under this state of affairs, and with additional official evidence furnished President Washington in regard to the insurrection, he, on the 7th day of August, 1794, issued the following

Proclamation.

WHEREAS, Combinations to defeat the execution of the laws levying duties upon spirits distilled in the United States and upon stills, have from the time of the commencement of those laws, existed in some of the western parts of Pennsylvania. And whereas, the said combinations, proceeding in a manner subversive equally of the just authority of the government, and of the rights of individuals, have hitherto effected their dangerous and criminal purpose by the influence of certain irregular meetings, whose proceedings have tended to encourage and uphold the spirit of opposition; by representations of the laws calculated to render them obnoxious; by endeavors to deter those who might be so disposed from accepting offices under them, through fear of public resentment and injury to person and property, and to compel those who had accepted such offices, by actual violence, to surrender or forbear the execution of them; by circulating vindictive menaces against all those who should otherwise directly or indirectly aid in the execution of said laws, or, who yielding to the dictates of conscience and to a sense of obligation, should themselves comply therewith by actually injuring and destroying the property of persons who were understood to have so complied, by inflicting cruel and humiliating punishment upon private citizens for no other cause than that of appearing to be the friends of the laws; by intercepting the public officers on the highways, abusing, assaulting, or otherwise ill-treating them; by going to their houses in the night, gaining admittance by force, taking away their papers, and committing other outrages; employing for their unwarrantable purposes the agency of armed banditti, disguised in such a manner as for the most part to escape discovery. And whereas, the endeavors of the legislature to obviate objections to the said laws, by lowering the duties and other alterations, conducive to the convenience of those whom they immediately affect (though they have given satisfaction in other quarters) and the endeavors of the executive officers to conciliate a compliance with the laws, by explanations, by forbearance, and even by particular accommodations founded on the suggestion of local considerations, have been disappointed of their effect by the machinations of persons whose industry to excite resistance has increased with every appearance of a disposition among the people to relax in their opposition and to acquiesce in the laws—insomuch that many persons in the said western parts of Pennsylvania have at length been hardy enough to perpetrate acts which I am advised amount to treason, being overt acts of levying war against the United States; the said persons having on the 16th and 17th of July last, proceeded in arms (on the second day amounting to several hundreds) to the house of John Neville, Inspector of the Revenue for the fourth survey of the District of Pennsylvania, having repeatedly attacked the said house with the persons therein, wounding some of them; having seized David Lennox, Marshal of the District of Pennsylvania, who previously thereto had been fired upon while in the execution of his duty by a party of armed men, detaining him for some time prisoner, till for the preservation of his life and liberty he found it necessary to enter into stipulations to forbear the execution of certain official duties touching processes issuing out of a court of the United States, and having finally obliged the said inspector of the revenue and the said marshal, from considerations of personal safety, to fly from that part of the country in order, by a circuitous route, to proceed to the seat of government, avowing as the motive of these outrageous proceedings an intention to prevent by force of arms the execution of the said laws, to oblige the said inspector of the revenue to renounce his said office, to withstand by open violence the lawful authority of the government of the United States, and to compel thereby an alteration of the measures of the legislature, and a repeal of the laws aforesaid.

And whereas, by a law of the United States entitled "An act to provide for calling forth the militia to execute the laws of the Union, suppress insurrections, and repel invasions, it is enacted that, whenever the laws of the United States shall be opposed, or the execution thereof obstructed in any State, by combinations too powerful to be suppressed by the ordinary course of judicial proceedings, or by the powers vested in the marshals by that act, the same being notified by an associate justice, or the district judge, it shall be lawful for the President of the United States to call forth the militia of such State to suppress such combinations, and to cause the laws to be duly executed.

And if the militia of a State where such combinations may happen shall refuse, or be insufficient to suppress the same, it shall be lawful for the President, if the legislature of the United States be not in session, to call forth and employ such members of the militia of any State or States most convenient thereto, as may be necessary, and the use of the militia so to be called forth may be continued, if necessary, until the expiration of thirty days after the commencement of the ensuing session; provided always, that whenever it may be necessary in the judgment of the President to use the military force hereby directed to be called forth, the President shall forthwith, and previous thereto, by proclamation, command such insurgents "to disperse and retire peaceably to their respective abodes within a limited time."

And whereas, James Wilson, an associate justice, on the 4th inst., by writing under his hand, did, from evidence which had been laid before him, notify to me "that in the counties of Washington and Allegheny, in Pennsylvania, laws of the United States are opposed, and the execution thereof obstructed by combinations too powerful to be suppressed by the ordinary course of judicial proceedings, or by the powers vested in the marshal of that district."

And whereas it is in my judgment necessary, under the circumstances of the case, to take measures for calling forth the militia, in order to suppress the combinations aforesaid, and to cause the laws to be duly executed, and I have accordingly determined to do so, feeling the deepest regret for the occasion, but withal the most solemn conviction that the essential interests of the Union demand it; that the very existence of government, and the fundamental principles of social order are materially involved in the issue; and that the patriotism and firmness of all good citizens seriously called upon, as occasion may require, to aid in the effectual suppression of so fatal a spirit.

Wherefore, and in pursuance of the proviso above recited, I, George Washington, President of the United States, do hereby command all persons being insurgents as aforesaid, and all others whom it may concern, on or before the 1st day of September next to disperse and retire peaceably to their respective abodes. And I do, moreover, warn all persons whomsoever against aiding, abetting, or comforting the perpetrators of the aforesaid treasonable acts. And I do require all officers and other citizens, according to their respective duties and the laws of the land, to exert their utmost endeavors to prevent and suppress such dangerous proceedings.

In testimony whereof, I have caused the seal of the United States of America to be affixed to these presents, and signed the same with my hand.

Done at the city of Philadelphia, the seventh day of August, one thousand seven hundred and ninety-four, and of the independence of the United States of America the nineteenth.

By the President: GEORGE WASHINGTON.
   EDM. RANDOLPH.

Washington, after he had learned that his proclamation of the 7th of August, 1794, was rejected, and after he had heard the report of the commissioners, determined to *crush out the rebellion*, and on the 25th of September, 1794, issued the following proclamation :—

BY THE PRESIDENT OF THE UNITED STATES :

WHEREAS, From a hope that the combinations against the constitution and laws of the United States in certain of the western counties of Pennsylvania would yield to time and reflection, I thought it sufficient, in the first instance, rather to take measures for the calling forth of the militia, than immediately to embody them, but the moment has now come when the overtures of forgiveness, with no other condition than a submission to law, have been only partially accepted; when every form of conciliation not inconsistent with the well-being of government has been adopted without effect; when the well-disposed in those counties are unable by their influence and example to reclaim the wicked from their fury, and are compelled to associate in their own defence; when the proper lenity has been misinterpreted into an apprehension that the citizens will march with reluctance; when the opportunity of examining the serious consequences of a treasonable opposition has been employed in propagating principles of anarchy, endeavoring through emissaries to alienate the friends of order from its support, and inviting its enemies to perpetrate similar acts of insurrection; when it is manifest that violence would continue to be exercised upon every attempt to enforce the laws; when, therefore, government is set at defiance, the contest being whether a small portion of the United States shall dictate to the whole Union, and, at the expense of those who desire peace, indulge a desperate ambition.

Now, therefore, I, George Washington, President of the United States, in obedience to that high and irresistible duty consigned to me by the constitution, "to take care that the laws be faithfully executed," deploring that the American name should be sullied by the outrages of citizens on their own government, commiserating such as remain obstinate from delusion, but resolved in perfect reliance on that gracious providence which so signally displays its goodness toward this country, to reduce the refractory to a due subordination to the laws, do hereby make known that, with a satisfaction which can be equalled only by the merits of the militia, surrounded with the service from the States of New Jersey, Pennsylvania, Maryland, and Virginia, I have received intelligence of their patriotic alacrity in obeying the call of the present, though painful, yet commanding necessity; that a force which, according to every reasonable expectation, is adequate to the exigency, is already in motion to the scene of disaffection; that those who have confided or shall confide in the protection of government shall meet full succor under the standard and arms of the United States; that those who, having offended against the law, have since entitled themselves to indemnity, will be treated with the most liberal and good faith, if they shall not have forfeited their claim by any subsequent conduct, and that instructions are given accordingly. And I do, moreover, expect all individuals and bodies of men to contemplate with abhorrence the measures leading directly or indirectly to those crimes which produce this military coercion; to check in their respective spheres the effort of misguided or designing men to substitute their misrepresentations in the place of truth, and their discontents in the place of stable government; and so call to mind that, as the people of the United States have been permitted under the divine favor, in perfect freedom, after solemn deliberation, and in an enlightened age, to elect their own government, so will their gratitude for this inestimable blessing be best distinguished by firm exertions to maintain the constitution and laws. And lastly, I again warn all persons whomsoever and wheresoever, not to abet, aid, or comfort the insurgents aforesaid, as they will answer the country at their peril; and I do also require all officers and other citizens, according to their several duties, as far as may be in their power, to bring under the cognizance of law all offenders in the premises.

In witness whereof, I have caused the seal of the United States of America to be affixed to these presents, and signed the same with my hand.

Done at the city of Philadelphia, the twenty-fifth day of September, one thousand seven hundred and ninety-four, and of the independence of the United States of America the nineteenth.

By the President: GEORGE WASHINGTON.
    EDM. RANDOLPH.

In accordance with this proclamation, troops from Eastern Pennsylvania, New Jersey, Maryland, and Virginia amounting to about fourteen thousand militia, consisting of artillery, cavalry, and infantry, were ordered to advance to quell the rebellion, under the command of Governor Henry Lee, of Virginia. Gen. Morgan led the Virginia troops; Gen. Smith, of Baltimore, the Maryland troops; Governor Howell the New Jersey troops, and Gov. Mifflin the Eastern Pennsylvania troops. The Virginia and Maryland troops composed the *left* wing of the army, their place of rendezvous was Cumberland, and their orders were to march across the mountains by Braddock's Road, through Uniontown.

The troops of New Jersey and Eastern Pennsylvania constituted the *right* wing; their place of rendezvous was Carlisle; their orders were to march to Bedford and take the northern route through Somerset. Judge Lobingier says the right wing halted in three divisions on this side of the Chesnut Ridge. The advance division encamped on the spot where Mount Pleasant, Westmoreland County, is built, the second division on Col. Bonnett's farm, and the rear division remained at Lobingier's Mills. They remained in their encampments about eight days; they then struck their tents and marched to the forks of Yough, in Washington County, where they were met by the *left* wing of the army, composed of the Maryland and Virginia troops, who had come through Cumberland and Uniontown. This occurrence took place early in October, 1794.

Let us now retrace our steps to inquire what the insurgents were engaged in from the departure of the National and State commissioners, to the arrival of the army in the forks of Yough, in October.

When the people of the four rebellious counties found so powerful an army advancing, a proposition was made by the members who called the first meeting at Parkinson's Ferry, to again assemble on the 2d of October, with the view to submit to the laws of the United States. The notice was published in the Pittsburg *Gazette*, and at the time designated the delegates assembled, and the following is the result of their deliberations:—

Parkinson's Ferry, Thursday, Oct. 2d, 1794.

A meeting of the delegates of the townships of the 14th of August, at Parkinson's Ferry, having been advertised in the Pittsburg *Gazette* of last Saturday, to be held here this day for the purpose of taking under consideration whether it be necessary that any armed force should advance on the part of government, for the purpose of assisting the civil authority in suppressing insurrection and preserving peace,

John Cannon was appointed Chairman ;

Alexander Addison was appointed Secretary.

Agreeably to the recommendation in the advertisement in the Pittsburg *Gazette*, several of the subscription papers with a number of names annexed in the form of submission prescribed by the commissioners, were produced by members and laid on the table.

The meeting having taken these papers into their consideration and communicated their respective knowledge of the sentiment of the people in their townships,

1. *Resolved*, That it is the unanimous opinion of the meeting that if the signature of the submission is not universal, it is not so much owing to any existing disposition to oppose the laws as to a want of time or information to operate a correspondent sentiment, and with respect to the greatest number, a prevailing consciousness of their having had no concern in any outrage, and an idea that their signature would imply a sense of guilt.

2. *Resolved*, Unanimously, that we will submit to the laws of the United States, that we will not directly or indirectly oppose the execution of the acts for raising a revenue on distilled spirits and stills, and that we will support as far as the law requires, the civil authority in affording the protection due to all officers and other citizens, reserving at the same time our constitutional rights of petition and remonstrance.

3. *Resolved*, Unanimously, that in our opinion in the four counties of Pennsylvania, westward of the Allegheny Mountains, there is a general disposition to submit to all laws of the United States, and a determination to support the civil authority in their execution.

4. *Resolved*, Unanimously, that Wm. Findley, of Westmoreland County, and David Reddick, of Washington County, be appointed commissioners to wait on the President of the United States, and the Governor of Pennsylvania, with a copy of these resolutions, and to explain to the government the present state of this country, and detail such circumstances as may enable the President to judge whether an armed force be now necessary to support the civil authority in these counties.

5. *Resolved*, Unanimously, that the secretary of the meeting transmit a copy of these resolutions by post to the President of the United States and to the Governor of Pennsylvania, and have a copy printed in the Pittsburg *Gazette*.

The people through their delegates having thus triumphed by the foregoing resolutions, a new state of affairs was about being inaugurated. Loyal men were emboldened in publicly declaring their attachment to the Constitution, the laws, and their country; while the disloyal cowered before the gaze of public indignation. Wilkeson, in his Recollections, says, in speaking of this subject, that Bradford and a few others who had the worst to fear, fled to the Spanish country on the Mississippi. Others equally guilty, but less notorious offenders, sought security in sequestered settlements.

According to the instructions of the meeting contained in the *fourth* resolution, Messrs. Findley and Reddick went to Carlisle to meet Gen. Washington and Alexander Hamilton, the Secretary of the Treasury, who had accompanied the right wing of the army thus far. After hearing the committee, their protestations and asseverations, declaring eternal fidelity to the Constitution and the laws, and that the people had been misled by designing, ambitious, and unprincipled men, General Washington remarked (says Gallatin) that he had two great objects in view in calling out the militia: *first*, to show not only to the inhabitants of the western country, but to the Union at large, and indeed to foreign nations, both the possibility of a republican government exerting its physical strength in order to enforce the execution of the laws when opposed, and the readiness of the American citizens to make every sacrifice and to encounter every difficulty and danger for the sake of supporting that fundamental principle of government. *Second*, to procure a full and complete restoration of order and submission to the laws, amongst the insurgents. The *first* object, the President said, was fully attained, and no doubt could remain, from the success of the experiment, of the practicability of a republican government, although extending over a large territory, supporting itself, even in the case of a disobedience of any part of the body politic. On the second head he observed that although the meeting of October 2, which they represented, had given it as their opinion that there was a unanimous disposition to submit to and support the laws, there was no *positive, unequivocal, and explicit declaration* that offices of inspection would be immediately and safely established. In the next place, that whatever might be the grounds of the opinion of the meeting, until the law was actually carried into operation, it was only an opinion, and that the general expenses of the campaign being already incurred, and the great sacrifices of individuals being already made, there remained no motive sufficiently strong to induce the magistrate, whose duty it was to enforce the execution of the laws, to run any unnecessary risk by intrusting that care to the exertions of the country itself, as long as any doubt might remain of their sincerity or power, the force embodied being fully competent to that object, and so far on the march to the intended spot. The President concluded by adding that as the amnesty which he had once offered through the commissioners had not been universally embraced by the offenders, some *atonement for past offences* had become necessary.

Thus ended the negotiation, and Messrs. Findley and Reddick returned and called another meeting of the committees of the townships of the four western counties of Pennsylvania and of sundry other citizens at Parkinson's Ferry, the 24th of October, 1794, when the following resolutions were adopted :—

1. *Resolved*, That in our opinion, the civil authority is now fully competent to enforce the laws and to punish both past and future offences, inasmuch as the people at large are determined to support every description of civil officers in the legal discharge of their duty.

2. *Resolved,* That in our opinion all persons who may be charged or suspected with having committed any offence against the United States or the State during the late disturbances (and who have not entitled themselves to the act of oblivion), ought immediately to surrender themselves to the civil authority in order to stand their trial; that if there be any such persons amongst us, they are ready to surrender themselves accordingly, and that we will unite in giving our assistance to bring to justice such offenders as shall not surrender.

3. *Resolved,* That in our opinion offices of inspection may be immediately opened in the respective counties of this survey without any danger of violence being offered to any of the officers, and that the distillers are ready and willing to enter their stills.

Messrs. William Findley, David Reddick, Ephraim Douglass, and Thos. Morton were then appointed to wait on the President of the United States with the foregoing resolutions.   JAMES EDGAR, *Chairman.*

Attest—ALBERT GALLATIN, *Secretary.*

Messrs. Findley and Reddick again recrossed the mountains and made fuller and stronger professions of loyalty and obedience to General Alexander Hamilton, the President having returned to Philadelphia, leaving him as his deputy. A proclamation of amnesty was afterwards issued, and the re-establishment of law and order was perfected by the citizens renewing their oath of allegiance and fealty to government.*

General Morgan, however, remained during the winter with the twenty-five hundred soldiers under his command. In the spring they were discharged and all returned to their homes.

On the 5th of February, 1796, Congress passed an act providing for citizens who had suffered in their property by the insurgents of Western Pennsylvania, thereby demonstrating both the justice and mercy of our government in upholding the government and providing for the sufferer.

We shall now examine into the political status of Washington County during the pending of this insurrection.

As the inhabitants of the four western counties were in a state of insurrection on the second Tuesday of October, 1794, the day of the general election, the question arose in the legislature, upon its assembling, whether the members elect were entitled to represent said counties. The case was referred to the consideration of a committee of the whole house. The following extracts from the minutes of the House of Representatives will explain themselves.

1794, Dec. 16. A motion was made by Mr. Kelly, seconded by Mr. Barton, and read as follows, viz :—

WHEREAS, It is declared by the 5th section of the 9th article of the constitution of this commonwealth, as one of the great and essential principles of liberty and free government, that elections shall be free and equal;

AND WHEREAS, A majority of the inhabitants of the counties of West-

---

* Upon the trial of the arrested persons two only were found guilty, one for arson for burning the collector's house, and the other for robbing the United States mail, who was sentenced to be hung, but the President pardoned them.

moreland, Washington, Fayette, and Allegheny were in a state of insurrection and opposition to the government and laws of this commonwealth on the second Tuesday in October last, the time appointed by the constitution for choosing representatives to the General Assembly of this State, to the terror of those who were friends to government and good order residing in the counties aforesaid;

AND WHEREAS, It is directed by the constitution that each House shall judge of the qualifications of its members, therefore

Resolved, That the persons chosen at the last general election held for the counties of Westmoreland, Washington, Fayette, and Allegheny to represent said counties in the House of Representatives in this State, are not duly qualified for said office.

1794. *Dec.* 20. Agreeably to the order of the day the motion made by Mr. Kelly and seconded by Mr. Barton, December 16, relative to the ineligibility of the persons elected to represent the counties of Westmoreland, Washington, Fayette, and Allegheny in the House of Representatives was read the second time.

And the resolution contained therein being under consideration, viz:—

Resolved, That the persons chosen at the last general election held for the counties of Westmoreland, Washington, Fayette, and Allegheny to represent the aforesaid counties in the House of Representatives in this State, are not duly qualified for said office.

A motion was made by Mr. Kelly, and seconded by Mr. Barton, to postpone the consideration of said resolution in order to introduce the following in lieu thereof.

Resolved, That the elections held during the late insurrection in the counties of Westmoreland, Washington, Fayette, and Allegheny for members to represent said counties in this House, were unconstitutional and they are hereby declared void.

On the question, "Will the House agree to postpone for the purpose aforesaid?" it was determined in the affirmative.

1795. *January* 9. On the question "Will the House agree to the following resolution," viz:—

Resolved, That the legislature of this commonwealth will adjourn on Thursday next to meet again on the first Tuesday of February next.

It was determined in the negative—yeas 37, nays 38.

The House proceeded to consider the resolution on the subject of the elections held during the late insurrection in the counties of Westmoreland, Washington, Fayette, and Allegheny, reported by the committee of the whole yesterday.

A motion was made by Mr. Gallatin, seconded by Mr. Nagle, to postpone the consideration of said resolution in order to introduce the following in lieu thereof:—

WHEREAS, it appears to this house, that during the month of July last the laws of the United States were opposed in the counties of Washington and Allegheny, in this State, and the execution of said laws obstructed by combinations too powerful to be suppressed by the ordinary course of law proceedings, or by the powers vested in the Marshal of that district; inasmuch as several bodies of armed men did, at sundry times, assemble in the county of Allegheny aforesaid, and commit various acts of riot and arson, and more particularly attacked the house of John Neville, Esq., Inspector of the Revenue for the fourth survey of the district of Pennsylvania, and after firing upon and wounding sundry persons employed in protecting and defending the said house, set fire to it and totally destroyed the same.

That the spirit of opposition to the revenue law of the United States soon after pervaded other parts of the fourth survey of Pennsylvania (which consists of the counties of Westmoreland, Washington, Fayette, Allegheny, and Bedford), inasmuch as all the officers of inspection established therein were violently suppressed.

That commissioners, having been appointed respectively by the President of the United States, and by the Governor of this State, in order to induce the inhabitants of the fourth survey aforesaid to submit peaceably to the laws, the assurance of submission required of the inhabitants aforesaid by said commissioners were not so general as to justify an opinion that offices of inspection could have been safely established there on the 11th of September last past. And the said commissioners of the United States did give it as their opinion, that on the 16th of September last past there was a considerable majority of the inhabitants of the fourth survey aforesaid who were disposed to submit to the execution of the laws; but that such was the state of things in the survey, that there was no probability that the revenue laws of Congress could at that time be enforced by the usual course of law; so that a more competent force was necessary to cause the laws to be duly executed, and to insure protection to the officers and well-disposed citizens.

And that in consequence of that information it became necessary for the President of the United States to cause to be embodied a large number of the militia of the United States, and to order the same to march into the fourth survey aforesaid, in order to aid the civil authority in causing the laws to be duly executed, in re-establishing order and peace, and in affording protection to the officers and citizens.

AND WHEREAS it also appears to this house that a majority of the inhabitants of the fourth district survey aforesaid did not at any time enter into a general combination against the execution of the laws of the United States;

That the meeting composed of delegates of the respective townships of the said survey never entered into any criminal resolution or combination, but, on the contrary, contributed by degrees to restore peace and order;

That no acts of violence were committed in the said survey after the 11th of September, 1794, nor did any combinations, meetings, or preparations take place tending to oppose future resistance to the laws of the United States, and to the militia then on their march to the said survey;

That from and after the 14th day of August last there was a gradual restoration and order of submission expressed by individual signatures or otherwise previous to the 16th of September aforesaid; by the answer of the grand jury of the county of Washington to the charge of the judge of the court for the said county, delivered at the September court, and by resolutions adopted by the committee of townships for the county of Fayette, on the 10th and 17th days of September, and by the resolutions adopted by the committee of townships for the counties of Westmoreland, Washington, Fayette, and Allegheny, on the 2d October last past, which resolutions expressed their disposition to submit to the laws of the United States, and to support the civil authority; and their opinion that the people at large were disposed to do the same, as also by resolutions, adopted by the people of the county of Fayette, on the day of the date of the late general election, the object of which was to provide for the accommodation of the militia of the United States, then on their march to the fourth survey aforesaid.

AND WHEREAS there are no proofs whatever before the house, either that the people of the fourth survey, or any of them, were in a state of insurrection on the day of the late general election, nor that any undue influence was used, or acts of violence committed on said day in any of the counties composing the said survey, nor that the late insurrection, riots, and opposition to the laws of the United States had any effect upon the said late general election.

AND WHEREAS it is represented to this house, by the representatives of the counties composing the fourth survey aforesaid, that they are able to prove by evidence that the late general elections held in the said counties were fairly conducted, uninfluenced by fear or violence, and perfectly free and equal.

AND WHEREAS the house wish to have full information upon the facts, in order that they may thereupon take such constitutional measures as to them will appear best—

Resolved, That in the opinion of this house it is proper for them to institute an inquiry on the subject of late general elections, held in the counties of Westmoreland, Washington, Fayette, and Allegheny, in order to ascertain whether the inhabitants of said counties, or any of them, were in a state of insurrection at the time of holding the said elections, and whether the late insurrection in the fourth survey of Pennsylvania had any effect on the said elections in the said counties.

Resolved, That a committee be appointed to devise and report to this house a plan of the manner in which the said inquiry should be conducted, with power to summon evidences on the subject.

On the question "Will the house agree to postpone for the purpose aforesaid?" it was determined in the negative.

The original question recurring, the previous question thereon was called for, and on the question being put, viz., "Shall the main question be now put," it was determined in the affirmative—yeas, 44; nays, 20.

Whereupon the eleven members of the counties of Westmoreland, Washington, Fayette, and Allegheny withdrew, and the main question, viz :—

"*Resolved*, That the elections, held during the late insurrection in the counties of Westmoreland, Washington, Fayette, and Allegheny, to represent said counties in this house, were unconstitutional, and they are hereby declared void," being put, it was determined in the affirmative—yeas, 43; nays, 20.

As I have given extracts from the minutes of the House of Representatives, I will now add those of the Senate on the same subject.

1795, January 2. Moved that the consideration of the following resolution, which is the order of the day, viz :—

Resolved, That the Senate will proceed to consider and determine whether the elections held in the districts composed of the counties of Allegheny, Washington, Westmoreland, and Fayette, during the insurrection in those counties, ought to be admitted as constitutional and valid, be postponed, in order to take into consideration the following resolution, to wit :—

Resolved, That it is necessary for the Senate to inquire

1st. Whether the Senate have any jurisdiction in the case of elections, and in what manner it can be exercised.

2d. Whether the inhabitants of the counties of Westmoreland, Washington, Fayette, and Allegheny, or a majority of them, were in a state of insurrection at the time of holding the late general election (and if so), what was the nature of the same and its effects upon the said election ?

And that ———— ———— be assigned to hear evidence on the subject of said insurrection.

The question on postponing for said purpose was put and carried in the negative.

1795, January 3. The following resolution, as reported by the committee of the whole, viz:—

Resolved, That the elections of Senators held in the counties of Washington, Allegheny, Westmoreland, and Fayette, during the late insurrection, were not constitutional and, therefore, not valid, being under consideration—

It was moved the further consideration of the resolution be postponed in order to take the evidence of the State Commissioners, and to bring forward testimony of persons who were present at the election in Westmoreland County. And the question on postponing for said purpose being put, was carried in the negative.

It was then moved that

WHEREAS, A resolution is now before the Senate which, if carried, will deprive the counties of Washington, Allegheny, Fayette, and Westmoreland, of any representation in the Senate of this Commonwealth; and whereas, it would be highly improper that a partial representation should legistate for the whole State, therefore

Resolved, That the Senate will, so soon as the said resolution is carried, adjourn to such time as will give the said four western counties an opportunity of holding elections and returning members in the stead of those now deprived of their seats, if the House of Representatives shall concur in such adjournment.

The question being put, it passed in the negative.

The question being afterwards put on the following motion, viz:—

Resolved, That in taking the votes of the Senate on the resolution relative to the validity of the elections from the four western counties, the clerk be directed not to call the names of the members of those counties, as their representative characters are involved in said resolution.

It passed in the affirmative.

And the original question, viz:—

Resolved, That the election of Senators held in the counties of Washington, Allegheny, Westmoreland, and Fayette, during the late insurrection, were not constitutional and, therefore, not valid, again recurring,

It passed in the affirmative.

Reasons of the vote of the subscribers on the question of the validity of the elections held in the counties of Westmoreland, Washington, Fayette, and Allegheny.

We are of opinion that the resolutions adopted by the Senate are unjust, unconstitutional, and impolitic.

UNJUST.

Because the documents, upon which the decision is grounded, were not legal evidence, inasmuch as they consisted only of written, vague, hearsay and newspaper information, and it was in the power of the Senate to procure oral, direct, and positive evidence.

Because the documents produced to support the resolutions do not contain any facts, subsequent to the 15th day of September, which was near one month previous to the election; nor does it appear by the said documents, or by any of the alleged facts therein contained, either that all the four western counties ever were declared to be in a state of insurrection, or that the majority of the inhabitants thereof, ever were concerned in any insurrection, criminal combination, or illegal opposition, against the laws of the Union.

Because every act of the people, or any part of the people of the western counties, subsequent to the 15th day of September, evinces a restoration of order and an universal determination to submit to the laws and to support the civil authority.

Because no testimony was adduced to prove that the spirit of the late insurrection had any effect on the elections, but on the contrary, the Senators representing those counties offered to prove, by evidence, that the said elections were fairly conducted and perfectly free and equal.

Because the Senate, by a positive vote, refused to hear the evidence of the commissioners appointed by the State, to confer with citizens of the western country, and also the evidence of persons (known friends to order and good government) who were present at the election of one of the said counties. And

Because there was not a single act (that might be considered as a sign of insurrection, opposition, or combination) committed in two of the western counties, which did not also take place in other counties of this State, and yet the counties of Westmoreland and Fayette are included in the decision of the Senate, while those others were not even hinted at.

UNCONSTITUTIONAL.

Because the Constitution expressly declares that contested elections shall be tried by a select committee, and not by the Senate, and expressly restrains the jurisdiction of either branch of the legislature, to judging the qualifications of their members. And

Because if this was not to be considered as a case of contested elections. it could only be a retrospective disfranchising act, an act which was expressly forbidden by that clause of the Constitution which declares that no *ex post facto* law shall be made, and which, if it could be enacted by any authority whatever, should have been the act of the *legislature*, and not of a *single branch*.

IMPOLITIC.

Because there was no apparent necessity for, or advantage resulting from the measure, but on the contrary, at a time when the inhabitants of the western country, who might have been deluded into criminal excesses, were brought to a sense of their duty, and when the whole body of the people of Pennsylvania had manifested their determination to support the laws and Constitution of the United States, we conceived it the duty of the legislature to *conciliate* and not *inflame* the minds of the citizens.

Because, by ordering special elections, in the middle of winter, and at a short notice, in a country the population of which is widely scattered, any change that may take place in the representation can only be the effect of a particular party, ever watchful to their own interest, and there is, therefore, a danger that the good citizens of the western counties may, for the term of four years, be unfairly and partially represented. And

Because the Senate, having refused to adjourn until new elections shall have take place, laws passed whilst one-sixth part of the State is unrepresented, may not be thought binding by those citizens who had no share in the enacting of the same, and the measure will, at least, tend to diminish that respect and obedience to the laws and government which is so essentially necessary under the present circumstances, to encourage and inculcate.

These, with many other, reasons have influenced our vote, and we trust we have discharged that duty which we owe to our country and our consciences, by voting and protesting against a measure which we think may be of the most pernicious and destructive consequences.

WILLIAM HEPBURNE, THOMAS JOHNSTON,
JOHN KEAN, GEORGE WILSON.

In a Philadelphia paper of February 16, 1795, is published a letter in which it is stated that the *eleven* members of the House, and the *four* Senators, who were deprived of their seats, have all been re-elected, except one Senator (Mr. Moore), who declined serving.

The members elected in pursuance of special writs of election held in February, 1795, for members to fill vacancies in the House of Representatives caused by the expulsion of the members elected at the stated election held in October, 1794, were as follows, viz: Westmoreland County, Benjamin Lodge, George Smith, and Michael Ruch; Washington County, William Wallace, Craig Ritchie, James Brice, and Benjamin White; Fayette County, Albert Gallatin, John Cunningham; Allegheny County, Pressley Neville and Dunning McNair.

Senators: Westmoreland and Fayette, William Todd and Pressley Carr Lane; Washington and Allegheny, Thomas Stokely and Absalom Baird (re-elected).

Pertinent to this whole subject is the legal opinion of Judge Addison, of Washington, Pennsylvania, delivered to the grand jury of Washington County on the necessity of submission to the excise law. In his preface the Judge says they were written at the time specified, and the man must be wise or insensible indeed, of whom the experience of seven years, in a period of most interesting novelty, varies no sentiment and corrects no judgment.

Judge Addison forwarded a copy of all his charges, published in Washington by John Colerick in 1800, to General Washington, and received in reply the following complimentary letter:—

MOUNT VERNON, March 4, 1799.

SIR: Your favor of the 30th of January, inclosing your charge to the grand juries of the county courts of the 5th Circuit of the State of Pennsylvania, has been duly received, and for the inclosure I thank you.

I wish sincerely that your good example, in endeavoring to bring the people of these United States more acquainted with the laws and principles of their government was followed. They only require a proper understanding of these to judge rightly on all great national questions, but unfortunately, infinite more pains is taken to blind them by one description of men than there is to open their eyes by the other, which, in my opinion, is the source of most of the evils we labor under.

With very great respect I am, sir,
Your most obedient servant,
GEORGE WASHINGTON.

ALEXANDER ADDISON, Esq.

At the September session of the Court of Quarter Sessions for Washington County in the year 1794, Hon. Alexander Addison delivered the following charge on the necessity of submission to the excise law :—

GENTLEMEN OF THE GRAND JURY:
The alarming and awful situation of this country at this time is too well known to require a statement. On the part of government we are now offered a forgiveness of all that is past, on condition that we sincerely submit to the excise law and all other laws. The question now is, whether we will submit to the terms proposed or not.

The decision of this question is of such importance that I am sure it will receive a solemn consideration from every citizen of a sober mind. If we accept the terms we shall have *peace;* if we reject them, we shall have *war.* There is no *medium* between these extremes, for, in the present state of this country, it is impossible to expect from government a repeal of the excise law. Government is the *whole* people, acting by their representatives. The will of those representatives must not be extorted by force or fear; otherwise those who thus constrain them exercise a tyranny over the rest of the people. We are a little more than the seventieth part of the United States. We ought not, therefore, to pretend to dictate laws to the whole. But whatever portion we may be of the people, if one law is repealed, at the call of armed men, government is destroyed; no law will have any force; every law will be disobeyed in some part of the union. Government is therefore now compelled to enforce submission to *this* law or to *none.* The whole force of the United States must be exerted to support its authority now, or the government of the United States must cease to exist. *Submission* or *war,* therefore, is the alternative.

War is so dreadful a calamity that nothing can justify its admission, but an evil against which no other remedy remains. That the colonies to relieve themselves from the tyranny of Britain should have roused to war, no man will wonder. They had to acquire the first principles of liberty, an equal voice in framing their laws. The same was the case of France. Its constitution was overthrown and one man had, by inheritance, acquired a power which he could transmit to his successor, of making laws for the whole nation. But our Constitution has already secured the most democratic principles of representation. Our complaint is against the ordinary exercise of legislation. We have now more than a just proportion of representation—one Senator and three Representatives in Congress. To fill our just proportion we may choose whom we please. And we ought not yet to despair that in a legal manner we shall receive redress for every just complaint. The principles of liberty are completely established in our Constitution. Those principles are, that the will of a majority should control the few. We wish now for a liberty destructive of those principles which we formerly sought, and the French now fight to establish. Our complaint is, that the *many* have not *yet* repealed a law at the request of the few, and therefore we rashly propose war.

If we determine on *war,* look forward to the consequences. Either we shall *defeat* the United States, or the United States will *subdue* us. If the United States subdue us we shall at the end of the war be certainly not in a better situation than we are in at present. For the same necessity, the preservation of the authority of government, will exist for enforcing the law *then* which exists for enforcing it *now.* We shall be in a worse situation, for government will then be under no obligation to grant us the favorable terms which are now offered, but may exact punishment for past offences, penalties for past delinquencies, compensation for past damages, and reimbursement of the expenses of the war. To these I might add the miseries attending the war; but as these will attend the war in either event, I shall particularly allude to them in the supposition of our defeating the United States. To me this event appears improbable in the last degree. A train of unfortunate delusions (for such I deem them) seems to occupy the minds of many in this country. It is said that no militia will come out against us; that if they do, we are so much superior in arms that we shall easily defeat them; that we can intercept them in the mountains and prevent their passage; that if they should come they will march peaceably along and not disturb the citizen engaged in the lawful occupations of life; and that, at the worst, we can throw ourselves under the protection of Britain.

On such notions, these are my remarks: From all that I have heard or seen there is a resentment in the people of the other side of the mountains against our conduct on two grounds—as being contradictory to the principles of democracy, which require obedience to a constitutional law; and as refusing to bear any part of a burden, to which they have submitted. This resentment will not only carry *vast numbers* to them, to comply with the regular call of the militia, but to step forward as volunteers. Supposing (which may yet be doubted) that they may at first be inferior to us in the art of fighting, the interests of the United States are so deeply involved in our submission, that no expense will be spared to accomplish it. And should the draught of the militia be insufficient, certainly the legislature will enable the Executive to raise and maintain a standing body of forces to accomplish the object of government. They will come at different times and in different directions and accumulated numbers; for the "whole force" of the United States will be directed against us: so has the President, who never speaks until he has determined, declared by his proclamation. If this county rejects the conditions offered, the whole country will be considered as in a state of rebellion; every man must be considered either as a citizen or an enemy. If he says he is a citizen, he may be called upon by the authority of the government to assist its force in subduing its enemies. If he refuse, he becomes an enemy and may be treated as such. The arm of government may live among us at free quarters, and reduce us to obedience by plunder, fire, and sword. Will the British receive us? The government of Canada dare not, without authority from London. And it is not to be supposed that Britain will risk the loss of the friendship and trade of the United States for so poor an object as our becoming her subjects. If she did, might we not expect that the United States would seize her dominions on the eastern part of Canada and Nova Scotia and intercept our communication with her? Against the "whole force" of the United States, exerted as we have reason to fear, what have we to rest on? Where are our arms? Where are our magazines of military stores? Or where can we obtain a supply of these articles, but from the United States, with whom we shall be at war? All communication between us and our fellow citizens on the east side of the mountains will be cut off. Even the supplies of the common articles of life, which we receive from them, will be prevented; and not a single article of food or clothing, much less of arms or ammunition, will be furnished to us from that quarter. Army after army will be sent against us. In a state of open war, we shall be considered as any other enemy, with the additional rancor attached to a civil war. Our agriculture will be destroyed; our fields laid waste; our houses burnt; and while we are fighting our fellow-citizens on one side, the Indians (and God knows how soon) will attack us on the other. The consciences of many among ourselves will shrink back with horror at the idea of drawing a sword against our brethren! They will call for neutrality. They will enter into associations for mutual defence. Many, who now from fear of danger or insult, put on the appearance of zeal and violence, will, when it comes to decisive exertion, draw back. But those who are for war will strive by force to draw in those who are for peace. We shall attack and destroy each other, and fall by our own hands. Our cornfields will be converted into fields of battle. No man will sow, for no man will be sure that he will reap. Poverty, distress, and famine will extinguish us. All mutual confidence will be at an end, and all the bonds of society will be dissolved. Every man will be afraid to speak to his neighbor. There will be no power of government to control the violence of the wicked. No man's life, no man's house, no man's goods, no man's wife, no man's daughter will be safe. A scene of general destruction will take place. And should government weary of chastising us, at last leave us to ourselves, we shall be a miserable remnant, without wealth, commerce, or virtue—a prey to the savages, or slaves to Britain.

Are we prepared for a separation from the United States, and to exist as an independent people? This is a question which ought to be settled previously to our taking up arms against government. For, to disobey government, while by remaining in it we admit its authority to command, is too absurd, and too contrary to the duty of citizens, for any man of reason and virtue to maintain; especially when that government, like ours, is created and changeable by the people themselves—that is, by the *whole* people, or a majority of the *whole* people. Our appeal to arms is, therefore, a declaration of independence, and must issue either in separation or submission. Government cannot recede farther than it has done. It has already made sacrifices which entitle it to grateful returns. It offers to forgive past offences and consider us as having never erred. It cannot, without a total extinction of all authority, repeal this law while we resist it. Government must either subdue us or cast us off. For, however we may flatter ourselves with the destructive hope of *defeating* government, we can have no prospect of *subduing* it, and compelling the United States to retain us in the Union. Suppose us, then, a separate people, what prospect have we of being able to secure those objects which are essential to the prosperity of this country, and of far more consequence than the repeal of the excise law? Shall we, at our own expense, subdue the Indians, seize the western posts, and open the Mississippi? Or will not the British, countenanced by the United States, retain the posts, and arm and protect the Indians against us? And will not the Spaniards, under the same countenance, block up the Mississippi, and refuse, perhaps, all trade with us? At present, there is a fair prospect of an accommodation with Britain, and, by the influence of the United States, we have reason to hope for a surrender of the western posts, and of consequence a peace with the Indians. There is also a negotiation industriously and not unpromisingly conducted with Spain, for the free navigation of the Mississippi. The continuance of our union with the United States may, therefore, in a short time secure us all our favorite objects. And there must be time; for we have to deal with sovereign and powerful nations, whose rights we cannot infringe: we must therefore solicit, and not extort. But separated from the United States, and of course from the friendship of France and the world, what hope have we to bend the haughty nations of Britain and Spain? We should be their sport or their slaves.

In rejecting the conditions now offered us by government, we cannot hope to extort a repeal of the excise law. If we would remove it by force, we must be able to cut ourselves off from the United States, with the loss of our prosperity, our happiness, and perhaps our existence. A rejection of the conditions is a declaration of war, and war is the sure road to ruin.

Let us next consider what will be the consequence of our submission to the government on the terms offered: We are restored to the peace and protection of government. We shall be tried for our offences or delinquencies by courts and juries in our neighborhood. But with these favorable terms we must submit to the excise law.

The peculiar objection which lay in the mouths of the people on this side of the mountains to this law was this: that from our *local* circumstances it drew from us a sum of money which was disproportioned to our wealth, and would soon exhaust our circulating medium. However necessary on these grounds an opposition to the excise law might be three years ago, it is *less* necessary now. Since that period, the progress of this country to wealth has been amazingly rapid. There have been more public and private buildings raised within this period, than for nine years preceding; and fewer sheriff's sales for debt in the whole three, than in any one of the nine. Three years ago, I believe, there was not a burr mill-stone in this county; now there are many. The quantity of money circulating among us is, since, greatly increased, and the value of all property is thereby greatly increased: in other words, the value of money is greatly lessened, and thereby the value of the excise to be paid by us is greatly lessened. *Then* there was hardly any trade to the Spanish settlements on the Mississippi; it was, at any rate, small, and confined to a few adventurers; the quantity of grain exported was but little—of course but little was withdrawn from our own consumption, and this little was generally bought with goods. Now a very respectable trade is carried on to the Spanish settlements; our traders are treated with great civility by the Spaniards; the duty on our trade is reduced to a mere trifle, and there is very little difficulty in bringing away dollars in return. We shall soon have the whole supply of that market to ourselves. Last spring our best flour was sold there for a dollar each barrel dearer than flour from New York. None of the traders *now* depend on goods for the purchase of wheat, but must purchase at a reasonable price in money. From this increased exportation of our grain, the necessity of distillation is greatly lessened in degree, and will every day lessen. Government does not *now*, as *formerly*, supply the army with whiskey, through contractors purchasing with goods, but employs agents to purchase it with money. Last year ten thousand dollars were laid out in this way by one agent in this county, and the execution of an order for ten thousand more was stopped only by the present troubles. The contractors themselves have, these two last years, purchased their supplies with cash. From these circumstances, and the pay and other expenses of the army, government sends *far* more money to this side of the mountains than it can draw back by the excise. At the commencement of this law a very great quantity of foreign spirits was consumed in this country; but so heavy is the duty which this law lays on foreign spirits, that the people on the east side of the mountains drink such spirits at a very increased price, and our storekeepers cannot afford to bring foreign spirits in any considerable quantity over the mountains.

As our circumstances are thus materially changed, so the law itself is changed also. Originally, the duty on a still was sixty cents per gallon, now it is fifty-four; originally, the duty on a gallon of whiskey was nine cents, now it is seven cents. Another material alteration is, granting a license by the month, at ten cents per gallon on the still—a provision peculiarly suited to a country where few distillers work in summer.

I do not say that by these alterations in our circumstances, and in the law, our objections to the excise law are *removed*, but they are surely *lessened*. We have reason also to believe, that our remonstrance would be listened to more effectually, if, by obedience, we put ourselves in a capacity of being heard; but it is natural to answer, "Why complain of a law which you have never obeyed?" I will go yet further, and state an opinion, that the easiest, the speediest, and I believe the only way to accomplish our object, a total repeal of this law, is instantly to accept the conditions offered by government, honestly comply with them, and come fairly before the legislature with our remonstrance.

I have before stated the impossibility that the legislature should repeal this law, so long as we resist it. I will now explain to you on what grounds I form the opinion, that they will repeal it as soon as possible after, by our submission, we have restored them to their authority, and you may judge of yourselves of the probability of this opinion.

The present prospect of French affairs, and the favorable reception which Mr. Jay, our ambassador, has met with in England, give reason to hope for a good understanding between us and Britain, and a consequent termination of the Indian war. I estimate two years as a reasonable period for these causes to operate and these effects to be produced. If the extraordinary expenses of the Indian war ceased, there is reason to expect—such is the increasing trade of America—that the imposts would suffice for the ordinary expenses of government. If this be true, so generally is the excise on domestic produce disliked, and so imperfectly paid, that we have no reason to presume that the legislature will keep it up longer than it is necessary. You have now the grounds on which I state the opinion that it may be repealed in two years. If repealed then, it will have lasted five years; of these five, we shall, perhaps, if we comply now, be compelled to pay for only two years; and supposing the tax so unequal, paying but two years out of five may correct the inequality; and while we pay a far greater sum for the expenses of the war is circulated among us. Thus the Indian war, occasioning the excise, bears with it a remedy; and when this remedy fails, there is reason to expect the evil may also fail.

Whether, therefore, we could avoid ruin, or whether we could obtain a repeal of the excise law, it appears evident to me that we have no way to gain our point but by immediately accepting and faithfully performing the conditions proposed.

If we do not, we shall get no more cash for our whiskey. The army will be supplied with whiskey from Kentucky, and regulations will doubtless be made and exerted, to seize and forfeit our whiskey, if carried anywhere out of this county. We shall therefore become its only consumers, and it will again cease to be a cash article and again become a mere drug.

But it is said, if we submit now, we have nothing to expect from a remonstrance; for our past remonstrances have been ineffectual. I say, it is too hasty to draw this conclusion. Besides what I have formerly observed, that we have never by obedience entitled ourselves to relief, I request your attention to the situation of the United States hitherto: The imposts have not been sufficient for the expenses of government, including those of the Indian war. The excise law, therefore, could not be repealed, unless some new fund were substituted in its stead. Now it is impossible to impose any tax whatever that will operate equally on all men. Suppose, therefore, some other tax imposed in lieu of this, while we continue to resist this, what would be the consequence? It might be as unpopular *here*, or in some other place, as this excise; the consequence would be, that from an experience of the weakness of government in failing to enforce the excise, the new tax would be resisted also, and *no* tax would ever be enforced. [A direct tax, imposed by a law of Congress, produced in 1799 an insurrection in Northampton County, Pennsylvania.]

Suppose a direct tax, on a general valuation of property, there would be great frauds. Suppose a direct tax on lands. The amount of all direct taxes in each State must be in proportion to its number of inhabitants (U. S. Court, i. 2); now unless lands or other property in quantity and value bear the same proportion in each State with the number of inhabitants to the whole, the direct tax would in some States be unconstitutional, and of course resisted. I am informed that in New England a direct tax would be as unpopular as the excise is here. Government, therefore, could not with safety substitute any other tax, instead of the excise, till it had first shown that its authority was sufficient to enforce the excise.

Attend, especially, to the situation of the United States during the last session of Congress and judge for yourselves: Was that a time to release any established subject of taxation and try a new experiment? The whole world seemed to lower upon us. The Indians attacked our back settlements. The Algerines plundered and the British captured our ships at sea. It was judged necessary, for safety and justice, to equip a fleet, to fortify our harbors, and to send out against the Indians two thousand volunteers from Kentucky. For all these purposes, the imposts (diminished by the spoliations and the embargo) would come too slowly in, and it was found necessary to anticipate the revenue by enabling the President to borrow a million of dollars. Was this a time to press a repeal of the excise law? From all these circumstances, the failure of our past remonstrances is no sufficient reason to conclude that after we have submitted to the authority of government, and after its embarrassments are removed, our future remonstrances will fail of a just effect.

On all these grounds I do most earnestly exhort to an immediate acceptance of the conditions offered by the commissioners, and a faithful performance of them on our part, as the only way in which we can hope for redress or escape ruin.

I have thus expressed my sentiments honestly and freely, as at this crisis it becomes every man who has any regard to the welfare of this country to take every occasion to do. This is not a time for concealment or dissimulation. Let every man speak out, and let us not by silence or falsehood deceive one another. Let a free currency of opinions restore mutual confidence and mutual safety; that the dagger of the assassin, the torch of the incendiary, and the tongue of the slanderer be not feared. Let the energy of government be restored; let the public peace and the rights of persons and property be preserved sacred; and let every individual repose with confidence and safety on the protection of the law. Let the power of punishment be exerted only as our principles prescribe by courts and juries; let offences be ascertained only by the volumes of our laws; while a man's words and actions are lawful, let his safety be untouched, and let not individuals assume the public duty of repaying vengeance.

Do you, gentlemen, who by your station can do it so effectually, unite with me in expressing, propagating, and supporting these sentiments; and through you, both now and hereafter, let them be felt to be the voice of your country.

They are mine; and were an angel from heaven to charge me to make to you, as I should answer it at the tribunal of God, a faithful declaration of my opinion of the interest of this country at this important period, I would, were it the last moment of my life, address you as I have now done. And oh, may the God of Wisdom and Peace inspire this people with discernment and virtue; remove from their minds blindness and passion, and save this country from becoming a field of blood!

[P. S.—The meeting at Redstone not having given the assurances required by the commissioners, but appointed a committee to obtain better terms the commissioners changed the terms, to individual subscriptions of assurance by every man in these counties. When these terms were declared, I exhorted to a compliance with them in the delivery of this charge in the several counties, adapting the expressions to the circumstances. The following paragraphs are as delivered at Washington, Sept. 22, 1794.]

It may not be amiss to suggest that, notwithstanding the limited time is expired, it may still be proper, for those who have not signed the form of acknowledgment of submission, yet to sign it before some magistrate. Signing it is no admission of past offence, nor any additional obligation of duty in any particular person. It is merely that criterion of civil duty, which our fellow-citizens have thought proper to require after a general appearance of departure from it. And to this duty we are equally bound, whether we sign or not.

You, gentlemen, are guardians of the public peace of this county. At this time, it is peculiarly incumbent on us to watch over the preservation of the peace. Notwithstanding the assembling of an army, under the discouraging view of our reluctance to return to our duty, and of our persisting in the acts of violence, we may yet, perhaps, save ourselves from the disgrace and injury of its entering among us, by manifesting to government plain proofs of our submission to its authority, and our firm determination to preserve the peace. Let us not have it said that our reformation has been accomplished by fear of an armed force, but from a generous reflection on past error, a sincere sense of duty and an honorable purpose of receiving the estimable character of good citizens. The people of this country, I always hoped, and still trust more and more to be convinced, have good sense and virtue sufficient to entitle them to the respect and good will of their fellow-citizens of the United States. One rash step may be obliterated by an uniform tenor of regular demeanor, and our name may be restored to its due credit. But if we would arrest the threatening hand of government, if we would honorably deserve the character of good citizens, let us now, at this critical moment, watch with peculiar care against the least symptoms of violence, outrage, or breach of the peace. Let all tumults, tumultuous assemblies, appearances, or words of sedition be instantly discouraged, suppressed, and if necessary brought under the coercion and punishment of the civil authority. This alone can secure to us that peace which we had lately lost, and preserve us from that fatal anarchy in which we were lately plunged; for if civil authority be not supported by ourselves, it must be supported by some other force. This alone can prevent an armed force from entering our country and exposing our peaceable citizens to the private plunder of troops not inured to discipline and irritated by our misconduct. This alone can secure to us that pardon and indemnity which the generosity of government has held out to our former offences, and of which another outrage would certainly deprive us. And this alone can restore to every man among us, that shield of protection against fear and danger, which law and government only can furnish, and make us sit securely in our houses and sleep soundly in our beds.

In the neighboring counties, resolutions have been entered into for preserving the public peace and supporting the civil authority. In two of the counties, persons uttering inflammatory and threatening expressions have been put in gaol. I trust the county of Washington will be behind none in duty and love of peace, and will show itself as respectable in the virtue, as it is in the number of inhabitants. We may especially expect from all peace officers, justices, sheriffs, and constables, watchful and earnest exertions of their duty and power, for the establishment of peace and tranquillity, and from all the well-disposed citizens ready aid and concurrence, in support of the authority of officers and the maintenance of the happiness, honor, and virtue of this country.

At the December Sessions of the Court of Quarter Sessions for Washington County, in the year 1794, Judge Addison delivered the following charge to the grand jury :—

GENTLEMEN : The late insurrection in this country, from the numbers concerned in it, the manner in which it was conducted, the object it proposed to accomplish, the fatal effects which it produced, and the melancholy prospects which it exhibited, may be considered as the most alarming event that has occurred in America for many years. When authority has been encountered with tumult, and laws have been suspended by armed men, when the rage of some citizens has attacked the lives of other citizens and destroyed their houses and property by fire; every man of a sober mind must be impressed with concern, and seriously consider to what these things tend.

That a people struggling against usurped powers should oppose oppression by violence, or that, in the state of inflammation which is produced by a revolution, occasional outbreaks should break forth, no man will wonder. But that a people living under a settled and free government of laws, established by their own will, and changeable when and to what they please, should have recourse to force to repeal or alter their laws, or to anything but authority to redress their grievances, is not less absurd in itself than destructive to liberty, and will more effectually promote arbitrary power, discredit democracy, and show the inefficacy of a free representative government, than all the arts and arguments which its enemies have ever invented.

All governments are liable to change, all have had their changes, for no human art or invention is perpetual. The freedom of the savage state is by degrees restrained by the rules which are necessary to preserve one man from the force or fraud of another. As wickedness becomes ingenious or daring restraints are multiplied, or in other words, the powers of government are enlarged. Every new act of violence in the people becomes an argument for a new accession of force to the government, till arbitrary power is gradually invested in one man, as the only remedy for preserving every man from the injustice of every other. Such *has been* the progress of governments, and such by the violence of passion *may be* the progress of ours.

We profess to admire liberty and to respect the principles of a demonstrative republic as the best source of government, and we consider our own government as founded on those principles. Will we be honest in our profession and act on the principles which we admire? The principles of a democracy are that the whole people, either personally or by their representatives, should have the power of making laws. But what law is it in which the whole people would concur? So various are the faculties and interests of men, that unanimity of many in any measure is seldom to be expected of a whole people, almost never. If no law were to be made, therefore, till the whole people should assent to it, no law would almost ever be made. But as laws must be made, there is a necessity that the will of some of the people should be constrained, and reason requires that the greater number should bind the less. In our government, therefore, the will of the majority is equivalent to the will of the whole, and as such must be obeyed, unless we will avow that we mean to change or destroy the principles of our government by violence and terror, and abandoning reason, the principle of action in man, degrade ourselves to the rank of brutes.

To permit or assume a power in any particular part of a State, to defeat or evade a law, is to establish a principle that every part of a State may make laws for itself, or in other words, that there shall be no law, no State, and no duty, but a complication of separate societies, acting each according to its pleasure. These societies will again be subdivided, for a majority of the whole of any society will have no authority to control any one refractory member. Each man in the State will be free from all law but his own will. Government and society are then destroyed, anarchy is established, and the wicked and the strong, like savages and wild beasts, prey on the whole and on one another.

Such are the natural and necessary consequences of opposing a law by force. This opposition persisted in, must terminate, either in anarchy, in the people, or tyranny in the government, and in either case must terminate in the destruction of those republican principles which we profess to admire and are bound to support. If the government yield, one example of successful violence will excite some other part of the people, for some other cause, to pursue the same unwarrantable means for the attainment of a favorite object. Every law will be opposed in some quarter by interested men. Indulgence to some will necessarily beget indulgence to all. There will be no law, the wicked will have no restraint, happiness will no longer exist; mutual jealousy, distrust, and terror will pervade all; thefts, robberies, and murders will spread over the country, and every man will be the enemy of every other. If the government exert its force, the resistance which it will experience, and the difficulty with which it will overcome it, will convince the whole people or the well-disposed, and the greater number, that there is a necessity of abridging the privileges of the citizens and arming the government with greater power. To repress improper violence in the people, powers, otherwise unnecessary, will be given to the government, and those powers will be increased by every new occasion of violence till a tyranny is established. And this is the most probable result of tumults, riots, and insurrections. For all good men are instantly impressed with indignation and resentment against them, and disposed to lend their aid to government to punish and restrain them. And in the choice of anarchy to tyranny the last as the least evil will be preferred.

I hold, therefore, that a forcible opposition to law, instead of favoring liberty, is the surest way to destroy it. Is then forcible resistance to law never justifiable? Never, if the law be consistent with the constitution. If a law be not contradictory to the principles of the constitution, however erroneous these principles be, it is entitled to obedience. If a law be bad, let those who dislike it apply, by petition to the legislature, for its repeal. If the legislature refuse, let the petitioners change their representatives. If a law be repugnant to the constitution, the constitution, being the paramount authority, silences the law and makes it void. To an unconstitutional law, therefore, forcible resistance may be justifiable, but even in this case it is not prudent, but highly dangerous, because the resister makes it at his peril, and has no other rule but his own opinion, which may be erroneous. For individuals to exercise the right of determining that a law is unconstitutional is dangerous to themselves and to the peace of the State. And even the exercise of this right by the judiciary (to whom it certainly belongs) may sometimes be insidious and occasion jealousies and resentments between them and the legislature. In the case of an unconstitutional law, an appeal to the judiciary ought not to be made without necessity, and to individual force never, till all other remedies are exhausted. Thus, according to the genius of our government, opposition even to an unconstitutional law ought to begin, as opposition to a bad law, by petition to the legislature for its repeal, or by a change of representatives. If those measures fail, the validity of the law must be questioned and established or annulled in a court of justice. In this manner it becomes us, as friends to liberty, to seek for every amendment either of a law or of the constitution, in a peaceable manner; for to attempt it by force implies an apprehension that the alteration attempted will not bear the test of reason, nor receive the approbation of a majority. If either the law or the constitution displease a majority, the majority can alter either. If either the law or the constitution displease a minority, the minority must submit, or retire from the territory of the State. These are the principles of democratic republics. By these principles, if we examine *our* resistance to the excise law, we shall find it as unjustifiable in its nature as it is outrageous in its degree. A power to lay and collect excises was explicitly vested in Congress by the constitution of the United States. This power received a very full discussion and deliberate sanction from all the States in their conventions. And four of the States (Massachusetts, South Carolina, New Hampshire, and New York) to the ratification of the constitution, annexed declarations of their opinions that Congress should not impose direct taxes, unless the amount of the imposts and excises should be insufficient for the public exigencies. According to the opinions of those States, therefore, Congress instead of being censurable for not preferring a direct tax to an excise, would have been censurable if they had not imposed a direct tax till the last extremity.

All our benefits are mingled with some degree of inconvenience. The union of the States under a general government, which, by combining the whole strength, renders the States respectable and prosperous, may be truly considered as essential to our safety and happiness, and as one of the greatest political benefits which we can possess. But it is necessarily attended with this inconvenience, that the laws, which from their nature must be general, will often be less adapted to the circumstances of some States than of others. The suffering States must seek consolation under this evil from the principles of mutual concession, and remedy for it from time, experience, and reciprocal inequality of taxation. If this tax bear peculiarly hard on this country, there may be other taxes which bear peculiarly hard on other parts of the United States, and affect us but little. I know not whether I ought to reckon of this number the taxation on property sold at auction; the tax on the manufacture of snuff and refined sugar, or the tax on licenses for selling wine or foreign fruits by retail; but of this number I surely may reckon, so far as it goes, the tax on carriages for the conveyance of persons. If all these taxes do not, the last certainly does affect others chiefly and us but little; the last, I may rather say, affects us not at all. They were all imposed in the last session of Congress, and if the progress be persisted in, all may correct the inequality of each, or the interests of all combining, for mutual protection, and instructed by observation and experience, may in time produce the repeal of all, if a new system more acceptable in its nature and more easy in practice can be introduced. In the mean time, while we murmur at the inconvenience of any law, let us seriously reflect on the difficulty of making laws equal and acceptable to so extended and varying a territory as that of the United States. And considering the fraternal band which ties us together and the source of our laws, from the appointment of the whole people, ought we rashly to abandon a confidence, that as soon as a law is plainly proved by experience to be oppressive to us, our brethren will relieve us? Would not we do so to others? And have others less virtue than we?

Together with these general principles, the particular circumstances of this country press upon us a faithful submission to this law as a point of conscience, honor, and safety. If we do not *yield*, an armed force will *compel* a punctual obedience. The law will be executed, and let us not render it impossible for government to execute it by proper persons. As a public office becomes necessary for our honor and safety, let us render its execution respectable and encourage and protect honest and respectable men in it. We may thus in some degree lessen the burden of the law, and render our obedience more pleasant to ourselves.

God forbid that any man among us should entertain the horrid idea that secret association should accomplish the work which it is found no longer safe for open insurrection to attempt. When danger to its very existence has once roused the power of government, no art of machination, nothing but implicit submission, can restore safety to the aggressor. Even for our own security from each other, such an idea is one of the most dreadful that can be conceived. Vices the most daring and destable need only a plausible introduction to render them familiar and general. One instance of assassination of the most odious person among us, would render the life of the most respectable altogether unsafe. For assassination is the work of a ruffian, and is there any person whom a ruffian will respect? Cast a moment's reflection on our late troubles, and tell me what kind of villany there is which all at once did not become fashionable. Chopping off heads was spoken of as easily as slicing a cucumber, and burning houses became as trivial as tearing waste paper. Introduce assassination or any other species of crime under a plausible pretence, and it will soon spread over the country and extend to every object.

The late troubles exhibit an awful lesson which it would be inexcusable to pass over without attention and improvement. During their existence the passions were too much excited and the mind too little at leisure to examine thoroughly their nature or effects, and terror debarred the exercise of freedom of opinion and expression. But now when the storm is over, it becomes our duty to look back on the past scenes to contemplate the ruins it made and speaking of the leading transactions freely and without disguise, to bestow some serious reflections on their nature and tendency. These reflections, while they afford us an opportunity of remarking how fatal to happiness is a resistance to lawful authority, will show us also how opposite to liberty anarchy is.

Some of the plainest dictates of personal liberty, if not its most essential principles, are that every man be free to think, to speak, and to act, as his inclination and judgment may lead him, provided he offend not against any law; that no man shall be tried or punished according to the arbitrary will of any individual, but according to the established forms and rules of the law, and that the enjoyment of every man's property shall be secured to him until he forfeit it by the sentence of the law, and that sentence be executed by the proper officer. With these maxims compare the effects of anarchy as we have experienced it. Because the interest or inclination of some men led them to accept and execute certain offices established by public authority, lawless bodies of men assembled for the purpose of riot and violence, seized, insulted, and abused their persons, entered their houses by force and destroyed both their houses and property by fire. If anything can place such transactions in a more detestable light than at first sight they must appear, it may be this, that if these things may be done for any cause, however good, there need no more for their execution for every cause, than that the party to execute them be of opinion that the cause is good. Let but a mob assemble, however small it be, if sufficient to accomplish its purpose, let them agree in opinion that such a man is dangerous, and therefore, that his property ought to be destroyed, and it is instantly done. Let but one man hate another and resolve to destroy him, he has only to assemble a few of similar sentiments, or over whom he has influence; they instantly pretend to be the people, and the work of malice is accomplished under the semblance of zeal for the public good.

The outrages of anarchy were not confined to public officers. They extended also to private citizens of respectable character and inoffensive manners. Variety of opinion seems to be as natural to the human mind as variety in shape, features, and complexion, is to the human body. Both seem to be the work of our Creator; neither can be a proper cause of punishment, and to punish for either is the grossest tyranny. Actions which some may think meritorious, others may think detestable, and a law which some may think bad, others may think good. But surely no man of sense and virtue will think that any man ought to be punished for entertaining or expressing either of these opinions, or for acting as if he thought a law good. Yet for such causes were men, who had offended against no law, severed from all the attachments of domestic life, driven from their families and homes, it might have been to wander they knew not where, and to subsist they knew not how, under the fear and peril of death if they should return. Is this liberty? Such is the liberty of anarchy.

To a private letter, a sacred respect, somewhat resembling the ancient mysteries of religion, has been usually annexed, and to violate its *secrecy* requires the suspicion of a coward and the villany of a traitor. Yet for no object that I can perceive of any public nature, but only to gratify the little revenge of a malignant mind, or to show that there was no crime which we were not ready to perpetrate, the public post was robbed and the letters in the mail were opened by a set of self-created inquisitors, who, advancing from one degree of guilt to a greater, assumed the authority of government, and called out the militia of the country to share and cover their crimes.

These transactions furnish us with this melancholy instruction, that when men have once transgressed the bounds of civil obligation and violated public authority, there is afterwards no restraint to their excess. They will do deeds which they never before intended, and from which, had they been suggested, they would have shrunk back with horror, and they will do them from no motive and to no end of interest to themselves or others, but merely from the rashness of the moment, a sally of wantonness, or an impulse of malice. Let us learn, therefore, to confine our conduct within the strict line of duty, and remember that the first transgression renders easy every subsequent one, however enormous.

I will state one or two causes, founded in ignorance and error, which contributed to the late unhappy insurrection or facilitated its progress.

I shall mention, first, *an opinion that riots and terror, banishing the officers of excise, would produce a repeal of the excise law, or its inactivity with regard to us ;* but I have said so much on this, on other occasions, that I shall but maintain it now, and pass it by without further notice. I shall next mention *a desire to cover the guilt of those who first attacked Gen. Neville's house.* As it seems an opinion generally prevailed that riots in this cause were proper, it appeared hard that those who engaged in them should suffer for their services in the public cause, and it seems to have been believed that the best way to protect them was by multiplying the number of offenders to make the punishment of any appear dangerous. Perhaps here one might find matter for questioning whether it be not desirable that wickedness should be accompanied with understanding, and whether folly be not the most mischievous of all qualities. Had the men who incited the second attack on Gen. Neville's house, and the subsequent transactions in the insurrection, been men of sound well-informed judgment, they would have reasoned in this manner: "The rioters have erred, but we have countenanced and shared the opinion from which their error proceeded, and we ought to endeavor to save them. Let the whole county now rise and seize and secure them for public justice. When this is done, let us go forward to government, with solemn and sincere assurances that we will submit to this law honestly and punctually, and that if required, we will pay for all past damages and delinquencies, and with these assurances, let us request that government forgive our offending brethren." If measures of this nature had been pursued, the issue would have been more fortunate to the offenders, to these counties and to the United States.

Another cause which I shall mention is *a mistaken use of the word* PEO-PLE. As, in a democracy, the people is the source of all authority, and as the people on this side of the mountains seemed all to agree in reprobating the excise law, declaimers never extending their views beyond their own neighborhood, but considering the people *here* as the *whole* people, took occasion to represent that the people *here* might lawfully correct any errors of their public servants. On these principles every neighborhood, considering itself as the people, thought it had a right to do as it pleased. Assuming as what needs no proof, that the union of all the States is necessary for the prosperity of each, and that separate from the union we should be insignificant and dependent; I would observe that it is the *whole* people of the union that is the source of all power, to argue that a very small portion of the people is the source of all power is absurd. If every small portion of the people were to assume the power of the whole, instead of a government, we should have a chaos of jarring authorities and conflicting wills. While the constitution subsists, even the whole people can speak only in the constitutional manner by their representatives. So that the only voice of the people is the laws. And the laws must be presumed to be the will of the people until the repeal of them declare that the people have changed their minds.

I shall mention but another cause which facilitated the progress of the late insurrection. The danger of this country from Indian incursions had rendered it often necessary to assemble the militia without waiting for the orders of government, which would come too late for the danger. From experience it was found that attack was the best defence. Hence voluntary expeditions into the Indian country were frequently undertaken, and government, from a sense of their utility, afterwards sanctioned them by defraying their expenses. In this manner *it had become habitual with the militia of these counties to assemble at the call of their officers without inquiring into the authority or object of the call.* This habit, well known to the contrivers of the rendezvous at Braddock's Field, rendered the execution of their plan an easy matter. They issued their orders to the officers of the militia, who assembled their men, accustomed to obey orders of this kind given on the sudden and without authority. The militia came together without knowing from whom the orders originated or for what purpose they met. And when met, it was easy to communicate from breast to breast, more or less of the popular frenzy, till all felt it or found it prudent to dissemble and feign that they felt it. This gave appearance at length of strength and unanimity to the insurrection, silenced the well-disposed, and emboldened ruffians to proceed with audacity to subsequent outrages, which there was no energy to restrain nor force to punish.

In these reflections we find nothing consolatory; all is sorrow and disgrace. Let us turn then to the other side of the picture, and consider the conduct of government and of our fellow-citizens in other parts of the Union. A measure no less prudent than generous was adopted by the government. Commissioners were sent to offer us a full pardon of all past offences on the simple condition of future obedience. Lest these terms offered generously at once, and the best that could be offered should fail in reclaiming us to duty, the president ordered that a competent number of our fellow-citizens should be ready in arms to compel that obedience which reason and mercy could not produce. While the terms were under our consideration, there appeared a manifest reluctance in our fellow-citizens to draw their swords against their brethren. But no sooner was it known that we rejected those terms and threatened the government with war and dissolution, than the contest among them was who should be foremost in the field. It was then no longer a doubt whether a sufficient number could be procured to go; but whether multitudes, beyond this number, could be persuaded to stay. The merchant abandoned his warehouse, the lawyer his office, the mechanic his shop, the gentleman his pleasures, and every man the gains and enjoyments of domestic life, to endure hardships which they had never experienced before, and hazard their lives in defence of the laws. At the call, "Your country is in danger," the rich and the poor met together, forgetting all distinctions of stations and circumstances, and blended in one common class of patriots. Even the pacific Quaker, whose principles restrain him from shedding blood, now assumed the garb and weapons of war, and marched in arms to maintain the peace and government of his country.

In this we receive a lesson of the power of government, and are taught that, however riot and anarchy may triumph for a while, there is an energy and struggle to crush them; that reason and the law are the only protection of free citizens; that violence only brings ruin on its authors; that, in times of sedition, it is the interest of all to be not lukewarm and indifferent, but firm and persevering on the side of public authority; and that the faithful friends of law and order, however borne down for a time, will in the end be protected and rise above oppression.

Even at this bright prospect of the generous and spirited conduct of our patriotic fellow citizens, a cloud intervenes, though none of them fell by our arms, yet some have fallen victims to a change of climate and manner of living, an inclement season, and severity of fatigue, over swamps and mountains. Some gallant youths will never return to their anxious parents. Some parents will never return to bless their children in their dying moments. And some husbands have expired without a wife to close their eyes. Can we think of this without suspicion that their blood may be upon our heads?

But, gentlemen, the past cannot be recalled; let us only study to improve it, and strive to make some compensation by our future conduct. For that purpose let us suppress the first seed of sedition and not allow it to grow up, as before, to a strength not to be resisted. Let even words tending to any violence or a breach of the peace be held criminal; let every witness of such things carry the offender before a magistrate, that justice may be executed. And let every magistrate take heed that he hear not the sound in vain. To permit criminals to escape from punishment is to encourage crimes. Impunity begets offences as corruption begets maggots. A few examples of punishment of the late disorderly conduct given among ourselves in each county, will perhaps secure our place for many years and prevent the existence of many crimes and the necessity of many and severe punishments.

To your particular and serious consideration, gentlemen, do I address these sentiments. You are the door, by which only justice may be come at. By you, a way may be opened up to justice. By you justice may be shut up. In your hands the laws of your country have placed this authority, and for the exercise of it strictly, according to law and truth, you are bound by your oaths, and answerable to your God. You have no discretion to do as you please—your opinion must be governed by the laws—your belief must be guided by testimony—and so you have seen. It is not for you to determine whether it be *expected* that punishment should be inflicted on any particular offender, but only whether it be *true* that any particular person is an offender.

There are reasons which ought, particularly at this time, to induce juries and all other officers concerned in the administration of justice, and all citizens to discharge their respective duties with precision, and carry the laws into execution with perfect exactness. An armed force is now in our country, for the purpose of enforcing submission to the laws. The sooner we give satisfactory evidence of our voluntary and exact conformity to the laws, the sooner will our country be cleared of the stain on its character. Further, a law has lately been passed directing that certain cases, which formerly were tried in the federal courts, *may* now be tried in the State courts, and experiments under this law are about to be made. We have now in many cases an opportunity of being tried in our own counties, instead of being carried for trial to York or Philadelphia. But if we show any backwardness or bias in doing justice, we cannot expect that we should be trusted with its administration in those cases. Government must require strict justice, and if this cannot be obtained in our own courts they will be shunned as corrupt, and we shall be taken for trial to a distance and have our cases decided by others. If we wish, therefore, to be delivered from a standing army, or if we wish to have trials in the cases offered to us in our counties—let us now at this critical time give specimens of our being ruled by law. If we do so now perhaps after some experience of our virtue, the federal government may trust us in all cases whatsoever, with trials in our own counties.

I therefore solemnly adjure you to deal faithfully and make presentment in all cases of any breach of the peace or other offence, especially respecting the late troubles. This will be the true test of our integrity, and will determine how far government ought to trust us with the management of ourselves. Whenever a bill is sent up to you, if it be proved true, I call upon you, as you regard your oaths and the interest of your county, to find it so. Where any offence is within the knowledge of any of you, I call upon you, by the same regard to your oaths and your country, that you present the facts to us or give information of them to the prosecutor for the State, that he may draw up a bill to be *found* on your knowledge.

One offence to which I would recommend your particular consideration is *the raising of liberty poles.* What is the liberty which those pole raisers wanted? A liberty to be governed by no law—a liberty to destroy every man who differed from them in opinion, or whom they hated—a liberty to do what mischief they pleased. It is not *acts* of violence alone which constitute offences. Offences may be commenced by writing, by words, or by other signs of an evil purpose. The mere act of raising a pole is in itself a harmless thing; the question is, what is the meaning of it? Those poles were evidently standards of rebellion, and signs of war against the government. They were raised by the seditious with an avowed intent to hold under fear all the well-disposed and peaceable part of the community; to keep alive the spirit of riot and confusion in the country, and to prevent the return of law, peace, and safety. And they produced all the ill-effects which were intended. They gave an opportunity to the violent to know their strength, and one another. What was it but these pole raisings and their attendant circumstances that prevented our return to submission and duty and a general acquiescence with the terms offered by the commissioners, and made it necessary for government to march an army into this country to subdue that spirit of sedition and riot which blind madness first excited, and those pole raisings kept alive? Will any man doubt, therefore, that raising those poles was criminal—that those were especially criminal who raised them after the arrival of the commissioners of government in this country? And those, above all, who raised them after the generous terms offered by government were made known.

Another class of offenders, perhaps yet more atrocious, consists of those who, by violence or threats, prevented, or endeavored to prevent, the signing of the acknowledgment of submission required by government as the condition of our pardon and peace. Besides the fatal effects of this violence to the country, it was a restraint on that freedom of will which every man has a right to exercise. Was it not a plain breach of the peace? Was it not a plain declaration of war against government? Need I, gentlemen, use words to convince you that it was a crime? I know I need not.

Neither need I tell you that those men are criminal, and ought to be subjected to prosecution, who took upon them to burn houses or abuse property or persons for supposed misconduct. Those also are criminal in a high degree, who assembled in parties for the purpose of doing such things, though they never did them. This is a clear offence, and a breach of the peace. It tended also to keep up the terrors against returning duty, and rendered an army necessary to remove those terrors, and restore the minds of the people to freedom and ease, and the country to peace.

Let me in the words of Scripture point out the certain difference between liberty and licentiousness. So is the will of God, that you submit to every ordinance of man; as free, and not using your liberty for a cloak of maliciousness, but as the servants of God. For, brethren, ye have been called unto liberty, only use not your liberty for an occasion to the flesh, but by love serve one another. (1 Peter ii. 13, 16; Gal. v. 13.) True liberty, like true religion, is known by its fruits. Liberty, the daughter of heaven, and the best gift of God to a favored people, a generous principle, whose object is the peace and prosperity of the human race, must produce fruits worthy of its divine origin. Licentiousness, the offspring of hell and the scourge of an offending nation, selfish in its nature, and seeking the degradation of all but itself, bears fruits of an opposite kind: sedition, fury, hatred, malice, and mischief. By its fruits judge whether our insurrection proceeded from a spirit of liberty or of licentiousness. Whether it was the work of God or of the devil.

Do your duty, gentlemen, and satisfy your own consciences. Present all offenders whatever, to the justice of your country. This you are bound by your oaths to do; whether those offenders shall be considered as proper objects of mercy or of punishment, it is not for you to decide. That question lies with others, and you cannot take it up without violating your oaths, and prostrating the principles of our laws and government.

I shall conclude with exhorting to a speedy and faithful compliance with the propositions made to us by the agents of government. *One* is, of taking an oath of fidelity and of submission to the laws, and the *other* is, entering into an association for supporting their authority, and protecting their officers.

It may be asked why should we do so? I will give two reasons. First. We have been great offenders, and we cannot give too strong assurances of our return to duty. The assurances required seem due to our own character, and to the satisfaction of our fellow citizens. Second. A temporary army is now, and a standing army will be established among us unless we can convince government and our fellow citizens by unequivocal proofs of our regular and sincere habits of submission to law, and of our exertions to enforce obedience to all authority. If we refuse compliance, government and our fellow citizens may suspect that there is a change only in our conduct, not in our hearts, that our submission is temporary and not dissembled, and that if we believed it safe we would again break out into riots. Let us prevent such suspicions by our conduct, and as we have rendered it necessary for government to establish a force to restrain us, let us render it proper to withdraw this force. Let us begin by taking this oath and entering into this association, and continue in a faithful adherence to both. We may thus repair our character, and relieve ourselves from the disgrace of being governed by force and a standing army.

I shall now add a list of the names of the citizens of Washington County, in their respective townships, which I have been enabled to procure from a variety of sources, who took the oath of allegiance, which was in these words:—

I do solemnly, in the presence of Almighty God, swear and declare that I will faithfully and sincerely support the Constitution of the United States, and obey all laws thereof, and will discontinue opposition thereto, except by way of petition and remonstrance, and all attempts to resist, obstruct, or illtreat the officers of the United States in the execution of their respective duties, so help me God.

Each person, in taking this oath, was required to subscribe his name thereto, as well as sign the following pledge:—

In pursuance of the oath hereto annexed, I do hereby engage and associate to and with all others who may subscribe these presents to countenance and protect the officers of the United States in the execution of their duties according to law, and to discover and bring to justice all persons who may be concerned, directly or indirectly, in illegally hindering or obstructing the said officers, or any of them, in the execution of their duty, or in doing any manner of violence to them, or either of them. In witness of all which I have hereunto subscribed my hand the day and year opposite my name.

Sworn and subscribed before me,   ELEAZER JENKINS.

Dec. 29, 1794.   *Bethlehem Township.*

David Enoch, John Smiley, Nathan Meck, David Sutton, James Braden, Abel McFarland, Samuel Meck, Daniel McFarland, Jr., James Gillespie, John James, Lemuel Cooper, David Evans, John Bockius, James Evans, Christopher Horn, Thomas Ijams, Daniel Cory, Valentine Kender, Bazel Barnet, Christopher Cox, John Horn, George Horn, James Graham, Aaron Davis, Caleb Ball, Jacob Young, John Meck, Jr., Isaac Pettit, Sampson Nicholls.

Dec. 30, 1794.   *Somerset Township.*

James Dawson, Samuel Ferguson, John Greenleas, Thomas Gill, Archibald Blue, John Huffman.

Dec. 30, 1794.   *Bethlehem Township.*

Wm. Guthrey, John Fusten, Christian Cockler, John Meck Johnson, Gabriel Nave.

Dec. 30, 1794. *Strabane Township.*
Samuel Fitch, James Collins, John Fitch.

Dec. 31, 1794. *Somerset Township.*

James Collams, Allen Olfer, Andrew Ault, Jacob Swagler, Henry McDonough, Samuel Crawford, George McIlwaine, Jno. McIlwaine, James Miller, Grier McIlwaine, Samuel Wier, Francis Keely, Jacob Myers, Henry Hewitt, James Cochran, Wm. McCombe, Patrick McCulloch, Robert McComb, Peter Black, Samuel Shuster, Samuel Moser, Michael Paker, James Leydy, John Leydy, Benjamin Leydy, Wm. Smith, David Huffman, Martin Huffman, Andrew Smith, John Stevenson, Martin Smith, William Thompson, Robert McFarland, John Chapman, Mathias Luse, Frederick Leydy, John Vance, John Kinney, James Dickson, Alex. Porter, Andrew Simons.

Bethlehem Township.

Thomas Wier, James Hill, Peter Drake, Joshua Drake, Jonathan Drake, James Beatty, Joseph Hill, Jr., Leonard Roberts, Dickinson Roberts, Daniel Driskel, Thomas Richardson, Wm. Campbell, Richard Richardson, John Weston, Sr., Fred. Dage, Sr., Frederic Dage, Jr., Adam Smith, Pat McDowell, Robert Ferguson, David Sutton, Sr., John Dage, Michael Letherman, John Weston, Jr., John Conkle, Jacob Conkle, Ezekier Bradon, Mich. Dage, And. Rogers, Thomas Caton, Mathias Dage, Gasper Pilts, George Dawson, Peter Hewitt, George Drister, Abm. Barber.

Fallowfield Township.

John Sutherland, Jr., George Young, Alex. Moore, Thomas Chambers, Joseph Weir.

Dec. 20, 1794. *Hanover Township.*

Taken before SAMUEL GLASGOW, J. P.

Miles Wilson, Thomas Moss, Adam Vinnage, John Moor, Augustus Moor, James Proudfoot, Lewis Sadler, Daniel McConnell, John Thompson, Thomas Dornan, John White, Christopher Walters, Elijah Devner, Patrick McDonald.

Dec. 29, 1794. Taken before WM. PARKER.

Jacob Book, Andrew Kintner, George Kintner, Daniel Hamilton, Geo. Parker, John Parkeson, Wm. Parker, Jr., James Parker, Wm. McEard, Christopher Elliott, George Stooday, Martin Zuzidant, Daniel Zuzidant, Isaac Lash, George McMillan, Jacob Zug, George Frend.

Dec. 9, 1794. Sworn before EBN. GOBLE, of Morris Township.

Demas Lindsly, Zeba Lindsly, David Johnson, Leonard Colman, Charles Kinlan, Cyrus Riggs, Mathias Roll, Abijah Leveridge, Joseph Riggs, Samuel Parkhurst, Caleb Lindsley, Jr., John Archer, Caleb Edy, Joseph Coe, Chr. McAlrath, Nathan Axtell, Samuel Ratan, Jno. Lindsly, Price Dille, Constant Rowlee, Caleb Winget, Alex. Scott, Darling Day, Thomas Palmer, Peter Rush, David Conduit, Archer Scott.

Nov. 2, 1794. Before JOSEPH VANCE, of Smith Township.

Robert Marquis, James Campbell, Hugh Lee, Thos. Pray, Robert Lyle, Adam Hayes, Charles Campbell, James Best, George Day, John Hamilton, John Dodds, James Edgar, Samuel Whitaker, John Coper, Nathan Kiniber, Wm. Hanon, Samuel Marquis, John Wilkins, Wm. Huse, Hugh Mont-

HISTORY OF WASHINGTON COUNTY. 109

gomery, James Miller, William Johnston, James Gaston, David McCreery, Hugh Dobbins, John McKibler, John Coners, Henry Fullerton, Robert Kennedy, George Meeaner, Geo. Miller, Samuel Marchant, William Lee, James Boggs, James Wiley, James D. Barr, Joseph Scott, Gorsham Hull, Thomas Elder, John Cook, Charles Murray, James Hammond, James Leech, Philip Burget, Rowland Rogers, James Allison, David Thompson, George Lee, George Burget, Wm. McGee, John McMillin, James Rankin, James Caldwell, John Riddle, Wm. Bay, Alex. McBride, Samuel Barr, Thomas Brice, James Ravenscraft, Moses Hays, John Marquis, Hugh Bays, John Bar, John Montgomery, Wm. McBride, Wm. Jackson, Philip Jackson, William Wallace, Thomas Hays, John Coventry, John Lyle, James Hayes, Robert Magee, James Moore, Thomas Phillips, Adam Glass, David Hays, John Bavington, James Cavert, And. Elliott, James Maxwell, William Leech, James Leech, Robert Stuart, Henry Cooper, Robert Pattridge, Joseph Hays, John McCuoy, Richard McKibben, David Marquer, William Campbell, Joseph Phillis, Robert Wallace, Samuel Strain, Wm. Thompson, Wm. Wilkin, Thomas Thompson, Robert Thompson, John Eakin, Sr., John Eakin, Jr., Samuel Eakin, Joseph Eakins, John Colter, John Duncan, James Moore, William Ferguson, Thomas Rogers, Edward Hatfield, John Shilber, Andw. McClean, James Dunbar, Abraham Russel, John Thinkerd, Sr., James Thinkerd, John Thinkerd, Jr., Wm. Wallace, Sr., John Strain, Alex Robertson, Henry Rankin, John Bell, Robert Holmes.

From the 18th of November to 29th of December, 1794, before DANIEL DEPUE, in *Fallowfield Township*—

Joseph Depue, Samuel Cole, Samuel Gunsalis, Joseph Parkinson, Thomas Nichols, John Rolston, Adam Wickersham, Jr., Thomas Beaty, Christian Stout, Jacob Stilwagon, Jacob Resasher, Peter Wickersham, Peter Wayant, Peter Erigh, Cornelius Wayant, Andrew Platter, James Coulter, Hammond Cole, Vincent Colvin, Thomas Shaver, Wm. Beemur, Isaac Cole, John Tannehill, Jr., Samuel Coulter, Nicholas Johnson, Robert Galloway, Jacob Rape, Jr., John Ammon, Andrew Cole, Wm. Jewell Benjamin Morrow, Thomas Legg, William Vanhorn, Edward Loder, Joseph Hall, Peter Bellefelt, Thomas Case, Geo. Grant, John Muller, Nicholas Depue, Samuel Moody, Jacob Rope, Symonds Bandwell, Christopher Reading, William Nitherfreed, Samuel Baxter, Massal Case, Martin Wirt, Samuel Quimby, Daniel McGuire, Thomas Fenton, Wm. Storer, James Baxter, John Lane, Henry Lane, John Johnston, Samuel Baxter, Jr., John Fenton, S. Storer, Richard Storer, Jonathan Hamilton, Nicholas Conley, Isaac Teeple, Richard Jackson, David Grant, Daniel Hickey, Lewis Chatfield, Robert George, Alexander George, Thomas Coulter, John Ruth, Benjamin Gunsalis, James Hill, Conrad Ammon, John Bind, Alex. Stelle, Daniel Hamilton, Jonathan Coulter, Nathan Woodbury, Peter Casner, Daniel Rice, Abraham Crabs, Philip Crabs, Robert Croskeny, Jas. Rice, Robert Williams, John Shouse, Jacob Ammon, Peter Jesseroon, Abraham Hickman, Samuel Lewis, Abraham Frye, Sr., Abraham Frye, Jr., Frederick Cooper, Samuel Willey, Samuel Frye, John Amlin, Jr., James Carson, Abraham Seevers, Abraham Brokow, Thos. Rape, John Slette, Sheddrack Hyatt, Robert Latta Robert Speers, Henry Falconer, William Ringland, John Cooper, John Stockton, Michael Power, Jacob Crabs, Daniel McComus, Henry Crabs, Jas. Davidson, James Rush, Samuel Vanvoorhis, Daniel Vanvoorhis, Wm. Guilleford, Daniel Brent.

Sworn before ELEAZER JENKINS, January 5, 1795. *Strabane Township*—
Pals. Frank, Wm. Nivin, John Chambers, John Whitehill, Jas. Duncan, N. Simons, Joshua Davis, John Munel, Jonathan Williams.

Sworn before WM. NAILER, from 15th of November to 30th of December, 1794. He says, "I do certify that these persons have taken the oath and subscribed the association prescribed by his excellency Gen. Henry Lee, to the inhabitants of the four western counties of Pennsylvania."

Thomas Cannon, Wm. Nailer, Shebazzar Bentley, James Chambers, John Cox, Benjamin Cox, John Hoven, Shadrack Hyatt, Thomas Thompson, Elisha Teeters, John McCaran, V. Ferguson, James Gelly, Gilbert Samuels, John Riddle, Jos. Blackburn, John Thompson, Edward Duffield, Jonathan Thompson, Abraham Fingby, J. Ferguson, John Happer, Wm. Ramage, Math. Hartford, John Kennedy, Charles Dailey. Isaac Dailey, Richard Sutton, Samuel Gallohar, Wm. Mitchell, John Cormy, Wm. Corn, Henry Newkirk, David Milender, Jacob Auld, A. Miller, Neil Murray, Abraham Southard, Jonas Segby, Jacob Fegley, Sr., Jacob Fegley, Jr., Jas. McCall, James Nailor, Alexander Armstrong, John Anderson, James Parkinson, Arthur Latimer, Henry Harsh, Abraham Frider, Abraham McNitt, Simon Waugh, Joseph Barkley, Christopher Fletcher, Lewis Stacher, J. Clotter, Jacob Repsher, Leonard Englar, Daniel Robbins, Robert Wallace, Matthew Myers, John McCormic, John Welch, John Baldwin, Henry Magner, Wm. Rodgers, Ralph Naylor, John Chambers, Samuel Gaston, John Crague, Moses Rodgers, Edmund Thomas, John Munn, Jr., Liverton Thomas, Thomas Thornley, Joseph Hagerty, Samuel Ogden, Andrew Crawford, Geo. Onstatt, Lewis Onstatt, John Todd, Wm. Armstrong, Benjamin Crawford, Samuel McGornaway, James Huston, Joseph Leweston, Joseph Barr, John Moore, William Fought, Joseph Fowler, Samuel Barr, Benjamin Merriner, Andrew Regan, John Shaw, Samuel Johnson, Benjamin Bebast, William Byers, Thomas Frazer, Benjamin Lyons, Joseph Gladden, David Munn, Benjamin Price, Andrew Wadell, William Dunshee, Robert Crouch, John Crouch, John Young, Wm. Kenney, Henry Morrison, Charles Fox, John Morrison, John Johnston, Amazariah Johnston, Abraham Johnston, Lemuel Sayers, Sr., Lemuel Sayers, Jr., Robert McGee, Andrew Devore, Shadrack Ruark, John Clark, Wm. Jolly, James Meleney, Thomas Patterson, John Patterson, Abraham Stevens, Joseph Calwell, Peter Sharp, James Glass, Lemuel Connelly, Eph. Sayers, James Price, Thomas Deusher, Peter Denburn, John Leedom, Samuel Bebout, William Stuart, Edward Magner, Sr., James Archby, Enoch McFanold, Thomas Bounds, Thomas Pollock, Wm. Pollock, John Pollock, Andrew Sullivan, Isaac Wilson, William Ayres, Matthew Logan, James Logan, John Mitchel, Joseph Scofield, John Hollcraft, A. McFarlane.

Persons sworn by DAVID HAMILTON, from November 24, to December 30, 1794—

Wm. Hannah, Hugh Hannah, Samuel Scott, Abner Biddle, Oliver Brennen, James O. Donnell, James Kobyon, John Scott, John Small, Arthur Gardner, Benjamin Shune, Michael Study, George Branan, Joseph Watt, James Parkinson, John Fune. Maxwell Earicson, James Taylor, Sr.. Jas. Taylor, Jr., Daniel Welch, William Parkinson, Joseph Phillips, Abner Lash, Allen Means, Reuben Rennyon, Jacob Shuster, Isaac Rose, Joseph Tuelleg.

Cross Creek, September 11, 1794.

William Rannalls, Henry Graham, Samuel McKibben, Thomas Patterson, Thomas Marshall, Gideon Gibson, John Morrison, Benjamin Bay, John Marshall, William McCaskey, Samuel Johnston, Robert Walker, Elijah Henwood, John Marshall, Robert Forsythe, Joseph Scott, William Campbell, Richard Wells, of James, William Rea, Elijah Robertson, Peter Coe, James Davison,

James Marshall, James How, John Leeper, Robert Marshall, Thomas Wiley, Alexander Wells, John Stevenson, George Wells, Wm. McKibben, Elisha Robertson, Robert Moore, James Jackson, Hugh Rogers, William Wells, Thomas Beaty, Isaac Cowan, John McClurg, James Linn, Joseph Riley, Thomas McKibben, William Caldwell, Nathaniel Pettit, Samuel Robertson, John Graham, Philemon Davis, William Young, James Todd, James Leeper, Thomas Graham, Samuel Davis, Robert McComb, Joseph Carter, John Scott, John Beaty, Adam Glass, William Smith, James Dunbar, Samuel Leeper, Thomas Ward, Alexander Johnson, James Clark, Ebenezer Smith, John Cowen, John Stevenson, William Hughs, James Smith, David Hays, John Moore, Samuel Carson, Ephraim Hart, Isaac Johnson, Joseph Reed, Daniel Cameron, Isaac Shannon, Daniel Johnson, Samuel Futhey, James Weaver, William Watson, Samuel Gilmore, Samuel Robb, Stephen Johnson, James Colville, Andrew Ferguson, Andrew McKinney, Richard Davis, Henry Wells, Bobert Colville, Hugh Newell, Timothy Spencer, James Riley, Robert Robb, John Tennille, William Vance, John Stevenson, John Morrison, John Criss, Robert Glass, John Robb, William McClurg, Nicholas Brown, Robert Armstrong, John Brown, John Campbell, John Marquis, John Wagoner, Sen., James Taylor, John Harriman, Jacob Romans, John Robinson, Samuel McMillan, John Wilken, Sen., James Patterson, Thomas Bay, John Lawther, Samuel Smith, James Watson, Sen., James Kirk, William Ayrs, Edward Brown, Cornelius Boyles, Wm. McGarrah, Alexander Ayrs, George Coffman, James Ward, Wm. Shearer, Robert McCready, Joseph Caldwell, John Gardner, William Caldwell, James Doudle, Hugh McClurg, James Satterfield, James Robinson, Joseph Colville, Bosten Burgett, Richard Wells, George Tennille, Daniel Tennille, Peter Linville, John Robb, Tarry McGarry, George Moore, Jacob Buxton, John Poagen.

Done in presence of .

WILLIAM REA,
AARON LYLE, } Commissioners.
THOMAS PATTERSON,

LIST OF STILLS seized by Robert Johnston, and left at William McAllister's, Peter Chessround's, Shesbazzar Bentley's, and John Baldwin's, Washington County, and Nathan Couch's, of Allegheny County.

TIME OF SEIZURE.	POSSESSOR.	STILLS.	CAPACITY OF STILLS.
1794, Nov. 14.	Vincent Colvin,	2	80 and 65.
	David Hamilton,	1	stole afterwards.
	Christopher Stacker,	1	76
	Benjamin Parkinson,	1	100
	James Parkinson,	2	80
	John Reed.	1	68
" " 15.	John Baldwin,	1	
	John Hamilton,	1	
	Samuel Scott,	2	
	Wm. Parker,	1	
	Peter Chessround,	2	
	Wm. Armstrong,	1	
	James Stuart	2	
	Peter Lyle,	1	
	Shezbazzar Bentley,	2	

112 APPENDIX TO

List of stills and liquor seized by Benjamin Wells, and left at Canonsburg, except those taken away by Gen. Neville.

Time of seizure.	Person's Name.	Liquor.	Stills.
1794, Nov. 14.	Abraham Singhorse,		3
	David Ralston,		2
	James Dohings,	75 gals.	1
	Joseph Beeler,		1
	William Wallace,		2
	Thomas McCeanel,		2
	James McElroy,		2
	Robert Thompson,		2
	Andrew Ritchie,		1
	Thomas Menary,		1
	William Cambell,		2
	John Sutherling,		2
	Samuel McBride,	25 "	1
	James Woodhen,	7 "	1
		107 gals.	23

The duty imposed on stills by the act of Congress was not paid in these counties, and the attempts to enforce its payment here having excited the insurrection, and been rendered effectual by the expedition of 1794, the Secretary of the Treasury, on the 17th November, 1794, considering the hardship of enforcing the payment of all the arrears of duty in these counties, from 30th June, 1791, instructed the collectors to receive entries of stills for the year beginning with the 1st July, 1794, and ending with the 30th June, 1795, without exacting the payment of any arrears of duty except for the year immediately preceding, that is, from the 30th June, 1793, to 1st July, 1794, ascertaining these arrears by the capacity of the stills; hence an inspection office was opened in Washington June, 1794.

To exhibit the number of stills which were in operation in the several townships of Washington County before the whiskey insurrection, I have prepared the following information from the original records. Thus, in 1791, were 272 licensed stills, while in 1869 there are but 18 distilleries.

Townships	1787. STILLS.	1788. STILLS.	1790. STILLS.	1791. STILLS.
1. Amwell,	11	8	3	5
2. Bethlehem,	22	12	9	16
3. Cecil,	17	27	14	10
4. Cumberland,	13	28	26	25
5. Donegal,	9	11	14	13
6. Fallowfield,	22	24	25	14
7. Hopewell,	16	21	28	27
8. Morgan,	4	8	6	7
9. Peters,	13	23	6	5
10. Robinson,	9	8	9	12
11. Smith,	9	11	4	14
12. Strabane,	3	8	4	22
13. Nottingham,	15	14	18	16
14. Somerset,	17	12	18	18
15. Green,	16	13	19	
16. Dickinson,	14	22		
17. Washington,	3	2		
18. Hanover,	6	2	5	5
19. Franklin,	9	21	6	6
20. Finley,		5	1	1
21. Morris,			2	6
22. East Bethlehem,			10	13
23. West Bethlehem,			12	9
24. Cross Creek,			9	12
25. Chartiers,			14	16
	228	280	262	272

We shall now proceed with the judicial view of the insurrection, by the publication of important letters:—

Pittsburg, November 24, 1794.

Sir : The judge of the district having spent several days in this town for the purpose of examining into the cases of persons accused, and taking the examination of witnesses relative to offences committed within the district against the United States, and his public business requiring his attendance in another part of the district, I am under the necessity of requesting your attention to the continuance of that inquiry, which public justice requires, relative to the offences committed as above mentioned.

The list inclosed, and the excepted cases in Governor Lee's proclamation, will indicate the persons in regard to whose conduct during the late convulsion it is desirable to establish the truth.

I will be obliged to you, sir, to reduce their testimony to writing, and to furnish me with the depositions, and to bind the witnesses over in a reasonable sum expressed in dollars to appear and testify in behalf of the United States, at the next circuit court of the United States, stated or special, to be holden within the district aforesaid.

The following cases I desire you to notice particularly:—

1. To bind over a certain Matthew Logan as a witness against Ebenezer Gallagher.

2. To take the recognizance of Thomas Hughes, Esq., if he shall offer bail and good securities in no less sum in the whole than 3000 dollars for his appearance to answer.

The charge against him is his having been one of the *blackened* party who attacked the house of Capt. Faulkner, and his having signed a contemptuous and improper paper on the 11th of September last. His offence, therefore, is of a bailable nature.

3. To send for and bind over as witnesses Major Richard Talbot and Rev. Philip Dodridge, of Hopewell township, and John Tennell of Cross Creek.

These instances are not mentioned as the exclusive cases in which your assistance is requested. To your judgment every other case is with great confidence committed. Truth will gradually reveal itself and testimony of which we are ignorant.

With great consideration and respect,
I have the honor to be
To JUDGE ADDISON. W. RAWLE.

The endorsement is as follows: Bound R. Talbot 22d Dec. 1794. Mr. Talbot says Rev. Dodridge's name is Joseph. Philip is a brother.
Bound John Tennell and A. Wells.
Bound Joseph Dodridge and John Buchanan.

Recognizances for appearance at Pittsburg and Washington.

Pennsylvania } Defendant turned over for bail by Gen. Lee, Commander-
vs. } in-Chief.
Moses Devore. }

Moses Devore, of Elizabeth township, Allegheny County, tent in £200,
Joseph Becket, " " " 100,
John Dailey, of Rostraver township, Westmoreland County, " 100,
Conditioned for appearance at next court of quarter sessions for county of Allegheny, to answer, &c., 25th Nov. 1794.
COR. ALEX. ADDISON.

Recognized in court of Allegheny County to keep peace and good behavior for twelve months, no bill having been found by grand jury.

Pennsylvania }
vs. } Turned over *ut supra.*
Henry McKinney. }

Joseph Becket and John Dailey each held in £100 for appearance of Henry McKinney, who is bound in the sum of £200.

No bill found, and bound by recognizance to keep the peace and good behavior for twelve months by Gen. Gibson.

Pennsylvania }
vs. } Turned over *ut supra.*
Andrew Holmes. }

Andrew Holmes, of Nottingham township, Washington Co., tent £200,
John Gaston, of Peters township, Washington County, tent £100,
Samuel McClean, of Nottingham township, Washington Co., tent £100,
Conditioned for appearance of Andrew Holmes at next court of quarter sessions for county of Allegheny and county of Washington, 25th November, 1794. COR. ALEX. ADDISON.

Recognized by Gen. Gibson to appear at circuit court. Dismissed by him till Washington court. No bill found by grand jury. Bound in recognizance to keep the peace and good behavior twelve months.

The same proceedings were held against John Gaston, of Peters township (Joseph Becket and John Dailey, securities).

David Donaldson, of Nottingham township (Robert Barr and John Gaston securities).

John Love, of Nottingham township (Robert Barr and Andrew McIntire, securities).

John McGill, of Canonsburg (with John Gaston and W. McMillan, securities).

Samuel Ewing,
Norris Morrison,
Against whom no bills were found, but each bound over for twelve months to keep peace and good behavior, on 25th Nov. 1794.

Fifth Circuit of Pennsylvania.

[L.S.] ALEXANDER ADDISON, President of the courts of common pleas of the fifth circuit, Pennsylvania,

To MICHAEL MOUNT and RICHARD LONGSTREET.

WHEREAS, Oath hath been made before me that Edward Wagner, of Peters township, the younger, did excite a number of riotous persons in the month of July last, to proceed with force and arms to the house of Gen. Neville in Allegheny County, there to commit sundry acts of violence and unlawful force, and did also, by menace and force in the month of September last, prevent the signing of the submission required by government. These are, therefore, to require you and each of you to take the said Edward Wagner the younger and bring him forthwith before me at the house of Wm. Amberson in the town of Pittsburg, county of Allegheny, to answer to the premises, and be dealt with according to law. Given under my hand and seal at Pittsburg, November 21, 1794.

ALEXANDER ADDISON.

The warrant is indorsed: Edward Wagner, Jr., lives with his father at Wagner's Mills, on Peters Creek, Washington County, fifteen miles from Pittsburg. Go up the road to Redstone, turning to the left on the top of the coal hill over Monongahela, about fourteen miles off, inquire for James Barclay, who lives near Wagner. Non est inventus.

MICHAEL MOUNT.

List of Prisoners sent to Philadelphia, November 24, 1794.

James Kerr, John Hamilton, James Stuart, John Lockray, John Corbely, John Black, Marmaduke Curtis, Robert Porter, Thomas Burney, David Bolton, Joseph Scott, Caleb Mountz, John Barnet, Thomas Miller, Isaac Walker, Thomas Sedgwick, and William Crawford.

Greensburg, November 26, 1794.

JUDGE ADDISON: Permit me to request you will be good enough to send for a Doctor Robinson, Wm. Parker, Esq., Daniel Depuy, and Wm. Irwin, and endeavor to ascertain from their examinations *from whom* they received instructions to harangue Col. John Hamilton's battalion on the 4th of July last, in opposition to excise law (as it is called), for it appears, on inquiry, that a regular plan has been formed to prevent the execution of the law by the extirpation of all the officers, and that the attack upon Gen. Neville's was an execution of their system.

I am, with great respect, your servant,
W. RAWLE.

It appears that the depositions were sent January 1, 1795.

Head Quarters, Pittsburg, November 26, 1794.

HON. ALEXANDER ADDISON:

SIR: Major-General Morgan, who will command the troops destined to continue in this district, will be always ready to support the civil authority when required.

To you, as the head of the judiciary, belongs the right of demanding this aid whenever in your judgment it shall be necessary. I am persuaded the wisdom and vigor which will be displayed by the officers of justice in their several stations will probably be found equal to all future exigencies. Should my hopes prove fallacious, the power of the protection established by me cannot fail in the immediate suppression of every irregularity, and will, I trust, be instantly resorted to.

Praying that this district may long enjoy peace and tranquillity, I return home with pleasing anticipations of their growing prospects and happiness, in which I cannot but feel myself deeply interested.

I have the honor to be, sir, with great respect,
Your obedient servant,
HENRY LEE.

1794, Nov. 30. Gen. Henry Lee, in general orders, directed the books containing the oath of allegiance to the United States to return the same to the following persons:—
In Washington, to Judge Addison.
In Allegheny, to Judge Wallace.
In Westmoreland, to Judge Jack.
In Fayette, to Judge Breading.

HEAD QUARTERS, December, 15, 1794.

JUDGE ADDISON, *Washington:*—

SIR: I am at a loss to know how to act with respect to the people charged with treasonable practices against the United States, who have come under my notice.

Since Judge Peters left this country he wrote to me that they were to come under your notice. I will thank you to inform me in what way I am to act. The inclosed petition from Shields and Lapsley with some depositions I think comes more under your notice than mine. A number of characters mentioned in Governor Lee's proclamation have delivered themselves to me, who I have parolled at my own risk upon their giving me their words to come in whenever called on. If Shields and Lapsley had given themselves up to me, I should have used the same lenity with them, as I believe the people of this county wish to come to order, and my intention is to encourage it as much as it lies in my power. Your immediate answer will particularly oblige Sir, your obedient servant,
DANIEL MORGAN.

About the 10th or 12th of November last I left home to visit a friend in Westmoreland County. I had no apprehension that I (a person who had signed the assurances of government) would be called for; but when hearing they were called for as well as others, I immediately came home, and finding the judges removed from Pittsburg, I gave myself up to Adamson Tannihill, Esq. This I certify in truth. JOHN SHIELDS.
December 4, 1796.

I do certify that I went abroad about the 10th or 12th day of November last to visit some friends, not knowing at the time of my departure that there was any charge against myself, as I had the submissive paper as prescribed by government; but hearing on my return that there had been a guard after me, I then proceeded as fast as possible and immediately delivered myself to justice before Adamson Tannihill, Esq., December ye 4th, 1794. THOMAS LAPSLEY.

TO WHOM CONCERNED :—

I do certify that I heard Jacob Ferree say he was willing to give testimony that he saw John Shield sign a submission to the laws as directed by commissioners on behalf of the United States on the 11th of September last. I do also certify that I saw the names of John Shields and Thomas Lapsley written on the paper of submission taken on that day, and that the name of Thomas Lapsley I believe to be in his own hand writing
A. TANNIHILL.

PENNSYLVANIA DISTRICT :—

Before me came William McMillan, of Peters township, Washington County, and declared on oath that Edward Wagner, Jr., of the said township, came to the deponent on the 16th of July last, and called on deponent to go to Gen. Neville's house on the day following, intimating that unless he went his property would be in danger—that on the day of signing the submission the deponent was deterred from signing it by the threats of the said Edward Wagner. WILLIAM MCMILLAN.

Sworn the 21st of November, 1794, before Alexander Addison.

HON. A. ADDISON :— *Philadelphia* December, 24, 1794.

DEAR SIR : I have just now the pleasure of receiving yours of the 5th inst. Agreeably to your request I proceed to make as full a statement of the reasons for excepting the persons specified in the proclamation as the present opportunity will admit.

The offences of †B. Parkinson, †John Holcross, †Daniel Hamilton, and David Bradford are too generally known to require a particular enumeration.

†ARTHUR GARDNER, one of those who on the 4th of July, at the meeting of Colonel Hamilton's battalion, agreed to oppose excise law by arms, etc., met at Couch's, united in the attack on Gen. Neville's, issued orders for the meeting at Braddock's Field, of assisting at Catfish the 14th of August in raising liberty pole.

THOMAS LAPSLEY, active at Neville's.

WILLIAM MILLER, active at Neville's and opposed to signing the paper, very contemptuous of the laws and processes of the United States.

EDWARD WRIGHT, at Neville's, at Braddock's Field, opposed to signing submission.

RICHARD NOLCROFT, set Neville's house on fire, active and acrimonious at Braddock's Field.

†JOHN MITCHELL, at Neville's and robbed the mail.

ALEXANDER FULTON, at Neville's, privy to robbing the mail, signed circular letter to convene the meeting at Braddock's Field.

THOMAS SPIERS, same as Fulton except being at Neville's.

WILLIAM BRADFORD, robbing the mail.

†GEORGE PARKER, at Couch's fort, Neville's, Braddock's, and Militia meeting July 4, at Col. John Hamilton's.

WILLIAM HANNA, atrocious conduct at Neville's house, shot at General Neville.

EDWARD WAGNER, at Neville's and menaces against those who signed the paper.

THOMAS HUGHES, one of the men with blackened faces who attacked Faulkner, etc.

JOHN SHIELDS, a principal in the affair at Neville's.

WILLIAM HAY, went to Couch's, and thence to Neville's, and menaced one man if he would not go, also at Braddock's.

WILLIAM MCILHENNY, at Neville's.

†THOMAS PATTON is, I fear, a mistake either of the clerk or the press, at least I do not at present recollect, nor can I lay my hands relative to such a person.

†PATRICK JACK, S. Jack and A. Hilands concerned in the outrage on Regan and the destruction of Wells'.

(Those marked with a † delivered themselves to General Morgan under the direction of Judge Peters.)

The others are the three fugitives already examined by Judge Peters, and ordered for trial, and the Virginians who will probably be apprehended in the State where they reside.

The youth of George Parker was not known when his name was inserted. In respect to his resignation it is understood not to avail those who fly from home. It cannot be a *bona fide* submission in such cases. This also applies to Shields and Lapsley, yet it is open to them all to explain the reasons of their absence; if proved to be of a justifiable nature, their right to present immunity will be restored.

I am with sincere respect, yours, etc.

W. RAWLE.

January 18, 1795.

H. H. BRACKENRIDGE, Esq.

SIR: I have been pursuing the plan for robbing the mail, and can trace it no higher than Bradford. It was proposed by him to Marshall on their way to the Mingo meeting-house. Baldwin and David Hamilton were in company, and it was put on them to execute it. The object to be obtained, was to know the opinions of the people on the business carried on. The post to be robbed was the post from Washington to Pittsburg, and it was only when Baldwin and Hamilton sent word that they could not perform their part, and when it was then too late to intercept the mail to Pittsburg, that the plan was changed to what was really executed. Bradford sent his cousin William, and David Hamilton, I believe, sent John Mitchel, who executed the business. My information is from a good source and may be depended on. The matter I believe was not talked of at the Mingo Creek meeting-house, nor did Edward Cook know anything of it.

ALEXANDER ADDISON.

April 10, 1795.

SIR: In respect to the recognizances, I apprehend that pursuant to the 33d section of the judiciary bill, the recognizances themselves, and not copies, should be produced, but although Judge Peters preferred the mode you state, during the western expedition from several motives, and I believe has continued the practice (whether he did so before I cannot tell), yet as the signature of the party is not essential to the effect of the recognizance, and is not generally practised by the State magistrates, I cannot suppose it would be deemed necessary in the courts of the United States.

While the law stands as it is, my duty (whatever may be my opinions) is to conform to it, and that duty being to *prosecute* every legal step conducive to a proper termination of such prosecution is to be pursued by me.

Yours, W. RAWLE.

JUDGE ADDISON.

Judge Turner to Judge Addison.

Cincinnati, May 17, 1795.

SIR: After an absence of fifty-three weeks on the western circuit I landed yesterday at this place, and found here your two letters of the 3d of Jan. and 22d of April. This must be my apology for not having answered the former at least before this time.

I have made some inquiries into the case of C. Cunningham, who is recognized it seems, to appear before our general court on the charge you last mention. The offence being committed against the United States alone (of which this territory is no part but only a dependency), our inferior court was wrong in binding Cunningham's appearance to the general court where the offence is not triable. It was imposing upon the accused a hardship not admissible in law, since his appearance could answer no other end than to extend his recognizance to the proper court within the United States, and to which the inferior court was competent in the first instance.

If, therefore, you will forward hither a certificate that Cunningham has entered into a fresh recognizance for that purpose, I shall take care to lay it before the general court whenever his case shall come up officially before it, so that he may be discharged from his present recognizance.

I am with respect, yours, G. TURNER.

Indorsed, took recognizance June 19, 1795, and transmitted to Judge Turner.

Letter of William Rawle to Hon. Alexander Addison.

DEAR SIR: *Philadelphia*, July 17, 1795.

In the expectation of seeing you at the court of errors and appeal this week I postponed answering your letter longer than I should otherwise have done.

Gen. Morgan was not very correct in the names he furnished; only the three last in the list came within the request, viz., Ewing, Paton, and McCall.

Arthur Gardner, George Parker, John Holcroft, having proved their signatures to submission, and accounted for their absence, are bound over as witnesses.

John Mitchell is under sentence.

Patrick Jack appeared, upon inquiry, not a fit object of prosecution, and no bill has been sent against him.

Ebenezer Gallagher and Daniel Hamilton are indicted.

Benjamin Parkinson surrendered himself; he continued however to avoid confinement, and the marshal has not yet been able to apprehend him— he is also indicted.

The marshal's officer, who is the bearer of this, has instructions to apply to you and to the magistrates where recourse cannot be had to you for advice, if necessary, in the execution of the duties he is going to perform.

Your active and able exertions in support of the laws (which have received so much public approbation) give me reason to hope you will not think this trouble too much. The event of Cunningham's case is, I flatter myself, conformable to your wishes.

I am, with great respect and esteem,
Your most obedient humble servant,
W. RAWLE.

See letter of December 24, 1794, on the same subject.

Judge Turner to Judge Addison.

SIR: Cincinatti, July 24, 1795.

I was honored a few days ago with your letter, inclosing proper certificate concerning Cunningham's recognizance, and shall in consequence take care by placing it on the files of the general court that no inconvenience shall arise to him in this quarter.

Either you have mistaken my meaning, or, what is more probable, I have not expressed myself clearly in my answer to your former communications. My letter-files are not this moment at hand. It was certainly not my intention to have the matter open to the general court, because it was, and yet is, my decided opinion that the offence is not properly triable here.

We have lately had some expresses from head quarters. It appears that a treaty of some sort will at length be the result; but how long this will last may easily be conjectured. It assuredly cannot be founded upon any decisive battle; for notwithstanding accounts respecting the last action wore a very florid complexion, that doubtless was little if any more than a skirmish in which the enemy lost seven and twenty men.

I beg you to believe me to be, with perfect and respectful esteem,
Your very, very obedient servant,
G. TURNER.

Wm. Rawle, Esq., to Hon. Alexander Addison.

DEAR SIR: Philadelphia, Aug. 15, 1795.

I must take the liberty of intruding once more upon a portion of your time on account of the trials, yet to take place, of persons charged with treasonable practice from your part of the State.

At the last sitting of the circuit court it was discovered that a great unwillingness in witnesses to say too much against their fellow-citizens, a reluctance in the jury to convict the smaller engine on the testimony of their ringleaders, and a natural repugnance to capital convictions, occasioned some unexpected acquittals, and, in some instances, bills were returned ignoramus equally contrary to what appeared a grounded expectation. Something particularly on the latter score must, I think, be attributed to the difficult distinctions necessary to be made between the different jurisdictions. There now remain to be tried, upon bills found, Edward Wright, James Stuart, and David Bolton, whose presence is not doubtful; and bills are found against David Bradford, Daniel Hamilton, William Miller, Benjamin Parkinson, Ebenezer Gallagher, William Hanna, Richard Holcroft, David Lock, Alexander Fulton, Peter Lisle, Thomas Spiers, and Samuel Hanna, some of whom may perhaps surrender themselves.

After the pains already taken to discover and produce testimony establishing the offence charged, I do not know that it would be reasonable to expect greater success from further inquiry.

But if, in the course of your judicial proceedings, any matters relative to and explanatory of the conduct of the persons before mentioned should occur, you will oblige me much by forwarding such information thereon as may appear to you likely to be useful. A circumstance not very pleasing occurred during the trial of Robert Porter. James Parker, when before you at Washington, stating in his affidavit the persons who had been at the destruction of Gen. Neville's house, included the name of Robert Porter, yet on the trial he denied that he saw him elsewhere than at Couch's before, and at Col. D. Phillips's after the attack. It appeared improper to avoid taking notice of this variance, as in one or the other case he must be forsworn. I was under the necessity of having him bound over to be prosecuted for perjury, to wit, on the false oath taken before you, and this, I fear, will render your attendance at Yorktown necessary, unless you can point out any means to do the business otherwise. I earnestly wish to terminate the whole of this business before next October, that the inhabitants of so remote a place may not again suffer the inconvenience of attending the federal court.

I am, with great respect and esteem,
Your obedient humble servant,
W. RAWLE.

Philadelphia, Aug. 31, 1795.
Wm. Rawle to Hon. A. Addison concludes his letter with these words: "This, I believe, sir, is all the trouble I am likely to give you concerning this unhappy business, equally disadvantageous to the county in its immediate existence and its inevitable consequences. To murmur and to obey the laws is the full extent of political dissatisfaction on the eastern side of the State; to murmur and to resist it will not again I hope be the characteristic of any part of it."

DEAR SIR: *Philadelphia,* Oct. 29, 1795.
Joseph Dorsey may rest easy as to his recognizance. The event of the trials at York fully verified your observation as to the impediments to conviction created by distance.

You have doubtless by this time been informed of the material circumstances, which I, therefore, will not encroach upon your time by repeating.

I consider the business as now nearly ended. It is not probable that many, if any, of those who have fled will return. My information in respect to Bradford was I find erroneous. The witnesses are, however, generally held under recognizance, and to be ready in any case of surrender.

I am, with respect and esteem,
W. RAWLE.

JUDGE ADDISON.

INDEX

-
Abraham, 362
Indian Peter, 235
Jonas, 362
Tecumseh, 295
Wingenund, 288

-A-

AASTON
S. M., 193
ABELL
John L., 325
Joseph E., 325
ABERLY
Charles, 316
ABRAHAM(S)
Henry, A9
Isaac M., 311
ACHESON
A. W., 144, 156, 169, 199, 340
Alexander W., 132, 133, 134, 143, 208, 255, 260, 261, 296, 318, 354
David, 130, 146, 252, 296, 303, 318, 343, 355
General, 293, 294
George, 261
George W., 256, 261, 351
Hannah, 195
J. C., 334, 344
J. W., 358
James C., 135, 139,

176, 178, 343
John W., 303, 312, 313
Joseph Mck., 335
Judge, 369
M. W., 160
Marcus, 261
Marcus W., 155, 261
Miss, 352
Sandie, 319
Thomas, 130, 133, 265, 291, 292, 296, 355, 358
ACKEY
Alfred, 306
ACKLESON
David, 307
ACKLEY
J., 324
ACTON
Thomas, 316
ADAMS
Alexander, 267, 316
George, A72
Jesse, 94
John, 97, 299, 315
John Quincy, 147
M., 357
Ross, 327
Samuel C., 328
Thomas, A20
W. H., 360
ADDISON
A., A121
Alexander, 56, 119, 130, 141, 142,173, 255, 261, A77, A82, A90,A114, A115,

A116, A117, A118, A119
Jane, 202
Judge, 97, A90, A98, A114, A116,A120
Mr., 84
Wilson, 202
AGNEW
-, 334
G. Holmes, 178
J. Holmes, 170
Samuel, 78, 219, 253
AIKEN
David, 5, 135, 149, 189, 197, 258, 333, 334, 345, 370
George W., 146
H. M., 334
J., 149
James, 316
John, 109, 135, 261
Joseph M., 316
William, 336
AILES
Isaac, 267
J. F., 333
AIMES
George, 314
Joseph, 314
ALDEN
Joseph, 227, 228
Rev. Dr., 224
T. J. Fox, 261
ALEXANDER
-, 334
Andrew J., 268
Edward, 322
Henry, 268

J. W., 254, 299, 336,
  343, 358
Joseph, 259, 268
Rev. Mr., 240
W. J., 248, 338
William J., 247
William S., 268
ALGEO
  Thomas, 328
ALISON
  James, 61
ALLEN
  Albert, 327
  Andrew, A14
  Ephraim, 305
  Francis, 304, 330
  Harrison, 306
  John, 345, A9
  Moses, 112
  S. P., 94
  Thomas G., 267
  William, 25, 203,
    334, 345, A26
ALLFREE
  Isaac H., 329
ALLHOUSE
  George, 310
ALLISON
  Adam, 268
  Alexander, 261
  James, 67, 69, 114,
    150, 155, 256, 259,
    264, 312, 321, A109
  James B., 322
  John, 77, A7
  Judge, 150
  Patrick, 268
  Thomas, 250
  William, 261
ALLMAN
  William, 314
ALMUND

John, 233
ALRICH
  J. C., 334
  W. P., 240
  William, 334
  William P., 169, 170,
    333
ALTER
  H. H., 334
  Henry H., 303
  Solomon, 261, 351
ALVEY
  Eleven, 316
AMALONG
  S., 333
AMBERSON
  William, A115
AMLIN
  John, A109
AMMON
  Conrad, A109
  Jacob, A109
  Jesse, 333
  John, A109
  Joshua M., 268
AMON
  William, 319, 334
AMOS
  Andrew, 330
  Vincent, 330
ANDERSON
  A., 101
  A. R., 101
  Abraham, 224, 225,
    226, 330
  Alfred W., 305
  B., 260
  B. L., 306
  Benjamin, 266
  Charles, 310
  D., 358
  F. H., 311

Isaac, 283
James, 83, 106
John, 107, 173, 175,
  223, 310, 358, A110
John A., 309
Joshua, 259
R., 296
Rev. Mr., 196
Robert, 126, 131, 133,
  173, 174, 253, 254,
  258, 292, 302
Samuel, 306
W. C., 121
William, 22
William C., 176
ANDRES
  Abraham, 322
  Peter, 322
ANDREW(S)
  A., 261
  Charles, 192
  James W., 312
  Joseph, 220, 315
  Milton, 361
  R. M., 334
  Robert, A21, A29,
    A31, A32, A33,
    A36
  Robert S., 216
  William H., 220
ANGUS
  James, 345
ANISANSEL
  Henry, 325
APPLETON
  George, 261
ARCHBY
  James, A110
ARCHER
  D., 324
  David T., 268
  Ebenezer, 268

James, 85, 268
John, A108
ARMSTRONG
Alexander, A110
Alexander R., 329
Captain, 334
Hugh, 268
James, 103, 303, 316, 321, 329, 333, 351
Jessie A., 329
John, 40, 64, 65, 124, 136, A23
Joseph, 328
Robert, A111
Samuel S., 328
William, 319, 321, A110, A111
ARNDT
John, 77
ARNOLD
H. H., 334
Hagan H., 324
Henry H., 335
John, 321
John A., 331
Simon, 321
ARTHRUS
James, 322
ARTHUR
Lewis, 325
M., 309
ARTIST
Alexander, 325
ASBURY
Francis, 181
ASHBROOK
Absalom, 328
James, 131, 260, 261
ASHBROOKE
Thomas, 20
ASHETON
Ralph, 35

ASHMAN
John, 327
ASHMEAD
Samuel, 235
ATCHESON
John, 330
Samuel, 330, 345
ATKINSON
Boyd E., 321
George, 68
John, 122
ATLEE
W. L., 306
AUBREY
Mr., 234
AUDRAIN
Peter, A72
AULD
Jacob, A110
AULT
Andrew, A108
Matthias, A47, A48
AVERY
Charles, 183
P. J., 261
AXTEL(L)
Nathan, A108
P., 193
Philip, 94
Thomas, 79, 260
AXTEN
Andrew, 327
AXTON
Matthew, 315
AYR(E)S
Alexander, A111
Benjamin A., 324
R., 238
Rev. Mr., 237
Robert, 237
William, 261, A110, A111

-B-

BABCOCK
Samuel E., 105
BACKUS
Rev. Mr., 210
BAER
John, 181
BAILEY
Eli, 268
Isaac, 261
Matthew, 112
Mr., A58
Silas M., 305
W. E., 326
W. K., 335
William, A58
BAIRD
A., A71
A. T., 141, 155, 178
Absalom, 78, 87, 130, 141, 142, 174, 251, 252, 258, 268, 341, A67, A73, A90
George, 133, 135, 138, 176, 178, 258, 268, 296, 342, 343, 358
James, 319
John, 189, 191, 260, 334, 357
Judge, 126, 362
Samuel, 319
Thomas H., 133, 138, 142, 143, 198, 255, 260, 261, 292, 296, 359, 368
William, 134, 260, 261, 264, 296, 368, 369

BAKER
 D. G. C., 269
 Enoch, 320
 J., 239
 J. B., 309
 Jacob, 330
 John, 369
 L. F., 269
 L. J., 269
 Lewis F., 268
 Lindsey, 331
 Mrs., 352
 Nelson F., 316
 W., 299
 Z., 320
 Zachariah, 320
BALDING
 Nathaniel, 333
BALDWIN
 -, A118
 David, 312
 G., 324
 Henry, 261
 Ira, 320
 J., 324
 John, A110, A111
 N., 333
 Thomas, 324
BALL
 Caleb, A107
BALPH
 J., 109
BAMBURGER
 David, 305
BANDWELL
 Symonds, A109
BANE
 J. N., 334
 John M., 305
 John W., 220
 Joseph E., 329
 Patrick, 326

 Sample S., 326
 Samuel D., 326
 Solomon S., 331
 Stephen P., 328
 William A., 326
BANKS
 John, 37
BAR
 John, A109
BARBER
 Abraham, A108
BARCLAY
 J., 346
 James, A115
 John, 345, A26
BARKER
 Cyrus J., 316
 James, 323
 John, 361
 Lewis, 182, 259, 370
BARKLEY
 Joseph, 360, A110
 William, 122
BARLOW
 F. Anika, 185
BARNARD
 Samuel B., 331
BARNES
 Amos, 180
 William, 181, 305
BARNET(T)
 Bazel, A107
 D. M., 327
 John, A115
 Samuel, 268
 W. G., 227
 William, 328
 William H., 305
BARNHART
 Henry, 333
BARR
 A. J., 326

 Bankhead B., 321
 Collin W., 312
 David, 359
 J. W., 140
 James, 49, 279, 303, 316
 James D., A109
 John, 268, 321
 John A., 268
 John S., 369
 Joseph, 265, A110
 Mr., 140, 141, 177
 Robert, A115
 S. Gailey, 261
 Samuel, 331, A109, A110
 Thomas J., 312
BARRACKMAN
 Peter, 20
BARRINGER
 George, 310
 John, 310
 William, 310
BARRINGTON
 John, 135, 196, 198, 296
BARRY
 George, 299
 James, 308
 Michael, 304
BARTON
 Mr., A84, A85
 Thomas, 49
BASSETT
 George W., 337
BATES
 John, 94
BATY
 Thomas, 316
BAUER
 J. H., 299

BAUMGARNER
George, 326
BAUSMAN
E. W., 316
Edwin W., 303
Jacob, 22
John, 134, 200, 351
BAVINGTON
Captain, 210
John, 118, A109
BAXTER
Cyrus, 329
James, A109
James W., 330
Mrs., 245
Samuel, A109
William, 304
BAY
Benjamin, A110
Elizabeth, 50
Thomas, 49, 50, 59, 232, A111
William, A109
BAYARD
George D., 307, 328
BAYHE
G. L., 335, 344, 346
George L., 346
BAYNE
G. L., 345
BAYS
Hugh, A109
BEACH
C., 345
BEACOM
J. J., 243
Minnie, 236
BEAL(L)
Gen., 294
Reasin, 130
Thomas B., 261
William, 311

Zephaniah, 265, 268
BEALLE
Zephaniah, 238
BEAM
Daniel, 86
BEAN
Isaac, 268
BEARKUS
Benjamin, 49
BEARLEY
Nicholas, 268
BEAT
James D., 134
BEAT(T)Y
C. C., 154, 160
Dr., 158
James, A108
John, A111
Jonathan, 312
S., 149
Samuel, 135, 176, 363
Stephen P., 325
Thomas, 232, A109, A111
William T., 334
BEAUMONT
Mr., 350
BEAVER
John, 40
Sampson, 20
BEAZELL
Isaac R., 304, 311
Luke P., 310
Samuel, 304
BEAZLE
Luke, 310
BEBAST
Benjamin, A110
BEBOUT
Beden, 320
Ira C., 268
J. L., 312

James A., 320, 346
Leicester, 320
Lester, 320
Mrs. E. J., 360
S. M. H., 312
Samuel, A110
William, 320
BECK
Jacob W., 330
James, 363
S., 306
BECKERMAN
Rev. Mr., 188
BECKET(T)
J. B., 261
Joseph, 13, 349, A114, A115
Joseph B., 170
Samuel, 260
BECKWITH
Cyrus, 341
BECROFT
George, 308
John, 308
BEDOUTE
Martha, 361
BEE
Thomas, 333
BEEBE
Walter B., 261
BEEKMAN
-, A57
BEELER
Joseph, 26, A112
Samuel, 67
BEEMUR
William, A109
BEHANNA
Alexander, 330
Charles, 330
David, 330
James, 335

John, 330
Samuel, 330
BEHOUT
Beden, 320
BELL
  Algernon C., 155
  Andrew, 193
  D. B., 261
  David, 110
  David W., 155
  Fulton, 320
  Fulton J., 320
  Hazlett M., 320
  J. B., 312
  J. Fulton, 319
  James, 83, 268
  John, 324, 368, A109
  John E., 149, 182,
    256, 264
  John F., 328
  Michael, 305
  Moses M., 316
  R. R., 345
  S. M., A50
  Sample F., 320
  Solomon, 261
  T. J., 260
  Thomas J., 140
  William A., 314
BELLAS
  John, 304
BELLEFELT
  Peter, A109
BENEDICT
  Sidney J., 333
BENHAM
  Robert, 77, 258
BENJAMIN
  John, 138
BENNER
  Jesse, 329
BENNETT

Benjamin, 297
BENNINGTON
  Demas, 267
  Harrison, 304, 327
  Moses, 268
  S. B., 336
  W., 310
BENNY
  Benjamin W., 331
BENSON
  Robert, 69
BENTLEY
  Ianthus, 260, 261, 310
  S., 260, 343
  Samuel B., 318
  Sashbazer, 81
  Shazbazzar, 268
  Shebazzar, A110
  Shesbazzar, 120,
    A111
  Sheshbazzar, 258
  Shezbazzar, A111
BERKINSHA
  James M., 346
BERRY
  David, 321
  James L., 321
  John M., 321
  M., 310
  William, 268
BERRYHILL
  James S., 322
BERWICK
  Alexander, 308
  Frank, 308
  James, 22
BEST
  Benjamin U., 316
  James, A108
  James D., 259
  John, 134, 343
BEUMONT

James, 309
BEVERIDGE
  Thomas, 101, 182,
    226
BIDDLE
  Abner, A110
  Frances, 204
  James, 101
  Mrs., 205
  Mrs. Francis, 200,
    201
  Richard, 261
BIERER
  Everhart, 19
BIGELOW
  James F., 333
BIGGART
  Thomas, 101
BIGGER
  Kate M., 107
  Thomas, 268
BIGHAM
  R. J., 261
  T. J., 155
BIGLER
  David, 369
  William, 38
BILLICK
  John, 319
BILLINGS
  Stephen, 316
  William H., 316
BILLINGSLY
  J. K., 332
  Jac. D., 333
  James R., 333
  William H. H., 333
BIND
  John, A109
BINGHAM
  John A., 308
  W. H. H., 321

BIRCH
  Abner, 320
  George, 109
  James, 320
  John, 260, 268
  Robert, 320
  S., 324
  Thomas L., 292, 345
  Thomas Ledlie, 173, 174
BIRD
  Milton, 94, 193
BIRKETT
  Edward, 180, 181
BISHOP
  J. K., 319
BITTING
  D. C., 310
BITTS
  Samuel F., 308
BLACHLEY
  H. H., 357
  S. L., 358
BLACHLY
  Milton, 320
BLACK
  Benjamin, 321
  Charles, 328
  George, 134, 198
  J. E., 265
  J. L., 261
  James, 109, 155, 169, 170, 218
  James L., 306
  John, A115
  John A., 320
  John E., 259
  Julius, 319
  Margaret, 297
  Milton O., 312
  Peter, A108
  Ross, 261
  S. W., 309
  Samuel, 330, 353
  T. J., 306
  William, 321
BLACKBURN
  Joseph, A110
  Madison, 325
BLACKENY
  Gabriel, 268
BLACKLY
  G., 313
BLACKMORE
  D., 130
BLACKSTONE
  Bridget, 26
BLACKWELL
  John, 34
BLAIM
  Ephraim, 192
BLAINE
  D. H., 363
  Ephraim L., 256, 268
  James, 132, 133, 144, 268, 296
  Justice, 365
BLAIR
  Alexander, 260
  David, 261
  Isaac S., 360
  Isaiah, 169
  James W., 333
  John, 299, 319
  W., 191
  William, 189, 190
  William C., 178
BLAKE
  James, 318, 319
  John, 316
  Matthew, 191
  S. W., 238
BLAKELY
  Gabriel, 86
BLAKEN(E)Y
  Col., A71, A72
BLOMBERG
  Peter A., 316
BLONBERG
  Peter, 303
BLOOMFIELD
  John, A9
BLUE
  Archibald, A107
BLYTHE
  James, 323
BOARDLEY
  J. Beale, A26
BOARDMAN
  James L., 305
  W. H., 306
BOATMAN
  H. J., 318
  Henry J., 319
BOBBETT
  Jacob, 42
BOCKIUS
  John, A107
BODY
  Milton R., 322
BOGGS
  Andrew, 268
  James, A109
  John, 227
BOICE
  -, A44
  Ebenezer, 261
BOLDEN
  George, 197
BOLEK
  C. H., 361
BOLLES
  Francis M., 328
BOLTON
  David, A115, A120
BONNETT
  Col., A81

BOOK
  Jacob, A108
BOON
  Hugh P., 303
  James, 176, 297
  Robert, 328
  Thomas F., 316
  William, 324
BOORD
  O. G., 324
BOOTH
  W. F., 327
BORELAND
  Mark, 345
  Samuel, 368
BOSTON
  Rev. Mr., 237
BOTETOURT
  Lord, A18
BOTKINS
  G. W., 268
  George W., 363
BOUNDS
  Thomas, A110
BOWEN
  B. F., 330
BOWER
  George R., 329
  John, 266, 360
  Lawrence W., 329
  William, 103
BOWERS
  Andrew, 268
  Benjamin F., 268
  George, 268
  John, 268
BOWLAND
  Robert, 114, 220, 265
BOWMAN
  A. B., 95
  J., 234
  J. L., 261

James, 187
John, 261
Michael, 345
Rev. Bishop, 186
William, 261
William L., 187
BOYCE
  D. W., 309
  David, 321
  Isaac N., 309
  John M., 309
  John W., 309
  Joseph, 309
  Robert, 309
  Thomas D., 309
  William, 308
BOYD
  Andrew W., 210
  Bankhead, 123
  Captain, 60, 66, 283
  Charles, 335
  D. M., 269
  David W., 321
  George D., 333
  George W., 268
  J., 95
  James, 330
  John, 196, 268, 283, 304
  John Q. A., 303
  R., 183
  Rees, 304
  Robert, 144, 181, 190, 310, 353
  Thomas, 261, 269
  Thomas J., 267
BOYER
  Leonard, 130
BOYLE
  Felix, 330
  John, 330
  John D., 133, 145,

146, 147, 148, 149, 370, 375
BOYLES
  Cornelius, A111
BOYNTON
  David J., 316
BRACKENRIDGE
  -, A73
  Alexander, 261
  H. H., 261, A71, A72, A75, A77, A118
  H. M., 261
  John, 268
  Mr., A67
  R. J., 224
  Robert J., 226, 228
BRACKER
  Thomas, 114
BRADDOCK
  Abner, 79
  C. G., 109
  Cyrus, 217
  Francis, 79
  John N., 331
  Norton, 334
BRADEN
  David, 331
  James, A107
  John D., 261
  Mrs. Samuel, 94
BRADFIELD
  John, 134
BRADFORD
  -, A118, A121
  B. Rush, 38
  D., A69, A70
  David, 219, 252, 260, 261, 265, A62, A69, A72, A73, A75, A76, A117, A120
  G. D., 104
  James, 113, 259

William, A75, A117, A118
BRADLEY
James, 331
Nathaniel, A62
BRADON
Ezekier, A108
BRADY
A., 145
Andrew, 133, 135, 145, 148, 189, 339
David, 303, 334
Freeman, 5, 134, 135, 139, 140, 146, 190, 207, 257, 261, 345, 357
J. S., 199
Jasper E., 261, 321
John, 321, 345
John S., 132, 133, 134, 144, 198, 200, 261, 369
Joshua, 306
Robert, 306
BRAKENY
Gabriel, 130
BRAMIN
Michael, 310
BRAMLEY
William, 268
BRANAN
George, A110
BRANDEBERRY
William, 180
BRANNER
Frederick, 327
BRANNON
John L., 320
Joseph, 320
BRANT
L. George, 326
BRATTON

John, 314
Josias, 314
BREADING
Judge, A116
BRECKENRIDGE
Hugh M., 101
Mr., A70
BRECKLE
John, 299
BRENNEN
Oliver, A110
BRENT
Daniel, A109
George, 19, 22
BRENTON
Joseph, 268
BREVARD
George W., 325
BREWER
William H., 170
BRICE
Charles, 20
George W., 132, 134, 135, 183, 268, 305
Henry, 268
James, 134, 175, 199, 201, 202, 203, 204, 205, 208, 252, 259, 358, A90
John, 103, 150
John G., 316
Rev. Mr., 245
Thomas, A109
BRICELAND
Garland, 306
James, 210
BRICKER
Jacob L., 343
BRIGGS
Lazarus, 322
Thomas, 312
BRIGHTWELL

Alonzo, 329
BRISON
James, A70, A71
BRISTER
Henry M., 135
BRISTOR
Thomas, 130
BROADHEAD
Col., A44
Daniel, 58, 81, 84
BROADMAN
William, 343, 344
BROBST
John B., 316
John V., 303
N. B., 334
N. F., 135, 200
BROCK
James P., 327
BROCKUNIER
S. R., 181
BRODHEAD
Daniel, 278
BROECK
Ten, 246
BROKOW
Abraham, A109
BROOKINS
Castle, 316
BROOKS
Enoch, 314
J., 324
V., 310
W., 310
William B., 304
BROTHERTON
John, 305
BROWN
A., 228
A. B., 224, 226
Abigail M., 185
Alexander, 74, 178, 228

Alexander A., 114
Alexander B., 111, 227
  B., 350, 351
  Basil, 23
  Curtis P., 185
  D. W., 261
  Daniel, 185
  David, 269
  Edward, A111
  Ephraim C., 319
  General, 171
  George, 181
  George W., 330
  Henry, 135, 303
  Isaiah, 345
  Israel, 179
  J. N., 312
  James, 110, 133, 134, 208, 256, 257, 266, 316, 334
  James A., 187
  John, 188, 323, 343, A111
  John C., 338
  John R., 193
  John W., 299
  Joseph, 72, 84, 269
  M., 358
  Mary C., 185
  Matthew, 111, 114, 143, 169, 175, 224, 225, 228, 229, 244
  Nicholas, A111
  Samuel, 84, 306, 309
  Stephen K., 311
  Thomas, 72, A8
  W., 327
  William, 109, 310, 327
  William F., 228
BROWNE
  Anne, 64
  Joseph, 344
BROWNFIELD
  William, 196
BROWNLEE
  Ariel, 312
  James, 86, 268
  James D., 305
  John, 259, 266, 268
  John T., 250
  Joseph W., 328
  Samuel C., 328
  W. C., 118, 241
  William, 198, 200
BROWNSON
  J. J., 168
  James I., 6, 154, 155, 156, 169, 173, 175, 177, 189, 200, 203, 205, 206
  James Irwin, 176
BRUBAKER
  B., 310
BRUCE
  Andrew, 258, 260
  David, 118
  Mr., 119
  R., 110
  William, 16
BRUGH
  W. J., 170, 218
BRUNSON
  Alfred, 181
BRYAN
  A., 193
  A. M., 94
  Alfred, 192, 193, 245
  George, A21
BRYANT
  Joseph, 365
BRYSLAND
  Thomas, 114
BRYSON
  Patrick, 126, 128, 130
  Peggy, A56
  Thomas B., 134, 135
BUBBET(T)
  Benjamin, 265
  Benjamin T., 269
BUCHANAN
  Andrew, 261
  Benjamin B., 322
  Captain, 293
  David, 269
  George, 257, 265
  George Watson, 309
  H., 200
  J. A. J., 261
  Jacob, 299
  James S., 269
  John, 269, 362, A114
  John H., 329
  Joseph, 104
  Miss, 352
  N., 361
  Thomas, 266
  Walter, 269
BUCK
  Thomas, 269
BUCKINGHAM
  Abel, 345
  John B., 331
  S., 261
  Thomas C., 325
BUCKLEY
  Philip, 355
BUFFINGTON
  A. J., 254, 255, 334
  Seth, 269
BULFORD
  John, 305
  Samuel, 145
  Samuel S., 305, 337
BULL
  John, 285
  Mr., 286

BULLARD
  Owen, 303
BULLING
  Harriet, 185
  John, 185
BUMGARNER
  David, 269
  Jesse, 269
BUNDHART
  H., 299
BUNNELL
  Samuel, 319
BUNTON
  William, 333
BUPP
  Augustus, 316
BURGAN
  Daniel, 269
  Frank, 310
  James W., 314
BURGESS
  Nelson, 183
BURGET(T)
  Bosten, A111
  George, 117, A109
  Philip, A109
BURK(E)
  Jonathan D., 329
  Martin, 316
  Richard, 17
  William, 305, 328, 331, 334
BURKEN
  Henry, A9
BURKETT
  Aurie T., 107
BURKHART
  Alfred, 329
BURNET(T)
  -, A51, A53
BURNEY
  Thomas, A115

BURNS
  Alexander, 79, 269
  John, 183, 266, 267, 269
  Richard, 22, 330
  Robert C., 265
  William, 305
BURNSIDE
  General, 315
BURROW
  R., 94
  Reuben, 192
BURSON
  Joseph, 314
BURTON
  Harriet, 185
  Rebecca, 185
  William, 210
BUSH
  Henry, 314
BUSHFIELD
  William, 183
BUSSELL
  James, 360
BUTLER
  Dennis, 305
  Ira, 245
  Ira R., 269
  Major, A70
  Richard, A42
  W., 310
  W. H., 313
BUTTERFASS
  John S., 312
BUTTERFOSS
  D. J., 322
BUTTS
  Charles, 191
  John L., 305
BUTZ
  David, 269
BUXTON

Jacob, 232, A111
BYERS
  David, 330
  J. M., 344
  James M., 258, 334, 343, 344
  Jerome, 330
  John, 357
  John A., 303
  Robert H., 312
  Samuel, 103
  Thomas, 260, 315
  William, A110

-C-

CAAR
  Howard, 314
CACK
  Hans, A8
CADY
  Mrs., 150
CAESBER
  Jonathan, 269
CAIN
  George, 306
  John, A52
  Robert, 309
  William, 306
CAIRNS
  C., 197
CALDWELL
  A. B., 135, 145, 146, 147, 149, 191
  Alexander, 261
  Charles, 312
  George B., 303, 316
  George W., 261
  J., 324
  J. C., 190, 241
  J. P., 311, 337
  J. T., 210

James, 324, A109
John, 269
John C., 317
Joseph, A111
Mr., 240
Rev. Mr., 177
Robert, 269, 312
Samuel, 330
Samuel R., 312
William, A111
William S., 306
CALHOON
J. Y., 210
CALLENDER
I., 228
Robert, 261
CALLIGAN
Charles A., 309
CALLOHAN
George, 345
Thomas, 220, 243
William S., 306
CALOHAN
William S., 338
CALVIN
William, 232
CALWELL
Joseph, A110
CAMBELL
William, A112
CAMERON
Daniel, A111
Simon, 315
CAMP
Peter, 372
CAMPBELL
Alexander, 195
Amelia, 355
Arthur, 49
Charles, 261, 279, A108
D. B., 105

David, 303, 331, 355
David R., 241
Edward, 311, 314, 315
Francis C., 261
Henry M., 261
J. D., 319
J. M., 360
James, 261, A108
James C., 210
James D., 318
John, 13, 23, 67, 269, A56, A111
Miss, 352
Parker, 133, 142, 143, 175, 197, 198, 223, 260, 261, 291, 292, 296, 353, 358, 368
Philip D., 329
R., 345
Richard, 225
Thomas, 194
William, 49, 68, 78, 259, 347, A108, A109, A110
CAMPSEY
James, 323
Joseph, 312
CANAHAN
James, 222
CANE
Charles H., 320
CAN(N)ON
Col., 219, 221
John, 15, 24, 57, 59, 60, 63, 64, 66, 67, 68, 81, 85, 86, 101, 219, 220, 252, 269, A69, A70, A82
Mrs., 224
Thomas, A110
CAPRON

H. N., 228
CAREY
E., 358
John, 94, 245
William J., 338
CARIER
Abraham, 178
CARLISLE
Robert, 368
CARMAC
J. W., 345
CARMICHAEL
John, 358
CARNAHAN
James, 227, A64
CAROTHERS
James, 312
John, 312
CARPENTER
Christopher, 22
D. O., 333
CARROL(L)
-, 214
Benjamin, 357
Josiah, 321
Mrs., 192
William, 269
William D., 324
CARRONS
Leslie, 185
CARSON
David, 182
James, 105, A109
James G., 220, 240
John, 261
Samuel, A111
Thomas, 269
Washington, 269
CARTER
George W., 322
J., 324
Jesse, 322

John, 95, 269
Joseph, A111
Nelson, 247
S., 324
Thomas J., 322
William, 259
CARTEY
  Captain, 293
CARUTHERS
  J. E., 156
CASE
  Massal, A109
  Thomas, A109
CASEBER
  Jonathan, 109
CASNER
  Peter, A109
CASS
  Lewis, 171
CASSEL
  I. C., 228
CASTNER
  Daniel, 269
CATFISH, 127, 128
CATON
  A. J., 135, 356
  Thomas, A108
CAVANAUGH
  James, 324
CAVEAT
  James, A18
CAVERT
  James, A109
CHALFANT
  H. S., 248, 269, 358
  Lucinda, 248
CHAMBERLAIN
  John, 16
CHAMBERLIN
  B. B., 255
CHAMBERS
  George R., 328

J. D., 188
J. R., 306
James, 74, 140, 174,
  179, 341, A110
James C., 256
John, 341, A109,
  A110
John C., 369
John D., 208
John G., 357
John S., 306
Josiah R., 306
Stephen, 77
Thomas, A108
CHAMP
  Stephen, 321
CHANEY
  George, 360
  James, 323
CHAPLAN
  Richard B., 368
CHAPLIN
  Richard B., 195
  Sophia, 195
CHAPLINE
  John H., 261
CHAPMAN
  A., 94
  John, A108
  Sarah, 204
CHARLTON
  J. P., 323
  John P., 257
  William, 326
CHARTIERS
  Peter, 46
CHASE
  Charles D., 317
  Joseph, 315
  Newton, 315
CHATFIELD
  Lewis, A109

CHEEKS
  William H., 312
CHEESE
  N., 324
CHERRY
  Thomas, 68
CHESSROUND
  James Y., 326, 330
  Peter, A111
CHESTER
  Andrew, 322
  John, 308
  Joseph W., 333
  L., 310
  Morrison, 269
  R., 324
  Rev. Dr., 155
  W., 324
CHEW
  Benjamin, A26
  Clark, 315
CHILDS
  W. A., 155
CHISLETT
  John, 206
  Mr., 208
CHRISHOLM
  Isaac W., 322
CHRISTIAN
  John, 22
CHRISTY
  Joseph W., 305
CHUTTER
  N. D., 324
CILDOO
  James, 350
CLAFFEY
  David, 327
  William, 316
CLARK(E)
  Andrew, 269, 360
  Augustus, 333

Brig. General, 8
Captain, A44
David, 58, 269, 330, 368
Ezekiel, 305
Francis M., 329
George, 277
H. H., 176, 189, 190, 191, 199
Harvey H., 269
J., 354
J. Murray, 261, 269
James, 169, 177, A111
James R., 338
Jane, 112
John, 112, 150, 315, 317, A110
John B., 219, 220, 227
John G., 182
John S., 328
M. H., 134, 182, 199, 200, 203, 206, 208, 334, 358
Mary, 204
Miss, 352
Munson, 345
Rev. Mr., A68
S. A., 334
Samuel, 81, 87, 182, 257, 258, 341, 353
Sandy, 335
William, 269, 368
CLAWSON
Peter, 74
Samuel, 183
CLAY
Henry, 149
CLEARY
William, 363
CLEAVER
David W., 319
Isaac J., 319
Isaac N., 269
Kimber, 38
Lewis M., 319
Nathan, 260
CLEAVINGER
Samuel, 261
CLEMENS
John, 269, 317
William, 269
CLEMENTS
Samuel, 186
CLEMINS
James B., 319
CLENDANIEL
John, 346
S., 314
CLENDENNEL
George W., 333
Jefferson, 333
CLINE
Amos P., 305
William, 185
CLINGMAN
Samuel, 247
CLOAKEY
John S., 269
CLOAN
John M., 50
CLOKEY
Samuel, 200, 360
CLOSSER
John, 320, 346
CLOTTER
J., A110
CLOUBY
John, 197
CLOW
James, A72
CLOYD
John, 261
CLUTTER
A., 324
G. W., 324
Milton, 320
Squire, 88
CLYDE
John, 308
CLYMER
George, 77
Hiester, 38
COATES
Isaac B., 324
COATSWORTH
Joseph, 345
Thomas, 345
COBURN
Captain, A8
COCAINE
J. W., 317
COCHERAN
William, 66
COCHRAN
A. G., 261
George R., 261
Hugh, 306
James, 322, A108
John P., 109
S. N., 261
William, 114
Wilson, 306
COCHRANE
Admiral, 295
COCK
John L., 329
COCKLER
Christian, A107
COCKS
Mr., 234
COE
Joseph, A108
Moses, 113
Peter, A110

COFFMAN
George, A111
COLE
Andrew, A109
Ellis J., 319
Freegrift C., 324
Hammond, A109
Isaac, A109
John, 269
Samuel, 261, 297, A109
COLEE
Charles C., 328
COLEMAN
A. A., 321
Charles, 261
Frank, 306
George, 247
James, 247, 321
Lieut., 306
William, 25, A26
COLERICK
John, 118, 260, 350, A90
COLLAMS
James, A108
COLLIER
F., 322
F. J., 156
Francis J., 111, 154, 155, 160, 162
John, 299
COLLINS
Elbridge, 315
James, A108
M., 130
Miss, 352
Patrick, 304, 317
S., 310
Sylvester, 304
Thomas, 246, 261, 270

COLMAN
Leonard, A108
COLMERY
John, 253, 265, 269
Maria, 266
Robert, 146, 175, 257, 258, 264, 266, 270
William, 265, 270
COLTER
John, A109
COLTON
John, 259
COLVILLE
Bobert, A111
James, A111
Joseph, A111
COLVIN
Vincent, 338, A109, A111
William, A8
COMPSEY
Thomas, 328
CONAN
Thomas H., 308
CONDIT(T)
Daniel W., 329
Jabez, 329
Samuel, 326
Simon S., 329
W. C., 346
William C., 329
CONDUIT
David, A108
CONERS
John, A109
CONGER
G. W., 324
CONGHBRAN
William, A65
CONKLE
Jacob, A108
John, A108

CONKLIN
O., 324
William, 270
CONLEY
Nicholas, A109
William, 305
CONLIN
John, 297
Joseph, 345
CONN
Gabriel, A8
Jacob, 270
CONNELLY
John, 13, 181
Joshua, 309
Lemuel, A110
CONNER
John, 59
Maria, 197
Thomas, 309
CONNOLLY
John, A10, A11, A12, A13, A14, A16, A19
CONWAY
Ezra, 322
COOK
Arthur, 34
Charles, 181, 245
Col., A75
D., 353
Edward, A62, A72, A73, A75, A118
H. J., 360
Jacob, 216, 347
John, A109
John V. H., 306
John W., 327
Moses, 86
Mr., 338
Mrs. Isabella, 129
O. P., 260

Samuel, 306, 334
Samuel R., 321
William B., 322
Zeba, 270
COOKE
  Catharine D., 266
  Charles, 181
  David, 341
  Edward, 63
  Isabella, 108, 130
  J. L., 334
  John, 198, 266, 316, 364
  John L., 266, 267, 303
  Miss, 352
  Silas, 322
COON
  Jacob, 225
  Mr., 234
COOPER
  D., 324
  D. B., 365, 366
  Frederick, A109
  George, 94
  H. D., 310
  Henry, A109
  Jesse, 260, 270
  John, 49, 178, A9, A109
  John W., 320
  Lemuel, A107
  Philip A., 319
  R. F., 208, 261
  Robert F., 258, 270, 303, 323, 337
  Sylvanus, 365, 366
  Thomas, 203
  W. S., 310
  William S., 304
  Zebulon, 365
COPER
  John, A108

CORBELY
  John, A115
CORBIN
  David W., 322
  Joseph, 322
CORBITT
  John S., 326
CORBL(E)Y
  Joh, 95
  John, A59
CORBY
  John, 150
CORE
  Michael H., 326
CORMY
  John, A110
CORN
  William, A110
CORNAGHAN
  John, 64
CORNPLANTER
  -, A40
CORNWALL
  William H., 257
CORT
  Jacob, 254
  Simon, 135, 207
CORY
  Daniel, A107
COTTON
  Hugh, 122
  John, 113
  Rachel, 69
COUBOY
  Thomas, 317
COUCH
  Nathan, A111
COULTER
  G. M., 309
  James, A109
  Jonathan, A109
  Raphael, 345

Robert, 345
Samuel, A109
Samuel L., 312
Thomas, A109
COUP
  George W., 309
  Jacob, 309
  W. F., 309
COUTER
  Thomas, A8
COVENTRY
  John, A109
COWAN
  Isaac, A111
  J. W., 306
  Joseph W., 99, 140, 260, 265
  Thomas H., 308
  William H., 328
COWDERY
  Oliver, 89
COWELL
  John, 183
COWEN
  John, 49, A111
  Joseph W., 270
  Mary, 49
  Robert, 345
  Samuel, 305
  Silas, 331
COX
  Abraham, 309
  Andrew, 270
  Benjamin, A110
  Christopher, A107
  Gabriel, 20
  Harvey, 314
  Isaac, 13, 16, 23, 24
  John, 20, A110
  William, 181
COXE
  John, 67

COYLE
  John, 376
CRAB(B)S
  Abraham, A109
  Henry, A109
  Jacob, 265, 270, A109
  Philip, A109
CRACRAFT
  J., 324
CRAFT(S)
  Eliza M., 185
  J., 324
  James S., 261
  W. S., 324
CRAFTY
  J. M. S., 312
CRAGG
  William H., 329
CRAGO
  Felix H., 329, 330
  Henry C., 329
  Thomas J., 329
  William H., 329
CRAGUE
  John, A110
CRAIG
  Benjamin F., 323
  David, 261
  Hugh, 254, 260, 270
  Hugh R., 215
  I. H., 261
  James, 346
  James S., 312
  John, 58, 72, 270
  Thomas B., 328
  Walter, 198, 252, 253, 259
  William, 270
CRAIGHEAD
  George, 113, 114, 270
CRALL
  E., 309

  J. S., 345
  Mrs. J. S., 346
CRAMER
  Margaret, 197
CRANAGE
  George W., 105
CRANE
  J. B., 196
CRANVILLE
  H., 324
CRASSON
  William, 312
CRAVEN
  Abner J., 330
  E., 310
  James, 330
  John W., 330
  Joseph F., 329
CRAWFORD
  Alexander, 357
  Andrew, A110
  Benjamin, A110
  Captain, 85
  Col., 287, 290
  Colonel, 80, 83
  David, 261
  Eli, 321
  James, 95, A8
  James M., 321, 329
  John, 114
  John M., 311
  Joseph, 211
  Josiah W., 315
  Josias, A8
  Richard, 329
  Samuel, A108
  Samuel R., 329
  Thomas, 232
  Vincent, 321
  William, 8, 13, 16, 19, 20, 22, 23, 74, 242, 270, 277, 287,

  368, A10, A13, A14, A18, A41, A44, A56, A115
CREACRAFT
  E. G., 252, 261, 267
  William, 270
CREIGH
  Alfred, 3, 5, 6, 132, 133, 135, 145, 146, 147, 148, 149, 334, 343, 344, 345, 354, 375, A50
  Dr., 148
  Samuel, 261
  Thomas, 261
  W. T., 149, 150
  William T., 335
CREIGHTON
  Edward, 270, 343
CRENSHAW
  G. B., 107
  T. A., 107, 196
CRESSAP
  Michael, A10
CRESSAY
  Michael, 22
CRIDER
  Daniel L., 328
  William, 308
CRISWELL
  R. W., 312
CRITTENDEN
  E. W., 246
CROGHAN
  George, 13, A5, A7, A8, A9
CROGHEN
  William, 71
CROMLOW
  Mr., 234
CROMWELL
  Oliver, 10

CROOK
  Thomas, 20
CROOKS
  Richard, 265, 295
  Thomas, 59, 259, 270
CROSKENY
  Robert, A109
CROSLAND
  Greenbury, 315
CROSS
  Col., 300
CROUCH
  A. V., 345
  Andrew, 308
  George, 270
  Hiram, 314
  James, 326
  John, 326, 330, A110
  Robert, A110
CROUGH
  Adah, 329
CROW
  -, A57
  Azariah, 270
  Benjamin, 270
  Frederick, 74
  John N., 333
  William G., 315
CRUM
  David, 306
CRUMRINE
  Alexander, 331
  Bishop, 261
  Boyd, 155, 160, 260, 261, 311, 333, 334, 340, 344, 369
  E. W., 314
  Jackson, 313
  Marion, 333
CULBERTSON
  Albert, 248
  Lafayette, 310
  S. D., 248
CULLY
  John, 318
  John P., 319
CULVER
  J. Z., 306
CUMMINS
  Benjamin H., 322
  David S., 328
  James, 296
  John L., 328
CUMSON
  Israel, 314
CUNDALL
  Edward G., 176
  W. B., 148, 189, 190
  William B., 145, 259
CUNNARD
  John, 333
CUNNINGHAM
  Alexander, 138
  Alpheus, 320
  C., A119
  Charles, 320
  J. W., 319
  John, 135, A90
  R. A., 228
  Samuel, 133, 135, 149, 199, 200, 202, 206, 207, 257, 258, 260, 362
  Thomas, 261
  Thomas S., 170
  W. J., 318
CURKINDALE
  Jacobus, 350
CURRAN
  Edward, 309
  Michael, 317
CURREN
  John, 312
CURRY
  Andrew, 320
  James, 70, 245
  Joseph M., 345
  Levi, 320
  Milton B., 270
  Samuel, 319
CURTIN
  Andrew G., 38
  Governor, 306, 327
CURTIS
  Marmaduke, A115
  William A., 308
CURTZ
  John, 299
CUST
  Miss, 352
CUSTARD
  John, 80
CUSWORTH
  J., 310
CUTTEN
  N. D., 319

-D-

DABBIN
  James, 49
DABINETT
  John, 327
DAGE
  Frederick, A108
  John, A108
  John A., 327
  Mathias, A108
  Michael, A108
DAGER
  Peter, 113
DAGG(S)
  G. Jackson, 135
  James S., 321
  James T., 183, 342
  John N., 134, 364

Thomas, 145
DAGUE
  Henry, 329
DAGUIN
  Michael, 317
DAIL(E)Y
  Andrew, 305
  Charles, 196, A110
  Isaac, A110
  J., 324
  John, A114, A115
  Peter, 74, 78
DALES
  George, 314
  Henry G., 314
DALTON
  James, 317
DANFORD
  Patrick, 317
DARBY
  William, 129, 226
DARLEY
  S., 130
DARRAGH
  Archibald D., 309
  Daniel, 266, 270
DAUGHERTY
  Michael, 322
DAVID
  James N., 329
  William, 184
DAVIDSON
  Andrew, 317
  James, A109
  Matilda, 93
  Mrs., 91
  Samuel, 324
  W., 255
  W. A., 147, 181, 358
DAVIS
  A. J., 215
  Aaron, A107
  Andrew B., 322
  Andrew J., 326
  Charles, 306, 307
  F. A., 184
  Fayette, 247
  George, 321
  George M., 305
  Jacob, 314, 315
  Jefferson, 302
  John, 345, 347
  John C., 321
  John M., 192, 342
  John Z., 326
  Joshua, A109
  Kennedy, 329
  Milton S., 328
  Mr., 180
  Philemon, A111
  Rev. Mr., 237
  Richard, A111
  Robert, 135
  Robert H., 145
  Samuel, A111
  Samuel A., 305
  William, 122, 176, 199, 266, 267
  William R., 313
DAVISON
  James, A110
DAWSON
  George, A108
  Isaac P., 325
  James, A107
  Jeremiah, 315
  John, 261
  John L., 251
  Richard W., 311
DAY
  Arvida, 361
  Charles H., 333
  Daniel, 305
  Darling, A108
  Edward, A70, A71
  F. A., 88
  George, A108
  H. P., 324
  Hannah, 297
  J. Miller, 267
  John, 322
  Jonathan R., 324
  Joseph, 335
  L. W., 320
  Leroy W., 320
  Lt., 324
  Luther, 270, 324
  Nathan A., 312
  Samuel, 365
  Stephen A., 327
  Theodore, 327
DE CAMP
  James, 18
DE FRANCE
  Hugh, 270
DE HASS
  Charles, 102, 241
DE HAVEN
  Abraham, 114, 220
  Peter, 178
DE PUE
  Daniel, 270
DEAN
  John, 315
DECKER
  Eleanor, 362
  M., 317
  Samuel M., 323, 335, 345
  Samuel T., 324, 335
  William ., 335
DEEDS
  Andrew, A55
DEEMS
  G. T., 309
  Harrison, 327

Joshua B., 327
Peter, 331
DEGARMO
  Hiram, 330
  W. H. H., 330
DEHAVEN
  Jehu, 333
DELANEY
  William, 328
DELONG
  John, A8
DENBURN
  Peter, A110
DENMAN
  J. W., 346
DENNISON
  James S., 305
DENNISTON
  William, 307
DENNY
  Harmar, 261
  J., 324
  S., 324
  William, 35
DEPUE
  Daniel, A109
  Joseph, A109
  Nicholas, A109
DEPUY
  Daniel, A115
DERUELLE
  Daniel, 176, 210
DESELLAM
  Jacob, 315
DEUSHER
  Thomas, A110
DEVALL
  William, 306
DEVAN
  Houston, 311
DEVER
  Chancey R., 326

DEVLIN
  W., 310
DEVNER
  Elijah, A108
DEVORE
  A. A., 332, 333
  Andrew, 315, A110
  Benton, 319
  Henry E., 333
  James, 20, 22
  Major, 349
  Moses, A114
  Samuel, 270
  Theophilus V., 333
DEWBERY
  J., 325
DEWIRE
  Monterville D., 316
DEWIT (DEWITT)
  Ezekiel, 18, 19, A9
DICKERSON
  Col., 293
  Joshua, 252, 253
  Samuel, 305
DICKEY
  Benjamin G., 304
  James, 245
  John, 251
  John A., 319
  Nathaniel E., 306
DICKINSON
  John, A23, A32, A36, A37
  Joshua, 265
DICKSON
  H., 325
  Henry, 322, 347
  J., 325
  J. G., 358
  Jacob, 325
  James, A108
  James G., 155

John, 35
DILKS
  Charles P., 309
DILL
  Matthew, 133
DILLE
  Ezra, 365, 368
  John A., 365
  Lewis, 320
  Price, A108
DILLEY
  J. M., 325
DILLON
  Frank, 312
DIMIT
  Jacob, 297
DIMLER
  John, 309
DINSMORE
  J. W., 334
  Robert W., 369
  William, 266, 267
DIXON
  Jeremiah, 8, A24, A26
DOAK(E)
  Joseph, 363
  Reed, 368
  Samuel, 135
  Samuel H., 331
DOANE
  Abraham, 367
DOBBINS
  Hugh, A109
  James, 150
DOBBS
  Angier, 326
DODD
  C. M., 170, 227
  Cephas, 216, 218, 227, 358
  Charles, 129, 136

Charles S., 226
Daniel, 88
E. F., 358
James F., 309
John, 49, 73, 129, 136
Samuel T., 327, 331
Sylvester F., 331
Thaddeus, 88, 122, 137, 150, 173, 216, 218, 358
DODGE
R. V., 190
DODRIDGE
-, 283
Joseph, 99, 184, 237, 238, 357, A114
Philip, 261, A114
Rev. Dr., 50, A45
Rev. Joseph, 284
DOHINGS
James, A112
DOLBY
Thomas, 270
DOLEN
John, 330
DONAGHHO
John N., 314
M. D., 314
DONAHEY
John, 49
DONAHOO
James, 270
DONALDSON
Charles R., 321
David, A115
Holliday, 330
Isaac, 322
James, 270
John W., 261
R., 265
Richard, 253, 254, 270, 296

Samuel, 328
William, 306
William G., 321
DONAN
Alexander, 241
DONAT
John, 78
DONAVAN
A. O. D., 304
Alexander D. O., 310
Colton, 323
DONEHOO
D. M., 256
J. R., 150
James, 254, 260, 372
John R., 5, 261, 334, 351
DONLEY
Thomas, 317
DONNAN
Alexander, 118
John W., 261
DONNEL(L)
Henry, 270
James O., A110
John, 114
R., 94
Robert, 192
Walter, 312
DONNELLY
J. B., 251
DONOVAN
Simon, 323
DORNAN
Thomas, A108
DORSEY
Benjamin, 197
James, 326
James V., 369
Joseph, A121
S. J., 184
DOSSMAN

John, 22
DOTTS
Zoliver, 331
DOTY
Thomas, 320
Wilson, 320
DOUBERT
Rev. Mr., 188
DOUDLE
James, A111
DOUDS
J. W., 264
Joseph W., 265
DOUGAN
H. M., 316, 317
Henry M., 303
John, 315
DOUGHERTY
G. A., 358
George W., 329
J., 325
James, 264, 296
John C., 304
M., 310
Michael, 74
Mr., 103
DOUGLASS
Ephraim, 367, A84
John, 58, 78, 261, 270, 309
Joseph, 73
DOVER
Chauncey R., 325
DOWAL
Jacob, 180
DOWLER
G., 346
Thomas E., 328
Thomas H., 270
DOWLING
David, 319
J. W., 319

James R., 333
Michael, 333
Thomas J., 308
DOWN
Thomas, A8
DOWNER
George, 315
J. W., 310, 335, 345, 346
James L., 338
DOWNEY
F., 95
R. W., 376
DRAKE
Jonathan, A108
Joshua, A108
Peter, 84, 95, A108
DREHLER
Frederick, 299
DRISKEL
Daniel, A108
DRISTER
George, A108
DRIVER
G. W., 334
George W., 345
DRUMM
Samuel, 327
Silas, 327
DRURY
R. M'Ilvaine, 149
W. H., 149
William H., 135, 136
DUDGEON
James A., 326
DUFF
J. B., 306
DUFFIELD
Edward, A110
DUFFY
Rev. Mr., 191
DUGAN

Henry, 283
Henry M., 262
Robert, 270
DUNBAR
James, A109, A111
Martha, 49
Robert, 49
DUNCAN
A. S., 319
J. W., 319
James, A109
John, A109
John M., 309
John S., 270
Thomas, 262
DUNDAS
John R., 217
DUNGAN
Robert B., 322
DUNHAM
Franklin, 195
DUNKLE
Hawthorn, 328
Thomas, 308
DUNLANEY
Francis, 150
DUNLAP
James, 181, 222, 225, 295, 296
John, 112
John R., 243
Major, 171
Rev. Dr., 223
Rev. Mr., 245
S. G., 244
DUNMORE
Earl of, A10
Governor, A11
John, A13, A14, A16
DUNN
Edmund, 324
J., 324

Washington L., 343
DUNSHEE
William, A110
DUNWOOD
James, 77
DURANT
H. B., 316
Horace B., 303, 316
Tertius A., 303, 317
William, 317
DURBIN
Sylvester S., 305
DUTTON
James, 310
DUVAL
Alexander B., 369
DWYER
Theodore, 327
DYE
Daniel, 356
George W., 305
J. M., 319
John, 145, 177
Mr., 180
Theodore J., 305
DYER
Rev. Mr., 184
DYSON
J., A38

-E-

EACHES
Theodore, 335
EAGLESON
Andrew S., 305
D. S., 358
John, 107, 169
EAGY
George W., 329
EAKIN
John, A109

Joseph, A109
Samuel, A109
EARE
  John, 13
EARICSON
  Maxwell, A110
EARL
  William, A72
EARNEST
  Benjamin F., 322
EATON
  Frank B., 306, 307
EBERHART
  W. H. H., 304
ECKELS
  Charles, 315
ECKER
  A. H., 5, 135, 150, 351
  Mr., 150
ECKERT
  David, 133, 198, 199, 200, 201, 204, 265
  James, 319
ECKLES
  Alfred, 310
  Amzi, 310
  James, 305
  James C., 317
  Samuel, 305
ECKLEY
  John, 34
EDDIE
  Alexander, 270
EDDY
  Alexander, 58
  Caleb, 197
  J., 193
EDGAR
  -, A73
  Catharine, 50
  James, 40, 47, 48, 49, 50, 56, 58, 59, 67, 68, 74, 103, 124, 136, 252, 256, 270, 297, A75, A84, A108
  Judge, 222
  Martha, 49
  Mary, 50
  Mr., 64, 370
EDGINGTON
  Jesse, 262
EDINGFIELD
  Milton, 315
EDMISTON
  John, 193
EDMONSTONE
  Charles, A41
EDWARDS
  C. H., 248
  Charles H., 105
  Jonathan, 158, 169, 227, 228
EDY
  Caleb, A108
EGAN
  Francis, 192
EGE
  Peter F., 262
EICHELBERGER
  Frank, 338
EICHER
  George, 329
EKIN
  John, 49
ELDER
  Thomas, A109
ELLER
  Harvey H., 331
ELLIOTT
  -, A58
  A. C., 307
  Andrew, 304, 331, A29, A31, A32, A35, A36, A109
  Christopher, A108
  Commodore, 360
  D., 201, 204
  David, 151, 169, 176, 199, 217
  George, 270
  H. B., 264
  J. J., 361
  James S., 260, 270
  Mr., 338
  Robert B., 303, 316
  Robert C., 308
  Sebastian B., 329
  William, A18
ELLMAKER
  Ellis E., 262
ELROD
  Johnston, 270
ELSON
  Richard, 68
ELWOOD
  John W., 326
ELY
  A., 93
  D. R., 93
  James, 265
  Nelson, 324
EMERY
  Boyd, 122, 358
  E. G., 321
EMORY
  Mr., 229
  Rev. Mr., 242
ENGLAND
  J., 324
  Joel, 324
  Samuel, 270
ENGLAR
  Leonard, A110
ENGLE
  Ashford, 135

ENLOW
  Henry, 270
  Thomas, 265
ENOCH
  Abner, 320
  David, A107
  H. D., 358
  Henry, 68
ENOCHS
  Thomas C., 331
ENSLOW
  Abraham, 74
  Henry, A9
  John, A9
  Mr., 214
ERDMAN
  Henry, 303
ERIGH
  Peter, A109
ERNEST
  Matthew, A71, A72
ERRET
  Mr., 145
  Russel, 351
  William, 192
  William E., 140
ERSKINE
  Robert, A50
ERVINS
  James, 62, 270
ESPY
  David, 262
ESSICK(S)
  Annie, 71
  Michael, 328
  Rudolph, 308
ESTEP
  Ephraim, 368
  Josiah, 345
  Robert, 143
ETWINE
  John, 286

EUWER
  James, 360
EVANS
  Abel M., 260, 270
  Benjamin, 306
  David, 94, A72, A107
  David J., 271
  Gabriel, 363
  James, A107
  James M., 305
  Jesse, 103
  John, 34
  John C., 333
  Joseph, 320
  Nathan P., 320
  Samuel, 320
EWART
  John, 271, 342
EWING
  -, A119
  J. Kennedy, 255, 376
  James, 176, 208, 309, A20
  John, 109, 254, A21, A26, A29, A31, A32, A34
  John H., 5, 155, 156, 199, 202, 204, 206, 208, 251, 252, 254, 262, 334, 354, 362, 364
  John K., 156
  Major, 147
  Mr., 148
  N., 155
  Nathaniel, 255, 262
  Rev. Dr., 370
  Samuel, A115
  Samuel P., 317
  Thomas, 155
  Thomas L., 262
  William, 114, 226, 309, 374

-F-

FALCONER
  Henry, A109
FANNING
  N. D., 262
FARCHAR
  James, 341
FARLEY
  Andrew, 79
  John, 271
FARMER
  Lewis, 59
  Terrance, 331
FARRABEES
  Captain, 325
FARRAN
  James, 191
FARRAR
  John, 256
FARRELL
  Dennis, 312
FARRER
  John, 369
FARRIER
  E. F., 170
FAULKNER
  -, A117
  Captain, A114
FAUQUIER
  Francis, A4, A6
FEATHER
  Joseph, 309
FEE
  Robert, 351
  William, 271
FEGLEY
  Jacob, A110
FELEBAUM
  George, A45
FENNERTY
  William J., 317

FENTON
  Aaron, 198
  John, A109
  Thomas, A109
FEREE
  William, 345
FERERO
  E., 262
FERGUS
  Hugh, 176, 271
  J. P., 182
  Samuel, 182, 319
  Thomas, 175
FERGUSON
  Andrew, 50, A111
  B. P., 95
  D., 170
  David, 220
  J., A110
  James, 307
  John, 271
  M., 310
  Robert, A108
  Samuel, A107
  V., A110
  William, 122, A109
FERREE
  Jacob, A117
FETTERMAN
  N. P., 262, 369
  W. W., 262
FIELDS
  John, 360
FIFE
  James, 266
FINCH
  Samuel, 22
FINDLEY
  Mr., 84
  S., 108
  William, 36, 77, 130,
    A82, A83, A84

FINGBY
  Abraham, A110
FINLEY
  Abraham, 314
  Henry B., 271
  J. B., 345
  James, 242, A37, A38
FINLEY
  John, 350
FINLEY
  Levi, 271
  Rev. Dr., 220
  S. M., 326
FINNEGAN
  John, 315
FISHER
  George, 315
  George W., 314
  Isaac, 315
  Jacob, A50, A54
  Mr., 348
  Richard, 328
FITCH
  John, A108
  Samuel, A108
FITTERER
  Joseph B., 309
FITZENBURG
  Benjamin, 327
FITZHUGH
  S. H., 262
FITZPATRICK
  John, 361
FITZSIMMONS
  Franklin, 326
  Hamilton, 333
  Thomas, 77
FITZWILLIAM(S)
  F. P., 262
  Frank, 345
  John, 297
  William, 135, 356

FLAKE
  John, 130
FLANAGAN
  Thomas, 330
FLAN(N)IGAN
  Hugh, 309
  James, 335
FLEMING
  F. W., 307
  J., 249
  Robert W., 271
  Samuel, 232, 271
  Thornton, 180, 181
  W. T., 135
  William, 192
  William T., 134, 135,
    334
FLEN(N)IKEN
  Elias A., 329
  John C., 252, 262
  R. P., 262
FLETCHER
  Benjamin, 34
  Christopher, A110
FLINDER
  John, 315
FLORA
  John, 74
  Robert, 74
FLOWERS
  John, 331
FLOYD
  Andrew J., 326
  Benjamin F., 329
FOGLER
  Robert, 369
FORBES
  Arthur, 121
  Frank C., 323
FORD
  Andrew, 145, 148
  Thomas, 307

FORDYCE
  James H., 322
  John, 315
  Rhoda, 213
FOREMAN
  Charles, 279
  P. M., 307
FOREST
  Joshua R., 141
  Richard R., 334
FORESTER
  Samuel C., 328
FORREST
  Joshua R., 262
  R. R., 355
  Robert R., 354
FORSYTHE
  Robert, A110
FORWARD
  Walter, 262
FOSTER
  Cyrus A., 324
  Henry, 334
  Henry A., 324
  James, 114
  R., 185
  Samuel, 334
  Sarah R., 205
  Thomas, 305, 338
  W. Alexander, 262
  William M., 309
FOUGHT
  William, A110
FOUST
  John F., 308
FOWLER
  Joseph, A110
  Leonidas A., 317
  Mary, 297
  Samuel M., 317
  Sylvestus G., 317
  William, 227

FOX
  Charles, A110
  Jonathan, 323
  Josiah, 309
FRANA
  G. W., 345
FRANCE
  John D., 317
FRANCIS
  Stephen John, 238
FRANK
  John W., 335
  Pals., A109
FRANKLIN
  Benjamin, 31, 35, 55, 101, 150, 370
FRASER
  John, 318, 321
FRAZEE
  Jacob, 320
FRAZ(I)ER
  A., 325
  Alexander, 114, 135, 214, 260, 271, 363, A56
  Andrew S., 326
  David, 254, 271
  John, 226, A9
  Joseph C., 322
  Martin V., 331
  Thomas, 271, A110
FREDERICK (S)
  C. G., 188
  J. T., 117
  James T., 118
  John T., 47
FREEBY
  George, 143, 149
  George W., 305
FREEMAN
  John, 256, 271
  Lewis M., 333

  Paul, 20
  Rev. Mr., 237
  Thomas, 24
FRENCH
  Andrew D., 305
  D. A., 155
  D. H., 220
  David, 240
  David Huston, 219
  David W., 326
  Enoch, 320
  James S., 327
  S. W., 328
  S. Webster, 326
  William H., 326
FREND
  George, A108
FREW
  Samuel, 262
FRIDER
  Abraham, A110
FRISBIE
  A. R., 135
  H. H., 343, 344
FROMAN
  Paul, 23
FROST
  W. H., 332
FRY(E)
  A., 310
  Abraham, 235, A109
  B., 325
  Lewis, 329
  Samuel, 105, A109
  Simon, 310
  Thomas, 310
FULLENWEIDER
  Peter, A45
FULLER
  A., 346
  Benjamin, 328
  Joseph, 328

FULLERTON
  Henry, A109
FULMER
  G. S., 314
  George S., 313
  William H., 314
FULTON
  A., A69, A70
  Alexander, A117,
    A120
  Elizabeth, 108
  Henry, 245
  Isabella, 108
  James P., 118
  John, 210, 322
  Mary, 108
  Robert, 108, 129, 130
  Thomas H., 312
FUNE
  John, A110
FURGUS
  Hugh D., 312
FURLONG
  Henry, 181
FURST
  Luther C., 307
FUSTEN
  John, A107
FUTHEY
  Samuel, A111

-G-

GABBY
  F., 334
  James, 137
  James F., 361
  John, 137
  William, 137, 182,
    200
  William A., 316
GABLE

  Z. H., 188
GAGE
  General, A4
  T. J., 314
GAITHER
  Edward, A47, A52
GALBRAITH
  James, 227
  Robert, 262, 329
  William, 271, 310
  William R., 329
  William, 271
GALBREATH
  Mr., 360
  William R., 328
GALLAGHER
  Ebenezer, A113,
    A119, A120
  J. M., 155
  M., 192
  Rev. Mr., 191
GALLATIN
  Albert, 250, A73,
    A75, A76, A77,
    A84, A90
  Mr., A62, A85
GALLOHAR
  Samuel, A110
GALLOWAY
  Charles, 310
  Rev. Mr., 210
  Robert, A109
GALT
  Alfred, 139
GAMBLE
  Hamilton R., 302
  John, 260, 266
  Josias, 78
  Samuel, 122
GANTZ
  Hardman, 303, 327
  Henry, 262

GAPEN
  Stephen, 74
  W. A., 262
  Zachariah, 259
GARBER
  George W., 314
  W. W., 314
GARDNER
  Arthur, A110, A117,
    A119
  David, 271
  Francis J., 245
  John, 328, A111
  John F., 322
  William, 329
GARNER
  Charles, 299
GARRET
  David, 220
  James, 133
  John S., 262
  Robert, 271
  Samuel, 271
  Samuel A., 308
GARRETSON
  Isaac R. W., 317
GARRETT
  Christian, 331
  Henry, 315
  O. L., 324
  Peter, 94
GARRETY
  William, 353
GARRITY
  William, 347
GARTON
  William, 333
GASCOYGNE
  B., A38
GASS
  George, 325
  John T., 329
  Patrick, 137, A36

GASTON
  Alexander, 321
  James, 114, A109
  James M., 308
  John, 321, A66,
    A114, A115
  John H., 307
  Joseph S., 271
  Samuel, 350, A110
  W. R., 271
  William, 103, 345,
    347
GATES
  Guerdon, 169
  Thomas, 10
GAULT
  John W., 309
  William, 114
GAUMER
  Moses F., 308
GAYMAN
  Jacob, 267
  Samuel, 331
GAZZAM
  E. D., 37
GEARY
  John W., 38
  William M., 322
GEE
  J. L., 345, 347
  R. M., 246, 345, 347
GEHO
  William, 333
GEIGER
  John, 70
GELLY
  James, A110
GEORGE
  Alexander, A109
  Jacob, 308
  Robert, A109
GETTIENS
  Hugh, 305
GETTYS
  John L., 303
GIBBER
  John M., 107
GIBBS
  Charles, 309
  J., 310
  John M., 304
  William, 309
GIBSON
  Col., 286
  G., 310
  General, A70, A114
  George, 77, 345
  Gideon, A110
  J. S., 98
  James, 330
  James B., 264
  John, 13, 15, 82, 308,
    A70, A71
  M. G., 345
  W. M. C., 240
  William, 230
GILBERT
  Nehemiah, 319
GILCHRIST
  J. C., 236
  Mrs. H. C., 236
GILDER
  John L., 299
GILFILLAN
  John, 345
GILKESON
  John, 321
GILKISOD
  A., 312
GILL
  Benjamin, 315
  Thomas, A107
GILLARD
  Tacitus, 25
GILLELAND
  Alexander, 171
GILLESPIE
  James, 271, A107
  Mr., 249
  Neal, 234
  Noble, 184
GILLFILLEN
  W., 358
GILLILAND
  William, 360
GILMER
  J., 310
  W. P., 310
GILMORE
  David, 305
  James, 130, 271
  John, 260, 262, 323
  Samuel, 255, A111
GILPIN
  Samuel, 113
GIRTY
  Simon, 23, A44
GIST
  George W., 308
  Thomas, 20, 24, 26
  William, 345
GLADDEN
  Joseph, A110
GLASS
  Adam, A109, A111
  James, A110
  William, 306
GLASSGOW
  Samuel, 74, 271
GLEN
  John, 101
GLENN
  John, 262
  Robert, 357
  Thomas, 320
  William, 254

GLENNER
  Francis, 299
GLOWERS
  J., 310
GLUM
  Charles, 334
GOBLE
  Ebenezer, 271
  Ebn., A108
GOE
  William, 13
GOLDEN
  Caleb H., 305
GOLDSMITH
  Jacob, 135, 149, 345, 347
GOOD
  J. G., 236
  Thomas, 133, 260, 264
GOODENOW
  John M., 262
GOOKIN
  Charles, 34
GORDON
  A. M. S., 193
  Abel M. S., 192
  Alexander, 259
  James, 245, 256, 257, 259, 265, 271
  James M. H., 333
  John A., 311
  Patrick, 34
  Robert, 317
  William, 94, 309
GORMLEY
  Samuel, 262
  William, A72
GOUDY
  James, 130
GOW
  Alexander M., 207, 262

G. L., 334
George L., 262
John L., 5, 125, 132, 134, 170, 200, 202, 206, 208, 256, 262, 321
GRABLE
  Joel, 343
GRACE
  Patrick, 327
GRAHAM
  DeWitt Clinton, 333
  Ebenezer S., 121
  G. S., 307
  Henry, 49, 85, 86, 230, 232, 271, A110
  J. Smith, 322
  James, A107
  John, 169, A111
  Mary, 49, 230
  Rev. Mr., 220
  S. H., 118
  Thomas, A111
  W., 310
  William, 70, 72, 254
  William J., 315
GRANT
  Andrew, 304
  Andrew B., 326
  David, A109
  George, A109
  Robert, 368
  U. S., 146, 147, 148
GRANVILLE
  Henry, 324
GRAVE
  David, 233
GRAY
  David, 271
  James, 326
  John W., 326
  Rev. Mr., 109

William, 138, 317
GRAYSON
  Alexander, 77
  John, 134, 149, 176, 189, 190, 191, 199, 200, 201, 202, 203, 204, 205, 206, 256, 257, 260, 271, 297, 341, 351, 362
  Judge, 143
  Martha, 358
  T. W., 134, 149, 351
  Thomas W., 5, 134, 135
  William, 262
  Wray, 358
GRAZER
  George, 156
GREEN
  Gabriel, 22
  Jacob, 225
GREENE
  Charles, 247
GREENFIELD
  A. J., 326, 327
GREENLEAS
  John, A107
GREENOUGH
  Rev. Mr., 243
GREER
  Augustus R., 247
  John W., 305
  Mathew H., 307
  Robert, 312
  Thomas, 317
  William, 317, 334
  William I., 321
GREGG
  A. T., 271, 345, 346
  Aaron T., 320
  Alexander, 304
  Andrew, 36, 271

Ellis, 262
Ellis B., 329
Harrison, 299
Henry, 271
Ivin, 326
John, 132, 135, 296, 326
John H., 334
Mrs., 362
Robert, 368
GRENAUGH
Ruth, 73
GREY
Joseph, 185
GRIER
Charles, 334
Charles V., 135, 141
David, 77
George, 321
James, 303
GRIEVES
Cyrus, 312
GRIFFIN
Cyrus, A20
Mat(t)hew, 132, 134, 193, 345
Peter, 345, 347
Peter S., 345
GRIFFITH(S)
David, 328
E. H., 346
Elisha, 271
Ellen, 149
Emmor H., 360
Jacob, 233
James W., 321
John M., 303, 305
John R., 132, 134, 143, 144, 179, 183, 259, 362, 363
Levi, 95, 215, 321
Samuel T., 303, 323, 334, 335

Thomas, 312
W., 184
W. E., 327
GRIFFITS
Thomas, 35
GRIM
Martin, 322
GRIST
Samuel, 317
GROFF
John H., 308
GROOMES
James B., 329
GROSS
Levan, 247
GROVER
Jacob, 315
GROVES
G. M., 345
GRUBER
Jacob, 180
GRUM
Samuel, 361
GUDGEON
Andrew, A8
GUESS(E)
Joseph, 322
Thomas, A9
GUILER
Absalom, 311
GUILLEFORD
William, A109
GUINEA
David, 334
I. J., 334
Joseph, 328
Stephen J., 331
GUNDY
J., 310
John, 306
GUNFORD
T. C., 95

GUNN
Aaron, 319
Alexander A., 324
GUNSALIS
Benjamin, A109
Samuel, A109
GUSEMAN
Jacob, 329
GUTHERY
John, 193
GUTHREY
John, 271
William, A107
GUTTERY
Charles, 320
James, 193
GUY
Henry, 82, 100
Shepherd L., 271
GWIN
Andrew, 121, 358

-H-

HAAGER
Lewis, 317
HAAS
G. S., 299
HADDEN
Thomas, 262
HADERMANN
C. J., 225
HAGARTY
H., 296
HAGERTY
Joseph, A110
HAINER
I. N., 372
J. N., 334
J. Nick, 181, 345
John, 334
HAINES
Josiah, 113

HAIR
  Greer, 312
  James, 245
  John, 271
  William, 328
HALE
  Richard, 80
HALER
  Henry, 327
HALEY
  G. W., 317
  J. B., 317
HALL
  Daniel, 317
  David, 140
  Edward M., 315
  George, 186
  John, 58, 208, 264, 271, 344
  Jonathan, A26
  Joseph, A109
  Milton S., 315
  R. T., 335
  S. M., 149
  Thomas M., 345
HALLAM(S)
  Charles, 303, 331
  John, 135, 141, 334
  Samuel S., 331
  William, 271
HALLAS
  Daniel, 307
  George, 307
  Mrs., 321
  William, 307
HAMAR
  Theodore, 299
HAMBRIGHT
  H. A., 310
HAMILL
  William S., 351
HAMILTON
  Alexander, 122, A61, A83, A84
  Alexander C., 303
  Andrew, 31, 34, 329
  Col., 243
  Colonel, A117
  D. J., 345
  Daniel, A108, A109, A117, A119, A120
  David, 271, A73, A110, A111, A118
  Gen., 222
  George, 258, 299
  Governor, 127
  H. T., 317
  I. Y., 146, 147, 149, 257, 369
  Isaac Y., 262
  J. W., 88, 90, 91, 111, 218
  J. Y., 133, 145
  James, 35, 192, 299, 312, 321, A26, A39
  John, 251, 253, 256, 258, 262, 330, 368, A70, A73, A108, A111, A115
  Jonathan, A109
  Joseph, 329
  Robert, 353
  Samuel, 109
  Thomas, 258
  William, 347, 357
  William T., 303
HAMLIN
  Rev. Bishop, 180
HAMMOND
  Daniel Hallas, 307
  George, 334
  George F., 347
  George T., 331, 332, 345
  James, A109
  R. J., 118
HAND
  Edward, 77
HANEY
  Alexander, 304
HANLIN
  Charles, 360
  George A., 322
  William, 322
HANNA
  Henry M., 315
  J., 325
  Jacob, 309, 315
  Mrs., 206
  Robert, A19
  Samuel, 78, A120
  Sarah R., 205
  Sarah R. F., 205
  Thomas, 49, 182, 200, 205, 208, 271
  W., 105
  William, 109, 315, A117, A120
HANNAH
  Hugh, A110
  William, A110
HANNEN
  Jeremiah L., 317
HANNEY
  John, 317
HANON
  William, A108
HAPPEL
  Frederick, 299
HAPPER
  A. G., 336
  Andrew G., 309
  John, A110
  John A., 254
HARBISON
  Adam, 343

HARDEE
  George, 328
HARDEN
  Benjamin, 331
HARDESTY
  Thomas, 318, 319
HARDGRAVE
  Rev. Mr., 246
HARDING
  V., 181, 200, 203,
    206, 370
HARDY
  James, 312
HARDZOTH
  Rev. Mr., 123
HARE
  Michael, 283
HARFORD
  Thomas M., 314
  William, 325
HARGRAVE(S)
  Mr., 177
  Rev. Mr., 242
  Samuel, 141, 187
HARRIMAN
  John, A111
HARRIS
  Andrew J., 333
  James S., 304
  Jonah, 329
  Joseph, 130
  Lemuel, 317
  Martin, 89
  William J., 333
HARRISON
  Catherine, 26
  James A., 326
  Lawrence, A9
  President, 147
  Richard, A9
  W. H., 295
  William, 22
HARROD
  W., 74
HARRY
  John, 22
HARSH
  Henry, A110
HARSHA
  William, 307
HARSHMAN
  Andrew, 305
HART
  Alexander, 305
  David, 271, 326
  Dunning, 321
  Ephraim, 232, A111
  George S., 5, 135,
    260, 262, 334, 351
  H. B., 310
  James, 317
  James G., 256, 271,
    339
  James P., 264, 325
  Joseph, 54
  Mason, 319
  William, 303, 305,
    333, 334, 343, 344
  William P., 334
HARTAPEE
  William, 114
HARTER
  James S., 335
  John, 149, 179, 180,
    181, 199, 200, 201,
    205, 362
  William, 345, 347
HARTFORD
  A. F., 319
  Mathew, A110
HARTLEY
  T., 188
  Thomas, 77
HARTMAN
  William, 315
HARTRANFT
  William, 326
HARTSTEIN
  Jacob, 317
HARTZELL
  Jeremiah, 315
HARVER
  Hiram, 314
HARVEY
  Captain, 244
  D. W. C., 271
  William, 262
HARVISON
  W. P., 218
HARWELL
  A., 247
HASBROUCK
  Cicero, 262
HASILL
  Samuel, 35
HASSINGER
  Peter, 104
HASSON
  Benjamin F., 331
HASTINGS
  John, 370
  John C., 135, 207
  Moses, 307
  Sally, 119, 120
  Thomas, 113
HATFIELD
  Edward, A109
  Jacob, 320
  Robert, 320
HATHAWAY
  James, 320
  John L., 320
HATHWAY
  Alexander, 314
  B. F., 314
  Richard, 314
  T. J., 314

HATTON
  Adam, A8
HAVELIN
  David, 321
  John W., 338
HAVER
  Jacob, 314
HAVLIN
  M. M., 307
  William, 307
HAWKINS
  Charles, 175, 178
  Elizabeth, A52
  Gideon H., 329
  John W., 329
  Miss, A53, A54
  W. G., 155
  William, 22, 267,
    A51, A52, A53
  William G., 252, 262
HAWTHORN
  Benjamin F., 322
HAWTHORNE
  W. W., 271
HAY
  George P., 154
  John, 271
  William, A118
HAYDEN
  George, 307
  James, 357
HAYES
  Adam, A108
  Charles, 133, 191
  Christopher, 61, 63
  Frederick, 185
  James, A109
  Marshal H., 347
  Morgan, 190, 347
  Mr., 175
  S. B., 149, 347
  William B., 315

William F., 246
HAYMOND
  W. C., 299
HAYNER
  W. P., 331
HAYS
  Alexander, 303
  C., 354
  Charles, 353
  Charles McClure, 262
  Charles W., 133, 134,
    135, 207, 354
  Christian, 280, 281
  Christopher, 66
  David, A109, A111
  G. W., 325
  George S., 304, 305
  James P., 316
  John, 219
  John B., 271, 323,
    361
  Joseph, 262, A109
  Marshal H., 345
  Morgan, 345, 353,
    354
  Moses, A109
  Mrs. S. C., 236
  S. B., 208, 354
  Sheldon B., 353, 354
  Thomas, 50, A109
  Thomas C., 322
  William, 113, 114,
    258, 271
HAYWARD
  M., 309
HAZARD
  Chill W., 336
  Joseph D. V., 304
HAZELHURST
  Isaac, 38
HAZLETT
  J., 109, 325

J. C., 183
Robert, 130, 131, 178,
  296
Samuel, 134, 135,
  145, 148, 178, 180,
  181, 199, 200, 202,
  203, 207, 334, 356,
  364, 370
HAZZARD
  C., 360
  Chill, 351
  J. D. V., 310
  Joseph D. V., 310
  T. R., 262, 271, 339,
    345, 347, 351
HEAD
  John, 233
HEADLEY
  Hiram, 328
HEALD
  John, 95
  Nathaniel, 95
HEATH
  A. P., 345
  Andrew, 15, 17, 20,
    22, 59
  Henry, 22
  W. H., 304
HEATON
  Hiram, 262
  John, 74
  William, 171
HECKARD
  John D., 315
HECKMAN
  Ezekiel, A9
HEDGE
  Hugh P., 325
  William, 271, 331
HEER
  Charles, 317
HEINES
  James, 309

HEISLEY
  F. A., 305
HELMICK
  B. F., 330
HELT
  William A., 321, 322
HEMLER
  Michael, 326
HEMPHILL
  Joseph, 322
HENDERSON
  Franklin, 312
  Henry, 305
  J. A., 299
  J. B., 327
  James, 181
  John, 272, 322
  Joseph, 134, 146, 151,
    176, 198, 199, 207,
    208, 254, 258, 262,
    265, 271, 297, 334,
    362, 374, 375
  Matthew, 220, 240
  Mr., 221
  Oliver, 315
  Rev. Mr., 150
  Robert, 319, 328
  S. M., 121
HENDRICK(S)
  J. W., 327
  James, 267, A10
HENDRICKSON
  Edward, 330
  Franklin, 330
  S., 310
  Samuel, 312
  Willis, 330
HENESY
  Thomas, 315
HENKINS
  Abraham, 272
HENNARD
  Jonathan, 70
HENNING
  William, 309
HENRY
  James F., 330
  Lewis, 319
  Noah, 330
  Patrick, A20, A21,
    A22
HENWOOD
  Elijah, A110
HEPBURNE
  William, A90
HERMILL
  John, 272
HERR
  J. D., 184
HERRICK
  Henry A., 305
HERRILL
  Wilson, 309
HERRIOTT
  I. V., 227
  James, 295
  John, 309
HERRON
  J. C., 110, 220
  James, 346
  Robert, 333
HERSEY
  Thomas, 357
HERTZOG
  G. G., 236, 346
HERVEY
  David, 241
  John C., 272
HERVIE
  John, A18
HESS
  Eli, 303
  Peter, 305
  W. W., 330
HEWIT(T)
  A. H., 325
  Henry, A108
  Isaac, 176
  John, 193
  Lewis, 188, 266
  Peter, A108
HICKENBOTTOM
  Ralph, A9
HICKEY
  Daniel, 191, A109
HICKMAN
  Abraham, A109
  Peter, 327
HIESTER
  Daniel, 77
  Joseph, 36
HIGBY
  Jame, 312
HIGGINS
  Jacob, 307, 326
  James, 317
HILANDS
  A., A118
HILES
  George, 307
HILL
  Antuban, 326
  B. F., 318
  Col., 171
  Eliza H., 185
  Emmer H., 329
  Isaac, 329
  James, A108, A109
  John, 83
  Joseph, 272, A108
  Joseph W., 327
  Rev. Mr., 98
  Robert, 113, 114
  S. E., 358
  S. G., 360
  Samuel, 256, 265

Stephen, 99, 272
William, 99
William A., 360
William McC., 315
HILLER
  Joseph, 299
HILLES
  Matthew, 49
HILLIARD
  John Wilkes, 272
HILLIER
  G. W., 351
HILLIS
  William, 101
HILLMAN
  Henry, 330
HILLSBOROUGH
  Lord, A38
HILTON
  James, 320
HIMMEGER
  James, 322
HINDMAN
  Samuel, 49, 245
HINES
  W. H., 312
HIPPLE
  George, 272
HIRST
  Francis M., 326
HISER
  Shed., 345
HITCHCOCK
  L. P., 132
HITE
  Daniel, 180
HITT
  Daniel, 180
HIXENBAUGH
  Charles S., 333
  Simon R., 324
HIXON

Jonathan, 297
HOBAUGH
  D., 310
HODGE
  J., 310
HODGENS
  Isaac, 256, 260, 272
  John, 272
  Samuel G., 306
  Thomas, 370
  Thomas J., 356
HODGINS
  T. J., 135
HOFFMAN
  Charles W., 305
  Cyrus, 329
  William J., 304
HOGDENS
  John W., 322
HOGE
  David, 40, 64, 65, 124, 125, 126, 129, 136, 147, 177
  John, 56, 69, 71, 72, 76, 78, 80, 84, 86, 87, 103, 124, 125, 129, 131, 178, 179, 188, 251, 267, 272, 341, 349
  Mr., 178, 179
  Thomas, 104, 198, 217, 358, 359, 362
  William, 124, 125, 129, 131, 150, 151, 188, 250, 252, 256, 257, 292
HOGELAND
  William, 81
HOGGMAN
  R. C., 262
HOLCROFT
  John, A119

Richard, A120
HOLCROSS
  John, A117
HOLLAND
  John, 266, 325, 343
  Samuel B., 325
  W. W., 326
HOLLCRAFT
  John, A110
HOLLINGSHEAD
  William, 307
HOLLINGSWORTH
  Mr., A57
HOLMES
  Andrew, A114
  Andrew H., 329
  Charles A., 181
  George S., 99, 181
  Hiram A., 332
  J. Y., 215
  Joseph, 70, 334
  Robert, A109
HOLT
  J., 299
HOMES
  Shipley, 357
HOOD
  F., 149
HOOK
  Ewing, 311
HOOKER
  George H., 311, 312
HOON
  John, 133, 176, 355
HOOTER
  Michael, A8
HOOTMAN
  David, 272, 368
HOOVER
  Jacob, 326
  Mr., 241

HOPKINS
  Andrew, 262, 344, 351
  James H., 376
  Mr., 148
  Richard, 83
  Thomas, 253, 259
  W., 191
  White F., 272
  William, 5, 132, 133, 134, 208, 252, 254, 265, 272, 304, 363
HOPPER
  Samuel, 309
HORN
  Charles, 307
  Christopher, A107
  Elias, 314
  George, A107
  Hezekiah, 314
  Hugh H., 327
  Jacob, 327
  John, 266, 314, A107
  John N., 329
  Jonas, 314
  Levi, 329
  W. H., 5, 316
  William H., 257, 303, 311, 313, 314, 343
HORNBAKE
  J., 332
  Jacob, 346
  William H., 333
HORNBECK
  George W., 235
HORNER
  Rev. Mr., 103
  William H., 329
HORNISH
  Christian, 188, 305
  Samuel, 362
  William, 272, 343

HORSEMAN
  Anthony, 130
HORTON
  Joseph, 22
  William, 129, 319
HOSACK
  John, 122
HOSKINSON
  W. N., 346
HOUDON
  Noble, 333
HOUSE
  J. M., 344
  James M., 343, 354, 355
HOUSEHOLDER
  Joseph, 325
HOUSEN
  Isaac, 317
  J., 317
HOUSTON
  A. B., 183, 185
  A. Y., 110
  Alexander, 307
  D., 200
  D. C., 167
  Daniel, 198, 199
  David C., 160, 162
  J. D., 346
  James, 177
  William S., 306
HOVEN
  John, A110
HOW
  James, A111
HOWARD
  William, 319
HOWE
  Daniel, 333
  George, 297
  John, 272
  Lemuel B., 333

  Mr., 248
  S. Bentley, 304
  Samuel J., 333
  William, 185
  William H., 304
HOWELL
  Abner, 58, 272
  Alexander, 317
  Alfred, 262
  Colonel, 314
  Governor, A81
  H., 325
  John, 271, 272
  Joshua B., 262, 311
HOWLAND
  E., 94
HOY
  Peter, 328
HOYT
  David, 327
HUBBARD
  W. B., 344
HUBBS
  James C., 332
HUDDLESTON
  Rev. Mr., 228
HUDSON
  Joshua, 299
  Rev., 99
  S. E., 193
  Samuel E., 245
  T. M., 105
  Thomas, 181
HUFF
  George, 299
HUFFMAN
  David, A108
  John, A107
  Martin, A108
HUFFNAGLE
  William, 262

HUGG
  Andrew J., 315
  James W., 315
HUGGINS
  Jacob G., 346
  R. C., 248
HUGGMAN
  Frederick, 195
HUGHES
  Captain, 68
  Elizabeth E., 49
  Ellis, 272
  J. W., 303
  James, 150, 272
  James M., 320
  James S., 306
  John, 49, 60, 61, 63,
    65, 66, 69, 70, A73
  Jonathan W., 320
  R. P., 338
  Remembrance, 272
  Robert, 114
  Robert P., 303, 311,
    313
  Samuel L., 95, 272,
    321
  Thomas, 227, 272,
    A113, A117
  W., 183
  Watson, 156
  William, 5, 49, 188,
    260, 264, 272
  Workman, 267, 272
HUGHS
  William, A111
HUGHY
  Edward, 24
HULBUT
  Philastus, 93
HULE
  Sarah, 211
  Solomon, 211

HULEE
  Henry, 350
HULL
  Gen., 294
  General, 293
  Gorsham, A109
  Robert W., 322
HUMBRICKHOUSE
  T. S., 262
HUMPHREYS
  James W., 135
  Robert, 103
HUNTER
  Abraham, 125, 127
  Alexander, 299
  Archibald, 272
  J. Joshua, 328
  John, 326
  Joseph, 125
  Joseph C., 328
  Joshua J., 308
  Martha, 125
  Mr., 350
  William, 133, 134,
    139, 183, 198, 199,
    200, 266, 296, 364
  William J., 307
HUPER
  J., 192
HUPP
  Alfred, A50
  Ann, A47, A48, A49
  Elizabeth, A46, A49
  Frank, A50, A51, A54
  J. C., 8, A38
  John, A46, A47, A49
  John C., A46, A50,
    A55
  Margaret, A46, A49
  Mary, A46
  P., A49
  Philip, A48

HURD
  Seth T., 185, 262, 351
HURFORT
  Annie M., 236
HURLEY
  William, 324
HUSBAND
  -, A73
HUSE
  William, A108
HUSTEIN
  John, 49
HUSTON
  Absalom, 180
  Cyrus, 369
  David A., 326
  Dixon, A73
  Eli, 315
  Hamilton, A73
  Hannah, 50
  Hugh, 321
  J., 360
  J. D., 346
  James, 135, 145, 146,
    147, A110
  John, 345, A56
  John W., 328
  William, 50, 126, A56
HUTCHESON
  Thomas, 317
HUTCHINS
  Thomas, A29, A31,
    A32, A34
HUTCHI(N)SON
  Andrew J., 312
  James M., 134, 345,
    347
  Osmond, 333
  Samuel P., 345
  Thomas, 130, 259
  W. S., 183
  William S., 183, 329

HUTSON
  Samuel, 145, 148, 334
  William, 128
HYATT
  Shadrack, A110
  Sheddrack, A109
HYDE
  Andrew J., 303
  Samuel, 272

-I-

IJAMS
  F. F., 346
  Frank, 320, 322
  Franklin, 320
  Thomas, A107
IMBRIE
  David, 227
IMMEL
  William, 305
IMSEN
  William, 245
INDIAN STEPHEN, A41
INGALL
  R. C., 262
ING(H)RAM
  A., 307
  Hamilton, 309
INGLES
  John W., 312
INGLIS
  Lieutenant, A41
INGMAN
  John, A18, A41
INKS
  Adolphus J., 315
INLOW
  Abraham, 79
IREY

Clarke, 319
IRISH
  Nathaniel, A72
IRONS
  John, 363
  Joseph, 272
IRVIN
  James, 37
IRVINE
  Brigadier-General, A37
  Gen., 290
  General, 283
  William, 58, 77, 286, A67, A75
IRWIN
  J. D., 265
  John, 24, A72
  Samuel, 22, 262
  Thomas S., 272
  William, 272, A115
ISENBERG
  J. G., 326
ISRAEL
  Charles H., 262
  John, 257, 350

-J-

JACK
  -, 351
  Judge, A116
  Patrick, A118, A119
  S., A118
JACKMAN
  J., 260
  Jehu, 254, 258, 265
  Robert, 235, 236
  Simeon, 272
  W. H., 314
  W. W., 235
JACKSON

A., 228
Agness, 49
Andrew, 296, 360
C. F., 335
George, 238, 272, 296
James, 49, 232, A111
James A., 320
James B., 322
Jehu, 139
John W., 307
Joseph, 307
Philip, A109
President, 147
Richard, A109
Robert, 260
Robert S., 322
Samuel, A77
Stonewall, 314
Thomas, 307, 321, 327
William, 307, A109
William H., 322
JACOB(S)
  D. H., 346
  J. G., A36
JACOBUS
  Rev. Dr., 158
JAMES
  John, 94, A107
  Robert, 350
JAMISON
  John, 272, 309
  William, 328
  William R., 335
JAY
  Mr., A95
JEFFEREY
  Samuel, 49
JEFFERS
  John, 307
JEFFERSON
  Mr., 229

Thomas, 278, 370,
372, A30
JEFFREY
John S., 317
William, 162, 166
JEFFRIES
Margaret, 82
JEFFRY
John, 272
JENKIN
Eleazer, 79
JENKINS
B., 315
Eleazer, 78, 265, 272,
A107, A109
G. W., 327
George W., 327
Thomas J., 315
William, 332
JENKINSON
Isaac, 95, 96, 272
JENNINGS
Benjamin, A9
David, 262
Ebenezer, 253
John C., 329
Joseph, 329
O., 352
Obadiah, 175, 176,
262, 358, 359
Samuel, 176
JESSEROON
Peter, A109
JESTER
S., 310
JEWELL
William, A109
JOB(E)S
Andrew N., 333
Joseph, 333
Patterson, 312
Robert, 333

Robert D., 317
Samuel, 333
William W., 333
JOHN
Joseph S., 329
JOHNSON
A., 310
Alexander, A111
Barnet, 314
C. T., 196
Daniel, A111
David, 252, A108
Esther, 362
Isaac, A111
J. B., 322
J. R., 177
James B., 323
James M., 333
John, 162, 266, 296
John Meck, A107
John S., 317
Joseph, 333
Judge, 165
Mary, 362
Matthew, 101
Nicholas, A109
Robert, A64, A66
S. A., 360
Samuel, 232, 320,
A110
Stephen, A111
Walter, 308
JOHNSTON
Abraham, 178, 179,
A110
Adam, 312
Amazariah, A110
B. W., 262
Charles, 299
David, 137, 150, 221,
222
Eleanor, 362

Elizabeth, 362
Ezekiel, A9
F. W., 262
George, 332
George W., 322
Henry, 328
J., A9
J. R., 169
J. Rankin, 182
Jacob, 362
James B., 323
Job, 235, 262, 272,
339
John, 20, 114, 259,
A109, A110
Mary, 49
Matthew, 82, 100
Richard, 272
Robert, 175, 227,
A67, A111
Samuel, 49, 58, 272,
A110
Thomas, A90
Thomas G., 262
W. F., 376
William, 272, A7,
A56, A109
William F., 37, 38
JOHNSTONE
William, 71
JOLIFF
Luke, 17
JOLLY
Martin, A56
William, A110
JONES
Ahira, 342
Charles E., 139, 183
David, 319
Edward, 333
G. O., 135, 334
George O., 145, 317

J. F., 228
James, 122
John, 105
John G., 22
John W., 247
Joseph, 334
Joseph A., 335
L. F., 314
M., 325
R. W., 150
Richard, 319
Robert, 330
S. T., 247
Samuel, 170, 226
Shugart T., 247
Sylvester, 228
Thomas, 131, 309, 319, 368
JORDAN
Ann, 192
Cardena, 330
Jacob, 297
Jesse, 145, 148, 149
John J., 319
John P., 330
Mary, 192
Mrs., 214
JORDON
Isaiah, 314
JUDSON
J. L., 5, 134, 135, 145, 146, 147, 207
J. Lawrence, 262, 272
JUSTICE
Isaac, 16

-K-

KAINE
C. C., 191, 351
Hiram, 128
Michael, 191

KALTERLEE
F., 324
KAMMERER, 109
KANE
Daniel, 262
KANN
John, 329
KARROD
Levi, 63, 272
KAUFFMAN
George, 332
KEAN
John, A90
KEARNEY
David, 304
Dennis, 191, 246
James, 191, 330
Jerome, 191
KEARSLEY
Jonathan, 170
KEELING
W. B., 189, 241
KEELY
Francis, A108
KEENAN
Michael, 315
KEENE
Lawrence, 77
KEENEY
D. L., 319
KEHR
Daniel, 130, 131, 259, 264
KEIFER
John C., 309
Samuel, 309
KEIHL
George, 329
KEITH
William, 34
KELLER
Samuel P., 310

KELLEY
J. R., 149, 254
James S., 319
KELLY
Freeman, 329
H., 310
James W., 351
John, 320
Mr., A84, A85
Samuel, 215
Samuel F., 328
William, 346
KELSEY
John, 299
KELSO
Charles W., 262
KENDALL
John, 303
John B., 317
Louis, 325
S., 95
KENDER
Valentine, A107
KENDREE
Rev. Dr., 181
KENNA
John, 266
KENNEDY
Benjamin K., 323, 335
D. S., 118
James B., 303
John, 262, 272, 360, 363, 368, 369, A110
John H., 111, 225
John M., 155
John T., 309
Joseph M., 309
Peter, 134, 183, 184, 305
Robert, A109
William A., 309
William G., 304

KENNER
  Frank, 324
KENNEY
  Wesley, 181
  William, A110
KENRICK
  Bishop, 192
  Francis Patrick, 191
KENSTWICK
  Amos, 320
KENT
  Jacob, 332
  Samuel, 332
  Z. B., 327
KEPPELLE
  George H., 262, 341
KERFOOT
  J. D., 187
KERNS
  Alexander, 317
  James, 330
  Samuel, 326
  Thomas, 326
KERR
  Aaron, 245, 253, 254
  Archibald, 130, 132, 133
  George, 329
  Huston, 329
  Isaac, 257, 260, 262, 264, 265, 296
  J., 145
  J. W., 105, 244
  James, 122, 133, 223, 252, 253, 260, 272, A115
  James P., 322
  John W., 112, 316
  Joseph, 312
  Robert, 215
  T. C., 334
  W. W., 312

William, 113, 114, 122, 311, 360
William A., 322
William W., 312
Willison, 272
Wilson, 272
KESNER
  Frederick, 319
KESSLER
  J. W., 105
  Jacob, 134
KETCHIM
  George, 314
KEYS
  David, 273
  Hugh, 258, 326, 329, 330, 342
  James, 253, 272
  John, 325, 326
  R. S. H., 330, 343
KIDD
  Alexander, 49, 83, 273
  Peter, 40, 112
  William, 273
  William A., 258
KIDDOO
  James, A65
  Joseph, 245
KIEHL
  John M., 330
KIESER
  J. C., 334
KIMBLE
  Andrew, 330
KIMMEGAR
  David, 315
KINCAID
  James, 363
  John, 363
  Lieutenant, A42
KINDER

Christian, 326
Harvey, 327
Valentine, 99
KING
  Al, 309
  Alvin, 257, 336
  H. B., 304
  James, 170
  R. C., 247
  Sampson S., 262
  W., 358
  W. C., 265
  W. W., 262
  William R., 305
KINGSTON
  J., 262
KINIBER
  Nathan, A108
KINLAN
  Charles, A108
KINNEY
  John, A108
KINTNER
  Andrew, A108
  George, A108
KIRCHNER
  Michael, 192
KIRK
  Cornelius D. B., 322
  J. T., 149
  James, A111
  James T., 306
  Tabitha, 50
KIRKPATRICK
  Abraham, A68, A71, A73
  Daniel, 114
  John, A75
  John M., 155
  Major, A70
KIRKWOOD
  D., 170

KISSLER
  Jacob, 134
KITSNER
  Frederick, 328
KLEIVES
  Ferdinand, 317
KLINE
  John R., 312
KLINEFELTER
  Jacob, 327
KLOTZBARKER
  John, 317
KNAPP
  Joseph M., 335
KNIGHT
  Dr., 288, 290
  Gideon, 315
  Jonathan, 143, 251, 252, 253, 259, 364
  Joseph, 327
KNOLE
  Peter, 299
KNOX
  General, A70
  Henry, 85
  John S., 360
KOBYON
  James, A110
KOECHLINE
  C. Z., 330, 345
  Jacob, 126
KOONTZ
  H., 309
  H. S., 309
  James W., 207
  John, 133, 199, 200, 201, 204
  John W., 317
  M. G., 191
  R. H., 5
  Robert H., 260, 262
KOOTE

  Ephraim, 262
KRAMER
  Louis, 308
KREIDER
  Christian, 238
KREPPS
  Christian A., 326
  John B., 262
  Samuel J., 254
  Solomon G., 336
KUHN
  James J., 155
  Mr., 180
  Philip, 134, 345
KUNTZ
  George, 127, 132, 133, 134, 135, 200, 362
  James W., 5, 133, 135
  John, 132, 296
  M. G., 135
  Michael G., 347
  Philip P., 303
KURTZ
  Henry, 358
  William K., 262
KUYKENDALL
  Benjamin, 22, 24
  Mr., 16

-L-

LABARRE
  George J., 308
LACEY
  B. W., 262, 351
LACKEY
  David, 345
  Thomas, 178, 179
LACLERC
  Lewis, 313
LACOCK

  Atlas, 332
  Ira, 135
  Ira J., 262
  Isaac, 320
  John, 259
  Oliver, 99
LAFFERTY
  William, 326
LAGGETT
  Lemuel, 328
LAIDLEY
  John, 311
LAIN
  John M., 227
LAING
  Robert, 240
LAKE
  Henry, 93
LAMB
  Mr., 244
LAMBDEN
  William, 180
LAMBERT
  William, 191
LANCASTER
  D. H., 313
  David H., 360
  Hugh, 333
LANE
  Henry, A109
  John, A109
  Joseph J., 303, 328, 329
  Pressley Carr, A90
  R. P., 185, 200
  Richard Carr, 262
LANERY
  John W., 317
LANG
  J. E., 307
  James, A75
  R. N., 307

LANGE
　William, 317
LANGFITT
　John W., 317
LANGLEY
　Henry, 134, 135, 143,
　　144, 151, 195, 198,
　　200, 264, 265
　James, 132, 200
LANK
　W. B., 345, 350
　William B., 320
LANUM
　William H., 322
LAP
　George, 327
LAPE
　M., 317
LAPSLEY
　Thomas, A116, A117
LARID
　Robert A., 327
LASH
　Abner, A110
　Isaac, A108
　William B., 314
LASHLEY
　Alexander, 84
LATIMER
　Arthur, A110
LATTA
　Alexander S., 333
　Robert, A109
　William L., 333
LATTIMER
　John A., 309
LATTIMORE
　Abraham, 130
　. James, 133
LAUGHLIN
　John, 221, 303
LAUGHRAN
　Cornelius, 217
LAWRENCE
　Captain, 293
　George V., 251, 252, 254
　Joseph, 122, 200, 202, 251, 253, 254
　Thomas, 35, 247
LAWS
　James, 181
LAWSON
　Joseph, 322
LAWTHER
　John, A111
LAWTON
　John, 303
LAYMAN
　F., 310
　Frederick, 304
LAYTON
　Henry, 354
LAZEAR
　Jesse, 251
　Thomas C., 155
LEACOCK
　James, 364
LEAKE
　F., 114
LEASURE
　Daniel, 315
　George, 317
LEATHERMAN
　D. M., 265, 372
　Jonathan, 254
LEAVER
　Henry, 330
LEDBEATER
　A., 332
LEE
　Anna E., 185
　Charles, 100
　Flora, 185
　Francis H., 185
　Francis Lightfoot, A20
　George, A109
　Governor, A113, A116
　Henry, A81, A110, A116
　Hugh, A108
　James, 260, 265, 373
　Professor, 185
　R. H., 170, 184, 185, 186, 201, 260, 262, 362
　Rev. Dr., 187
　Richard H., 204
　Richard Henry, 185, 186
　Robert, 227
　William, 329, A109
　William M., 232
LEECH
　David, 118
　James, 273, A109
　William, A109
LEEDOM
　John, A110
LEEDS
　John, A26
LEEPER
　James, A111
　John, A111
　Samuel, 49, A111
LEET (LITE)
　Daniel, 22, 40, 58, 61, 65, 69, 124, 130, 136, 252, 267, 273, 288
　Daniel W., 262
　David, 57
　Isaac, 19, 103, 132, 134, 251, 252, 259, 260, 262, 264, 347

43

Jonathan, 130, 267, 273
Jonathan D., 146, 254, 262, 345
Mr., 138
William, 81
William V., 267
LEFFER
  George, A45
  Jacob, A45
LEFFLER
  Jacob, 273
LEGG
  Thomas, A109
LEIGHTY
  George C., 304
LEINBACH
  Mr., 285
LEIPER
  James, 182
LEMAN
  John, 81
LEMES
  Christopher, A7
LEMOYNE
  F. J., 171, 191, 198, 199, 200, 201, 202, 203, 204, 205, 206, 207, 362, A56
  F. Julius, 37, 296
  Francis J., 145, 324
  Frank J., 336
  John Julius, 357
LENNING
  S. Kendall, 95
LENNOM
  Joseph M., 305
LENNOX
  David, A78
  H., 317
LEONARD
  Abner, 178

B. F., 330
Benjamin, 363
Caleb, 368
Isaac, 273
LESCALLETT
  Eli, 308
LESNET(T)
  John, 79
  Richard, 309
LESTER
  W. H., 103
LETHERMAN
  Michael, A108
LEVER
  James H., 326
  John S., 326
  Joseph, 326
LEVERIDGE
  Abijah, A108
LEVIS
  John C., 311
LEWELLEN
  James S., 346
LEWELLYN
  George, 307
LEWESTON
  Joseph, A110
LEWIS
  Col., A41, A44
  Ira, 320
  John W., 320
  R. P., 262
  Samuel, 346, A109
  Simon W., 303, 317
  W., 325
  William H., 317
LEYDA
  John, 122, 330
LEYDY
  Benjamin, A108
  Frederick, A108
  James, A108

John, A108
LICHTEBERGER
  Elijah, 333
LIGGETT
  Addison, 317
LIGHTNER
  N., 325
LILLY
  Ellis N., 304
LIMERICK
  Daniel, 181
LINCOLN
  Mordecai, 315
  President, 302
LINDKEA
  J. B., 246
LINDL(E)Y
  Cyrus, 320
  Daniel, 150
  Demas, 67, 122, 216, 259
  Demus, 68, 82
  Isaac, 82
  Jacob, 217, 227
  James E., 273
  Milton, 320
  S., 325
  Stephen, 227
  William, 266, 273
LINDSAY
  George, 334
  James, 311
LINDSEY
  Charles, A9
  Eleanor, 26
  James, 255, 262
  John, 114
  Oliver, 134, 259
  Robert, 319
  William C., 262
LINDSL(E)Y
  Caleb, A108

Demas, A108
John, A108
Zeba, A108
LINK
  Dallas, 332
  Jonathan, A50, A51,
    A53, A54
  W. H. Harrison, 305
LINLEY
  Henry H., 317
LINN
  Alonzo, 155, 170, 227
  Andrew, A8
  Edward P., 328
  George A., 358
  Harrison, 326
  James, 273, A111
  John, 326, 334
  Mathew, 334
  Matthew, 139, 254,
    260, 273
  Matthew P., 303
  Moses, 259
  Thomas M., 326
  William, A8
LINNVILLE
  George, 273
LINSKED
  John B., 215
LINSLEY
  Demus, 85
  Elijah, 317
LINT
  Samuel, 299
LINTON
  Benjamin, 368
  C. L., 320
  Charles L., 303, 318,
    319
  E. H., 318
  Edward, 328
  Joseph, 265

Samuel, 260
LINVILLE
  Peter, A111
LISLE
  Peter, A120
LITLE
  A. H., 181
LITTELL
  D. S., 123
LITTIMORE
  George, 36
LITTLE
  A. H., 334
  David, 143
  H., 325
  J. H., 358
  Joseph W., 361
  L. R. W., 135
  L. R. Woods, 369
  Le Roy Woods, 262
  Moses, 193, 259
  Mr., 125
  N., 325
  Nicholas, 58, 219,
    273
LIVES
  Hark, 197
LIVINGSTON
  Samuel, 254, 360
LLOYD
  Thomas, 34
  William, 320
LOAFMAN
  John, 320
  William, 305
LOBING(I)ER
  C. C., 317
  Judge, A66, A81
LOCHMAN
  J., 130
LOCHRY
  Archibald, 280

LOCK
  David, A120
LOCKE
  Melancthon, 299
LOCKHART
  John W., 135
LOCKNY
  L., A69, A70
LOCKRAY
  John, A115
LODER
  Edward, A109
LODGE
  Benjamin, A90
LOGAN
  James, 35, 273, A110
  James K., 360
  John, 266
  Matthew, A110, A113
  Samuel, 114
  Thomas, 134, 345,
    347
LOMAS
  John, 360
LONG
  Christopher, 329
  James, 304
  James L., 346
  John, 363
  Mr., 366
  Thomas, 319
  Warren, 105
  William, 365
LONGDON
  Isaac H., 260
LONGSTREET
  Richard, A115
LONGSTRETH
  Morris, 37
LONKERT
  George, 134, 180,
    200, 208

Gust, 334
Mrs. G., 149
LOOP
  James, 49
LOPP
  John, 332
LORRISON
  John, 94
LOSKIEL
  -, 284
LOUDERBECK
  Andrew, 304
LOUGHEAD
  John B., 308
LOUGHMAN
  Jacob, 328
  John, 303
  Robert, 328
LOUTED
  James, 345, 346
LOVE
  James, 359
  John, A115
  Robert, 254, 260
LOVEJOY
  Andrew A., 312
LOW
  John, 312, 345
LOWARY
  David P., 176, 207, 260
LOWE
  Jefferson, 315
  John, 319, 334
LOWERY
  E., 325
LOWMAN
  Isaac, 345
LOWR(E)Y
  Frederick, 315
  Jack, 300
  James W., 317

William J., 308
LUCAS
  Gen., 294
  J. E., 334
  John B. C., A75
  Thomas B., 319
  Val., 184
LUCE
  M., 196
  Matthias, 193
LUDINGTON
  Captain, 328
  Hagan Z., 311
LUELLAN
  A. J., 305
LUELLEN
  Charles, 329
  Francis I., 329
LUKENS
  John, 124, A26, A29, A31, A33, A34
LUKER
  A. R., 314
LUSE
  Mathias, A108
  Matthias, 196, 259
LUTES
  George, 330
  John, 330
LUTHER
  Martin, 135, 354
LYLE
  Aaron, 78, 232, 251, 252, 253, 259, A111
  David, 46
  James C., 322
  John, 259, A109
  Moses, 259, 364
  Peter, A111
  Robert, 322, A108
LYNCH
  Edward, 124, 130

Thomas W., 329
W. R., 326
LYNN
  James, 322, A9
  John, 315, A64, A67
  Matthew, 312
  William, 22, 260, 262, 315
LYON(S)
  Benjamin, A110
  George W., 308, 345
  Hamilton, 312
  Harvey, 360
  John, 262
  N. B., 189, 217
  Oscar F., 312
  Samuel, 257, 262
  William, 325
LYT(T)LE
  Alexander, 128, 273
  Harriet, 128
  Isaac, 273, 345

-M-

MC ADOO
  James, 323
  Sylvanus, 323
MC AFEE
  Henry, 274
  J. B., 346
  Jacob, 320
  James, 320
  John, 346
MC AL(L)ISTER
  Benjamin, 315
  Henry J., 315
  James, 274, 345
  John, 135, 258, 260
  John L., 309
  Thomas, 331
  William, A111

MC ALRATH
  Charles, A108
MC BAY
  C. H., 324
MC BETH
  James W., 130
MC BRIBE
  Joseph S., 323
MC BRIDE
  Alexander, A109
  Archibald, 263
  Henry, 49
  James, 101, 326, 360
  John S., 303, 310
  M., 309
  Samuel, 101, A112
  Samuel B., 322
  William, A109
MC BURNEY
  Ebenezer, 274
  James, 260, 274
  Robert, 274
MC CABE
  John D., 322
  Joseph E., 312
MC CADDEN
  James, 199, 200, 259
MC CAHAN
  A., 220
  Alexander, 220
  James, 307
MC CAIN
  Charles, 304
  H., 310
  Isaac S., 333
  James P., 333
MC CALL
  -, A119
  James, A110
  Thomas, 198, 251, 253
  William, 308

MC CALMANT
  Alexander, 369
MC CALMO(N)T
  James, 274
  John A., 322
  John S., 306
MC CAMANT
  William, 173, 174
MC CANDLESS
  Alex, 49
  Alexander, 362
  Janet, 49
  Judge, 160
  William, 49, 112
MC CANN
  Daniel, 317
MC CARAN
  John, A110
MC CARREL(L)
  Alexander, 104
  L., 263
  William, 308
MC CARROL
  Thomas, 256, 260, 274
MC CARTNEY
  Washington, 225
MC CARTY
  William, 328
MC CASHEM
  John, 61
MC CASKEY
  William, A110
MC CASLIN
  M., 252
MC CAUSLAND
  Maxwell, 317
MC CAY
  Daniel, A8
MC CEANEL
  Thomas, A112
MC CLAIN(E)

Archibald, A26
  Daniel, 319
  Jefferson, 309
  John, 114, 355
  M. Wilson, 176
  William, 274, 334
MC CLAIR
  George W., 331
MC CLANAHAN
  Joseph, 309
MC CLANE
  James, 109
MC CLAREN
  Joseph, 360
MC CLASKEY
  Hugh, 274
  James, 266, 274
MC CLAY
  Mr., 77
MC CLEAN
  Alexander, 62, 267, A22, A23, A36
  Andrew, A109
  Hans, 114
  Joseph, A8
  Samuel, A114
MC CLEARY
  Alexander, 274
  William, 60, 64, 68, 215, 252, 372
MC CLEES
  Alexander, 274
MC CLEL(L)AN(D)
  A. C., 155
  Archibald, 328
  Elias, 260
  George W., 317
  Hugh, 190, 274
  James, 78, 265, 274, 297
  John, 135
  Robert, 258, 369

John, 182
William, 329
MC CLERRACHAN
Blair, 77
MC CLINTOCK
John, 178
MC CLOSKY
John, 307
MC CLOUD
James, 329
MC CLUNEY
Captain, 171
John, 143, 258
MC CLURE
Andrew F., 308
Benjamin F., 317
Boyce Irvin, 305
Captain, A42
John R., 317
Joseph A., 331
R. B., 274
Rev., 105
William, A73
William J., 309
MC CLURG
Hugh, A111
John, A111
Robert, 322
William, A111
MC CLUSKEY
John, 103, 217
MC COLLUM
A. J., 346
B., 191
Charles B., 317
H. B., 193, 334, 345
James, 191
M., 346
Moses, 319, 320
MC COMB(E)
General, 171
John H., 263

Mr., 174
Robert, A108, A111
William, 59, 67, 72, A108
MC COMBS
George W., 176
John, 297
Mathew, 309
William, 69, 71, 173, 178, 232, 258
MC COMUS
Daniel, A109
MC CONAUGHY
D., 177, 200, 202
David, 169, 205
J. K., 360
James K., 274
R., 274
Rev. Dr., 201, 204, 205
MC CONKEY
Isaac, 308
S., 308
MC CONN
John, 319
MC CONNEL(L)
Alexander, 297
Alexander W., 328
Daniel, A108
Harrison, 322
Matthew, 58, 274
R. A., 263
W. A., 241
MC CONOUGH
J. B., 336
MC COOK
George, 114
George W., 263
MC COOMBS
Thomas, 309
MC COON
William, 315

MC CORD
George T., 343
James P., 265
John A., 274
John P., 307
MC CORKLE
Thomas, 232
MC CORMIC(K)
George, 18, 22, 64, 211, 259
John, A110
Patrick, 49
W. S., 308
William, 309
MC COY
Alexander, 104
Daniel, 220
Daniel C., 49
David, 319
Hugh, 324
James, 200
John, 368, 369
John C., 344
John F., 315
O. H. P., 274
Robert, 333
William, 333
William A., 303
MC CRACKEN
Clara, 149
John, 330
M. L. A., 149, 257, 263, 305
MC CREADY
Captain, 293
D. A., 228
Edward R., 369
James, 259, 260
Robert, 49, 259, A111
MC CREARY
James, 334
Joseph, 305

Peter, 305
William, 251, 253, 259, 274
MC CREEDY
James, 113
MC CREERY
David, A109
MC CULLO(C)H
George, 49
James, 254
Jean, 64
Patrick, A108
Richard S., 226
MC CULLOUGH
-, 313
Benjamin, 322
Elizabeth, 49
J., 307
J. E., 334
Jacob L., 317
James, 274
John, 265, 274
John E., 319
John L., 317
Joseph E., 317
Nathaniel, 317
Patrick, 48, 58, 121, 122, 274
Samuel, 317
William, 49
MC CUNE
James H., 312
Thomas, 319
MC CUOY
John, A109
MC CURDY
Elisha, 210, 227
James K., 322, 337
MC DANIEL
Charles W., 259, 306
Riddle W., 322
S., 325

William, 254, 339, 373
MC DAVID
G. W., 324
MC DERMOT
James, 297
Jane, 195
MC DONALD
-, 214
Col., 112
Edward, 254, 274
H. A., 220
James A., 332
John, 263, 309
John B., 320
John N., 254
Mr., 223
Patrick, A108
Robert, 333
W. K., 362
William, 309
William K., 170, 263
MC DONELL
Andrew, 330
MC DONOUGH
Henry, 274, A108
I., 358
J., 342
MC DOW
James, 326
MC DOWELL
J., 150
J. W., 263
Jacob C., 309
James, 193, 274
John, 20, 56, 59, 67, 68, 113, 121, 252, 256, 259
Mr., 370
Pat, A108
Samuel, 368
Stephen, 315

MC EARD
William, A108
MC EDDINGTON
Daniel, 263
MC ELFISH
Owen, 322
Sylvester, 323
MC ELHENY
O. T., 360
Robert, 345
MC ELREE
A. S., 358
James, 193
MC ELROY
Archibald, 180
Ebenezer, 317
James, 274, A112
John, 133, 135, 145, 334, 356, 370
Patrick, 22
Thomas, 309
William, 260, 308
MC ENRUE
Thomas, 192
MC EWEN
John, 328
Joseph W., 321
William J., 309
MC FADDEN
Eliza, 107
G., 361
James, 274, 307
John B., 364
O. B., 208, 254, 256, 263, 274, 345
Thomas, 131, 274
MC FAIT
James, 328
MC FANOLD
Enoch, A110
MC FARLAND
A., 360

Abel, 94, 251, 253,
    A107
Andrew, 347, A13
Daniel, A107
Francis, 169, A73
James, 94, A68
James H., 319
M. Taylor, 305
Major, A73
Robert, 245, A108
Samuel, 193, 198,
    199, 200, 203, 264,
    369
Taylor, 303
W. V., 369
William, 258, 274
MC FARLANE
    A., A110
    George W., 317
    Samuel, 263
    William, 59, 64, 67,
        74, 76, 140
MC FARREN
    James, 254, 274, 294
    S. J., 336
MC FEELY
    George, 309
MC GARRAH
    William, A111
MC GARROUGH
    Thomas, 357
MC GARRY
    Tarry, A111
MC GARVEY
    W. B., 317
MC GAUGH
    Samuel, 274
MC GEE
    Robert, A110
    Thomas, 336
    William, A109
MC GEHAN

Brice, 101
MC GIBBONY
    G. W., 322
    George, 274
MC GIFFEN
    Thomas, 99
MC GIFFIN
    George, 314
    George W., 263
    Nathaniel, 94
    Norton, 189, 258,
        264, 300, 303, 311,
        333, 334
    Thomas, 132, 133,
        142, 143, 144, 145,
        198, 254, 263, 296
    W. H., 314
MC GILL
    Alexander T., 225
    John, A115
    Joseph, 317
    W. T., 317
MC GINNIS
    Elizabeth A., 360
    G. Harold, 321
MC GLAUGHLIN
    Edward, 323
    William, 72
MC GLUMPHEY
    James S., 322
MC GORNAWAY
    Samuel, A110
MC GOVERN
    John, 326
MC GOWAN
    Hugh, 308
    Rev. Mr., 191
MC GOWEN
    Alfred, 345
MC GREERY
    P., 310
MC GREGOR

H. C., 308
S., 312
S. M., 312
T. C., 308
MC GREW
    H., 310
    James, 245, 309
MC GUFFIN
    Ebenezer, 328
MC GUGIN
    David, 308
    James D., 264
MC GUIRE
    Daniel, A109
    Father, 246
    John B., 274
    Latshaw, 228
MC HENRY
    S. L., 312
    Samuel L., 337
MC ILHENNY
    William, A118
MC ILVAINE
    G. W., 263
    Greer, 122
    Grier, 265
    James, 187, 199, 316
    John, 305, 314
    John A., 263
    R. F., 263, 274
    S. B., 274
    William, 192
MC ILWAINE
    George, A108
    Grier, A108
    John, A108
MC INTIRE
    Andrew, A115
    J. C., 238
MC INTOSH
    -, A56
    General, A44

MC INTYRE
  Andrew, A72
MC JAMES
  H., 307
MC JENKIN
  Henry C., 326
MC JUNKIN
  John, 274
  Milton, 314
  Robert R., 322
MC KAHAN
  John D., 303
  Thomas, 215
MC KAIG
  Clement N., 112
MC KAY
  Alexander, 314
MC KEA
  Alexander, A42
MC KEAG
  David, 315
  Moses, 315
MC KEAN
  Maria, 178
  T., 309
  Thomas, 35, 36, 54, 56, 135, 176, 178, 188, 189, 199, 200, 203, 206, 334, 354, 372, A67, A75
MC KEE
  Alexander, 331
  J. A., 216
  James, A.
  James W., 308
  John, 254, 263
  Joseph A., 135, 260, 370
  Robert, 274
  Samuel W., 307
  W. R., 113
MC KEEHAN
  David, 260, 263
MC KEEN
  Matthew, 274
MC KEEVER
  A. B., 275
  Alexander C., 317
  C. B., 328
  Ella E., 107
  John, 303
  John B., 317
  Martha, 107
  Morris B., 316
  Thomas, 256, 275, 317
  Thomas M., 303
MC KENNAN
  J. B., 334
  Jacob B., 187
  James W., 170, 210, 218, 263
  John, 170
  Miss, 352
  T. M. T., 169, 198, 199, 200, 201, 202, 203, 204, 206, 354, 368
  Thomas, 151, 155, 176, 178, 200, 203, 206, 334, 340, 358
  Thomas M. T., 133, 134, 251
  Thomas T. M., 263
  W., 156
  William, 132, 134, 155, 185, 187, 200, 208, 256, 258, 260, 263, 275, 291
  William B., 187
MC KENNEY
  D., 156
MC KIBBEN
  Richard, A109

Samuel, A110
Thomas, A111
William, A111
MC KIBLER
  John, A109
MC KINLEY
  G. W., 309
  Hugh B., 324, 335
  James, 135, 345
  John, 308
  Robert, 275
  T. S., 135
  Thomas S., 345, 347
  Thompson, 326
  William, A75
MC KINNEY
  Andrew, A111
  David, 155
  H., 346
  Henry, A114
  Isaac N., 227
  Winder, 320
MC KNIGHT
  Joseph, 151
MC LANE
  Samuel B., 329
  Thomas H., 329
MC LAUGHLIN
  John, 333
MC LEAN
  H. B., 260, 275
  John, 315
  Robert, 171
MC LEOD
  J., 310
MC LONEY
  John, 275, 368
MC MAHON
  James, 19
  M., 325
  Peter B., 263

MC MANNIS
  John, 275
MC MASTERS
  John, A72
  R., 346
MC MEANS
  John W., 322
MC MEILLIN
  William, 335
MC MILLAN
  Dr., 222, 223
  George, A108
  J. T., 309
  Jane, 115
  John, 114, 115, 121,
    122, 150, 222, 225,
    A37
  Margaret, 115
  Mr., 221
  Rev. Dr., 173, 223,
    224
  Rev. Mr., 221
  Samuel, A111
  W., A115
  William, 225, 230,
    338, A117
MC MILLEN
  Elizabeth, 50
  James D., 305
  John, 49, 113, 216
  Robert, 305
MC MILLIN
  John, A109
  John A., 312
MC MUHN
  Thomas, 350
MC MURRAY
  Henry, 323
  William, 309
  Wilson, 323
MC NAIR
  Dunning, A90

MC NALL
  Joseph, 275
MC NARY
  David, 121
  James, 275
  Joseph, 182
  Matthew, 275
  Oliver R., 303
  T. M., 322
  Thomas, 275
  W. H., 321
  W. Pollock, 307
  William P., 337
MC NEAR
  Frank B., 319
MC NEIL(L)
  Hugh B., 315, 319
  Nelson R., 305
MC NICKLE
  Andrew, A72
MC NITT
  Abraham, A110
MC NULTY
  C. J., 328
  Caleb J., 303
  P. H., 307
  W. W., 307, 308
MC NUTT
  John, 322
MC PEAK
  Andrew, 317, 323
  J., 307
  J. H., 307
  J. O., 307
  R. N., 307
  Thomas J., 323
MC PHERSON
  John, 104
  Robert, 109
  Samuel, 275
MC QUOW(E)N
  James, 265, 267

MC VAY
  Jacob, 275
  Oliver, 314
MC VEHIL
  James, 305
MC VEY
  S., 360
MC WHIRTER
  Moses, 259
MC WILLIAMS
  J. M., 338
  J. W., 351
  John W., 263
  Wallace, 254, 260,
    265
  William, 307
MC WREATH
  Catharine, 360
M'CANDLESS
  Judge, 167
M'CONAUGHY
  David, 176
M'CORKLE
  James, 185
M'CORMICK
  George, 13
M'DERMOT
  James, 146
M'ELROY
  G. B., 184
M'KINSTRY
  Mrs., 92
M'NARY
  John H., 306
  W. P., 306
M'NEILL
  J., 376
MACAHEY
  John, 114
MACK
  Thomas, 304
  William, 304

MACKAY
  Aeneas, A13, A19, A42
  Alexander, A5
  H., 246
MACKEY
  James, 300
  James L., 307
  Samuel, 307
MACOY
  John, 259, 265
MADISON
  James, A21, A29, A31, A33
  Rev. Dr., A36
MAGEE
  Robert, A109
MAGGS
  William, 306
MAGILL
  Fulton, 210
  James K. P., 322
MAGNER
  Edward, A110
  Henry, A110
MAHAFFEY
  Amelia, 192
  Martha, 192
MAHON
  Robert, 253, 259, 273
  Samuel S., 262
MAKEOWN
  John, 322
MALLUM
  George, 305
MALONE
  Carson, 324
  Peter, 329
MALOY
  J., 309
MANCHA
  Eli W., 331

MANNING
  Andrew J., 326
  John D., 326
  John W., 332
MANNON
  James, 319
MANOWN
  William, 246
MANSFIELD
  John A., 312
MARCHAND
  J. A., 334
MARCHANT
  Samuel, A109
MAREOWN
  John S., 331
MARGERUM
  James S., 332
MARKER
  George, 333
  Joseph, 331
  Samuel, 331
MARKHAM
  William, 28, 31, 34
MARKLE
  John S., 246
  Joseph, 37
MARLOW
  Mrs. F. A., 185
MARQUER
  David, A109
MARQUIS(S)
  George, 49, 232
  Jean, 50
  John, 49, 232, A109, A111
  John S., 122
  Mary, 49
  Mr., 48
  Mrs., 230
  Robert, A108
  Samuel, A108

  Sarah, 50
  Thomas, 49,107, 232, 259
MARSH
  E. B., 265
  John, 317
  L. M., 370
  Nathan B., 332
  Roswell, 262
MARSHAL(L)
  -, A73
  Benjamin, 314
  Col., A69
  Colonel, 86, 150
  George, 109
  Gilbert C., 324
  Hannah, 195
  J., A70
  James, 49,57, 59, 60, 62, 65, 67, 68, 69, 71, 72, 73, 74, 79, 84, 129, 138, 232, 257, 258, 259, 281, 296, 367, A22, A62, A73, A75, A111
  Jeremiah, 145
  John, 58, 64, 135, 198, 199, 200, 202, 205, 232, 253, 258, 262, 273, 322, A69, A73, A110
  Margaret, 50
  Mr., 208
  Robert, 50, 150, A111
  Samuel, 151, 195, 264, 315, 352
  T. J., 325
  Thomas, A110
  Thomas H., 305
  William, 70, 74, 220, 259
MARSHEL
  Jerry, 334

MARSHMAN
  A. G., 273
  Alexander G., 258
  B., 325
  R., 325
MARTIN
  Charles, 226
  David, 324
  E. H., 321
  Ebenezer, 368
  George, 305, A8
  Hugh, 279
  James, 335
  James L., 319
  Jesse, 245, 254, A8
  John, A8
  John D., 192
  John S., 318, 319
  Jonathan, 259, 273
  Joseph, 193
  Philip, 312
  Robert, 193
  W. J., 170
MARTINDALE
  Thomas, 96, 264
MARUS
  John, 283
MASON
  Charles, 8, A24, A26
  Samuel, 58, 273, A43
  Thomas, 327
  William, 326
MASSEY
  M. B., 262
MATHEWS
  William J., 334
MATTHEWS
  James, 49
  Paul, 16
  Prudence, 49
  William J., 189, 370
MATTOX

E., 325
MAXWELL
  Jacob R., 329
  James, A109
  N. J., 315
MAY
  John, A49
MAYBELL
  William, 16
MAYER
  B., A3
MAYES
  Isaac, 273
  Joseph T., 273
MAYHORN
  James, 315
  Joseph, 333
  Robert, 333
MAZZUCHELLI
  S., 191
MEANOR
  William H., 309
MEANS
  Allen, A110
  Andrew, 328, 366
  John, 315
MEARS
  C., 325
  Hugh, 130
MEASON
  Isaac, 26, 279
  Thomas, 262
MECK
  John, A107
  Nathan, A107
  Samuel, A107
MEEANER
  George, A109
MEEKS
  James, 314
  John A., 326
  Joseph, 320

MEETKIRKE
  William, 130, 146,
    259, 273, A70, A71,
    A73
MEHAFF(E)Y
  James, 304
  William, 315
MELCHIE
  E. M., 273
MELDOON
  Robert A., 322
MELENEY
  James, A110
MELHOM
  Rev. Mr., 242
MELLINGER
  Marcus, 331
  Mr., 242
  W. S., 310, 345
  William S., 310, 336
MELLON
  Edward, 324
MELONE
  John, 266
  Mary, 266
MELOY
  John, 254, 257, 273,
    322
MELVIN
  Mr., 125
  Samuel J., 317
MENARY
  Thomas, 219, A112
MENDENHALL
  J. K., 187
  Jonathan, 267
MENDLEN
  William, 325
MERCER
  Boyd, 121, 173, 217,
    256, 368
  John, 113

MERCHANT
  Samuel, 360
MEREDITH
  John, 309
  William, 262
  William T., 304
MERRICK
  J., 310
  John, 304, 317
MERRIMAN
  James C., 306
MERRINER
  Benjamin, A110
MESSENGER
  E. J., 185
  John C., 122, 123
MESSINGER
  John, 262
MESSNER
  S., 346
  Samuel, 345
METCALFE
  Norris, 322
METTAMMICONT
  Richard, 28
METZLER
  Jacob, 334
METZNER
  George, 149, 150, 316
  Michael, 192
MEYER
  George, 299
MICHENER
  J. E., 314, 337
  John E., 311, 313
MICKEY
  W. A., 5
  William A., 257, 273
MIDDLETON
  William M., 305
MIFFLIN
  Governor, A70, A81

Thomas, 35, 56
MILENDER
  David, A110
MILES
  Col., 77
  James, 320
  Mr., 84
  William, 305
MILLAN
  Dr., 114
  William W., 227
MILLER
  A., A110
  A. H., 324
  Aaron, 266
  Abraham, 314
  Adam, 82
  Alexander, 263
  Anthony, 299
  Augustus J., 304
  B., 245
  Capt., 229
  Captain, A43, A55
  David, 273
  David M., 210
  Edward C., 328
  Eli A., 331
  Emmor H., 329
  Frederick, A47, A49, A50
  G. W., 5
  George, 315, A109
  George V., 305
  George W., 170, 252, 263
  H. B., 188
  Henry, 299
  Hillery, 304
  Hiram, 245
  Hugh Q., 187
  Isaac, 322
  J., 217

J. H., 310
J. Madison, 342
J. S., 310
J. W., 325
Jacob, 8, 135, 145, 207, A38, A45, A46, A47, A48, A49, A50, A51, A53, A54
Jacob H., 155
Jacob S., 304
James, 260, 308, 320, A108, A109
James M., 320
James P., 230
John, 273, 363, A55
John B., 176, 324
John W., 254
Joseph, 90, 91, 297
Julius P., 317
Mary, 130
Mr., 222, A67
Nicholas, 327
O. H., 155
Prof., 223
R. L., 228
Richard, 319
Robert, 84, 228
Samuel, 222, 225, 230
Sanson, 333
Thomas, 273, 317, A115
W., 310
William, A46, A117, A120
William H., 322
MILLIGAN
  I., 325
  I. M., 263
  J., 325
  J. W., 325
  John F., 328

Robert, 170, 196
William, 312
MILLIKEN
　Abel, 94
　J. C., 93, 343
　James, 94
　John, 314
MILLS
　Benjamin, 150
　Elisha, 80
　James, 181
　Samuel, 319
　William, 263
MILSACH
　Philip, 130
MINKS
　Henry, 331
MINOR
　John, 63, 81, 252, 273
　L., 376
　William, 65
MINTON
　J. N., 324
　J. Newton, 324
　Mathias, 273
　Matthias, 319
MISHNER
　Samuel, 317
MITCHEL(L)
　D. G., 130, 357
　David, 273
　Esquire, 110
　George, 151, 334
　George W., 328
　Henry, 326
　Isaac I., 329
　James, 85, 86, 273,
　　349, 357
　John, A110, A117,
　　A118, A119
　John R., 321, 322
　March, 273

Mark, 363
Robert, 315
W., 358
W. S., 149
William, 331, A110
MITCHENER
　M. W., 326
MITCHENOR
　Milton W., 330
MOCKBEE
　Daniel, 304
MOFFIT(T)
　Eli, 327
　George W., 357
　Hopkins, 325
　James, 273
　Thomas H., 331
MOLDEN
　Horatio, 297
　Jacob, 331
　Robert, 331
MOLONEY
　John, 317
MONESMITH
　Rev. Mr., 188
MONINGER
　George W., 332
MONNIGER
　John, 335
MONROE
　Andrew, 273
　James, 171, 229
　John, 180
　Joshua, 181, 273
　President, 147, 172
MONTEUR
　-, 283
MONTFORD
　James H., 316
MONTGOMERY
　Hugh, A108
　J. B., 332

James, 263, 320
James B., 333
John, A42, A109
William, 77, 251,
　260, 263, 273
MOODY
　D., 130
　R. S., 263
　Samuel, A109
MOON
　Robert, 122
MOOR
　Augustus, A108
　John, A108
MOORE
　Abel, 332
　Alexander, A108
　Allen, 333
　Andrew, 273
　Daniel, 130, 132, 133,
　　135, 146, 151, 175,
　　198, 200, 364
　David, 245, 359
　Dr., 129
　Franklin, 181
　George, 320, A111
　Hugh, 305
　J., 263
　Jacob D., 315
　James, 273, A109
　Jesse S., 314
　John, 241, 273, 319,
　　362, A110, A111
　John M., 312
　Joseph L., 322
　Leet S., 332
　Martin, 317
　Michael, 332
　Mr., 244, A90
　President, 283
　Robert, 259, 260, 263,
　　266, A111

Russel, 368
Samuel, 327
Thomas, 216, 218
W. S., 5, 154
W. W., 273
William, 35
William S., 155, 256, 263, 264, 351
MO(O)R(E)HEAD
Jane, 115
John, 273
Samuel, 279
W., 227
William, 115
MORELAND
W. C., 263
MORELEY
Thomas, 337
MORETON
David, 304
Thomas, 251
MORGAN
A. C., 314
Anastasie, 191
B., 309
Daniel, A116
David T., 116
Frances, 64
Francis S., 307
General, A70, A81, A84, A118, A119
George, 116, A43
George W., 300
Jacob, 149, 265
Jasper, 314
John, 94, 192, 198, 245, 266, 274, 291, 361
John H., 309
Robert, 50
Samuel W., 309
T. J., 149

Thomas, 146, 198, 199, 200, 256, 263, 274, 304, 351
Thomas Gibbs, 263
Thomas J., 300
Thomas Jefferson, 297, 299, 351
W. Duane, 149
William, 247
Zachwell, 19
MORILES
Antonio, 305
MORMON, 89
MORRELL
Josiah P., 336
MORRIS
David, 130, 132, 133, 171, 292, 296
J. J., 322
John, 55, 311
Jonathan, 324, 353
Mary, 108
Mrs. David, 129
R. H., 370
Robert Hunter, 35
Samuel C., 54
William M., 303
MORRISON
A. P., 155, 263
F. Cooper, 257
G. W., 265
George, 257, 342, 345
George L., 134
H. R., 309
Henry, A110
J. L., 274
J. N., 312
J. S., 155
James, 60, 61, 63, 65, 69, 70, 113, 220, 263, 345
John, A110

Joseph, 309
Joseph S., 263
M. P., 335, 337, 358
Norris, A115
R. L., 263
Samuel, 274, 359
William, 312
William M., 325
MORROW
A. C., 135, 145, 146, 147, 149, 370
Adam C., A69
Benjamin, A109
Charles, 308
George, 322
John, 134, 366
MORTIMER
W. H., 310
MORTON
Adam S., 329
Joseph B., 326
R. W., 240
Samuel, 309
Thomas, A62, A75, A84
Thomas P., 326
MOSE
Mr., 177
MOSER
Mr., 140, 141
Samuel, A108
MOSIER
William H., 329
MOSS
J. R., 317
J. W., 263, 351
Thomas, A108
MOUCK
Edward, 323
James M. G., 309
W. M., 345
MOUK
J. P., 309

MOUNT
  Michael, A115
  Samuel, 198, 199, 200
MOUNTAIN
  A. S., 263
  James, 222, 263
MOUNTS
  Samuel, 180
MOUNTZ
  Caleb, A115
  Enoch, 317, 322
  P., 20
  Richard, 328
MOURIE
  Tellinghast, 319
MOWRY
  Daniel B., 316
MUCKLE
  Alexander, 170
MUHLENBERG
  Frederick A., 77
  H. A., 37
  Peter, 77
MUHLENBURG
  F. A., 35
MULL
  Anthony, 319
MULLEN
  Josiah, 317
MULLER
  John, A109
MULLIGAN
  Peter, 308
MULLIKEN
  John, 357
MUNEL
  John, A109
MUNFORD
  James, 303
MUNN
  David, A110

John, A110
Samuel A., 331
MUNNEL
  Hugh, 193
MUNROE
  Andrew, 70, 220
  William, 180
MURCH
  James, 104
  James C., 215
MURDOCH
  Alexander, 125, 132, 133, 142, 143, 198, 208, 223, 256, 258, 263, 274, 292, 296, 370
  Samuel, 198, 223, 357
MURDOCK
  Alexander, 358
  S., 193
MURPH(E)Y
  Alphew, 135
  G. W., 334
  John, 265, 274, 311, 338, 343
  Martin, 332
MURRAY
  Alfred W., 323
  Charles, A109
  Chester P., 308
  George H., 327
  George R., 322
  John H., 328
  Neil, A110
  Nicholas, 170, 217
MUSSER
  Alexander M., 307
  J. B., 150, 342, 343, 344, 351
MUSTARD
  John L., 307
MYERS

-, 310
Edward A., 305
F. M., 345
H. S., 314
Henry, 327
Henry A., 325, 326
Hiram, 330
Jacob, A108
Jeremiah, 331
John, 303
John M., 326
Matthew, A110
W. H., 314
William H., 313

-N-

NAFFEE
  C. G. W., 299
NAGHTAN
  John, 135
NAGLE
  Mr., A85
NAILER
  William, A110
NAILOR
  James, A110
  William, 275, A73
NATHANIEL
  Rev., 285
NAUGTAN
  John, 135
NAVE
  Gabriel, A107
NAYLOR
  Ralph, A110
NEAL(L)
  John, 139, 197, 296, 359
  Miss, 352
NEBLING
  S. M., 109

NEDROW
Jacob, 329
NEEDHAM
Hugh, 319
NEELY
Joseph, 315
Robert, 275
NEFF
H., 228
Henry, 105
Thomas, 329
NEGELY
James S., 303
NEIL
John, 312
Joseph, 122
NEILSON
Frank, 260
NELSON
Francis, 246, 275
NESBITT
John, 275
Thomas, 263
NEVILLE
Col., A70
Gen., 238
General, 70, A67, A68, A102, A112, A115, A117, A120
John, 67, 78, 82, A43, A65, A78, A85
Joseph, A22, A23, A35, A36
Morgan, 263
Mr., 71
Presley, 81, 82
Pressley, A90
Pressly, 267
NEVIN
R. P., 156
Robert P., 155
NEWALL

Mr., 16
NEWBIT
Robert D., 328
NEWBOLD
Ebert, 335
NEWCOMER
Clark, 327
NEWELL
Archibald, 308
Hugh, A111
NEWKIRK
Elias, 49
Enoch J., 331
Henry, A110
Isaac, 265
Isaac J., 265
NEWLAND
Harrod, 74
NEWMAN
Alfred, 247
Alvin, 319
William, 247
NEWWEL
Hugh, 49
NICHOL
Franklin, 208
Thomas, A56
NICHOLAS
Sampson, 80
NICHOL(L)S
Atkinson, 275
J. A., 327
James, 275
John, 68, 263
Sampson, A107
Thomas, A109
NICHOLSON
Thomas, 254
W. F., 299
NICKERSON
Colin R., 322
Henry W., 312

John W., 322
William, 263
NIMMONS
William, A56
NIMON
William C., 329
NISER
George, 286
NITHERFREED
William, A109
NIVIN
William, A109
NOAH
James L., 322
NOBLE
Isaac B., 299
James, 275
John, 357
T. C., 267
Thomas L., 322
NOEL
Lewis, 326
NOLAND
William, 191
NOLCROFT
Richard, A117
NORCROSS
William, 333
NORRIS
George, 319
Leah, 64
NUTT
Thomas, 325

-O-

OBENBAUGH
Henry C., 317
OBONY
S. C., 309
OCER
Robert, 134

O'CONNER
  Father, 246
ODDBERT
  Arthur, 360
ODENBAUGH
  Henry C., 303
ODEY
  Thomas, 323
O'DONALD
  Thomas B., 328
O'DONNEL
  Walter, 312
OFFICER
  James, 114
  Robert, 132, 134, 144,
    175, 183, 198, 199,
    201, 258, 265, 368
  Thomas, 131, 132,
    133, 134, 175, 256,
    258, 296, 358
OGDEN
  Samuel, A110
O'HARA
  James, 77, 159
  Joseph, 135
  Thomas, 135
  Thomas D., 265., 334,
    345
OKER
  William, 316
OLDS
  Davis, 324
OLFER
  Allen, A108
OLIPHANT
  E. H., 311
  Ethelbert P., 263
  John, A62
OLIVER
  Addison, 263
  Charles, 304
  Frank L., 335

George M., 263
J. Warren, 305
John M., 305
Warren Joseph, 328
William, 304
William L., 125, 328
William R., 134, 260
ONG
  William, 304
ONSTATT
  George, A110
  Lewis, A110
ORLEANS
  Duke of, 348
ORR
  David, 323, 345
  Francis W., 305
  James, 130, 132, 133,
    142, 175, 179, 265,
    296
  Robert W., 226
  Thomas, 79, 317
  W. H., 111
OSBURN
  Robert C., 360
O'SHEA
  Francis Joseph, 191
OSTRANDER
  J., 310
OTTIA
  Anne, 95
OWEN
  George W., 331
OWENS
  William, 263
OZENBAUGH
  L. E., 305

-P-

PACE
  H., 310

PACKER
  Asa, 38
  William F., 38
PADEN
  Edward, 122
  Judson W., 320
  W., 122
PAGE
  Andrew, 171
  Hiram, 89
  James, 171
  John, A29, A31, A33
PAKER
  Michael, A108
PALMER
  Anthony, 35
  Daniel, 275
  Elizabeth, 64
  Henry, 184
  James, 260
  Joseph, 312
  Thomas, A108
PANE
  George A., 263
PARK(E)
  Annie, 49
  John, 254, 312, 323
  Mr., 230
  Susannah, 50
PARKER
  Albert G., 320
  David R., 315
  George, A108, A117,
    A118, A119
  Hamilton, 320
  James, A108, A120
  John, 58, 275
  Mr., 213
  Silas, 275, 319
  William, 60, 62, 67,
    77, 81, 275, A108,
    A111, A115

PARKES
  Thomas, 308
PARKESON
  John, A108
PARKHURST
  Samuel, A108
PARKIN
  Mr., 208, 209
PARKINSON
  -, A73
  B., A69, A70, A117
  Benjamin, 58, 275,
    A111, A119, A120
  Captain, 328
  I., 310
  James, A110, A111
  Joseph, 58, 243, 275,
    A109
  Mr., 244
  R. W., 324
  Robert B., 322
  Washington, 275
  William, A110
PARSHALL
  George E., 326
  James S., 326
  William, 325
PARSONS
  Abraham, 275
PASCAL
  David G., 312
PASSMORE
  George, 258, 260,
    275, 342
PATON
  -, A119
PATTEN
  James R., 337
PATTERSON
  A. O., 171
  Col., 294
  D. F., 207, 351

David F., 263
David S., 147
Elliott, 215
James, 326, 357,
  A111
James L., 275
Jean, 49
John, 110, 309, 312,
  328, A110
Joseph, 49, 112
M., 325
Mary, 50, 64, 230
Mr., 89, 92, 148
Nathaniel, 333
R., 155
R. B., 154, 263, 334
Robert, 226, 259, 275,
  319
Stewart, 329
Susannah, 50
T., 309
Thomas, 198, 251,
  265, 293, 294, 308,
  332, 336, A110,
  A111
Thomas M., 275
William, 104, 232,
  253, 254, 265, 295
PATTISON
  Albertus, 319
  J. H., 144
  James H., 134
  John, 319
PATTON
  Benjamin, 263
  J., 296
  James M., 321
  James R., 307
  Joseph, 265
  Samuel R., 309
  Thomas, A118
  William F., 308

William J., 263
William J. P., 322
William P., 308
PATTRIDGE
  Robert, A109
PAUL
  Col., 289
  George, 263
  James, 289
  Philo, 320
PAULL
  Alfred, 217
  David, 220
  William, 334
PAXTON
  Captain, 322
  John, 321
  John R., 321, 322
  John W., 346
  Samuel B., 304
  Thomas, 306
  Wilson N., 263, 321
PEAK
  -, A53
  Presley, A51
PEASE
  Nicholas, 23
PECAS
  Catharine, 64
PECK
  Harmon M., 321
PECKEROL
  Nancy, 64
PECKHAM
  S. F., 170
PEDEN
  Alexander, 233
  David, 275
PEES
  James B., 275
PEESE
  Zechariah, 122

PEIFFER
  Rev. Mr., 237
PEIRCE
  John N., 311
PENDLETON
  Philip, 19, 22
PENN
  John, 35, A4, A5, A6, A7, A8, A12
  Richard, 35, A9
  T. J., 324
  William, 27, 28, 29, 30, 31, 34, A10, A24, A26
PENNELL
  William P., 307
PENN(E)Y
  J. P., 155
  John P., 263
  John W., 319, 332
PENNOCK
  Joseph, 233
PENSE
  Henry, 328
PENTECOST
  Dorsey, 13, 20, 23, 24, 58, 59, 60, 61, 62, 63, 65, 66, 67, 70, 71, 72, 255, 259, 281, 285, 286, 290
  Dorsey B., 263
  J., 368
  J. Ross, 263
  Joseph, 263
  Joseph H., 316
PEPPER
  Samuel G., 263
PERRET(T)
  George A., 303, 306
PERRINE
  Thomas A., 322

PERRY
  James, 307
PETER
  Indian, 22
PETERS
  James, 315
  Judge, A116, A118
  Richard, 25, A26, A77
PETERSON
  Gabriel, 60, 61, 63, 65, 70
  Josiah, 215
PETHEL
  Henry, 305
PETITT
  Henry H., 307
PETTET
  Isaac, 215
PETTIT
  Charles, 77
  Elymas, 331
  Isaac, A107
  Nathaniel, A111
PEYTON
  Henry, 22
PHELPS
  W. C., 326
PHILLIP(S)
  Betsy, 197
  D., A120
  David, 196, 275, 349, A62
  David B., 322
  David R., 333
  J. F., 307
  James, 300
  James M., 329
  Jesse, 360
  John C., 309
  John L., 265
  Joseph, 196, A110

Perry, 317
Peter, 320
R. O., 314
Rolla O., 311
Rollin O., 303
Rollo O., 313
T. H., 358
Theophilus, 19
Thomas, A109
Thomas H., 310, 336
Wayne J., 322
William, 334
PHILLIS
  Catharine, 50
  Joseph, A109
PHIPPS
  W. H., 184
PICKERING
  Timothy, 116
PIER
  John, 317
PIERCE
  D. A., 228, 235, 236
  Elizabeth, 362
  Jacob L., 326
PIERREPONT
  Governor, 325
PIERSON
  John J., 263
  Thomas, A27
PILTS
  Gasper, A108
PINNEY
  John B., 176
PIPER
  John, 60
PIPES
  S., 325
  Stephen, 361
PLANTS
  Andrew, 319
PLATTER
  Andrew, A109

PLUM(M)ER
  George, 275
  William, A62
PLUMSTEAD
  Clement, 35
PLYMIRE
  James, 305
  W. H., 327
POAGEN
  John, A111
POE
  Adam, 62, 210
POLAND
  Robert M., 305
POLK
  Elias B., 305
  President, 147, 300
POLLOCK
  A. W., 182, 264, 312
  A. Wilson, 361
  D., 307
  Dr., 342
  H. C., 263
  James, 38, 66, 139,
    260, 264, 265, 275
  James W., 322
  John, A110
  Thomas, 108, A110
  William, 319, 322,
    A110
  William H., 319
POMROY
  John, 279
POOLE
  Letitia, 185
POPE
  Harvey, 320
  Levi H., 332
  Martin, 315
PORT
  John T., 347
PORTER

Alexander, A108
Andrew, A35, A36
Col., A33
David R., 37
Elizabeth, 297
George A., 305
George D., 244
Governor, A35
Hugh, 328
J. Noble, 145, 148
James, 183
James L., 139, 183
John, 263
Joseph, 328
Robert, A115, A120
S., 325
Vear R., 331
William, 322, A50,
  A54
William M., 308
POST
  Charles, 345
  Henrietta M., 204,
    205
  J., 149, 325
  S., 149
  W. E., 193
  William, 334
  William B., 319
POTTER
  Alonzo, 186, 246
  Bishop, 187
  Curtus R., 317
  James, A7
  Philip, 143
  S., 325
  Samuel, 173, 185,
    317, 327
  W., 325
POTTS
  G. W., 310
  George W., 304

Samuel, 77
POWELL
  Albert G., 329
  Alexander C., 329
  Esau, 319
  James, 275
POWELSON
  Benjamin F., 322
  Elmore, 308
  William R. H., 322
POWER
  James, 122
  Jesse T., 320
  John, 245
  Michael, A109
  Thomas J., 251
POWERS
  James, 48, A55
  John, A75
  N., 243
PRALL
  Henry, 332
  John A., 332
  John N., 332
  Joshua C., 336
PRATT
  Amos, 297
PRAUL(L)
  Jackson, 319
  William, 176
PRAY
  Thomas, A108
PRESTON
  Clark, 331
  Samuel, 35
PRICE
  Benjamin, A110
  James, A110
  Mr., 138
  R. T., 241
PRIGG(S)
  John, 135, 356

John F. A., A26
Mr., 180
PRINGLE
  John S., 234
PRISSER
  Henry, A8
PRITCHARD
  Samuel, 304
  T., 310
PROCTOR
  Captain, A13
  Gen., 295
  Jackson, 299
  John, 279
PROUDFIT
  James A., 312
  John L., 275
  Moses, 210
PROUDFOOT
  James, A108
PROVINCE
  Benjamin S., 326
  Joseph R., 332
PROWITT
  Alexander, 307
PRY
  David Mc C., 322
  Jacob C., 317
  Robert A., 322
  William Lewis, 322
PRYOR
  Robert, 314
  Wilson, 314
PUMPHREY
  Reason, 362
PURCIL
  I., 310
PURDY
  James L., 210
PURMAN
  Andrew A., 263
PURSELL

Dennis, 348
PURSLEY
  Benjamin, A9
PURVIANCE
  H. A., 5, 314, 315, 351
  Henry, A71
  Henry A., 303, 311
  J., 130
  John, 143, 260, 263
  Thomas S., 314
  Thompson S., 315
PUSEY
  Nathan, 198
PYLE
  Nathan, 368
  Taylor, 329

-Q-

QUAIL
  Charles, 319
  David, 275
  Huston, 263
  J. W., 275
  James, 307
  Robert, 275, 363
  William, 338
QUALK
  Hiram, 333
  Jacob, 332
QUAY
  M. S., 254
QUEEN
  Amos, 326
QUIGG
  Frederick, 309
  James, 335
QUIGLEY
  William, 357
QUILLAND
  Lewis W., 308

QUIMBY
  Samuel, A109
QUINN
  George A., 305
QUIVEY
  James M., 329

-R-

RADCLIFFE
  William J., 319
RAFFERTY
  P., 191
RAHN
  John, 299
RAIL
  John E., 330
RALEIGH
  Walter, 9
RALPH
  John, 263
RALSTON
  David, A112
  David H., 328
  Dr., 245
  George, 322
  John C., 316
  Rev. Mr., 242
  Robert, 78
  Samuel, 243, 244
  Samuel N., 309
  Thomas, 299
RAMAGE
  William, A110
RAMALEY
  David, 351
RAMSAY
  Rev. Dr., 219
RAMSEY
  Alexander, 139, 193, 199
  Calvin, 320

George W., 328
J. C., 160
James, 220, 225
John, 228, 275, 351
Robert, 204
Thomas, 296
William, 122
RANDOLPH
Edm., A79
W. H., 312
RANKIN
Alexander, 303, 306
Christopher, 169
Henry, A109
J. C., 113
James, 122, 275, A109
James G., 113
James S., 322
John, 78
Samuel, 294
Thomas, 68, 81
William, 68, 112
RANNALLS
William, A110
RANNELLS
David, 49
Martha, 50
Ruth, 49
William, 49
RANSEY
Alexander, 175
RAPE
Jacob, A109
Thomas, A109
RATAN
Samuel, A108
RAU
Frederick, 317
RAUHAUSER
H. J., 265
RAVENSCRAFT

James, A109
RAWLE
W., A114, A115, A118, A121
William, A119
RAY
E. A., 361
J. M., 319
J. Milton, 318
John, 335
John M., 318
John Milton, 318
William, 276
REA
A. M., 358
Alexander M., 338
J. L., 338
William, A110, A111
William M., 322
READ
Alexander, 360
Coleman, 77
Collin M., 134
James, 82
John, 26
Joseph, 35
READER
F. Francis, 276
Francis, 267, 276
Frank S., 333
James, 333
READING
Christopher, A109
REAGER
Joseph, 311
Joseph G., 304
REARDON
James, 317
REDD
George, 320
RED(D)ICK
David, 56, 71, 72, 73,
74, 76, 79, 80, 84,
124, 125, 136, 256,
258, 263, 264, 267,
353, 370, 372, A82,
A83, A84
Jonathan, 263
Mr., 78
REED
Agnes, 64
Alexander, 126, 130,
132, 133, 135, 198,
199, 200, 201, 202,
203, 265, 296, 341,
358, 359, 362, 364
C. M., 5, 149, 198,
199, 203, 207
Collin M., 132, 134,
151, 188, 189, 199,
202, 204, 206, 207,
334, 354
Collon M., 200
David, 155, 219, 263
George, 334
George B., 303
George W., 309
James, 100, 101, 138,
169, 199, 200, 201,
267, 296
John, 58, 76, 83, 101,
138, 143, 169, 253,
259, 276, A65, A66,
A111
Joseph, 8, 57, 276,
A20, A21, A22,
A30, A111
President, 278
R. R., 155, 176, 202,
203, 204
Robert R., 154, 178,
200, 202, 219, 251,
254, 276, 318, 319
Samuel, 49

Sarah, 204
Simon H., 317
Thomas B., 336
Thomas R., 276
William, 138
REES(E)
  A. T., 193
  Boon, 314
  John, 314
  Russel, 94
  William, 109
REEVES
  Thomas, 326
REGAN
  Andrew, A110
  P., A65
  Philip, A67
REGESTER
  Isaac M., 329, 330
  John R., 329
REGISTER
  Isaac, 342
REICHTER
  Thomas, 317
REIGART
  E. C., 37
REIGNAMAN
  John M., 309
REIHL
  Egelbert, 299
REILEY
  James, 180
REIMOND
  J. P., 334
REIMUND
  Peter, 132
REMLEY
  John, 311
REMPLETON
  William H., 277
REN(N)O
  Francis, 238

William, 24, 49
RENNYON
  Reuben, A110
RENOLDS
  David, 232
  William, 232
RENTZ
  Charles, 319
RENZ
  Anthony, 192
  Marie Jane, 192
REPSHER
  Jacob, A110
RESASHER
  Jacob, A109
RETTIG
  Samuel, 319
REYNERD
  J., 310
REYNOLDS
  Alexander, A56
  D. L., 276
  H. H., 187
  H. T., 312
  H. W., 135
  Henry T., 312
  Hugh H., 185, 345
  Hugh W., 133
  James, A56
  John, 327
  John H., 332
  Joseph, 180
  Rev. Mr., 191
  Zachariah, 264
RHIENHARDT
  P. H., 351
RHINEHART
  J. H., 307
RHORER
  Daniel, 326
RIAL
  S. H., 334

RICE
  Daniel, A45, A109
  George, 22, A38
  James, A109
  Lorenzo A., 308
RICHARDS
  Henry, 319
  M. Austin, 319
  Thomas S., 307
  William C., 328
RICHARDSON
  A. B., 326
  Richard, 276, A108
  Stephen C., 329
  Thomas, 68, 136, 360,
    366, 367, A108
  William, 179, 299
RICHEY
  William C., 307
RICHIE
  J. B., 308
  Joseph B., 308
  Matthew, 81, 82, 100,
    101
RICHISON
  Jacob, 312
RICHMOND
  -, 214
  David, 308
  Isaac H., 316
  John, 307, A58
  Thomas, 308
RICKEY
  A. D., 334
  Samuel B., 303
RIDDLE
  D. H., 155, 169, 228
  David, 122, 254
  David H., 227
  Hugh, 276
  Isaac V., 122
  John, 276, A109,
    A110

M. B., 227
S. P., 260
Samuel P., 276
RIDER
Daniel, 254
John, 276
Rev. Mr., 246
William A., 314
RIDOUT
J., A26
RIGBY
Titus, 178
RIGDEN
Napoleon B., 325
Sidney, 89
RIGDON
Henry J., 315
Sidney, 92
RIGGS
Cyrus, A108
H. N., 236
Joseph, A108
Mr., 245
William T., 332
RILEY
Edward, 317
J., 325
J. Z., 325
James, A111
Joseph, A111
RIMMEL(L)
Frederick, 333
John, 333
William, 315
RINARD
John, 304
RINE
D. I. K., 184
RINGLAND
George S., 337
J. B., 265
John, 235

Thomas, 252, 253
William, A109
RIPPEY
W. J., 308
RITCHEY
Samuel, 122
Washington, 328
William, 327
RITCHIE
Andrew, A112
Andrew S., 199, 276, 339
C. Frank, 306
Craig, 68, 70, 113, 114, 220, 222, 230, 252, 276, A90
Matthew, 22, 24, 60, 64, 65, 67, 68, 69, 130, 220, 252, 256, 267, 276, 341
RITMAN
Joseph, 332
RITNER
John B., 303
Joseph, 37, 170, 253, 293
RITTENHOUSE
David, A21, A29, A31, A32, A33, A34, A35, A36
RITTER
John, 297
RIZER
David, 328
ROACH
James M., 314
ROBB
Ebenezer, 276
George W., 331
James, 159, 351
John, A111
Robert, A111

Samuel, A111
William L., 276
ROBBINS
Daniel, A110
L., 217
ROBERTS
Dickerson, 253, 258
Dickinson, 265, 276, A108
Edward, 314
J. B., 183
J. D., 363
J. S., 170
John T., 323
Leonard, A108
Leonard A., 326
Lewis, 263
Richard P., 318
Samuel, 255
William, 307, 309
ROBERTSON
A. S., 193
Alex, A109
Elijah, A110
Elisha, A111
George, 317
J. L., 308
Samuel, A111
Theodore, 317
ROBINSON
Alexander, 94, 245, 319
Doctor, A115
George, A72
James, 183, 325, 326, A111
John, 49, A111
Marshall, 331
R. T., 246
S. B., 183, 351
Terry, 197
Tyre, 324
William, 134

ROBSON
George, 330
H., 330
ROCKWELL
Elijah, 315
Jacob, 315
Rev. Mr., 243
ROCKY
George C., 315
RODE
J. G., 334
RODGERS
Charles, A51
Ebenezer, 182
Elizabeth, A49
H. Gould, 263
Moses, A110
Richard, A8
Thomas B., 318
Thomas L., 263
William, A110
ROE
Ezekiel, 58
ROGERS
Andrew, A108
Charles, 327
Hugh, A111
Joseph H., 329
Rev. Dr., A59
Rowland, A109
S. S., 338
Samuel, 238
Samuel J., 327
Thomas, 81, A109
ROLL
Mathias, A108
ROLLISON
B., 310
ROLSTON
John, A109
ROMANS
Jacob, A111

RONEY
Alexander, 341
Hercules, 79, A57
J., 325
James, 109
ROOP
Samuel, 319
ROOT
Captain, 171
ROOTES
George, 22
ROPE
Jacob, A109
ROSE
Charles E., 331
Franklin A., 317
Gales S., 319
Isaac, A110
J., 310
William B., 135
William H., 308, 328
ROSENBERGER
A. B., 308
ROSS
A. M., 312
Andrew, 22
General, 295
George, 55
Hugh, 263
James, 35, 36, 56, 78, 100, 130, 263, 347, 348, 368, A75
John, 308
Jonathan, 79
Josephus, 332
Major, 290
Matthew, 312
Moses, 312
Mr., 84, 202
Nancy, A57
Robert E., 329
Thomas W., 324

Timothy, 276
ROSSEL
Job, 215
ROSWELL
Henry B., 192
ROTHRICK
William, 317
ROWE
Adam, A48, A49
Daniel, A49
Jacob, A48, A49, A55
Mrs., A49
ROWLAND
James, 169
ROWLEE
Constant, A108
ROWLEY
John, 311, 312
ROYALL
Captain, 349
RUARK
Shadrack, A110
RUBLE
David, 70, 319
RUCH
Michael, A90
RUDGE
George, 317
RUF(F)NER
J., 335
William, 322
RUNYAN
Hill, 263
RUPLE
C. M., 141
Charles H., 345
Charles M., 263
I. Goodrich, 135
J. B., 149
J. C., 149
J. G., 334

James, 132, 143, 198,
199, 201, 204, 258,
259, 295, 364, 368
James B., 5, 133, 256,
342, 347, 351
John G., 263
W. L., 149
RUSH
Benjamin, 357
James, 133, 134, 192,
A109
Michael, 305
Peter, A108
Randolph, 305
Robert G., 328
RUSSEL(L)
Abraham, A109
Andrew, A56
Andrew K., 169
Felix, 333
Hannah, 64
James A., 320
Simon S., 317
Thomas, 317
W., 183
RUTAN
J. S., 263
James S., 252
William, 320
RUTH
James R., 260, 263,
334, 369
John, A109
Samuel, 258, 323
RUTMAN
John, 93
RYAN
B. F., 307
Cephas A., 305
George, 323
James, 321
Joseph, 215

Thaddeus, 335
RYDER
Rev. Mr., 242
RYERSON
Mr., 84
Thomas, 80, 85, 276

-S-

SADLER
Lewis, A108
ST. CLAIR
Arthur, 35, 264, A10,
A11, A12, A16,
A41
David, 264
Jesse, 277
ST. THOMAS
JENIFER
Dan of, A26
SAMLLEY
John, 319
SAMMS
John, 233
SAMPLE
Cunningham, 263
David, 260, 263
George, 330
Joseph M., 309
Matthew, 359
William, 199, 256,
258, 265, 293, 295,
350, 351
SAMPSON
A. C., 345
John, 266
John P. C., 263
SAMUELS
Gilbert, A110
John, 276
SANDERS
John, 50

John W., 320
M., 345
Michael, 276, 345
Silas A., 319
Simeon S., 320
William, 276
SANSOM
Iram F., 320
J. G., 105, 181
Joseph G., 181
SAPPINGTON
J., 299
SARGENT
Hiram, 327
Thomas, 327
SARRAT(T)
James F., 345, 347
SARVER
John, 307
SATTERFIELD
James, 227, A111
SAUNDERS
J., 325
John, 331
Mr., 366
S., 324
William, 317
SAUPPE
John G., 308
SAWHILL
Thomas H., 312
SAYER(S)
Ephraim, A110
James, 319
James P., 263, 318
Lemuel, A110
SAYRES
Ezra, 376

SCANLON
John, 192
John O. G., 246
SCHAFFER
David, 309
Jacob, 334
SCHELL
Joseph, 312
SCHMIDT
Charles, 276
SCHOENTHAL
Henry, 345
SCHOONMAKER
James M., 323
SCHULTZ
David, 183
SCOFIELD
Joseph, A110
SCOTT
A. B., 267
A. D., 276
Alexander, 79, 87, 228, 256, 257, 259, A108
Alexander W., 303
Andrew, 332
Archer, A108
Benjamin F., 304
Brown, 307
Col., 296
David, 328
Elizabeth, 108
Finley, 48
George K., 126
Henderson, 322
Hugh, 40, 48, 65, 76, 122, 124, 136, 276
J. H., 334
J. W., 155
James, 79, 101
James D., 307
James M., 307

James S., 304
John, 113, 122, 133, 184, 215, 276, A110, A111
John W., 169, 170, 178, 189, 334
Joseph, 40, 74, 276, A109, A110, A115
Joseph A., 330
Joseph L., 361
Josiah, 77, 175, A58
Josiah N., 276
Levi, 327, 328
Margaret, 130
Miss, 352
Moses T., 334
Mr., 108
Mrs. Peggy, 129
Parker, 276, 369
Patrick, 121, 122
Robert M., 305
Samuel, 265, 276, A110, A111
T. R., 309
Thomas, 57, 63, 64, 66, 69, 72, 76, 77, 78, 79, 80, 86, 87, 150, 250, 252, 256, 257, 263, 276, 281, 367, A19, A43 W., 95
W. Wallace, 307
William, 19, 58, 59, 215, 276, 312, 322
Winfield, 300
SCRIBER
F., 324
SCULL
John, A72
Mr., A66
SEAMAN
Alexander, 135, 199

SEAMAN
Alexander, 207
SEAMAN(S)
J. W., 334
James, 334
James S., 306
John, 181
John W., 144
Joseph, 130
Thomas, 135
SEARIGHT
William, 363
SEARS
William, 328
SEATON
I. D., 183
Rev. Mr., 238
William, 259
SEDGWICK
Thomas, 276, A73, A115
SEDICKER
David, 188
SEES(E)
James, 323
Nathaniel, 322
SEEVERS
Abraham, A109
SEGBY
Jonas, A110
SEIGRIST
George W., 307
SELDEN
George, 263
SEMPLE
David, 22
SEMULT
James B., 328
SENEY
Joshua, 263
SERGE(A)NT
Edward, 79

John, 36, 57
Mr., 211, 212, 213
SHAFFER
  Augustus, 333
  Joseph E., 317
  Joseph M., 309
  William, 327
SHALER
  Charles, 263
  S., 149
SHALLENBERGER
  John B., 329, 330
SHANAFEET
  Thomas, 324
SHANER
  David, 358
SHANKS
  Elizabeth, 64
SHANNON
  Dutton, 105, 260
  Isaac, A111
  James, 132, 134, 179
  James R., 185
  John, 263
  Robert K., 135
  Samuel, 276
  William K., 345
SHARP
  Cephas D., 303, 319, 320
  Christopher, 368
  Edward, 22
  George, 85
  Isaac, 276, 320, 346
  Peter, A110
  W. W., 346, 358
SHARPE
  David, 105
  Horatio, A26
  Thomas, 299
  W. W., 318
SHAVER

Thomas, A109
SHAW
  John, A110
  Joseph, 104, 215, 312
  W. D., 312
  William, 26, 104
SHEAFF
  H. H., 307
  Henry, 343
SHEAFFER
  J. S., 180
  John, 151, 180
SHEALER
  Samuel, 334
SHEARER
  Andrew, 134, 139, 200, 260
  Captain, 282
  Henry, 139, 203
  William, 71, A111
SHEBOSH
  Minister, 285
SHEETS
  J. B., 325
  William, 322, 329
  William, 330
SHEHAN
  Patrick, 191, 192
SHELBY
  Captain, A27
SHEPHARD
  David, 317, A43
SHEPHERD
  David, 16, 68, 303
SHEPLAR
  Robert C., 324
SHEPLER
  James, 246
  Robert C., 335
SHERER
  Hugh, 49
SHERHOLTZ

Herman, 326
SHERLEY
  Widow of John, 26
SHERMAN
  W. T., 315
SHERRARD
  William, 131, 175
SHERRICK
  Joseph, 320
SHIELD(S)
  B. F., 309
  David, 132, 135, 138, 139, 151, 185, 198, 359
  John, A116, A117, A118
  Mr., A57
  Thomas L., 263
  W., 311
SHILBER
  John, A109
SHINDLES
  Samuel K., 322
SHINN
  Asa, 181
SHIPLEY
  Presley H., 319
  Richard P., 328
SHIPPEN
  Edward, 25, 34
  Joseph, A9
  Judge, 86
SHIRAS
  George, 160, 263
SHIVELY
  William, 330
SHOOK
  J., 193
SHOTWELL
  Rev. Mr., 243
SHOUSE
  Captain, 293
  John, A109

SHOWALTERS
  William, 333
SHRECKONGOST
  L., 346
SHULTZ
  J. Andrew, 36
SHUNE
  Benjamin, A110
SHUNK
  Francis R., 37
SHUSTER
  Jacob, A110
  Lewis F., 299
  Samuel, A108
SHUTTERLY
  John J., 323, 343
  Lewis, 376
SIBERT
  James, 320
  John, 320
SICKLES
  R. H., 317
SICKMAN
  Alafred M., 304
SIEGFRED
  Simeon, 215
SIKES
  Nehemiah, 333
SILVEY
  Adam, 134, 260
  George W., 305
SIMCOX
  William S., 317
SIMISON
  James C., 263
SIMMONS
  Laura, 205
SIMMS
  Charles, 22
SIMON(S)
  Andrew, A108
  Michael, 95
  N., A109
  Samuel, 332
SIMONSON
  John, 131, 175, 291
SIMONTON
  J. S., 170
  Professor, 168
SIMPKINS
  R., 309
SIMPSON
  Dr., 214
  G. F., 324
  J. Taylor, 324, 335
  James, 232
  Jeremiah, 219
  Mr., 118
  R. L., 276
SIMS
  Charles, A18
  James, 323
SINCLAIR
  Charles, 327
  James B., 327
  John Casper, 130
  John M., 326
  Leander, 305
  Mr., A23
  Samuel, 22, 327
SINGER
  John, 49
SINGHORSE
  Abraham, A112
SINSABAUGH
  Hiram, 181
SIRES
  William, 312
SKINNER
  Rev. Mr., 123
  W. B., 95
SLAGLE
  Jacob, 133, 134, 175,
    198, 199, 200, 202,
    203, 205, 206, 207,
    256, 264, 339, 362
SLANGER
  John S., 303
SLATER
  Theodore F., 133
  William, 103
SLAVE
  Ben, 362
  Dinah, 362
  Lot, 362
  Suke, 362
  Zelph, 362
SLEIGHTER
  Henry, 305
SLEMENS
  William, 259, 276
SLETTE
  John, A109
SLOAN
  James, 121
  James G., 322
  John C., 254
  Rev. Dr., 313
SLOPPY
  Henry, 317
SLUSHER
  Henry, 332
  Thomas, 332
SMALL
  John, A110
SMALLEY
  Emmor, 320, 3320
SMALLMAN
  Thomas, 13, 15, 22
SMILEY
  James, 308
  James E., 333, 334
  John, A107
  William, 49, 76, 276
SMILIE
  John, 70, 251

SMITH
A. V., 326
Abraham, 95
Adam, A108
Alexander V., 332
Amos, 327
Andrew, 122, 327, A108
Col., 77
D., A42
David S., 263
Dennis, 93
Devereaux, A13, A19
E. R., 99
Ebenezer, 49, 360, A111
Edward R., 258, 361, A56
Eli, 314
Frank, 326
Frank B., 332
General, A81
George, A75, A90
George E., 276
George W., 317
Hannah, 197
Henry, 276, 299, 315
Hiram, 89
J. P. K., 325
J. W., 313
James, 122, 176, 276, 279, 328, A19, A111
James B., 331
James C., 328
James M., 217, 243
James W., 345
Jehu P., 265
John, 68, 276, 330, 357
John H., 276, 327, 360
John M., 156, 360
Jonathan B., 54, 263
Joseph, 19, 89, 90, 91, 106, 108, 137, 150, 227, 232
Lewis E., 276, 332, 369
Martin, A108
Mays, 169
Merriweather, A20
Mr., 77
Nicholas, 114
Rev., 220
Rev. Dr., 19
Robert, 276
Rudolph, 315
Samuel, 277, A111
Samuel H., 89
Sheriff, 369
Thomas, 264
W., 104, 148, 149
W. M., 184
W. T., 311
William, 49, 83, 103, 122, 125, 133, 134, 144, 147, 148, 155, 193, 193, 198, 199, 207, 224, 225, 277, 321, 343, 344, 347, A108, A111
William D., 170
William F., 308
William W., 187, 334
SMURR
Reason, 311
SMYLIE
William, 174
SNEE
J. M., 345
Thomas, 345
SNELL
Frederick, 345

SNODGRASS
Rev., 175
Samuel, 360
SNYDER
Christian, 326
David M., 329
Demas S., 327
George W., 326
H., 228
Henry, 226, 330
John, 331
Peter, 188
Samuel, 36
Simon, 36, 296
SOUGHERLAND
William, A75
SOULSBY
Cuthbert, 333
SOUTHARD
Abraham, A110
SOWERS
Andrew J., 332
Daniel W., 320
George, 259
SPARKS
S. M., 245
Samuel M., 245
SPAULDING
John, 92
Mr., 91, 92
Mrs., 91
Solomon, 89, 90, 91, 92, 93
SPAYD
John, 36
SPEAR(S)
Hugh, 78
Joseph, A19
T., A69, A70
Thomas L., 220
William, 223
William F., 332

SPEER(S)
  Jacob B., 314
  John, 322
  Rev., 193
  Rev. Mr., 249
  Robert, A109
  Robert L., 322
SPENCE
  George, 297
SPENCER
  James, A9
  John, 105
  Timothy, 83, 106, A111
SPIERS
  Thomas, A117, A120
SPOHN
  H. S., 314
SPOTTSWOOD
  Alexander, 11
SPRIGG(S)
  J. M., 334
  Jackson, 135, 176, 188
  James, 133, 257, 258
  James C., 305
  Joseph M., 181, 345
SPRINGER
  C. J., 277
SPROULS
  Arthur W., 305
  Hugh, 72
SPROWLS
  Alexander, 267
  Cyrus, 315
  George, 323
  Jesse M., 323
SQUIER
  Odel, 193, 257
STACHER
  Lewis, A110
STACKER

Christopher, A111
  John, 331
  Peter, 330
STAGLE
  Jacob, 133
STALEY
  Oliver, 323
STANDLEY
  John, 130
  Rachel, 361
STANLEY
  Samuel, 99
STANSBERRY
  James, 320
STANTON
  Thaddeus, 135
  Thadeus, 264
STAPLES
  John L., 338
STAR
  George, 323
STARER
  Thomas R., 307
STARR
  Joseph, 328
  W. P., 331
STATTERS
  W. H., 327
STAUB
  Adam, 314
STAUNTON
  David, 357
STECK
  J. F., 334
STEDMAN
  Alexander, 25
STEEL(E)
  David, 22
  John, A7, A8
  Rev. Dr., 235
  Rev. Mr., A9
STEEN

Isaiah, 131
STEEP
  Francis J. L., 305
  Thomas M., 305
STELLE
  Alexander, A109
STEPHENS
  Alexander H., 302
STEPHENSON
  George N., 317
  James, 253
  John, 13, 24, 26, 49, 67, 170, 252, 265
  John E., 317
  Joseph, 358
  Moses, 277
  Rev. Mr., 103
  William, 20
STERLING
  Hugh, 22
STERRET
  James, 140
STERRITT
  James P., 155, 159
STEVENS
  Abraham, A110
  James, 133, 199, 357
  William, 198
STEVENSON
  D. K., 343
  J., 104
  James, 103, 251
  John, 58, 62, 69, 122, 277, A108, A111
  Josias, 104
  Robert, 277, A75
STEWART
  Andrew, 170, 311
  Arabella, 9
  B. S., 351
  Benjamin S., 264
  Dr., 321

George, 304, A26
J., 264, 325
J. D., 311
James A., 277
John, 199, 260
John G., 328
John M., 322
Joseph, 328
K. J., 184
R. L., 322
Rev., 185
Samuel, 321
Samuel S., 335
Thomas, 328, 334
Thomas H., 335
Thomas M., 324
William, 78, 101, 309
William B., 322
STICK IN THE MUD
  Tom, 130
STILES
  Joseph, 60, 61, 66
STILLEY
  John B., 226
STILLWELL
  A., 325
STILWAGON
  Jacob, A109
STOCKDALE
  John, 264
  Robert, 277
STOCKING
  James, 303
STOCKLEY
  Thomas, 73
STOCKTON
  John, 48, 169, 217,
    232, A55, A109
  Joseph, 222
  L. W., 135
  Mr., 174
  Robert, 173

T. C. M., 337
Thomas, 175
William A., 322
STOCKWELL
  James, 319
  John, 319
  William, 319
STOEFUL
  John, 345
STOELZLE
  David, 299
STOKELEY
  Thomas, A73
STOKELY
  Captain, 66, 281
  Nehemiah, A62
  Samuel, 264
  Thomas, 69, 78, 81,
    86, 101, 103, 130,
    251, 252, 257, 267,
    277, 283, A90
STOKES
  William A., 264
STOLLARD
  William, 323
STONE
  Edmund, 327
  Elias, 123
  Elizabeth, 123
  John, 49
  Thomas A., 320
STONEROAD
  Joel, 118, 210
STOODAY
  George, A108
STOOPS
  W. H., 309
STORER
  Frank R., 345, 360
  Henry, 327
  John, 254
  Richard, A109

S., A109
T. R., 358
Thomas, 337
William, A109
STORK
  William, 317
STORMENT
  John, 307
STORY
  John, 71
STOUT
  Christian, A109
STOVER
  Francis R., 320
STOY
  W. H., 135
  William H., 306
STRAIGHT
  Anne, 64
STRAIN
  John, 49, A109
  R. F., 334
  Samuel, A109
  Thomas, 49
STRANGER
  Isaac N., 317
STRAWHAN
  Robert, A65
STREAM
  James G., 366
STREAN
  James G., 129, 136,
    200, 351, 354
  R. F., 351
  Robert F., 129, 188,
    376
STREATER
  L. P., 196
STREATOR
  L. P., 207
STREINER
  John, 325

STROOP
  Solomon, 317
STROSNIDER
  A. J., 307
STROUD
  James, 267, 277
STROUS
  S. S., 358
STUART
  James, 366, A111,
    A115, A120
  John, A38
  Mr., 366
  Robert, A109
  William, A110
STUDY
  Michael, A110
STULL
  William, 314
STUMP
  Irwin C., 338
STUNTZNER
  Lewis, 299
SULLIVAN
  Andrew, A110
  Samuel, 331
SUMMEY
  Boyd E., 331
SUMNEY
  David, 322
  John T., 322, 360
SUNDERLAND
  Angas, 50
  Jane, 50
SUNEDECKER
  J., 314
SURG
  Frederick, 331
SURGEON
  M. D., 324
SUTCHELL
  J. S., 244

SUTE
  Philip, A8
SUTHERLAND
  John, 277, A108
  W. R., 369
SUTHERLING
  John, A112
SUTMAN
  Aaron, 331
  John M., 331
SUTTON
  Andrew, 253
  David, 95, A107,
    A108
  General, 171
  I., 228
  James, 94
  John, 307
  R. R., 246
  Reuben, 304
  Richard, A110
  William B., 330
SWABE
  Samuel, 277
SWAGLER
  Jacob, A108
SWAIN
  Thomas, 196
SWAN
  Mr., 150
  William, 5, 150, 351
SWART
  A. J., 320
  Amos, 320
  H. C., 320
  Henry C., 319
SWARTZ
  A. J., 346
  Andrew J., 303
  H. C., 346
  Henry, A8
SWARTZWELDER

  Marshal, 264
SWEARINGEN
  Andrew, 24, 59, 64,
    67, 70, 84, 86, 101,
    173, 175, 264, 277
  Mr., 174
  Thomas, 260
  Van, 40, 59, 64, 65,
    67, 70, 124, 130,
    136, 175, 258, 367
SWEEN(E)Y
  Alexander, 180, 198,
    199, 200, 201, 203,
    205, 322
  John, 334
  John R., 303
  Sample, 132, 134,
    182, 200, 204, 334
SWEIGERT
  P., 188
SWEITZER
  Bowman, 264
  J. Bowman, 185
SWENGER
  G., 311
SWICKARD
  Daniel, 260
SWIFT
  Elisha P., 177
SWIHART
  Joseph, 320
SWISSLER
  Charles, 188
SYMCOCK
  John, 34

-T-

TAGGART
  David L., 321
  James, 265
  M. R., 335
  Robert J., 317, 337

TAGGERT
S., 108
TALBERT
Richard, 277
TALBOT
Richard, A114
TANNEHILL
John, A109
Josiah, A72
TANNIHILL
A., A117
TAPPAN
Kake, 28
TARPINE
William, 74
TARR
John, 264
TATE
Samuel, 227
TAYLOR
A. W., 252
B. F., 317
Benjamin L., 330
George, 99, 260, 277, 295
Griffith, 330
Griffith D., 305
Henry, 58, 61, 65, 68, 74, 76, 81, 84, 85, 87, 136, 174, 255, 256, 277, 305, A43
Henry M., 315
Isaac, A27
James, 264, A110, A111
Jesse C., 303, 317, 337
John, 99
John B., 330
Malachi, 196
Mr., 82, 84, 338
President, 147

Robert, 83
Robert G., 314, 315
Samuel, 277
Samuel O., 264
William, 135, 145
William H., 126
Z., 300
TEAGARDEN
A., 325
Eberhardt, 332
George W., 320
William, 20, 320
William H., 320
TEAL
Isaac, 343
TEEDYUSCUNG, 127
TEEPLE
Clinton, 330
Isaac, A109
J. M., 330
Thomas W., 331
TEETERS
Elisha, A110
TEEVES
John S., 329
TELFORD
Robert, 196
TEMPLE
Rev. Mr., 237
TEMPLETON
Aaron, 317
David A., 316
J. A., 149
John, 135, 145
John A., 149
Joseph, 200
Joseph H., 303, 316
M., 312
Matthew, 338
S. M., 149, 334
Samuel M., 303
Thomas B., 317

W. F., 303
William F., 264, 316
TENBROOKE
Rev. Mr., 237
TEN(N)ELL
John, 232, A114
TENNEY
John P., 192
TENNILLE
Daniel, A111
George, A111
John, A111
TERRY
James, A73
William R., 345
THARP
Ezekiel, 193
Hiram, 320, 332
THINER
Louis, 299
THINKERD
James, A109
John, A109
THIRKIELD
Alfred, 134
THOMAS
Captain, 293
Edmund, A110
George, 35
Governor, 46
James, 322
John, 215
Liverton, 109, A110
Philip, 333
S. O., 314
W. H., 247
William, 109
THOMPSON
Allen, 297
Andrew, 312, 317
Armour, 327
Charles, 285

David, 49, 250, A109
Dr., 220
Elizabeth, 50
George, 309
George W., 317
H. H. B., 305
Isaac, 260
Israel, 23
J. C., 193, 331
J. H., 307
J. Ross, 334
Jacob L., 312
James B., 317
John, 345, A9, A108, A110
Jonathan, A110
Joseph R., 241
Parker, 178
R. B., 312
R. L., 334
Robert, 58, 277, 303, 332, A109, A112
Robert L., 303
Samuel, 342
Samuel F., 317
Scheffer, 334
Thomas, 312, A109, A110
W. R., 358
William, 49, A108, A109
William W., 303
THORN
  Charles, 181
THORNBURG
  Adam A., 328
  John S., 328
THORNLEY
  Thomas, A110
THRONGMORTEM
  J., 325
THROP

Samuel, 317
TIBBY
  George, 307
TILGHMAN
  James, A14
  William, 36
TILTON
  C. W., 95
  Daniel, 215
  John, 215
TINGOOCQUA, 127
TIPTON
  William, 105
TISDELL
  J. B. W., 196
TITUS
  Margaret, A49
TODD
  A. M., 178, 334
  Alexander M., 264
  Edward, 259, 291
  James, 264, A111
  John, 220, A110
  M. L., 357
  Oliphant M., 210
  Robert K., 264
  W. C., 309
  William, A90
TOM THE TINKER, A65, A66
TOMLINSON
  W. F., 264
TOMPOH
  George, 83
TOPPIN
  John, 323
TOWER
  E. W., 245
TOWN
  Edward O., 215
  Eli C., 215
  Ezra, 215

TOWNSEND
  Cyrus, 322
  Elijah, 277
  John, 95
  Joseph, 95
  Mrs. Joseph, 95
TREACLE
  Stephen, 68
TRE(A)DWELL
  James B., 312, 313
TRIMBLE
  John, 309
TROESHER
  Charles F., 330
TROXALL
  Elias S., 326
TRUSLER
  Samuel, 332
TRUSSEL
  George W., 323
  Manson, 215
TRUSSLER
  John, 331
TRUXAL
  Foster H., 333
  John W., 333
  N. W., 332, 333
TUCKER
  Isaac, 320
  Jonathan, 319
TUELLEG
  Joseph, A110
TURNER
  E. H., 126
  G., A120
  Judge, A119
  Robert, 34
  Samuel, 328
  Theodore, 334
  Theodore M., 335
TURVEY
  John, 83

TWEED
William, 259
TWINING
E. H., 170
TYGARD
Abraham, A8

-U-

UL(L)ERY
Jacob, 332
Stephen, 99
UNDERWOOD
Cyrus, 257
Elihu, 333
G., 332
H. C., 345
William, 181
William H., 303
UPPERMAN
Lewis, 327
URIE
John, 256, 259, 297
Samuel, 252, 277

-V-

VALENTINE
D. C., 334
VALLANDI(N)GHAM
George, 13, 59, 60, 259, 264
VAN DYKE
James, 320
James B., 319
VAN GILDER
J. G., 332
S. J., 337
VAN HORN
John S., 346

VAN METRE
Henry, 347
VAN VOORHIS
Abraham, 335
I. S., 358
VANCE
Alexander H., 312
Anne, 49
David, 232
Henry, 122, 309
Isaac, 259, 277, 303
Isaac N., 318
James, 122
John, 79, 122, 293, 294, A108
Joseph, 49, 253, A108
Joseph Colville, 50
Major, 294
Samuel, 176, 200
Sarah, 50
William, 49, 253, 259, 294, A111
William M., 334
VANDYKE
J. B., 346
VANEMAN
Joseph, 277
L., 361
Thomas, 105
VANEWAN
Joseph, 266
VANGILDER
George J., 311
Jefferson G., 304
VANHORN
William, A109
VANKIRK
Andrew J., 320
H. J., 5, 133, 190, 191, 254, 255, 267, 312, 338, 369
Harvey J., 257, 264, 311

Henry, 195
Joseph, 260, 266
Mr., 141
Nelson, 135, 140, 177
Simeon, 319
Theophilus, 304
William, 5, 256, 319, 332
VANMETRE
Henry, 70, 259, 277
Jesse, 74
VANSBINDER
John, 277
VANVOORHIS
Abraham, 277, 327
Daniel, A109
Isaac, 245
J. S., 254
Samuel, A109
VARNDELL
Charles, 315
VARRO
F. P., 334
VAUGHN
Joseph, 122
VEATCH
N. X., 343
VEECH
James, 6, 155, 160, 264, A26, A27, A30, A38
VERNON
Persifor F., 277
VERVALSON
John, A8
VINNAGE
Adam, A108
VIRGIN
W. H., 314
VIRTUE
A., 105
Robert, 323

VISINER
  Charles, 352
VOLTENBURG
  James, 321
VORE
  Isaac W., 277
VOSE
  George B., 170
  Professor, 168
VOWELL
  J. B., 191
  John B., 190
  John D., 226

-W-

WADDIE
  S. D., 324
WADDINGTON
  William, 317
WADELL
  Andrew, A110
WADSWORTH
  General, 293
WAGNER
  Edward, A115, A117
WAGONER
  John, A111
WAIBLE
  John, 312
  William, 312
WAKEFIELD
  Rev., 99
WALBOLD
  F., 299
WALDRON
  John, 135
  P., 135
WALKER
  -, A41
  A. E., 265
  Alexander E., 277

Conrad, 20
David, 264
Gabriel, 49
George J., 303
Isaac, A115
J., 325
James, 140, 260
John H., 341
John N., 260
Mrs., A44
Robert, 83, A110
Stephen D., 264
Thomas, 135, 333, 345, 347, 356
Thomas J., 133
William H., 316
WALL
  Brisben, 310
  Frederick, 193
  Isaac, 319
WALLACE
  George, A71, A72
  Joseph, 307
  Judge, A70, A116
  Moses, 49
  Oliver M., 277, 361
  Richard, 283
  Robert, A109, A110
  Samuel, 309
  W., 184, 311
  William, 40, 49, 72, 74, 81, 87, 108, 220, 226, 252, 258, 277, A90, A109, A112
WALLANDINGHAM
  George, 70
WALLER
  James, A8
WALTER(S)
  Christopher, A108
  Conrad, 20

WALTON
  Ames, 314
  Henry, 314
  James, 135
  S. M., 346
WALTZ
  Colin, 319
WARD
  Edward, 13, 22
  Henry B., 299
  James, A111
  John W., 361
  Stephen, 333
  Stephen H., 333
  Thomas, A111
WARFIELD
  Chloe, 197
WARNER
  A. J., 306
WARNOCK
  William, 357
WARRAN
  H. A., 346
WARREN
  John, 311
  Thomas, 24
WARRICK
  George M., 356
  George W., 370
  W. W., 356
WARRING
  John, 357
WASHINGTON
  General, 82, 126, 177, 278
  George, 63, 100, 101, 341, A79, A83, A90
  Martha, 177
WATERMAN
  John, 181
WATERS
  Rev. Mr., 242

WATKINS
  James, 315
  Lewis, 311, 314, 315
  W. B., 181
  William H., 327
WATSON
  -, 310
  Andrew, A72
  David, 334, 335
  David T., 264
  George, 264
  Henry, 320
  J. A., 311
  J. H., 311
  James, 198, 199, 208, 264, 332, A111
  John, 115, 222, 225, 227, 264, 266, 313
  John M., 322
  Margaret, 115
  Robert, 283
  Thomas, 254, 265
  William, A111
  William S., 320
WATT
  Joseph, A110
WAUGH
  John H., 264
  Joseph, 170
  Simon, A110
  William, 253, 254, 260, 264, 369
WAY
  Stephen, 130
WAYANT
  Cornelius, A109
  Peter, A109
WAYNE
  Anthony, 149
  Isaac, 36
WEAVER
  Abraham, 333
  F., 326
  Isaac, 251, 252
  J., 333
  J. W., 105
  James, A111
  James M., 327
  James P., 322
  John, 333, 338
  Joshua, 322
  Mr., 249
  Rev., 193
  T. J., 321
  Thomas, 322
WEBB
  Edward, 359
  Theodore S., 305
WEBSTER
  John, A67
WEEMS
  -, 290
WEIBLEY
  William, 312
WEIGLEY
  Joseph, 264
WEILLS
  Abraham, 188
  John S. C., 264
WEIR
  Joseph, A108
WEIRICH
  Jacob, 188, 253
  John S., 317
  Samuel, 140, 334
  Samuel K., 260, 277
WEISS
  Anthony, 299
  L., 285
WELCH
  Andrew M., 323
  Daniel, A110
  J. M., 312
  James M, 312
  John, A110
  Joseph, 312
  Louis, 345
  Lt., 329
  R. C., 240
  Robert, 114
  Robert C., 328
  William, 114
WELLS
  A., A114
  Alexander, 232, A111
  Benjamin, A64, A67, A112
  George, A111
  Grafton, 308
  Henry, A111
  Hiram, 333
  James I., 314
  Jefferson, 277
  John, A65
  John G., 307, 308
  Joseph, 78
  Richard, A111
  Richard of James, A110
  William, 277, A111
WELSH
  Christopher C., 320
  Christy, 315
  Joseph, 254
  Joseph B., 277
  Thomas, 327
  William, 265, 277
WELTNER
  John R., 311
WEST
  John, 181, 317, 327
  Mr., 237
  Samuel K., 332
  W. C., 247
  W. W., 226

WESTERMAN
J. H., 309
Thomas, 309
WESTLEY
John P., 334
WESTON
John, A108
WEYGANDT
Henry, 188
WHANN
Samuel, 174
WHARTON
Thomas, 35, A20
WHEATLEY
Francis L., 305
WHEELER
Charles, 95, 193, 196, 197
James N., 330
Ulysses, 323
WHEELIN
Rev. Bishop, 192
WHERRY
David, 135
James, 277
John, 317
Joseph, 72, 173, 175
Mr., 99, 174
Samuel, 175
WHITAKER
Samuel, A108
WHITE
Alexander, 277
Benjamin, 252, 277, A90
Bishop, 370
Charles, 334
David, 139, 140, 322
David A., 330
Francis M., 326
J., 99
J. W. F., 180, 264, 351
James, 130, 277, 297, 323, 327
James A. S., 329
James S., 304
John, 58, 67, 103, 180, 219, 264, 277, 315, A108
John C., 317
Richard, 332
Right Rev. Bishop, 184
Robert, 114, 330
Robert M., 226
Rt. Rev. Bishop, 238
S. F., 264
Samuel H., 330
Thomas, 323
Thomas J., 328
William, 31
William H., 330
William P., 330
William T., 328
William, 331
Z. A., 338
WHITEEYES
George, 370
WHITEHEAD
William, 95
WHITEHILL
John, A109
Robert, 77, 264
WHITELY
Frederick, 121
WHITESIDE
James, 341
WHITLACK
Rev. Mr., 249
WHITMER
Christian, 89
David, 89
Jacob, 89
John, 89
Peter, 89
WHITTAKER
R., 309
WHITTEN
J. B., 110
WICK
William, 227
WICKERHAM
Adam, 244
William, 245
WICKERSHAM
Adam, 325, A109
James S., 330
Peter, A109
W. H. H., 304
William H., 329
WIER
Adam, 121, 175, 368
Hugh, 322
Joseph, 266
Samuel, 121, A108
Thomas, A108
WILBY
R., 309
WILES
J. C. S., 334
W. M. L., 334
William, 305
WILEY
Cephas, 330
Elizabeth, 192
Hugh, 130
James, A109
John, 134, 176
John W., 318
John Wishart, 264
Joseph, 50
Martha, 178
Thomas, A111
W. C., 149
William, 180
William C., 361

WILGUS
  Lorenzo D., 317
WILKEN
  John, A111
WILKIN(S)
  Abraham H., 328
  Edward, 334
  General, A70
  George W. C., 305
  John, 232, 277, A71, A72, A108
  Joseph S., 346
  R. D., 307
  Thomas, 323
  William, 164, 333, A109
WILKINSON
  John C., 311
WILLEY
  Samuel, A109
WILLIAMS
  A., 155
  A. G., 181
  A. L., 308
  Aaron, 155, 226, 228
  Abraham, 277
  Anthony, 307
  D., 182
  D. H., 330
  David D., 326
  E., 264
  Eli, 363
  Henry, 143, 178
  J., 228
  J. B., 345
  J. R., 333
  James, 309
  James M., 331
  Jonathan, A109
  Joseph H., 308
  L., 326
  R. M., 299

  Robert, A109
  S. R., 226
  Samuel, R.
  Samuel O., 334
  Thomas, 326
  W. H., 320
  William, 307
WILLIAMSON
  Col., 288, 291
  David, 8, 77, 81, 101, 258, 277, 283, 287
  James, 178
  Samuel, 58, 277, 328
WILLING
  Thomas, A26
WILLS
  John A., 334, 376
WILMOT
  David, 38
WILSON
  A. Wiley, 264
  Alexander, 5, 6, 110, 123, 207, 260, 264
  Alexander M., 321
  Andrew W., 303
  Catharine A., 297
  D. S., 149, 155, 160, 188, 208
  Daniel H., 328
  David S., 6, 97, 126, 140, 151, 208
  David Shields, 264
  George, 198, A19, A90
  Hilleary, 308
  Hugh, 133, 175, 196
  Hugh W., 200, 203
  Isaac, A110
  J., 325
  J. B., 334
  J. E., 307
  J. R., 135, 358

  James, 20, 77, 136, A78
  James B., 303, 369
  John, 126, 130, 132, 133, 134, 144, 149, 151, 174, 176, 179, 193, 199, 242, 258, 259, 265, 277, 334, 341, 345
  John F., 320, 321
  John K., 134, 176, 198, 199, 265, 364
  John M., 356
  John V., 277
  Jonathan R., 323
  Joseph, 322
  Joseph R., 114, 226
  Judge, 86
  Miles, A108
  Mr., 219, 356
  Robert, 307
  Robert S., 304
  S., 325
  S. J., 155, 156
  Samuel, 332, 360
  Samuel J., 155, 169, 170, 332
  Selden L., 337
  Simon, 244
  T., 346
  Theophilus, 314
  Thomas, 345
  W. J., 181, 207, 312
  W. L. S., 343
  W. S., 309
  William, 113, 323, 346
  William H., 338
  William J., 135, 199, 259, 345, 347
  William W., 266
WIMER
  Jackson, 317

WINES
  E. C., 170, 217
WINGE
  Isaiah, 264
WINGET
  Caleb, A108
  F., 325
  S., 325
  Stephen, 94
WINN
  Isaac, 215
WINNET(T)
  Adam, 265
  Hiram, 99
  Rev. Mr., 249
WINSWORTH
  J. G., 334
WINTER(S)
  A., 191
  Abraham, 188
  David, 277
  Robert, 191
WIRT
  Martin, A109
WISE
  Finley, 333
  Frederick, 96
  Freeman, 277
  Henrietta M., 204
  Jacob L., 332
  James, 319
  Joseph, 266
  Samuel, 319
  Uriah W., 264, 351
WISEMAN
  John, A8
WISHART
  A., 304
  Alexander, 207, 305, 343, 344
  David, 331, 332
  J. D., 319

J. W., 188
James, 114
John, 175, 200, 202, 203, 296, 357, 358, 362
John D., 318
John W., 189, 200, 208
John Wilson, 176 203, 318
Marcus, 155
R. T., 312
Robert T., 303, 312
WITHEROW
  John, 343
  S. R., 135
WITHEY
  Griffith, 264
WITHREW
  Robert, 294
WOLF
  A. B., 180
  Alfred D., 333
  David, 135
  George, 37, 265, 352
  J. S., 334
  J. W., 311
  Jacob, 171, 308
  James S., 357
  John B., 305
  Nancy J., 297
  Peter, A58
  Samuel C., 323
  Simon, 183, 362
  T. G., 334
  Wesley, 135, 303, 334
  Westley, 264
  William, 343, 344, 345, 347
WOLFE
  David, 134
  Jacob, 277, A55, A56

  Peter, 134, 193, 258
WONDER
  John, 317
WOOD
  Col., 77
  Henry, 190, 217, 358
  Israel, 277
  J., 311
  John, 235, 313
  John J., 22
  Mr., 77
  Samuel, 315
  Stephen, 130, 143, 265
  William, 196, 227
WOODBURN
  James R., 328
  William, 328
WOODBURY
  Nathan, A109
WOODHEN
  James, A112
WOODRUFF
  H., 160
  J., 183
  Nehemiah, 94
  W. S., 160
WOODS
  A. S., 184
  Henry, 170, 264, 300
  J. G., 264
  John, 250, 251, 264, A62
  M., 324
  Professor, 168
  Robert, 264
  Stephen, 266, 267
WOODWARD
  Enos, 183, 184, 185
  George W., 38
  John, 315
  John H., 304

T., 130
Thomas, 188
W., 310
William, 304, 335
WOOTRING
Abraham, 200
WORCESTER
William, 327
WORK
Captain, 324, 328
G. T., 328
George T., 308, 326, 327, 328, 369
Samuel C., 307
WORKMAN
Hugh, 130, 132, 133, 134, A56
James, 170, A56
Jamy, A56
M., 309
S., 309
Samuel, 146, 253, 258, 264, 350
William, 133, 257, 264
WORKMEN
Hugh, 130, 131
Samuel, 130
WORM
Francis, 22
WORRELL
William, 333
WORSTELL
James, 323
WORTH
John, 277
Major, 171
WOTRING
Abraham, 256, 265, 277
F. R., 334
Jonathan, 337

WRIGHT
Aaron, 93
Alexander, 49, 62, 65, 112, 277
E. N., 345
Edward, A117, A120
Enoch, 198, 243, 266
J., 325
J. O., 91
J. T. F., 289
John, 243, 245
John C., 264
Johnson, 20
Joseph, 309
Joshua, 20
Marshall, 323
Samuel, 330
Silas, 309
William, 327
WYAND
David, 299
WYETH
A. R., 338
WYLIE
A., 242
Andrew, 121, 169, 171, 217, 223, 224, 225
F. J. L., 334
Hugh, 146, 175, 296
J. S., 210
J. W., 334
John, 334, 370
President, 223
R. D., 170
Robert, 198, 200
T. M., 334
William, 140, 182, 266, 267, 334
William C., 146
Wright Tappan, 334
WYNKOOP

Henry, 77
WYTHE
A. B., 307

-Y-

YARNALL
J. B., 121, 123, 233
Rev., 99
YATES
Daniel D., 304
Jasper, A75
YEATES
Richard, 19, 59
YEHO
E. S., 346
YERTY
Henry, 228
YODERS
Jacob, 320
YODES
Jacob, 320
YOHE
David D., 245
J. M., 311
John S., 330
YOKE
Daniel, 277
YORTY
Henry C., 314
Mrs. J., 361
YOUMANS
Israel, 326
YOUNG
Abraham, 277
George, A108
George W., 196
H. H., 326
Harvey H., 326, 329
Henry, 317
J. S., 334, 344
Jacob, 180, A107

James, 307, 317, 322
James P., 324, 360
John, 264, 309, A62, A110
John M., 330
Loyal, 156
Nathaniel, 333
Peter, 331, A8
R. H., 345
Robert, 333
Samuel, 174, 235, 304
Thomas, 332, 346
William, 311, A111
William A., 337
YOUNKIN
Jefferson, 319

-Z-

ZEDIKER
John, 277
ZELLARS
Morgan W., 312
ZELT
William, 335
ZOLLARS
Morgan W., 311
ZUG
Jacob, A108
ZUZIDANT
Daniel, A108
Martin, A108

www.ingramcontent.com/pod-product-compliance
Lightning Source LLC
Chambersburg PA
CBHW071712300426
44115CB00010B/1391